State Constitutions of the United States

State Constitutions of the United States

ROBERT L. MADDEX

CONGRESSIONAL QUARTERLY INC.

WASHINGTON, D.C.

Produced by Archetype Press, Inc.
Washington, D.C.

Project Director: Diane Maddex
Editor: Gretchen Smith Mui
Editorial Assistant: John Hovanec
Designer: Robert L. Wiser

Library of Congress Cataloging-in-Publication Data

Maddex, Robert L.
    State constitutions of the United States / Robert L. Maddex
        p.   cm.
    Includes bibliographical references and index.
    ISBN 1-56802-373-1
    1. Constitutional law—United States—States. 2. Constitutions—United States—States. I. Title.
    KF4530.M33   1998
    342'.02—dc21   98-36835
                                                                                CIP
                                                                                r98

Printed in the United States of America

Cover: The Fundamental Orders of Connecticut (1638–39), a colonial document that is believed to be the world's first written constitution. [Photograph by John Wareham; courtesy Museum of Connecticut History, Connecticut State Library]

Robert L. Maddex is the author of *Constitutions of the World* and *The Illustrated Dictionary of Constitutional Concepts,* both published by Congressional Quarterly Books. An attorney in the Washington, D.C., area, he has served as chief counsel of the Foreign Claims Settlement Commission of the United States and as an adviser on constitutional issues.

Contents

State Constitutions of the United States

Constitutions of U.S. Territories

Appendixes

Preface

The United States, like Australia, Brazil, Germany, and other federal nations, juggles two tiers of government: one sovereign government at the national level and fifty semi-sovereign governments at the state level. As coequal political entities within the federal system, the American states retain all the residual rights guaranteed to them by the U.S. Constitution. This concept of federalism provides for ongoing constitutional innovation in the states and in the territories (which remain under the federal government's jurisdiction) as well as between the states and the national government. Through trial and error in response to changing times, such innovation has led to new systems and procedures of government and to new rights on both the federal and state levels.

Although much has been written about the U.S. Constitution, and deservedly so, the constitutions of the states also play a vital role in the day-to-day lives of U.S. citizens. Their domain may lie beneath that of the national constitution, but their influence on the shape of American government and politics has been and continues to be significant.

Even though it would be impossible for any state constitution to match the worldwide acclaim and emulation of the U.S. Constitution, the states have been occupied for two hundred years in trying to perfect their own supreme laws. As of 1995, 230 state constitutional conventions have been held, 146 constitutions adopted, and some 6,000 amendments made to them. The average state constitution today numbers nearly 30,000 words, while the U.S. Constitution contains about 3,500 words and has been amended just twenty-seven times since it went into effect in 1789. One reason state constitutions have been rewritten and revised so much is that they are the means by which the people can restrict the extensive residual powers left to the states by the Tenth Amendment (1791) to the U.S. Constitution, which contains more limited specific powers.

The purpose of a state constitution, according to John J. Parker, chief judge of the U.S. Court of Appeals from 1931 to 1958, "is two-fold: (1) to protect the rights of the individual from encroachment by the State; and (2) to provide a framework of government for the State and its subdivisions." If all the framers of state constitutions had kept such a succinct definition in mind, succeeding generations might not have felt the need to revise them so much—to remove statutory-type provisions, to better phrase and organize them, to integrate their numerous amendments into the original text—so that understanding and comparing state constitutions would be much easier today.

State Constitutions of the United States was written to simplify this task. It gives a broad general picture of the constitutional development of the United States below the national level, a topic often misunderstood or even ignored in discussions of federal constitutional law. In summary form the book presents the current constitutions of the fifty states and the three U.S. territories that have constitutions. Bearing in mind Judge Parker's criteria for state constitutions, the book focuses on topics of major importance and interest, from fundamental citizen rights to the roles of the legislature and its presiding officers, the governor, and the supreme court. Some less significant provisions are generally not included—for example, sections dealing with state elections, voting requirements, apportionment of the legislature, compensation for public officials, and requirements for officials and institutions of lesser importance to the basic system of state government. In addition, not all the same types of provision are covered in each state, especially where more unusual items in one state also warrant attention.

Each profile begins with a brief statement of general information: the date of the state or territory's admission to the Union or territorial status, its nickname, its size, the states or areas bordering it, its population and rank in population, and key industries and crops. Next come an overview of the three branches of the state government and the date or dates of its constitutions, followed by a summary of the constitutional history of each state or territory. These historical summaries generally begin at the time of European contact with the New World, continue through attainment of statehood or territorial status, and describe the various constitutions adopted. Next is an introduction to the state's current constitution itself, including any pertinent comparisons and historical insights.

A summary of key provisions of the state's constitution follows, using actual text in many instances and, in general, mirroring the order typical of most constitutions. After the preamble the constitution's fundamental rights provisions are outlined. Although in some instances the items included under this rubric may not seem to be fundamental rights, they are noted to indicate the range of concepts that have been brought under this heading by the framers of state constitutions. After a statement of the division of powers within the state, the text moves to an outline of the government structure created by the constitution—the legislative, executive, and judicial branches, presented in the order of their relative importance in state government. The section on the legislative branch focuses on the structure of the state legislature, the officers and members, their privileges and immunities, legislative rules, and procedures for enacting legislation. For the executive branch, the discussion centers on the role and responsibilities of the governor, including qualifications, term, succession to office, and other elected statewide officials with whom the governor shares power. The summary of the judicial branch features the state supreme court, noting its composition, selection of members, and jurisdiction.

Subsequent sections present excerpts from other key provisions: impeachment and a variety of items that appear in some but not all documents, such as direct democracy procedures (initiative, referendum, and recall), local government, taxation and finance, education, the official language, health and welfare, and the environment. Finally, the state's constitutional amendment procedures are summarized.

In presenting the excerpts from and discussions of the state constitutions, a balance has been struck in each state's entry between retaining the general form and structure of the document itself and organizing material in standardized locations where it will be more helpful to the reader.

Selected rulings of federal and state courts are noted throughout to show how state constitutional provisions have affected the rights and interests of individuals, businesses, and public and private institutions; such decisions also illuminate constitutional language, explain or limit the meaning of constitutional provisions, and provide a general sense of the relationships among the branches of state government and between state and federal constitutional law. A table of the cases cited is provided on pages 482–89.

Comments on and comparisons with historic predecessor constitutions, earlier forms of a constitution before amendments, other state constitutions, or the U.S. Constitution (see pages 467–81) are included where appropriate. Another aid in comparing state constitutions, beginning on page xxiv, is a set of quick reference charts that give general information about state constitutions as well as the structure and processes of state governments, provisions relating to new individual rights, and special constitutional provisions. A glossary of terms and concepts begins on page 490.

The texts of the constitutions included in the book were obtained from the states and territories. These documents vary in form, style, and readability, both from constitution to constitution and within each constitution. Because state constitutions are amended far more frequently than the U.S. Constitution, each one is presented here subject to later amendment; those amendments adopted through January 1, 1998, have been noted where applicable. In states where the amendments have been integrated into the constitution, dates of amendments may not be given.

In addition to the helpful staff members of the offices of governors, attorneys general, secretaries of state, state courts, and state legislatures, I am grateful for the assistance of Gretchen Smith Mui, editor, John Hovanec, editorial assistant, and Robert L. Wiser, designer, Archetype Press; Shana Wagger, acquisitions editor, and Nancy Lammers, director of operations, Congressional Quarterly Books; A. E. Dick Howard, White Burkett Miller Professor of Law and Public Affairs, University of Virginia School of Law, for his continued support and assistance; and my wife, Diane Maddex, president of Archetype Press, for her dedication in producing my latest reference work on constitutions.

Introduction

It may be a reflection on human nature, that such devices [constitutions] should be necessary to controul the abuses of government. But what is government itself but the greatest of all reflections on human nature?   —James Madison, Essay 51, *The Federalist* (1788)

Constitutional democracy—the concept enshrined in the U.S. Constitution and the constitutions of its fifty constituent states, some of which predate the federal document itself—is spreading around the globe. Today most nations can be categorized as constitutional democracies, even if they are imperfect in some respects, and approximately ninety percent of the countries of the world select their legislators by free and open elections.

The honor of having the world's oldest written constitution that is still in force, however, goes not to the United States or another nation but to one of the original American states: the Commonwealth of Massachusetts (1780). A number of other states can also claim constitutional "firsts." The Fundamental Orders of Connecticut, an early colonial government document dating from 1638–39, has been hailed as the world's first written constitution. The document that revolutionary New Hampshirites drafted in 1776 is considered the first written for an independent state, although it remained in effect only until 1784. And in 1778 New Hampshire assembled the first constitutional convention—a body of delegates, not members of a legislature, specially selected to revise or draft a constitution. Since then, its method of drafting a constitution has been used the world over, including by the United States in 1787.

The constitutions of the original thirteen American colonies and their antecedents during the colonial period played a key role in the constitutional development of the nation as a whole and, in turn, of most of the world's democracies. In fact, it is doubtful that the U.S. Constitution would have taken the form it did had it not been for the experience of the thirteen colonies, which used written constitutions as the basis for their governments when they became independent states.

Laboratories of Democracy

The influential role of state constitutions did not end with the drafting of the U.S. Constitution in Philadelphia beginning in the summer of 1787. Part of the genius of our constitutional form of government lies in the ability of the state governments to evolve and influence each other as well as the national government. Far from being simply mirror images of the U.S. Constitution on a smaller scale, all of our state constitutions have become experiments—as they should be in a federal democracy—in human rights and systems of government. U.S. Supreme Court Justice Louis D. Brandeis, who served on the Court from 1916 to 1939, called the states "laboratories of democracy." This ongoing experimentation in self-government and the relationship among the states and between them and the federal government is made possible by the concept of federalism embodied in the U.S. Constitution. A grant of specific powers by the people of the states of the Union, the Constitution leaves to the states, as expressed in the Tenth Amendment (1791), significant residual powers of government. State constitutions, therefore, are limitations placed on those residual powers by the citizens of the states. They are necessary to protect individuals from unchecked political power at the state level, in the same way that the federal Constitution shields the citizens and the states themselves from unbridled national political power.

Before the Fourteenth Amendment (1868), the federal courts had no basis for enforcing in the states the guarantees of the Constitution's Bill of Rights (1791). For much of the early federal period, therefore, state constitutions and state courts were citizens' major sources of protection against infringement of rights by state government. Building on the Fourteenth Amendment, the U.S. Supreme Court embarked on an expansion of civil and individual rights vis-à-vis state government, culminating after World War II in a number of important precedents. The Court's decision in *Brown v. Board of Education of Topeka* (1954), voiding the "separate but equal" doctrine on which school segregation had been based, is one of the best-known examples of this expansion of rights. Other rights found by the Court during this era include the right of privacy and the right to an abortion during the early stages of pregnancy, neither of which is expressly mentioned in the U.S. Constitution.

Beginning in the 1970s, however, the federal courts began to slow the growth of citizen rights. Once again, the slack is being taken up by the constitutions and courts of many of the states and territories. As the "new federalism" or "judicial federalism" has evolved over the past three decades, state constitutions have come to play an increasingly important role. Using new individual rights guaranteed in state constitutions and statutes, many state courts are taking an activist stance in interpreting rights that the U.S. Supreme Court now circumscribes. From the states also come a variety of innovations in self-government that have not yet found their way into the U.S. Constitution:

New Rights. The states have also recorded a number of "firsts" in the area of individual rights: in 1776 Virginia was the first to produce a constitutional declaration of rights; Vermont added the first antislavery provision in 1777; the Wyoming Territory in 1869 became the first government anywhere to allow women to vote. Current concerns at the national level—equal rights, accessibility for the disabled, welfare, treatment of crime victims, abuses of taxpayers, and environmental protection—have already been addressed in many state constitutions although none is enumerated in the U.S. Constitution. Nineteen state constitutions have prohibitions against discrimination on the basis of sex, and five have similar provisions relating to the disabled. A number have welfare rights provisions, bills of rights for crime victims, and guarantees of environmental rights. More than half the states have either a constitutional or a statutory bill of rights for taxpayers. To date eight constitutions have incorporated an express right of privacy, and nineteen states have adopted some form of statutory privacy right. Many states have enacted other analogous statutory provisions relating to fundamental rights.

Not only do state constitutions include new rights not guaranteed by the federal constitution—a 1974 amendment to the California constitution even asserts that "[r]ights guaranteed by this Constitution are not dependent on those guaranteed by the U.S. Constitution"—many state constitutions and state courts also have a policy of more vigorous enforcement of fundamental rights.

Initiative, Referendum, and Recall. A majority of the states now provide some type of direct democratic procedures whereby citizens may bypass the traditional legislative process of representative democracy and initiate legislation and constitutional amendments, approve or reject proposed laws and government actions through referendums, and recall elected and appointed state officials. Several restrict direct democracy to the right to recall certain officials.

Item Veto Power and Balanced Budgets. All but six states grant the governor power to veto individual items in appropriations bills. Although Congress tried to provide the president with limited line-item veto power, this grant was overturned by the U.S. Supreme Court in mid-1998. At least thirty-five state constitutions mandate a balanced budget—an issue debated perennially on the national level—and half of the remaining states adddress the issue through state laws.

Term Limits. Term limits for governors were in place in many state constitutions before the Twenty-second Amendment to the U.S. Constitution, limiting the president to two terms, was ratified in 1951. A dozen states, however, have no limitations on how often the governor may be elected. Sixteen state constitutions have also set term limits for state legislators, while Congress grapples with pressure to propose a constitutional amendment on this subject. Some have also attempted to restrict the terms of their members of Congress as well.

Election of Judges. About forty state constitutions now require approval by the voters for supreme court justices and judges to attain or be retained in office. Rarely do states permit their justices to serve simply "during good behavior" until they retire, as is the rule in the federal judiciary, whose members are appointed by the president.

Constitutional Amendments. In addition to the more traditional ways of amending their constitutions, eighteen states now permit constitutional amendments to be proposed by popular initiative. Fourteen states mandate that conventions be called at regular intervals or at least that the question of whether to call a convention be regularly submitted to the electorate. Several states, unlike the federal government, periodically integrate amendments into the text of their constitutions, bringing them up-to-date and making them more understandable to citizens.

Just as laboratory experiments test the laws of chemistry and physics, these experiments are assessing current political and government theories. The results are not always perfect. Item vetoes, for example, have been used on occasion to change the intention of legislation, not merely to reduce the amount of appropriations in a bill. The election of supreme court judges has led to punishment of jurists by the electorate for what may be valid but unpopular decisions. Initiatives, referendums, and recall petitions can create complicated ballots that confuse voters and produce inequities for minorities. Term limits may result in the loss of effective political leaders. Nonetheless, the constructive evolution of the democratic process seems to be taking place more and more in the laboratory of the states before progressive or new ideas reach the national level.

State constitutions also continue to have an impact on other states, just as their predecessors did in forming the Union two centuries ago. Constitution makers in one state often look to provisions and court rulings on constitutional issues in others during their deliberations to amend, revise, or rewrite their own state's constitution. Many state courts also review constitutional language and judicial rulings in other states to analyze questions brought before them about their own state's supreme laws.

The constant interaction between constitutional development in the states and at the national level is what makes our federal system of government so complex and yet so creative. Americans are innovators, and the system of government designed in 1787 in Philadelphia for a new nation continues to provide opportunities for further innovation.

The Beginnings of State Constitutions

All written national and state constitutions, including the U.S. Constitution, can trace their lineage to the governing charters of the American colonies that declared their independence from Great Britain on July 4, 1776. Before the U.S. Constitution, the only written constitutions were those of the thirteen British colonies in America, and since then nearly all the other nations of the world have adopted similar written documents.

In some cases the early charters and frames of government of these British colonies were granted to or imposed on the colonists by the Crown. In others they were bestowed by colonial proprietors, such as William Penn, who had received territorial rights in the New World from the English government. In a few instances, they were drawn up by the colonists themselves—the Mayflower Compact of 1620, for example, was an agreement among some of the English Pilgrims to "covenant and combine ourselves together into a civil Body Politick, for our better Ordering and Preservation...." Although most colonies had governors appointed by the Crown, the colonists were often granted the right to participate in governing the colony along with rights to which English subjects were entitled.

After American independence was declared, the colonists' early charters significantly influenced the constitution making of the thirteen original states. In addition to borrowing ideas from one another, their constitutions, dating to 1776, also served as a starting point for the drafters of the Articles of Confederation, which was adopted in 1781, and then the U.S. Constitution when it was written six years later. State constitutions thus predate by thirteen years the effective date of the U.S. Constitution itself in 1789.

When planters in the Connecticut Colony met in 1638–39 to "frame a social compact ... constituting a new and independent commonwealth, with definite officers, executive and legislative, and prescribed rules and modes of government," they created what is believed to be the world's first written constitution. The colony's Fundamental Orders of 1638–39 and the royal charter of 1662 were adopted together as the state's constitution after it entered the Union on January 9, 1788. Rhode Island also used its colonial charter of 1663 as its constitution once it became a state. Six months before the Declaration of Independence was signed, New Hampshire launched the process of writing constitutions. Seven more of the first thirteen independent American states adopted new written constitutions in 1776 and two did so the following year. Because Connecticut, Rhode

Island, New Hampshire, and the other states with early constitutions have all since replaced their first constitutions, the prize for the oldest written constitution still in effect goes to the 1780 constitution of Massachusetts.

Both the Pilgrims in Plymouth and the framers of the U.S. Constitution had been exposed to the British constitution initiated in 1215 when King John had the great charter of liberties—Magna Carta—thrust on him by his unbowed barons. This unwritten constitution encompassed both the structure of the government and succeeding monarchs' acknowledgments that their subjects and the Parliament possessed certain liberties and rights. At the time of the Declaration of Independence in 1776, no other nation in the world extended to its enfranchised subjects anywhere near the democratic rights to which those under the British Crown were entitled. Although derived for the most part from the British constitution, the basic concepts of constitutional democracy embodied in the early American state constitutions, however, had been forged in the Athens of Plato and Aristotle and the Rome of Cincinnatus and Cicero. The history of all written constitutions begins in these two cities of the distant past.

From the government of Athens between 508 and 338 B.C. came the basic ideas of democracy: majority rule, popular sovereignty, regular elections, and accountability of government officials. From the Roman republic between 509 and 27 B.C. came the notion of representative government as epitomized by the Roman senate—a term still used today in the federal and state constitutions to designate the upper house of the legislature. The next link in the chain of modern democratic government was forged in Iceland, where a parliamentary-type body called the Althing was established in A.D. 930.

The story of constitutional government then moves to England. Beginning with Magna Carta in 1215, England began moving away from rule by a monarch in consultation with representatives of the nobles and commoners toward rule by a parliament consisting of an upper chamber of the clergy and nobility and a lower chamber of representatives of the commoners; the monarch's consent would become an impotent formality. Today even the powers of the House of Lords, the upper chamber, have been eroded by the lower House of Commons, to the extent that the Lords can only delay some legislative actions.

When the newly independent states of the United States began to form their own governments, not all of their constitutions—as might be expected with any new invention—worked as well as their framers expected. The major flaw in most of these early supreme laws stemmed from the lack of institutional checks and balances among the government's legislative, executive, and judicial branches and too much reliance on frequent elections of legislators to curb excesses and remedy government inadequacies. Perhaps the model of the all-powerful British Parliament, which technically includes the two houses of Parliament as well as the monarch, had an overriding influence on the first state constitutions. As the eighteenth-century English jurist Sir Edward Coke is said to have commented: "The power and jurisdiction of parliament is so transcendent and absolute, that it cannot be confined, either for causes or persons, within any bounds." With experience, however, the documents were replaced by new constitutions that increased the authority of the governor at the expense of the legislature and the independence of the judiciary.

In addition to informing the drafters of the U.S. Constitution, the early state constitutions had an influence beyond America's shores. The documents were translated into

French and made available in France almost immediately after their adoption. At the urging of Benjamin Franklin, then the American minister to France, a compilation sanctioned by the French government and entitled *Constitutions des Treize Etats de l'Amerique,* was published in France in 1783. There is no doubt that the early American state constitutions affected those who drew up the constitution of the first French Republic of 1791 as well as other constitutions modeled on this and later French constitutions. The drafters of the first French constitution, for example, included a declaration of rights, called the Declaration of the Rights of Man and of the Citizen, as well as guarantees of natural and civil rights; expressly separated the legislative, executive, and judicial powers of government; established a national legislature elected indirectly by the citizens that could not be dissolved by the French monarch, who headed the executive branch; and enumerated the legislature's powers.

The Constitutions of the States

Unlike national constitutions, state constitutions do not simply stand alone at the apex of a system of laws but are part of an interactive organization of federal and state governments. Federalism, which is an attempt to solve the problems that arise from this interaction between national and state laws, has continued to evolve since the nation was founded. As Delaware Supreme Court Justice Randy J. Holland observes in *The Delaware Constitution of 1897: The First One Hundred Years* (1997), "A knowledge of the origins and history of state constitutions is essential to understanding federalism in the United States."

Together with the federal and state constitutions, the other major component of America's federal system is the body of constitutional law created by the courts as they interpret these constitutions in individual cases. In seven states the supreme court is also constitutionally authorized to give advisory opinions to other branches of government, and in many states the attorney general in addition may render advisory opinions, but neither carries the same weight as a legal opinion of a court in an actual case.

State constitutions differ from the U.S. Constitution in that the federal document makes specific grants of authority to the national government, while the states retain residual power that is generally considered to be broad and unfettered. Article 1, section 8, of the U.S. Constitution, for example, itemizes the powers of Congress. If Congress tries to enact inappropriate legislation, the courts can declare it unconstitutional. State legislatures, on the other hand, are not subject to any restraints on the legislative matters they may address, except those that are delegated exclusively to the federal government by the U.S. Constitution (such as coining money) or prohibited by it (such as entering into any treaty, alliance, or confederation) and matters expressly barred by the state's constitution. Because state constitutions are considered to be limitations on the states' residual power rather than grants of authority by the sovereign citizens, state courts have often found it difficult to restrain state legislatures within the bounds of their constitutions and, until recently, to enforce individual rights under them.

All state constitutions have some elements in common with one another and with the U.S. Constitution. They all, like the federal document, create three major branches of government—legislative, executive, and judicial. The U.S. Constitution and all but one of the states establish bicameral legislatures. The highest executive officer in each state is called the governor. And most states have a hierarchical judiciary, with a supreme court at the top and a chief justice as the head of the judicial administration. A statement of fundamental rights similar to the U.S. Constitution's Bill of Rights is a feature common to all.

But in many more respects state constitutions differ from the federal document. One obvious difference is length. State constitutions range from 8,300 words (Vermont's) to 220,000 words (Alabama's), and the average is about 30,000 words, compared to the succinct 3,500 words in the U.S. Constitution. The number of amendments also varies greatly. Whereas the U.S. Constitution has been amended a mere twenty-seven times since 1789—ten of the amendments forming the Bill of Rights two years later—amendments to state constitutions run as high as 618 in Alabama.

Also unlike the U.S. Constitution, most state constitutions create a plural executive branch in which a number of statewide elected officers—a secretary of state, a treasurer, and an attorney general, among others—share power with the governor. Many governors, but not the U.S. president, have power to veto items in appropriations bills, and many states require balanced budgets, a goal that has yet eluded the federal government. Most state constitutions, but not the federal document, provide for the election of judges, including the justices of the state supreme court. State constitutions, on the other hand, vary widely among themselves with respect to rights expressly granted, the detail with which they are written, the inclusion of direct democracy procedures, and the ways in which their constitutions may be amended or revised.

Many of the documents can be grouped together, beginning with the late-eighteenth-century constitutions reflecting the earliest constitutional forms—Massachusetts (1780), New Hampshire (1784), Vermont (1793)—which in turn influenced those of Maine (1820) and Rhode Island (1843). Southern constitutions of the late nineteenth century—Texas (1876), Mississippi (1890), and South Carolina (1896), for example—evince a reaction to the negative experiences of the post–Civil War era. The Midwest and Northwest tend toward progressive constitutions, the less-populated western states toward businesslike documents. At the opposite end of the spectrum are the modern constitutions—New Jersey (1948), Puerto Rico (1952), and Alaska and Hawaii (both 1959), which are modeled more on the U.S. Constitution. Some constitutions came close to being modernized— New York (1894), New Mexico (1911), and Maryland (1867), for example—except that the voters in these states indicated a willingness to keep the devil they know.

All state constitutions nonetheless adhere to a basic format, one that is followed closely in *State Constitutions of the United States*, as the outline below summarizes.

Preamble. Derived from the Latin words *pre* (before) and *ambulo* (to walk), a constitution's preamble generally contains an introductory statement of the basis, reasons, or goals for the constitution as well as language intended to make the it operative, such as: "We, the people … do ordain and establish this constitution." Preambles, which differ in length, style, and content, do not appear in all constitutions and are not considered enforceable by a court in the same way that the language in the body of the document is.

Fundamental Rights. Fundamental rights are guarantees made by a government to its citizens. Such rights—to speak freely, profess individual religious beliefs, obtain due process under and equal protection of the law, and be safe from inhumane treatment at the hands of government officials—are generally enumerated in a separate section of a constitution, usually at the beginning. This section may be called a "bill of rights," as are the first ten amendments of the U.S. Constitution, or a "declaration of rights."

The fundamental rights found in the Bill of Rights, such as freedom of speech, religion, and the press and the right to assemble peaceably and petition the government for redress of grievances, are often recited. Other typical provisions include probitions against quartering soldiers in private homes without the owners' consent, excessive bail, and cruel and (in the case of some states, *or*) unusual punishment. In addition to many of the basic federal rights and freedoms, state constitutions may contain provisions ensuring rights of women, the disabled, crime victims, and taxpayers as well as guarantees of welfare and privacy, to name a few. Whereas the federally guaranteed fundamental rights are in a sense a minimum floor of government protection for the individual, the enumerated rights in state constitutions can represent another layer.

That a state constitution does not enumerate certain rights does not necessarily mean that the state does not recognize those rights. States disagree on which rights are fundamental and which fundamental rights should be included in a constitution. Many states have choosen to establish fundamental rights—or, perhaps for them, less than fundamental rights—by statute instead. Some states consider welfare, protection of the environment, and privacy as fundamental rights worthy of inclusion in their constitutions. Others either make no provision for such rights or deal with them only by statute. The fact that a provision is raised to the level of a constitutional right, however, may indicate just how much importance the state places on it.

All fundamental rights in a constitution may not even be contained in the bill or declaration of rights. Alabama's constitution, for example, describes property rights of women in article x, Exemptions, rather than in article i, Declaration of Rights. And all the provisions in the rights section may not relate directly to individual rights. A number of states, such as West Virginia, proclaim that a free government can be preserved "only by a firm adherence to justice, moderation, temperance, frugality and virtue, and by frequent recurrence to fundamental principles." In a strict sense this language is not a guarantee of any right or freedom for citizens but serves as an admonition to them.

In general, the trend in state constitutions and statutes is to expand the nature and scope of fundamental rights over what has been and is currently considered a right at the federal level. State courts also act to expand the scope of these rights. Of course, exceptions occur: in 1982, after the Florida supreme court extended state constitutional protection against unreasonable searches and seizures beyond that afforded by the Fourth Amendment (1791) of the U.S. Constitution, the Florida constitution was amended to indicate that this right would be "construed in conformity with the 4th Amendment to the United States Constitution, as interpreted by the United States Supreme Court."

Division of Powers. A tenet of constitutionalism is that the basic powers of a constitutional government must be kept largely separate. Plato noted in the fourth century B.C. that a balance of power is needed among a state's ruling elements; and Charles-Louis de Secondat, baron de La Brède et de Montesquieu, author of *The Spirit of the Laws* (1748), identified the executive, legislative, and judicial functions as the separate powers common to all sovereign governments.

Like the U.S. Constitution, some state constitutions do not articulate the separation of powers principle, but most do. The concept does not require absolute separation, and, as James Madison pointed out in essay 47 of *The Federalist* (1788), it does not preclude one branch of government from having some control over another through checks and balances. The question of whether the principle has been violated by a particular branch of government is generally a matter that is settled by the courts. But even the courts sometimes have a hard time drawing a line between branches of government. As U.S. Supreme Court Justice Oliver Wendell Holmes noted in a dissenting opinion in 1928, "[H]owever we may disguise it by veiling words we do not and cannot carry out the distinction between the legislative and executive branches with mathematical precision and divide the branches into watertight compartments...."

Legislative Branch. The legislature has tended to be the dominant branch of state government. Reasons for this may stem from the people's historic distrust of the executive branch and a lack of aggressive judicial review at the state level. Many states, however, are experimenting with ways to circumvent and circumscribe their state legislators through direct democracy provisions such as the popular initiative, referendum, and recall as well as limits on the number of years legislators can serve. More than one-half of all state constitutions now include some direct democracy provisions, and nearly as many limit legislators' terms. Such changes indicate that some citizens are not totally satisfied with the traditional form of representative state government.

Except for Nebraska, all states and the three U.S. territories with constitutions have bicameral legislatures, but bicameralism has little real significance at the state level. It was important when the parliamentary system of government was evolving in England because it required the agreement of the aristocracy and the commoners for laws to be passed; in the United States at the national level it allows states to be represented in the Senate and individuals to be represented in the House of Representatives. A bicameral state legislature, however, does create the possibility of greater checks on the legislative process, especially when each house is controlled by a different political party.

State constitutions generally provide basic procedures for enacting legislation, which vary from state to state and according to the type of legislative action specified. They also define the quorum necessary for doing business and the majorities needed for approval of various types of legislation. Also addressed are the ways in which legislative business is conducted, such as the selection of the legislature's officers, and legislators' privileges and immunities, including the legislature's power to discipline members (and sometimes the public) for improper behavior.

Executive Branch. The head of the executive branch in each state and territory with a constitution is invariably called the governor. The term *governor* was used in the British colonial system to denote an intermediate executive position between a superior governor general and an inferior lieutenant governor. All governors are popularly elected for a term of four years except in New Hampshire and Vermont, where the governor serves for two years. Most states have a lieutenant governor, who may be elected jointly with the governor or separately, in which case the two may represent different political parties. In the majority of the forty-two states that elect both a governor and a lieutenant governor, the two are elected jointly. Where the lieutenant governor must act as or succeed to the governor's position, this ensures political continuity. In some states, however, the desire to keep the executive branch from becoming dominated by one party outweighs the potential benefits of political party continuity.

The constitutions of several states, notably Alaska, Hawaii, and New Jersey, closely follow the U.S. Constitution in that they concentrate all executive power in the hands of a single elected official, the governor; in those states there are no other statewide elected officials in the executive branch with whom power must be shared. The governor is a true chief executive who, like the American president, can appoint the heads of the executive departments, such as the secretary of state, treasurer, and attorney general.

In most other states, the constitutions provide for a number of elected officials in the executive branch who share power with the governor. In such cases the state's chief executive, unlike the president, has to work with a secretary of state, an attorney general, or other elected officials who may be from an opposition party, thus making full implementation of the governor's programs difficult. This plural form of government is desirable in many states because it diffuses power throughout the executive branch rather than concentrating it in a single person.

Like the president, each governor oversees the executive branch, makes certain appointments as authorized by the constitution or a statute, informs the legislature about "the state of the state," and is responsible for preparing and executing the state budget. The governors of some states are required to submit a balanced state budget, while in others this task falls to the legislature.

State constitutions detail age and additional qualifications for the governor and other statewide elected officials, along with their terms of office and the manner in which the governor is elected. Most states restrict the governor's service to two consecutive terms or two terms only. Indiana and Oregon, however, limit it to eight of twelve years and Montana and Wyoming to eight of sixteen years. The lieutenant governor often serves as president of the upper house of the state legislature, just as the vice president of the United States presides over the Senate. The incumbent may also act for the governor when the governor is incapacitated or simply out of the state and succeeds to the governorship in the case of resignation, conviction on impeachment, or death.

Judicial Branch. The judicial branch in state governments has not been truly coequal with the other two branches and has tended to be more deferential to them than the federal judiciary has been to the president and Congress. A number of state constitutions, especially in the Northeast, provide little detail about the judiciary, which is true of the U.S. Constitution as well. The courts were not the focus of the American Revolution, and the framers of the early state constitutions were more concerned with the legislative and executive branches, letting the judiciary take care of itself to a great extent.

But this tendency has changed. Many state constitutions now go to great lengths to describe the structure, jurisdiction, and duties of their state court system. During this century state judges have also become increasingly subject to regular scrutiny by the electorate. In contrast to the selection process for justices of the U.S. Supreme Court and other federal courts, the vast majority of state constitutions today provide for some form of popular input into the selection or retention of the state judiciary. Justices and judges may be either elected for fixed terms or initially appointed by the governor, with the approval of the legislature (generally the senate), and then subjected to popular approval at fixed intervals through partisan or nonpartisan elections. In South Carolina and Virginia, justices are elected by the legislature, whereas in Connecticut they are appointed by the legislature. Only three states—Massachusetts, New Jersey, and Rhode Island—still mandate virtually life tenure for appointed justices.

The highest state court is usually called the supreme court, but in a few cases it is known as the court of appeals. This court generally consists of a chief justice and an even number of other justices. Some states, including Delaware and Indiana, have just five members on their supreme courts, while others, such as Mississippi and Oklahoma, have as many as nine justices. Qualifications for the supreme court generally include admission to the state bar and a period of time spent either practicing law or serving on a lower court. Procedures for disciplining and removing judges vary, but they are often subject to impeachment, and some special commissions may recommend disciplinary action. The state supreme court may be given constitutional authority to hear disciplinary charges.

The jurisdiction of a state supreme court is generally limited to hearing cases on appeal from lower courts, issuing writs necessary to carry out their judicial functions, and overseeing the state bar. Seven state constitutions authorize the state's highest court, unlike the U.S. Supreme Court, to give advisory opinions to the other branches of government.

Impeachment. All state constitutions except Oregon's have provisions for impeachment of executive branch officials; in some, officials in another branch are also subject to removal in this fashion. Impeachment procedures are found in different parts of constitutions and generally follow the language of the U.S. Constitution. These rules are derived from the British Parliament, the highest court in the United Kingdom, where impeachment is the prosecution by the House of Commons before the House of Lords of any person, peer or commoner, for treason or other high crimes and misdemeanors. In most state constitutions, as in the U.S. Constitution, impeachment charges are brought against a government official by the lower house of the legislature and then tried before the upper house. In Nebraska, because of its unicameral legislature, the procedure has been modified.

In addition to formal impeachment proceedings, many state constitutions provide for other means of disciplining and removing government officials, including recall by the voters—an action that puts democratic power directly in the hands of citizens.

Other Provisions. Other provisions that are often included in state constitutions and that are generally highlighted in *State Constitutions of the United States* include direct democracy procedures, local government (such as home rule), taxation and finance, education, and, less frequently, health and welfare and environmental protection.

Direct democracy procedures include popular initiatives for state legislation or constitutional amendments; referendums on legislation or statewide issues; and recall of state officials. Although not focused on in this book, a few state constitutions provide for initiative, referendum, and recall only with respect to special matters or to issues below the state level, such as municipal officers or decision making.

Most state constitutions provide for local management of government affairs by cities or counties, often referred to as home rule. The state constitution may also prescribe the methods by which home rule charters are obtained by municipalities.

Education policy varies only slightly from constitution to constitution: all states generally undertake to provide for the education of children, and some go further, promoting higher education for high school graduates. All states have some sort of welfare policy, but to date only about a dozen include welfare in their constitutions. All states also have some environmental protection policy—a growing area of public concern about clean air and water and preservation of wildlife, wilderness, and historic areas—but not many spell out such policy in their constitutions.

Addressing contentious current issues, a handful of states, among them Arizona, California, Florida, and Nebraska, have adopted constitutional provisions making English their official language; others have statutory provisions to this effect. Several—Arkansas, Colorado, and Rhode Island—have inserted language regarding abortions; all other states have adopted statutory language on the subject.

Amendment Procedures. State constitutions provide for the constitution itself to be amended or revised. Typically included are procedures for the legislature to propose amendments, which often require a supermajority vote by both houses and in some cases a vote at two separate sessions, the second after a general election. All but nine state constitutions also provide for amendments and major revisions of the constitution by convention and contain procedures for selecting delegates. New York is one of the fourteen states that require regular conventions or voter choice as to whether a convention should be convened. Forty-nine states submit amendments to the voters for ratification; only Delaware does not.

In states where amendments may be made by popular initiative, the proposals must have a requisite number of signatures, in addition to other requirements. As signatories, Massachusetts requires three percent of the total vote cast for governor in the preceding election, while at the other end of the spectrum Arizona demands fifteen percent of the total votes cast for all gubernatorial candidates in the last election.

State constitutions are amended far more frequently than is the U.S. Constitution. The reasons for this vary, but at least the procedures for amending state constitutions are not so difficult that they inhibit changes. Citizens and particularly state legislators clearly view their state constitution as a work in progress rather than a nearly immutable document, as so many regard the U.S. Constitution. Making amendments easy is not a bad idea. An outdated constitution—and a number of state constitutions can be considered outdated by their own standards—is a hindrance to better government. Although some may say that state amendment procedures are too easy, the processes of amending or revising a constitution and writing a completely new constitution are a major part of the democratic nature of constitutional government. Thomas Jefferson believed that each generation should have the opportunity to rewrite the U.S. Constitution. This may seem extreme, but constitutions, like other organizational plans, must change because times change. And constitutions can always be improved.

One problem with the proliferation of amendments to state constitutions, however, is that the more amendments a constitution has, the more difficult it is for the average citizen or even the average lawyer to understand what effect the amendments have had on the original document. This is particularly true for states such as Alabama and Massachusetts, for example, which have no provision for integrating the text of amendments into the body of the original constitution. Like the U.S. Constitution, Massachusetts's even earlier 1780 constitution keeps its historic form because its 117 current amendments are simply appended rather than integrated into the original text. In 1917 Massachusetts tried to update its constitution and called a constitutional convention that corrected technical errors and integrated the amendments into the old text. Although the convention's efforts were approved at the polls in 1919, the state supreme court ruled that only the original version and individual amendments were controlling. Most other states integrate their amendments into the basic document, making reference to the current constitution much easier for citizens and lawyers alike.

As James Madison intimated in his *Federalist* essay quoted at the beginning of this introduction, human nature can be both destructive and creative. This dualism has frustrated the efforts of humankind to live in peace, harmony, and cooperation. But as the "Father of the Constitution" obviously understood, constitutions, especially written ones, provide the noble side of our nature with the means to take charge of ourselves and to limit the ignoble side. With such a document people can thus resolve to control baser instincts that lead to absolutist rule, persecution of minorities and political dissenters, and arbitrary and capricious government decision making. Constitutional restraints facilitate a better society of human beings, thereby increasing both our chances for survival and opportunities for more citizens to have a materially richer and happier life.

Like the constitutions of nations, state constitutions are similar in their fundamental aspects but varied in many of their details. The concept of federalism allows the great democratic experiment envisioned by the framers of the U.S. Constitution to be carried out a little differently in fifty jurisdictions at the same time. Each state has the freedom to make incremental adjustments to the nature of its constitutional democracy. These differences do not weaken the fabric of our national democracy; instead, they strengthen it by allowing innovation and change to occur incrementally without great nationwide debates or massive campaigns.

Tinkering with the process of constitutional democracy in the American states has become a national pastime. The signals being sent by the citizens of the states are unclear. Obviously, efficient, just, honest, and responsive state government is the goal of the electorate, but just how to ensure this outcome through constitutional language is proving elusive. State constitutions have been subjected in some cases to hundreds of amendments, indicating that many of them are being called on to do more than just protecting the rights of the people and providing a basic structure and operational plan of government.

The question being asked in the states, as in many countries, is, How can a constitution best be written to implement government of the people, for the people, and by the people? A single answer to this question may never be possible, but given their two centuries of constitutional democracy, Americans are uniquely qualified to work on this problem. Now that many rights and provisions that can improve the measure of justice and the quality of life for all are increasingly found only in state constitutions, the importance of these documents to all citizens has risen dramatically.

State Government Structure

Executive Branch

State	Term of Governor (Years)	Term Limit[1]	Joint Election with Lt. Governor	Veto Power	Item Veto Power	Statewide Elected Officials
Alabama	4	2c	No	Yes	Yes	8
Alaska	4	2c	Yes	Yes	Yes	2
Arizona	4	2c	No Lt. Governor	Yes	Yes	5
Arkansas	4	2	No	Yes	Yes	6
California	4	2c	No	Yes	Yes	6
Colorado	4	2c	Yes	Yes	Yes	5
Connecticut	4	No	Yes	Yes	Yes	6
Delaware	4	2	No	Yes	Yes	6
Florida	4	2c	Yes	Yes	Yes	8
Georgia	4	2c	No	Yes	Yes	8
Hawaii	4	2c	Yes	Yes	Yes	2
Idaho	4	No	No	Yes	Yes	7
Illinois	4	No	Yes	Yes	Yes	6
Indiana	4	8 of 12 years	Yes	Yes	No	5
Iowa	4	No	Yes	Yes	Yes	6
Kansas	4	2	Yes	Yes	Yes	4

Legislative Branch _____   # Judicial Branch _____

State	Upper House Members	Lower House Members	Term Limits	Supreme Court Members	Justices Appointed	Justices Elected	Advisory Opinions
Alabama	35	105	No	9	No	Yes	Yes[3]
Alaska	20	40	No	5	Yes	Yes	No
Arizona	30	60	Yes	5	Yes	Yes	No
Arkansas	35	100	Yes	7	No	Yes	No
California	40	80	Yes	7	Yes	Yes	No
Colorado	35	65	Yes	7	Yes	Yes	Yes
Connecticut	36	151	No	7	Yes[2]	No	No
Delaware	21	41	No	5	Yes	No	Yes[3]
Florida	40	120	Yes	7	Yes	Yes	Yes
Georgia	56	180	No	7	No	Yes	No
Hawaii	25	51	No	5	Yes	No	No
Idaho	35	70	No	5	No	Yes	No
Illinois	59	118	No	7	No	Yes	No
Indiana	50	100	No	5	Yes	Yes	No
Iowa	50	100	No	9	Yes	Yes	No
Kansas	40	125	No	7	Yes	Yes	No

Executive Branch

State	Term of Governor (Years)	Term Limit[1]	Joint Election with Lt. Governor	Veto Power	Item Veto Power	Statewide Elected Officials
Kentucky	4	2c	Yes	Yes	Yes	7
Louisiana	4	2c	No	Yes	Yes	9
Maine	4	2c	No Lt. Governor	Yes	Yes	1
Maryland	4	2c	Yes	Yes	Yes	4
Massachusetts	4	No	Yes	Yes	Yes	6
Michigan	4	2	Yes	Yes	Yes	4
Minnesota	4	No	Yes	Yes	Yes	6
Mississippi	4	2	No	Yes	Yes	5
Missouri	4	2	No	Yes	Yes	6
Montana	4	8 of 16 years	Yes	Yes	Yes	6
Nebraska	4	2c	Yes	Yes	Yes	6
Nevada	4	2	No	Yes	No	6
New Hampshire	2	No	No Lt. Governor	Yes	No	1
New Jersey	4	2c	No Lt. Governor	Yes	Yes	1
New Mexico	4	2c	Yes	Yes	Yes	7
New York	4	No	Yes	Yes	Yes	4
North Carolina	4	2c	No	Yes	No	10
North Dakota	4	No	Yes	Yes	Yes	13
Ohio	4	2	Yes	Yes	Yes	6
Oklahoma	4	2	No	Yes	Yes	9

Legislative Branch _____ Judicial Branch _____

State	Upper House Members	Lower House Members	Term Limits	Supreme Court Members	Justices Appointed	Justices Elected	Advisory Opinions
Kentucky	38	100	No	7	No	Yes	No
Louisiana	39	105	Yes	7[4]	No	Yes	No
Maine	35	151	Yes	7	Yes	No	Yes
Maryland	47	141	No	7	Yes	Yes	No
Massachusetts	40	160	No	7	Yes	No	Yes
Michigan	38	110	Yes	7	No	Yes	Yes
Minnesota	67	134	No	7	No	Yes	No
Mississippi	52	122	No	9	No	Yes	No
Missouri	34	163	Yes	7	Yes	Yes	No
Montana	50	100	Yes	7	No	Yes	No
Nebraska	49 (unicameral)		No	7	Yes	Yes	No
Nevada	21	42	Yes	5	No	Yes	No
New Hampshire	24	400	No	5	Yes	No	Yes
New Jersey	40	80	No	7	Yes	No	No
New Mexico	42	70	No	5	Yes	Yes	No
New York	61	150	No	7	Yes	No	No
North Carolina	50	120	No	7	No	Yes	No
North Dakota	49	98	No	5	No	Yes	No
Ohio	33	99	Yes	7	No	Yes	No
Oklahoma	48	101	Yes	9	Yes	Yes	No

Executive Branch

State	Term of Governor (Years)	Term Limit[1]	Joint Election with Lt. Governor	Veto Power	Item Veto Power	Statewide Elected Officials
Oregon	4	8 of 12 years	No Lt. Governor	Yes	Yes	3
Pennsylvania	4	2c	Yes	Yes	Yes	5
Rhode Island	4	2c	No	Yes	No	5
South Carolina	4	2	No	Yes	Yes	9
South Dakota	4	2c	Yes	Yes	Yes	7
Tennessee	4	2c	No Lt. Governor	Yes	Yes	1
Texas	4	No	No	Yes	Yes	5
Utah	4	12 years[3]	Yes	Yes	Yes	5
Vermont	2	No	No	Yes	No	5
Virginia	4	1c	No	Yes	Yes	3
Washington	4	8 of 14 years[3]	No	Yes	Yes	8
West Virginia	4	2c	No Lt. Governor	Yes	Yes	6
Wisconsin	4	No	Yes	Yes	Yes	5
Wyoming	4	8 of 16 years[3]	No Lt. Governor	Yes	Yes	5

Legislative Branch   Judicial Branch

State	Upper House Members	Lower House Members	Term Limits	Supreme Court Members	Justices Appointed	Justices Elected	Advisory Opinions
Oregon	30	60	Yes	7	No	Yes	No
Pennsylvania	50	203	No	7	No	Yes	No
Rhode Island	50	100	No	5	Yes	No	Yes
South Carolina	46	124	No	5	No	Yes[5]	No
South Dakota	35	70	Yes	5	Yes	Yes	Yes
Tennessee	33	99	No	5	No	Yes	No
Texas	31	150	No	9	No	Yes	No
Utah	29	75	Yes[3]	5	Yes	Yes	No
Vermont	30	150	No	5	Yes	No	No
Virginia	40	100	No	7	No	Yes[5]	No
Washington	49	98	No	9	No	Yes	No
West Virginia	34	100	No	5	No	Yes	No
Wisconsin	33	99	No	7	No	Yes	No
Wyoming	30	60	Yes[3]	5	Yes	Yes	No

Notes

[1] the letter *c* indicates consecutive terms; in some states, however, eligibility is restored after an interval of one term

[2] appointed by the legislature

[3] authorized by statute or otherwise

[4] excludes one judge assigned from the court of appeals

[5] elected by the legislature

State Constitutions and Amendments

General Information

State	Date of Statehood	Current Constitution	Number of Constitutions
Alabama	December 14, 1819	November 28, 1901	6
Alaska	January 3, 1959	January 3, 1959	1
Arizona	February 14, 1912	February 14, 1912	1
Arkansas	June 15, 1836	October 30, 1874	5
California	September 9, 1850	July 4, 1879	2
Colorado	August 1, 1876	August 1, 1876	1
Connecticut	January 9, 1788	December 30, 1965	3
Delaware	December 7, 1787	June 10, 1897	4
Florida	March 3, 1845	January 7, 1969	6
Georgia	January 2, 1788	July 1, 1983	10
Hawaii	August 21, 1959	August 21, 1959	1
Idaho	July 3, 1890	July 3, 1890	1
Illinois	December 3, 1818	July 1, 1971	4
Indiana	December 11, 1816	November 1, 1851	2
Iowa	December 28, 1846	September 3, 1857	2
Kansas	January 29, 1861	January 29, 1861	1

Amendments

State	Number of Amendments	Legislative Vote for Amendments	Constitutional Convention	Popular Initiative for Amendments
Alabama	618	3/5	Yes	No
Alaska	26	2/3	Yes	No
Arizona	121	1/2 + 1	Yes	Yes
Arkansas	97	1/2 + 1	No	Yes
California	493	2/3	Yes	Yes
Colorado	133	2/3	Yes	Yes
Connecticut	29	3/4 or 1/2 + 1[1]	Yes	No
Delaware	130	2/3[2]	Yes	No
Florida	74	3/5	Yes	Yes
Georgia	48	2/3	Yes	No
Hawaii	95	2/3 or 1/2 + 1[3]	Yes	No
Idaho	115	2/3	Yes	No
Illinois	10	3/5	Yes	Yes
Indiana	40	1/2 + 1	No	No
Iowa	47	1/2 + 1	Yes	No
Kansas	90	2/3	Yes	No

General Information

State	Date of Statehood	Current Constitution	Number of Constitutions
Kentucky	June 1, 1792	September 28, 1891	4
Louisiana	April 30, 1812	December 31, 1974	11
Maine	March 15, 1820	March 15, 1820	1
Maryland	April 28, 1788	October 5, 1867	4
Massachusetts	February 6, 1788	October 25, 1780	1
Michigan	January 26, 1837	January 1, 1964	4
Minnesota	May 11, 1858	May 11, 1858	1
Mississippi	December 10, 1817	November 1, 1890	4
Missouri	August 10, 1821	March 30, 1945	4
Montana	November 8, 1889	July 1, 1973	2
Nebraska	March 1, 1867	November 1, 1875	2
Nevada	October 31, 1864	October 31, 1864	1
New Hampshire	June 21, 1788	June 2, 1784	2
New Jersey	December 18, 1787	January 1, 1948	3
New Mexico	January 6, 1912	January 6, 1912	1
New York	July 26, 1788	January 1, 1895	4
North Carolina	November 21, 1789	July 1, 1971	3
North Dakota	November 2, 1889	November 2, 1889	1
Ohio	March 1, 1803	September 1, 1851	2
Oklahoma	November 16, 1907	November 16, 1907	1

Amendments

State	Number of Amendments	Legislative Vote for Amendments	Constitutional Convention	Popular Initiative for Amendments
Kentucky	35	3/5	Yes	No
Louisiana	79	2/3	Yes	No
Maine	167	2/3	Yes	No
Maryland	212	3/5	Yes	No
Massachusetts	117	1/2 + 1[4]	No	Yes
Michigan	22	2/3	Yes	Yes
Minnesota	115	1/2 + 1	Yes	No
Mississippi	119	2/3	No	Yes
Missouri	90	1/2 + 1	Yes	Yes
Montana	21	2/3	Yes	Yes
Nebraska	199	3/5	Yes	Yes
Nevada	117	1/2 + 1	Yes	Yes
New Hampshire	143	3/5	Yes	No
New Jersey	48	3/5 or 1/2 + 1[5]	No	No
New Mexico	134	1/2 + 1[6]	Yes	No
New York	216	1/2 + 1	Yes	No
North Carolina	30	3/5	Yes	No
North Dakota	137	1/2 + 1	No	Yes
Ohio	158	3/5	Yes	Yes
Oklahoma	152	1/2 + 1	Yes	Yes

State	Date of Statehood	Current Constitution	Number of Constitutions
Oregon	February 14, 1859	February 14, 1859	1
Pennsylvania	December 12, 1787	April 23, 1968[7]	5
Rhode Island	May 29, 1790	May 3, 1843	2
South Carolina	May 23, 1788	January 1, 1896	7
South Dakota	November 2, 1889	November 2, 1889	1
Tennessee	June 1, 1796	May 5, 1870	3
Texas	December 29, 1845	February 15, 1876	5
Utah	January 4, 1896	January 4, 1896	1
Vermont	March 4, 1791	July 9, 1793	3
Virginia	June 25, 1788	July 1, 1971	6
Washington	November 11, 1889	November 11, 1889	1
West Virginia	June 20, 1863	August 22, 1872[8]	2
Wisconsin	May 29, 1848	May 29, 1848	1
Wyoming	July 10, 1890	July 10, 1890	1

Amendments

State	Number of Amendments	Legislative Vote for Amendments	Constitutional Convention	Popular Initiative for Amendments
Oregon	210	1/2 + 1 or 2/3[9]	Yes	Yes
Pennsylvania	24	1/2 + 1 or 2/3[10]	No	No
Rhode Island	59	1/2 + 1	Yes	No
South Carolina	474	2/3 and 1/2 + 1[11]	Yes	No
South Dakota	103	1/2 + 1	Yes	Yes
Tennessee	32	1/2 + 1 and 2/3[12]	Yes	No
Texas	377	2/3	No	No
Utah	90	2/3	Yes	No
Vermont	52	2/3 and 1/2 + 1[13]	No	No
Virginia	31	1/2 + 1	Yes	No
Washington	91	2/3	Yes	No
West Virginia	67	2/3	Yes	No
Wisconsin	128	1/2 + 1	Yes	No
Wyoming	65	2/3	Yes	No

Notes

[1] requires three-fourths vote at one session or majority at two successive sessions

[2] requires two successive sessions, no popular ratification

[3] requires two-thirds vote at one session or majority at two successive sessions

[4] requires majority of both houses in joint session

[5] requires three-fifths vote at one session or majority at two successive sessions

[6] requires a supermajority in certain cases

[7] effective dates of provisions varied

[8] date of popular ratification

[9] requires majority vote to amend and two-thirds to revise

[10] requires two-thirds vote for emergency amendments

[11] requires two-thirds vote to initiate amendment and majority after popular ratification

[12] requires majority for first passage, two-thirds for second

[13] requires two-thirds vote in upper house and majority in lower house for first passage and majority in both for second passage

New State Rights and Special Provisions

New Rights

State	Privacy	Sexual Discrimination	Disabled Persons	Victims	Taxpayers
Alabama	No	No	Statute	No	Statute
Alaska	Constitution	Constitution	Statute	Constitution	No
Arizona	Constitution	Statute	Statute	Constitution	Statute[2]
Arkansas	Statute	Statute	Statute	Statute	Statute
California	Constitution	Constitution	Statute	Constitution	Statute
Colorado	No	Constitution	Statute	Constitution	Constitution
Connecticut	No	Constitution	Constitution	Constitution	Statute
Delaware	Statute	Statute	Statute	Statute	No
Florida	Constitution	Statute	Constitution	Constitution	Constitution
Georgia	Statute	Statute	Statute	Statute	Statute
Hawaii	Constitution	Constitution	Statute	Statute	No
Idaho	No	Statute	No	Constitution	Statute
Illinois	Constitution	Constitution	Constitution	Constitution	Statute
Indiana	Statute	Statute	Statute	Constitution	No[6]
Iowa	No	No	Statute	No	Statute
Kansas	No	No	Statute	Constitution	No

Special Provisions

State	Balanced Budget	Direct Democracy[1]	Health and Welfare	Home Rule	Environment	Official Language	Abortion
Alabama	Statute	No	Statute	No	Statute	Constitution	Statute
Alaska	Statute	Constitution	Constitution	Constitution	Constitution	No	Statute
Arizona	Constitution	Constitution	Statute	Constitution	Statute	Constitution	Statute
Arkansas	Statute	Constitution	Statute	Statute	Statute	Statute	Constitution
California	Constitution	Constitution	Constitution	Constitution	Statute	Constitution	Statute
Colorado	Constitution	Constitution	Statute	Constitution	Statute	Constitution	Constitution
Connecticut	Constitution	Statute	Statute	Constitution	Statute	No	Statute
Delaware	Constitution	Constitution[3]	Statute	Statute	Statute	No	Statute
Florida	Constitution	Constitution	Statute	Constitution	Statute	Constitution	Statute
Georgia	Constitution	Statute[4]	Statute	Constitution	Statute	Statute	Statute
Hawaii	Constitution	No	Constitution	Constitution	Constitution	Constitution	Statute
Idaho	Constitution	Constitution	Statute	No	Statute	No	Statute
Illinois	Constitution	Constitution[5]	Statute	Constitution	Constitution	Statute	Statute
Indiana	No	No	Statute	Statute	Statute	Statute	Statute
Iowa	Statute	No	Statute	Constitution	Statute	No	Statute
Kansas	Constitution	Constitution[7]	Constitution	Constitution	Statute	No	Statute

New Rights

State	Privacy	Sexual Discrimination	Disabled Persons	Victims	Taxpayers
Kentucky	No	Statute	Statute	Statute	Statute
Louisiana	Constitution	Constitution	Constitution	Statute	No
Maine	Statute	Statute	Statute	Statute	No
Maryland	No	Constitution	No	Constitution	No
Massachusetts	Statute	Constitution	Constitution	Statute	Statute
Michigan	Statute	Statute	Statute	Constitution	No
Minnesota	Statute	No	Statute	Statute	Statute
Mississippi	No	No	No	Statute	No
Missouri	No	Statute	Statute	Constitution	Statute
Montana	Constitution	Constitution	Statute	Statute	Statute
Nebraska	Statute	No	No	Constitution	No
Nevada	No	No	No	No	Statute
New Hampshire	Statute	Constitution	No	Statute	Statute
New Jersey	No	Constitution[9]	No	Constitution	No
New Mexico	No	Constitution	Statute	Constitution	No
New York	Statute	Statute	Statute	Statute	Statute
North Carolina	No	No	Statute	Constitution	No
North Dakota	No	Statute	Statute	Statute	No
Ohio	No	No	No	Constitution	Statute
Oklahoma	Statute	Statute	No	Constitution	No

Special Provisions

State	Balanced Budget	Direct Democracy[1]	Health and Welfare	Home Rule	Environment	Official Language	Abortion
Kentucky	Constitution	No	Constitution	Constitution	Statute	Statute	Statute
Louisiana	Constitution	Constitution[7]	Statute	Constitution	Constitution	No	Statute
Maine	Constitution	Constitution	Statute	Constitution	Statute	No	Statute
Maryland	Constitution	Constitution	Statute	Constitution	Statute	No	Statute
Massachusetts	Constitution	Constitution	Statute	Statute	Constitution	No	Statute
Michigan	Constitution	Constitution	Statute	Constitution	Statute	No	Statute
Minnesota	Statute	Constitution[7]	Statute	Constitution	Statute	No	Statute
Mississippi	Statute	Constitution[8]	Statute	No	Statute	Statute	Statute
Missouri	Constitution	Constitution	Constitution	Constitution	Statute	No	Statute
Montana	Constitution	Constitution	Statute	Constitution	Constitution	Statute	Statute
Nebraska	Constitution	Constitution	Statute	Constitution	Statute	Constitution	Statute
Nevada	Constitution	Constitution	Statute	Statute	Statute	No	Statute
New Hampshire	No	No	Statute	Constitution	Statute	Statute	Statute
New Jersey	Constitution	Constitution[7]	Statute	Statute	Statute	No	Statute
New Mexico	Constitution	Constitution	Statute	Constitution	Statute	No	Statute
New York	Constitution	No	Constitution	Constitution	Constitution	No	Statute
North Carolina	Constitution	No	Constitution	Statute	Statute	Statute	Statute
North Dakota	Constitution	Constitution	Statute	Constitution	Statute	Statute	Statute
Ohio	Constitution	Constitution	Statute	Constitution	Statute	No	Statute
Oklahoma	Constitution	Constitution	Constitution	Constitution	Statute	No	Statute

New Rights

State	Privacy	Sexual Discrimination	Disabled Persons	Victims	Taxpayers
Oregon	No	No	Statute	Constitution	Statute
Pennsylvania	No	Constitution	Statute	Statute	Statute
Rhode Island	Statute	Constitution	Constitution	Constitution	No
South Carolina	No	Statute	Statute	Statute	Statute
South Dakota	Statute	Statute	Statute	Statute	Statute
Tennessee	Statute	Statute	Statute	Statute	Statute
Texas	No	Constitution	Statute	Constitution	No
Utah	Statute	Constitution	Statute	Constitution	Statute
Vermont	Statute	Statute	Statute	Statute	No
Virginia	No	Statute	Statute	Constitution	Statute
Washington	Statute	Constitution	Statute	Constitution	Statute
West Virginia	No	Statute	Statute	Statute	No
Wisconsin	Statute	Statute	Statute	Constitution	No
Wyoming	No	Constitution	Statute	Statute	Statute

Special Provisions

State	Balanced Budget	Direct Democracy[1]	Health and Welfare	Home Rule	Environment	Official Language	Abortion
Oregon	Constitution	Constitution	Statute	Constitution	Statute	No	Statute
Pennsylvania	Constitution	No	Constitution	Constitution	Constitution	No	Statute
Rhode Island	Constitution	Constitution[7]	Statute	Constitution	Statute	No	Constitution
South Carolina	Constitution	No	Constitution	Constitution	Statute	No	Statute
South Dakota	Constitution	Constitution	Statute	Constitution	Statute	Statute	Statute
Tennessee	Constitution	No	Statute	Constitution	Statute	Statute	Statute
Texas	Constitution	No	Constitution	Constitution	Constitution	No	Statute
Utah	Constitution	Constitution	Statute	Constitution	Statute	No	Statute
Vermont	No	No	Statute	No	Statute	No	Statute
Virginia	No	No	Statute	Constitution	Constitution	Statute	Statute
Washington	No	Constitution	Statute	Constitution	Statute	No	Statute
West Virginia	Constitution	No	Statute	Constitution	Statute	No	Statute
Wisconsin	Constitution	Constitution[7]	Statute	Constitution	Statute	No	Statute
Wyoming	Constitution	Constitution	Statute	Constitution	Statute	Statute	Statute

Notes

[1] applicable only at the state level

[2] effective January 1, 1999

[3] applicable only to oppose bingo

[4] applicable only to certain referendums

[5] applicable only to constitutional amendments regarding the structure of the legislative branch

[6] only a taxpayer rights advocate authorized by statute

[7] applicable only to the recall of public officials

[8] applicable only to constitutional amendments by initiative

[9] as interpreted by the state's supreme court

State Constitutions of the United States

Alabama became the twenty-second state of the United States on December 14, 1819. The capital of the "Heart of Dixie" is Montgomery. Some 52,420 square miles in area, Alabama is bounded by Tennessee on the north, Georgia on the east, Mobile Bay (which provides access to the Gulf of Mexico) on the south, and Mississippi on the west. With approximately 4.2 million residents, Alabama is the twenty-second most populous state in the nation. Among the state's principal industries are pulp and paper, chemicals, and electronics; its chief crops include cotton, peanuts, corn, and sweet potatoes.

ALABAMA

General Information

Government: The governor and lieutenant governor are elected on separate tickets for four years and are limited to two successive terms. Alabama's legislature consists of thirty-five senators and 105 representatives, all of whom serve identical terms of four years for both chambers. The supreme court includes a chief justice and eight other justices elected for six-year terms.

Dates of Constitutions: 1819, 1861, 1865, 1868, 1875, and 1901

Constitutional History

When Europeans arrived in the New World at the beginning of the sixteenth century, the territory that would become the state of Alabama was inhabited by the Creek, Cherokee, Chickasaw, Choctaw, and Alabama peoples. Spanish seamen who had scouted the coast of this region as early as 1505 told tales of a country where "people wore hats of gold." In 1539 Hernando de Soto, the Spanish explorer, mounted an expedition that landed on the west coast of the Florida peninsula, proceeded inland due north, and then turned west, crossing the Alabama territory. Eventually de Soto located the Mississippi River but found no gold hats.

The first Spanish settlement on Mobile Bay, established in 1559 by the explorer Tristan de Luna, was abandoned two years later, after which the Alabama territory attracted little attention. Much of the land was included in the 1629 and 1663 Carolina charters granted respectively by Charles I and Charles II of England, and the 1669 Fundamental Constitutions of the Carolina Colony also applied to the Alabama area.

When England established its Georgia colony in 1732, it became the first of the European powers who were vying to dominate North America to settle the territory between Carolina, an English colony, and Florida, which belonged to Spain. Spain lost Florida to England after the French and Indian War (1754–63) but received the Louisiana territory in 1762 from France for being its ally in the conflict. From 1777 to 1790 the Alabama territory was under the jurisdiction of Georgia, which adopted constitutions in 1777 and 1789. In 1798 some of the Alabama region came under the control of the U.S. territorial government of Mississippi.

Spain returned the Louisiana territory to France in 1800, and on March 30, 1803, the United States purchased it from France for 60 million francs, then the equivalent of $15 million. Following President Thomas Jefferson's famed Louisiana Purchase, the U.S. government in 1808 officially extended the right of suffrage for electing representatives to the general assembly and a delegate to Congress from the Mississippi Territory, which included the Alabama region and Mobile. During the War of 1812, the United States took possession of Mobile and part of Spanish Florida.

The Territorial Government of Alabama Act of 1817 carved the separate jurisdiction of Alabama out of the Mississippi Territory. Its first governor, appointed by President James Monroe, was William Wyatt Bibb, who later was elected the first governor of the new state. A document drafted by the constitutional convention that met in Huntsville from July 5 to August 2, 1819, was approved by the voters and went into effect on December 14 of that year, when Alabama joined the Union. The 1819 constitution drew heavily on the 1817 constitution of Mississippi. The capital of Alabama was moved from Huntsville to Cahaba in 1820, then to Tuscaloosa in 1827, and finally Montgomery was designated the capital in 1846.

In 1861, at the beginning of the Civil War, a state constitutional convention voted to secede from the Union and amended the 1819 constitution to reflect the state's inclusion in the Confederacy. A constitutional convention meeting in Montgomery produced a third constitution in 1865, which attempted to continue white supremacy. Another convention called in 1867 pursuant to the congressional Reconstruction Acts drafted a fourth document, which was ratified by the voters and became effective in 1868. This constitution eliminated racial qualifications for legislative office, enfranchised newly freed black men, and incorporated a major innovation for Alabama—an article on education based on a similar provision in Iowa's 1857 constitution.

A fifth constitution, prepared by a convention meeting in Montgomery and approved by the electorate, went into effect in December 1875. The major features of this document included the reenfranchisement of former secessionist leaders and a reduction in state representatives from the "black belt" counties. With the exception of North Carolina and Tennessee, each of the former Confederate states has had at least five constitutions.

Alabama's current constitution was prepared by a constitutional convention held in Montgomery from May 21 to September 3, 1901. On approval by the voters it went into effect on November 28, 1901.

The Constitution

The 1901 Alabama constitution, like many other southern states' constitutions of this period, was designed to perpetuate what remained of the antebellum social system. Article VIII, section 182, was eventually found by the U.S. Supreme Court in *Hunter v. Underwood* (1985) to have been "enacted with the intent of disenfranchising blacks." Similarly, a federal district court in 1966 invalidated the poll tax authorized in section 194 of the same article, finding it a means of subverting the Fifteenth Amendment (1870) of the U.S. Constitution, which guarantees black citizens the right to vote.

The Alabama constitution was crafted to diffuse power among many authorities to moderate conflicts between the entrenched white power structure and the liberal and populist factions prevalent in southern state politics. The document also vests greater discretion and authority in the executive than its predecessor and makes the amendment process relatively easier.

The detailed nature of Alabama's constitution, its limitations on government authorities, and its less stringent amendment procedures have resulted in the adoption of 618 amendments as of January 1, 1998, making it by far the longest state constitution with some 220,000 words. Many of these amendments have an extremely narrow focus. For example, some amendments are entitled Special Property Tax for Educational Purposes in Lee County and City of Opelika, Bonds for Courthouse and Jail in Henry County, and Fire Protection or Garbage and Trash Disposal Districts in Jefferson County. Some of the amendments, such as that to article VI, The Judicial Department, nonetheless have general applicability.

The preamble, although not originally designated as such in the constitution, reads as follows: "We, the people of the State of Alabama, in order to establish justice, insure domestic tranquillity, and secure the blessings of liberty to ourselves and our posterity, invoking the favor and guidance of Almighty God, do ordain and establish the following constitution and form of government for the State of Alabama."

Preamble

Article I, Declaration of Rights, proclaims: "That the great, general, and essential principles of liberty and free government may be recognized and established, we declare: **Section 1.** . . . That all men are equally free and independent; that they are endowed by their Creator with certain inalienable rights; that among these are life, liberty, and the pursuit of happiness."

Fundamental Rights

Section 2 acknowledges the concept of popular sovereignty, while **section 3** forbids establishing any religion by law or giving preference to any "religious sect, society, denomination, or mode of worship." **Section 4** guarantees freedom of speech and the press, as long as such liberty is not abused, and **section 5** prohibits unreasonable searches and seizures in language similar to the Fourth Amendment (1791) of the U.S. Constitution.

Sections 6, 7, 8, and **9,** respectively, extend rights to those accused of a crime; declare that "no person shall be accused or arrested, or detained, except in cases ascertained by law. . ."; provide that "no person shall be proceeded against criminally, by information," except in certain enumerated cases; and prohibit double jeopardy. Sections **10** through **17** include the right to a jury trial; a guarantee of open courts; and prohibitions against excessive fines, cruel or unusual punishment, excessive bail, and the suspension of the writ of habeas corpus. A 1995 amendment added provisions granting rights to crime victims.

Sections 18 through **22** provide a definition of treason in terms similar to those in the U.S. Constitution and prohibit attainder for treason by the legislature, imprisonment for debt, suspension of the laws except by the legislature, and ex post facto laws and laws impairing the obligation of contracts. **Section 23** requires just compensation for the taking of private property; and **section 24** proclaims that "all navigable water shall remain forever public highways. . . ."

Sections 25 through **34** identify the right to peaceably assemble, petition for the redress of grievances, and bear arms. Exile and slavery are prohibited, and the privilege of suffrage and the property rights of aliens are protected.

Section 35 states that "the sole object and only legitimate end of government is to protect the citizen in the enjoyment of life, liberty, and property, and when the government assumes other functions it is usurpation and oppression."

Article X, Exemptions, section 209, confirms certain property rights of women, stating: "The real and personal property of any female in this state, acquired before marriage, and all property, real or personal, to which she may afterwards be entitled by gift, grant, inheritance, or devise, shall be and remain the separate estate and property of such female...."

Division of Powers

Article III, Distribution of Powers of Government, sections 42 and **43,** divide the government into three distinct departments—legislative, executive, and judicial—and prohibit any one department from exercising the powers of another unless expressly directed or permitted by the constitution.

Legislative Branch

Article IV, Legislative Department, section 44, declares: "The legislative power of this state shall be vested in a legislature, which shall consist of a senate and a house of representatives." **Section 46** specifies in part: "In the year nineteen hundred and six, and in every fourth year thereafter, all the senators and representatives shall be elected." Thus, unlike most other state constitutions except those of Louisiana, Maryland, Mississippi, and North Dakota, Alabama's constitution provides that members of both houses of its legislature serve four-year terms.

Section 47 requires that senators be at least twenty-five years old at the time of their election, and representatives at least twenty-one years old. **Section 50** limits the legislature to "not more than thirty-five senators, and not more than one hundred and five members of the house of representatives." Currently the total for each house is thirty-five and 105, respectively.

Sections 51 through **59** authorize the election of a president pro tempore of the senate and a speaker of the house of representatives; require a majority of each house for a quorum; grant each house the power to determine its own rules; require a journal of proceedings of each house; and extend to legislators immunity from arrest during sessions and travel to or from sessions, except in cases of treason, felony, violation of the oath of office, and breach of the peace. **Section 60** bars people "convicted of embezzlement of the public money, bribery, perjury, or other infamous crime" from the legislature or other state offices of trust or profit.

Sections 61 through **64** focus on the procedure for passing laws. Bills may not be altered during passage to change their original purpose and may not become laws unless referred to and returned from a standing committee. They must be read on three separate days, must be voted on by yeas and nays (the names of the members voting for and against are recorded in the journals), and must receive a majority of the votes in each house, except, as noted in **section 63,** "as otherwise provided in this Constitution."

Section 70 mandates that revenue bills originate in the house of representatives. Under **section 71,** a general appropriations bill must be restricted to the ordinary expenses of the executive, legislative, and judicial branches, and no official's salary may be increased in such a bill, unless otherwise provided for by law.

Section 86, reflecting century-old mores, states: "The legislature shall pass such penal laws as it may deem expedient to suppress the evil practice of dueling." The constitutions of several other states, including Kentucky and Tennessee, retain similar provisions that seem equally out-of-date.

Article V, Executive Department, section 112, indicates that Alabama's executive officers "shall consist of a governor, lieutenant governor, attorney-general, state auditor, secretary of state, state treasurer, superintendent of education, commissioner of agriculture and industries, and a sheriff for each county." A 1969 amendment now requires the superintendent of education to be appointed by and serve at the pleasure of an elected board of education. **Section 113** vests supreme executive power in a "chief magistrate, who shall be styled 'The Governor of the State of Alabama.'" "Supreme executive power" implies that other officers in the executive branch also exercise some executive power, and therefore the governor of Alabama, unlike the U.S. president and some state governors, is not vested with sole executive authority but must share it with other constitutional officers.

Section 114 requires that all executive department officials except sheriffs be elected "at the same time and places appointed for the election of members of the legislature." **Section 116,** as amended in 1968, restricts the enumerated executive officers to a four-year term each. They may run again, but "no person shall be eligible to succeed himself for more than one additional term." The governor is ineligible for any other state office or the U.S. Senate during his or her term "and within one year after the expiration thereof." **Section 117** specifies that the governor and lieutenant governor, who are elected separately, be at least thirty years old, citizens of the United States for ten years, and residents of the state "at least seven years next before the date of their election." The lieutenant governor is ex officio president of the senate but has no vote except in the case of a tie.

Section 120 authorizes the governor to "take care that the laws be faithfully executed"; and **section 121** directs the governor to require reports from other executive branch officers. **Section 122** empowers the governor to convene the legislature on extraordinary occasions. Under **section 123,** the governor is required to provide reports and information to the legislature: "[H]e shall account to the legislature . . . for all moneys received and paid out by him or by his order; and at the commencement of each regular session he shall present to the legislature estimates of the amounts of money required to be raised by taxation for all purposes."

Section 124, as amended in 1939, authorizes the governor to "grant reprieves, paroles, commutations of sentence, and pardons." **Section 125** gives him or her the power to veto legislation, which may be overridden by "a majority of the whole number elected" to each house. Only a simple majority of a quorum, however, is required for initial passage of a bill. **Section 126** states that the governor has authority to veto individual items in legislation. According to **section 131,** the governor also serves as commander in chief of the state's militia and volunteer forces, "except when they shall be called into the service of the United States. . . ."

Section 127 provides that if the governor is removed from office, dies, or resigns, the lieutenant governor assumes the position, as he does if the governor is impeached, disabled, or absent from the state for more than twenty days.

Judicial Branch

Article VI, The Judicial Department, was repealed and a new article added by amendment in 1973. **[Section] 6.01** declares: "**(a)** Except as otherwise provided by this Constitution, the judicial power of the state shall be vested exclusively in a unified judicial system which shall consist of a supreme court, a court of criminal appeals, a court of civil appeals, a trial court of general jurisdiction known as the circuit court, a trial court of limited jurisdiction known as the district court, a probate court and such other municipal courts as may be provided by law."

[Section] 6.02(a) establishes the supreme court as "the highest court of the state"; it consists of "one chief justice and such number of justices as may be prescribed by law" (currently nine). According to **[section] 6.02(b),** the supreme court's responsibilities are to "have original jurisdiction **(1)** of cases and controversies as provided by this Constitution, **(2)** to issue such remedial writs or orders as may be necessary to give it general supervision and control of the courts of inferior jurisdiction, and **(3)** to answer questions of state law certified by a court of the United States." **[Section] 6.02(c)** notes that the supreme court "shall have such appellate jurisdiction as may be provided by law."

[Section] 6.07 notes the qualifications of judges: "Judges of the supreme court, courts of appeals, circuit court and district court shall be licensed to practice law in this state and have such other qualifications as the legislature may prescribe. Judges of the probate court shall have such qualifications as may be provided by law." **[Section] 6.10** designates the chief justice of the supreme court as the administrative head of the judicial system. **[Section] 6.11** empowers the supreme court to "make and promulgate rules governing the administration of all courts and rules governing practice and procedure in all courts...." According to **[section] 6.13,** all judges are to be elected "by vote of the electors within the territorial jurisdiction of their respective courts." The term of office for each judge, as stated in **[section] 6.15,** is six years.

Impeachment

Article VII, Impeachments, section 173, sets forth the procedure for impeachment of the governor, lieutenant governor, attorney general, auditor, secretary of state, treasurer, and commissioner of agriculture and industries. Impeachment charges brought by the house for willful neglect of duty, corruption in office, incompetency, intemperate use of intoxicating liquors or narcotics, or an offense involving "moral turpitude" are tried by the senate. By amendment in 1969, the superintendent of education now serves at the pleasure of the board of education, and under a 1973 amendment, supreme court justices now come under the disciplinary provisions of the revised article VI.

Taxation and Finance

Article XI, Taxation, section 212, mandates that "[t]he power to levy taxes shall not be delegated to individuals or private corporations or associations." In *Opinion of the Justices* (1980), the Alabama supreme court declared that it would be unconstitutional for the savings and loan commissioner to fix the rate of taxation on the assets of savings and loan associations. **Section 214** restricts the legislature's power to set tax rates in any one year to not more than "sixty-five one-hundredths of one per centum on the value of the taxable property within the state."

Article XIV, Education, section 256, as amended in 1956, declares in part: "It is the policy of the state of Alabama to foster and promote the education of its citizens in a manner and extent consistent with its available resources, and the willingness and ability of the individual student, but nothing in this Constitution shall be construed as creating or recognizing any right to education or training at public expense, nor as limiting the authority and duty of the legislature, in furthering or providing for education, to require or impose conditions or procedures deemed necessary to the preservation of peace and order." The legislature is expressly given authority to provide for the establishment and operation of schools.

Education

Amendment 509, adopted in 1990, specifies that "English is the official language of the state of Alabama" and indicates that "[t]he legislature and officials of the state of Alabama shall take all steps necessary to insure that the role of English as the common language of the state of Alabama is preserved and enhanced." Adds the amendment: "The legislature shall make no law which diminishes or ignores the role of English as the common language of the state of Alabama." It further notes that "[a]ny person who is a resident of or doing business in the state of Alabama shall have standing to sue the state of Alabama to enforce this amendment, and the courts of record of the state of Alabama shall have jurisdiction to hear cases brought to enforce this provision. . . ."

Official Language

Article XVIII, Mode of Amending the Constitution, section 284, as amended in 1933, specifies the procedure for amending Alabama's constitution. Amendments must be proposed by the legislature by reading them in the house in which they originate "on three several days." If voted on favorably by at least three-fifths of the elected members of that house on the third day, they are sent to the other house, where the procedure is repeated. If the proposed amendments are approved by the legislature, it orders an election on them by the voters to be held not later than three months after the legislature's adjournment; and if a majority of the voters favor the amendments, they become a part of the constitution. In *Gafford v. Pemberton* (1982), the Alabama supreme court declared: "The legislature can only propose a constitutional amendment; it cannot enact one." The last sentence of section 284 states that "[r]epresentation in the legislature shall be based on population, and such basis of representation shall not be changed by Constitutional amendments." In *Opinion of the Justices* (1955), four of the seven justices of the Alabama supreme court concluded that, despite the language in this section, the legislature had the authority to propose an amendment repealing the last sentence.

Amendment Procedures

Section 286 gives the legislature the authority to call a convention "for the purpose of altering or amending the Constitution" if the call is approved by a majority of the members of each house of the legislature and if the measure receives a majority of the votes of those voting. Once the convention is assembled, its power is unrestricted with respect to "altering, revising, or amending the existing Constitution."

ALASKA

On January 3, 1959, Alaska became the forty-ninth state of the United States. The capital of this state, nicknamed the "Last Frontier" and "Land of the Midnight Sun," is Juneau. With its 656,424 square miles, Alaska is the largest in area of the fifty states. It is bordered by the Arctic Ocean on the north, the Yukon Territory of Canada on the east, the Pacific Ocean on the south, and the Bering Sea on the west. The state ranks forty-eighth in population with approximately 600,000 residents. Alaska's principal industries include oil, gas, tourism, and commercial fishing; among its chief crops are barley, oats, potatoes, and lettuce.

General Information

Government: The governor is elected for a four-year term and is limited to two consecutive terms. The lieutenant governor runs on the same ticket. The legislature consists of a twenty-member senate and a forty-member house of representatives. Senators serve four-year terms, with one-half elected every two years, while representatives serve two-year terms. The supreme court includes a chief justice and four additional justices who are appointed by the governor from nominations by a judicial council and are subject to voter approval after the first three years and every ten years thereafter.

Date of Constitution: 1959

Constitutional History

The New World claimed by Christopher Columbus in 1492 had been discovered thousands of years earlier by gatherers and hunters from Asia who crossed a land bridge into what is now Alaska. These peoples formed tribes such as the Tlingits, Haidas, Tsimshians, and Inuits, whose word *alaska* meant "the object toward which the sea's action is directed." The next wave of immigrants also came from the west—the Russians. In 1741 the Dane Vitus Bering led a Russian fur-trading expedition along the southern Alaskan coast. Attempts at colonization were limited, however, and Catherine the Great, empress of Russia from 1762 to 1796, was chary of giving much government support to a commercial venture so far from home.

During the American Revolution, the English explorer Captain James Cook mapped the Alaskan coastline and warned that Russia and Spain, through their aggressive exploration, might claim the entire Pacific coast of North America. In 1789, the year of the French Revolution, the first Americans sailed to Alaska to compete in the fur-trading business.

To provide a government for its Alaskan territory, in 1799 Russia chartered the Russian American Company, whose managers in North America also served as governors of the settlements. Generally established along the coastline, these small colonies extended as far south as Fort Ross, just north of San Francisco Bay. As Spain lost interest in the northern Pacific coast, the Czarist government began entering into treaties with the United States and Britain in 1824 and 1825 regarding rival trade interests in Alaska and western Canada.

By 1841, however, when the Russian American Company sought to renew its twenty-year charter for the second time, there were only 633 Russians in all of Alaska. As the United States began seeing its "manifest destiny" as a nation stretching from sea to sea, the U.S. government became more interested in Alaska. Russia, which had been defeated by Great Britain, France, Turkey, and Sardinia in the Crimean War (1853-56), decided to cut its losses in North America. Negotiations with the United States over the disposition of Alaska, however, were interrupted by the Civil War.

On June 20, 1867, Russia ceded its North American territory to the United States for $7 million plus a reimbursement of $200,000 to the Russian American Company for a contract with a U.S. company in San Francisco. Derided by some newspapers as "Seward's Folly" or "Seward's Ice Box"—U.S. Secretary of State William H. Seward had negotiated the Alaska purchase agreement—the territory did not formally come under federal authority until the Civil Government of Alaska Act of 1884.

At the urging of John C. Brady, who had been appointed governor of Alaska in 1897, President William McKinley proposed upgrading the territory's status as a preliminary step toward statehood. The Carter Act of June 6, 1900, accomplished this, and legislation in 1906 allowed Alaska an elected but nonvoting delegate in the House of Representatives. Home rule was granted on August 24, 1912, but Alaska did not become a state until forty-seven years later.

A constitution for the proposed new state was drafted by a constitutional convention held between November 8, 1955, and February 5, 1956, on the campus of the University of Alaska in Juneau and was approved in an election held in April 1956. Adopting a strategy used by Tennessee to expedite admission to the Union, a delegation of two elected senators and a representative tried to present their credentials to Congress immediately after the draft constitution was ratified by the voters. But Congress delayed admission to ensure that a number of federal interests in Alaska would be guaranteed after statehood was acquired. In another election held in August 1958 Alaskans approved a list of accommodations pledged by the state to the national government. Finally, on January 3, 1959, Alaska became a state, and its constitution went into effect.

The Constitution

During Alaska's long history as a territory of the United States, three major organic laws developed, and these provided a basis for the state constitution: the Civil Government of Alaska Act of 1884, the Carter Act of 1900, and the Alaska Home Rule Act of 1912. Influenced also by a model constitution prepared by the National Municipal League, Alaska's constitution is similar to Hawaii's, which was adopted in 1950, although Hawaii did not become a state until March 18, 1959. Both these modern state constitutions have been described as managerial in style, granting broad powers to the executive branch and providing few structural limits on the legislature. Unlike the Hawaiian constitution, however, which mirrors the U.S. Constitution's procedures for selection of judges, Alaska requires that judges be named by the governor from a judicial council's list and that they be approved by the voters after three years. Alaska's constitution, like Hawaii's, also contains articles dealing with local government, natural resource conservation, and social programs, including health, education, and welfare. As of January 1, 1998, the relatively short 16,000-word constitution has been amended twenty-six times.

Preamble

The preamble to Alaska's constitution reads: "We the people of Alaska, grateful to God and to those who founded our nation and pioneered this great land, in order to secure and transmit to succeeding generations our heritage of political, civil, and religious liberty within the Union of States, do ordain and establish this constitution for the State of Alaska."

Fundamental Rights

Article I, Declaration of Rights, section 1, declares: "This constitution is dedicated to the principles that all persons have a natural right to life, liberty, the pursuit of happiness, and the enjoyment of the rewards of their own industry; that all persons are equal and entitled to equal rights, opportunities, and protection under the law; and that all persons have corresponding obligations to the people and to the State."

Section 2 asserts in part: "All political power is inherent in the people." **Section 3,** as amended in 1972, posits the civil rights of citizens: "No person is to be denied the enjoyment of any civil or political right because of race, color, creed, sex, or national origin. The legislature shall implement this section." A 1981 opinion of the attorney general indicates that this section prohibits special hunting privileges for Native Americans in Alaska.

Sections 4, 5, and **6,** respectively, guarantee freedom of religion, speech, and assembly and petition. **Section 7** ensures due process of law; and **sections 8** through **13** deal with criminal law rights. In *Blue v. State* (1977), the Alaska supreme court held that the state constitution may have broader safeguards for those accused of crimes than the minimum federal level. **Section 14** restricts searches and seizures; **section 15** prohibits certain state actions with respect to contracts, corruption of the blood (a provision of English law that declared the property of a criminal forfeited to the state), or forfeiture of estates; and **section 16** addresses civil suits and trial by jury.

Sections 17, 18, 19, and **20,** respectively, cover other fundamental issues—imprisonment for debt, eminent domain, the right to keep and bear arms, and the quartering of soldiers. A 1994 amendment to section 19 added: "The individual right to keep and bear arms shall not be denied or infringed by the State or a political subdivision of the State." Notes **section 21,** "The enumeration of rights in this constitution shall not impair or deny others retained by the people."

Section 22, which was created by amendment in 1972, addresses the right of privacy: "The right of the people to privacy is recognized and shall not be infringed. The legislature shall implement this section." In *Ravin v. State* (1975), the Alaska supreme court held that the right of privacy extends to the home and "encompasses the ingestion of such substances as marijuana in a purely personal, noncommunal context in the home unless the state can meet its substantial burden and show that proscription of possession of marijuana is supportable by achievement of a legitimate state interest."

Section 23 authorizes the state to grant preferences to residents over nonresidents to the extent permitted by the U.S. Constitution. **Section 24,** added by amendment in 1994, extends certain rights to crime victims, such as protection from the accused, consultation with the prosecution, and dignified, respectful, and fair treatment.

Division of Powers

The Alaska constitution does not expressly recite the concept of separation of government powers but does divide the basic structure of the state government into the legislature, executive, and judiciary. **Article XII, General Provisions, section 8,** however, notes that the "enumeration of specified powers in this constitution shall not be construed as limiting the powers of the State." This language reflects the fact that, unlike the federal constitution, which is a grant of powers to the national government, state constitutions limit and organize the residual inherent powers of the states.

Article II, The Legislature, section 1, proclaims: "The legislative power of the State is vested in a legislature consisting of a senate with a membership of twenty and a house of representatives with a membership of forty." According to **section 3,** legislators must be elected at general elections; the term of representatives is two years and that of senators is four years, with one-half of the senators being elected every two years.

Legislative Branch

Section 2 provides that any qualified voter who is twenty-one years old and has been a resident of the state for three years and of his or her district for one year is eligible for election to the house; senators must be twenty-five years old. In *Alaskans for Legislative Reform v. State* (1994), the Alaska supreme court found that the lieutenant governor was justified in denying a popular initiative for legislation to place term limits on legislators because such proposed new qualifications would be at variance with section 2 and therefore unconstitutional.

Section 5 precludes a legislator from simultaneously holding any other office of the United States or the state. And **article XII, General Provisions, section 4,** declares: "No person who advocates, or who aids or belongs to any party or organization or association which advocates, the overthrow by force or violence of the government of the United States or of the State shall be qualified to hold any public office of trust or profit under this constitution."

Article II, The Legislature, section 8, specifies that the legislature must convene on the fourth Monday of January, unless otherwise changed by law, and adjourn after 120 days, unless extended for up to ten days. **Section 9** allows special legislative sessions, limited to thirty days, to be called by the governor or by a two-thirds vote of the legislators.

Section 14 authorizes the legislature to establish procedures for the enactment of bills into laws, providing: "No bill may become law unless it has passed three readings in each house on three separate days, except that any bill may be advanced from second to third reading on the same day by concurrence of three-fourths of the house considering it." This section also specifies that no bill "may become law without an affirmative vote of a majority of the membership of each house."

Section 15 permits the governor to veto bills and to "veto, strike or reduce items in appropriations bills." **Section 16** states that the veto of money bills (making appropriations or raising revenue), however, may be overridden by a vote of three-fourths of the legislature meeting in joint session; other vetoes may be overturned by a two-thirds vote.

Article III, The Executive, section 1, declares: "The executive power of the State is vested in the governor."

Executive Branch

Section 2 stipulates that the governor be thirty years old and a qualified voter, a U.S. citizen, and a resident of Alaska for at least seven years preceding the election. **Sections 3** through **6** provide that the candidate receiving the greatest number of votes will be elected to a four-year term; no person may be elected to more than two consecutive terms; and the governor may hold no other position in the U.S. or state government.

Sections 7 through **11** outline the lieutenant governor's qualifications and duties. He or she is to have the same qualifications and serve for the same term as the governor, run jointly in the election with the governor, perform such duties as prescribed by law or delegated by the governor, serve as acting governor in the temporary absence of the governor, and succeed to the remainder of the governor's term in the event of the governor's death or any other vacancy in the office. Before the adoption of a 1970 amendment, which created the position of lieutenant governor, the secretary of state performed the functions of the lieutenant governor. **Section 12** declares that whenever the governor's duties are not performed for six months, the office is declared vacant.

Section 16 indicates that the governor "shall be responsible for the faithful execution of the laws." The officeholder "may, by appropriate court action or proceeding brought in the name of the State, enforce compliance with any constitutional or legislative mandate, or restrain violation of any constitutional or legislative power, duty, or right by any officer, department, or agency of the State or any of its political subdivisions." The governor is precluded from taking any action against the legislature, however. In *Bradner v. Hammond* (1976), the Alaska supreme court ruled that this section, taken together with section 1, gives the governor "the power to appoint subordinate officers to aid him in carrying out the laws of Alaska."

Section 19 authorizes the governor to serve as commander in chief of the state's armed forces. According to **section 20,** the executive may proclaim martial law in the case of rebellion or actual or imminent danger, although it may not remain in effect for more than twenty days without the legislature's approval. **Section 21** allows the governor to grant pardons, commutations, and reprieves.

Section 22 restricts the executive branch to no more than twenty principal departments, although **section 23** allows the governor to reorganize the branch and the assignment of functions. Pursuant to **sections 24** and **25,** the executive branch department heads, whose appointment requires legislative confirmation and who serve at the pleasure of the governor, are under the governor's supervision.

Judicial Branch

Article IV, The Judiciary, section 1, declares: "The judicial power of the State is vested in a supreme court, a superior court, and the courts established by the legislature. The jurisdiction of courts shall be prescribed by law. The courts shall constitute a unified judicial system for operation and administration. Judicial districts shall be established by law."

Section 2(a) notes that the supreme court "shall be the highest court of the State, with final appellate jurisdiction" and that it "shall consist of three justices, one of whom is chief justice." Moreover, "[t]he number of justices may be increased by law upon the request of the supreme court." In *Wharton v. State* (1979), the Alaska supreme court held that "final appellate jurisdiction" under this section inherently includes review of criminal sentences. **Section 2(b),** added by amendment in 1970, states: "The chief justice shall be selected from among the justices of the supreme court by a majority vote of the justices. His term of office as chief justice is three years. A justice may serve more than one term as chief justice but he may not serve consecutive terms in that office."

Section 4 stipulates that supreme court justices and superior court judges be citizens of the state and the United States, be licensed to practice law in the state, and possess additional qualifications as prescribed by law. **Section 5** authorizes the governor to fill supreme court and superior court vacancies by appointing one of two or more persons nominated by a judicial council. According to **section 6,** supreme court justices and superior court judges are subject to approval or rejection by the voters at the first general election held more than three years after their appointments and afterward at general elections every tenth year for supreme court justices and every sixth year for superior court judges.

Section 15 authorizes the supreme court to "make and promulgate rules governing the administration of all courts ... [and] rules governing practice and procedure in civil and criminal cases in all courts." These rules, however, may be changed by a two-thirds vote of the members elected to each house of the legislature. **Section 16** designates the chief justice as the administrative head of all courts; he or she is authorized "with the approval of the supreme court, [to] appoint an administrative director to serve at the pleasure of the supreme court and to supervise the administrative operations of the judicial system."

Section 8 establishes a judicial council that, as specified in **section 9,** "shall conduct studies for improvement of the administration of justice, and make reports and recommendations to the supreme court and to the legislature ...," among other duties. **Section 10** establishes a commission on judicial conduct, which has the power to recommend discipline and removal of supreme court judges. Some other state constitutions, such as Kentucky's, create a similar body. **Section 11** requires justices and judges to retire "at the age of seventy ... except for special assignments [of retired judges] as provided by court rule." **Section 12** provides for the impeachment of any judge or justice for malfeasance or misfeasance of official duties in the same manner as for other civil officers.

Impeachment

Article II, The Legislature, section 20, specifies that all civil officers of the state are subject to impeachment by the legislature. Impeachment proceedings must originate in the senate and be approved by a two-thirds vote of its members. A trial on impeachment charges is conducted in the house of representatives and presided over by a supreme court justice designated by the court. A judgment of impeachment requires a two-thirds vote of the members of the house, and punishment extends only to removal from office, although further proceedings in a court of law are not precluded.

Direct Democracy

Article XI, Initiative, Referendum, and Recall, sets forth the procedure for citizens to participate directly in the democratic government of the state. **Section 2** stipulates that an application for a legislative initiative or referendum must be filed by at least one hundred voters as sponsors with the lieutenant governor, who prepares a summary of the subject matter of the proposed law or referendum. Pursuant to **section 3**, this summary is then circulated by the sponsors to obtain the signatures of at least ten percent of those "who voted in the preceding general election and [who are] resident in at least two-thirds of the election districts of the state." **Section 4** authorizes the lieutenant governor to prepare the proposal to be placed on the ballot of the next statewide election. If a majority of the votes cast are in favor of the popularly initiated measure, it is enacted. According to **section 8**, recall applies to all elected state officials except judicial officers, and procedures and grounds for recall are to be prescribed by the legislature.

Local Government

Article X, Local Government, section 2, provides: "All local government powers shall be vested in boroughs and cities. The State may delegate taxing powers to organized boroughs and cities only." According to **section 11**, "A home rule borough or city may exercise all legislative powers not prohibited by law or by charter." In *Jefferson v. State* (1974), the Alaska supreme court ruled that a municipal ordinance is not invalid unless it contravenes the constitution or the legislature has expressly preempted the particular area of law.

Taxation and Finance

Article IX, Finance and Taxation, section 1, mandates: "The power of taxation shall never be surrendered. This power shall not be suspended or contracted away, except as provided in this article." **Section 6** states: "No tax shall be levied, or appropriation of public money made, or public property transferred, nor shall public credit be used, except for a public purpose." **Section 12** requires that the governor "submit to the legislature, at a time fixed by law, a budget for the next fiscal year setting forth all proposed expenditures and anticipated income of all departments, offices, and agencies of the State." At the same time he or she is to submit a general appropriations bill to authorize proposed expenditures.

Education

Article VII, Health, Education and Welfare, section 1, authorizes the legislature to "establish and maintain a system of public schools open to all children of the State, and … provide for other public educational institutions. Schools and institutions so established shall be free from sectarian control. No money shall be paid from public funds for the direct benefit of any religious or other private educational institution."

Health and Welfare

Article VII, Health, Education, and Welfare, sections 4 and **5**, state that the legislature provides for the promotion and protection of public health and for the public welfare. In *Gray v. Gray* (1974), the Alaska supreme court decided that the right of privacy may be subordinate to the legislature's constitutional power to protect the public health and provide for the general welfare if a compelling interest is shown.

Environment

Article VIII, Natural Resources, section 1, asserts: "It is the policy of the State to encourage the settlement of its land and the development of its resources by making them available for maximum use consistent with the public interest." **Section 2** directs the legislature to "provide for the utilization, development, and conservation of all natural resources belonging to the State…." **Section 3** notes that "[w]herever occurring in their natural state, fish, wildlife, and waters are reserved to the people for common use," and **section 17** requires that "laws and regulations governing the use or disposal of natural resources shall apply equally to all persons similarly situated...."

Article XII, General Provisions, section 14, added in 1996, provides in part: "A federal statute ... that affects an interest of this State under the Act admitting Alaska to the Union is ineffective as against the State interest unless approved by a two-thirds vote of each house of the legislature or approved by the people of the State." If implemented, this provision's constitutionality under the U.S. Constitution may be questioned.

Article XIII, Amendment and Revision, section 1, as amended in 1970 and 1974, provides that amendments to the constitution must be proposed by a two-thirds vote of each house of the legislature and approved by a majority of voters at the next general election. **Section 2** authorizes the legislature to call a constitutional convention at any time. **Section 3,** as amended in 1970, specifies that if during any ten-year period no convention is called, the ballot at the next general election must include the question: "Shall there be a Constitutional Convention?" According to **section 4,** constitutional conventions are given "plenary power to amend or revise the constitution, subject only to ratification by the people."

ARIZONA

Arizona, the "Grand Canyon State," became the forty-eighth state of the United States on February 14, 1912. Its capital is Phoenix. With approximately 4.2 million residents, Arizona ranks twenty-fifth among the states in population. Some 114,000 square miles in area, it is bordered by Utah on the north, New Mexico on the east, Mexico on the south, and California and Nevada on the west. Arizona's principal industries include manufacturing, tourism, and mining; cotton, lettuce, and broccoli are among its chief crops.

General Information

Government: The governor is elected for a four-year term and is limited to two consecutive terms. There is no lieutenant governor. The legislature consists of thirty senators and sixty members of the house of representatives, all of whom are elected for two-year terms and restricted to four consecutive terms. The supreme court is composed of a chief justice, a vice chief justice, and three additional justices initially appointed by the governor from nominees submitted by an appointments commission; thereafter they are elected for six-year terms.

Date of Constitution: 1912

Constitutional History

Early inhabitants of the area of southwestern North America that would become Arizona included the Anasazi ("the ancient ones" in the Navajo language), Hohokam, and Mogollon peoples. The state name Arizona comes from *aleh-zon*, a Papago Indian term for "little spring." Lured by tales of cities of silver and gold, Spaniards including Francisco Vásquez de Coronado traversed the area beginning in the 1500s but found little of value.

A Pueblo Indian revolt against the Spaniards in 1680 resulted in a campaign by an Italian Jesuit, Father Eusebio Francisco Kino, to systematically explore and map the territory and establish missions among the native inhabitants beginning in 1692. (Father Kino is one of two Arizonans commemorated with a statue in Statuary Hall in the U.S. Capitol in Washington, D.C.) Sixty years later a *presidio* (Spanish military administration) was set up in Tubac. The Jesuits were expelled in 1767, and the headquarters of the military administration moved to Tucson. Spain's interest in the region waned after Yuma Indians massacred military and mission personnel in 1781.

After Mexico declared its independence from Spain in 1821, American fur traders and trappers moved into the Arizona territory. As the American presence increased, so did clashes with the Mexican colonists. In 1846 the United States declared war on Mexico, and American troops occupied Tucson. Under the terms of the 1848 Treaty of Guadalupe Hidalgo ending the war, the Arizona territory north of the Gila River was ceded to the United States. A disputed southern strip of land was acquired by the United States from Mexico several years later for $10 million pursuant to a settlement known as the Gadsden Purchase.

Arizona became a part of the New Mexico Territory in 1850, but residents drafted a provisional constitution in 1860 and sought separate recognition and a nonvoting delegate in the House of Representatives, without success. Recognizing an opportunity to acquire western territory, the Confederate States of America established the Territory of Arizona in 1862 and seated an Arizona delegate in its congress in Richmond, Virginia. A Confederate unit occupied Tucson, but U.S. General James E. Carleton proclaimed the territory to be under martial law, and on February 20, 1863, a Federal Territorial Act established a separate government for Arizona.

After the Civil War the population of the Arizona Territory grew slowly but steadily, partly because of the discovery of a rich silver lode at what would become the town of Tombstone. By 1890 more than 88,000 people were living in the territory, prompting an attempt by the territorial legislature to call a constitutional convention. This first attempt was thwarted by the territorial governor, but a second one led to a convention that met in 1891 in Phoenix, where the delegates struggled with major issues such as polygamy and free silver. Voters approved the convention's draft constitution by a margin of 5,440 to 2,280.

Admission to the Union did not follow swiftly. On June 20, 1910, however, Congress finally passed a statehood bill requiring that another constitutional convention be held, and the voters approved a new constitutional document on February 9, 1911. But an unusual provision of the enabling act required Congress and the president, or the president alone if Congress failed to act, to approve Arizona's constitution, and President William Howard Taft, objecting to a provision for the popular recall of judges, withheld his approval. He gave his assent only after a joint resolution of Congress made statehood contingent on the removal of the offending provision. On February 14, 1912, Arizona was admitted to the Union, and its revised constitution went into effect.

The Constitution

The drafters of the Arizona constitution looked to the constitutions of recently admitted states such as Idaho, Montana, Washington, and Wyoming to create a relatively liberal document, although it made no provision for women's suffrage as did the Wyoming model. Of average length, with approximately 28,900 words, the Arizona constitution has been amended 121 times as of January 1, 1998.

As with other state constitutions of the late nineteenth and early twentieth centuries, a major focus was curbing the abuses of corporate power. The 1912 constitution of Arizona and the 1889 constitutions of Montana and Wyoming, for example, abrogated the common law principle known as the "fellow-servant" rule, which often precluded workers from obtaining compensation for injuries on the job. Furthermore, both Arizona and Wyoming prohibited labor contracts that waived employers' responsibility for work-related injuries.

Preamble

The preamble to the Arizona constitution reads: "We, the people of the State of Arizona, grateful to almighty God for our liberties, do ordain this Constitution."

Fundamental Rights

Article II, Declaration of Rights, section 1, observes: "A frequent recurrence to fundamental principles is essential to the security of individual rights and the perpetuity of free government." Adds **section 2:** "All political power is inherent in the people, and governments derive their just powers from the consent of the governed, and are established to protect and maintain individual rights." Echoing the Declaration of Independence, it continues: "Governments are instituted among Men, deriving their just Powers from the Consent of the Governed."

Section 2.1, added in 1990, provides that the rights of crime victims include the rights "[t]o be treated with fairness, respect, and dignity, and to be free from intimidation, harassment, or abuse, throughout the criminal justice process; ... [t]o be informed, upon request, when the accused or convicted person is released from custody or has escaped; ... [t]o be present at and, upon request, to be informed of all criminal proceedings where the defendant has the right to be present; ... [t]o be heard at any proceeding involving a post-arrest release decision, a negotiated plea, and sentencing; ... [and] [t]o confer with the prosecution, after the crime against the victim has been charged, before trial or before any disposition of the case and to be informed of the disposition...." In *State ex rel. Hance v. Arizona Bd. of Pardons* (1993), the Arizona court of appeals stated that the linchpin of the Victims' Bill of Rights is the victims' right to be informed of their constitutional rights and that the state has an affirmative obligation to so inform them.

Sections 2.2 and **2.3,** respectively, provide, among other basic principles, that the U.S. Constitution is the supreme law of the land and that no person may be deprived of life, liberty, or property without due process of law. **Sections 2.4** through **2.10** guarantee the right of petition and peaceable assembly "for the common good"; freedom of speech and the press; the right of privacy; liberty of conscience and religious freedom; the subordination of the military to civil authority; free and equal elections; and the right to bear arms.

Section 24, one of several sections in article II that relate to the rights of the accused, guarantees that anyone accused of a crime has the right "to appear and defend in person, and by counsel, to demand the nature and cause of the accusation against him, to have a copy thereof, to testify in his own behalf, to meet the witnesses against him face to face"; to compel witnesses to testify on his or her behalf; to obtain "a speedy public trial by an impartial jury"; and to appeal. In *Miranda v. Arizona* (1966), the U.S. Supreme Court announced a far-reaching and important right of the accused under the Sixth Amendment (1791) of the U.S. Constitution: before questioning by officials of the state—police officers, for example—the accused must be informed that he or she has the right to remain silent, that statements made may be used against him or her, and that he or she has the right to have an attorney present, one retained by the accused or appointed by the court.

Section 32 states: "The provisions of this constitution are mandatory, unless by express words they are declared to be otherwise." The South Carolina constitution has a similar provision. According to **section 33,** "The enumeration in this constitution of certain rights shall not be construed to deny others retained by the people." **Section 34,** added by amendment in 1912, reads: "The state of Arizona and each municipal corporation within the state of Arizona shall have the right to engage in industrial pursuits."

Article XX, Ordinance, addresses further rights and responsibilities of citizens, among them: "**First.** Perfect toleration of religious sentiment shall be secured to every inhabitant of the state.... **Second.** Polygamous or plural marriages, or polygamous cohabitation, are forever prohibited within this state...." The article notes that the ordinance is made a part of the state constitution and its provisions "shall be irrevocable without the consent of the United States and the people of this state.... [N]o future constitutional amendment shall be made which in any manner changes or abrogates this ordinance in whole or in part without the consent of congress."

Article III, Distribution of Powers, states: "The powers of government of the State of Arizona shall be divided into three separate departments, the Legislative, the Executive, and the Judicial; and, except as provided in this Constitution, such departments shall be separate and distinct, and no one of such departments shall exercise the powers properly belonging to either of the others."

Article IV, Legislative Department, part 1, section 1, as amended in 1914, provides in part that the state's legislative authority is vested in a legislature consisting of a senate and a house of representatives. **Part 2, section 1,** as amended eight times between 1918 and 1972, states that the senate "shall be composed of one member elected from each of the thirty legislative districts established by the legislature, [and] [t]he house of representatives shall be composed of two members elected from each of [those districts]." Section 1 also directs the governor to call a special session of the legislature on the request of two-thirds of the members of each house.

Section 2 notes: "No person shall be a member of the legislature unless he shall be a citizen of the United States at the time of his election, nor unless he shall be at least twenty-five years of age, and shall have been a resident of Arizona at least three years and of the county from which he is elected at least one year before his election." **Section 4** generally disqualifies persons holding a state or federal office from also serving as members of the legislature, with the exception of positions in the state militia, notaries public, and postmasters "of the fourth class."

Sections 6 and **7,** respectively, exempt members of the legislature from arrest, except in cases of "treason, felony, and breach of the peace," as well as from "any civil process during the session of the legislature [and] for fifteen days next before the commencement of each session" and from liability "in any civil or criminal prosecution for words spoken in debate." Other procedural matters set forth in **sections 8** through **16** include authorizing each house to choose its own officers and judge its elections and the qualifications of its members; defining a quorum as a majority of the members of each house; granting each house the power to punish its members for disorderly conduct and expel a member by a vote of two-thirds of the members; requiring, except in the case of emergency, every bill to be "read on three different days" and every measure when finally passed by a "majority of all members elected to each house" to "be presented to the governor for his approval or disapproval"; and expressly permitting any members of the legislature "to protest and have the reasons of his protest entered on the journal" of the respective house.

Section 18 states: "The legislature shall direct by law in what manner and in what courts suits may be brought against the state." **Section 19** prohibits local and special laws in a number of specific instances and "[w]hen a general law can be made applicable." In *Tucson Elec. Power Co. v. Apache County* (1996), the Arizona court of appeals announced three criteria for "general laws": there must be a rational basis for classification of those citizens affected; classification must be by population, geography, or time limitation; and classification must be elastic, allowing members to be classified differently as their circumstances change.

Section 21, as amended in 1992, restricts state senators and representatives from serving "more than four consecutive terms in that office."

Executive Branch

Article V, Executive Department, section 1, was amended in 1948, 1968, 1988, and 1992. **Section 1(A)** states: "The executive department shall consist of the governor, secretary of state, state treasurer, attorney general, and superintendent of public instruction . . . ," who are elected for four-year terms and are limited to two consecutive terms. "The officers of the executive department during their terms of office," notes **section 1(C),** "shall perform such duties as are prescribed by the constitution and as may be provided by law." The fact that four constitutional officers of the executive branch are named in addition to the governor and that their duties, according to **sections 1** and **9,** may be changed as "provided by law" or as "prescribed by law" augments the legislature's power vis-à-vis the executive branch. In this respect the Arizona constitution is similar to the Minnesota constitution and some others.

Section 2 requires persons seeking constitutionally defined executive department offices to be "not less than twenty-five years" of age, a citizen of the United States "for ten years next preceding his election," and a citizen of Arizona "for five years next preceding his election."

Section 3 makes the governor the "commander-in-chief of the military forces of the state, except when such forces shall be called into the service of the United States." **Section 4** requires the governor to "take care that the laws be faithfully executed" and empowers the office holder to "require information in writing from officers in the executive department upon any subject relating to the duties of their respective offices" and to "convene the legislature in extraordinary session." Under **section 5,** the governor is also vested with authority "to grant reprieves, commutations, and pardons, after conviction for all offenses except treason and cases of impeachment, upon such conditions and with such restrictions and limitations as may be provided by law."

Section 6, as amended in 1948 and 1968, provides in part: "In the event of the death of the governor, or his resignation, removal from office, or permanent disability . . . the secretary of state, if holding [office] by election, shall succeed to the office of governor until his successor shall be elected and shall qualify." Because the state has no lieutenant governor, the secretary of state also performs the duties of the governor in case of the chief executive's impeachment or absence from the state. In *McClusky v. Hunter* (1928), the Arizona supreme court held that when the governor is absent from the state, the acts of the secretary of state are as valid and binding as though they had been performed by the governor.

Section 7 stipulates that the governor has five days in which to veto legislation but that the veto may be overridden "by an aye and nay vote on roll call of two-thirds of the members elected to each house." If the legislature by its final adjournment prevents the governor from returning a bill, "it shall be filed with his objections in the office of the secretary of state within ten days after such adjournment (Sundays excepted), or become a law. ..." The governor is granted item veto power in the case of appropriations bills, but the veto power "shall not extend to any bill passed by the legislature and referred to the people for adoption or rejection." **Section 8** empowers the governor to fill vacancies in offices not otherwise provided for by the constitution or law.

Article VI, Judicial Department, was completely revised in 1960. **Section 1** declares: "The judicial power shall be vested in an integrated judicial department consisting of a supreme court, such intermediate appellate courts as may be provided by law, a superior court, such courts inferior to the superior court as may be provided by law, and justice courts." **Section 2** prescribes that "[t]he supreme court shall consist of not less than five justices ... [and it] shall sit in accordance with rules adopted by it, either in banc or in divisions of not less than three justices, but the court shall not declare any law unconstitutional except when sitting in banc." Section 2 continues: "The court shall be open at all times, except on nonjudicial days, for the transaction of business."

Section 3, as amended in 1974, states: "The supreme court shall have administrative supervision over all the courts of the state. The chief justice shall be elected by the justices of the supreme court from one of their number for a term of five years, and may be reelected for like terms." A vice chief justice, a position found in the constitutions of several other states including Oklahoma, is similarly elected "for a term determined by the court." The chief justice, or in his or her absence the vice chief justice, "shall exercise the court's administrative supervision over all the courts of the state." **Section 4,** as amended in 1974, generally limits the term of justices to six years, although **section 37** provides: "Each justice or judge ... appointed [by the governor] shall initially hold office for a term ending sixty days following the next regular general election after the expiration of a term of two years in office."

Section 5 grants to the supreme court the following powers: "**1.** Original jurisdiction of habeas corpus, and quo warranto, mandamus, injunction and other extraordinary writs to state officers. **2.** Original and exclusive jurisdiction ... [in] causes between counties concerning disputed boundaries. ... **3.** Appellate jurisdiction in all actions and proceedings except civil and criminal actions originating in courts not of record, unless the action involves the validity of a tax, impost, assessment, toll, statute or municipal ordinance. **4.** Power to issue injunctions and writs of mandamus, review, prohibition, habeas corpus, certiorari [and all other writs]. **5.** Power to make rules relative to all procedural matters in any court. **6.** Such other jurisdiction as may be provided by law."

Section 6 provides that "[a] justice of the supreme court shall be a person of good moral character and admitted to the practice of law in and a resident of the state of Arizona for ten years next preceding his taking office." **Section 7** empowers the supreme court to "appoint a clerk of the court and assistants thereto who shall serve at its pleasure ... [and] an administrative director and staff to serve at its pleasure to assist the chief justice in discharging his administrative duties." Other sections provide for intermediate appellate courts and superior courts in each county.

Section 20, as amended in 1974, generally prescribes that "justices and judges of courts of record be retired upon reaching the age of seventy." **Section 37,** added in 1974 and as amended in 1992, requires that a "vacancy in the office of a justice or a judge be filled by appointment by the governor without regard to political affiliation...." In the case of a justice or judge of an intermediate appellate court of record, such appointment is to be made from a list of "names of not less than three persons nominated to fill such vacancy, no more than two of whom shall be members of the same political party unless there are more than four such nominees" submitted to the governor by a nonpartisan commission on appellate court appointments.

Article VI.I, added in 1970, creates a commission on judicial conduct and gives the procedures for disqualifying, suspending or removing, and forcing the retirement of a judge. In *Matter of Marquardt* (1989), the Arizona supreme court held that the conviction of a judge for possession of less than nine-tenths of a gram of marijuana did not warrant summary removal from office, especially when his prior record was unblemished.

Impeachment

Article VIII, Removal from Office, part 2, section 1, gives the house of representatives the sole power of impeachment, by a "concurrence of a majority of all the members." **Section 2** directs that the trial be held in the senate, with a "concurrence of two-thirds of the senators elected" necessary for conviction and provides for the impeachment of the "governor and other state and judicial officers, except justices of courts not of record ... for high crimes, misdemeanors, or malfeasance in office...."

Direct Democracy

Arizona has some of the earliest constitutional provisions implementing procedures for direct democracy in response to voter dissatisfaction with the legislature. It is one of eighteen states with initiative provisions.

Article IV, Legislative Department, part 1, section 1(1), as amended in 1914, states in part that "the people reserve the power to propose laws and amendments to the constitution and to enact or reject such laws and amendments at the polls, independently of the legislature...." Under **section 1(2),** "ten per centum of the qualified electors shall have the right to propose any measure, and fifteen per centum shall have the right to propose any amendment to the constitution." **Section 1(3)** stipulates that with certain exceptions "the legislature, or five per centum of the qualified electors, may order the submission to the people at the polls of any measure, item, section, or part of any measure, enacted by the legislature...." **Section 1(4)** requires that initiative petitions be filed with the secretary of state "not less than four months preceding the date of the election at which the measures so proposed are to be voted upon," and referendum petitions "shall be filed with the secretary of state not more than ninety days after the final adjournment of the session of the legislature which shall have passed the measure to which the referendum is applied."

Section 1(5) specifies that any measure or amendment referred to the people becomes law "when approved by a majority of the votes cast thereon and upon proclamation of the governor …," but **section 1(6)** notes that "[t]he veto power of the governor, or the power of the legislature, to repeal or amend, shall not extend to initiative or referendum measures approved by a majority vote of the qualified electors."

Article VIII, Removal from Office, part 1, section 1, as amended in 1912, provides: "Every public officer in the state of Arizona, holding an elective office, either by election or appointment, is subject to recall from such office by the qualified electors of the electoral district from which candidates are elected … [and] [s]uch number of said electors as shall equal twenty-five per centum of the number of votes cast at the last preceding general election for all of the candidates for the office held by such officer, may by petition, which shall be known as a recall petition, demand his recall."

In *Adams v. Bolin* (1952), the Arizona supreme court declared that the effect of Arizona's direct democracy provisions is that the state's legislative authority is vested in the legislature and the people and may be exercised by both; therefore, the legislature had authority to submit to the people a referendum to repeal a law enacted by the initiative method that had received only a majority of the votes cast and not a majority of the votes of all qualified voters.

Article XII, Counties, section 1, provides: "Each county of the state, now or hereafter organized, shall be a body politic and corporate." **Section 5,** as amended in 1992, states that any county with a population of "more than five hundred thousand persons" may seek and obtain a county charter, which gives such counties certain powers, including the power, noted in **section 7(C)(1),** to "[tax] on a countywide basis to provide services on a countywide basis…."

Local Government

Article IX, Public Debt, Revenue, and Taxation, section 1, declares: "The power of taxation shall never be surrendered, suspended, or contracted away. All taxes shall be uniform upon the same class of property within the territorial limits of the authority levying the tax, and shall be levied and collected for public purposes only."

Taxation and Finance

Section 3 in part mandates a balanced budget: "The Legislature shall provide by law for an annual tax sufficient, with other sources of revenue, to defray the necessary ordinary expenses of the State for each fiscal year. And for the purpose of paying the State debt, if there be any, the Legislature shall provide for levying an annual tax sufficient to pay the annual interest and the principal of such debt within twenty-five years from the final passage of the law creating the debt."

Article X, State and School Lands, addresses the holding and sale or lease of lands by the state in trust. **Article XI, Education, section 1,** mandates: "The legislature shall enact such laws as shall provide for the establishment and maintenance of a general and uniform public school system." **Section 2** directs that "general conduct and supervision of the public school system shall be vested in a state board of education, a state superintendent

Education

of public instruction, county school superintendents, and such governing boards for the state institutions as may be provided by law."

Official Language

Article XX, Ordinance, specifies in part: "**Eighth.** The ability to read, write, speak, and understand the English language sufficiently well to conduct the duties of the office without the aid of an interpreter, shall be a necessary qualification for all state officers and members of the state legislature."

Article XXVIII, English as the Official Language, added in 1988, declares English to be the state's official language for "the ballot, the public schools and all government functions and actions." Under **section 4,** "A person who resides in or does business in this state shall have standing to bring suit to enforce this article in a court of record of the state."

Amendment Procedures

Article XXI, Mode of Amending, section 1, provides that amendments to the constitution "may be proposed in either house of the legislature, or by initiative petition signed by a number of qualified electors equal to fifteen per centum of the total number of votes for all candidates for governor at the last preceding general election." After approval by "a majority of the members elected to each ... house" or after electors file an amendment together with a petition presenting the required signatures with the secretary of state, the amendment is placed on the ballot at the next general election, unless the legislature requests a special election. A proposed amendment becomes a part of the constitution if "a majority of the qualified electors voting thereon shall approve [it]...."

Section 2 states that a convention to alter, revise, or amend the constitution may be called by the legislature, if "laws providing for such convention shall first be approved by the people on a referendum vote at a regular or special election...." Proposals of the convention must "be approved by the majority of the electors voting thereon" at a general or special election.

Arkansas became the twenty-fifth state of the United States on June 15, 1836. Little Rock is the capital of the "Land of Opportunity." Some 53,182 square miles in area, Arkansas is bordered by Missouri on the north, Tennessee and Mississippi on the east, Louisiana on the south, and Oklahoma on the west. Arkansas ranks thirty-third among the states in population with approximately 2.5 million residents. The state's principal industries include manufacturing, agriculture, tourism, and forestry; among its chief crops are soybeans, rice, cotton, and tomatoes.

Government: The governor and lieutenant governor are elected separately for four-year terms and are limited to two terms. The legislature, called the general assembly, is made up of thirty-five senators, elected for four-year terms and limited to two terms, and 100 members of the house of representatives, elected for two-year terms and limited to three terms. The supreme court is composed of a chief justice and six additional judges, all of whom are elected for eight-year terms.

Dates of Constitutions: 1836, 1861, 1864, 1868, and 1874

In the summer of 1541, the Spanish explorer Hernando de Soto crossed the Mississippi River, most likely a few miles south of the present-day town of Helena, and remained in the region that would become the state of Arkansas until the spring of 1542. In 1673 the Frenchmen Louis Joliet and Father Jacques Marquette set out to explore this region but turned back at the mouth of the Arkansas River, warned by the Quapaw, or Arkansas, people of hostile tribes farther south. However, just nine years later, in 1682, Robert Cavelier, sieur de La Salle, met with Quapaw villagers and claimed the lands west of the Mississippi for France.

In 1686 Henri de Tonti, another Frenchman, established the first European settlement in the Arkansas territory near the confluence of the Arkansas and Mississippi Rivers. Called Arkansas Post, this settlement became an active trading center for indigenous peoples and English settlers from the east. To encourage more permanent settlements, France designated Arkansas Post the administrative capital of the Upper Louisiana Territory in 1721. Still, immigration was slow, and in 1762 France ceded its territory west of the Mississippi to Spain.

Spain did little to extend its colonization into the territory, and in 1800 it ceded the trans-Mississippi region back to France. In 1803, under the terms of the Louisiana Purchase, engineered by President Thomas Jefferson, the lands became a part of the United States. According to a 1799 Spanish census, only 368 white residents lived in the Arkansas region, but after the American flag was raised over Arkansas Post in the spring of 1804, the population began to increase rapidly. An act of Congress in March of that year provided for the governance of the trans-Mississippi territory, treating the local indigenous tribes as sovereign nations.

In 1818 the Quapaw ceded their lands between the Red and Arkansas Rivers to the United States, and Arkansas, a part of the Missouri Territory since 1812, became a separate territory by an act of Congress on March 2, 1819. An 1820 census reported a population of 14,276 in the territory, but by 1835 the number had grown to more than 50,000. In 1833 a delegate from the Arkansas Territory proposed a statehood enabling act in the House of

Representatives, but statehood supporters—aware that having a written constitution had paved the way to statehood for Kentucky in 1792 and Maine in 1820—urged the creation of a constitutional convention before action by Congress. The Louisiana Purchase treaty in any case obligated the U.S. government to grant statehood to any territory organized within the lands of the purchase when the residents had established the basic instruments for self-government. The Arkansas territorial legislature, therefore, called for a convention to meet in Little Rock on January 4, 1836.

Arkansas's first constitution, which was delivered to the U.S. secretary of state on March 8, 1836, became effective on June 15, 1836, when Arkansas was admitted to the Union. Modeled closely on the U.S. Constitution, the 1836 constitution was concise and adaptable. It provided for the popular election of the governor, legislators, and county officers but stipulated that other officials of the state's executive branch and judges were to be selected by a joint legislative session. It also recognized slavery. Arkansas's secession from the Union and alignment with the Confederacy necessitated a second constitution, enacted in 1861.

Federal troops occupied Little Rock on September 10, 1863, and a new constitution was framed by a convention, including some delegates designated by the military government, meeting there in January 1864. President Abraham Lincoln personally endorsed the convention's effort by letter, and in March 1864 the new constitution was overwhelmingly approved by the voters, 12,177 to 266. Congress deemed the southern states not yet capable of managing their internal affairs, so on March 2, 1867, as part of the Reconstruction Acts, the governments of Arkansas and nine other states were voided. This legislation created five military jurisdictions, with Arkansas and Mississippi designated as the fourth district. Under the military government, all blacks were enfranchised and all ex-Confederates were disenfranchised.

A fourth constitutional convention meeting in Little Rock in 1868 produced a new document designed to undermine white supremacy and the political leadership of Confederate sympathizers. It was approved by the voters, and Arkansas was readmitted to the Union on June 22, 1868, although Congress had to override a veto by President Andrew Johnson to do so. In an attempt to counteract the effects of Reconstruction, a constitutional convention meeting in Little Rock from July 14 to September 7, 1874, produced a new constitution that, among other things, focused on taxation, elections, and patronage. It was approved by the voters on October 13, 1874, and went into effect on October 30.

The Constitution

The 1874 Arkansas constitution, written at a time when the state consisted of mostly rural communities and rooted in the rejection of the post–Civil War Reconstruction government administered by the Republican Party, is sometimes viewed as anti-government. Although three constitutional conventions have been called since then to rewrite the document and modernize Arkansas's organic law, these attempts have been unsuccessful. Eighty-one amendments have been adopted since 1874, but, as with the Massachusetts constitution, these have not been fully integrated with the original text of the document.

Somewhat longer than average at approximately 40,700 words, the 1874 Arkansas constitution as of January 1, 1998, contains only eighty-four amendments; eight superseded amendments and five other amendments adopted since statehood are not included.

Nine new amendments, three proposed by the legislature and six by initiative, were scheduled to be voted on in 1998. The document creates a relatively typical structure of state government: a plural executive branch headed by a governor elected for a four-year term; a bicameral legislature with the members of the upper house elected for four years and members of the lower house for two years; and an elected judiciary. Like the constitutions of several other southern states, including South Carolina, the Arkansas document requires belief in "a God" to hold any state office or to be considered a competent witness in court.

The preamble to the 1874 Arkansas constitution proclaims: "We, the people of the State of Arkansas, grateful to Almighty God for the privilege of choosing our own form of government, for our civil and religious liberty, and desiring to perpetuate its blessings and secure the same to our selves and posterity, do ordain and establish this Constitution."

Preamble

Article 2, Declaration of Rights, section 1, declares: "All political power is inherent in the people and government is instituted for their protection, security and benefit; and they have the right to alter, reform or abolish the same in such manner as they may think proper." According to **section 2,** "All men are created equally free and independent, and have certain inherent and inalienable rights, amongst which are those of enjoying and defending life and liberty; of acquiring, possessing and protecting property and reputation, and of pursuing their own happiness. To secure these rights governments are instituted among men, deriving their just powers from the consent of the governed." The language of this section owes an obvious debt to the Declaration of Independence. **Section 3** asserts: "The equality of all persons before the law is recognized, and ever shall remain inviolate; nor shall any citizen ever be deprived of any right, privilege or immunity, nor exempted from any burden or duty, on account of race, color or previous condition."

Fundamental Rights

Sections 4, 5, and **6,** respectively, guarantee the right to assemble and to petition the government; the right to bear arms; and liberty of the press and speech, provided that there is responsibility for abuse of the right and that truth, good motives, and justifiable ends are absolute defenses to libel. **Section 7,** as amended in 1928, states in part: "The right of trial by jury shall remain inviolate...." **Sections 8, 9,** and **10** extend certain rights to those accused of crimes, including prohibition against self-incrimination and double jeopardy, a guarantee of due process of law and reasonable bail, and an assurance of a "speedy and public trial by impartial jury of the county in which the crime shall have been committed." An amendment in 1936 provides in part: "All offenses heretofore required to be prosecuted by indictment may be prosecuted either by indictment by a grand jury or information filed by the Prosecuting Attorney." **Sections 11** and **12** limit the suspension of the writ of habeas corpus and the laws of the state.

Section 13 states: "Every person is entitled to a certain remedy in the laws for all injuries or wrongs he may receive in his person, property or character; he ought to obtain justice freely, and without purchase, completely, and without denial, promptly and without delay, conformably to the laws." A number of state constitutions, including those of New York and Rhode Island, have similar provisions. **Section 14** addresses treason in language similar to that in the U.S. Constitution. **Sections 15, 16,** and **17,** respectively, prohibit unreasonable searches and seizures; imprisonment for debt; and bills of attainder, ex post facto laws, and laws "impairing the obligation of contracts." **Article 19, Miscellaneous Provisions, section 13,** prescribes that the maximum rate of interest "on any contract ... shall not exceed five percent (5%) per annum above the Federal Reserve Discount Rate at the time of the contract." In *McInnis v. Cooper Communities, Inc.* (1981), however, the Arkansas supreme court held that an act of Congress could suspend the state's usury laws as expressed in article 19, section 13.

Article 2, section 18, mandates that the legislature "shall not grant to any citizen or class of citizens privileges or immunities which upon the same terms shall not equally belong to all citizens." **Section 19** states: "Perpetuities and monopolies are contrary to the genius of a republic, and shall not be allowed; nor shall any hereditary emoluments, privileges or honors ever be granted or conferred in this State." **Section 20** provides: "No distinction shall ever be made by law between resident aliens and citizens in regard to the possession, enjoyment or descent of property." **Section 21** guarantees to the accused "the judgment of his peers [and] the law of the land" and prohibits exile from the state "under any circumstances."

Section 22 proclaims that the right of property "is before and higher than any constitutional sanction" and mandates compensation for private property "taken, appropriated or damaged for public use." **Section 23** notes: "The State's ancient right of eminent domain and of taxation is herein fully and expressly conceded; and the General Assembly may delegate the taxing power, with the necessary restriction, to the State's subordinate political and municipal corporations to the extent of providing for their existence, maintenance and well being, but no further." **Section 28** provides, as does the Mississippi constitution: "All lands in this State are declared to be allodial; and feudal tenures of every description, with all their incidents, are prohibited."

Section 24 guarantees religious liberty, and **section 25** states: "Religion, morality and knowledge being essential to good government, the General Assembly shall enact suitable laws to protect every religious denomination in the peaceable enjoyment of its own mode of public worship." **Section 26** prohibits religious tests for voting, holding office, or being a competent witness, but **article 19, Miscellaneous Provisions, section 1,** declares: "No person who denies the being of a God shall hold any office in the civil departments of this State, nor be competent to testify as a witness in any court." In *Flora v. White* (1982), the U.S. Court of Appeals held that two atheists failed to prove that they suffered an injury sufficient enough to give them standing in court to challenge this provision.

Article 2, section 27, prohibits slavery and involuntary servitude, "except as a punishment for crime," and also prohibits standing armies in peacetime; it further limits the quartering of soldiers on private property and subordinates the military to civil power. A 1944 amendment states: "No person shall be denied employment because of membership in or affiliation with or resignation from a labor union, or because of refusal to join or affiliate with a labor union...."

Article 4, Departments, section 1, declares: "The powers of the government of the State of Arkansas shall be divided into three distinct departments, each of them to be confided to a separate body of magistracy, to wit: Those which are legislative to one, those which are executive to another, and those which are judicial to another." **Section 2** states: "No person, or collection of persons, being one of these departments, shall exercise any power belonging to either of the others, except in the instances hereinafter expressly directed or permitted." The language of article 4 is similar to that found in the Mississippi constitution regarding the separation of powers.

Exercising judicial deference to the legislature, the Arkansas supreme court in *Mears v. Hall* (1978) declared that if a constitutional provision is reasonably subject to more than one meaning the legislature's choice is conclusive. Under **article 5, Legislative Department, section 20,** proclaims: "The State of Arkansas shall never be made defendant in any of her courts."

Article 5, Legislative Department, section 1, as amended in 1920, places legislative power in a general assembly encompassing a senate and a house of representatives. **Section 2,** as amended in 1992, specifies: "**(a)** The Arkansas House of Representatives shall consist of members to be chosen every second year by the qualified electors of the several counties. No member of [that body] may serve more than three such two year terms." **Section 3,** as amended in 1992, now reads: "The Arkansas Senate shall consist of members to be chosen every four years by the qualified voters of the several districts. No member of [that body] may serve more than two such four year terms. At the first session of the Senate the Senators shall divide themselves into two classes by lot, and the first class shall hold their places for two years only, after which all shall be elected for four years."

Section 4 stipulates: "No person shall be a Senator or Representative who, at the time of his election, is not a citizen of the United States, nor any one who has not been for two years next preceding his election a resident of the State, and for one year next preceding his election a resident of the county or district whence he may be chosen. Senators shall be at least twenty-five years of age and Representatives at least twenty-one years of age." **Section 7** declares certain officers of the state and federal government to be ineligible for a seat in the legislature but exempts militia officers, justices of the peace, postmasters, officers of public schools, and notaries. **Sections 8** and **9** make ineligible for office certain persons who are responsible for public funds until they "have accounted for and paid over all sums for which [they] may have been liable" as well as persons "convicted of embezzlement of public money, bribery, forgery or other infamous crime...."

Section 11 provides: "Each house shall appoint its own officers, and shall be sole judge of the qualifications, returns and elections of its own members. A majority of all the members elected to each house shall constitute a quorum ..., but a smaller number may adjourn from day to day, and compel the attendance of absent members...." **Section 12**

empowers each house "to determine the rules of its proceedings; ... punish its members or other persons for contempt or disorderly behavior in its presence; enforce obedience to its process; [and] ... protect its members against violence or offers of bribes or private solicitations...." Each house may expel members by a "concurrence of two-thirds" of its members, and a "member expelled for corruption shall not thereafter be eligible to either house...."

Section 15 states that general assembly members "shall, in all cases except treason, felony and breach or surety of the peace, be privileged from arrest during their attendance at the sessions of their respective houses, and in going to and returning from the same; and for any speech or debate in either house they shall not be questioned in any other place." According to **section 18,** "Each house, at the beginning of every regular session of the General Assembly, and whenever a vacancy may occur, shall elect from its members a presiding officer to be styled, respectively, the President of the Senate and the Speaker of the House of Representatives...."

Section 21 stipulates: "No law shall be passed except by bill, and no bill shall be altered or amended on its passage through either house as to change its original purpose." **Section 22** requires that "[e]very bill shall be read at length on three different days in each house, unless the rules be suspended by two-thirds of the house, when the same may be read a second or third time on the same day; and no bill shall become a law unless on its final passage the vote be taken by yeas and nays, the names of the persons voting for and against the same be entered on the journal, and a majority of each house be recorded thereon as voting in its favor." Under **section 23**, "No law shall be revived, amended, or the provisions thereof extended or conferred by reference to its title only; but so much thereof as is revived, amended, extended or conferred shall be reenacted and published at length." A 1926 constitutional amendment regarding special laws stipulates: "The General Assembly shall not pass any local or special act. This amendment shall not prohibit the repeal of local or special acts."

Section 27 prohibits extra compensation or the payment of claims not provided for by preexisting laws without a "bill passed by two-thirds of the members elected to each branch of the General Assembly." **Section 30** provides: "The general appropriation bill shall embrace nothing but appropriations for the ordinary expense of the executive, legislative and judicial departments ...; all other appropriations shall be made by separate bills, each embracing but one subject." **Section 34** requires that "[n]o new bill shall be introduced into either house during the last three days of the session."

[Section 37], added by amendment in 1934, states: "Not less than a majority of the members of each House of the General Assembly may enact a law." **[Section 38],** also added by amendment in 1934, addresses rates of taxation statewide: "None of the rates for property, excise, privilege or personal taxes, now levied shall be increased by the General Assembly except after the approval of the qualified electors voting thereon at an election, or in case of emergency, by the votes of three-fourths of the members elected to each House...."

Article 6, Executive Department, section 1, as amended in 1992, declares: "**(a)** The Executive Department of this State shall consist of a Governor, Lieutenant Governor, Secretary of State, Treasurer of State, Auditor of State, Attorney General, and Commissioner of State Lands, all of whom shall keep their offices at the seat of government, and hold their offices for the term of four years, and until their successors are elected and qualified. **(b)** No elected officials of the Executive Department of this State may serve in the same office more than two such four year terms." **Section 2,** as amended in 1914, provides in part: "The executive power shall be vested in a Governor. . . ." **Section 5** indicates that the governor must be a citizen of the United States who is at least thirty years old and has been a resident of the state for seven years.

Section 6 states: "The Governor shall be commander-in-chief of the military and naval forces of this State, except when they shall be called into the actual service of the United States." **Section 7** notes that the governor "may require information in writing from the officers of the executive department on any subject relating to the duties of their respective offices, and shall see that the laws are faithfully executed." **Section 8** directs the governor to "give to the General Assembly from time to time, and at the close of his official term to the next General Assembly, information by message concerning the condition and government of the State, and recommend for their consideration such measures as he may deem expedient."

Section 15 provides that bills passed by both houses of the general assembly "shall be presented to the Governor; if he approves it, he shall sign it; but if he shall not approve it, he shall return it, with his objections, to the house in which it originated. . . ." If "a majority of the whole number elected to" each house of the legislature agree to pass a bill, "it shall be a law." **Section 16** states that "[e]very order or resolution in which the concurrence of both houses of the General Assembly may be necessary, except on questions of adjournment," must also be approved by the governor; if not approved, it must be repassed, as in the case of a bill. **Section 17** grants the governor item veto power in "any bill making appropriation of money," but items vetoed may be restored if repassed, as in the case of bills.

Section 18 provides in part: "In all criminal and penal cases, except in those of treason and impeachment, the Governor shall have power to grant reprieves, commutations of sentence and pardons after conviction; and to remit fines and forfeitures under such rules and regulations as shall be prescribed by law." **Section 19** authorizes the governor "by proclamation, on extraordinary occasions [to] convene the General Assembly at the seat of government. . . ." **Section 20** grants the governor the power to adjourn the two houses "to a time not beyond the day of their next meeting," if they cannot agree to a time of adjournment. A 1938 amendment provides: "Vacancies in the office of United States Senator, and in all elective state, district, circuit, county, and township offices except those of Lieutenant Governor, Member of the General Assembly and Representative in the Congress of the United States, shall be filled by appointment by the Governor."

Sections 2 through **6,** as amended in 1914, address the position of lieutenant governor. **Section 2** requires that the lieutenant governor be chosen "at the same time and for the same term [as the governor],” although they are elected on separate tickets. **Section 4** notes that in case of the governor's impeachment, removal from office, death, inability to discharge the powers and duties of the office, resignation, or absence from the state, “the powers and duties of the office, shall devolve upon the Lieutenant Governor for the residue of the term, or until the disability shall cease.” According to **section 5,** the lieutenant governor must have the same qualifications as the governor; “[h]e shall be President of the Senate, but shall have only a casting vote therein in case of a tie vote.”

Judicial Branch

Article 7, Judicial Department, section 1, vests judicial power “in one Supreme Court, in circuit courts, in county and probate courts, and in justices of the peace. The General Assembly may also vest such jurisdiction as may be deemed necessary in municipal corporation courts, courts of common pleas, where established, and, when deemed expedient, may establish separate courts of chancery.” **Sections 2** and **3,** as amended in 1924, provide: “The Supreme Court shall be composed of five judges, one of whom shall be styled Chief Justice and elected as such, any three of whom shall constitute a quorum.... Provided, if it should hereafter become necessary to increase the number of judges of the Supreme Court, the Legislature may provide for two additional judges and may also provide for the court sitting in divisions under such regulations as may be prescribed by law; provided, further, that ... in all cases where the construction of the Constitution is involved, the cause shall be heard by the court in banc....” Currently the Arkansas supreme court consists of seven members.

Section 6 requires that “[a] judge of the Supreme Court shall be at least thirty years of age, of good moral character, and learned in the law; a citizen of the United States and two years a resident of the State, and who has been a practicing lawyer eight years, or whose service upon the bench of any court of record, when added to the time he may have practiced law, shall be equal to eight years. The judges of the Supreme Court shall be elected ... and shall hold their offices during the term of eight years....” The elections are staggered.

Section 4, as amended in 1938, states: “The Supreme Court, except in cases otherwise provided by this Constitution, shall have appellate jurisdiction only, which shall be co-extensive with the State, under such restrictions as may from time to time be prescribed by law. It shall have a general superintending control over all inferior courts of law and equity; and, in aid of its appellate and supervisory jurisdiction, it shall have power to issue writs of error and supersedeas, certiorari, habeas corpus, prohibition, mandamus and quo warranto, and, other remedial writs.... Its judges shall be conservators of the peace ... and shall severally have power to issue any of the aforesaid writs.” In *Miller v. State* (1977), the Arkansas supreme court declared that its rule-making authority is an inherent power of the judicial branch of the government.

Section 20 prescribes that “[n]o judge or justice shall preside in the trial of any cause in ... which he may be interested, or where either of the parties shall be connected with him by consanguinity or affinity, within such degree as may be prescribed by law; or in which he may have been of counsel or have presided in any inferior court.” A 1988 constitutional amendment created a judicial discipline and disability commission that "may initiate, and shall receive and investigate, complaints concerning misconduct of all justices and judges, and requests and suggestions for leave or involuntary disability retirement."

By amendment in 1978, the legislature was "empowered to create and establish a Court of Appeals and divisions thereof ... [with] such appellate jurisdiction as the Supreme Court shall by rule determine, and shall be subject to the general superintending control of the Supreme Court."

Article 15, Impeachment and Address, section 1, provides: "The Governor and all State officers, judges of the supreme [court, and other judicial officers] shall be liable to impeachment for high crimes and misdemeanors and gross misconduct in office, but the judgment shall go no further than removal from office and disqualification to hold any office ... under this State. An impeachment whether successful or not, shall be no bar to an indictment." According to **section 2,** "The House of Representatives shall have the sole power of impeachment. All impeachments shall be tried by the Senate." A two-thirds vote of the members is required for conviction.

Impeachment

Section 3 adds: "The Governor, upon the joint address of two-thirds of the members elected to each house of the General Assembly, for good cause, may remove the Auditor, Treasurer, Secretary of the State, Attorney General, judges of the supreme [court and other judicial officers]."

Amendment 7, Initiative and Referendum, added in 1920, provides that "the people reserve to themselves the power to propose legislative measures, laws and amendments to the Constitution, and to enact or reject the same at the polls independent of the General Assembly; and also reserve the power, at their own option, to approve or reject at the polls any entire act or any item of an appropriation bill."

Direct Democracy

Article 12, Municipal and Private Corporations, section 3, grants the general assembly authority to provide, "by general laws, for the organization of cities (which may be classified) and incorporated towns, and restrict their powers of taxation, assessment, borrowing money and contracting debts, so as to prevent the abuse of such power."

Local Government

Article 14, Education, section 1, as amended in 1968, notes in part: "Intelligence and virtue being the safeguards of liberty and the bulwark of a free and good government, the State shall ever maintain a general, suitable and efficient system of free public schools and shall adopt all suitable means to secure to the people the advantages and opportunities of education."

Education

Article 2, Declaration of Rights, section 27, as amended in 1988, denies funds "to pay for any abortion, except to save the mother's life," noting that "[t]he policy of Arkansas is to protect the life of every unborn child from conception until birth, to the extent permitted by the Federal Constitution."

Abortion

Amendment Procedures   **Article 19, Miscellaneous Provisions, section 22,** authorizes in part: "Either branch of the General Assembly at a regular session thereof may propose amendments to this Constitution, and, if the same be agreed to by a majority of all members elected to each house, such proposed amendments shall be entered on the journals [of each house] with the yeas and nays, and published in at least one newspaper in each county, where a newspaper is published, for six months immediately preceding the next general election for Senators and Representatives, at which time the same shall be submitted to the electors of the State for approval or rejection; and if a majority of the electors voting at such election adopt such amendments the same shall become a part of this Constitution, but no more than three amendments shall be proposed or submitted at the same time." The constitutions of several other states restrict the number of amendments that may be presented to the voters at the same election; one of these, Kansas, allows up to five amendments to be submitted at once.

The Arkansas constitution, as amended in 1920, also affirms that "the people reserve to themselves the power to propose . . . amendments to the constitution." Ten percent of legal voters may "propose a Constitutional Amendment by initiative petition. . . ."

On September 9, 1850, California became the thirty-first state of the United States. Its capital is Sacramento. California, nicknamed the "Golden State," is some 163,707 square miles in area and is bordered by Oregon on the north, Nevada and Arizona on the east, Mexico on the south, and the Pacific Ocean on the west. With approximately 32 million inhabitants, California ranks first among the states in population. Its principal industries include agriculture, entertainment, and manufacturing; its chief crops are grapes, cotton, flowers, and oranges.

CALIFORNIA

Government: The governor and lieutenant governor are elected separately for four-year terms and are limited to two terms. The legislature consists of a senate, which has forty members, and an assembly, which has eighty members. Senators are elected for four-year terms and are limited to two terms; one-half are elected every two years. Assembly members are elected for two-year terms and are limited to three terms. The supreme court is composed of a chief justice and six associate justices initially appointed by the governor and confirmed by a commission on judicial appointments; at the next general election they stand for election to a twelve-year term.

Dates of Constitutions: 1849 and 1879

Fifty years after Christopher Columbus discovered the New World, Spanish explorers landed on the coast of California and found the region inhabited by many peoples, including the Modocs, Yumans, and Klamaths. On learning that the native population lacked agricultural skills and metals, the Spanish colonial government in Mexico quickly lost interest in the region. In 1579 the English buccaneer Sir Francis Drake, on his voyage from London around the world, refurbished his ship, the *Golden Hind*, near San Francisco Bay.

California, which was named by the Spanish explorers Hernán Cortéz and Fortún Ximenez for an island in an early-sixteenth-century novel by Garciá Ordóñez de Montalvo, *Las Sergas de Esplandián,* attracted little attention until after the Seven Years War in Europe, which ended in 1763. José de Gálvez, on the orders of Charles III of Spain, began planning the colonization of California using Roman Catholic missions to convert and educate the indigenous peoples. News of Russian settlers advancing from the north spurred him to enlist the help of Father Junipero Serra, a Franciscan missionary, in the colonization effort. By 1769 Spain had occupied California, and the same year Father Serra established a mission at San Diego de Alcala. Spanish administration of the territory was divided between the *presidio* (military) and the *pueblo* (civilian).

By 1822, when Mexico won its independence from Spain, more than twenty missions had been founded in California, and the Russians had built a trading post, Fort Ross, just north of San Francisco Bay. When the Russians pulled out in 1841, they sold it to John Sutter. The U.S. government, envisioning its "manifest destiny" as a nation extending from the Atlantic Ocean to the Pacific, encouraged Americans to settle in the area, a policy that led to tensions with Mexico. In April 1846 American revolutionaries in Sonoma attempted to establish a separate republic under their own flag, bearing a star and a grizzly bear. U.S. Army Captain John C. Frémont, on his own initiative, led his troops to help defend the "Bear Flaggers." The month-old Bear Flag Republic ceased to exist on May 13, 1846, when the United States declared war on Mexico and U.S. naval forces occupied every port in California. Two years later, by the terms of the Treaty of Guadalupe Hidalgo of May 30, 1848, which ended the war with Mexico, the territory of the future state of California was transferred to the United States.

Earlier that month, on May 12, 1848, Sam Brannan, hoping to stimulate business for his store at John Sutter's fort, announced to San Franciscans, and provided compelling proof, that gold had been found on Sutter's land. The gold rush that followed brought many settlers to California—at least 80,000 in 1849 alone. In June of that year, a proclamation by the governor, U.S. Army General Bennet Riley, called for the formation of a state constitution. The first constitution for the California Territory was adopted by a convention that met in Monterey from September 1 to October 13, 1849, and was ratified by the people on November 13.

California was admitted to the Union on September 9, 1850, as a free state in accordance with the Compromise of 1850, proposed by Henry Clay of Kentucky and supported by Daniel Webster of Massachusetts and Stephen A. Douglas of Illinois. Under the compromise, New Mexico and Utah were organized as U.S. territories and permitted to determine for themselves whether to permit the holding of slaves.

California's 1849 constitution, the only state constitution to be written in both English and Spanish, contained a declaration of rights and was amended in 1857 and 1871. It was the first state constitution to expressly recognize the separate property rights of women. A new constitution adopted in March 1879 by a convention held in Sacramento was approved by the voters that May 7. This constitution, which was more than twice as long as the old document, regulated the legislature's powers and included new articles on local government, corporations, revenue and taxation, and Chinese immigrants. It went into effect with respect to the election of state officials on July 4, 1879, and became completely effective on January 1, 1880. A lawsuit in 1879 to force Hastings College of Law to admit two women students influenced the inclusion of language prohibiting discrimination in college admissions and employment on the basis of sex, although suffrage would not be extended to women until an amendment in 1911.

The Constitution

California's second constitution is still in effect today, although as of January 1, 1998, it has been amended 493 times, making it second only to Alabama's constitution in number of amendments. Significant amendments to the provisions regarding the legislative, executive, and judicial branches and the civil service system were approved in 1966. An "omnibus" revision proposed by the legislature was defeated at the polls in 1968.

The current constitution of California, like other state constitutions, is basically a restriction on the residual powers of the state guaranteed by the Tenth Amendment (1791) of the U.S. Constitution. Thus, the state legislature may exercise any powers not limited by the federal and state constitutions. But California, a state whose economy dwarfs that of most nations of the world, has been independent in its approach to state constitutional issues. At the 1879 constitutional convention, a delegate declared that "the State Constitution is much more a charter of our liberties than the Constitution of the United States." And a 1974 amendment to that century-old document asserts that rights under the California constitution "are not dependent on those guaranteed by the United States Constitution."

The structure of the state government created by the California constitution, however, is typical of that of most other states. The plural executive branch has four elected state officers in addition to the governor and lieutenant governor. In the 1960s the bicameral legislature, like the U.S. Congress but unlike the legislatures of most other states, became a nearly full-time body continuously in session. The state supreme court, whose members are elected for twelve-year terms, has been an activist tribunal. The addition of an intermediate appellate court in 1904 has made the supreme court's jurisdiction largely discretionary today.

The preamble to the California constitution reads: "We the People of the State of California, grateful to Almighty God for our freedom, in order to secure and perpetuate its blessings, do establish this Constitution."

Preamble

In 1974 most sections of article 1, relating to fundamental rights, were repealed and new ones were adopted. All sections referred to here are those adopted in 1974, unless otherwise noted.

Fundamental Rights

Article 1, Declaration of Rights, section 1, proclaims: "All people are by nature free and independent and have inalienable rights. Among these are enjoying and defending life and liberty, acquiring, possessing, and protecting property, and pursuing and obtaining safety, happiness, and privacy." **Section 2,** as amended in 1980, states in part: "**(a)** Every person may freely speak, write and publish his or her sentiments on all subjects, being responsible for the abuse of this right. A law may not restrain or abridge liberty of speech or press." Under **section 3,** "The people have the right to instruct their representatives, petition government for redress of grievances, and assemble freely to consult for the common good."

Sections 4, 5, and **6,** respectively, guarantee the free exercise of religion; subordinate the military to civil power and limit the quartering of soldiers in private homes; and prohibit slavery. **Section 7,** as amended in 1979, states in part: "**(a)** A person may not be deprived of life, liberty, or property without due process of law or denied equal protection of the laws.... **(b)** A citizen or class of citizens may not be granted privileges or immunities not granted on the same terms to all citizens." In *Gay Law Students Association v. Pacific Telephone and Telegraph Company* (1979), the California supreme court held that under article 1, section 7(a), a state-protected utility may not arbitrarily discriminate against a class of citizens, including homosexuals. As provided in **section 8,** "A person may not be disqualified from entering or pursuing a business, profession, vocation, or employment because of sex, race, creed, color, or national or ethnic origin."

Section 9 prohibits bills of attainder, ex post facto laws, and laws impairing the obligations of contracts; **section 10** disallows the unreasonable detention of witnesses; **section 11** limits the suspension of habeas corpus; and **section 12,** as amended in 1982 and 1994, with some exceptions, guarantees bail to persons accused of a crime. **Section 13** prohibits unreasonable searches and seizures, and **section 14** sets forth in part: "Felonies shall be prosecuted as provided by law, either by indictment or, after examination and commitment by a magistrate, by information." **Section 15** provides rights for those accused of a crime, including the right to a speedy public trial and the right to compel witnesses in the defendant's behalf. **Section 16,** as amended in 1980, guarantees trial by jury, and **section 17** prohibits "cruel or unusual punishment." In *People v. Anderson* (1972), the California supreme court found that the use of the word *or* in this phrase rather than *and,* which is used in the U.S. Constitution, provided a basis for finding that the death penalty in California violated this state provision. However, **section 27,** added by initiative in 1972, provides in part: "All statutes of this state in effect on February 17, 1972, requiring, authorizing, imposing, or relating to the death penalty are in full force and effect, subject to legislative amendment or repeal by statute, initiative, or referendum."

Section 28, added in 1996, creates a victims' bill of rights. **Section 31,** added in 1996, declares in part: "The state shall not discriminate, or grant preferential treatment to any individual or group on the basis of race, sex, color, ethnicity, or national origin in the operation of public employment, public education, or public contracting."

Section 24, a rare provision as indicated earlier, asserts: "Rights guaranteed by this Constitution are not dependent on those guaranteed by the United States Constitution." One of the rights enumerated in this section is the right to privacy.

Division of Powers

Article III, State of California, was added by amendment in 1972. **Section 3** states: "The powers of state government are legislative, executive, and judicial. Persons charged with the exercise of one power may not exercise either of the others except as permitted by this Constitution." In *Serrano v. Priest* (1976), the California supreme court recognized that the separation of powers principle prohibits the courts from ordering the legislature to legislate and the governor to sign legislation even if such legislation is required by the constitution.

Legislative Branch

Article IV, Legislative, was completely revised in 1966. **Section 1** reads: "The legislative power of this State is vested in the California Legislature which consists of the Senate and Assembly, but the people reserve to themselves the powers of initiative and referendum." **Section 1.5** authorizes limits to legislators' terms by stating in part: "The people find and declare that the Founding Fathers established a system of representative government based upon free, fair, and competitive elections. The increased concentration of political power in the hands of incumbent representatives has made our electoral system less free, less competitive, and less representative.... To restore a free and democratic system of fair elections ... the people find and declare that the powers of incumbency must be limited...."

Section 2(a) provides for a senate membership of forty senators who are elected for four-year terms, twenty of whom stand for election every two years. "No Senator may serve more [than] 2 terms," it adds. The assembly's eighty members are elected for two-year terms, and "[n]o member of the Assembly may serve more [than] three terms." **Section 2(c)** mandates: "A person is ineligible to be a member of the Legislature unless the person is an elector and has been a resident of the legislative district for one year, and a citizen of the United States and a resident of California for 3 years, immediately preceding the election."

Section 5(a) directs that "[e]ach house shall judge the qualifications and elections of its Members and, by rollcall vote entered in the journal, two thirds of the membership concurring, may expel a Member." **Sections 5(b), (c),** and **(d)** ban legislators from accepting honoraria, gifts, or compensation for appearing on behalf of another person. Under **section 7(a),** "Each house shall choose its officers and adopt rules for its proceedings. A majority of the membership constitutes a quorum, but a smaller number may recess from day to day and compel the attendance of absent members." **Section 22,** a unique provision, declares: "It is the right of the people to hold their legislators accountable. To assist the people in exercising this right, at the convening of each regular session of the Legislature, the President pro Tempore of the Senate, the Speaker of the Assembly, and the minority leader of each house shall report to their house the goals and objectives of that house during that session and, at the close of each regular session, the progress made toward meeting those goals and objectives."

Section 8(a) stipulates: "At regular sessions no bill other than the budget bill may be heard or acted on by committee or either house until the 31st day after the bill is introduced unless the house dispenses with this requirement by rollcall vote ..., three-fourths of the membership concurring." Under **section 8(b),** "The Legislature may make no law except by statute and may enact no statute except by bill. No bill may be passed unless it is read by title on 3 days in each house except that the house may dispense with this requirement by a rollcall vote ..., two thirds of the membership concurring. No bill may be passed until the bill with amendments has been printed and distributed to the members...." A majority of the membership of each house must concur for a bill to be passed. **Section 9** requires that each "statute shall embrace but one subject, which shall be expressed in its title."

Section 10(a) provides: "Each bill passed by the Legislature shall be presented to the Governor. It becomes a statute if it is signed by the Governor. The Governor may veto it by returning it with any objections to the house of origin...." The legislature may override the veto "by rollcall vote ..., two-thirds of the membership concurring." **Section 10(b)(3)** stipulates: "Any other bill presented to the Governor that is not returned within 12 days becomes a statute." **Section 10(d)** adds that the legislature "may not present any bill to the Governor after November 15 of the second calendar year of the biennium of the legislative session." **Section 10(e)** gives the governor the power to "reduce or eliminate one or more items of appropriation while approving other portions of a bill."

Article V, Executive, was completely revised in 1966. According to **section 1,** as amended in 1974, "The supreme executive power of this State is vested in the Governor. The Governor shall see that the law is faithfully executed." **Section 2** provides: "The Governor shall be elected every fourth year ..., [and he or she] shall be an elector who has been a citizen of the United States and a resident of this State for 5 years immediately

Executive Branch

preceding the Governor's election. The Governor may not hold other public office. No Governor may serve more than 2 terms." Under **section 11,** the lieutenant governor, attorney general, controller, secretary of state, and treasurer are to be elected at the same time and places and for the same term as the governor. They are similarly limited to two terms.

Section 3, as amended in 1972, directs: "The Governor shall report to the Legislature each calendar year on the condition of the State and make recommendations." Under **section 4,** the governor is permitted to "require executive officers and agencies and their employees to furnish information relating to their duties." **Section 5,** as amended in 1976, authorizes the governor to "fill a vacancy in office by appointment until a successor qualifies." In the case of certain enumerated positions, including the lieutenant governor, secretary of state, and attorney general, the governor's appointee must be confirmed by a majority of both houses of the legislature. **Section 6** empowers the governor to "assign and reorganize functions among executive officers and agencies and their employees, other than elective officers and agencies administered by elective officers."

Section 7, as amended in 1974, provides: "The Governor is commander in chief of a militia that shall be provided by statute. The Governor may call it forth to execute the law." **Section 8,** as amended in 1974, states in part: "Subject to application procedures provided by statute, the Governor, on conditions the Governor deems proper, may grant a reprieve, pardon, and commutation, after sentence, except in case of impeachment. The Governor shall report to the Legislature each [action] ... and the reasons for ... it."

Article IV, Legislative, section 3(b), as amended in 1976, grants the governor the power "[o]n extraordinary occasions" to call the legislature "to assemble in special session." **Section 12,** as amended in 1974, further directs the governor: "Within the first 10 days of each calendar year, the Governor shall submit to the Legislature, with an explanatory message, a budget for the ensuing fiscal year containing itemized statements for recommended state expenditures and estimated state revenues. If recommended expenditures exceed estimated revenues, the Governor shall recommend the sources [of] additional revenues...."

Article V, Executive, section 9, as amended in 1974, sets out responsibilities for the state's lieutenant governor: "The Lieutenant Governor shall have the same qualifications as the Governor. The Lieutenant Governor is President of the Senate but has only a casting vote." **Section 10,** as amended in 1974, provides: "The Lieutenant Governor shall become Governor when a vacancy occurs in the office of Governor. The Lieutenant Governor shall act as Governor during the impeachment, absence from the State, or other temporary disability of the Governor or of a Governor-elect who fails to take office." The lieutenant governor is not elected jointly with the governor, so he or she may be of another political party. Because actions taken in the governor's temporary absence may be inconsistent with the governor's policies, the constitutions of almost half of the states require that the two be elected jointly on a single-party ticket, as are the U.S. president and vice president. Section 10 continues: "The Legislature shall provide an order of precedence after the Lieutenant Governor for succession.... The Supreme Court has exclusive jurisdiction to determine all questions arising under this section. Standing to raise questions of vacancy or temporary disability is vested exclusively in a body provided by statute."

Article VI, Judicial, was completely revised in 1966. **Section 1,** as amended in 1994, declares: "The judicial power of this State is vested in the Supreme Court, courts of appeal, superior courts, and municipal courts." **Section 2,** as amended in 1974, outlines the composition and responsibilities of the state supreme court: "The Supreme Court consists of the Chief Justice of California and 6 associate justices. The Chief Justice may convene the court at any time. Concurrence of 4 judges present at the argument is necessary for a judgment. An acting Chief Justice [an associate justice selected by the chief justice, or if he or she fails to do so, the court] shall perform all functions of the Chief Justice when the Chief Justice is absent or unable to act."

Section 16, as amended in 1974, provides in part: "**(a)** Judges of the Supreme Court shall be elected at large … at the same time and places as the Governor. Their terms are 12 years … except that a judge elected to an unexpired term serves the remainder of the term." **Section 16(d)** notes: "Within 30 days before August 16 preceding the expiration of the judge's term, a judge of the Supreme Court or a court of appeal may file a declaration of candidacy to succeed to the office…. If the declaration is not filed, the Governor before September 16 shall nominate a candidate. At the next general election, only the candidate so declared or nominated may appear on the ballot…. A candidate not elected may not be appointed to that court but later may be nominated and elected." Section 16(d) continues: "The Governor shall fill vacancies in [the] courts by appointment. An appointee holds office until the Monday after January 1 following the first general election at which the appointee had the right to become a candidate or until an elected judge qualifies. A nomination or appointment by the Governor is effective when confirmed by the Commission on Judicial Appointments."

Section 15, as amended in 1994, states: "A person is ineligible to be a judge of a court of record unless for 5 years immediately preceding selection to a municipal court or 10 years immediately preceding selection to other courts, the person has been a member of the State Bar or served as a judge of a court of record in this State…." **Section 17** provides in part: "A judge of a court of record may not practice law and during the employment or public office, except a judge of a court of record may accept a part-time teaching position that is outside the normal hours of his or her judicial position and that does not interfere with the regular performance of his or her judicial duties…."

Section 10 sets out the jurisdiction of the courts: "The Supreme Court, courts of appeal, superior courts, and their judges have original jurisdiction in habeas corpus proceedings. Those courts also have original jurisdiction in proceedings for extraordinary relief in the nature of mandamus, certiorari, and prohibition." **Section 11,** as amended in 1994, states in part: "The Supreme Court has appellate jurisdiction when judgment of death has been pronounced." **Section 12,** as amended in 1985, provides in part: "**(a)** The Supreme Court may, before decision, transfer to itself a cause in a court of appeal … or from one court of appeal or division to another. The court to which the cause is transferred has jurisdiction. **(b)** The Supreme Court may review the decision of a court of appeal in any cause."

Section 8, as amended in 1994, creates a commission on judicial performance. **Section 18,** adopted in 1994, addresses disqualification, suspension, removal, and retirement of judges, authorizing the commission on judicial performance to disqualify a judge from acting as a judge, suspend a judge without salary, and remove a judge from office. **Section 18(d)** provides that, in general, the commission may: **"(1)** retire a judge for disability that seriously interferes with the performance of the judge's duties and is or is likely to become permanent, or **(2)** censure . . . or remove a judge for [among other things] willful misconduct in office . . . or **(3)** publicly or privately admonish a judge . . . found to have engaged in an improper action or dereliction of duty." **Section 20** directs the legislature to "provide for retirement, with reasonable allowance, of judges of courts of record for age or disability."

Impeachment

Article IV, Legislative, section 18, added in 1966, sets forth impeachment procedures: **"(a)** The Assembly has the sole power of impeachment. Impeachments shall be tried by the Senate. A person may not be convicted unless, by rollcall vote . . . , two-thirds of the membership of the Senate concurs. **(b)** State officers elected on a statewide basis, members of the State Board of Equalization, and judges of state courts are subject to impeachment for misconduct in office. Judgment may extend only to removal from office and disqualification to hold any office under the State, but the person convicted or acquitted remains subject to criminal punishment according to law."

Direct Democracy

Article II, Voting, Initiative and Referendum, and Recall, which was repealed in 1972 and revised in 1976, declares in **section 1:** "All political power is inherent in the people. Government is instituted for their protection, security, and benefit, and they have the right to alter or reform it when the public good may require."

Section 8(a) provides: "The initiative is the power of the electors to propose statutes and amendments to the Constitution and to adopt or reject them." **Section 9(a)** states: "The referendum is the power of the electors to approve or reject statutes or parts of statutes except urgency statutes, statutes calling elections, and statutes providing for tax levies or appropriations for usual current expenses of the State." **Section 13,** adopted in 1976, affirms: "Recall is the power of the electors to remove an elective officer."

Local Government

Article XI, Local Government, as amended in 1974, states in part in **section 3:** **"(a)** For its own government, a county or city may adopt a charter by majority vote of its electors voting on the question. The charter is effective when filed with the Secretary of State. A charter may be amended, revised, or repealed in the same manner. . . . The provisions of a charter are the law of the State and have the force and effect of legislative enactments."

Taxation and Finance

Article XIII, Taxation, was added in 1974. **Section 1** indicates in part: "Unless otherwise provided by this Constitution or the laws of the United States: **(a)** All property is taxable and shall be assessed at the same percentage of fair market value." **Article XIII-B, Government Spending Limitation,** was adopted by initiative in 1979. **Section 1** provides: "The total annual appropriations subject to limitation of the state and of each local government shall not exceed the appropriations limit of the entity of government for the prior year adjusted for the change in the cost of living and the change in population, except as otherwise provided in this article."

Article IX, Education, section 1, declares: "A general diffusion of knowledge and intelligence being essential to the preservation of the rights and liberties of the people, the Legislature shall encourage by all suitable means the promotion of intellectual, scientific, moral, and agricultural improvement."

Article III, State of California, was added in 1972. **Section 6,** the result of a 1986 initiative, mandates an official state language and provides in part: "**(a)** English is the common language of the people of the United States of America and the State of California. This section is intended to preserve, protect and strengthen the English language, and not to supersede any of the rights guaranteed to the people by this Constitution. **(b)** English is the Official Language of the State of California."

Article XVI, Public Finance, section 11, added in 1938 and amended in 1962, empowers the "Legislature or the people by initiative ... to amend, alter, or repeal any law relating to the relief of hardship and destitution...."

Article XVIII, Amending and Revising the Constitution, was added in 1970. Under **section 1,** "The Legislature by rollcall vote ... [with] two-thirds of the membership of each house concurring, may propose an amendment or revision of the Constitution and in the same manner may amend or withdraw its proposal." **Section 2** similarly empowers the legislature, with "two-thirds of the membership of each house concurring," to submit to the voters the question of calling "a convention to revise the Constitution." Section 2 continues: "If the majority vote yes on that question, within 6 months the Legislature shall provide for the convention."

Section 3 states: "The electors may amend the Constitution by initiative." In *Amador Valley Joint Union High School Dist. v. State Bd. of Equalization* (1978), the California supreme court recognized that while the legislature was authorized to propose "an amendment or revision" to the constitution, the language in section 3 permitted amendment only by initiative, not by revision. As specified in **section 4,** "A proposed amendment or revision shall be submitted to the electors and if approved by a majority of votes thereon takes effect the day after the election unless the measure provides otherwise."

COLORADO

Colorado became the thirty-eighth state of the United States on August 1, 1876. Denver is the capital of the "Centennial State," which encompasses some 104,200 square miles and is bordered by Wyoming and Nebraska on the north, Nebraska and Kansas on the east, Oklahoma and New Mexico on the south, and Utah on the west. Colorado ranks twenty-fifth among the states in population with approximately 3.7 million residents. The state's principal industries include manufacturing, construction, aerospace, and electronics equipment; corn, wheat, and hay are among its chief crops.

General Information

Government: The governor and lieutenant governor are elected jointly for four-year terms and are limited to two consecutive terms. The legislature, called the general assembly, consists of thirty-five senators elected for four-year terms and sixty-five representatives elected for two-year terms; senators are limited to two consecutive terms and representatives to four consecutive terms. The supreme court is composed of a chief justice and six additional justices appointed by the governor from a list prepared by a supreme court nominating commission for an initial two-year term; justices may stand for reelection for additional ten-year terms.

Date of Constitution: 1876

Constitutional History

Two thousand years ago the Anasazi people lived near the present site of Durango among the *colorado* (red or ruddy) Rocky Mountains in the southwestern part of what is now the state of Colorado. Around A.D. 700 the cliff-dwelling Pueblo people took their place. As early as the sixteenth century, conquistadors advised the Spanish colonial authorities in Mexico City about the Colorado territory north of their explorations, and by 1700 Spanish traders were visiting local villages near the present site of La Junta. At the same time French explorers reached the Rockies.

At the beginning of the seventeenth century the Spanish colonial government laid claim to an area east of Pueblo, but in 1739 a French expedition led by Pierre and Paul Mallet crossed the Colorado region on their trek from the Nebraska plains to present-day New Mexico. French and Spanish rivalry for the area continued throughout most of the century. In 1803, however, under the Louisiana Purchase negotiated with France, the United States acquired the eastern portion of the Colorado territory, which originally encompassed parts of the territories of Utah, Kansas, Nebraska, and New Mexico.

In 1806 Lieutenant Zebulon Pike set out with sixteen soldiers to cross the Rocky Mountains, but he, like other Americans, knew next to nothing about the newly acquired Colorado territory. Although the experience was a harrowing one, Pike and his party traversed the mountains and discovered for the United States the 14,110-foot-high peak that bears his name. Trappers and mountain men followed Pike, and in 1829 four brothers named Bent established a trading post in the La Junta region. But not until 1858, ten years after the California gold rush, did a significant number of permanent settlers arrive in the Colorado region, lured by the promise of gold in the Rocky Mountains.

As a result of the 1850 political compromise in Congress over the admission of slave and free states, the vast Territory of Utah was established west of the summit of the Rocky Mountains and the 1854 Kansas-Nebraska Act created the Territory of Kansas from the Missouri Territory. In 1858 a group of miners with the West Denver Company drafted a constitution and petitioned Congress for separate territorial status, but a bill to create the Territory of Jefferson, as the Colorado region was to be called, was not acted on. Local promoters seized on the name, and the Constitution of Jefferson Territory, although not authorized by any legitimate government authority and thus illegal, was approved by a vote of 1,852 to 280. A territorial legislature convened under its provisions on November 7, 1859.

On February 28, 1861, President James Buchanan signed the act of Congress officially creating the autonomous Territory of Colorado out of parts of Kansas and Utah and establishing a separate temporary government for the region. The Civil War impelled the statehood movement because Republicans in Congress wanted the additional votes that they believed would be contributed by newly admitted western states.

A statehood enabling act was passed in the spring of 1864, but the first draft of a state constitution was rejected handily at the polls. A second draft was barely approved in 1865, but President Andrew Johnson vetoed attempts by Congress to admit Colorado on the grounds that the proposed state constitution differed significantly from the requirements of the enabling statute.

A constitution was drafted by a convention held in Denver from December 20, 1875, to March 14, 1876. Ratified by the voters in July, it became effective when Colorado was admitted to the Union on August 1, 1876, the year of the U.S. centennial.

The Constitution

With nearly 46,000 words, the Colorado constitution is one of the longest state constitutions (only six are longer). As of January 1, 1998, it has been amended 133 times. When approved in 1876, the constitution gave black males the right to vote but denied the same right to women, even though women's suffrage had been granted in the neighboring Territory of Wyoming in 1869. The plural executive structure created by the Colorado constitution is found in most other states, but not in the U.S. Constitution or the more recent constitutions of Alaska and New Jersey, for example.

An underlying distrust of representative government is reflected in the document— for example, in its detailed instructions for and restrictions on legislative committee procedures and party caucuses, together with direct democracy provisions and term limitations on elective state offices. Furthermore, a constitutional amendment enacted by the people in 1996 supports term limits on the national level, authorizing voters to instruct state legislators and members of Congress to support an amendment to the U.S. Constitution allowing such limits. In a term limits case involving another state the previous year, the U.S. Supreme Court in *U.S. Term Limits, Inc. v. Thornton* (1995) struck down an amendment to the Arkansas constitution that tried to limit the terms of that state's congressional delegates, noting that state-imposed restrictions on the qualifications for U.S. congressional offices violate the concept that the people, not the states, have the right to choose representatives.

Preamble

The preamble to the 1876 Colorado constitution proclaims: "We, the people of Colorado, with profound reverence for the Supreme Ruler of the Universe, in order to form a more independent and perfect government; establish justice; insure tranquillity; provide for the common defense; promote the general welfare and secure the blessings of liberty to ourselves and our posterity, do ordain and establish this constitution for the 'State of Colorado.'"

Fundamental Rights

Article II, Bill of Rights, begins: "In order to assert our rights, acknowledge our duties, and proclaim the principles upon which our government is founded, we declare: **Section 1.** ... All political power is vested in and derived from the people; all government, of right, originates from the people, is founded upon their will only, and is instituted solely for the good of the whole." According to **section 2,** "The people of this state have the sole and exclusive right of governing themselves, as a free, sovereign and independent state; and to alter and abolish their constitution and form of government whenever they may deem it necessary to their safety and happiness, provided, such change be not repugnant to the constitution of the United States."

Section 3 recites the inalienable rights of individuals, and **section 4** guarantees religious freedom. **Section 5** states: "All elections shall be free and open; and no power, civil or military, shall at any time interfere to prevent the free exercise of the right of suffrage." **Section 6** declares that "[c]ourts of justice shall be open to every person, and a speedy remedy afforded for every injury to person, property or character; and right and justice should be administered without sale, denial or delay." The constitutions of a number of other states, including Delaware, contain similar language.

Sections 7 and **8,** respectively, prohibit unreasonable searches and seizures and require prosecutions "[u]ntil otherwise provided by law" to be by indictment or information. **Section 9,** in language similar to that used in the U.S. Constitution, defines treason and the method of conviction for treason and guarantees that the estates of suicides "shall descend or vest as in cases of natural death." **Section 10** guarantees freedom of speech and the press; **section 11** prohibits ex post facto laws and laws impairing the obligation of contracts; and **section 12** prohibits imprisonment for debt. **Section 13** states: "The right of no person to keep and bear arms in defense of his home, person or property, or in aid of the civil power when thereto legally summoned, shall be called in question; but nothing herein contained shall be construed to justify the practice of carrying concealed weapons."

Section 14 stipulates that an owner's consent is required for taking private property for private use "except for private ways of necessity, and except for reservoirs, drains, flumes or ditches on or across the lands of others, for agricultural, mining, milling, domestic or sanitary purposes." The Idaho constitution has a similar provision fostering the state's interest in mining that permits the taking of private property for private as well as public use and the development of the state's mining interests among others. **Section 15** states in part: "Private property shall not be taken or damaged, for public or private use, without just compensation."

Sections 16, 17, and **18,** respectively, provide for rights of the defendant in criminal prosecutions and rights of victims of crime (added by amendment in 1993); limitations on imprisonment of witnesses; and protections against self-incrimination and double jeopardy. **Section 19,** as amended in 1983 and 1995, guarantees all persons the right to bail with certain exceptions—for example, in "capital offenses when proof is evident or presumption is great." Bail may also be denied in cases when proof is evident or presumption is great and the court finds that "the public would be placed in significant peril if the accused were released on bail," and the accused is charged with any of three specified types of violent crimes. **Section 20** prohibits excessive bail, fines, and punishment.

Section 21 prohibits the suspension of habeas corpus, "unless when in case of rebellion or invasion, the public safety may require it." **Sections 22** through **27,** respectively, provide for subordination of the military to civilian power, trial by jury and grand juries, the right to assemble and petition for redress of grievances, due process of law, the prohibition of slavery, and the property rights of aliens. **Section 29** declares: "Equality of rights under the law shall not be denied or abridged by the state of Colorado or any of its political subdivisions on account of sex." The constitutions of roughly a third of the states have similar equal rights provisions.

Section 30b, added by amendment in 1993, states in part: "Neither the State of Colorado [nor any of its instrumentalities] shall enact, adopt or enforce any statute, regulation, ordinance or policy whereby homosexual, lesbian or bisexual orientation, conduct, practices or relationships shall constitute or otherwise be the basis of or entitle any person or class of persons to have or claim any minority status, quota preferences, protected status or claim of discrimination." In *Romer v. Evans* (1996), the U.S. Supreme Court found section 30b to be unconstitutional under the U.S. Constitution on the grounds that a law declaring in essence that it is more difficult for one group to seek aid from the government is itself a denial of equal protection of the laws guaranteed by the U.S. Constitution.

Article III, Distribution of Powers, proclaims: "The powers of the government of this state are divided into three distinct departments,—the legislative, executive and judicial; and no person or collection of persons charged with the exercise of powers properly belonging to one of these departments shall exercise any power properly belonging to either of the others, except as in this constitution expressly directed or permitted."

Division of Powers

Article V, Legislative Department, section 1, as amended in 1910, 1980, and 1995, provides in part: "**(1)** The legislative power of the state shall be vested in the general assembly consisting of a senate and house of representatives, both to be elected by the people…." **Section 45,** as amended in 1966, limits the general assembly to "not more than thirty-five members of the senate and … not more than sixty-five members of the house of representatives, one to be elected from each senatorial and each representative district, respectively." **Section 3(1)** prescribes four-year terms for senators and two-year terms for representatives, while **section 3(2)** states: "In order to broaden the opportunities for public service and to assure that the general assembly is representative of Colorado citizens, no senator shall serve more than two consecutive terms in the senate, and no representative shall serve more than four consecutive terms in the house of representatives."

Legislative Branch

Section 4 requires that representatives and senator be twenty-five years old, citizens of the United States, and residents of their electoral county or district for one year. **Section 5,** as amended in 1974, directs that the "senate shall be divided so that one-half of the senators, as nearly as practicable, may be chosen biennially."

Section 10, as amended in 1974, provides that "[a]t the beginning of the first regular session after a general election ... the senate shall elect one of its members president, and the house of representatives shall elect one of its members as speaker...." **Section 11** defines a quorum as a majority of each house. **Section 12,** as amended in 1974, authorizes each house to determine its own rules and punish its members or other persons "for contempt or disorderly behavior in its presence...." Each house may expel a member "with the concurrence of two-thirds ..., but not a second time for the same cause...." Under **section 16,** as amended in 1974, legislators are exempt from arrest except for treason or felony "during their attendance at the sessions of their respective houses, or any committees thereof"; furthermore, "in going to and returning from the same; and for any speech or debate in either house, or any committees thereof, they shall not be questioned in any other place."

Section 17 provides that "[n]o law shall be passed except by bill, and no bill shall be so altered or amended on its passage through either house as to change its original purpose." **Section 20,** as amended in 1989, states in part: "No bill shall be considered or become a law unless referred to a committee, returned therefrom, and printed for use of the members." This section also sets forth detailed guidelines for committee consideration of bills and the legislature's proceedings regarding committee actions. Most other state constitutions do not address this issue. **Section 21** mandates that "[n]o bill, except general appropriation bills, shall be passed containing more than one subject, which shall be clearly expressed in its title ..."; and **section 22,** as amended in 1950, requires: "Every bill shall be read by title when introduced, and at length on two different days in each house; provided, however, any reading at length may be dispensed with upon unanimous consent of the members present."

Section 22a, added by amendment in 1989, directs: "**(1)** No member or members of the general assembly shall require or commit themselves or any other member or members[,] through a vote in a party caucus or any other similar procedure, to vote in favor of or against any bill, appointment, veto, or other measure or issue pending or proposed to be introduced...." This attempt to micromanage political party organization in the state legislature is a unique provision. **Section 22a(2),** however, exempts votes in party caucuses "on matters directly relating to the selection of officers of a party caucus and the selection of the leadership of the general assembly." Most state constitutions, like the U.S. Constitution, do not expressly address the matter of political parties or their procedures.

Section 25 prohibits local or special legislation in certain enumerated cases, including granting divorces and regulating county or township affairs. **Section 25a,** added by amendment in 1902 and amended in 1989, requires the legislature to "provide by law, and ... prescribe suitable penalties for the violation" of employment exceeding eight hours within any twenty-four hours, except in certain emergencies, "for persons employed in underground mines or other underground workings...."

Section 26, as amended in 1974, states that all bills and joint resolutions passed by the general assembly must be signed by the presiding officer of each house. **Section 31** provides that revenue bills must originate in the house of representatives, although "the senate may propose amendments, as in the case of other bills." **Section 35** prohibits the legislature from delegating "to any special commission, private corporation or association, any power to make, supervise or interfere with any municipal improvement, money, property or effects...." According to **section 39,** "Every order, resolution or vote to which the concurrence of both houses may be necessary, except on the question of adjournment, or relating solely to the transaction of business of the two houses, shall be presented to the governor, and before it shall take effect, be approved by him, or being disapproved, shall be repassed by two-thirds of both houses, according to the rules and limitations prescribed in case of a bill."

Section 49, as amended in 1974, authorizes the legislature, "by a majority vote of the members elected to and serving in each house ... [and] without regard to political affiliation," to appoint a state auditor. The office holder must be a certified public accountant, and duties include conducting "post audits of all financial transactions and accounts kept by or for all departments, offices, agencies, and institutions of the state government...."

Article IV, Executive Department, section 1, as amended in 1964 and 1991, declares: "**(1)** The executive department shall include the governor, lieutenant governor, secretary of state, state treasurer, and attorney general, each of whom shall hold his office for the term of four years.... **(2)** In order to broaden the opportunities for public service and to guard against excessive concentrations of power, [none of these officials] shall serve more than two consecutive terms...." **Section 2** vests the state's supreme executive power in the governor, "who shall take care that the laws be faithfully executed."

Executive Branch

Section 3, as amended in 1968 and 1985, states in part: "The governor and the lieutenant governor shall be chosen jointly by the casting by each voter of a single vote applicable to both offices." **Section 4,** as amended in 1964, requires that the governor and lieutenant governor be thirty years old. The other statewide constitutional executive branch officers must be twenty-five years old, and the attorney general must be "a licensed attorney of the supreme court of the state in good standing." All executive officers must be citizens of the United States "and have resided within the limits of the state two years next preceding [their] election."

Section 5 mandates: "The governor shall be commander-in-chief of the military forces of the state, except when they shall be called into actual service of the United States. He shall have power to call out the militia to execute the laws, suppress insurrection or repel invasion." **Section 6** authorizes the governor to "nominate, and, by and with the consent of the senate, appoint all officers whose offices are established by this constitution, or which may be created by law, and whose appointment or election is not otherwise provided for …"; the governor may also remove these officers for "incompetency, neglect of duty, or malfeasance in office."

Section 7 empowers the governor to grant reprieves and pardons "for all offenses except treason, and except in case of impeachment, subject to such regulations as may be prescribed by law …," although the chief executive must send to the general assembly at its next session "a transcript of the petition, all proceedings, and the reasons for [this] action." **Section 8** directs the governor to "require information in writing from the officers of the executive department upon any subject relating to the duties of their respective offices…." According to **section 9,** the governor may convene the legislature or the senate "on extraordinary occasions," and **section 10** states that "in case of a disagreement between the two houses as to the time of adjournment," the governor may adjourn them.

Section 11 provides: "Every bill passed by the general assembly shall, before it becomes a law, be presented to the governor. If he approve, he shall sign it, and thereupon it shall become a law; but if he do not approve, he shall return it, with his objections, to the house in which originated…." The governor's veto may be overridden by a vote of two-thirds of the elected members in each house. If a bill is not signed and not returned by the governor within ten days, it becomes law without a signature, "unless the general assembly shall by their adjournment prevent its return, in which case it shall be filed with his objections in the office of the secretary of state, within thirty days after such adjournment, or else become a law." In *Romer v. Colorado General Assembly* (1992), the Colorado supreme court held that vetoed bills returned to the legislature with the words "disapproved and vetoed" written on each did not satisfy the constitutional requirement that bills be returned by the governor "with his objections." **Section 12** grants the governor the item veto power in "any bill making appropriations of money [and] embracing distinct items…."

Section 13, as amended in 1974, designates the lieutenant governor to become governor "**(1)** [i]n the case of the death, impeachment, conviction of a felony, or resignation of the governor…." If a similar vacancy occurs in the office of the lieutenant governor, the governor nominates a replacement "who shall take office upon confirmation by a majority vote of both houses of the general assembly." And **section 13(5)** provides that when the offices of both the governor and the lieutenant governor are vacant temporarily—for example, because of their absence from the state or because of a mental or physical disability—their duties are to be performed by "the first named member of the general assembly [president of the senate, speaker of the house of representatives, minority leader of the senate, and so forth] who is affiliated with the same political party as the lieutenant governor…." This provision ensures that the political party affiliation of the person filling the position of governor and lieutenant governor even temporarily will remain unchanged.

Judicial Branch

Article VI, Judicial Department, was extensively revised by amendments effective in 1965. Dates are noted only for later amendments. **Section 1** declares: "The judicial power of the state shall be vested in a supreme court, district courts, a probate [and juvenile] court in the city and county of Denver, … county courts, and such other courts or judicial officers with jurisdiction inferior to the supreme court, as the general assembly may, from time to time establish; provided, however, that nothing herein contained shall be construed to restrict or diminish the powers of home rule cities and towns … to create municipal and police courts."

Section 2 states in part: "**(1)** The supreme court, except as otherwise provided in this constitution, shall have appellate jurisdiction only, which shall be coextensive with the state, and shall have a general superintending control over all inferior courts, under such regulations and limitations as may be prescribed by law. **(2)** Appellate review by the supreme court of every final judgment of the district courts, the probate court … and the juvenile court … of Denver shall be allowed, and the supreme court shall have such other appellate review as may be provided by law." In *Colorado v. Nunez* (1984), the U.S. Supreme Court concluded that the Colorado supreme court had relied on independent and adequate state grounds in ruling on the rights of a defendant accused of a crime, thus precluding a basis for the federal court to act on the matter as in previous cases where it had determined that a state court's decision "fairly appeared to rest primarily on federal law or [was] interwoven with federal law."

Section 3 authorizes the supreme court to issue writs of habeas corpus, mandamus, quo warranto, certiorari, injunction, and "such other original and remedial writs as may be provided by rule of court with authority to hear and determine the same…." The court also renders advisory opinions on important questions "upon solemn occasions" at the request of the governor or general assembly. **Section 21** directs the supreme court to "make and promulgate rules governing the administration of all courts and … rules governing practice and procedure in civil and criminal cases, except that the general assembly shall have the power to provide simplified procedures in county courts [in some cases]."

Section 5, as amended in 1967, provides: "**(1)** The supreme court shall consist of not less than seven justices, who may sit en banc or in departments…. [N]o decision of any department shall become judgment of the court unless concurred in by at least three justices, and no case involving construction of the [state or federal] constitution … shall be decided except by the court en banc." If two-thirds of the members of the senate and house of representatives concur, the court may be increased to a maximum of nine members. **Sections 5(2)** and **5(3)**, respectively, direct the supreme court to select from among the members a chief justice, who shall "serve at the pleasure of a majority of the court … [and] who shall be the executive head of the judicial system," and to appoint a court administrator "and such other personnel as the court may deem necessary…."

Section 7, as amended in 1967, sets the term of office for supreme court justices at ten years. According to **section 8**, as amended in 1962, supreme court justices must be "qualified electors" of the state and must have been "licensed to practice law in this state for at least five years."

Section 20, as amended in 1967, states: "**(1)** A vacancy in any judicial office in any court of record shall be filled by appointment of the governor, from a list of three nominees for the supreme court ... [and] shall hold office for a provisional term of two years." A justice must then stand for election to a full ten-year term. **Section 6,** which was repealed in 1967, had provided for the election of judges. **Section 20(2)** stipulates that "[r]etention in office ... shall be by election...." **Section 23,** as amended in 1967 and 1983, sets an age limit for justices: "**(1)** On attaining the age of seventy-two a justice or judge of a court of record shall retire...."

Impeachment

Article XIII, Impeachments, as amended in 1991, gives the house of representatives the sole power of impeachment and the senate the power to try all impeachments. The governor and other state and judicial officers may be impeached "for high crimes or misdemeanors or malfeasance in office...." Impeachment requires a majority of all the representatives, and conviction requires two-thirds of all the senators. Judgment extends only to removal from office and disqualification from holding other state offices and does not insulate a person from further prosecution under the law.

Direct Democracy

Article V, Legislative Department, section 1, as amended in 1910, 1980, and 1995, underscores citizen rights to participate in the legislative process, asserting that "**(1)** ... the people reserve to themselves the power to propose laws and amendments to the constitution and to enact or reject the same at the polls independent of the general assembly and also reserve power at their own option to approve or reject at the polls any act or item, section, or part of any act of the general assembly."

Sections 1(2) and **1(3)** outline the procedures for implementing popular initiatives and referendums. In *Meyer v. Grant* (1988), the U.S. Supreme Court held that a Colorado state law making it a felony to pay people to circulate "initiative petitions" required to place a proposed law or amendment on the ballot was a violation of a citizen's right to political free speech under the First Amendment (1791) and Fourteenth Amendment (1868) of the U.S. Constitution. **Section 1(4)** provides: "The veto power of the governor shall not extend to measures initiated by or referred to the people. All elections on measures initiated by or referred to the people ... shall be held at the biennial regular general election, and all such measures shall become the law or a part of the constitution, when approved by a majority of the votes cast thereon...." According to **section 1(9),** "The initiative and referendum powers reserved to the people by this section are hereby further reserved to the registered electors of every city, town, and municipality...."

Taxation and Finance

Article X, Revenue, section 2, declares: "The general assembly shall provide by law for an annual tax sufficient, with other resources, to defray the estimated expenses of the state government for each fiscal year." **Section 3,** as amended in 1956, 1982, and 1989, states in part: "**(1)(a)** Each property tax levy shall be uniform upon all real and personal property not exempt from taxation under this article...." **Section 20** constitutes a taxpayers' bill of rights, which includes spending limits, a provision similar to one in the Florida constitution.

Article IX, Education, section 2, directs the legislature to "provide for the establishment and maintenance of a thorough and uniform system of free public schools throughout the state, wherein all residents of the state, between the ages of six and twenty-one years, may be educated gratuitously."

Education

Article II, Bill of Rights, section 30a, added in 1989, asserts: "The English language is the official language of the State of Colorado. This section is self executing; however, the General Assembly may enact laws to implement this section."

Official Language

Article V, Legislative Department, section 50, added in 1985, provides: "No public funds shall be used ... to pay or otherwise reimburse ... any person, agency or facility for the performance of any induced abortion...." An exception, however, is made "to prevent the death of either a pregnant woman or her unborn child under circumstances where every reasonable effort is made to preserve the life of each."

Abortion

Article XIX, Amendments, section 1, prescribes how the constitution may be revised, altered, or amended by a constitutional convention, if "two-thirds of the members elected to each house, recommend to the electors ... to vote at the next general election for or against a convention...." The convention's revision, alterations, or amendments then must be ratified by "a majority of the electors voting" on them.

Amendment Procedures

Section 2, as amended in 1900, 1980, and 1995, provides in part: "**(1)** Any amendment or amendments to this constitution may be proposed in either house of the general assembly, and, if [approved] by two-thirds of all the members elected to each house ... [they] shall be published with the laws of that session...." The amendment then becomes a part of the constitution if it is approved at the next general election "by a majority of those voting thereon."

Article V, Legislative Department, sections 1(5) through **1(7.5),** as amended in 1910, 1980, and 1995, describe detailed procedures for proposing and ratifying amendments by popular initiative. Any petition for a proposed initiated amendment must be signed by a number of voters equivalent to at least five percent of the votes cast for all candidates for secretary of state at the last general election and be presented no less than three months before the election at which it is to be voted on. The text, limited to one subject, is submitted to the general assembly's research and drafting offices for review and comment. Within two weeks, comments are to be aired during a public meeting. The text and title of each measure are then published throughout the state at least fifteen days before voter registration closes for the next election. Thirty days before the election takes place, a ballot information booklet, containing a "fair and impartial analysis of each measure," including a summary of arguments for and against it, must be distributed to "active registered voters statewide." Once put before the electorate, the measure requires a majority vote for approval.

CONNECTICUT

Connecticut became the fifth state of the United States on January 9, 1788. Hartford is the capital of the "Constitution State," which ranks twenty-eighth in population with approximately 3.3 million residents. Some 5,544 square miles in area, Connecticut is bordered by Massachusetts on the north, Rhode Island on the east, Long Island Sound on the south, and New York on the west. The state's principal industries include manufacturing, retail trade, finance, and insurance; among its chief crops are nursery stock, Christmas trees, and mushrooms.

General Information

Government: The governor and lieutenant governor, who run on the same ticket, are elected for four-year terms. The legislature, called the general assembly, consists of thirty-six senators and 151 members of the house of representatives, all elected for two-year terms. The supreme court includes a chief justice and six other justices nominated by the governor and appointed by the legislature for eight-year terms.

Dates of Constitutions: 1776 (charters of 1638–39 and 1662 continued in force after statehood), 1818, and 1965

Constitutional History

When the first Europeans arrived in the region that would become Connecticut, it was inhabited by the Mahicans and Pequots, among other members of the Algonkian nation. In 1614 Adriaen Block, a Dutchman, sailed up the Connecticut River, but the Dutch had established no settlements in the territory by 1630, when the first English colonists landed at what is today the town of Dorchester. In March 1632 the earl of Warwick granted the English settlers dubious title to the land, and in 1633 the Dutch built a fort at the present site of Hartford.

In exchange for confirmation of their title, the growing number of English settlers acknowledged the jurisdiction of the Massachusetts Bay Colony. The first general court, or legislature, was established in Hartford in 1636, and by the terms of the Fundamental Orders of Connecticut, a document dated January 14, 1638, the settlements of Windsor, Hartford, and Wethersfield formed a compact. In 1639 the New Haven colony adopted a fundamental government document, or constitution, and four years later the general court in New Haven adopted a more detailed plan of government. The Fundamental Orders of 1638–39 have been called the world's first written constitution (accordingly, in 1959 the legislature designated Connecticut the "Constitution State").

Charles II granted the colonists a Charter of Connecticut, which was formally received on October 9, 1662. The provisions of the charter were suspended by the Crown in 1687, and the document itself survived an attempted confiscation by agents of James II, having been hidden by Captain John Wadsworth in a giant tree since called the "Charter Oak." The charter was reinstated after 1689.

Other British colonies such as New Jersey and Pennsylvania rushed to draft new constitutions after declaring their independence in 1776, but the government of Connecticut adopted a Constitutional Ordinance, which declared: "PARAGRAPH 1.... the Charter from *Charles* the Second ... shall be and remain the Civil Constitution of this State, under the sole authority of the People thereof, independent of any King or Prince whatever [a]nd ... this Republic is, and shall forever be and remain, a free, sovereign and independent State, by the Name of the STATE OF CONNECTICUT."

A dispute between Connecticut and Pennsylvania, which had broken out before the Revolutionary War over the lands encompassed in their respective charters, raged until 1782, when an arbitration committee created by the Continental Congress gave the disputed territory to Pennsylvania. Connecticut became a state of the Union on January 9, 1788, and Connecticut's colonial charter, as did Rhode Island's, continued to serve as its constitution.

A constitutional convention that met in Hartford from August 26 to September 16, 1818, drafted a new constitution. It was ratified by the voters on October 5 of that year and went into effect on October 12. The document contained a declaration of rights generally based on the Declaration of Rights included in Virginia's 1776 constitution. Moving away from the legislative supremacy of the 1662 charter, the 1818 constitution enshrined the independence of the three basic branches of government.

By 1902 the 1818 constitution had thirty-one articles of amendment, but a legislative proposal that year to revise the document was rejected. Amendments increasing the independent powers of the executive and judicial branches in the early 1930s continued the process of changing the structure of the state government. Finally, in 1953 the electorate approved a proposed revision of the document entitled Constitutional Amendment to Incorporate Forty-Seven Amendments in the Constitution of the State, without Other Revision, which went into effect on January 1, 1955.

At a special session of the state legislature in November 1964, an act was passed calling for a constitutional convention for the limited purposes of making the senate electoral districts consistent with federal constitutional standards, reapportioning the house of representatives, and simplifying the amendment procedures. As can happen with constitutional conventions, the delegates went beyond the mandate of the act calling for the convention and added articles on home rule and mandatory periodic referendums on whether to convene a new constitutional convention. The new constitution framed by the convention, which met in Hartford from July 1 through October 28, 1965, was approved by the voters on December 14 and took effect on December 30 of that year.

The Constitution

The 1965 Connecticut constitution, with only 9,564 words, is the third shortest state constitution, after Vermont's and New Hampshire's. It is also one of the least amended constitutions, with only twenty-nine amendments as of January 1, 1998. As with the U.S., Massachusetts, and some other state constitutions, however, amendments are not integrated into the basic text.

The state government structure created by the 1965 document is fairly typical, consisting of a plural executive branch, with three statewide officers elected in addition to the governor and lieutenant governor, and a bicameral legislature, both houses of which are elected biennially. A unique feature is that supreme court judges are appointed by the legislature from nominations made by the governor and based exclusively on candidates submitted by a judicial selection committee.

Major changes in the 1965 constitution include the addition of an article on home rule, which grants a high degree of autonomy to local governments; a requirement that the question of whether to call a constitutional convention be posed to the voters every twenty years; and changes in the article on the judiciary, such as renaming the state's highest court the supreme court rather than the supreme court of errors. Also added in

1965 were a guarantee of free primary and secondary education, a "trailer" legislative session to deal with last-minute vetoed bills, and a two-thirds requirement for overriding a veto (formerly only a simple majority was necessary).

Preamble

The preamble to Connecticut's 1965 constitution reads: "The People of Connecticut acknowledging with gratitude, the good providence of God, in having permitted them to enjoy a free government; do, in order more effectually to define, secure, and perpetuate the liberties, rights, and privileges which they have derived from their ancestors; hereby, after a careful consideration and revision, ordain and establish the following constitution and form of civil government."

Fundamental Rights

Article First, Declaration of Rights, proclaims: "That the great and essential principles of liberty and free government may be recognized and established, WE DECLARE: **Section 1.** All men when they form a social compact, are equal in rights; and no man or set of men are entitled to exclusive public emoluments or privileges from the community." In *Barnes v. New Haven* (1953), the Connecticut supreme court of errors stated that the clause "no man or set of men are entitled to exclusive public emoluments ..." has the same meaning as the equal protection clause of the Fourteenth Amendment (1868) to the U.S. Constitution. Much earlier, however, the court, in interpreting this same provision in Connecticut's 1818 constitution, had found that, although broad in scope, section 1 was limited to those who were parties to the social contract and thus did not apply to slaves.

Section 2 declares that "[a]ll political power is inherent in the people, and all free governments are founded on their authority, and instituted for their benefit; and they have at all times an undeniable and indefeasible right to alter their form of government in such manner as they may think expedient."

Section 3 guarantees freedom of religion, "provided, that the right hereby declared and established, shall not be so construed as to excuse acts of licentiousness, or to justify practices inconsistent with the peace and safety of the state." Religion is also addressed in the single paragraph of **article Seventh, Of Religion:** "It being the right of all men to worship the Supreme Being, the Great Creator and Preserver of the Universe, and to render that worship in a mode consistent with the dictates of their consciences, no person shall by law be compelled to join or support, nor be classed or associated with, any congregation, church or religious association. No preference shall be given by law to any religious society or denomination in the state. Each shall have and enjoy the same and equal powers, rights and privileges, and may support and maintain the ministers or teachers of its society or denomination, and may build and repair houses for public worship."

Section 4 grants liberty of speech and the press, and **section 5** prohibits laws limiting liberty of speech or the press. In *State v. Andrews* (1962), the Connecticut supreme court of errors held that obscenity is not protected under the First Amendment (1791) to the U.S. Constitution or under the state constitution, but in *State v. Martin* (1965), the same court found that nudist magazines, more than half the contents of which were photographs of nude females, were not suppressible as "obscene."

Section 6 states: "In all prosecutions or indictments for libels, the truth may be given in evidence, and the jury shall have the right to determine the law and the facts, under the direction of the court." Sections 7 through 14, respectively, provide for security from searches and seizures, rights of the accused in criminal prosecutions (as amended in 1982), the right of personal liberty, the right of redress for injuries, the right of private property, the writ of habeas corpus, a prohibition against attainder, and the right to assemble and petition the government for redress of grievances. Although the Connecticut constitution does not contain an express right of privacy, the state played a role in developing the federal privacy right. In *Griswold v. Connecticut* (1965), the U.S. Supreme Court found that the state's birth control law unconstitutionally intruded on the marital right of privacy. Section 8 was amended in 1996 to include rights for victims of crime.

Section 15 affirms that "[e]very citizen has a right to bear arms in defense of himself and the state." Sections 16 and 17, respectively, provide for the subordination of the military to civil power and limit the quartering of troops in private homes; and section 18 prohibits hereditary emoluments. Section 19, as amended in 1972, asserts: "The right of trial by jury shall remain inviolate." In *Williams v. Coppola* (1986), the Connecticut superior court for New Haven ruled that the constitutional right to a trial by an impartial jury guarantees a fair chance of a jury composed of a cross section of the population. Section 20, as amended in 1974 and 1984, states that "[n]o person shall be denied the equal protection of the law nor be subjected to segregation or discrimination in the exercise or enjoyment of his or her civil or political rights because of religion, race, color, ancestry, national origin, sex or physical or mental disability."

Article Second, Of the Distribution of Powers, as amended in 1982, divides the powers of government into "three distinct departments ... each of them confided to a separate magistracy": the legislative, the executive, and the judicial. It notes: "The legislative department may delegate regulatory authority to the executive department; except that any administrative regulation of any agency of the executive department may be disapproved by the general assembly or a committee thereof in such manner as shall by law be prescribed." Although in general the separation of powers doctrine prohibits the legislature from delegating its powers to another branch, courts will allow it where the legislative body has declared a policy and set specific standards, leaving to the administrative authority the responsibility only for the details of carrying out the legislature's policy.

Division of Powers

Article Third, Of the Legislative Department, as amended in 1970, 1976, 1980, and 1992, declares in **section 1**: "The legislative power of the state shall be vested in two distinct houses or branches; the one to be styled the senate, the other the house of representatives, and both together the general assembly."

Legislative Branch

Section 2, as amended in 1970, provides for, among other things, convening the legislature "on the Wednesday following the first Monday of the January next succeeding the election of its members" and adjourning it "in odd-numbered years not later than the first Wednesday after the first Monday in June and in even-numbered years not later than the first Wednesday after the first Monday in May." It also requires the secretary of state to reconvene the legislature if the mandated adjournment prevents the reconsideration of bills not signed by the governor.

Section 3, as amended in 1970, states that the senate shall consist of "not less than thirty and not more than fifty members, each of whom shall have attained the age of twenty-one years and be an elector residing in the senatorial district from which he is elected. Each senatorial district shall be contiguous as to territory and shall elect no more than one senator." **Section 4,** as amended in 1980, limits the number of representatives to between 125 and 225, who must be eighteen years of age and reside "in the assembly district from which [they are] elected." Currently there are thirty-six senators and 151 representatives.

Section 12 provides: "The house of representatives, when assembled, shall choose a speaker, clerk and other officers. The senate shall choose a president pro tempore, clerk and other officers, except the president [according to **article Fourth, Of the Executive Department, section 17,** the lieutenant governor is the president of the senate]. A majority of each house shall constitute a quorum to do business; but a smaller number may adjourn from day to day, and compel the attendance of absent members…."

Section 13 allows each house to "determine the rules of its own proceedings, and punish members for disorderly conduct, and, with the consent of two-thirds, expel a member…." **Section 14** requires each house to keep a journal of its proceedings. **Section 15** extends the privilege of immunity from arrest "in all cases of civil process" to members of the legislature during any session "and for four days before the commencement and after the termination of any session" and provides that "for any speech or debate in either house, they shall not be questioned in any other place." **Section 16** requires that "debates of each house shall be public, except on such occasions as in the opinion of the house may require secrecy."

Executive Branch

Article Fourth, Of the Executive Department, section 1, as amended in 1970, specifies that the general election for governor, lieutenant governor, secretary of state, treasurer, comptroller, and attorney general shall be held "on the Tuesday after the first Monday of November, 1974, and quadrennially thereafter." The amendment added the attorney general to the list of constitutional executive branch officers elected statewide. **Section 3** requires that voting for the governor and lieutenant governor "shall be as a unit."

Section 5 mandates: "The supreme executive power of the state shall be vested in the governor. No person who is not an elector of the state, and who has not arrived at the age of thirty years, shall be eligible." **Section 6** requires the lieutenant governor to possess the same qualifications as the governor.

Section 8 stipulates that the governor "shall be captain general of the militia of the state, except when called into the service of the United States." Most states use the term *commander in chief* for the governor's command of the state militia; Rhode Island, however, uses both terms. **Sections 9** through **13,** respectively, provide that the governor "may require information in writing from the officers in the executive department, on any subject relating to the duties of their respective offices"; may adjourn the two houses of the legislature "in case of a disagreement between [them] respecting the time of adjournment ..."; "shall, from time to time, give to the general assembly, information of the state of the government, and recommend to their consideration such measures as he shall deem expedient"; "shall take care that the laws be faithfully executed"; and "shall have the power to grant reprieves after conviction, in all cases except those of impeachment, until the end of the next session of the general assembly, and no longer." In *Palko v. Walker* (1938), the Connecticut supreme court of errors declared that the limitation on the period during which a reprieve may operate runs from the time it is issued, not the day of conviction.

Section 15 directs the governor, when approving a bill passed by the legislature, to "sign it and transmit it to the secretary of the state...." If it is disapproved, the governor is required to transmit the bill to the secretary with objections, and the secretary then returns the bill with the governor's objections to the house in which it originated. The constitutions of most states require the governor to transmit approved and disapproved bills directly to the legislature. **Section 16** allows the governor to veto separate items in appropriations bills.

Section 17 states that the lieutenant governor "shall by virtue of his office, be president of the senate, and have, when in committee of the whole, a right to debate, and when the senate is equally divided, to give the casting vote." The lieutenant governor's express right of debate in the committee of the whole—when a legislative body dissolves itself into a committee that includes all members so that committee procedures rather than the formal parliamentary rules apply—is unusual.

Section 18 provides: "In case of the death, resignation, refusal to serve or removal from office of the governor, the lieutenant-governor shall, upon taking the oath of office of governor, be governor of the State until another is chosen at the next regular election for governor...." In other cases of the governor's inability to perform the duties of the office—for example, when impeached or absent from the state—the lieutenant governor is empowered to temporarily exercise the powers of the governor. According to **section 19,** the president pro tempore succeeds to the office of lieutenant governor under like circumstances. In constitutions such as Kansas's, however, the position of lieutenant governor remains vacant when he or she assumes the governor's duties.

Sections 22 through **24** briefly outline the responsibilities of the treasurer, secretary of state, and comptroller. The Connecticut courts have held that clerks of the legislature were the proper custodians for records during sessions but that records of the secretary of state were evidence of acts passed by the legislature.

Like the Massachusetts constitution's article on the judiciary, the Connecticut constitution's basic judicial article is short, consisting of only six sections. However, it is supplemented by a 1976 amendment that addressed removal and suspension of judges and allowed the general assembly to establish a judicial review council.

Judicial Branch

Article Fifth, Of the Judicial Department, section 1, as amended in 1982, vests the judicial power of the state in "a supreme court, an appellate court, a superior court, and such lower courts as the general assembly shall, from time to time, ordain and establish. The powers and jurisdiction of these courts shall be defined by law." In *Calder v. Bull* (1798), the U.S. Supreme Court noted that the Connecticut courts were the proper tribunals to decide whether state laws contrary to the state constitution were void. Five years later, in *Marbury v. Madison* (1803), the U.S. Supreme Court announced its power of judicial review to nullify legislation contrary to the U.S. Constitution. And in *H. A. Bosworth & Son, Inc. v. Tamiola* (1963), the Connecticut superior court, Hartford County, stated that courts must approach the question of the constitutionality of a statute with caution, examine it with care, and sustain it unless its invalidity is clear.

Section 2, as amended in 1986, states: "Judges of all courts, except those courts to which judges are elected, shall be nominated by the governor exclusively from candidates submitted by the judicial selection commission.... Judges so nominated shall be appointed by the general assembly in such manner as shall be prescribed by law. They shall hold their offices for the term of eight years...." Judges may be removed by impeachment, by the governor "on the address of two-thirds of each house of the general assembly," and by the supreme court "as is provided by law." Before the 1986 amendment, judges were nominated solely by the governor before being appointed by the legislature. **Section 3** provides for the appointment and terms of lower court judges; **sections 4** and **5,** respectively, provide for the election and terms of probate judges and justices of the peace; and **section 6,** as amended in 1974, prohibits a judge, with some exceptions, from holding office "after he shall arrive at the age of seventy years...."

Impeachment

Article Ninth, Of Impeachments, sections 1, 2, and **3,** respectively, grant the "house of representatives ... the sole power of impeaching"; grant the senate the power to try all impeachments with "the concurrence of at least two-thirds of the members present" to convict; and make the "governor, and all other executive and judicial officers ... liable to impeachment."

Taxation and Finance

Article Third, Of the Legislative Department, section 18a, as amended in 1992, mandates a balanced budget: "The amount of general budget expenditures authorized for any fiscal year shall not exceed the estimated amount of revenue for such fiscal year."

Local Government

Article Tenth, Of Home Rule, empowers the legislature to delegate by general law "such legislative authority as from time to time it deems appropriate to towns, cities and boroughs relative to the powers, organization, and form of government of such political subdivisions" and permits the legislature to "prescribe the methods by which towns, cities and boroughs may establish regional governments" and the methods by which these subdivisions of the state "may enter into compacts." In *State v. Miller* (1993), the Connecticut supreme court held that constitutional home rule provisions limit only the legislative powers of municipalities.

Article Eighth, Of Education, section 1, proclaims: "There shall always be free public elementary and secondary schools in the state. The general assembly shall implement this principle by appropriate legislation." **Section 2** provides in part: "The state shall maintain a system of higher education, including The University of Connecticut, which shall be dedicated to excellence in higher education." According to **section 3**, "The charter of Yale College, as modified by agreement with the corporation thereof, in pursuance of an act of the general assembly, passed in May, 1792, is hereby confirmed." **Section 4** creates a "SCHOOL FUND" exclusively for "the encouragement and support of public schools."

Article Twelfth, Of Amendments to the Constitution, as amended in 1974, provides: "Amendments to this constitution may be proposed by any member of the senate or house of representatives." Two types of amendment procedures prevail depending on whether the proposed amendment is passed by at least three-fourths or by a majority "of the total membership of each house." An amendment approved by just a majority, but not three-fourths, "shall be published with the laws which have been passed at the same session and be continued to the [next] regular session...." At the next session, if the proposed amendment is again passed by at least a majority, it and any amendment passed by "a yea and nay vote of at least three-fourths of the total membership of each house" are to be presented "to the electors ... for their consideration at the general election to be held on the Tuesday after the first Monday of November in the next even numbered year." A proposed amendment becomes a part of the constitution if approved by "a majority of the electors present and voting...."

Article Thirteenth, Of Constitutional Conventions, section 1, authorizes the legislature, by a vote of at least two-thirds of the total membership of each house, to provide for calling a constitutional convention to "amend or revise the constitution of the state not earlier than ten years from the date of convening any prior convention." **Section 2** requires that the question "'Shall there be a Constitutional Convention to amend or revise the Constitution of the State?'" be submitted to the electorate every twenty years. The constitutions of thirteen other states, including New York and Hawaii, for example, have similar provisions, and the Florida constitution calls for a constitutional revision commission every twenty years. The first time this question was voted on, in 1986, a majority of the electors said no. **Section 3** directs the legislature by a vote of "at least two-thirds of the total membership of each house" to "prescribe by law the manner of selection of the membership of such convention, the date of convening [it] ... and the date for final adjournment of such convention." Under **section 4**, the amendments proposed by the convention become effective thirty days after approval by a majority of electors voting, unless otherwise provided in the proposed amendments.

DELAWARE

On December 7, 1787, Delaware became the first state of the United States. The capital of the "First State," which encompasses some 2,489 square miles in area, is Dover. Delaware is bordered by Pennsylvania on the north, New Jersey on the east (beyond the Delaware River and Delaware Bay), and Maryland on the south and west. With approximately 717,000 inhabitants, Delaware ranks forty-sixth in population. Its principal industries include chemicals, agriculture, finance, and poultry; soybeans, potatoes, corn, and mushrooms are among its chief crops.

General Information

Government: The governor and lieutenant governor are elected separately for four-year terms, and the governor may not be elected to a third term. The legislature, called the general assembly, consists of twenty-one senators elected for four-year terms and forty-one members of the house of representatives elected for two-year terms. The supreme court is made up of a chief justice and four additional justices appointed by the governor with the consent of the senate for twelve-year terms.

Dates of Constitutions: 1776, 1792, 1831, and 1897

Constitutional History

The region that would become the state of Delaware was inhabited by the Lenni-Lenape people of the Algonquin nation when Europeans began arriving there in the early seventeenth century. On August 28, 1609, Henry Hudson, sailing for the Dutch East India Company, became the first European known to navigate the Delaware Bay and River. The following August, Captain Samuel Argall of the Virginia colony named the point of land at the entrance to the bay Cape La Warre, for Lord de la Warre, Sir Thomas West, the governor of Virginia. In 1631 the Dutch established on the bay a colony named *Zwaanendael* (Valley of Swans), but it was later destroyed by the local inhabitants.

In 1655 the Dutch captured Fort Christina, effectively eradicating the colony of New Sweden, which had been founded in 1638. Shortly after the duke of York acquired title to the land encompassing Connecticut and Maryland around 1676, his agents asserted jurisdiction over the Delaware territory, Dutch power there having greatly diminished. The territory was divided into the counties of New Castle, Kent, and Sussex, which would become the state of Delaware. These counties joined with William Penn's province of Pennsylvania pursuant to the 1682 Act of Union and spent the rest of the colonial period as part of Pennsylvania.

A frame of government, or constitution, went into effect in 1683. Devised by William Penn, it had an elected council to assist the governor in preparing legislation and a larger assembly to approve laws. A royal frame of government was imposed in 1696, and five years later Penn granted the Delaware counties a Charter of Privileges similar to one given earlier to Pennsylvania, in effect creating two colonies.

The British colonists' fervor for independence from Great Britain in 1776 spurred the inhabitants of New Castle, Kent, and Sussex Counties to declare their independence from Pennsylvania. A constitutional convention that assembled in New Castle on August 27, 1776, produced a declaration of rights and a constitution, both of which were promulgated in September of that year. Similar constitutional conventions were being held in nearby Philadelphia and Annapolis at about the same time, and this fact probably accounts for similar language in the earliest constitutions of Pennsylvania,

Maryland, and Delaware after they declared independence from Britain. The 1776 Delaware document, however, was unique in providing for a privy council to assume some of the oversight duties previously handled by Pennsylvania agencies.

The relatively simple 1776 constitution soon proved inadequate, and in November 1791 a constitutional convention was called in Dover. Changes incorporated into the 1792 constitution included restyling the declarations of rights in the form used in the Maryland constitution and making the legislative provisions more consistent with the same provisions of the U.S. Constitution and the 1790 Pennsylvania constitution. Delaware's 1792 constitution remained in force for thirty-nine years. A convention meeting in Dover from November 8 to December 2, 1831, adopted a new constitution, which, like its two predecessors, was not submitted to the people for ratification. Delaware's fourth and current constitution was adopted by a convention in Dover and went into effect on June 10, 1897, again without being submitted to the people for approval.

Historically, the Delaware legislature, like that of other states, was the most powerful institution created by the constitution. The 1897 constitution, however, shifted some of the legislature's power to the governor, the courts, and the people by giving the governor the power to veto bills and line items in appropriations bills, transferring the power to grant divorce and create corporations from the legislative branch to the judicial and executive branches, respectively, and taking the power to select the secretary of state from the legislature and giving it to the people.

Delaware's current constitution is some 19,000 words in length, less than average for state constitutions. It provides for a "supreme executive" type of governor who shares power with five other statewide elected officials, including the lieutenant governor. Unlike most other state constitutions, however, it gives extensive and detailed attention to the judicial branch, which was the subject of a comprehensive amendment in 1951. As of January 1, 1998, the 1897 Delaware constitution has been amended 130 times. Like the document itself, none of these amendments has been submitted to the voters for ratification because Delaware is the only state that does not require such approval.

The Constitution

The 1897 Delaware constitution begins with this statement, which precedes the preamble: "WE THE PEOPLE, HEREBY ORDAIN AND ESTABLISH THIS CONSTITUTION OF GOVERNMENT FOR THE STATE OF DELAWARE[.]"

Preamble

The preamble reads in part: "Through Divine goodness, all men have by nature the rights of worshipping and serving their Creator according to the dictates of their consciences, of enjoying and defending life and liberty, of acquiring and protecting reputation and property, and in general of attaining objects suitable to their condition, without injury by one to another...."

Article I, Bill of Rights, section 1, declares in part: "[N]o man shall or ought to be compelled to attend any religious worship, to contribute to the erection or support of any place of worship, or to the maintenance of any ministry, against his own free will and consent...." **Section 2** specifies that "[n]o religious test shall be required as a qualification to any office, or public trust, under this State." **Sections 3, 4,** and **5,** respectively, guarantee free and equal elections, trial by jury, and freedom of the press and

Fundamental Rights

truth as admissible evidence in trials for libel. **Section 6** prohibits unreasonable searches and seizures.

Sections 7 and **8** provide rights for those accused of crimes. **Section 9,** as amended in 1977, states in part: "All courts shall be open; and every man for an injury done to him in his reputation, person, movable or immovable possessions, shall have remedy by the due course of law, and justice administered according to the very right of the cause and the law of the land, without sale, denial, or unreasonable delay or expense." In *Couch v. Delmarva Power & Light Co.* (1991), the Delaware supreme court declared that when the government violates its own rules, without justifying an emergency, people adversely affected may obtain relief on the basis of either the Fourteenth Amendment (1868) to the U.S. Constitution or this section of the Delaware constitution. **Section 12** provides that "[a]ll prisoners shall be bailable by sufficient sureties, unless for capital offences when the proof is positive or the presumption great; and when persons are confined on accusation for such offences their friends and counsel may at proper seasons have access to them."

Section 16 addresses the people's right to petition the government: "Although disobedience to laws by a part of the people, upon suggestions of impolicy or injustice in them, tends by immediate effect and the influence of example not only to endanger the public welfare and safety, but also in governments of a republican form contravenes the social principles of such governments, founded on common consent for common good; yet the citizens have a right in an orderly manner to meet together, and to apply to persons intrusted with the powers of government, for redress of grievances or other proper purposes, by petition, remonstrance or address."

Section 17 stipulates that "[n]o standing army shall be kept without the consent of the [legislature], and the military shall in all cases and at all times be in strict subordination to the civil power"; and **section 18** prohibits quartering soldiers in peacetime without a homeowner's consent. **Section 19** bars granting hereditary distinctions or the acceptance of "any office or title of any kind whatever from any king, prince, or foreign State." **Section 20,** as amended in 1987, affirms that "[a] person has the right to keep and bear arms for the defense of self, family, home and State, and for hunting and recreational use."

Article I concludes with this statement: "WE DECLARE THAT EVERYTHING IN THIS ARTICLE IS RESERVED OUT OF THE GENERAL POWERS OF GOVERNMENT HEREINAFTER MENTIONED."

Division of Powers

Like the U.S. Constitution and the constitutions of some other states, including New York and Hawaii, the Delaware constitution contains no express provision declaring the separation of powers principle, but it is implicit in the structure of the government described in the constitution.

Legislative Branch

Article II, Legislature, section 1, proclaims: "The legislative power of this State shall be vested in a General Assembly, which shall consist of a Senate and a House of Representatives." **Section 2** originally provided in part that the house of representatives was to be composed of thirty-five members, elected for two years, and the senate of seventeen members, elected for four years." In *Roman v. Sincock* (1964), however, the U.S. Supreme Court declared sections 2 and 2(a) unconstitutional on the grounds that they improperly apportioned the state legislators. Currently the composition of the state legislature, which has twenty-one senators elected for four-year terms and forty-one representatives elected for two-year terms, is regulated by statute.

Section 3 specifies that a senator must be twenty-seven years old and must have been a citizen and inhabitant of Delaware for "three years next preceding the day of his election and the last year of that term an inhabitant of the Senatorial District in which he shall be chosen...." A representative must be twenty-four years old, a citizen and inhabitant for three years, and during the third year "an inhabitant of the Representative District in which he shall be chosen...." In *Cassidy v. Willis* (1974), the Delaware supreme court determined that a statute requiring a filing fee in primary elections did not unconstitutionally add to the qualifications for elective office.

Section 4 provides: "The General Assembly shall convene on the second Tuesday of January of each calendar year unless otherwise convened by the Governor, or by mutual call of the presiding officers of both houses." Pursuant to **section 7,** at the first annual session the senate is to choose one of its members as president pro tempore, "who shall preside in the absence of the Lieutenant-Governor," and its other officers. At the same session the house of representatives is to choose from among its members a speaker and other officers.

Section 8 authorizes each house of the legislature to be "the judge of the elections, returns, and qualifications of its own members" and requires "a majority of all the members elected to each House" for a quorum. **Section 9** provides that each house may "determine the rules of its proceedings, punish any of its members for disorderly behavior, and with the concurrence of two-thirds of all the members elected thereto expel a member; moreover, each house shall have "all other powers necessary for a branch of the Legislature of a free and independent State." **Section 13** states that legislators are privileged from arrest during attendance at and travel to and from their respective chambers, except in the case of treason, felony, or breach of the peace; furthermore, "for any speech or debate in either House they shall not be questioned in any other place."

Section 16 provides that no bill or joint resolution, except money bills, may "embrace more than one subject, which shall be expressed in its title." **Section 17,** as amended in 1983 and 1991, prohibits all forms of gambling, with certain enumerated exceptions; **section 18** states: "No divorce shall be granted, nor alimony allowed, except by the judgment of a court ..."; and **section 19,** as amended in 1984, prohibits the legislature from passing any local or special law concerning certain subjects including fences, the straying of livestock, and ditches.

Sections 20 through **22** require legislators to disclose personal or private interests in pending measures and impose certain restrictions and qualifications on legislators and other state officials. In *State ex rel. Wier v. Peterson* (1976), the Delaware supreme court held that under **section 21** conviction of an "infamous crime" prevents a person from holding public office and this disqualification obtains in spite of a pardon. **Section 23** states: "Every statute shall be a public law unless otherwise declared in the statute itself." **Section 24** requires the state treasurer to settle accounts annually with "the General Assembly or a joint committee thereof"; a person who has served in the office of state treasurer is not eligible to be a member of the legislature until after making "a final settlement of his accounts as treasurer and [discharging] the balance, if any, due thereon."

Executive Branch

Article III, Executive, section 1, declares: "The supreme executive powers of the State shall be vested in a Governor." **Section 2** directs that the governor "shall be chosen by the qualified electors of the State, once in every four years, at the general election." According to **section 5,** "The Governor shall hold his office during four years from the third Tuesday in January next ensuing his election; and shall not be elected a third time to said office."

Section 6 specifies that the governor must be at least thirty years old and must have been a citizen and inhabitant of the United States "twelve years next before the day of his election, and the last six years of that term an inhabitant of this State, unless he shall have been absent on public business of the United States or of this State."

Section 8 mandates that the governor is to be "commander-in-chief of the army and navy of this State, and of the militia, except when they shall be called into the service of the United States." **Section 9** authorizes the governor, "unless herein otherwise provided, to appoint, by and with the consent of a majority of all the members elected to the Senate, such officers as he is or may be authorized by this Constitution or by law to appoint ..." and "to fill all vacancies that may happen during the recess of the Senate ... except in the offices of Chancellor, Chief Justice and Associate Judges...." Pursuant to **section 10,** the governor has the power to appoint, "by and with the consent of a majority of all the members elected to the Senate, a Secretary of State, who shall hold office during the pleasure of the Governor."

Section 13 states in part that the governor may "for any reasonable cause remove any officer, except the Lieutenant-Governor and members of the General Assembly, upon the address of two-thirds of all the members elected to each House of the General Assembly." **Section 14** allows the governor to "require information in writing from the officers in the executive department, upon any subject relating to the duties of their respective offices." According to **section 15,** the governor "shall, from time to time, give to the General Assembly information of affairs concerning the State and recommend to its consideration such measures as he shall judge expedient." **Section 16** authorizes the governor "on extraordinary occasions [to] convene the General Assembly by proclamation ..."; and **section 17** mandates that "[h]e shall take care that the laws be faithfully executed."

Section 18 provides in part that every bill passed by both houses of the legislature be presented to the governor; "if he approves, he shall sign it; but if he shall not approve, he shall return it with his objections to the House in which it shall have originated...." The governor's veto may be overridden by a vote of three-fifths of the members elected to each house, but the vote may not be taken on the same day that the bill is returned. If the governor does not sign or return a bill within ten days, excepting Sundays, it becomes law without his signature, "unless the General Assembly shall, by final adjournment, prevent its return...." Section 18 continues: "The Governor shall have power to disapprove of any item or items of any bill making appropriations of money, embracing distinct items, and the part or parts of the bill approved shall be the law, and the item or items of appropriation disapproved shall be void...." In *Perry v. Decker* (1983), the Delaware supreme court held that the governor's item veto power extends only to bills containing more than one appropriation and that a partial veto (a veto of only a single appropriation in a single bill) is invalid and, therefore, necessarily results in failure of the bill to be enacted.

Section 19 stipulates that the lieutenant governor is chosen "at the same time, in the same manner, for the same term, and subject to the same provisions as the Governor," although they are elected on separate tickets. In addition, "he shall possess the same qualifications of eligibility for office as the Governor; he shall be President of the Senate, but shall have no vote unless the Senate be equally divided." Some other states, including Virginia, Michigan, and Idaho, give the lieutenant governor the same role in the upper house of the legislature as the vice president of the United States has in the Senate.

Section 20(a) provides that if the governor dies, is disqualified, refuses to take office, is removed from office, resigns, or is unable to discharge the powers and duties of the office, "the same shall devolve on the Lieutenant-Governor...." Next in line of succession are the secretary of state and the attorney general. **Section 20(b)** designates the lieutenant governor to serve as "Acting Governor" when the governor transmits a written declaration to the president pro tempore of the senate and the speaker of the house "that he is unable to discharge the powers and duties of his office." Section 20(b) also provides that when the "Chief Justice of the Delaware Supreme Court, the President of the Medical Society of Delaware and the Commissioner of the Department of Mental Health, acting unanimously," inform the same officials of the legislature in writing that "the Governor is unable to discharge the powers and duties of his office because of mental or physical disability," the lieutenant governor becomes acting governor until the governor is able to resume the position.

Section 21, as amended in 1980, specifies that the other elected state officials—the attorney general, insurance commissioner, auditor of accounts, and treasurer—are to be elected for four years and are to be chosen "by the qualified electors of the State at general elections, and be commissioned by the Governor."

Article VII, Pardons, section 1, empowers the governor "to remit fines and forfeitures and to grant reprieves, commutations of sentence and pardons, except in cases of impeachment; but no pardon, or reprieve for more than six months, shall be granted, nor sentence commuted, except upon the recommendation in writing of a majority of the Board of Pardons...." **Section 2** provides: "The Board of Pardons shall be composed of the Chancellor, Lieutenant-Governor, Secretary of State, State Treasurer and Auditor of Accounts";

and **section 3** authorizes the board to "require information from the Attorney General upon any subject relating to the duties of said board."

Judicial Branch

Article IV, Judiciary, section 1, declares: "The judicial power of this State shall be vested in a Supreme Court, a Superior Court, a Court of Chancery, an Orphans' Court [since abolished], a Register's Court, Justices of the Peace, and such other courts as the General Assembly, with the concurrence of two-thirds of all the Members elected to each House, shall ... by law [establish]." In *Delaware v. Van Arsdall* (1986), the U.S. Supreme Court reversed a judgment of the Delaware supreme court because the state court had not made a "plain statement" that its decision rested on state grounds. In his dissent, Justice John Paul Stevens commented: "State courts remain primarily responsible for reviewing the conduct of their own executive branches, for safeguarding the rights of their citizenry, and for nurturing the jurisprudence of state constitutional rights which it is their exclusive providence to expound."

Section 2 states in part that the Delaware supreme court is to consist of five justices, citizens of the state and "learned in the law." One of these is the chief justice, "who shall be designated as such by his appointment and who when present shall preside at all sittings of the Court." In his absence the justice with the greatest seniority presides. Section 2 also provides for seven state judges similarly qualified and designated, among others, as chancellor, vice chancellor, and president judge of the superior court. As **section 3** indicates: "The Justices of the Supreme Court, the Chancellor and the Vice-Chancellor or Vice-Chancellors, and the President Judge and Associate Judges of the Superior Court shall be appointed by the Governor, by and with the consent of a majority of all the members elected to the Senate, for the term of twelve years each...." Section 3 adds that "three of the five Justices of the Supreme Court in office at the same time, shall be of one major political party, and two of said Justices shall be of the other major political party."

Section 11, as amended in 1997, sets forth the supreme court's jurisdiction, the first being "**(1)(a)** To receive appeals from the Superior Court in civil causes and to determine finally all matters of appeal in the interlocutory or final judgments and other proceedings of said Superior Court in civil causes: Provided that on appeal from a verdict of a jury, the findings of the jury, if supported by evidence, shall be conclusive. **(1)(b)** To receive appeals from the Superior Court in criminal causes, upon application of the accused in all cases in which the sentence shall be death, imprisonment exceeding one month, or fine exceeding One Hundred Dollars, and in such other cases as shall be provided by law; and to determine finally all matters of appeal on the judgments and proceedings of said Superior Court in criminal causes...." **Sections 11(4)** through **11(9)** also grant the state supreme court jurisdiction to receive appeals from the court of chancery; issue writs of prohibition, quo warranto, certiorari, and mandamus; issue temporary writs and orders in causes pending on appeal or on writ of error; exercise other jurisdiction "by way of appeal, writ of error or of certiorari as the General Assembly may from time to time confer upon it"; and "hear and determine questions of law certified to it by other Delaware courts, the Supreme Court of the United States, a Court of Appeals of the United States, a United States District Court, or the highest appellate court of any other state, where it appears ... that there are important and urgent reasons for an immediate determination of such questions by it." Pursuant to **article V, Elections,** the supreme court also hears appeals from convictions for election offenses. However, in *State v. Hollinger* (1975), the Delaware superior court held that **section 8,** regarding prosecution for election offenses, violated the right of a defendant to a jury trial under the U.S. Constitution.

Section 12, among other provisions, defines a quorum of the supreme court as consisting "of not less than three Justices. The entire Court shall sit in any criminal case in which the accused has been sentenced to death and in such other civil and criminal cases as the Court, by rule, or the General Assembly, upon the concurrence of two-thirds of all the members elected to each house, shall determine." **Section 13** states in part: "The Chief Justice of the Supreme Court, or in the case of his absence from the State, disqualification, incapacity, or if there be a vacancy in that office, the next qualified and available Justice who by seniority is next in rank to the Chief Justice shall be administrative head of all the courts in the State, and shall have general administrative and supervisory powers over all the courts."

Section 10 provides that "[t]he Chancellor and Vice-Chancellor or Vice-Chancellors shall hold the Court of Chancery. One of them, respectively, shall sit alone in that court. This court shall have all the jurisdiction and powers vested by the laws of this State in the Court of Chancery." In *Beals v. Washington Int'l., Inc.* (1978), the Delaware court of chancery explained that its jurisdiction is the same as that of Great Britain's high court of chancery at the time of the separation of the American colonies.

Section 37 creates a "court on the judiciary" consisting of the justices of the supreme court, the chancellor, and the president judge of the superior court. It states in part: "Any judicial officer appointed by the Governor may be censured or removed by virtue of this section for wilful misconduct in office, wilful and persistent failure to perform his duties, the commission after appointment of an offense involving moral turpitude, or other persistent misconduct in violation of the Canons of Judicial Ethics as adopted by the Delaware Supreme Court from time to time. A judicial officer may be retired by virtue of this section for permanent mental or physical disability interfering with the proper performance of the duties of his office."

Article VI, Impeachment and Treason, section 1, vests the house of representatives with "the sole power of impeaching," noting that two-thirds of the members must concur in an impeachment. Impeachments are tried by the senate, and conviction requires "concurrence of two-thirds of all the Senators." **Section 2** states: "The Governor and all other civil officers under this State shall be liable to impeachment for treason, bribery, or any high crime or misdemeanor in office." Conviction results only in loss of office and disqualification from any future state office; it does not provide immunity from prosecution under the law. **Section 3** defines treason in terms similar to those used in the U.S. Constitution.

Impeachment

Direct Democracy   **Article II, Legislature, section 17A.1,** sets out the only direct democracy procedure available to the citizens of Delaware: a vote (held in 1958) on whether bingo was to be "licensed or prohibited within the limits" of Wilmington and the state's three counties.

Local Government   **Article II, Legislature, section 25,** directs the legislature to "enact laws under which municipalities and [the three counties] may adopt zoning ordinances, laws or rules limiting and restricting to specified districts and regulating therein buildings and structures according to their construction and the nature and extent of their use...."

Taxation and Finance   **Article VIII, Revenue and Taxation, section 1,** provides in part: "All taxes shall be uniform upon the same class of subjects within the territorial limits of the authority levying the tax, except as otherwise permitted herein, and shall be levied and collected under general laws passed by the General Assembly." In most other state constitutions, uniformity is limited to property taxes; although this provision has a broad reach, the Delaware courts have interpreted this language restrictively. In *Conard v. State* (1940), the Delaware supreme court found that the same reasonableness standard used in analyzing cases brought under the equal protection clause of the U.S. Constitution applied to analyses under this section. In contrast, in *Kelly v. Kalodner* (1935), the Pennsylvania supreme court construed similar language in its state constitution more liberally to prohibit a graduated income tax.

Section 6(b) states in part: "No appropriation, supplementary appropriation or budget act shall cause the aggregate State General Fund appropriations enacted for any given fiscal year to exceed 98 percent of the estimated State General Fund revenue for such fiscal year from all sources...."

Education   **Article X, Education, section 1,** mandates that the general assembly "provide for the establishment and maintenance of a general and efficient system of free public schools, and may require by law that every child, not physically or mentally disabled, shall attend the public school, unless educated by other means."

Amendment Procedures   **Article XVI, Amendments and Conventions, section 1,** provides that amendments to the constitution may be proposed in either house of the legislature; if they are agreed to by two-thirds of the members of each house, "the Secretary of State shall cause [them] to be published three months before the next General Election in at least three newspapers...." After the election, if the amendments are again agreed to by two-thirds of the members, they become a part of the constitution. Delaware is alone among the states in not requiring that amendments be ratified by the voters.

Section 2 outlines procedures for the legislature, "by a two-thirds vote of all the members elected to each House," to ask the voters if they wish a constitutional convention. A convention to be composed of forty-one delegates chosen by qualified electors takes place "if a majority of those voting on said question shall decide in favor of a Convention for such purpose...." **Section 4** exempts any bill or resolution under this section from requiring the governor's approval.

Florida was admitted to the Union on March 3, 1845, as the twenty-seventh state. Talla-hassee is the capital of the "Sunshine State," which consists of some 65,756 square miles of land bounded by Alabama and Georgia on the north, the Atlantic Ocean on the east, the Straits of Florida on the south, and the Gulf of Mexico and Alabama on the west. Florida ranks fourth among all the states with a population of more than 12 million. Tourism, agri-culture, manufacturing, and construction are among Florida's principal industries; its chief crops are citrus fruits, greenhouse and nursery plants, vegetables, and sugarcane.

Government: The governor and lieutenant governor are elected on a single ticket for four-year terms, the governor being limited to two consecutive terms. The legislature consists of forty senators elected for four-year terms and 120 members of the house of representatives elected for two-year terms; all are limited to eight years in office. The supreme court is composed of a chief justice and six additional justices, each of whom is initially appointed for a six-year term by the governor from nominees submitted by a judicial nominating commission; thereafter, the justices must stand for election.

General Information

Dates of Constitutions: 1845, 1861, 1865, 1868, 1887, and 1969

Constitutional History

The first Floridians included the Panzacola, Apalachee, and Calusa peoples, descen-dants of the immigrants from Asia who arrived via the Alaskan land bridge. At the time of the European discovery of the New World, many of these Native Americans lived in communities protected by walls made of tree trunks; they gathered in meeting houses that could accommodate more than a thousand people. Juan Ponce de León, who searched for the fabled fountain of youth, is generally credited with discovering the Florida peninsula for Spain in April 1513 and giving it its name, which means "the flowering land."

In 1565 Pedro Menéndez, a Spaniard, succeeded in establishing St. Augustine, the first permanent European settlement on what would become the continental United States. The Spanish founded Catholic missions throughout northern Florida, built an immense fort, Castillo de San Marcos, at St. Augustine between 1672 and 1695, and settled Pensa-cola in 1698.

Spanish Florida was ruled by a royal governor who was under the regional supervi-sion of the viceroy of Mexico and the governor-general of Cuba. An ad hoc *junta* (council) composed of the military commander, treasury officials, and the head of the principal church could be called on for advice. St. Augustine had its own *cabildo* (town council). During the seventeenth century the Spaniards exercised authority sparingly over the native villages, which they referred to as "the Republic of the Indians."

In 1761 Spain weighed in against the British in the French and Indian War and, as a result of the French defeat, was forced to cede Florida to Britain in order to retain the more valuable port of Cuba. The British ruled Florida from 1763 to 1783, dividing it into two colonies—West Florida, which extended from the Mississippi to the Apalachicola River, and East Florida.

Spain's intervention against the British during the American Revolution earned it the return of Florida. But American victories in the War of 1812 and later in the wars against the Seminole Indians frightened Spain into relinquishing Florida to the United States in 1819 on the best terms obtainable—the assumption of $5 million in Spanish debts to American citizens.

Congress, through an act approved on March 3, 1821, authorized the United States to take possession of East and West Florida as its territories. Andrew Jackson, who had played a key role in the War of 1812 and the Seminole Wars, was appointed to occupy the new territory and establish a government. By an act approved on March 30, 1822, Congress combined the two Floridas and created a territorial government, providing for a governor, a secretary, and a unicameral legislature with limited powers.

In 1823 Florida's territorial legislative council decided to create a new capital in Tallahassee, roughly halfway between Pensacola and St. Augustine. A territorial constitutional convention met in 1838 in St. Joseph, and after a draft state constitution was narrowly ratified by the people, the legislature, called the general assembly, petitioned Congress for admission to the Union. The territory's delegate to Congress, David Levy, who later adopted the Moorish title Yulee as his family name and became the first Jewish U.S. senator, lobbied extensively and skillfully, and on March 3, 1845, President John Tyler signed the bill making Florida the twenty-seventh state—a slave state whose admission was paired with the free state of Iowa.

Florida's first constitution, which went into effect when statehood was attained in 1845, established a system of government similar to that of other states. Among its provisions, it affirmed slavery and denied public offices to bank officers, clergymen, and anyone who had participated in a duel. Following the election of Abraham Lincoln in 1860, a constitutional convention was called, and on January 10, 1861, it adopted an Ordinance of Secession for the independent "nation of Florida." The convention also revised the state's constitution; the new version was patterned on its predecessor but tied the state to the Confederacy.

A third constitution, drafted and adopted in 1865, abolished slavery but denied the vote to blacks and women. Superseded by the military rule imposed by the Union, it never became law. After military law was terminated, an 1868 constitution extended voting rights to all males and even allocated seats in the legislature to Seminole Indians. Local officials were to be appointed by the governor, not elected.

The 1887 constitution, the state's fifth, sought to correct the abuses of the Reconstruction government by weakening the authority of the executive branch through elected cabinet officials and county officers, reducing the salaries of state officials, and limiting the governor to one term. It also imposed a poll tax, which lasted until 1937, effectively disenfranchising poor black and white citizens. By 1968, when the state's current constitution was adopted, the 1887 document had been amended 149 times and had grown to more than 50,000 words in length.

In a special session in 1968 the Florida legislature adopted three joint resolutions proposing a revision of the 1887 constitution. The voters ratified the new constitution on November 5, 1968, and it became effective on January 7, 1969.

The Constitution

The landmark U.S. Supreme Court ruling in *Baker v. Carr* (1962) required state legislatures to reapportion electoral districts more equitably and thus ensure a closer approximation of the "one man, one vote" concept encompassed in the equal protection clause of the U.S. Constitution's Fourteenth Amendment (1868). The court's decision forced state legislatures to redraw electoral districts. Before this ruling, state courts were unwilling to force legislatures to act on such matters. The issue of reapportionment awakened interest in state constitutions, especially in the southern states. With Florida's reapportionment came new state legislators elected in a special election in 1967, Democrats and Republicans alike, who agreed that the state government needed restructuring. Working with a constitutional revision committee created by statute, they framed a new constitution that strengthened each of the state's three branches of government.

The 1969 constitution is a complete change from the 1887 constitution, except for article v, which relates to the judiciary and had undergone significant alteration by amendment in 1956. It also has eight fewer articles and fifty percent less text. The new constitution is a more modern basic document, recognizing the expansion of civil rights and eliminating redundant and obsolete language. Unlike the U.S. Constitution, which specifies that cabinet members serve at the pleasure of the chief executive, and several other state constitutions, it retains a plural executive branch, in which six officials in addition to the governor and lieutenant governor are elected statewide. Since January 1, 1998, the Florida constitution has been amended seventy-four times.

"We, the people of the State of Florida," begins the preamble to the Florida constitution, "being grateful to Almighty God for our constitutional liberty, in order to secure its benefits, perfect our government, insure domestic tranquility, maintain public order, and guarantee equal civil and political rights to all, do ordain and establish this constitution." **Preamble**

Article I, Declaration of Rights, section 1, begins with this proclamation: "All political power is inherent in the people." The second sentence states that "[t]he enunciation herein of certain rights shall not be construed to deny or impair others retained by the people." This makes clear that the traditional rule of interpretation—*expressio unius est exclusio alterius* (any item not specifically enumerated is therefore excluded)—does not apply to fundamental rights listed in the constitution. In *State ex rel. Moodie v. Bryan* (1905), the Florida supreme court found that this rule should be applied with great caution in constitutional interpretation in general. However, in *Interlachen Lake Estates, Inc. v. Snyder* (1973), the same court used the rule to ensure that the intent of a particular constitutional provision was carried out. **Fundamental Rights**

Section 2, as amended in 1974, sets forth basic individual rights: "All natural persons are equal before the law and have inalienable rights, among which are the right to enjoy and defend life and liberty, to pursue happiness, to be rewarded for industry, and to acquire, possess and protect property; except that the ownership, inheritance, disposition and possession of real property by aliens ineligible for citizenship may be regulated or prohibited by law. No person shall be deprived of any right because of race, religion, or physical handicap." **Sections 4** through **9,** respectively, provide for freedom of speech and the press, the right to assemble, the right to work, civil control of military power, the right to bear arms, and due process of law. **Section 10** prohibits bills of attainder, ex post facto laws, and laws impairing contracts, while **section 11** forbids imprisonment for debt.

Section 12, as amended in 1982, addresses protection against unreasonable searches and seizures. This section is similar to the Fourth Amendment (1791) of the U.S. Constitution except for the last two sentences added in 1982. Before then the Florida supreme court had extended protection against unreasonable searches and seizures beyond the federal constitution's guarantee as interpreted by the U.S. Supreme Court. The penultimate sentence now reads: "This right shall be construed in conformity with the 4th Amendment to the United States Constitution, as interpreted by the United States Supreme Court." In *Florida v. Casal* (1983), Chief Justice Warren E. Burger in a concurring opinion commented on this amendment: "But when state courts interpret state law to require more than the Federal Constitution requires, the citizens of the state must be aware that they have the power to amend state law to ensure rational enforcement."

Sections 13 through **22** provide for rights of the accused, and **section 16(b),** adopted in 1988, provides for victims' rights. **Sections 23, 24,** and **25,** added by amendments effective in 1980, 1992, and 1993, respectively, create a right of privacy, grant access to public records and meetings, and establish a taxpayers' bill of rights.

Division of Powers

Article II, General Provisions, section 3, declares: "The powers of the state government shall be divided into legislative, executive and judicial branches. No person belonging to one branch shall exercise any powers appertaining to either of the other branches unless expressly provided herein." In *Brown v. State* (1978), the Florida supreme court, exhibiting judicial deference to the legislative branch, held that the judicial branch could not rewrite an overbroad or ambiguous statute "where there was no statutory language to support restructuring" the law. Earlier, however, in *Mitchem v. State ex rel. Schaub* (1971), the same court had no qualms about rewriting a state obscenity statute to include elements missing from the legal definition of obscenity, which were required by the U.S. Supreme Court in its decision in *A Book Named "John Cleland's Memoirs of a Woman of Pleasure" v. Attorney General of Commonwealth of Massachusetts* (1966).

Legislative Branch

Article III, Legislature, section 1, mandates: "The legislative power of the state shall be vested in a legislature of the State of Florida, consisting of a senate composed of one senator from each senatorial district and a house of representatives composed of one member elected from each representative district." This language in effect prevents the creation of multimember districts. Under **section 15(a),** senators' terms are set at four years, while **section 15(b)** indicates that house members serve two years. **Article VI, Suffrage and Elections, section 4(b),** limits all legislators to eight consecutive years.

Article III, Legislature, section 2, regarding members and officers, states in part: "Each house shall be the sole judge of the qualifications, elections, and returns of its members, and shall biennially choose its officers, including a permanent presiding officer selected from its membership, who shall be designated in the senate as President of the Senate, and in the house as Speaker of the House of Representatives."

Section 3, as amended in 1990 and 1994, prescribes the organization of regular and special legislative sessions, the latter convened by the governor or "as provided by law."

Section 4, as amended in 1990, establishes a quorum as "[a] majority of the membership of each house," and **section 5** authorizes investigations.

Section 6 stipulates that "[e]very law shall embrace but one subject and matter properly connected therewith. . . ." In *North Ridge General Hospital, Inc. v. City of Oakland Park* (1979), the Florida supreme court found that one subject can encompass a number of separate objects. **Section 7,** as amended in 1980, outlines the procedure for passage of bills: "Any bill may originate in either house and after passage in one may be amended in the other. It shall be read in each house on three separate days, unless this rule is waived by two-thirds vote. . . . On each reading, it shall be read by title only, unless one-third of the members present desire it read in full. On final passage, the vote of each member voting shall be entered on the journal. Passage of a bill shall require a majority vote in each house."

Section 8 requires every bill to be presented to the governor for signature or veto, and he or she may veto any specific appropriation in a general appropriations bill. If the governor does not sign or veto a bill, it still becomes law. A pocket veto occurs when the legislature adjourns after presenting a bill to the governor but before the seven days have passed. The bill then does not become law if the governor fails to sign it. In *Green v. Rawls* (1960), the Florida supreme court concluded that the only way to avoid a pocket veto was for the legislature to submit bills to the governor in a timely manner. A veto may be overridden by a two-thirds vote in each house of the legislature. **Section 9** prescribes that laws "shall take effect on the sixtieth day after adjournment sine die of the session of the legislature in which enacted or as otherwise provided therein."

Section 11 expressly prohibits certain special laws. However, unlike many other state constitutions, it does not prevent the legislature from passing a special law where a general law can be made applicable; the Florida legislature may thus enact any special law not otherwise expressly prohibited. **Section 19,** adopted in 1992, prescribes the state budgeting, planning, and appropriations processes, including a budget stabilization fund not to exceed "an amount equal to 10% of the last completed fiscal year's net revenue collections" to be used in emergencies as defined by general law.

Article IV, Executive, section 1, as amended in 1992, delineates the governor's role: "**(a)** The supreme executive power shall be vested in a governor. He shall be commander-in-chief of all military forces of the state not in active service of the United States. He shall take care that the laws be faithfully executed, [and] commission all officers of the state and counties. . . . He may require information in writing from all executive or administrative state, county or municipal officers upon any subject relating to the duties of their respective offices." As the state's chief administrative officer, the governor is responsible for the state's planning and budgeting and is also authorized to enforce officials' compliance with their duties or restrain them by legal means, to request advisory opinions from the supreme court, and to call out the militia in certain instances. The governor is required to present a message on the condition of the state annually to the legislature and is granted the power of appointment, except as otherwise provided for in the constitution.

Executive Branch

Section 2 creates the position of lieutenant governor, who is to perform duties as assigned by the governor or as may be prescribed by law. As provided in **section 3,** the lieutenant governor serves as governor when that office becomes vacant and acts as governor during a trial for impeachment of the governor. Further succession to the office of governor is to be provided for by law. **Section 4,** as amended in 1986, creates a constitutional cabinet composed of six members—the secretary of state, attorney general, comptroller, treasurer, commissioner of agriculture, and commissioner of education—and defines their major duties, noting that additional responsibilities may be prescribed by law. This definition of duties is quite general compared to more explicit definitions in some other state constitutions; Maryland's, for example, devotes two pages to the attorney general's duties.

Section 5 sets forth the procedures for the election, qualifications, and terms of office for officials of the executive branch elected statewide. **Section 5(a)** specifies that the governor, the lieutenant governor (who must be elected on the same ticket as the governor), and members of the cabinet are elected in statewide general elections "in each calendar year the number of which is even but not a multiple of four." According to **section 5(b),** each must be "an elector not less than thirty years of age who has resided in the state for the preceding seven years." The attorney general must have been a member of the Florida bar for the preceding five years.

Section 6 restricts the number of executive departments to twenty-five; **section 7** gives the governor the authority to suspend for certain enumerated reasons state officials not otherwise removable by impeachment; and **section 8** empowers the governor to grant reprieves, not exceeding sixty days, and full or conditional pardons with the approval of three members of the cabinet. **Sections 11** and **12,** respectively, added by amendment in 1988, establish departments of veterans and elderly affairs.

Judicial Branch

Article V, Judiciary, section 1, as amended in 1972 and 1988, declares in part: "The judicial power shall be vested in a supreme court, district courts of appeal, circuit courts and county courts." The statement that "[n]o other courts may be established by the state, any political subdivision or any municipality" indicates an intent to maintain a unified court system, in which all courts are supervised by the highest court. A similar judicial structure has been adopted in many other states. In this section the legislature is given the authority to divide the state into judicial districts and circuits following county lines, and officers and bodies may be granted quasi-judicial powers in matters connected with the functions of their offices.

Section 2(a), as amended in 1972, directs the supreme court to "adopt rules for the practice and procedure in all courts ... [which] may be repealed by general law enacted by two-thirds vote of the membership of each house of the legislature." Unlike the Alaska constitution, which permits the legislature to amend judicial rules by a two-thirds vote, this section allows the Florida legislature only to repeal judicial rules. According to **section 2(b),** the chief justice of the supreme court is chosen by a majority of the members of the court and is the chief administrative officer of the judicial system.

Section 3(a), as amended in 1972, 1976, 1980, and 1986, specifies: "The supreme court shall consist of seven justices. Of the seven justices, each appellate district shall have at least one justice elected or appointed from the district ... who is a resident of the district at the time of his original appointment or election." Five justices constitute a quorum, while the concurrence of four justices is required for a decision.

Section 3(b) establishes the supreme court's jurisdiction. Pursuant to **section 3(b)(1),** it may "hear appeals from final judgments of trial courts imposing the death penalty and from decisions of district courts of appeal declaring invalid a state statute or a provision of the state constitution." According to **section 3(b)(2),** the supreme court may be further authorized by general law to "hear appeals from final judgments entered in proceedings for the validation of bonds or certificates of indebtedness and ... [to] review action of statewide agencies relating to rates or service of utilities providing electric, gas, or telephone service." **Section 3(b)(3)** extends the supreme court's jurisdiction to certain expressly defined cases. Moreover, as specified in **section 3(b)(10),** the court may render advisory opinions "when requested by the attorney general" in accordance with the constitution.

Section 8, as amended in 1972 and 1985, stipulates that a justice or judge must be "an elector of the state," must reside "in the territorial district of his court," and must also have been a member of the Florida bar for the preceding ten years. Judges of a circuit or county court in a county having a population of more than 40,000, however, must have been members of the bar for only the preceding five years; in counties with a smaller population, only membership in good standing in the Florida bar is required. **Section 11,** as amended in 1972, 1976, and 1984, provides that the governor is to fill each vacancy on the supreme court or a district court of appeal "**(a)** ... by appointing[,] for a term ending on the first Tuesday after the first Monday in January of the year following the next general election occurring at least one year after the date of appointment, one of three persons nominated by the appropriate judicial nominating commission." **Section 10,** as amended in 1971 and 1976, provides for election following the initial appointment, specifying that a justice or judge "may qualify for retention by a vote of the electors in the general election next preceding the expiration of his term...."

Section 12, as amended in 1972, 1974, and 1976, establishes a judicial qualifications commission "**(a)** ... to investigate and recommend to the Supreme Court of Florida the removal from office of any justice or judge whose conduct ... demonstrates a present unfitness to hold office...." **Section 13,** as amended in 1972, requires judges to devote full time to their judicial duties for the state and not to practice law or hold office in any political party.

Article III, Legislature, section 17, as amended in 1988, declares: "**(a)** The governor, lieutenant governor, members of the cabinet, justices of the supreme court [and other judges] shall be liable to impeachment for misdemeanor in office. The house of representatives by a two-thirds vote shall have the power to impeach an officer.... **(c)** All impeachments ... shall be tried by the senate.... No officer shall be convicted without

Impeachment

the concurrence of two-thirds of the members of the senate present. Judgment of conviction ... shall remove the offender from office and, in the discretion of the senate, may include disqualification to hold any office. ... Conviction or acquittal shall not affect the civil or criminal responsibility of the officer."

Direct Democracy

Article XI, Amendments, section 3, as amended in 1972 and amended by initiative in 1994, provides in part: "The power to propose the revision or amendment of any portion or portions of this constitution by initiative is reserved to the people, provided that, any such revision or amendment, except for those limiting the power of government to raise revenue, shall embrace but one subject and matter directly connected therewith."

Local Government

Article VIII, Local Government, section 1(a), as amended in 1974 and 1984, mandates: "The state shall be divided by law into political subdivisions called counties. Counties may be created, abolished or changed by law, with provision for payment or apportionment of the public debt." This section is more flexible than the similar provision in the Washington state constitution that expressly continues the county boundaries in force before statehood. Regarding Dade County, **section 6(f)** provides: "To the extent not inconsistent with the powers of existing municipalities or general law, the Metropolitan Government of Dade County may exercise all the powers conferred now or hereafter by general law upon municipalities." Such provisions recognizing special requirements of a local jurisdiction frequently conflict with more general constitutional provisions. For example, in *State ex rel. Dade County v. Dickinson* (1969), the Florida supreme court addressed Dade County's special status in light of statewide ad valorem tax limitations contained in article VII, section 9.

Taxation and Finance

Article VII, Finance and Taxation, section 1, as amended in 1994, states: "**(a)** No tax shall be levied except in pursuance of law. No state ad valorem taxes shall be levied upon real estate or tangible personal property. All other forms of taxation shall be preempted to the state except as provided by general law." **Section 1(d)** mandates a balanced budget: "Provision shall be made by law for raising sufficient revenue to defray the expenses of the state for each fiscal period." **Section 11** requires state bonds to be approved by the voters but expressly exempts revenue bonds if the project is authorized by law.

Education

Article IX, Education, section 1, declares: "Adequate provision shall be made by law for a uniform system of free public schools and for the establishment, maintenance and operation of institutions of higher learning and other public education programs that the needs of the people may require." **Section 6** restricts the income derived from the state school fund to the support and maintenance of free public schools.

Official Language

Article II, General Provisions, section 9, added in 1988, declares English to be "the official language of the state" and empowers the legislature to enforce this provision.

Amendment Procedures

Article XI, Amendments, section 1, authorizes the Florida legislature to propose amendment or revision of the constitution by a "joint resolution agreed to by three-fifths of the membership of each house of the legislature." **Section 2,** as amended in 1988, provides for a constitutional revision commission to be established ten years after the date of the current constitution and then again every twenty years thereafter to hold public hearings and file with the secretary of state a proposal, if any, for revising the constitution. The first Florida Constitution Revision Commission conducted hearings in 1997 and was scheduled to file its recommendations in 1998.

Section 3, as amended in 1972 and 1994, provides for revision or amendment by initiative, and **section 4** authorizes a constitutional convention. The request to call a constitutional convention may be put to the voters only by a petition signed by at least fifteen percent of the voters. No provision is made for the legislature to propose a constitutional convention, presumably because of the provision for a revision commission every twenty years. Under **section 5,** as amended in 1988, any proposed amendment or revision must be submitted to the electorate at a general election.

Section 6, as amended in 1988, provides for a taxation and budget reform commission to meet in 1990 and every ten years thereafter; it too may propose revisions to the state constitution.

Article X, Miscellaneous, section 1, regarding amendments to the U.S. Constitution, directs the legislature not to "take action on any proposed amendment to the constitution of the United States unless a majority of the members thereof have been elected after the proposed amendment has been submitted for ratification." In *Trombetta v. State of Florida* (1973), a federal district court found this provision to be repugnant to article v of the U.S. Constitution and therefore invalid; the court ruled that the function performed by a state legislature in ratifying a federal constitutional amendment is "a purely Federal function" and accordingly not subject to restrictions by the states.

GEORGIA

Georgia, the "Empire State of the South," became the fourth state of the United States on January 2, 1788. Its capital is Atlanta. Encompassing some 59,441 square miles, Georgia is bordered by Tennessee and North Carolina on the north, South Carolina and the Atlantic Ocean on the east, Florida on the south, and Alabama on the west. It ranks tenth among the states in population with approximately 7.2 million residents. The state's principal industries include services, manufacturing, and retail trade; its chief crops are peanuts, cotton, corn, and tobacco.

General Information

Government: The governor and lieutenant governor are elected separately for four-year terms and may serve two consecutive terms and additional terms if four years intervene. The legislature, called the general assembly, consists of fifty-six senators and 180 members of the house of representatives, all elected for two-year terms. Although nine justices are permitted, the supreme court comprises a chief justice and six additional justices elected on a nonpartisan basis for six-year terms.

Dates of Constitutions: 1777, 1789, 1798, 1861, 1865, 1868, 1877, 1945, 1977, and 1983

Constitutional History

Searching for gold in the New World in 1540, the Spanish explorer Hernando de Soto and his followers were the first Europeans to cross the territory that would become the state of Georgia. French Huguenots led by Gaspard de Coligny traveled north from Florida along Georgia's Atlantic coast in 1562, but fierce resistance by the local inhabitants and France's lack of support doomed attempts to build permanent settlements. The Spanish, however, were able to establish Catholic missions on the islands of Cumberland, Jekyll, and St. Simon between 1573 and 1595.

In 1663 Charles II of England granted lands south of the Virginia colony to the proprietors of the Carolina colony. The territory included in the grant extended as far south as the thirty-first parallel, the present boundary between Alabama and Florida, and thus challenged Spanish claims to lands north of Florida. By the Treaty of Madrid in 1670, Spain agreed that England could keep all land it then held in North America, creating ambiguity about the territory between the English settlement of Charles Town and the Spanish settlement of St. Augustine, which became known as the "debatable lands."

By 1689, however, the Spanish had abandoned their missions in the "debatable lands" because of continual attacks by American natives and coastal pirates. Twelve years later an English expedition from southern Carolina invaded Florida, destroying Spanish missions on the Atlantic side of the peninsula. The first British settlement in Georgia, Fort King George, was built in 1721, and a treaty with the Cherokees in 1730 opened new trade routes and permitted more British settlements in the area.

In July 1730 the British humanitarian James Edward Oglethorpe and the earl of Egmont petitioned the British Crown for a grant of land "on the South-west of Carolina for settling poor persons of London." On January 27, 1732, the privy council in London approved a charter for the Georgia colony, the last British colony in North America. Signed by George II, it became effective on June 9, 1732. The charter created "the Trustees for Establishing the Colony of Georgia in America ... to be a body Politick and Corporate in Deed and name for ever." Oglethorpe landed at the site of present-day Savannah on February 12, 1733, and in May the Creek and Cherokee peoples granted him all the land between the Savannah and Altamaha Rivers.

In 1741 the Georgia colony was divided into two counties and given a new constitution by its trustees. After Oglethorpe retired as military governor, the second county was abolished and a government consisting of a president and five counsellors installed. The trustees surrendered the colonial charter in 1752, and in January 1755 the colony's first provincial congress met in Savannah. On June 5, 1775, with revolutionary fever in the air, Georgia declared its independence from Great Britain and replaced its colonial government with a provincial congress and a "council of safety" as its executive branch.

A third provincial congress adopted a temporary constitution on April 15, 1776, and on February 5, 1777, Georgia's first state constitution was approved and John Adams Treutlen became governor. A decade later, a constitutional convention was called to ratify the U.S. Constitution, which it did on January 2, 1788, and to revise the 1777 document, which had been based on Georgia's colonial form of government. As sometimes happens, the convention went beyond its mandate and drafted a wholly new constitution, which was adopted in May 1789. Again in 1798 a convention called simply to amend the constitution produced an entirely new document, one that expanded suffrage and abolished the African slave trade.

With Georgia's secession from the Union in 1861 came a fourth constitution, which, in anticipation of war, provided for a popularly elected governor with increased powers. After the Civil War, on November 7, 1865, a new constitution was adopted by a convention, but it was abrogated by Congress when the Georgia legislature refused to ratify the Fourteenth Amendment to the U.S. Constitution in November 1866. Two years later a Reconstruction constitution was ratified by the voters. Like other southerners, Georgians resented their Reconstruction constitution, and a convention to draft a new document was called in July 1877. The result, a detailed constitution bent on limiting government officials and institutions, was overwhelmingly approved by the voters and became effective on December 21, 1877.

Georgia's eighth constitution was drafted by a commission that met in Atlanta in 1943–44. This document incorporated a number of previous amendments to the 1877 constitution and, among other things, established the position of lieutenant governor. It was approved by the legislature and the voters in 1945. The draft of a new constitution prepared by a constitutional revision commission and approved by the legislature in 1964 was invalidated by a 1966 federal court ruling that held that the legislature was malapportioned. In the 1970s Governor George Busbee directed his staff to prepare a new draft constitution, which was approved by the electorate in 1976. Containing no major substantive revisions, it became effective on January 1, 1977. Georgia's current constitution, its tenth, took effect on July 1, 1983.

Like most southern states, Georgia has had numerous constitutions; its ten constitutions are second only to Louisiana's eleven. At approximately 25,000 words, Georgia's 1983 constitution is a little less than average in length, the result of the framers' avowed intent to avoid excessive verbiage. One of twelve states that elect legislators to the upper house for terms of only two years, Georgia is also one of thirteen states that choose the members of the state supreme court strictly on the basis of nonpartisan elections.

Georgia's 1983 constitution retains the flavor of the 1877 post-Reconstruction document in that it contains detailed grants of powers to and numerous restrictions on

The Constitution

the instruments of government. The biennial election of members of both houses of the legislature represents a way to increase popular oversight and limit continuity in the legislative branch, which gets the lion's share of attention in the 1983 document. Article III, which deals with the legislative branch, is far more voluminous and detailed than article V, dealing with the executive branch, and article VI, dealing with the judicial branch. A Georgia appellate court judge, Dorothy T. Beasley, once remarked, "The 1983 Constitution is a new and revitalized organic law, which speaks to the current people's will and understanding. . . ." As of January 1, 1998, it has been amended forty-eight times.

Preamble

The preamble to the 1983 Georgia constitution reads: "To perpetuate the principles of free government, insure justice to all, preserve peace, promote the interest and happiness of the citizen and of the family, and transmit to posterity the enjoyment of liberty, we the people of Georgia, relying upon the protection and guidance of Almighty God, do ordain and establish this Constitution."

Fundamental Rights

Article I, Bill of Rights, section I, paragraph I, proclaims: "No person shall be deprived of life, liberty, or property except by due process of law." **Paragraph II** affirms: "Protection to person and property is the paramount duty of government and shall be impartial and complete. No person shall be denied the equal protection of the laws." **Paragraphs III** through **VI,** respectively, guarantee freedom of conscience; freedom of religious opinion and religion; freedom of speech and of the press; and truth as a defense in libel actions.

Paragraph VII provides: "All citizens of the United States, resident in this state, are hereby declared citizens of this state; and it shall be the duty of the General Assembly to enact such laws as will protect them in the full enjoyment of the rights, privileges, and immunities due to such citizenship." The U.S. Supreme Court's decision in *Chisolm v. Georgia* (1793) that it had jurisdiction to hear a controversy between a citizen of one state against another state led to the Eleventh Amendment (1798) of the U.S. Constitution, which abrogated that jurisdiction.

Paragraph VIII guarantees the right to keep and bear arms; **paragraph IX** ensures the right to peaceably assemble and petition the government for redress of grievances; and **paragraph X** prohibits bills of attainder and retroactive laws. **Paragraphs XI** through **XVIII** provide for rights of those accused of crimes, beginning with the right to trial by jury. In *Williams v. State* (1955), the last in a series of cases involving the same criminal defendant, the Georgia supreme court declared that, even though the U.S. Supreme Court had held earlier in *Williams v. Georgia* (1955) that the use of white slips of paper for the names of white jurors and yellow slips of paper for the names of black jurors "as a matter of substantive law violated the defendant's constitutional rights" to a fair trial, there was sufficient procedural grounds under Georgia law to deny the defendant a new trial.

Paragraph XIX defines treason against the state of Georgia, in language similar to that used in the U.S. Constitution, as "insurrection against the state, adhering to the state's enemies, or giving them aid and comfort." **Paragraph XXI** provides: "Neither banishment beyond the limits of the state nor whipping shall be allowed as a punishment for crime." Pursuant to **paragraph XXII**, "There shall be no involuntary servitude within the State of Georgia except as a punishment for crime after legal conviction thereof or for contempt of court."

Paragraph XXV asserts that "[t]he social status of a citizen shall never be the subject of legislation." And **paragraph XXVII** states: "The separate property of each spouse shall remain the separate property of that spouse except as otherwise provided by law."

Section II, paragraph I, declares: "All government, of right, originates with the people, is founded upon their will only, and is instituted solely for the good of the whole. Public officers are the trustees and servants of the people and are at all times amenable to them." **Paragraph II** defines the object of government to include "the protection, security, and benefit of the people"; and **paragraph VII** underscores the separation of church and state: "No money shall ever be taken from the public treasury, directly or indirectly, in aid of any church, sect, cult, or religious denomination or of any sectarian institution." **Paragraph IX** provides for the waiver of the state's sovereign immunity in certain cases.

Article I, Bill of Rights, section II, paragraph III, states: "The legislative, judicial, and executive powers shall forever remain separate and distinct; and no person discharging the duties of one shall at the same time exercise the functions of either of the others except as herein provided."

Division of Powers

Article III, Legislative Branch, section I, paragraph I, vests the state's legislative power in "a General Assembly which shall consist of a Senate and a House of Representatives." **Section II, paragraph I,** specifies that "**(a)** [t]he Senate shall consist of not more than 56 Senators, each of whom shall be elected from single-member districts," while "**(b)** [t]he House of Representatives shall consist of not fewer than 180 Representatives apportioned among representative districts of the state." **Paragraph II** directs the general assembly to apportion the senate and house districts so that they are composed of "contiguous territory"; furthermore, apportionment must be changed "as necessary after each United States decennial census."

Legislative Branch

Paragraph III requires that at the time of their election senators be twenty-five years old, state citizens for two years, and legal residents of their district for one year. Representatives must meet the same qualifications except that they may be twenty-one years old. Pursuant to **paragraph IV,** disqualifications include serving on active duty in the U.S. armed forces or holding a government position. **Paragraph V** provides that legislators are elected "by the qualified electors of their respective districts for a term of two years...."

Section III, paragraphs I and **II,** respectively, provide for the senate to elect from among its members a president pro tempore (as stipulated in **article V, Executive Branch, section I, paragraph III,** the lieutenant governor is president of the senate) and the house of representatives to elect a speaker and speaker pro tempore. As noted in **paragraph III,** the other legislative officers are the secretary of the senate and the clerk of the house of representatives.

Section IV, paragraph I, mandates that the legislature "shall organize each odd-numbered year and shall be a different General Assembly for each two-year period." **Paragraph III** defines a quorum as "[a] majority of the members to which each house is entitled," although "[a] smaller number may adjourn from day to day and compel the presence of its absent members."

Paragraph IV allows each house to determine its procedural rules, provide for its employees, and create interim committees. **Paragraph VII** empowers each house to judge the election and qualifications of its members and punish them "for disorderly behavior or misconduct by censure, fine, imprisonment, or expulsion"; expulsion, however, requires "a vote of two-thirds of the members of the house to which such member belongs." According to **paragraph IX,** legislators are exempt from arrest "during sessions of the General Assembly, or committee meetings thereof, and in going thereto or returning therefrom" except in cases of treason, felony, or breach of the peace; furthermore, "[n]o member shall be liable to answer in any other place for anything spoken in either house or in any committee meeting of either house."

Section V, paragraph II, states: "All bills for raising revenue, or appropriating money, shall originate in the House of Representatives." **Paragraph V** stipulates that passage of a bill requires "a majority of the votes of all the members to which each house is entitled...." Pursuant to **paragraph VII,** "The title of every general bill and of every resolution intended to have the effect of general law or to amend this Constitution ... shall be read three times and on three separate days in each house before such a bill or resolution shall be voted upon; and the third reading of such bill and resolution shall be in their entirety when ordered by the presiding officer or by a majority of the members voting on such question in either house."

Paragraph X requires that "[a]ll Acts ... be signed by the President of the Senate and the Speaker of the House of Representatives." **Paragraph XI** notes: "No provision in this Constitution for a two-thirds' vote of both houses of the General Assembly shall be construed to waive the necessity for the signature of the Governor as in any other case, except in the case of the two-thirds' vote required to override the veto or to submit proposed constitutional amendments or a proposal for a new Constitution." In *Capitol Distrib. Co. v. Redwine* (1950), the Georgia supreme court held that the legislative journal and copies of bills could not impeach an act of the legislature signed by the principal officers of both houses and the governor. According to **paragraph XIII(a),** "... if the Governor approves or fails to veto [a bill or resolution] within six days [it shall become law] unless the General Assembly adjourns sine die or adjourns for more than 40 days prior to the expiration of said six days...." **Paragraph XIII(e)** allows the governor to "approve any appropriation and veto any other appropriation in the same bill...."

Section VI, paragraph I, directs the general assembly "to make all laws not inconsistent with this Constitution, and not repugnant to the Constitution of the United States, which it shall deem necessary and proper for the welfare of the state." In *Plumb v.*

Christie (1898), the Georgia supreme court determined that, although Congress may exercise only the powers delegated to it by the states in the U.S. Constitution, the state legislature may do anything not prohibited by the state constitution.

Paragraph II authorizes the legislature to enact laws concerning, among other things, "**(2)** [a] militia and … trial by courts-martial …"; "**(3)** [t]he participation by the state and political subdivisions and instrumentalities of the state in federal programs …" and "**(4)** [t]he continuity of state and local governments in periods of emergency. …" With respect to special legislation, **paragraph IV(a)** requires that "[l]aws of a general nature shall have uniform operation throughout this state and no local or special law shall be enacted in any case for which provision has been made by an existing general law. …"

Article V, Executive Branch, section I, paragraph I, provides in part: "There shall be a Governor who shall hold office for a term of four years and until a successor shall be chosen and qualified. Persons holding the office of Governor may succeed themselves for one four-year term of office." Governors who have served two consecutive terms, however, are eligible to run again after an interval of four years and may again serve two consecutive terms. In *Maddox v. Fortson* (1970), the Georgia supreme court held that the requirement to skip a term before being eligible to hold office as governor again did not violate the U.S. Constitution. **Paragraph III** establishes the position of lieutenant governor, who is elected "at the same time, for the same term, and in the same manner as the Governor" although not on the same ticket. He or she serves as president of the senate and has "such executive duties as prescribed by the Governor and as may be prescribed by law not inconsistent with the powers of the Governor or other provisions of this Constitution."

Paragraph IV requires that candidates for both governor and lieutenant governor be U.S. citizens for fifteen years, legal residents of the state for six years, and thirty years old "by the date of assuming office." Pursuant to **paragraph V(a)**, if the governor is temporarily disabled, the lieutenant governor assumes the powers and duties of the office until the disability ends; and, under **paragraph V(b),** the lieutenant governor succeeds to the office in the event of the governor's death, resignation, or permanent disability.

Section II, paragraph I, states in part: "The chief executive powers shall be vested in the Governor. The other executive officers shall have such powers as may be prescribed by this Constitution and by law." According to **paragraphs II** through **VII,** respectively, the governor must "take care that the laws are faithfully executed and … be the conservator of the peace throughout the state"; serve as the commander in chief of the state's military forces; "veto, approve, or take no action on any … bill or resolution … passed by the General Assembly"; issue "writs of election" to fill vacancies in the legislature; give to the general assembly information on "the state of the state" and recommend any necessary or expedient measures; and convene special sessions of the legislature "by proclamation. …" **Paragraph VIII(a)** authorizes the governor to fill vacancies in public offices, and according to **paragraph X,** he or she "may require information in writing from constitutional officers and all other officers and employees of the executive branch on any subject relating to the duties of their respective offices or employment."

Section III, paragraph I, designates the other executive officers who "shall be elected at the same time and hold their offices for the same term as the Governor." These are the secretary of state, attorney general, state school superintendent, and commissioners of insurance, agriculture, and labor. The attorney general's duties are described in **paragraph IV**, while **paragraph III** notes that the legislature is to prescribe the "powers, duties, compensation, and allowances" of the other officers. **Section IV** addresses the disability of executive officers.

Judicial Branch

Article VI, Judicial Branch, section 1, paragraph I, declares: "The judicial power of the state shall be vested exclusively in the following classes of courts: magistrate courts, probate courts, juvenile courts, state courts, superior courts, Court of Appeals, and Supreme Court." The legislature, however, is authorized to establish municipal courts and has "authority to confer 'by law' jurisdiction upon municipal courts to try state offenses." **Paragraph II** directs that "[a]ll courts of the state shall comprise a unified judicial system."

Paragraph IV establishes the courts' jurisdiction: "Each court may exercise such powers as necessary in aid of its jurisdiction or to protect or effectuate its judgments; but only the superior and appellate courts shall have the power to issue process in the nature of mandamus, prohibition, specific performance, quo warranto, and injunction. Each superior court, state court, and other courts of record may grant new trials on legal grounds." **Paragraph VII** authorizes the legislature to "abolish, create, consolidate, or modify judicial circuits and courts and judgeships," although specifying that "no circuit shall consist of less than one county." According to **paragraph IX**, "All rules of evidence shall be as prescribed by law."

Section VI, paragraph I, states in part: "The Supreme Court shall consist of not more than nine Justices who shall elect among themselves a Chief Justice as the chief presiding and administrative officer of the court and a Presiding Justice to serve if the Chief Justice is absent or is disqualified. A majority shall be necessary to hear and determine cases." According to **paragraph II**, "The Supreme Court shall be a court of review and shall exercise exclusive jurisdiction in . . . : **(1)** [a]ll cases involving the construction of a treaty or of the Constitution of the State of Georgia or of the United States and all cases in which the constitutionality of a law, ordinance, or constitutional provision has been drawn in question; and **(2)** [a]ll cases of election contest." **Paragraph III** provides that the supreme court's general appellate jurisdiction extends to cases involving title to land, equity, wills, habeas corpus, extraordinary remedies, divorce and alimony, and sentence of death, as well as cases certified to it by the court of appeals.

Paragraph IV confers on the supreme court jurisdiction to "answer any question of law from any state or federal appellate court" and "review by certiorari cases in the Court of Appeals which are of gravity or great public importance." **Paragraph VI** states: "The decisions of the Supreme Court shall bind all other courts as precedents."

Section VII, paragraph I, specifies: "All superior court and state court judges shall be elected on a nonpartisan basis for a term of four years. All Justices of the Supreme Court and the Judges of the Court of Appeals shall be elected on a nonpartisan basis for a term of six years." **Paragraph II** requires: "**(a)** Appellate and superior court judges shall have been admitted to practice law for seven years ... [and] **(d)** [all] judges shall reside in the geographical area in which they are selected to serve"; in addition, **paragraph II(e)** notes that "[t]he General Assembly may provide by law for additional qualifications...." **Paragraph III** directs the governor to fill vacancies by appointment "except as otherwise provided by law in the magistrate, probate, and juvenile courts." **Paragraph VI** creates a judicial qualifications commission to "discipline, remove, and cause involuntary retirement of judges."

Article III, Legislative Branch, section VII, paragraph I, grants the house of representatives "the sole power to vote impeachment charges against any executive or judicial officer of this state or any member of the General Assembly." Most state constitutions limit impeachment to government officials other than members of the legislature. **Paragraph II** provides in part: "The Senate shall have the sole power to try impeachments." Unless disqualified, the chief justice of the supreme court presides at impeachment trials; conviction requires concurrence of "two-thirds of the members to which the Senate is entitled." As noted in **paragraph III,** conviction extends only to removal and disqualification from holding any office and receiving any pension therefrom and does not "relieve any party from any criminal or civil liability."

Impeachment

Article II, Voting and Elections, section III, paragraph I, outlines other procedures for suspending or removing public officials, including "the Governor, the Lieutenant Governor, the Secretary of State, the Attorney General, the State School Superintendent, the Commissioner of Insurance, the Commissioner of Agriculture, the Commissioner of Labor, and any member of the General Assembly."

Article IX, Counties and Municipal Corporations, section I, paragraph I, asserts: "Each county shall be a body corporate and politic with such governing authority and with such powers and limitations as are provided in this Constitution and as provided by law...." **Section II, paragraph 1(a),** provides for home rule for counties and municipalities, stating in part: "The governing authority of each county shall have legislative power to adopt clearly reasonable ordinances, resolutions, or regulations relating to its property, affairs, and local government for which no provision has been made by general law and which is not inconsistent with this Constitution or any local law applicable thereto.... This, however, shall not restrict the authority of the General Assembly by general law to further define this power or to broaden, limit, or otherwise regulate the exercise thereof."

Local Government

Article VII, Taxation and Finance, section I, paragraph I, declares: "The state may not suspend or irrevocably give, grant, or restrain the right of taxation and all laws, grants, contracts, and other acts to effect any of these purposes are null and void. Except as otherwise provided in this Constitution, the right of taxation shall always be under the complete control of the state." **Paragraph II(a)** provides: "The annual levy of state ad valorem taxes on tangible property for all purposes, except for defending the state in an emergency, shall not exceed one-fourth mill on each dollar of the assessed value of

Taxation and Finance

property." **Paragraph III** states in part: "**(a)** All taxes shall be levied and collected under general laws and for public purposes only."

Article III, Legislative Branch, section IX, paragraph IV(b), specifies a balanced budget: "The General Assembly shall not appropriate funds for any given fiscal year which, in aggregate, exceed a sum equal to the amount of unappropriated surplus expected to have accrued in the state treasury at the beginning of the fiscal year together with an amount not greater than the total treasury receipts from existing revenue sources anticipated to be collected in the fiscal year...."

Education

Article VIII, Education, section I, mandates: "The provision of an adequate public education for the citizens shall be a primary obligation of the State of Georgia. Public education for the citizens prior to college or postsecondary level shall be free and shall be provided for by taxation. The expense of other public education shall be provided for in such manner and in such amount as may be provided by law."

Environment

Article III, Legislative Branch, section VI, paragraph II, directs the legislature to enact laws concerning "**(1)** [r]estrictions on land use in order to protect and preserve the natural resources, environment, and vital areas of this state."

Amendment Procedures

Article X, Amendments to the Constitution, section I, paragraph I, provides that amendments to the constitution may be proposed by the legislature or by a constitutional convention, noting: "Only amendments which are of general and uniform applicability throughout the state shall be proposed, passed, or submitted to the people." This requirement precludes the type of amendments that made up the majority of the amendments adopted before the 1983 constitution and that make up the majority of amendments to the current Alabama constitution, for example.

Paragraph II requires that proposed changes to the constitution "originate as a resolution in either the Senate or the House of Representatives and, if approved by two-thirds of the members to which each house is entitled in a roll-call vote entered on their respective journals, ... be submitted to the electors of the entire state at the next general election which is held in the even numbered years." A proposed amendment or new constitution is approved if "ratified by a majority of the electors qualified to vote for members of the General Assembly voting thereon in such general election." In *Towns v. Suttles* (1952), the Georgia supreme court ruled that a proclamation by the governor declaring that an amendment was properly ratified and adopted is not conclusive and that the courts may determine the amendment's validity.

Paragraph IV authorizes the legislature to call a constitutional convention "by the concurrence of two-thirds of the members to which each house ... is entitled." **Paragraph V** states: "The Governor shall not have the right to veto any proposal by the General Assembly or by a convention to amend this Constitution or to provide a new Constitution." **Paragraph VI** indicates that changes to the constitution "become effective on the first day of January following [ratification]."

On August 21, 1959, Hawaii became the fiftieth state of the United States. The capital of the "Aloha State" is Honolulu. Some 10,932 square miles in area, Hawaii consists of a chain of volcanic islands in the northern Pacific Ocean about 3,000 miles west of California. With approximately 1.2 million residents, it ranks fortieth among the states in population. Hawaii's principal industries include tourism and military defense; sugar, pineapples, macadamia nuts, and coffee are among the islands' chief crops.

Government: The governor and lieutenant governor are elected on a single ticket for a four-year term and are limited to two consecutive terms. The legislature consists of twenty-five senators elected for four-year terms and fifty-one members of the house of representatives elected for two-year terms. The supreme court includes a chief justice and four associate justices appointed by the governor with the consent of the senate from a list prepared by a judicial selection commission; the justices serve for ten-year renewable terms.

Date of Constitution: 1959

Around 3000 B.C. island people of Southeast Asia who spoke variations of the Malay-Polynesian, or Austronesian, language began spreading eastward in seagoing outrigger canoes. Within two thousand years their descendants had colonized Fiji, Tonga, and Samoa, and by A.D. 800 they had settled central Polynesia and the northernmost Hawaiian Islands.

The structure of Polynesian society and government varied, but political authority generally resided in a chief, a senior ranking male, who was believed to possess a super-natural power *(mana)* that gave him superior abilities in war and diplomacy and even in catching fish. Its invisible force made the chief taboo, or above contact with mere mortals, not unlike the status accorded to some Chinese and Roman emperors.

Polynesian societies have been categorized either as open—organized along more secular, military, and political lines—or as stratified. The latter type, found among the Polynesians in Hawaii, Tahiti, and Tonga, had a more hierarchical class structure with subordinate chiefs *(alii)* and a paramount chief *(alii nui)* at the apex who possessed all lands. Hawaii had the most highly developed stratified social and political system, probably because of its larger population and greater amount of available land. The Hawaiian *alii nui*, who was often despotic, had eleven *alii* under him, as well as a land manager *(kalaimoku)* who ran the government.

Captain James Cook, commander of a British naval squadron, is credited with the European discovery of the Hawaiian Islands on January 18, 1778. The following year, however, he was killed by Hawaiians while trying to retrieve a stolen boat. By 1787 the ships of European fur traders were plying the waters around the islands. In 1791 a high-ranking warrior who became known as Kamehameha I unified the inhabitants of the island of Hawaii under his rule, adding most of the other islands by 1796.

Hawaii's first constitution, promulgated by Kamehameha III in 1840, reflected the monarchical structure of Hawaiian government but did create a lower house of elected representatives. The Declaration of Rights, both of the People and Chiefs in the document reflected the moral influence of the Protestant missionaries from New England, who had come to the islands beginning in 1820. Other monarchical-style constitutions were issued in 1852, 1864, and 1887. In 1893 a group of local American businessmen, aided by the U.S. Marines, overthrew the monarchy of Queen Liliuokalani, and on July 4, 1894, a new constitution of the Republic of Hawaii, closely modeled on various U.S. state constitutions, was promulgated, and Sanford B. Dole became president.

Early attempts to persuade the United States to annex Hawaii met with opposition, particularly from President Grover Cleveland, but on August 12, 1898, annexation became official during President William McKinley's term. The Hawaiian Territorial Act of April 30, 1900, which incorporated much of the constitution of the Republic of Hawaii, became the organic act for the new territory.

Serious proposals for statehood began in 1940, but World War II delayed the process. Postwar fears of communist infiltration slowed progress again, but in 1950 hopeful Hawaiians called a constitutional convention. It produced the "hope chest" constitution, which was approved by the voters on November 7, 1950. Congress required three additional provisions: that Hawaii be admitted immediately as a state; that its boundaries be clearly stated (Palmyra Island, the Midway Islands, Johnston Island, Sana Island, and Kingham Reef were excluded); and that all provisions of the act reserving rights or powers to the United States as well as those prescribing terms or conditions of grants of land to the state be fully consented to. After Hawaiian voters approved these as amendments, President Dwight D. Eisenhower signed the proclamation admitting Hawaii as the fiftieth state of the Union on August 21, 1959. Its constitution became effective on that date.

The Constitution

Hawaii's constitution is similar to Alaska's, which also went into effect in 1959. Both states had similarly long histories as U.S. territories. In addition, Hawaii, like Texas, was briefly an independent republic before being annexed by the United States.

Hawaii's relatively modern constitution reflects an effort to balance the powers of the legislative, executive, and judicial branches, although the document does not expressly refer to the separation of powers principle. The governor is vested with complete executive authority and does not have to share executive power with other statewide elected officials. The document contains an extensive article on reapportionment.

As of January 1, 1998, Hawaii's constitution, which contains approximately 28,000 words, has been amended ninety-five times. Certain amendments proposed by a constitutional convention and presented for ratification to the voters on November 7, 1978, were later found by the Hawaii supreme court in *Kahalekai v. Doi* (1979) not to have been validly ratified. The text of the 1959 constitution was subsequently revised under the authority of a resolution by the convention in anticipation that some or all of the proposed amendments would not be approved by the voters in 1978. Most of the many 1978 amendments to the constitution were valid; thus, only the dates of amendments approved later than 1978 are noted here.

Preamble

The preamble to the 1959 Hawaiian constitution begins: "We, the people of Hawaii, grateful for Divine Guidance, and mindful of our Hawaiian heritage and uniqueness as an island State, dedicate our efforts to fulfill the philosophy decreed by the Hawaii State motto, 'Ua mau ke ea o ka aina i ka pono'" (The life of the land is perpetuated in righteousness).

Federal Constitution Adopted, a brief section that follows the preamble, states: "The Constitution of the United States of America is adopted on behalf of the people of the State of Hawaii."

Article I, Bill of Rights, section 1, proclaims: "All political power of this State is inherent in the people and the responsibility for the exercise thereof rests with the people. All government is founded on this authority." **Section 2** affirms: "All persons are free by nature and are equal in their inherent and inalienable rights. Among these rights are the enjoyment of life, liberty and the pursuit of happiness, and the acquiring and possessing of property. These rights cannot endure unless the people recognize their corresponding obligations and responsibilities." **Section 3** provides that equal rights under the law "shall not be denied or abridged by the State on account of sex" and states that "[t]he legislature shall have the power to enforce, by appropriate legislation, the provisions of this section."

Section 4 guarantees freedom of religion, speech, and the press and the right "peaceably to assemble and to petition the government for a redress of grievances." **Section 5** ensures due process of law and provides that no person "shall be denied the equal protection of the laws, nor be denied the enjoyment of the person's civil rights or be discriminated against in the exercise thereof because of race, religion, sex or ancestry." In *Baehr v. Lewin* (1993), the Hawaii supreme court ruled that, while the Hawaii constitution does not establish a fundamental right of marriage for same-sex couples, nevertheless a statute restricting marital relations to male and female establishes a sex-based classification that is subject to the "strict scrutiny" test for equal protection challenges. As a result of this decision, plans were developed to present to the voters of Hawaii in November 1998 a constitutional amendment banning same-sex marriages.

Section 6 states: "The right of the people to privacy is recognized and shall not be infringed without the showing of a compelling state interest. The legislature shall take affirmative steps to implement this right." **Section 7** addresses searches, seizures, and invasion of privacy; and **section 8** provides: "No citizen shall be disenfranchised, or deprived of any of the rights or privileges secured to other citizens, unless by the law of the land." **Section 9** prohibits segregation or denial of enlistment in the military "because of race, religious principles or ancestry."

Sections 10 through **14** provide for rights of those accused of a crime, including in **section 14** the right to "a public trial by an impartial jury." In *State v. Mabuti* (1991), the Hawaii supreme court held that a jury was not tainted by anonymous phone calls to some jurors where no threat was made and there was no actual reference to the trial. **Sections 15** through **20,** respectively, cover habeas corpus writs, the supremacy of civil power over the military, the right to bear arms, restrictions on quartering soldiers in private homes, prohibition against imprisonment for debt, and the right to compensation for private property taken or damaged for public use. **Section 21** declares: "The power of the State to act in the general welfare shall never be impaired by the making of any irrevocable grant of special privileges or immunities." According to **section 22,** "The enumeration of rights and privileges shall not be construed to impair or deny others retained by the people."

Division of Powers	Like the U.S. Constitution and the constitutions of Kansas, New York, and Alaska, for example, the Hawaii constitution has no general provision asserting the formal separation of state government powers. The internal structure of the document, however, creates separate legislative, executive, and judicial branches.
Legislative Branch	**Article III, The Legislature, section 1,** declares: "The legislative power of the State shall be vested in a legislature, which shall consist of two houses, a senate and a house of representatives. Such power shall extend to all rightful subjects of legislation not inconsistent with this constitution or the Constitution of the United States." **Section 2** limits the senate to twenty-five members, and **section 3** limits the house of representatives to fifty-one members. A provision allocating to Kauai a twenty-sixth senator was deleted when the 1978 constitutional convention revised **article XVIII, Schedule,** which in part addresses districting and apportionment.

Article III, The Legislature, section 4, as amended in 1988, stipulates that the "term of office of a member of the house of representatives shall be two years and the term of office of a member of the senate shall be four years." **Section 5** provides that a vacancy in the legislature is to be filled "in such manner as may be provided by law, or, if no provision be made by law, by appointment by the governor for the unexpired term."

Section 6 requires that a legislator must "have been a resident of the State for not less than three years, have attained the age of majority and be a qualified voter of the senatorial [or representative] district from which the person seeks to be elected." In *Hayes v. Gill* (1970), the Hawaii supreme court ruled that these qualifications must be met by the date of the general election. According to **section 8,** members of the legislature are disqualified from holding "any other public office under the State" during their term of office or being "elected or appointed to any public office or employment which shall have been created, or the emoluments whereof shall have been increased, by legislative act during such term."

Section 7 states: "No member of the legislature shall be held to answer before any other tribunal for any statement made or action taken in the exercise of the member's legislative functions; and members of the legislature shall, in all cases except felony or breach of the peace, be privileged from arrest during their attendance at the sessions of their respective houses, and in going to and returning from the same." In *Abercrombie v. McClung* (1974), the Hawaii supreme court determined that slander of a person by a legislator during an interview about a speech made earlier in the senate was not actionable because the legislator was exercising his legislative function and was therefore exempted from having to answer before the judiciary.

Section 11 provides that "neither house shall adjourn during any session of the legislature for more than three days, or sine die, without the consent of the other." **Section 12,** as amended in 1984, in part allows each house to judge the elections, returns, and qualifications of its members; punish any member for "misconduct, disorderly behavior or neglect of duty" by censure or, with a two-thirds vote, by suspension or expulsion;

and "choose its own officers, determine the rules of its proceedings and keep a journal." Section 12 continues: "Twenty days after a bill has been referred to a committee in either house, the bill may be recalled ... by the affirmative vote of one-third of the members...." Section 13 defines a quorum as "[a] majority of the number of members to which each house is entitled...."

Section 14 mandates that "[n]o law shall be passed except by bill." Section 15 provides in part that to become law a bill must pass three readings in each house on separate days; furthermore, "[n]o bill shall pass third or final reading in either house unless printed copies of the bill in the form to be passed shall have been made available to the members of that house for at least forty-eight hours."

Section 16 requires in part that every bill passed by the legislature be "certified by the presiding officers and clerks of both houses and ... presented to the governor." The governor must sign the bill or return it to the legislature with his or her objections. Continues section 16: "Except for items appropriated to be expended by the judicial and legislative branches, the governor may veto any specific item or items in any bill which appropriates money for specific purposes by striking out or reducing the same; but the governor shall veto other bills, if at all, only as a whole. The governor has ten days to consider a bill, and if he or she does not sign or return it in that time it becomes law "as if the governor had signed it." Under section 17, the governor's veto may be overridden "by a two-thirds vote of all members to which each house is entitled."

Article V, The Executive, section 1, states in part: "The executive power of the State shall be vested in a governor.... The term of office of the governor shall begin at noon on the first Monday in December next following the governor's election and end at noon on the first Monday in December, four years thereafter. No person shall be elected to the office of governor for more than two consecutive full terms. No person shall be eligible for the office of governor unless the person shall be a qualified voter, have attained the age of thirty years and have been a resident of this State for five years immediately preceding the person's election." In *Hankins v. State of Hawaii* (1986), the U.S. District Court determined that the durational residency requirement for gubernatorial candidates does not violate the equal protection clause of the U.S. Constitution.

Executive Branch

Section 2 specifies that the lieutenant governor must have the same qualifications as the governor and must be elected "at the same time and in the same manner" as the governor, "provided that the votes cast in the general election for the nominee for governor shall be deemed cast for the nominee for lieutenant governor of the same political party." The lieutenant governor may serve only two consecutive full terms and "shall perform such duties as may be provided by law." According to section 4, "When the office of governor is vacant, the lieutenant governor shall become governor. In the event of the absence of the governor from the State, or the governor's inability to exercise and discharge the powers and duties of the governor's office, such powers and duties shall devolve upon the lieutenant governor during such absence or disability." If impeached, neither the governor nor the lieutenant governor may perform his or her duties until acquitted.

Section 5 outlines the governor's powers, beginning: "The governor shall be responsible for the faithful execution of the laws." The governor also serves as commander in chief of the state's armed forces and "may call out such forces to execute the laws, suppress or prevent insurrection or lawless violence or repel invasion." At the beginning of each session and at other times, the governor may "give the legislature information concerning the affairs of the State and recommend to its consideration such measures as [he or she] shall deem expedient." Section 5 also empowers the governor to grant "reprieves, commutations, and pardons, after conviction, for all offenses, subject to regulation by law as to the manner of applying for the same"; the legislature may also authorize the governor "to grant pardons before conviction, to grant pardons for impeachment and to restore civil rights denied by reason of conviction of offenses by tribunals other than those of this State." Section 5 additionally directs the governor to "appoint an administrative director to serve at the governor's pleasure." Most state constitutions do not have such a provision; Vermont's constitution, however, authorizes a "Secretary of Civil and Military Affairs, to be appointed during [the governor's] pleasure...."

Section 6 provides: "All executive and administrative offices, departments and instrumentalities of the state government and their respective powers and duties shall be allocated by law among and within not more than twenty principal departments in such a manner as to group the same according to common purposes and related functions. Temporary commissions or agencies for special purposes may be established by law and need not be allocated within a principal department." Similarly, North Carolina's constitution excludes regulatory and quasi-judicial agencies and Michigan's constitution excludes the governing bodies of higher education from the basic constitutionally created executive departments. Section 6 continues: "Each principal department shall be under the supervision of the governor and, unless otherwise provided in this constitution or by law, shall be headed by a single executive [who] shall be nominated and, by and with the advice and consent of the senate, appointed by the governor." Such heads of departments serve during the term of the governor unless the governor removes them, except that the "removal of the chief legal officer of the State shall be subject to the advice and consent of the senate."

Judicial Branch

Article VI, The Judiciary, section 1, declares: "The judicial power of the State shall be vested in one supreme court, one intermediate appellate court, circuit courts, district courts and in such other courts as the legislature may from time to time establish. The several courts shall have original and appellate jurisdiction as provided by law and shall establish time limits for disposition of cases in accordance with their rules."

Section 2, as amended in 1986, provides: "The supreme court shall consist of a chief justice and four associate justices. The chief justice may assign ... judges of the intermediate appellate court or a circuit court to serve temporarily on the supreme court...." **Section 6** states that the chief justice is to be the administrative head of the courts; moreover, with the approval of the supreme court, "the chief justice shall appoint an administrative director to serve at the chief justice's pleasure."

Section 3, as amended in 1994, authorizes the governor with the consent of the senate to fill vacancies in the office of the chief justice, supreme court, intermediate appellate court, and circuit courts "by appointing a person from a list of not less than four, and not more than six nominees for the vacancy, presented to the governor by the judicial selection commission"; moreover, "[i]f the governor fails to make any appointment within thirty days of presentation, or within ten days of the senate's rejection of any previous appointment, the appointment shall be made by the judicial selection committee from the list with the consent of the senate." Supreme court justices, intermediate appellate court judges, and circuit court judges must be residents and citizens of Hawaii and of the United States and licensed to practice law for ten years, while district court judges must be licensed for five years. Similarly, Arizona, for example, requires a justice of the supreme court to have been admitted to practice for ten years, while Kentucky requires that a justice be a licensed attorney for eight years. Section 3 also specifies that the term of office for justices and judges of the supreme court, intermediate appellate court, and circuit courts is to be ten years and provides: "At least six months prior to the expiration of [such term], every justice and judge shall petition the judicial selection commission to be retained in office [and unless retiring, and if it so determines] the commission shall renew the term of office ... for the period provided in this section or by law." Justices and judges must retire when seventy years old.

Section 4, as amended in 1994, describes the judicial selection commission; and **section 5** grants the supreme court "the power to reprimand, discipline, suspend with or without salary, retire or remove from office any justice or judge for misconduct or disability, as provided by rules adopted by the supreme court. The supreme court shall create a commission on judicial discipline which shall have authority to investigate and conduct hearings concerning allegations of misconduct or disability and to make recommendations to the supreme court...."

Article IV, Reapportionment, section 10, gives the supreme court original jurisdiction to implement reapportionment "on the petition of any registered voter."

Article III, The Legislature, section 19, states: "The governor and lieutenant governor, and any appointive officer for whose removal the consent of the senate is required, may be removed from office upon conviction of impeachment for such causes as may be provided by law." The house of representatives "has the sole power of impeachment of the governor and lieutenant governor and the senate the sole power to try such impeachments." A two-thirds vote in the senate is required for conviction.

Impeachment

Article VIII, Local Government, section 2, provides for home rule: "Each political subdivision shall have the power to frame and adopt a charter for its own self-government within such limits and under such procedures as may be provided by general law. Such procedures, however, shall not require the approval of a charter by a legislative body.... Charter provisions with respect to a political subdivision's executive, legislative and administrative structure and organization shall be superior to statutory provisions...."

Local Government

Taxation and Finance

Article VII, Taxation and Finance, section 2, provides: "In enacting any law imposing a tax on or measured by income, the legislature may define income by reference to provisions of the laws of the United States as they may be or become effective at any time or from time to time...." **Section 3** creates a tax review commission beginning in 1980 and every five years afterward to "submit to the legislature an evaluation of the State's tax structure, recommend revenue and tax policy and then dissolve." **Section 5** mandates a balanced budget: "...General fund expenditures for any fiscal year shall not exceed the State's current general fund revenues and unencumbered cash balances, except when the governor publicly declares the public health, safety, or welfare threatened...."

Education

Article X, Education, section 1, as amended in 1994, declares: "The State shall provide for the establishment, support and control of a statewide system of public schools free from sectarian control, a state university, public libraries and such other educational institutions as may be deemed desirable, including physical facilities therefor. There shall be no discrimination in public educational institutions because of race, religion, sex or ancestry; nor shall public funds be appropriated for the support or benefit of any sectarian or private educational institution, except [in certain cases] not for profit corporations that provide early childhood education and care facilities serving the general public."

Health and Welfare

Article IX, Public Health and Welfare, section 1, declares: "The State shall provide for the protection and promotion of the public health." **Section 2** directs the state "to provide for the treatment and rehabilitation of handicapped persons," while **section 3** instructs it "to provide financial assistance, medical assistance and social services for persons who are found to be in need of and are eligible for such assistance and services as provided by law." **Sections 4, 5, 6,** and **7**, respectively, provide for economic security for the elderly; housing, slum clearance, development, and rehabilitation; management of state population growth; and public beauty and good order. Hawaii is one of eleven states, including Alaska and New York, that specifically provide for the public welfare in their constitutions.

Environment

Article XI, Conservation, Control and Development of Resources, section 9, affirms: "Each person has the right to a clean and healthful environment, as defined by laws relating to environmental quality, including control of pollution and conservation, protection and enhancement of natural resources. Any person may enforce this right against any party, public or private, through appropriate legal proceedings, subject to reasonable limitations and regulations as provided by law."

Hawaiian Culture

Article X, Education, section 4, mandates: "The State shall promote the study of Hawaiian culture, history and language. The State shall provide for a Hawaiian education program consisting of language, culture and history in the public schools. The use of community expertise shall be encouraged...."

Article XII, Hawaiian Affairs, section 5, establishes an office of Hawaiian affairs, "which shall hold title to all the real and personal property now or hereafter set aside or conveyed to it which shall be held in trust for native Hawaiians and Hawaiians. There shall be a board of trustees for the [office] elected by qualified voters who are Hawaiians...." According to **section 7,** "The State reaffirms and shall protect all rights, customarily and traditionally exercised for subsistence, cultural and religious purposes and possessed by *ahupua'a* tenants who are descendants of native Hawaiians who inhabited the Hawaiian Islands prior to 1778...."

Article XV, State Boundaries; Capital; Flag; Language and Motto, section 4, states: "English and Hawaiian shall be the official languages of Hawaii, except that Hawaiian shall be required for public acts and transactions only as provided by law."

Official Languages

Article XVII, Revision and Amendment, section 1, indicates: "Revisions of or amendments to this constitution may be proposed by constitutional convention or by the legislature." According to **section 2,** as amended in 1980, "The legislature may submit to the electorate at any general or special election the question, 'Shall there be a convention to propose a revision of or amendments to the Constitution?' If any nine-year period shall elapse during which the question shall not have been submitted, the lieutenant governor shall certify the question, to be voted on at the first general election following the expiration of such period." Section 2 also provides for a constitutional convention and notes: "The revision or amendments shall be effective only if approved at a general [or special] election by a majority of all the votes tallied upon the question ...," provided that the majority vote constitutes "at least thirty per cent of the total number of registered voters."

Amendment Procedures

Section 3 authorizes the legislature to propose amendments "by a two-thirds vote of each house on final reading at any session ... [or] by a majority vote of each house on final reading at each of two successive sessions." The procedure for voter ratification of amendments proposed by the legislature is the same as for those proposed by convention.

IDAHO

Idaho became the forty-third state of the United States on July 3, 1890. Boise is the capital of the "Gem State," which encompasses some 83,574 square miles and is bordered by the Canadian province of British Columbia and Montana on the north, Montana and Wyoming on the east, Nevada and Utah on the south, and Washington and Oregon on the west. Idaho ranks forty-first in population with some 1.2 million inhabitants. The state's principal industries include agriculture, manufacturing, lumber, and mining; among its chief crops are potatoes, peas, sugar beets, and alfalfa seed.

General Information

Government: The governor and lieutenant governor are elected separately for four-year terms. The legislature consists of thirty-five senators and seventy members of the house of representatives, all elected for two-year terms. The supreme court is made up of a chief justice and four additional justices elected for six-year terms.

Date of Constitution: 1890

Constitutional History

Idaho's name, signifying "gem of the mountains," is believed to have been coined from local Indian terms. The Shoshone and Nez Percé peoples were among the early inhabitants of Idaho, which was not settled by the early Europeans. In 1805 Meriwether Lewis and William Clark crossed the Idaho panhandle on their trek to the Pacific coast, and four years later a Canadian fur trading company built a trading post on the eastern shore of Lake Pend Oreille. In 1818 the United States and the United Kingdom agreed to jointly occupy the Pacific Northwest, including the Idaho area.

The actual boundaries and jurisdiction of the Idaho region shifted, and at various times it was considered part of the regions that produced the states of Montana, Oregon, Washington, and Wyoming. The first permanent settlement was Franklin, established on June 15, 1860, by Mormons from Utah, and gold was discovered near the Clearwater River the same year. The population and economy of the Idaho region began to grow, and on March 3, 1863, by an act of Congress, the Territory of Idaho was established with a temporary government.

After the Civil War, the Idaho Territory was the scene of hostilities between Mormons and anti-Mormons and against the growing Chinese labor population. Additional, separate territories were created out of the Idaho Territory—Montana in 1864 and Wyoming in 1868. In 1869 Congress authorized a delegate to represent Idaho in that body, but for several years afterward Congress debated whether to simply divide up Idaho between the Washington and Nevada Territories. By 1890, however, the population had increased to approximately 143,000 inhabitants, and on July 3, 1890, an act admitting Idaho as a state of the Union was approved.

A constitutional convention had met in Boise from July 4 to August 6, 1889, and the document drafted by the delegates was ratified at the polls on November 5 of that year. This constitution went into effect on the same day that Idaho became a state.

The Constitution

The Idaho constitution has been amended 115 times as of January 1, 1998, but its amendments are fully integrated, unlike the U.S. Constitution and the constitutions of many states, including Massachusetts; those documents retain the original text and simply attach amendments as they are adopted. Once the citizens of Idaho approve an amendment, it is incorporated directly into the constitution's text and the superseded language is deleted. In 1902 and 1970 voters rejected new constitutions, choosing instead to further amend the 1890 document. Thus, like a number of other states, including New Mexico, Idaho has updated its original constitution through amendments rather than revised it wholesale.

A relatively short document containing some 23,239 words, the Idaho constitution has not changed drastically since 1890. The amendments adopted have, however, expanded democracy and equality. The right to vote, for example, was extended formally in the constitution to women in 1896, to Native Americans in 1950, to Chinese Americans in 1962, and to Mormons in 1982 (although their right to vote had been acknowledged by the legislature in 1895). The basic structure of the government is fairly typical, with a plural, or divided, executive branch, elected justices and judges, and a bicameral legislature that shares its authority to make laws with the people through the right of popular initiative and referendum procedures.

The preamble to the 1890 Idaho constitution reads: "We, the people of the State of Idaho, grateful to Almighty God for our freedom, to secure its blessings and promote our common welfare do establish this Constitution."

Preamble

Article I, Declarations of Rights, section 1, proclaims that "[a]ll men are by nature free and equal, and have certain inalienable rights, among which are enjoying and defending life and liberty; acquiring, possessing and protecting property; pursuing happiness and securing safety." This provision reflects the historic declarations of rights of Virginia and Massachusetts, and its language is similar to that of the California and Montana constitutions. **Section 2** declares: "All political power is inherent in the people. Government is instituted for their equal protection and benefit, and they have the right to alter, reform or abolish the same whenever they may deem it necessary; and no special privileges or immunities shall ever be granted that may not be altered, revoked, or repealed by the legislature." **Section 3** states that "Idaho is an inseparable part of the American Union, and the Constitution of the United States is the supreme law of the land."

Fundamental Rights

Section 4 guarantees religious freedom; however, "the liberty of conscience hereby secured shall not be construed to dispense with oaths or affirmations, or excuse acts of licentiousness or justify polygamous or other pernicious practices, inconsistent with morality or the peace or safety of the state...." **Section 9** ensures the freedom to speak, write, and publish on all subjects, "being responsible for the abuse of that liberty." **Section 10** affirms the right to assemble and petition the legislature for the redress of grievances. **Section 11,** with a number of exceptions, guarantees the right to bear arms, and **section 12** subordinates the military to civil power and restricts the quartering of soldiers in private homes.

Section 5 limits the suspension of the writ of habeas corpus. In *Marks v. Vehlow* (1973), the Idaho supreme court rejected a journalist's claim to confidentiality of his sources in a habeas corpus proceeding, ruling that the "sanctity of the writ of habeas corpus ... outweighed any public interest in an unfettered press." **Section 6** guarantees the right to bail, "except for capital offenses, where the proof is evident or the presumption great," and prohibits excessive bail, excess fines, and cruel and unusual punishment. **Section 7** provides in part: "The right of trial by jury shall remain inviolate; but in civil actions, three-fourths of the jury may render a verdict, and the legislature may provide that in all cases of misdemeanors five-sixths of the jury may render a verdict." **Section 8** mandates: "No person shall be held to answer for any felony or criminal offense of any grade, unless on presentment or indictment of a grand jury or on information of the public prosecutor, after a commitment by a magistrate, except in cases of impeachment, in cases cognizable by probate courts or by justices of the peace, and in cases arising in the militia when in actual service in time of war or public danger...."

Section 13 guarantees a person accused of a crime the right "to a speedy and public trial; to have the process of the court to compel the attendance of witnesses in his behalf, and to appear and defend in person and with counsel"; prohibits double jeopardy and self-incrimination; and guarantees that no one "shall be deprived of life, liberty or property without due process of law." **Sections 15, 16,** and **17**, respectively, prohibit imprisonment for debt "except in cases of fraud"; bills of attainder, ex post facto laws, and laws impairing the obligation of contracts; and unreasonable searches and seizures. **Section 18** provides that every person has access to courts of justice, and "a speedy remedy afforded for every injury of person, property or character, and right and justice shall be administered without sale, denial, delay, or prejudice."

Section 14 states in part: "The necessary use of lands for the construction of reservoirs or storage basins, for the purpose of irrigation, or for rights of way for the construction of canals, ditches, flumes or pipes, to convey water to the place of use for any useful, beneficial or necessary purpose..., is hereby declared to be a public use, and subject to the regulation and control of the state. Private property may be taken for public use, but not until a just compensation, to be ascertained in the manner prescribed by law, shall be paid therefor."

Section 19 guarantees the right of suffrage. **Section 20** prohibits property qualifications "to vote or hold office except in school elections, or elections creating indebtedness, or in irrigation district elections, as to which last-named elections the legislature may restrict the voters to landowners." **Section 21** provides: "This enumeration of rights shall not be construed to impair or deny other rights retained by the people." **Section 22** enumerates rights for victims of crime, including the right "**(1)** To be treated with fairness, respect, dignity and privacy throughout the criminal justice process; **(2)** To timely disposition of the case; ... [and] **(8)** To refuse [an] interview, ex parte contact, or other request by the defendant, or any other person acting on behalf of the defendant, unless such request is authorized by law...."

Division of Powers

Article II, Distribution of Powers, section 1, declares: "The powers of the government of this state are divided into three distinct departments, the legislative, executive and judicial; and no person or collection of persons charged with the exercise of powers properly belonging to one of these departments shall exercise any powers properly belonging to either of the others, except as in this constitution expressly directed or permitted."

Article III, Legislative Department, section 1, vests the legislative power of the state in the senate and house of representatives. **Section 2** states in part: "**(1)** Following the decennial census of 1990 and in each legislature thereafter, the senate shall consist of not less than thirty nor more than thirty-five members. The legislature may fix the number of members of the house of representatives at not more than two times as many representatives as there are senators." Currently, the senate and house of representatives have the maximum number of members. **Section 3** specifies that the term of senators and representatives is two years. According to **section 6,** senators and representatives, at the time of their election, must be citizens of the United States, electors of the state, and electors of their county or district for at least one year.

Section 7 provides that legislators are privileged from arrest during attendance at and travel to and from their respective chambers, except in the case of treason, felony, or breach of the peace; furthermore, they "shall not be liable to any civil process during the session of the legislature, nor during the ten days next before the commencement thereof; nor shall a member, for words uttered in debate in either house, be questioned in any other place." **Section 9** authorizes each house of the legislature to choose its own officers; judge the election, qualifications, and returns of its members; determine its procedural rules; and adjourn itself; however, "neither house shall, without the concurrence of the other, adjourn for more than three (3) days, nor to any other place than that in which it may be sitting." According to **section 10,** a quorum consists of a majority of each house, but "a smaller number may adjourn from day to day, and may compel the attendance of absent members...." **Section 11** states: "Each house may, for good cause shown, with the concurrence of two-thirds (⅔) of all the members, expel a member."

Section 14 states that bills may originate in either house, although they may be amended or rejected in the other, except for money bills, which must originate in the house of representatives. This requirement for revenue bills is similar to that in the U.S. Constitution and the constitutions of a number of other states, including Alabama, for example. **Section 15** directs in part: "No law shall be passed except by bill, nor shall any bill be put upon its final passage until the same, with the amendments thereto, shall have been printed for the use of the members; nor shall any bill become a law unless the same shall have been read on three several days in each house previous to the final vote thereon: provided, in case of urgency, two-thirds (⅔) of the house where such bill may be pending may ... dispense with this provision." At final passage a bill must be read at length, and to become law a bill must be approved by "a majority of the members present." The constitutions of Oregon and a number of other states generally require that a majority of all elected members approve legislation.

Section 16 specifies that each act "shall embrace but one subject and matters properly connected therewith, which subject shall be expressed in the title...." Only the part of the act not expressed in the title is void, however. According to **section 17,** "Every act or joint resolution shall be plainly worded, avoiding as far as practicable the use of technical terms." While this provision, which is also found in the Oregon constitution, is commendable, it is difficult to enforce mainly because lawyers who draft and interpret legislation prefer legal language. **Section 18** requires that an amended section "shall be set forth and published at full length." **Section 19** prohibits local and special laws in certain enumerated cases including granting divorces, changing the names of persons or places, and authorizing the adoption and legitimization of children. **Section 21** stipulates that "all bills and joint resolutions passed shall be signed by the presiding officers of the respective houses"; but, according to **section 22,** none is to take effect for sixty days from the end of the session at which each was passed, "except in case of emergency, which emergency shall be declared in the preamble or in the body of the law."

Section 24 declares: "The first concern of all good government is the virtue and sobriety of the people, and the purity of the home. The legislature should further all wise and well directed efforts for the promotion of temperance and morality." To this end, **section 26** grants to the legislature "[f]rom and after [December 31, 1934] … [the] full power and authority to permit, control and regulate or prohibit the manufacture, sale, keeping for sale, and transportation for sale, of intoxicating liquors for beverage purposes." One year earlier, the Twenty-first Amendment (1933) to the U.S. Constitution, repealing Prohibition, had been ratified.

Executive Branch

Article IV, Executive Department, section 1, provides that "the executive department shall consist of a governor, lieutenant governor, secretary of state, state controller, state treasurer, attorney general and superintendent of public instruction, each of whom shall hold his office for four years …, commencing with those elected in the year 1946, except as otherwise provided in this Constitution.… They shall perform such duties as are prescribed by this Constitution and as may be prescribed by law, provided that the state controller shall not perform any post-audit functions." **Section 2** specifies that these officers "shall be elected by the qualified electors of the state.…" **Section 3** provides that the governor and lieutenant governor, who are elected on separate tickets, must be thirty years old at the time of their election and all the executive officers must be citizens of the United States and must have resided in the state for two years.

Section 5 mandates: "The supreme executive power of the state is vested in the governor, who shall see that the laws are faithfully executed." According to **section 4,** "The governor shall be commander-in-chief of the military forces of the state, except when they shall be called into actual service of the United States. He shall have power to call out the militia to execute the laws, to suppress insurrection, or to repel invasion."

Section 6 provides in part that the governor "shall nominate and, by and with the consent of the senate, appoint all officers [under] this constitution, or which may be created by law, and whose appointment or election is not otherwise provided for." If there is a vacancy in state offices, including a supreme court justice or elected executive department official, except that of lieutenant governor, the governor is authorized "to fill the same by appointment, as provided by law.…" **Section 7** empowers the governor to "grant respites or reprieves in all cases of convictions for offenses against the state, except treason or conviction on impeachment, but such respites or [reprieves] shall not extend beyond the next session of the board of pardons; and such board shall at such session continue or determine such respite or reprieve, or they may commute or pardon the offense. . . ."

Section 8 authorizes the governor to "require information in writing from the officers of the executive department upon any subject relating to the duties of their respective offices . . ."; furthermore, the incumbent may "at any time . . . appoint a committee to investigate and report to him upon the condition of any executive office or state institution." Section 8 continues: "The governor shall at the commencement of each session, and from time to time, by message, give to the legislature information of the condition of the state, and shall recommend such measures as he shall deem expedient." In addition, the governor is to provide the legislature with information on expenditures of money and "present estimates of the amount of money required to be raised by taxation for all purposes of the state."

Section 9 states that "the governor may, on extraordinary occasions, convene the legislature by proclamation . . . , [and] he may also . . . convene the senate in extraordinary session for the transaction of executive business." **Section 10** provides in part: "Every bill passed by the legislature shall, before it becomes a law, be presented to the governor. If he approve, he shall sign it . . . , but if he do not approve, he shall return it with his objections to the house in which it originated. . . ." The veto may be overridden by "two-thirds (⅔) of the members present" in each house. If the governor does not return a bill to the legislature within five days (excepting Sundays), it becomes a law "as if he had signed it." If the legislature prevents the return of the bill by adjourning, "it shall be filed, with [the governor's] objections, in the office of the secretary of state within ten (10) days after such adjournment (Sundays excepted) or become a law." **Section 11** grants the governor "power to disapprove of any item or items of any bill making appropriations of money embracing distinct items," which may be overridden as in the case of the veto of a bill.

Section 12 provides that "[i]n case of the failure to qualify, the impeachment, or conviction of treason, felony, or other infamous crime of the governor, or his death, removal from office, resignation, absence from the state, or inability to discharge the powers and duties of his office, the powers, duties and emoluments of the office for the residue of the term, or until the disability shall cease, shall devolve upon the lieutenant governor." The constitutions of most other states distinguish between cases in which the lieutenant governor becomes acting governor temporarily and cases in which he or she succeeds fully to the office of governor, as in the death of the governor. **Section 13** states that the lieutenant governor is to serve as president of the senate "but shall vote only when the senate is equally divided." In the event of the lieutenant governor's inability to carry out these duties, the president pro tempore of the senate is authorized to do so. In *Sweeny v. Otter* (1990), the Idaho supreme court concluded that section 13 empowered the lieutenant governor to vote even in organizational meetings of the senate to choose officers, including the president pro tempore, when the members were equally divided. In this particular case the tie was the result of partisan affiliations; of the forty-two senators then serving, twenty-one were Democrats and twenty-one were Republicans.

Section 20 stipulates that except for the constitutional offices "[a]ll executive and administrative officers, agencies, and instrumentalities of the executive department ... shall be allocated by law among and within not more than twenty departments...."

Judicial Branch

Article V, Judicial Department, section 1, declares: "The distinctions between actions at law and suits in equity, and the forms of all such actions and suits, are hereby prohibited; and there shall be in this state but one form of action for the enforcement or protection of private rights or the redress of private wrongs.... Feigned issues are prohibited, and the fact at issue shall be tried by order of the court before a jury."

Section 2 provides in part that "[t]he judicial power of the state shall be vested in a court for the trial of impeachments, a Supreme Court, district courts, and such other courts inferior to the Supreme Court as established by the legislature. The courts shall constitute a unified and integrated judicial system for administration and supervision by the Supreme Court."

Section 6 specifies: "The Supreme Court shall consist of five justices, a majority of whom shall be necessary to make a quorum or pronounce a decision." The justices are to be elected statewide for six-year terms, staggered by lot for two, four, and six years. "The chief justice," section 6 continues, "shall be selected from among the justices ... by a majority vote of the justices. His term of office shall be four years. When a vacancy in the office of chief justice occurs, a chief justice shall be selected for a full four year term. The chief justice shall be the executive head of the judicial system." Like the U.S. Constitution, the Idaho constitution does not specify qualifications for supreme court justices. But a statute last amended in 1996 requires that supreme court justices be thirty years old when elected, admitted to practice law for ten years, and admitted to practice in Idaho. **Section 7** prohibits justices from holding "any other office of trust or profit under the laws of this state" during their term.

Section 9 outlines the supreme court's jurisdiction: "The Supreme Court shall have jurisdiction to review, upon appeal, any decision of the district courts, or the judges thereof, any order of the public utilities commission, any order of the industrial accident board, and any plan proposed by the commission for reapportionment...." In addition, the supreme court has "original jurisdiction to issue writs of mandamus, certiorari, prohibition, and habeas corpus, and all writs necessary or proper to the complete exercise of its appellate jurisdiction." **Section 10** grants the supreme court "original jurisdiction to hear claims against the state, but its decision shall be merely recommendatory; ... [and it] shall be reported to the next session of the legislature for its action."

Section 13 states that "the legislature shall have no power to deprive the judicial department of any power or jurisdiction which rightly pertains to it as a coordinate department of the government...." But the legislature is required to "provide a proper system of appeals, and regulate by law, when necessary, the methods of proceeding in the exercise of their powers of all courts below the Supreme Court, so far as the same may be done without conflict with this Constitution, provided, however, that the legislature can provide mandatory minimum sentences for any crimes, and any sentence imposed shall be not less than the mandatory minimum sentence so provided." Section 13 continues: "Any mandatory minimum sentence so imposed shall not be reduced." **Section 28** notes that "[p]rovisions for the retirement, discipline and removal from office of justices and judges shall be as provided by law."

Article V, Judicial Department, section 3, designates the senate as the court for the trial of impeachments, which require the concurrence of a majority of the members. Furthermore, "judgment shall not extend beyond removal from, and disqualification to hold office in this state; but the party shall be liable to indictment and punishment according to law." **Section 4** provides in part: "The house of representatives solely shall have the power of impeachment. No person shall be convicted without the concurrence of two-thirds (⅔) of the senators elected."

Impeachment

Article III, Legislative Department, section 1, states in part: "The people reserve to themselves the power to approve or reject at the polls any act or measure passed by the legislature. This power is known as the referendum, and legal voters may, under such conditions and in such manner as may be provided by acts of the legislature, demand a referendum vote on any act or measure passed by the legislature and cause the same to be submitted to a vote of the people for their approval or rejection." Section 1 continues: "The people reserve to themselves the power to propose laws, and enact the same at the polls independent of the legislature. This power is known as the initiative ... [and as in the case of the referendum the] legal voters may ... cause the same to be submitted to the vote of the people at a general election for their approval or rejection." In *Luker v. Curtis* (1943), the Idaho supreme court ruled that the legislature had the power to repeal a law enacted by popular initiative.

Direct Democracy

Article VI, Suffrage and Elections, section 6, provides that "[e]very public officer in the state of Idaho, excepting the judicial officers, is subject to recall by the legal voters of the state or of the electoral district from which he is elected. The legislature shall pass the necessary laws to carry this provision into effect."

Article VII, Finance and Revenue, section 2, states in part: "The legislature shall provide such revenue as may be needful, by levying a tax by valuation, so that every person or corporation shall pay a tax in proportion to the value of his, her, or its property, except as in this article hereinafter otherwise provided." **Section 5** mandates that "[a]ll taxes shall be uniform upon the same class of subjects within the territorial limits, of the authority levying the tax, and shall be levied and collected under general laws, which shall prescribe such regulations as shall secure a just valuation for taxation of all property, real and personal: provided, that the legislature may allow such exemptions from taxation from time to time as shall seem necessary and just...."

Taxation and Finance

Section 11 requires a balanced budget: "No appropriation shall be made, nor any expenditure authorized by the legislature, whereby the expenditure of the state during any fiscal year shall exceed the total tax then provided for by law...."

Education	**Article IX, Education and School Lands, section 1,** proclaims: "The stability of a republican form of government depending mainly upon the intelligence of the people, it shall be the duty of the legislature of Idaho, to establish and maintain a general, uniform and thorough system of public, free common schools." **Section 2** vests supervision of the state's educational institutions and public school system in a state board of education, "the membership, powers and duties of which shall be prescribed by law." One ex officio member of this board is the state superintendent of public instruction.
Health and Welfare	**Article XVI, Livestock, section 1,** directs in part: "The legislature shall pass necessary laws to provide for the protection of livestock against the introduction or spread of pleuro pneumonia, glanders, splentic or Texas fever, and other infectious or contagious diseases."
Amendment Procedures	**Article XX, Amendments, section 1,** specifies that amendments to the Idaho constitution may be proposed in either branch of the legislature. If agreed to by "two-thirds (⅔) of all the members of each of the two (2) houses, voting separately, . . . it shall be the duty of the legislature to submit such amendment or amendments to the electors of the state at the next general election. . . ." If ratified by a majority of the voters, "such amendment or amendments shall become a part of this Constitution."

Section 3 addresses the issue of a constitutional convention: "Whenever two-thirds (⅔) of the members elected to each branch of the legislature shall deem it necessary to call a convention to revise or amend this Constitution, they shall recommend to the electors to vote at the next general election, for or against a convention, and if a majority of all the electors voting at said election shall have voted for a convention, the legislature shall at the next session provide by law for calling the same. . . ." **Section 4** notes that "[a]ny Constitution adopted by such convention, shall have no validity until it has been submitted to, and adopted by, the people."

On December 3, 1818, Illinois became the twenty-first state of the United States. Springfield is the capital of the "Prairie State," also known as the "Land of Lincoln," which encompasses some 57,918 square miles. Illinois is bordered by Wisconsin and Lake Michigan on the north, Indiana on the east, Kentucky and Missouri on the south, and Missouri and Iowa on the west. With approximately 12 million inhabitants, Illinois ranks sixth among the states in population. Its principal industries include services, manufacturing, travel, and wholesale and retail trade; corn, soybeans, wheat, and hay are among its chief crops.

ILLINOIS

Government: The governor and lieutenant governor are elected jointly for four-year terms. The legislature, called the general assembly, consists of fifty-nine senators, some elected for four-year terms and some for two-year terms (with the entire senate up for reelection every ten years), and 118 representatives elected for two-year terms. The supreme court is composed of a chief justice and six additional judges elected for ten-year terms.

General Information

Dates of Constitutions: 1818, 1848, 1870, and 1971

Constitutional History

When Father Jacques Marquette and Louis Joliet in 1673 and Robert Cavelier, sieur de La Salle, around the same time, began exploring the territory that would become the state of Illinois, seminomadic Algonkian peoples, including the Kaskaskia, Tamaroa, Illinois, and Peoria, inhabited the region. *Illini* was the Peoria people's word for "man" or "warrior," and the plural *Illiniwek* simply meant "the people." To ensure their control of the region, the French built outposts and forts including Fort Crevecoeur, near what is now the city of Peoria, and Fort de Chartres, near Kaskaskia on the Mississippi River. After the French and Indian War (1754–63), however, the British annexed this area to Quebec in 1774.

Four years later, Kaskaskia, about fifty miles south of the present-day St. Louis, was captured by the Virginia militia, led by George Rogers Clark. The 1778 Virginia Act for Establishing the County of Illinois brought the territory under the jurisdiction of the state of Virginia. By the terms of the 1783 Treaty of Paris, which formally ended the Revolutionary War, the vast territory extending west to the Mississippi River and north to Canada, including the Illinois territory, was transferred to the United States. The Virginia Act of Cession, passed by the Virginia Assembly on December 20, 1783, authorized the state's delegates in Congress to cede control of the Illinois territory to the U.S. government.

Many new settlers found their way to southern Illinois via the Ohio, Wabash, Mississippi, and Illinois Rivers. The population growth led to the creation in 1801 of a separate Indiana Territory, which included what would become the states of Indiana, Illinois, Michigan, and Wisconsin. Illinois Territory, including Wisconsin, became a territory eight years later. By the time Illinois became a state in 1818, some 4,600 families were living there, most of whom were of Scots-Irish and English descent and had previously lived in Kentucky, Tennessee, the Carolinas, and Virginia. In 1819 an unsettled tract of land was chosen for the site of the state's capital, called Vandalia, but in 1837 the capital was moved to Springfield.

The quest for statehood began in earnest in 1817, when the Illinois delegate to Congress, Nathaniel Pope, asked Congress to define the future state's northern border to include frontage on Lake Michigan. In the spring of 1818, Congress officially sanctioned a statehood convention, which met in Kaskaskia in August of that year. The document produced by the delegates to that convention, only one of whom had been born in the Illinois Territory, became effective when the state was admitted to the Union on December 3, 1818, without having been submitted to the voters. Because most of the settlers had come from Indiana, Kentucky, and Tennessee, the constitutions of those states, not surprisingly, served as models for the 1818 Illinois document, although the executive branch article was based on that of the 1802 Ohio constitution.

As the population of the state grew to more than 400,000, economic and social changes led to a constitutional convention held in Springfield in 1847. The document it produced, which was nearly three times the length of its predecessor, was approved by the voters on March 5, 1848, and took effect on April 1. Some of the provisions of the 1848 constitution, however, soon became obsolete, but a new draft constitution was voted down in June 1862, criticized as secessionist in principle if not in words.

A convention meeting in Springfield from December 13, 1869, to May 13, 1870, undertook again to rewrite the state's supreme law. The new document and certain separately submitted provisions were approved at the polls on July 2 and went into effect on August 8. The 1870 constitution deleted the qualification "white" from voting requirements, but a proposal for including women was turned down. The document also focused on eliminating the legislature's passage of private bills (which affect only a few citizens rather than the general public), a reaction to the 1867 legislative session, which produced some 2,500 pages of private acts compared to 205 pages of public laws.

The 1870 Illinois constitution was in effect for more than a century. The debacle of the 1968 Democratic Party national convention in Chicago, however, fueled by intense reactions to the cold war era and the Vietnam War in particular, rocked the state and led to demands for changes in the state constitution. A constitutional convention held in 1969 included a greater diversity of delegates than in the past, including thirteen blacks and fourteen women. The delegates took a year to produce a new constitution, which was ratified by the voters on December 15, 1970, and went into effect July 1, 1971.

The Constitution

The 1971 Illinois constitution is a relatively short state constitution, containing only some 13,700 words. By its terms the governor's powers were increased to include item veto power and the authority to recommend specific changes in bills. Such changes are treated by the legislature in the same manner as a gubernatorial veto, except that they may be adopted by the legislature by a smaller majority than that required to override the governor's regular veto of a bill. The governor and lieutenant governor run jointly, as do the candidates for U.S. president and vice president.

By 1970 Illinois was burdened with some 6,400 government divisions and subdivisions, more than any other state. The new document therefore included an innovative home rule provision that reduced the legislature's burden by giving municipalities with more than 25,000 inhabitants the power to handle their own affairs more flexibly and efficiently. In keeping with the social developments of the times, the 1971 Illinois constitution added provisions banning discrimination "on the basis of race, color, creed, national ancestry and sex" in all hiring and promotion decisions and the sale or rental of property and added equal protection provisions for women and the disabled.

As of January 1, 1998, the 1971 Illinois constitution has been amended only ten times. A 1988 referendum on calling a new constitutional convention was defeated at the polls.

The preamble to the 1971 Illinois constitution reads in part: "We, the People of the State of Illinois—grateful to Almighty God for the civil, political and religious liberty which He has permitted us to enjoy . . .—in order to provide for the health, safety and welfare of the people; maintain a representative and orderly government; eliminate poverty and inequality; assure legal, social and economic justice; provide opportunity for the fullest development of the individual . . .—do ordain and establish this Constitution for the State of Illinois."

Article I, Bill of Rights, section 1, proclaims: "All men are by nature free and independent and have certain inherent and inalienable rights among which are life, liberty and the pursuit of happiness. To secure these rights and the protection of property, governments are instituted among men, deriving their just powers from the consent of the governed." This language, which is similar to that in a number of state constitutions, reflects the influence of the Declaration of Independence. **Section 2** states: "No person shall be deprived of life, liberty or property without due process of law nor be denied the equal protection of the laws."

Section 3 provides: "The free exercise and enjoyment of religious profession and worship, without discrimination, shall forever be guaranteed, and no person shall be denied any civil or political right, privilege or capacity, on account of his religious opinions. . . ." **Sections 4, 5,** and **6,** respectively, guarantee freedom of speech; the right to assemble in a peaceable manner and apply for redress of grievance; and the right of the people "to be secure in their persons, houses, papers and other possessions against unreasonable searches, seizures, invasions of privacy or interceptions of communications by eavesdropping devices or other means. . . ." The enumeration of invasions of privacy and interception of communications goes well beyond the federal constitutional guarantee incorporated into most other state constitutions.

Sections 7 and **8,** the latter amended in 1994, pertain to rights of the accused, requiring an indictment by a grand jury in most cases involving a criminal offense and extending to the accused "the right to appear and defend in person and by counsel; to demand the nature and cause of the accusation and have a copy thereof; to be confronted with the witnesses against him or her and to have process to compel the attendance of witnesses in his or her behalf; and to have a speedy public trial by an impartial jury. . . ." **Section 8.1,** added in 1992, on the other hand, sets forth the rights of victims of crime, including, among others, the right to "be treated with fairness and respect . . .; [be notified] of court proceedings; communicate with the prosecution; [and] make a statement to the court at sentencing."

Section 9, as amended in 1986, with some exceptions guarantees to the accused the right to bail and limits the suspension of the writ of habeas corpus to "cases of rebellion or invasion when the public safety may require it." **Section 10** states: "No person shall be compelled in a criminal case to give evidence against himself nor be twice put in jeopardy for the same offense." **Section 11** begins: "All penalties shall be determined both according to the seriousness of the offense and with the objective of restoring the offender to useful citizenship." This statement is rare in state constitutions. Section 11 continues: "No conviction shall work corruption of blood or forfeiture of estate. No person shall be transported out of the State for an offense committed within the State."

Section 12 mandates: "Every person shall find a certain remedy in the laws for all injuries and wrongs which he receives to his person, privacy, property or reputation. He shall obtain justice by law, freely, completely, and promptly." The constitutions of a number of states, including Connecticut and Kansas, have similar provisions, although without the express mention of privacy. Section 13 guarantees trial by jury; section 14 prohibits imprisonment for debt "unless there is a strong presumption of fraud"; and section 15 guarantees: "Private property shall not be taken or damaged for public use without just compensation as provided by law. Such compensation shall be determined by a jury as provided by law." Section 16 prohibits ex post facto laws and laws impairing the obligation of contracts.

Section 17 states in part: "All persons shall have the right to be free from discrimination on the basis of race, color, creed, national ancestry and sex in the hiring and promotion practices of any employer or in the sale or rental of property." Section 18 guarantees that equal protection of the laws will not be denied on account of sex; and section 19 provides: "All persons with a physical or mental handicap shall be free from discrimination in the sale or rental of property and shall be free from discrimination unrelated to ability in the hiring and promotion practices of any employer." Only four other state constitutions expressly prohibit discrimination based on physical impairment. According to section 20, "To promote individual dignity, communications that portray criminality, depravity or lack of virtue in, or that incite violence, hatred, abuse or hostility toward, a person or group of persons by reason of or by reference to religious, racial, ethnic, national or regional affiliation are condemned." This "sensitivity" provision is rare in state constitutions.

Section 21 limits the quartering of soldiers in private homes, and section 22 provides: "Subject only to the police power, the right of the individual citizen to keep and bear arms shall not be infringed." In *Kalodimos v. Village of Morton Grove* (1984), the Illinois supreme court noted that the language of section 22 varied significantly from the language in the U.S. Constitution regarding the right to bear arms and found that a reasonable prohibition on handguns was permissible under the state constitution. Section 23 recites: "A frequent recurrence to the fundamental principles of civil government is necessary to preserve the blessings of liberty. These blessings cannot endure unless the people recognize their corresponding individual obligations and responsibilities." Section 24 confirms that the enumeration of rights in the constitution "shall not be construed to deny or disparage others retained by the individual citizens of the State."

Division of Powers

Article II, The Powers of the State, section 1, proclaims: "The legislative, executive and judicial branches are separate. No branch shall exercise powers properly belonging to another." Section 2 declares: "The enumeration in this Constitution of specified powers and functions shall not be construed as a limitation of powers of state government."

This language reflects the theory that, unlike the federal government, which may exercise only the powers delegated to it, a state government may exercise any powers not prohibited by the state constitution.

Article IV, The Legislature, section 1, as amended in 1980, states: "The legislative power is vested in a General Assembly consisting of a Senate and a House of Representatives, elected by the electors from 59 Legislative Districts and 118 Representative Districts." In *Munn v. Illinois* (1877), the U.S. Supreme Court held that the state legislature had the power to regulate maximum charges by grain storage warehouse operators and that such regulations were intended to promote the public good and did not violate the U.S. Constitution's commerce clause. **Section 2,** as amended in 1980, states in part: **"(a)** ... Immediately following each decennial redistricting, the General Assembly by law shall divide the Legislative Districts as equally as possible into three groups. Senators from one group shall be elected for terms of four years, four years and two years; ... the second group, for terms of four years, two years and four years; and ... the third group for terms of two years, four years and four years.... **(b)** Each Legislative District shall be divided into two Representative Districts. In 1982 and every two years thereafter one Representative shall be elected from each Representative District for a term of two years." **Section 4** provides: "Members of the General Assembly shall be elected at the general election in even-numbered years."

Section 6 specifies: **"(a)** A majority of the members elected to each house constitutes a quorum. **(b)** On the first day of the January session ... in odd-numbered years, the Secretary of State shall convene the House of Representatives to elect from its membership a Speaker ... as presiding officer, and the Governor shall convene the Senate to elect from its membership a President of the Senate as presiding officer.... **(d)** Each house shall determine the rules of its proceedings, judge the elections, returns and qualifications of its members and choose its officers. No member shall be expelled by either house, except by a vote of two-thirds of the members elected to that house. A member may be expelled only once for the same offense."

Section 6(d) continues: "Each house may punish by imprisonment any person, not a member, guilty of disrespect to the house by disorderly or contemptuous behavior in its presence. Imprisonment shall not extend beyond twenty-four hours at one time unless the person persists in [such] behavior." **Section 12,** in contrast, guarantees certain immunities for legislators: "Except in cases of treason, felony or breach of peace, a member shall be privileged from arrest going to, during, and returning from sessions of the General Assembly. A member shall not be held to answer before any other tribunal for any speech or debate, written or oral, in either house. These immunities shall apply to committee and legislative commission proceedings."

Section 8 states in part: **"(b)** The General Assembly shall enact laws only by bill. Bills may originate in either house, but may be amended or rejected by the other. **(c)** No bill shall become a law without the concurrence of a majority of the members elected to each house. **(d)** A bill shall be read by title on three different days in each house. A bill and each amendment thereto shall be reproduced and placed on the desk of each member before final passage. Bills, except bills for appropriations and for the codification, revision or rearrangement of laws, shall be confined to one subject. Appropriation bills shall be limited to the subject of appropriations. A bill expressly amending a law shall set forth completely the sections amended. The Speaker of the House of Representatives and the President of the Senate shall sign each bill that passes both houses. . . ."

Section 9 requires in part: "**(a)** Every bill passed by the General Assembly shall be presented to the Governor within 30 calendar days after its passage. The foregoing requirement shall be judicially enforceable. If the Governor approves the bill, he shall sign it and it shall become law. **(b)** If the Governor does not approve the bill, he shall veto it by returning it with his objections to the house in which it originated." If the bill is not returned within sixty days, it becomes law without the governor's signature. Each house then has fifteen days in which to override the veto by "a record vote of three-fifths of the members elected. . . ." **Section 9(d)** grants to the governor the power to veto items in appropriations bills. A vetoed item may be restored by the legislature in the same manner as in the case of vetoed bills. Section 9(d) also notes that a reduction in an item of appropriation may be overridden by a "required record vote . . . [of] a majority of the members elected to each house." **Section 9(e)**, an unusual provision noted earlier, provides in part: "The Governor may return a bill together with specific recommendations for change . . . [which] shall be considered in the same manner as a vetoed bill but the specific recommendations may be accepted by a record vote of a majority of the members elected to each house."

Section 13 requires: "The General Assembly shall pass no special or local law when a general law is or can be made applicable. Whether a general law is or can be made applicable shall be a matter for judicial determination." Unlike the constitutions of a number of other states, including Washington, for example, the Illinois constitution has abandoned the practice of listing specific types of provisions that may not be the subject of private or special laws. In *In re Belmont Fire Protection District* (1986), the Illinois supreme court interpreted this provision to mean that it was no longer bound to defer to the legislature in questions involving private or special laws versus general laws, although it will still resolve all reasonable doubt in favor of the legislature.

Executive Branch

Article V, The Executive, section 1, states: "The Executive Branch shall include a Governor, Lieutenant Governor, Attorney General, Secretary of State, Comptroller and Treasurer elected by the electors of the State. They shall keep the public records and maintain a residence at the seat of government during their terms of office." **Section 2** provides in part: "These elected officers . . . shall hold office for four years beginning on the second Monday of January after their election and, except in the case of the Lieutenant Governor, until their successors are qualified."

Section 3 specifies: "To be eligible to hold [these executive branch offices] a person must be a United States citizen, at least 25 years old, and a resident of this State for the three years preceding his election." **Section 4** states in part: "In the general election for Governor and Lieutenant Governor, one vote shall be cast jointly for the candidates nominated by the same political party or petition." **Section 6(a)** sets forth the order of succession to the office of the governor: the lieutenant governor, attorney general, and secretary of state. **Section 6(d)** directs the legislature to "specify [by law] by whom and by what procedures the ability of the Governor to serve or to resume office may be questioned and determined," noting that the supreme court is given "exclusive jurisdiction to review such a law. . . ." **Section 7** authorizes the governor to fill vacancies in the offices of the attorney general, secretary of state, and comptroller or treasurer. If the office of the lieutenant governor becomes vacant, "it shall remain vacant until the end of the term."

Section 8 declares: "The Governor shall have the supreme executive power, and shall be responsible for the faithful execution of the laws." **Section 9** sets forth in part: "**(a)** The Governor shall nominate and, by and with the advice and consent of the Senate, a majority of the members elected concurring by record vote, shall appoint all officers whose election or appointment is not otherwise provided for. Any nomination not acted upon by the Senate within 60 session days . . . shall be deemed [confirmed]." According to **section 10,** "The Governor may remove for incompetence, neglect of duty, or malfeasance in office any officer [he or she appoints]."

Section 11 provides in part: "The Governor, by Executive Order, may reassign functions among or reorganize executive agencies which are directly responsible to him." If the action would "contravene a statute," the legislature must be given an opportunity to reject it. **Section 12** states: "The Governor may grant reprieves, commutations and pardons, after conviction, for all offenses on such terms as he thinks proper. The manner of applying therefore may be regulated by law." The constitutions of some other states, including Massachusetts and New Jersey, for example, provide exceptions to the governor's pardoning power for impeachment and treason.

Section 13 mandates: "The Governor, at the beginning of each annual session of the General Assembly and at the close of his term of office, shall report to the General Assembly on the Condition of the State and recommend such measures as he deems desirable." **Sections 14** through **18,** respectively, set forth the duties of the other elected officers of the executive branch: the lieutenant governor's duties may be delegated by the governor or prescribed by law; the attorney general is the legal officer of the state, whose duties may be prescribed by law; the secretary of state maintains records of the acts of the legislature, among other responsibilities, and has such other duties as may be prescribed by law; the comptroller is to maintain the state's central fiscal accounts; and the treasurer "shall be responsible for the safekeeping and investment of monies and securities deposited with him, and for their disbursement upon order of the Comptroller." **Section 19** provides: "All officers of the Executive Branch shall keep accounts and shall make such reports as may be required by law. They shall provide the Governor with information relating to their respective offices, either in writing under oath, or otherwise, as the Governor may require."

Judicial Branch

Article VI, The Judiciary, section 1, declares: "The judicial power is vested in a Supreme Court, an Appellate Court and Circuit Courts." **Section 3** specifies: "The Supreme Court shall consist of seven Judges. Three shall be selected from the First Judicial District [Cook County] and one from each of the other Judicial Districts. Four Judges constitute a quorum and the concurrence of four is necessary for a decision. Supreme Court Judges shall select a Chief Justice from their number to serve for a term of three years." **Section 16** states in part: "General administrative and supervisory authority over all courts is vested in the Supreme Court and shall be exercised by the Chief Justice in accordance with its rules."

Section 4 provides: "**(a)** The Supreme Court may exercise original jurisdiction in cases relating to revenue, mandamus, prohibition or habeas corpus and as may be necessary to the complete determination of any case on review. **(b)** Appeals from judgments of Circuit Courts imposing a sentence of death shall be directly to the Supreme Court as a matter of right. The Supreme Court shall provide by rule for direct appeal in other cases. **(c)** Appeals from the Appellate Court to the Supreme Court are a matter of right if a question under the Constitution of the United States or of this State arises for the first time in and as a result of the action of the Appellate Court...." In analyzing constitutional questions, the Illinois supreme court in *Coalition for Political Honesty v. State Board of Elections* (1976) decided that the rules of statutory construction should be distinguished from the rules of constitutional interpretation. Some legal commentators believe, however, that the rules for interpreting both types of laws are similar.

Section 10 stipulates: "The terms of office of Supreme and Appellate Court Judges shall be ten years...." **Section 11** mandates: "No person shall be eligible to be a Judge ... unless he is a United States citizen, a licensed attorney-at-law of this State, and a resident of the unit which selects him...." **Section 12** states in part: "**(a)** Supreme, Appellate and Circuit Judges shall be nominated at primary elections or by petition. Judges shall be elected at general or judicial elections as the General Assembly shall provide by law.... **(c)** A vacancy occurring in the office ... shall be filled as the General Assembly may provide by law." Advises **section 13**: "**(a)** The Supreme Court shall adopt rules of conduct for Judges.... **(b)** Judges ... shall devote full time to judicial duties...."

Section 15 states in part: "**(a)** The General Assembly may provide by law for the retirement of Judges ... at a prescribed age." **Section 15(b)** creates a judicial inquiry board, and **section 15(e)** creates a courts commission to hear complaints filed by the judicial inquiry board and "to remove from office, suspend without pay, censure or reprimand a Judge...." According to **section 18(a)**, "The Supreme Court and the Appellate Court Judges of each Judicial District, respectively, shall appoint a clerk and other non-judicial officers...."

Impeachment

Article IV, The Legislature, section 14, mandates: "The House of Representatives has the sole power to conduct legislative investigations to determine the existence of cause for impeachment and, by the vote of a majority of the members elected, to impeach Executive and Judicial officers. Impeachments shall be tried by the Senate.... No person shall be convicted without the concurrence of two-thirds of the Senators elected. Judgment shall not extend beyond removal from office and disqualification to hold any public office of this State. An impeached officer … shall be liable to prosecution … according to law."

Article VII, Local Government, section 1, states: "'Municipalities' means cities, villages and incorporated towns. 'Units of local government' means counties, municipalities, townships, special districts, and units, designated as units of local government by law, which exercise limited governmental powers or powers in respect to limited governmental subjects, but does not include school districts." **Section 6** provides in part: "**(a)** A County which has a chief executive officer elected by the electors of the county and any municipality which has a population of more than 25,000 are home rule units…. **(f)** A home rule unit shall have the power subject to approval by referendum to adopt, alter or repeal a form of government provided by law, except [for] Cook County…."

Local Government

Article IX, Revenue, section 1, declares: "The General Assembly has the exclusive power to raise revenue by law except as limited or otherwise provided in this Constitution. The power of taxation shall not be surrendered, suspended, or contracted away." **Section 3(a)** provides in part: "A tax on or measured by income shall be at a non-graduated rate. At any one time there may be no more than one such tax imposed by the State for State purposes on individuals and one such tax so imposed on corporations." **Article VIII, Finance, section 2(a),** states in part: "The Governor shall prepare and submit to the General Assembly, at a time prescribed by law, a State budget for the ensuing fiscal year…. Proposed expenditures shall not exceed funds estimated to be available for the fiscal year as shown in the budget."

Taxation and Finance

Article X, Education, section 1, proclaims in part: "A fundamental goal of the People of the State is the educational development of all persons to the limits of their capacities. The State shall provide for an efficient system of high quality public educational institutions and services. Education in public schools through the secondary level shall be free. There may be such other free education as the General Assembly provides by law."

Education

Article XI, Environment, section 1, declares: "The public policy of the State and the duty of each person is to provide and maintain a healthful environment for the benefit of this and future generations. The General Assembly shall provide by law for the implementation and enforcement of this public policy."

Environment

Article XIV, Constitutional Revision, section 1(a), stipulates: "Whenever three-fifths of the members elected to each house of the General Assembly so direct, the question of whether a Constitutional Convention should be called shall be submitted to the electors at the general election next occurring at least six months after such legislative direction." **Section 1(b)** directs that if the question is not submitted in a twenty-year period, the secretary of state is to submit it automatically. **Section 1(c)** notes that a convention must be "approved by three-fifths of those voting on the question or a majority of those voting in the election." And, according to **section 1(g),** revisions or amendments

Amendment Procedures

proposed by the convention become effective "if approved by a majority of [the electors] voting on the question."

Section 2(a) provides in part: "Amendments to this Constitution may be initiated in either house of the General Assembly." They must be read in full on three different days and reproduced before final passage and approved by three-fifths of the members of each house. **Section 2(b)** states that the amendment becomes effective if "approved by either three-fifths of those voting on the question or a majority of those voting in the election." A majority of the members of each house, however, may vote to withdraw a proposed amendment before the election. According to **section 2(c)**, the legislature may not submit "amendments to more than three Articles of the Constitution at any one election."

Section 3 prescribes the process for submitting amendments by popular initiative but only for "structural and procedural subjects contained in Article IV [relating to the legislature]."

Section 4 requires the "affirmative vote of three-fifths of the members elected to each house of the General Assembly … to call a Federal Constitutional Convention, to ratify a proposed amendment to the [U.S.] Constitution, or to call a State Convention to ratify [such a] proposed amendment.…"

Indiana, the "Hoosier State," became the nineteenth state of the United States on December 11, 1816. Its capital is Indianapolis. Some 36,420 square miles in area, Indiana is bordered by Lake Michigan and Michigan on the north, Ohio on the east, Kentucky on the south, and Illinois on the west. Indiana ranks fourteenth among the states in population with approximately 5.8 million residents. The state's principal industries include manufacturing, services, and agriculture; its chief crops include corn, wheat, and soybeans.

Government: The governor and lieutenant governor are elected jointly for four-year terms; the governor is limited to eight of any twelve years in office. The legislature, called the general assembly, consists of fifty senators elected for four-year terms and 100 representatives elected for two-year terms. The supreme court is composed of a chief justice and four associate justices appointed by the governor from a list prepared by a judicial nominating commission; they are subject to voter approval after the first two years and every ten years thereafter.

Dates of Constitutions: 1816 and 1851

The presence of humans in what is today the state of Indiana dates to at least 8000 B.C. From 1000 B.C. to A.D. 900, the region was inhabited by members of the Woodland culture. They were succeeded by the Mississippians, whose culture survived until the sixteenth century. The Miami, Kickapoo, and Illinois peoples, among others, were living in the region when the first Europeans arrived.

Robert Cavelier, sieur de La Salle, who reached the site of present-day South Bend on December 5, 1679, is credited as the first European to enter Indiana territory. In May 1681, on a second trip, La Salle met with representatives of the Miami and Illinois to negotiate trade relations and enlist their support against the British. Facing constant pressure from British colonists contending for land and trade, the French established a number of outposts, including Fort Miami, built in 1722 on the present site of Fort Wayne.

Under the treaty ending the French and Indian War in 1763, France ceded to Great Britain land in North America that included the Indiana territory. In the winter of 1778–79, George Rogers Clark, while leading an expedition of Virginia militia during the Revolutionary War, captured Vincennes, a French settlement founded around 1708, in the Indian stronghold later known as Indiana. Virginia then incorporated the territory into its Illinois County but in 1783 ceded it to the Continental Congress.

A territorial land policy act approved by Congress in 1785 and the famous Northwest Ordinance of July 13, 1778, paved the way for American expansion into Indiana territory, as did General Anthony Wayne's defeat of an Indian alliance at the Battle of Fallen Timbers in 1794. The availability of smaller homestead lots to those who could not afford large-acreage farms and negotiation of Indian treaties by William Henry Harrison, the territorial governor, also encouraged settlement. The Territorial Act of May 7, 1800, provided a temporary government for a separate Indiana Territory, and by acts passed in 1805 and 1809 the present boundaries of Indiana were basically defined.

On December 11, 1815, the territorial legislature petitioned Congress for admission to the Union. Congress passed an enabling act on April 19, 1816, and a constitutional convention assembled on June 10. The document produced was modeled largely on the 1803

Ohio constitution with respect to the legislative article in particular, while the executive article was modeled on the 1799 Kentucky constitution; the judicial article was a combination of both. The constitution went into effect on December 11, 1816, when Indiana became a state.

With the rise of the Democratic Party under Andrew Jackson in the then-western states, Indiana's 1816 constitution came under criticism for hindering popular control of the government. Its luster was further tarnished by failed economic policies, including overpromotion of state banks. On October 7, 1850, a constitutional convention assembled in Indianapolis and produced a new document that was ratified by the people on August 4 and went into effect on November 1, 1851.

The Constitution

The Indiana constitution's bill of rights contains a number of sections relating to religion that reflect the revival of religious fervor of the time and the interest in religious freedom and humanitarian guarantees. Restrictions on the legislative process and popular election of the judiciary to curb its independence—a principle of Jacksonian democracy—was typical of other state constitutions adopted during this period. The article on the judiciary, although completely modernized in 1970, retains the requirement for voter approval of judges two years after their appointment by the governor and every ten years afterward.

The procedure for amending the Indiana constitution is particularly difficult. A 1962 study revealed that of the more than five hundred amendment proposals introduced in the legislature since 1851, only thirty-eight amendments had passed in two separate sessions of that body, as required by the constitution, and of these only twenty had been ratified by the people. As of January 1, 1998, Indiana's 1851 constitution, a relatively short document containing only some 10,230 words, has been amended just forty times. The only nineteenth-century state constitutions with fewer amendments are Kentucky's 1891 and Tennessee's 1870 documents.

Preamble

The preamble to the 1851 Indiana constitution reads: "TO THE END, that justice be established, public order maintained, and liberty perpetuated; WE, the People of the State of Indiana, grateful to ALMIGHTY GOD for the free exercise of the right to choose our own form of government, do ordain this Constitution."

Fundamental Rights

Article 1, Bill of Rights, section 1, as amended in 1984, proclaims: "WE DECLARE, That all people are created equal; that they are endowed by their CREATOR with certain inalienable rights; that among these are life, liberty, and the pursuit of happiness; that all power is inherent in the people; and that all free governments are, and of right ought to be, founded on their authority, and instituted for their peace, safety, and well-being. For the advancement of these ends, the people have, at all times, an indefeasible right to alter and reform their government." **Sections 2** through **7** affirm aspects of freedom of religion and conscience. **Section 8** states: "The mode of administering an oath or affirmation shall be such as may be most consistent with, and binding upon, the conscience of the person, to whom such oath or affirmation may be administered."

Section 9 mandates that "[n]o law shall be passed, restraining the free interchange of thought and opinion, or restricting the right to speak, write, or print, freely, on any subject whatever"; however, "for the abuse of that right, every person shall be responsible." **Section 10** provides: "In all prosecutions for libel, the truth of the matters alleged to be libelous, may be given in justification." **Section 11** guarantees freedom from unreasonable searches and seizures.

Sections 12 through **18** acknowledge rights of those accused of crime, while **section 13(b)**, added by amendment in 1996, establishes rights for victims. **Section 15** states that "[n]o person arrested, or confined in jail, shall be treated with unnecessary rigor"; and **section 18** provides that "[t]he penal code shall be founded on the principles of reformation, and not of vindictive justice." **Sections 19** and **20**, respectively, relate to juries in criminal and civil trials.

Section 21, as amended in 1984, requires compensation for services or property taken by the state; **section 22** guarantees to debtors that the "privilege … to enjoy the necessary comforts of life, shall be recognized by wholesome laws"; and **section 23** mandates: "The General Assembly shall not grant to any citizen, or class of citizens, privileges or immunities, which, upon the same terms, shall not equally belong to all citizens." **Sections 24** through **27**, respectively, prohibit ex post facto laws and laws impairing the obligation of contracts; laws made in accordance with "any authority, except as provided in this Constitution"; the suspension of the laws "except by the authority of the General Assembly"; and the suspension of the writ of habeas corpus "except in case of rebellion or invasion; and then, only if the public safety demand it."

Section 31 guarantees the people's right to assemble "in a peaceable manner, to consult for their common good," to instruct their representatives, and to apply "to the General Assembly for redress of grievances." **Sections 32** through **36**, respectively, assert the right to bear arms, subordinate the military to civilian power, restrict the quartering of soldiers, prohibit the legislature from granting "any title of nobility [or] hereditary distinctions," and allow emigration from the state. **Section 37**, as amended in 1984, states: "There shall be neither slavery, nor involuntary servitude, within the State, otherwise than for punishment of crimes, whereof the party shall have been duly convicted."

Article 3, Distribution of Powers, section 1, declares: "The powers of the Government are divided into three separate departments; the Legislative, the Executive including the Administrative, and the Judicial: and no person, charged with official duties under one of these departments, shall exercise any of the functions of another, except as in this Constitution expressly provided."

Division of Powers

Article 4, Legislative, section 1, mandates: "The Legislative authority of the State shall be vested in a General Assembly, which shall consist of a Senate and a House of Representatives. The style of every law shall be: 'Be it enacted by the General Assembly of the State of Indiana'; and no law shall be enacted, except by bill." In *Tucker v. State* (1941), the Indiana supreme court held that the management of state property was an executive rather than a legislative function.

Legislative Branch

Section 2, as amended in 1984, stipulates: "The Senate shall not exceed fifty, nor the House of Representatives one hundred members; and they shall be chosen by the electors of the respective districts into which the State may, from time to time, be divided." **Section 3,** as amended in 1984, provides that senators are elected for four-year terms and representatives for two-year terms "from the day next after their general election"; furthermore, "[o]ne half of the Senators, as nearly as possible, shall be elected biennially."

Section 4, as amended in 1881 and 1984, authorizes the legislature to "provide by law for the filling of such vacancies as may occur in the General Assembly." **Section 5,** as amended in 1984, requires: "The General Assembly elected during the year in which a federal decennial census is taken shall fix by law the number of Senators and Representatives and apportion them among districts according to the number of inhabitants in each district, as revealed by the . . . census. The territory in each district shall be contiguous." According to **section 7,** as amended in 1984, legislators must, "at the time of [their] election," be U.S. citizens, state residents for two years, and district residents for one year; in addition, "[s]enators shall be at least twenty-five, and Representatives at least twenty-one years of age."

Section 8 exempts legislators from arrest during or on their way to and from legislative sessions, except in cases of treason, felony, and breach of the peace. They may not be subject "to any civil process, during the session . . . nor during the fifteen days next before the commencement thereof"; furthermore, "[f]or any speech or debate in either House, a member shall not be questioned in any other place." Pursuant to **section 10,** "Each House, when assembled, shall choose its own officers, the President of the Senate excepted. . . ." Under **article 5, Executive, section 21,** the lieutenant governor is designated as president of the senate, and its **section 11** authorizes the senate to "elect one of its own members as President for the occasion" when the lieutenant governor is unable to preside over that body.

Article 4, Legislative, section 10, also allows each house to judge the election, qualifications, and returns of its members; to determine its procedural rules; and to "sit upon its own adjournment," although "neither House shall, without the consent of the other, adjourn for more than three days. . . ." **Section 11** defines a quorum as two-thirds of each house. Most state constitutions require only a majority of each house for a quorum. **Section 12** instructs both houses to keep a journal, and **section 13** mandates: "The doors of each House, and of Committees of the Whole, shall be kept open, except in such cases, as, in the opinion of either House, may require secrecy." **Section 14** authorizes each house to punish members "for disorderly behavior" and "with the concurrence of two-thirds" to expel them, while **section 15** further allows each house to punish "by imprisonment, any person not a member, who shall have been guilty of disrespect to the House, by disorderly or contemptuous behavior, in its presence. . . ." **Section 16** states: "Each House shall have all powers, necessary for a branch of the Legislative department of a free and independent State."

Section 17 provides that "[b]ills may originate in either House, but may be amended or rejected in the other; except that bills for raising revenue shall originate in the House of Representatives." **Section 18,** as amended in 1984, requires: "Every bill shall be read, by title, on three several days, in each House . . . ," but in an emergency this requirement can be dispensed with by a two-thirds vote, except on final passage of a bill. The vote on every bill or joint resolution "shall be taken by yeas and nays." **Section 22,** as amended in 1881 and 1984, enumerates topics that may not be the subject of local or special laws, including granting divorces and changing the names of persons; and **section 23** states: "In all the cases enumerated in the preceding section, and in all other cases where a general law can be made applicable, all laws shall be general, and of uniform operation throughout the State."

Section 25 requires a "majority of all the members elected to each House" for passing bills and joint resolutions; moreover, "all bills and joint resolutions so passed, shall be signed by the Presiding Officers of the respective Houses." In *Roeschlein v. Thomas* (1972), the Indiana supreme court found that the doctrine of the separation of powers requires that courts do not inquire into the actual manner of the passage of bills duly authenticated by officials of the legislature. **Section 28** states: "No act shall take effect, until the same shall have been published and circulated in the several counties of the State, by authority, except in case of emergency, which emergency shall be declared in the preamble, or in the body, of the law."

Article 5, Executive, section 1, as amended in 1972, declares: "The executive power of the State shall be vested in a Governor. He shall hold his office during four years, and shall not be eligible more than eight years in any period of twelve years." This is a variation of the more standard language, such as that used in the Alaska constitution, for example, that limits a governor to two consecutive terms. **Section 2** establishes the position of lieutenant governor, "who shall hold his office during four years." According to **section 4,** as amended in 1974, "Each candidate for Lieutenant Governor shall run jointly in the general election with a candidate for Governor, and his name shall appear jointly on the ballot with the candidate for Governor."

Executive Branch

Section 7 describes the qualifications for governor and lieutenant governor: "No person shall be eligible to the office of Governor or Lieutenant Governor, who shall not have been five years a citizen of the United States, and also a resident of the State of Indiana during the five years next preceding his election; . . . [or] who shall not have attained the age of thirty years." **Section 10(a),** as amended in 1978, provides that if the governor-elect fails to assume office, dies, resigns, or is removed from office, the lieutenant governor becomes governor. If the governor "is unable to discharge the powers and duties of his office," the lieutenant governor becomes acting governor. **Section 21** states: "The Lieutenant Governor shall, by virtue of his office, be President of the Senate; have a right, when in committee of the whole, to join in debate, and to vote on all subjects; and, whenever the Senate shall be equally divided, he shall give the casting vote." If the lieutenant governor's office becomes vacant, **section 10(b),** as amended in 1978, authorizes the governor to nominate a replacement "who shall take office upon confirmation by a majority vote in each house of the general assembly. . . ."

Sections 12 through **18** address the governor's powers and duties. **Section 12,** as amended in 1984, designates the governor "commander-in-chief of the armed forces," which he or she may call out "to execute the laws, or to suppress insurrection, or to repel invasion." **Section 13,** as amended in 1984, provides that he or she "shall, from time to time, give to the General Assembly information touching the condition of the State, and recommend such measures as he shall judge to be expedient." **Section 14(a),** as amended in 1972 and 1990, requires that all bills that pass the general assembly be presented to the governor. The governor has seven days to sign a bill into law, veto it, or "refuse to sign or veto such bill in which event it shall become a law without his signature on the eighth day after presentment to the Governor." If the governor vetoes a bill, **section 14(a)(2)(A)** requires that "he shall return such bill, with his objections, within seven days of presentment, to the House in which it originated." Pursuant to **section 14(a)(2)(C),** the veto may be overridden if "a majority of all the members elected to [each] House shall approve the bill. . . ." The governor has no item veto power.

Section 15 authorizes the governor to transact "all necessary business with the officers of government" and to require "information in writing from the officers of the administrative department, upon any subject relating to the duties of their respective offices." **Section 16** states: "The Governor shall take care that the laws are faithfully executed." **Sections 17** and **18,** respectively, empower the governor to "grant reprieves, commutations, and pardons, after conviction, for all offenses except treason and cases of impeachment, subject to such regulations as may be provided by law" and to fill vacancies, including those for which the general assembly has the power of appointment, when it is in recess, as well as vacancies "in any other State office, or in the office of Judge of any Court." And **section 20** adds that if "the seat of government becomes dangerous from disease or a common enemy, the Governor may convene the General Assembly at any other place."

Article 6, Administrative, section 1, as amended in 1970, states: "There shall be elected, by the voters of the state, a Secretary, an Auditor and a Treasurer of State, who shall, severally, hold their offices for four years. They shall perform such duties as may be enjoined by law; and no person shall be eligible to either of said offices, more than eight years in any period of twelve years." In *Tucker v. State* (1941), the Indiana supreme court determined that the word "administrative" is not synonymous with "executive" but is synonymous with "ministerial." **Section 7** provides: "All State officers shall, for crime, incapacity, or negligence, be liable to be removed from office, either by impeachment by the House of Representatives, to be tried by the Senate, or by a joint resolution of the General Assembly; two-thirds of the members elected to each branch voting, in either case, therefor."

Judicial Branch

Article 7, Judicial, was generally amended in 1881 and 1970, so only dates of later amendments are given. **Section 1** vests the state's judicial power in "one Supreme Court, one Court of Appeals, Circuit Courts, and such other courts as the General Assembly may establish." **Section 2** notes that "[t]he Supreme Court shall consist of the Chief Justice of the State and not less than four nor more than eight associate justices; a majority of whom shall form a quorum"; in addition, "The court may appoint such personnel as may be necessary."

Section 3 states: "The Chief Justice of the State shall be selected by the judicial nominating commission from the members of the Supreme Court and he shall retain that office for a period of five years, subject to reappointment in the same manner, except that a member of the Court may resign the office of Chief Justice without resigning from the Court." Section 3 also directs the chief justice to appoint "such person as the General Assembly by law may provide for the administration of his office" and to have prepared and submit to the legislature "regular reports on the condition of the courts and such other reports as may be requested."

Section 4, as amended in 1988, outlines the supreme court's jurisdiction: "The Supreme Court shall have no original jurisdiction except in admission to the practice of law; discipline or disbarment of those admitted; the unauthorized practice of law; discipline, removal and retirement of justices and judges; supervision of the exercise of jurisdiction by the other courts of the State; and issuance of writs necessary or appropriate in aid of its jurisdiction. The Supreme Court shall exercise appellate jurisdiction under such terms and conditions as specified by rules except that appeals from a judgment imposing a sentence of death, life imprisonment or imprisonment for a term greater than fifty years shall be taken directly to the Supreme Court. The Supreme Court shall have, in all appeals of criminal cases, the power to review all questions of law and to review and revise the sentence imposed."

Section 5 stipulates: "The Court of Appeals shall consist of as many geographic districts and sit at such locations as the General Assembly shall determine to be necessary. Each geographic district of the Court shall consist of three judges." According to **section 6,** "The Court [of Appeals] shall have no original jurisdiction, except that it may be authorized by rules of the Supreme Court to review directly decisions of administrative agencies."

Section 10 authorizes the governor to fill vacancies on the supreme court and court of appeals "... without regard to political affiliation, from a list of three nominees presented to him by the judicial nominating commission." If the governor does not make an appointment from the list within sixty days, the appointment is made by the chief justice. To be qualified to serve as a supreme court justice or court of appeals judge, "... a person must be domiciled within the geographic district, a citizen of the United States, admitted to the practice of law in the courts of the State for a period of not less than ten (10) years or must have served as a judge of a circuit, superior or criminal court of the State of Indiana for a period of not less than five (5) years."

Section 11 sets terms for justices and judges, noting that they "shall serve until the next general election following the expiration of two years from the date of appointment, and subject to approval or rejection by the electorate, shall continue to serve for terms of ten years." Justices and judges are to retire "at the age specified by statute in effect at the commencement of [their] current term."

Article 6, Administrative, section 7, provides: "All State officers shall, for crime, incapacity, or negligence, be liable to be removed from office, either by impeachment by the

Impeachment

House of Representatives, to be tried by the Senate, or by a joint resolution of the General Assembly; two-thirds of the members elected to each branch voting, in either case, therefor." Similarly, **section 8** provides that "[a]ll State, county, township, and town officers, may be impeached, or removed from office, in such manner as may be prescribed by law."

Taxation and Finance

Article 10, Finance, section 1, as amended in 1966, directs in part: "**(a)** The General Assembly shall provide, by law, for a uniform and equal rate of property assessment and taxation and shall prescribe regulations to secure a just valuation for taxation of all property, both real and personal." **Section 3** states: "No money shall be drawn from the Treasury, but in pursuance of appropriations made by law." According to **section 4,** "An accurate statement of the receipts and expenditures of the public money, shall be published with the laws of each regular session of the General Assembly."

Education

Article 8, Education, section 1, mandates: "Knowledge and learning, generally diffused throughout a community, being essential to the preservation of a free government; it shall be the duty of the General Assembly to encourage, by all suitable means, moral, intellectual, scientific, and agricultural improvement; and to provide, by law, for a general and uniform system of Common Schools, wherein tuition shall be without charge, and equally open to all." **Section 3** stipulates: "The principal of the Common School fund shall remain a perpetual fund, which may be increased, but shall never be diminished; and the income thereof shall be inviolably appropriated to the support of Common Schools, and to no other purpose whatever." In *Evans v. Tuttle* (1993), the Indiana court of appeals held that where the state provides education to nondisabled children older than eighteen, it must also provide education to disabled children of the same age.

Health and Welfare

Article 9, State Institutions, section 1, mandates: "It shall be the duty of the General Assembly to provide, by law, for the support of institutions for the education of the deaf, the mute, and the blind; and for the treatment of the insane." **Section 3** encourages counties to "provide farms, as an asylum for those persons who, by reason of age, infirmity, or other misfortune, have claims upon the sympathies and aid of society."

Amendment Procedures

Article 16, Amendments, section 1, provides that amendments may be proposed in either house of the legislature and must be agreed to by a majority of the members of each house. They are then "referred to the General Assembly to be chosen at the next general election. . . ." If that assembly agrees to the amendments "by a majority of all the members elected to each House," they are then submitted to the voters. If "a majority of said electors" ratify them, the amendments "shall become a part of this Constitution." **Section 2,** as amended in 1966 and 1984, states: "If two or more amendments shall be submitted at the same time, they shall be submitted in such manner that the electors shall vote for or against each of such amendments separately."

Iowa was admitted to the Union on December 28, 1846, as the twenty-ninth state. Des Moines is the capital of the "Hawkeye State," which encompasses 56,276 square miles and is bordered by Minnesota on the north, Wisconsin and Illinois on the east, Missouri on the south, and Nebraska and South Dakota on the west. Iowa ranks thirtieth among the states with a population of approximately 2.8 million. Agriculture, communications, and insurance are among the state's principal industries; its chief crops include silage and grain corn, soybeans, oats, and hay.

Government: The governor and lieutenant governor are elected jointly for four-year terms. The legislature, called the general assembly, consists of fifty senators elected for four-year terms, one-half every two years, and 100 members of the house of representatives elected for two-year terms. The supreme court consists of a chief justice and eight additional judges initially appointed by the governor from a list prepared by a judicial nominating commission; they stand for election after the first year and at the end of eight-years terms.

Dates of Constitutions: 1846 and 1857

The vast stretch of grassland between the Mississippi and Missouri Rivers that would become the state of Iowa was occupied by nomadic hunters of mammoths and bisons as early as 12,000 years ago. When Father Jacques Marquette and Louis Joliet first explored the region for France in 1673, it was sparsely inhabited by the Yankton Sioux and Iowa peoples. The name Iowa is derived from the tribal name *ayuxwa* (one who puts one to sleep); the English spelled it *Ioway* and the French *Ayoua*.

By a secret treaty in 1762, France ceded its territory west of the Mississippi River to Spain, and in 1788 Julien Du Buque, a French Canadian, settled permanently near the present-day site of the city bearing his name, reportedly to mine lead. Napoleon took back the territory in 1800 only to transfer it to the United States three years later under the terms of the Louisiana Purchase agreement. By then approximately 8,000 Sauk, Fox, Winnebago, Iowa, Sioux, Omaha, Oto, and Missouri peoples were living in the Iowa region.

Eager to learn more about his purchase, President Thomas Jefferson commissioned Meriwether Lewis and William Clark in 1804 to explore the Missouri River. Lieutenant Zebulon Pike, commissioned by the governor of the Louisiana Territory to locate the source of the Mississippi River, reached the mouth of the Des Moines River on August 20, 1805. Military and trading outposts were established, and in 1830 new settlers began working the abandoned Du Buque mine. In 1833, a year after the defeat of Black Hawk, chief of the Sauk, the settlements of Dubuque, Burlington, Fort Madison, Peru, and Bellevue were established.

Until 1812 the Iowa region had been incorporated into the Indiana Territory, with St. Louis in the Louisiana Territory as the administrative center. From 1812 to 1821 Iowa was part of the Missouri Territory. After being designated simply an unorganized territory of the Northwest, Iowa in 1834 came under the administration of the Michigan Territory and in 1836 under the Wisconsin Territory. Eager to regulate their own rights and duties, Iowa settlers began drafting local constitutions; the first one, adopted on

February 17, 1838, was known as the Constitution of the Citizens of the North Fork of the Maquoketa.

In November 1837 an unofficial territorial constitutional convention had met in Burlington, and a bill to create the Territory of Iowa out of part of the Wisconsin Territory was signed by President Martin Van Buren on June 12, 1838. A conflict arose between the first territorial governor, Robert Lucas of Ohio, and the territorial legislature regarding the governor's veto power. In response, Congress passed three acts relating to Iowa's status, all of which became effective on March 3, 1839. The acts did not solve all of Iowa's problems, and attempts to get voter approval for an official constitutional convention failed in 1840 and 1842.

A convention was finally approved, and the delegates met in Iowa City in October 1844. The draft they produced was rejected by the voters because of a provision concerning the size of the state as defined by Congress. A second draft constitution, specifying Iowa's present-day boundaries, was approved and accepted by Congress. This document eliminated the position of lieutenant governor established in the 1844 version and attempted to simplify the judicial provisions. Ratified by the voters on August 3, 1846, it became effective on Iowa's admission as a state on December 28 of that year. Iowa's constitution and New York's of the same year were the first state constitutions to provide for election of judges; by 1861 twenty-four of the thirty-four states had adopted similar provisions.

Dissatisfaction with the 1846 constitution was evident as early as February of the following year, when a proposal to rewrite the document was debated in the state legislature. A new convention did not assemble until 1857, however, when delegates met in Iowa City from January 19 to March 5. Narrowly approved by the voters in August, the new constitution went into effect by proclamation of the governor on September 3, 1857.

The Constitution

Iowa's relatively short 1857 constitution contains approximately 13,400 words and, as of January 1, 1998, has been amended only forty-seven times (three other amendments were voided). Like many other older state constitutions, the Iowa document grants the lion's share of power to the legislature: the governor administers an executive branch that has four other statewide elected officials, not including the lieutenant governor, and the judicial branch is dependent on the legislature for much of its jurisdiction and many of its rules and is answerable to the voters in periodic elections. An unusual feature is that the provision for an elected attorney general is placed in the judicial branch section rather than with the provisions relating to the executive branch.

There are two versions of the 1857 Iowa constitution: the original version and the codified version, which incorporates all the amendments through the 1994 general election and omits certain provisions superseded or obsolete. The following discussion is based on the codified version.

Preamble

The preamble to the 1857 Iowa constitution begins: "WE THE PEOPLE OF THE STATE OF IOWA, grateful to the Supreme Being for the blessings hitherto enjoyed, and feeling our dependence on Him for a continuation of those blessings, do ordain and establish a free and independent government, by the name of the State of Iowa...." There follows a description of the boundaries of the state. In *Missouri v. Iowa* (1849–50), the U.S. Supreme Court determined a boundary dispute between the two states in favor of Iowa.

Article I, Bill of Rights, section 1, declares: "All men are, by nature, free and equal, and have certain inalienable rights—among which are those of enjoying and defending life and liberty, acquiring, possessing and protecting property, and pursuing and obtaining safety and happiness." For Aristotle, known as the father of political science, the concept of happiness or the good life as the highest goal of the human political animal was embraced in the Greek word *eudaimonia*. **Section 2** affirms: "All political power is inherent in the people. Government is instituted for the protection, security, and benefit of the people, and they have the right, at all times, to alter or reform the same, whenever the public good may require it."

Section 3, mirroring language in the U.S. Bill of Rights but going somewhat further, mandates: "The general assembly shall make no law respecting an establishment of religion, or prohibiting the free exercise thereof; nor shall any person be compelled to attend any place of worship, pay tithes, taxes, or other rates for building or repairing places of worship, or the maintenance of any minister, or ministry." **Section 4** prohibits religious tests for public office or giving evidence in court. **Section 6** directs that "[a]ll laws of a general nature shall have a uniform operation"; furthermore, "the general assembly shall not grant to any citizen, or class of citizens, privileges or immunities, which, upon the same terms shall not equally belong to all citizens." In *Beirkamp v. Rogers* (1980), the Iowa supreme court used section 6 to invalidate a state "guest statute" that exempted the owner or operator of a motor vehicle, with some exceptions such as the driver's being under the influence of alcohol, from liability for damages to nonpaying passengers resulting from an accident.

Section 7 extends to every person freedom of speech and publication and guarantees that in "all prosecutions or indictments for libel, the truth may be given in evidence to the jury...." **Section 8** prohibits unreasonable seizures and searches; **section 9** guarantees the right of trial by jury and due process of law; and **section 10** provides: "In all criminal prosecutions, and in cases involving the life, or liberty of an individual the accused shall have a right to a speedy and public trial by an impartial jury; to be informed of the accusation against him, to have a copy of the same when demanded; to be confronted with the witnesses against him; to have compulsory process for his witnesses; and, to have the assistance of counsel." In determining the constitutionality of a law in light of section 10, the Iowa supreme court declared in *State v. Todd* (1991) that a statute is overbroad for constitutional purposes if it not only forbids conduct constitutionally subject to proscription but also sweeps within its ambit those actions ordinarily deemed to be constitutionally protected.

Sections 11 and **12** guarantee other rights of the accused, including the requirement of indictment by a grand jury for serious criminal offenses as well as the prohibition against double jeopardy and the right to bail "except for capital offences where the proof is evident, or the presumption great." **Section 13** prohibits the suspension of the writ of habeas corpus "unless in case of rebellion, or invasion the public safety may require it." **Sections 14, 15,** and **16,** respectively, subordinate the military to civil power; limit the quartering of soldiers in private homes; and define treason in terms similar to those used in the U.S. Constitution. Pursuant to **section 17,** "Excessive bail shall not be required; excessive fines shall not be imposed, and cruel and unusual punishment shall not be inflicted."

Section 18 requires compensation for the taking of private property for public use but, by amendment in 1908, provides: "The general assembly, however, may pass laws permitting the owners of lands to construct drains, ditches, and levees for agricultural, sanitary or mining purposes across the lands of others...." Similar language is found in some other state constitutions, including Colorado's, for example. **Section 19** prohibits imprisonment for debt, except in the case of fraud; **section 20** guarantees the rights to assemble and "to petition for a redress of grievances"; and **section 21** prohibits bills of attainder, ex post facto laws, and laws impairing the obligation of contracts. According to **section 22,** alien residents in the state "enjoy the same rights in respect to the possession, enjoyment and descent of property, as native born citizens."

Section 23 prohibits slavery and involuntary servitude "unless for the punishment of crime." **Section 24** states that "[n]o lease or grant of agricultural lands, reserving any rent, or service of any kind, shall be valid for a longer period than twenty years." Regarding article I, **section 25** provides: "This enumeration of rights shall not be construed to impair or deny others, retained by the people."

Division of Powers

In the Iowa constitution the provisions relating to both the distribution of powers and the legislative department are contained in article III.

Article III, Of the Distribution of Powers, section 1, proclaims: "The powers of the government of Iowa shall be divided into three separate departments—the legislative, the executive, and the judicial: and no person charged with the exercise of powers properly belonging to one of these departments shall exercise any function appertaining to either of the others, except in cases hereinafter expressly directed or permitted." In *Gamel v. Veterans Memorial Auditorium Commission* (1978), the Iowa supreme court ruled that the legislature was precluded from delegating its lawmaking power by the separation of powers doctrine in the state's constitution and not by any language in the U.S. Constitution.

Legislative Branch

Article III, Legislative Department, section 1, declares: "The legislative authority of this state shall be vested in a general assembly, which shall consist of a senate and house of representatives...." In *In the Interest of C.S.* (1994), the Iowa supreme court held that in determining whether the power exercised by the legislature is a proper legislative function, the court looks not to what the constitution authorizes but to what it prohibits.

Section 34, as amended in 1968, limits the senate to "not more than fifty" members and the house of representatives to "not more than one hundred members." **Section 22** disqualifies a person from holding a seat in the legislature if he or she also holds "any lucrative office under the United States, or this state;" exceptions, however, include positions in the militia, for which there is no annual salary, and justices of the peace and postmasters, "whose [annual salary] does not exceed one hundred dollars per annum."

Section 3 provides that "[t]he members of the house of representatives shall be chosen every second year, by the qualified electors of their respective districts ... and continue two years, and until their successors are elected and qualified." **Section 4,** as amended in 1880 and 1926, requires that house members be twenty-one years old, U.S. citizens, state residents for one year, and district or county residents for sixty days.

Section 5 provides: "Senators shall be chosen for the term of four years, at the same time and place as representatives; they shall be twenty-five years of age, and [otherwise] possess the qualifications of representatives...." **Section 6,** as amended in 1968, specifies: "The number of senators shall total not more than one-half the membership of the house of representatives. Senators shall be classified so that as nearly as possible one-half of the members of the senate shall be elected every two years."

Section 7 allows each house to choose its own officers and judge the qualifications and elections of its members, noting that "[a] contested election shall be determined in such manner as shall be directed by law." **Section 8** defines a quorum as "[a] majority of each house," although "a smaller number may adjourn from day to day, and may compel the attendance of absent members...." According to **section 9,** "Each house shall sit upon its own adjournments ...; determine its rules of proceedings, punish members for disorderly behavior, and, with the consent of two-thirds, expel a member, but not a second time for the same offense; and shall have all other powers necessary for a branch of the general assembly of a free and independent state."

Section 10 grants "[e]very member of the general assembly ... the liberty to dissent from, or protest against any act or resolution which he may think injurious to the public, or an individual...." **Section 11** exempts legislators from arrest "during the session of the general assembly, and in going to and returning from the same," except in instances of treason, felony, or breach of the peace.

Section 15 states that "[b]ills may originate in either house...." According to **section 17,** bills must be passed by "a majority of all the members elected to each branch of the general assembly...." **Section 16,** as amended in 1968, addresses the governor's role in the passage of bills: "Every bill which shall have passed the general assembly, shall, before it becomes a law, be presented to the governor. If he approve, he shall sign it; but if not, he shall return it with his objections, to the house in which it originated...." The governor's veto may be overridden "by a majority of two thirds of the members of each house...." Most state constitutions that similarly require a majority of all the elected legislators to pass laws—for example, Minnesota's—require a two-thirds vote of all the elected legislators to override the governor's veto. Indiana, however, requires an absolute majority of all the elected legislators for both passing laws and overriding a veto. Section 16 also provides that the governor has three days, Sundays excepted, to act on a bill. A bill submitted to the governor during the last three days of a legislative session "shall be deposited [with] the secretary of state, within thirty days after the adjournment ...," either approved or with the governor's objections. In the case of appropriations, the governor may exercise the item veto power. Pursuant to **section 26,** as amended in 1986,

"An act of the general assembly passed at a regular session ... shall take effect on July 1 following its passage unless a different effective date is stated in an act...." Acts passed at a special session take effect ninety days after adjournment unless otherwise specified.

Section 27 prohibits the legislature from granting a divorce, and **section 29** stipulates: "Every act shall embrace but one subject, and matters properly connected therewith; which subject shall be expressed in the title." **Section 30** restricts the legislature from passing "local or special laws in [certain] cases," including laws for "the assessment and collection of taxes for state, county, or road purposes" and for "changing the names of persons."

Executive Branch

Article IV, Executive Department, section 1, vests the state's supreme executive power in "a chief magistrate, who shall be styled the governor of the state of Iowa." **Section 2,** as amended in 1988, specifies that "[t]he governor and lieutenant governor shall ... hold office for four years from the time of installation in office and until a successor is elected and qualifies." **Section 3,** as amended in 1988, provides: "The electors shall designate their selections for governor and lieutenant governor as if these two offices were one and the same"; and **section 4,** as amended in 1988, states in part: "The nominees for governor and lieutenant governor jointly having the highest number of votes cast for them shall be declared duly elected."

Section 6 requires that eligible candidates for governor and lieutenant governor be U.S. citizens, state residents for two years, and thirty years old at the time of the election. **Section 14** prohibits the governor and lieutenant governor from simultaneously holding a federal or other state office "except as hereinafter expressly provided."

Section 7 designates the governor "commander in chief of the militia, the army, and the navy of this state." **Sections 8, 9,** and **10** describe other duties of the governor, including, respectively, transacting "all executive business with the officers of government, civil and military, and [requiring] information in writing from the officers of the executive department upon any subject relating to the duties of their respective offices"; "[taking] care that the laws are faithfully executed"; and filling any vacancies for which neither the constitution nor the laws of the state provide. In *State ex rel. Halbach v. Claussen* (1933), the Iowa supreme court held that a statute that implicitly prohibited filling a vacancy in an elective office at a general election held less than thirty days after a vacancy occurs was not unconstitutional.

Section 11 authorizes the governor to convene the legislature "on extraordinary occasions ... by proclamation," although he or she must "state to both houses, when assembled, the purpose for which they shall have been convened." **Section 12** directs the governor to "communicate, by message, to the general assembly, at every regular session, the condition of the state, and recommend such matters as he shall deem expedient." Pursuant to **section 13,** "In case of disagreement between the two houses with respect to the time of adjournment, the governor shall have power to adjourn the general assembly to such time as he may think proper...." **Section 16** empowers the governor to "grant reprieves, commutations and pardons, after conviction, for all offenses except treason and cases of impeachment, subject to such regulations as may be provided by law."

Section 18, as amended in 1988, describes the lieutenant governor's duties as those "provided by law and those ... assigned ... by the governor." **Section 17** specifies that "[i]n case of the death, impeachment, resignation, removal from office, or other disability of the governor, the powers and duties of the office for the residue of the term, or until he shall be acquitted, or the disability removed, shall devolve upon the lieutenant governor." **Section 19,** as amended in 1988, provides in general that in the event of a vacancy in the office of the governor and the lieutenant governor, "the president of the senate shall act as governor. . . ."

Section 22, as amended in 1972, enumerates other statewide elected officers: "A secretary of state, an auditor of state and a treasurer of state shall be elected by the qualified electors at the same time that the governor is elected and for a four-year term . . . , and they shall perform such duties as may be provided by law." **Article V, Judicial Department, section 12,** as amended in 1972, directs the legislature to provide "by law, for the election of an attorney general by the people, whose term of office shall be four years, and until his successor is elected and qualifies."

Article V, Judicial Department, section 1, declares: "The judicial power shall be vested in a supreme court, district courts, and such other courts, inferior to the supreme court, as the general assembly may, from time to time, establish." In 1983 the state legislature established the Iowa court of appeals as an intermediate appeals court. **Section 2** provides: "The supreme court shall consist of three judges, two of whom shall constitute a quorum to hold court." However, **section 10,** as amended in 1884, authorizes the legislature to "increase the number of judges of the supreme court. . . ." Currently there are nine judges on the Iowa supreme court, including a chief justice choosen by the court.

Judicial Branch

Section 4, as amended in 1962, establishes the supreme court's jurisdiction: "The supreme court shall have appellate jurisdiction only in cases in chancery, and shall constitute a court for the correction of errors at law, under such restrictions as the general assembly may, by law, prescribe; and shall have power to issue all writs and process necessary to secure justice to parties, and shall exercise a supervisory and administrative control over all inferior judicial tribunals throughout the state." **Section 7** charges judges of the supreme and district courts with being "conservators of the peace throughout the state."

Section 14 directs the legislature "to provide for the carrying into effect of this article, and to provide for a general system of practice in all the courts of this state." Although this section appears to allocate exclusive judicial rule-making authority to the legislature, the Iowa supreme court decided in *Iowa Civil Liberties Union v. Critelli* (1976) that it also possessed its own inherent rule-making powers.

Section 15, added in 1962, instructs the governor to fill vacancies in the supreme court and district court "by appointment ... from lists of nominees submitted by the appropriate judicial nominating commission"; specifically, "[t]hree nominees shall be submitted for each supreme court vacancy, and two nominees . . . for each district court vacancy." If the governor does not make an appointment within thirty days, "it shall be made from such nominees by the chief justice of the supreme court." **Section 17**, added by amendment in 1962, provides that "[m]embers of all courts shall have such tenure in office as may be fixed by law, but terms of supreme court judges shall be not less than eight years. . . ." Currently the term of Iowa supreme court judges is eight years. Section 17 continues: "Judges shall serve for one year after appointment and until the first day of January following the next judicial election after the expiration of such year. They shall at such judicial election stand for retention in office on a separate ballot which shall submit the question of whether such judge shall be retained in office for the tenure prescribed for such office and . . . shall, at the judicial election next before the end of each term, stand again for retention on such ballot."

Section 18, added by amendment in 1962, requires that supreme court and district court judges be members of the Iowa bar and possess "such other qualifications as may be prescribed by law." The legislature is to set the mandatory retirement age for judges and provide for "adequate retirement compensation." **Section 19**, added by amendment in 1962, provides: "In addition to the legislative power of impeachment of judges as set forth in article three (III), sections nineteen (19) and twenty (20) . . . , the supreme court shall have power to retire judges for disability and to discipline or remove them for good cause, upon application by a commission on judicial qualifications. The general assembly shall provide by law for the implementation of this section."

Impeachment

Article III, Legislative Department, section 19, grants the house of representatives "the sole power of impeachment" and the senate the right to try all impeachments. Conviction requires "the concurrence of two thirds of the members present." **Section 20** stipulates that "[t]he governor, judges of the supreme and district courts, and other state officers, shall be liable to impeachment for any misdemeanor or malfeasance in office"; however, judgment extends only to removal from office and disqualification to hold any state office. Anyone charged with impeachment is still liable under the law. Furthermore, "[a]ll other civil officers shall be tried for misdemeanors and malfeasance in office, in such manner as the general assembly may provide."

Local Government

Article III, Legislative Department, section 38A, added by amendment in 1968, provides: "Municipal corporations are granted home rule power and authority, not inconsistent with the laws of the general assembly, to determine their local affairs and government, except that they shall not have power to levy any tax unless expressly authorized by the general assembly. The rule or proposition of law that a municipal corporation possesses and can exercise only those powers granted in express words is not a part of the law of this state." **Section 39A**, added in 1978, states in part: "Counties or joint county-municipal corporation governments are granted home rule power and authority, not inconsistent with the laws of the general assembly, to determine their local affairs and government, except that they shall not have power to levy any tax unless expressly authorized by the general assembly."

Article IX, Education and School Lands, section 1, as revised in 1864 when the state board of education was abolished, mandates that "[t]he educational and school funds and lands shall be under the control and management of the general assembly of this state." Section 2 prescribes: "The university lands, and the proceeds thereof, and all monies belonging to said fund shall be a permanent fund for the sole use of the state university. The interest arising from the same shall be annually appropriated for the support and benefit of said university."

Education

Article X, Amendments to the Constitution, section 1, provides: "Any amendment or amendments to this Constitution may be proposed in either house of the general assembly; and if the same shall be agreed to by a majority of the members elected to each of the two houses, such proposed amendment shall be ... referred to the legislature to be chosen at the next general election...." The proposed amendments must be published for three months before the election, and if agreed to "by a majority of the members elected to each house," they are then submitted to the people "in such manner, and at such time as the general assembly shall provide...." If "a majority of the electors qualified to vote for members of the general assembly, voting thereon" approve the amendments, they "shall become a part of the Constitution of this state."

Amendment Procedures

Section 3, as amended in 1964, states in part: "At the general election ... held in the year one thousand nine hundred and seventy, and in each tenth year thereafter, and also at such times as the general assembly may, by law, provide, the question, 'Shall there be a convention to revise the Constitution, and propose amendment or amendments to same?' shall be decided by the electors qualified to vote for members of the general assembly...." If "a majority of the electors so qualified" voting on the question decide in favor of it, the legislature provides for a constitutional convention. The results of the convention must be submitted to the people for ratification.

KANSAS

On January 29, 1861, Kansas became the thirty-fourth state of the United States. The capital of the "Sunflower State" is Topeka. Some 82,282 square miles in area, Kansas is bordered by Nebraska on the north, Missouri on the east, Oklahoma on the south, and Colorado on the west. With approximately 2.6 million inhabitants, it ranks thirty-second among the states in population. Its principal industries include manufacturing, finance, and insurance; its chief crops are wheat, sorghum, corn, hay, and sunflowers.

General Information

Government: The governor and lieutenant governor are elected jointly on a single ticket for four-year terms and are limited to two successive terms. The legislature consists of forty senators elected for four-year terms and 125 members of the house of representatives elected for two-year terms. The supreme court comprises a chief justice and six additional justices who are initially appointed by the governor from a list of names submitted by a supreme court nominating commission; the justices must stand for election after the first year and every six years thereafter.

Date of Constitution: 1861

Constitutional History

In 1541, when Francisco Vásquez de Coronado entered the territory that would become the state of Kansas in search of gold, silver, and precious stones, he found the Quivira, or Wichita, people, who shared the land with the Pawnee, Kansa, and Osage Indians, among others. When Coronado returned to Mexico the following year, the Franciscan priest Juan Padilla stayed behind, only to become, at the hands of the indigenous peoples of central Kansas, the first Christian martyred in middle North America.

In 1682 the explorer Robert Cavelier, sieur de la Salle, claimed the "country of Louisiana," which included the Kansas territory, for France, and shortly afterward the French began building trading posts in the area. In 1719, while exploring the upper Louisiana Territory for France, Charles Claude du Tisné traversed Osage country, and in 1722 the French built Fort Orléans near the mouth of the Osage River. The French and Spanish rivalry in the area ended when France ceded the Louisiana Territory to Spain after the French and Indian War, which ended in 1763.

Spain returned the Louisiana Territory to France in 1800, and three years later the United States acquired the territory under the terms of the Louisiana Purchase. Meriwether Lewis and William Clark, commissioned by President Thomas Jefferson to explore the nation's new possession, made a landing at the mouth of the Kansas River on July 4, 1804. Zebulon Pike's expedition traveled through Kansas on its way west to Colorado two years later.

On June 4, 1812, Kansas became a part of the new Territory of Missouri. Three missions were established in Osage country in 1820, and the Santa Fe Trail was laid out across the future state the following year. The U.S. government discouraged settlement in Kansas, however, because it was used to a large extent for Indian reservations. In 1853 the Wyandot people sent a delegate to Congress asking permission to organize the Kansas-Nebraska Territory, but the proposal was rejected.

As more and more states were created out of western lands, the pressure to allow settlement of Kansas and Nebraska increased. In 1854 Congress was persuaded to repeal the Missouri Compromise, which required the admission of one slave state for every free state, in favor of "popular" or "squatter" sovereignty. The Kansas-Nebraska Act of May 30, 1854, opened the way for development of these territories by settlers and the builders of the transcontinental railroad. But the question of slavery was not solved, resulting in subsequent bloody conflicts over the issue and use of the epithet "Bleeding Kansas."

In anticipation of statehood, both the pro-slavery and the abolitionist movements attempted to influence draft constitutions. The Kansas "Free State" or "Free Soil" advocates held a constitutional convention in Topeka in the fall of 1855 and produced a draft constitution that prohibited slavery and involuntary servitude except as punishment for a crime. This document incited further clashes between the pro-slavery and abolitionist forces, culminating in John Brown's massacre of pro-slavery settlers in Pottawatonie in May 1856 after a center of abolitionist activities in Lawrence had been attacked by pro-slavery groups. A new constitutional convention assembled in Lecompton in September 1857 and produced a document that guaranteed owners protection for their slave property already in the territory and required full compensation for the emancipation of any slaves. While Congress debated the question of Kansas's admission to the Union, another convention meeting in Leavenworth produced another constitution, similar to the Topeka document, which was sent to Congress in January 1859.

Congress took no action, so a fourth constitutional convention was assembled in Wyandotte, later called Kansas City, on July 5, 1859. The major issue was still slavery and the status of blacks. The convention easily approved the prohibition of slavery in the new state and provided for the "protection of the rights of women, in acquiring and possessing property" and "their equal rights in the possession of their children." A proposal for maintaining segregated schools was tabled, but the requirement that one had to be white in order to vote was retained. This constitution was approved by the voters by about a two-to-one margin on October 4, 1859, and went into effect on January 29, 1861, when President James Buchanan signed the act granting statehood to Kansas.

The Constitution

Kansas's 1861 constitution was modeled generally on Ohio's 1851 document, which basically followed the U.S. Constitution. However, in the Kansas document the provisions for the executive branch precede those for the legislative branch, the treason provision is based on the federal model, and the requirement for a grand jury is omitted. Also, unlike the Ohio constitution but similar to the constitutions of Indiana, Kentucky, and Oregon, the Kansas document includes an office of superintendent of public instruction in the executive branch.

One of the shortest state constitutions, with only approximately 11,900 words, the Kansas constitution has been revised substantially (albeit gradually) rather than rewritten. Three constitutional commissions, beginning in 1957, contributed to the many reforms adopted by amendment. The third commission, a citizens committee created by the legislature in 1968, proposed increasing the number of amendments that could be voted on at one time from three to five and allowing special elections, rather than only general elections, for the people to consider amendments. In *Moore v. Shanahan* (1971), the chief justice of the Kansas supreme court wrote both the majority opinion (it being his turn in a since-abandoned custom of seniority rotation to write the majority opinion) and a dissenting opinion on the question of the proposed procedural amendments. The majority opinion held the proposal valid, but the dissent argued that, although the Kansas constitution allows revision by both amendment and convention, the effect of the proposal to amend the constitution's amendment provisions was to make the convention method of revision superfluous. As of January 1, 1998, the 1861 Kansas constitution has been amended ninety times, resulting in a number of significant structural changes.

Preamble

Preceding the preamble to the 1861 Kansas constitution is an Acceptance of Grant from Congress and an Ordinance relating to school sections, university lands, lands for public buildings, lands for benevolent institutions, salt springs and mines, proceeds to schools, school lands, and selection of lands. The preamble itself begins: "We, the people of Kansas, grateful to Almighty God for our civil and religious privileges, in order to insure the full enjoyment of our rights as American citizens, do ordain and establish this constitution of the state of Kansas, with the following boundaries...." In *Kansas v. Colorado* (1907), a suit brought by Kansas against Colorado for diverting waters from the Arkansas River before they reached Kansas, the U.S. Supreme Court declared that the federal government has no legislative powers not specifically granted by the U.S. Constitution over matters simply because they affect the nation as a whole.

Fundamental Rights

Bill of Rights, section 1, proclaims: "All men are possessed of equal and inalienable natural rights, among which are life, liberty, and the pursuit of happiness." The framers settled for this language from the Declaration of Independence rather than a more specific statement guaranteeing the rights of former slaves. **Section 2** declares in part: "All political power is inherent in the people, and all free governments are founded on their authority, and are instituted for their equal protection and benefit."

Section 3 ensures the right "to assemble, in a peaceable manner ... and to petition the government, or any department thereof, for the redress of grievances," while **section 4** guarantees the right to bear arms and subordinates the military to civil power. **Section 5** asserts: "The right to trial by jury shall be inviolate."

Section 6 prohibits slavery and "involuntary servitude, except for the punishment of crime, whereof the party shall have been duly convicted." **Section 7** provides in part: "The right to worship God according to the dictates of conscience shall never be infringed ... [and no] religious test or property qualification shall be required for any office of public trust, nor for any vote at any election, nor shall any person be incompetent to testify on account of religious belief."

Section 8 limits the suspension of the writ of habeas corpus, and **section 9** guarantees citizens bail "except for capital offenses, where proof is evident or the presumption great," and prohibits excessive fines and unusual punishment. **Section 10** outlines the rights of the accused: "In all prosecutions, the accused shall be allowed to appear and defend in person, or by counsel; to demand the nature and cause of the accusation against him; to meet the witness face to face, and to have compulsory process to compel the attendance of the witnesses in his behalf, and a speedy public trial by an impartial jury of the county or district in which the offense is alleged to have been committed. No person shall be a witness against himself, or be twice put in jeopardy for the same offense."

Section 11 affirms liberty of the press and freedom of speech, noting that "the truth may be given in evidence to the jury" in "all civil or criminal actions for libel." Pursuant to section 12, "No conviction within the state shall work a forfeiture of estate." Section 13 defines treason and describes the basis for conviction in terms similar to those used in the U.S. Constitution. Sections 14, 15, and 16, respectively, limit the quartering of soldiers in private homes, prohibit unreasonable searches and seizures, and limit imprisonment for debt to cases of fraud.

Section 17 declares: "No distinction shall ever be made between citizens of the state of Kansas and the citizens of other states and territories of the United States in reference to the purchase, enjoyment or descent of property. The rights of aliens in reference to the [same] may be regulated by law." This language is similar to that in the Florida constitution but more restrictive than in the Iowa constitution.

Section 18 guarantees that "[a]ll persons, for injuries suffered in person, reputation or property, shall have remedy by due course of law, and justice administered without delay." This section, a paraphrase of the language in Ohio's 1851 constitution, is another way of expressing the requirement of due process of law, although the courts generally prefer to base their decisions on the Fourteenth Amendment (1868) of the U.S. Constitution. In *Kansas Malpractice Coalition v. Bell* (1988), however, the Kansas supreme court struck down as violative of sections 5 and 18 statutes that capped recovery amounts in malpractice suits. Section 19 prohibits the state from granting "hereditary emoluments, honors, or privileges." And section 20 declares: "This enumeration of rights shall not be construed to impair or deny others retained by the people; and all powers not herein delegated remain with the people."

Article 15, Miscellaneous, section 6, mandates that "[t]he legislature shall provide for the protection of the rights of women, in acquiring and possessing property, real, personal and mixed, [and] shall also provide for their equal rights in the possession of their children." Section 15 provides for certain rights of victims, including the right to be informed of and be present at public hearings and to be heard at sentencing.

Division of Powers

Like the U.S. Constitution and the constitutions of Alaska, Hawaii, New York, and a number of other states, the Kansas constitution does not expressly declare the separation of powers principle. However, the document does divide the government into executive, legislative, and judicial branches. The principle is recognized and applied by the Kansas courts. In *State v. Reed* (1991), the Kansas supreme court reiterated a previous holding that the four factors to be considered when determining a violation of the principle were the essential nature of the power being exercised, the degree of control by one department over another, the objective sought by the legislature, and the practical result of the blending of powers as shown by experience over time.

Article 2, Legislative, section 1, provides: "The legislative power of this state shall be vested in a house of representatives and senate." **Section 2** specifies that the number of legislators may not exceed "one hundred twenty-five representatives and forty senators." At present the two houses of the legislature have the maximum number of members. Section 2 also specifies term lengths: "Representatives shall be elected for two year terms. Senators shall be elected for four year terms."

Section 4 requires that "[d]uring the time that any person is a candidate for nomination or election to the legislature and during the term of each legislator, such candidate or legislator shall be and remain a qualified elector who resides in his or her district." **Section 5** states that any "member of congress and ... civil officer or employee of the United States or of any department, agency, or instrumentality thereof" may not serve in the legislature.

Section 8 provides: "The legislature shall be organized concurrently with the terms of representatives [that is, every two years] except that the senate shall remain organized during the terms of senators [that is, for four years]. The president of the senate shall preside over the senate, and the speaker of the house of representatives shall preside over the house." A quorum is defined as "[a] majority of the members then elected (or appointed) and qualified...." Section 8 also allows each house to expel or censure members "in appropriate cases" and be the judge of elections and qualifications of its members. Pursuant to **section 9,** "All vacancies occurring in either house shall be filled as provided by law." **Section 18** authorizes the legislature to "provide for the election or appointment of all officers and the filling of all vacancies not otherwise provided for in this constitution." **Section 22** notes that "[f]or any speech, written document or debate in either house, the members shall not be questioned elsewhere"; and that "[n]o member ... shall be subject to arrest—except for treason, felony or breach of the peace—in going to, or returning from, the place of meeting, or during the continuance of the session; neither shall he be subject to the service of any civil process during the session, nor for fifteen days previous to its commencement."

Section 12 states: "Bills and concurrent resolutions may originate in either house, but may be amended or rejected by the other." The constitutions of a number of other states, however, restrict the origination of revenue or money bills to the house with the shorter legislative term, as does the U.S. Constitution.

Section 14 addresses the governor's approval of bills: "**(a)** Within ten days after passage, every bill shall be signed by the presiding officers and presented to the governor. If the governor approves a bill, he shall sign it. If the governor does not approve a bill, [he] shall veto it by returning the bill, with a veto message of the objections, to the house of origin of the bill.... If two-thirds of the members then elected (or appointed) and qualified [in each house] shall vote to pass the bill ... it shall become a law, notwithstanding the governor's veto." Section 14(a) continues: "If any bill shall not be returned within ten calendar days (excluding the day presented) after it shall have been presented ..., it shall become a law ... as if it had been signed by the governor." **Section 14(b)** grants the governor the power to veto items in "any bill [containing] several items of appropriation of money"; however, this item veto may be overridden by the legislature in the same manner as with any other vetoed bill.

Section 15 prohibits a bill from being passed on the day that it is introduced "unless in case of emergency declared by two-thirds of the members present. . . ." **Section 16** provides in part: "No bill shall contain more than one subject, except appropriation bills and bills for revision or codification of statutes. The subject of each bill shall be expressed in its title." In *Brickell v. Board of Education* (1973), the Kansas supreme court declared that it was not necessary for the title to contain all the specific details included in the law itself. **Section 17** mandates that "[a]ll laws of a general nature shall have a uniform operation throughout the state. . . ." According to **section 19**, "No act shall take effect until the enacting bill is published as provided by law." Unlike the U.S. Constitution, the constitutions of some states and foreign nations require laws to be officially published before they enter into force.

Article 1, Executive, section 3, vests the state's supreme executive power in the governor, "who shall be responsible for the enforcement of the laws of this state." According to **section 12**, "The lieutenant governor shall assist the governor and have such other powers and duties as are prescribed by law."

Executive Branch

Section 1 enumerates other statewide executive officers: "The constitutional officers of the executive department shall be the governor, lieutenant governor, secretary of state, and attorney general, who shall have such qualifications as are provided by law. Such officers shall be chosen by the electors of this state at the time of voting for members of the legislature in the year 1974 and every four years thereafter. . . ." The governor and lieutenant governor are "nominated and elected jointly in such manner as is prescribed by law so that a single vote shall be cast for a candidate for governor and a candidate for lieutenant governor running together. . . ." Section 1 continues: "No person may be elected to more than two successive terms as governor nor to more than two successive terms as lieutenant governor." **Section 11** stipulates that "[w]hen the office of governor is vacant, the lieutenant governor shall become governor." He or she assumes the duties of the governor "[i]n the event of the disability of the governor . . . until the disability is removed." Section 11 also provides: "When the office of secretary of state or attorney general is vacant, the governor shall fill the vacancy by appointment for the remainder of the term."

Section 4 addresses reports to the governor: "The governor may require information in writing from the officers of the executive department, upon any subject relating to their respective duties. The officers of the executive department, and of all public state institutions, shall, at least ten days preceding each regular session of the legislature, severally report to the governor, who shall transmit such reports to the legislature." The requirement to transmit these reports to the legislature is rare in state constitutions. **Section 5** states in part: "The governor may, on extraordinary occasions, call the legislature into special session by proclamation . . . and . . . upon petition signed by at least two-thirds of the members elected to each house. At every session of the legislature the governor shall communicate in writing information in reference to the condition of the state, and recommend such measures as he deems expedient."

Section 6(a) states: "For the purpose of transferring, abolishing, consolidating or coordinating the whole or any part of any state agency, or the functions thereof, within the executive branch … when the governor considers the same necessary for efficient administration, he may issue one or more executive reorganization orders, each bearing an identifying number, and transmit the same to the legislature within the first thirty calendar days of any regular session." **Section 6(c)** provides that, unless the legislature disapproves of the proposed reorganization "by a majority vote of the members elected" to each house, it goes into effect "on the July 1 following its transmittal to the legislature…."

Section 7 states: "The pardoning power shall be vested in the governor, under regulations and restrictions prescribed by law." **Article 8, Militia, section 4,** designates the governor "commander in chief," with the power to "call out the militia to execute the laws, to suppress insurrection, and to repel invasion."

Judicial Branch

Article 3, Judicial, section 1, declares: "The judicial power of this state shall be vested exclusively in one court of justice, which shall be divided into one supreme court, district courts, and such other courts as are provided by law…. The supreme court shall have general administrative authority over all courts in this state."

Section 2 specifies that "[t]he supreme court shall consist of not less than seven justices" who are appointed by the governor, pursuant to **section 5(a)**, from a list of three persons submitted by the nonpartisan supreme court nominating commission. **Section 5(c)** directs: "Each justice [so appointed] shall hold office for an initial term ending on the second Monday in January following the first general election that occurs after the expiration of twelve months in office." To remain in office a justice must stand for election after the first year and every six years thereafter. **Section 2** designates as chief justice "[t]he justice who is senior in continuous term of service"; if he or she becomes incapacitated, "the office shall devolve upon the justice who is next senior in continuous service."

Section 7 requires that supreme court justices and district court judges be at least thirty years old and "duly authorized by the supreme court of Kansas to practice law in the courts of this state"; in addition, they must possess "such other qualifications as may be prescribed by law." **Section 8** prohibits justices and judges from making "any contribution to or [holding] any office in a political party or organization or [taking] part in any political campaign."

Section 3 establishes the supreme court's jurisdiction: "The supreme court shall have original jurisdiction in proceedings in quo warranto, mandamus, and habeas corpus; and such appellate jurisdiction as may be provided by law. It shall hold one term each year at the seat of government and such other terms at such places as may be provided by law, and its jurisdiction shall be co-extensive with the state."

Section 15 provides that supreme court justices "may be removed from office by impeachment and conviction as prescribed in article 2 of this constitution." In addition, they may be retired "after appropriate hearing, upon certification to the governor, by the supreme court nominating commission that such justice is so incapacitated as to be unable to perform adequately his duties." Other judges are also "subject to retirement for incapacity, and to discipline, suspension and removal for cause by the supreme court after appropriate hearing."

Article 2, Legislative, section 27, states: "The house of representatives shall have the sole power to impeach. All impeachments shall be tried by the senate; and ... [n]o person shall be convicted without the concurrence of two-thirds of the senators then elected (or appointed) and qualified." According to section 28, "The governor and all other officers under this constitution, shall be removed from office on impeachment for, and conviction of treason, bribery, or other high crimes and misdemeanors."

Impeachment

Article 4, Elections, section 3, mandates: "All elected public officials in the state, except judicial officers, shall be subject to recall by voters of the state or political subdivision from which elected. Procedures and grounds for recall shall be prescribed by law."

Direct Democracy

Article 2, Legislative, section 17, indicates that although laws are to be uniform state-wide, "[t]he legislature may designate areas in counties ... 'urban areas' and enact special laws giving [them] such powers of local government and consolidation of local government as the legislature may deem proper." Section 21 states: "The legislature may confer powers of local legislation and administration upon political subdivisions." And section 30 provides: "The legislature may confer legislative powers upon inter-state bodies, comprised of officers of this state or its political subdivisions acting in conjunction with officers of other jurisdictions, relating to the functions thereof. Any such delegation, and any agreement made thereunder shall be subject to limitation, change or termination by the legislature, unless contained in a compact approved by the congress."

Local Government

Article 12, Corporations, section 5, as amended in 1961, declares that "[c]ities are hereby empowered to determine their local affairs...."

Article 11, Finance and Taxation, section 4, mandates a balanced budget: "The legislature shall provide, at each regular session, for raising sufficient revenue to defray the current expenses of the state for two years."

Taxation and Finance

Article 6, Education, section 1, declares: "The legislature shall provide for intellectual, educational, vocational and scientific improvement by establishing and maintaining public schools, educational institutions and related activities which may be organized and changed in such manner as may be provided by law." Section 2 authorizes the legislature to provide for "(a) ... a state board of education which shall have general supervision of public schools, educational institutions and all the educational interests of the state, except educational functions delegated by law to the state board of regents"

Education

and "**(b)** ... a state board of regents and ... its control and supervision of public institutions of higher education."

Kansas has figured in what is probably the most important case involving education in America: *Brown v. Board of Education of Topeka* (1954). In that case the U.S. Supreme Court held that racial segregation of public schools violated the equal protection of the laws guaranteed by the Fourteenth Amendment (1868) to the U.S. Constitution.

Health and Welfare

Article 7, Public Institutions and Welfare, sections 1, 4, and **5,** respectively require that "[i]nstitutions for the benefit of mentally or physically incapacitated or handicapped persons ... be fostered and supported ..."; that "[t]he respective counties ... provide ... for those inhabitants who, by reason of age, infirmity or other misfortune, may have claims upon the aid of society"; and that "[t]he state may provide by law for unemployment compensation and contributory old-age benefits...."

Amendment Procedures

Article 14, Constitutional Amendment and Revision, section 1, provides in part: "Propositions for the amendment of this constitution may be made by concurrent resolution originating in either house of the legislature, and if two-thirds of all the members elected (or appointed) and qualified of each house shall approve such resolution, the secretary of state [must publish it] in the manner provided by law." At the next general election or a special election called by the legislature, "[i]f a majority of the electors voting on any such amendment shall vote for the amendment, the same shall become a part of the constitution." Moreover, "[n]ot more than five amendments shall be submitted at the same election." The constitutions of several other states, including Arkansas, limit the number of amendments that may be voted on at any one election.

Section 2 directs the legislature "by the affirmative vote of two-thirds of all the members elected to each house, [to] submit the question 'Shall there be a convention to amend or revise the article(s) _____ of the constitution of the state of Kansas?,' to the electors at the next election for representatives...." If "a majority of all electors voting on the question" approve it, the voters then elect delegates, who must have "the same qualifications as provided by the constitution for members of the legislature...."

Section 2 also empowers the convention to "amend or revise all or that part of the constitution indicated by the question voted upon to call the convention...." The convention's proposals are then submitted "to the electors at the first general or special statewide election occurring not less than two months after final action thereon by the convention" and must be approved by "a majority of the qualified electors voting thereon."

Article 2, Legislative, section 13, requires "[t]wo-thirds (⅔) of the members then elected (or appointed) and qualified in each house, voting in the affirmative, ... to ratify any amendment to the Constitution of the United States or to make any application for congress to call a convention for proposing amendments to [it]." Congress has never called for a constitutional convention.

The Commonwealth of Kentucky became the fifteenth state of the United States on June 1, 1792. Frankfort is the capital of the "Bluegrass State," which encompasses some 40,411 square miles. Kentucky is bounded by Indiana and Ohio on the north, West Virginia and Virginia on the east, Tennessee on the south, and Missouri and Illinois on the west. In population the commonwealth ranks twenty-fourth among the states with approximately 3.8 million residents. Kentucky's principal industries include manufacturing, finance, insurance, and real estate; tobacco, corn, and soybeans are among its chief crops.

Government: The governor and lieutenant governor are elected on a single ticket for four-year terms and are limited to two consecutive terms. The legislature, or general assembly, consists of thirty-eight senators elected for four-year terms and 100 members of the house of representatives elected for two-year terms. The supreme court comprises a chief justice and six associate justices elected for eight-year terms.

Dates of Constitutions: 1792, 1800, 1850, and 1891

A hunting ground for the Cherokees, who called it *Ken-tah-teh* (the land where we will live), as well as the Shawnee, Wyandot, and Delaware peoples, the region that would become the state of Kentucky was first mapped by Colonel Abraham Wood and others in 1654. Originally included under the charters of the Virginia Company, the area remained unsettled by colonists and largely unknown until the second quarter of the eighteenth century.

In 1682 Robert Cavelier, sieur de La Salle, claimed the Louisiana territory, including the Kentucky region, for France. But nearly seventy-five years passed before the first French trading post was built in the northeast portion of the territory across the Ohio River from what is today Portsmouth, Ohio, in 1756. Earlier, Virginia had given the Loyal Land Company a grant of 800,000 acres in Kentucky territory, and a company expedition had passed through Cumberland Gap on its way to the region in 1750.

Daniel Boone and others began exploring parts of the Kentucky territory in 1769 in spite of boundary restrictions imposed after the French and Indian War (1754–63). North Carolina chartered the Transylvania Company to settle the same territory that Virginia had granted, and in 1774 the company negotiated for a large tract of the land of Kentucky from the Cherokees, a purchase formalized in the Treaty of Sycamore Shoals. Virginia settlers in the area quickly elected representatives to seek support for their interests in the Virginia legislature in Williamsburg, and by an act dated December 6, 1776, Kentucky became a county of Virginia.

After the American Revolution, the settlers in Kentucky demanded an independent government under a provision of Virginia's 1776 constitution, which permitted the legislature to establish one or more governments in the territory "westward of the Allegheny Mountains." However, it took ten conventions of delegates elected by settlers in the region and four enabling acts of the Virginia legislature before Kentucky was admitted to the Union. Congress passed an act "for the Government of the Territory of the United States, south of the river Ohio" in 1790 and another in 1791 admitting Kentucky as a state, effective June 1, 1792.

KENTUCKY

General Information

Constitutional History

In preparation for statehood, a constitutional convention had been held in April 1792 in Danville. The constitution promulgated when Kentucky became a state was a relatively short, general document allowing few elective positions. To reflect the people's desire for a more direct voice in their government, a convention met in Frankfort seven years later and adopted a new constitution that took effect on January 1, 1800. It provided for the direct election of the governor by qualified voters, rather than by the senate as in the earlier version, and increased the authority of the position.

A third constitution, ratified by the voters and made effective on June 11, 1850, limited the indebtedness of the state and increased the number of elected officials. A delegate to the convention remarked, "We have provided for the popular election of every public official except dog catcher, and if dogs could vote, we should have that as well." These changes to the document more than doubled the number of words to about 21,000.

The current constitution was drafted by a convention that met in Frankfort from September 1890 to April 1891 and was ratified by the people on August 3, 1891. A month later, however, the convention reassembled and made a number of significant changes to the document, which the convention proclaimed to be effective on September 28, 1891. Although the altered document was not resubmitted to the people for approval, the Kentucky courts have nevertheless declared it valid.

The Constitution

Kentucky's 1891 constitution was, in part, a response to the increased power of large corporations and the railroads as well as to abuses by government officials. The legislature had often passed laws serving special interests, rather than general laws, and the state treasurer had absconded with most of the funds in the Kentucky treasury. Therefore, like many other state constitutions written during this era, it reflected a distrust of the legislature and a desire for greater popular control over state officials.

The current constitution is a complex, technical document, at 27,200 words much longer and with more provisions than its predecessors. But unlike similar state constitutions in force for so long, it has been amended just thirty-five times as of January 1, 1998. Only in 1996 were Kentucky voters given the opportunity to approve an amendment that removed a provision permitting local governments to levy a poll or voting tax (the federal courts had declared such taxes invalid in Alabama and Texas thirty years earlier) and a provision requiring racially segregated schools, which were declared unconstitutional by the U.S. Supreme Court in 1954.

Preamble

The preamble to the 1891 Kentucky constitution, unlike that of its three predecessors, uses the term *commonwealth* instead of *state* and includes reference to *Almighty God*. The preamble reads: "We, the people of the Commonwealth of Kentucky, grateful to Almighty God for the civil, political and religious liberties we enjoy, and invoking the continuance of these blessings, do ordain and establish this Constitution."

Fundamental Rights

Bill of Rights proclaims: "That the great and essential principles of liberty and free government may be recognized and established, we declare that: **Section 1.** All men are, by nature, free and equal, and have certain inherent and inalienable rights, among which may be reckoned: First: The right of enjoying and defending their lives and liberties. Second: The right of worshipping Almighty God according to the dictates of their consciences. Third: The right of seeking and pursuing their safety and happiness. Fourth: The right of freely communicating their thoughts and opinions. Fifth: The right of acquiring and protecting property." The sixth and seventh rights, respectively, are the rights to assemble and to bear arms. Nebraska and North Dakota also place the right to bear arms in the first section of their bill of rights.

Section 2 states: "Absolute and arbitrary power over the lives, liberty and property of freemen exists nowhere in a republic, not even in the largest majority." **Section 3** provides that "[a]ll men, when they form a social compact, are equal ..."; and **section 4** affirms: "All power is inherent in the people, and all free governments are founded on their authority and instituted for their peace, safety, happiness and the protection of property." **Sections 5** through **10**, respectively, concern religious freedom, free and equal elections, trial by jury, freedom of speech and the press, libel, and security from unreasonable searches and seizures. **Sections 11** through **20** address the rights of the accused.

Section 21, in reference to suicide, provides that "[t]he estate of such persons as shall destroy their own lives shall descend or vest as in the cases of natural death...." According to **section 24**, "Emigration from the State shall not be prohibited." **Section 25** forbids "[s]lavery and involuntary servitude in this State ... except as a punishment for crime, whereof the party shall have been duly convicted." This section was revised by the 1891 constitutional convention after the document had been ratified by the people. The section of the 1850 constitution that it replaced read: "The right to property is before and higher than any constitutional sanction; and the right of the owner of a slave to such slave, and its increase, is the same, and as inviolable as the right of the owner of any property whatever."

Distribution of the Powers of Government, section 27, divides "[t]he powers of the government of the Commonwealth of Kentucky ... into three distinct departments," each "confined to a separate body of magistracy, to wit: Those which are legislative, to one; those which are executive, to another; and those which are judicial, to another." **Section 28** prohibits any "person or collection of persons, being of one of those departments, [from exercising] any power properly belonging to either of the others, except in the instances hereinafter expressly directed or permitted." In *Ex parte Auditor of Public Accounts* (1980), the Kentucky supreme court acknowledged the legislature's authority to enlarge the duties of members of the executive branch but ruled that the legislature violated the constitutional principle of separation of powers when it assigned the auditor functions under the jurisdiction of the judicial branch.

Division of Powers

The Legislative Department, section 29, declares: "The legislative power shall be vested in a House of Representatives and a Senate, which, together, shall be styled the General Assembly of the Commonwealth of Kentucky." Nineteen other states call their state legislature the general assembly. **Section 30**, as amended in 1979, provides that "[m]embers of the House of Representatives and Senators shall be elected at the general election in even-numbered years for terms of four years for Senators and two years for members of the House of Representatives."

Legislative Branch

Section 32 requires a member of the house of representatives to be a "citizen of Kentucky," twenty-four years old, and a resident "in this State two years next preceding his election, and the last year thereof in the county, town or city for which he may be chosen." In *Grantz v. Grauman* (1957), the Kentucky courts of appeals held that a representative must actually reside in the district for which he or she is elected, not merely in the county or city in which that district and other districts are located. Section 32 also requires a senator to be a "citizen of Kentucky," thirty years old, and a resident "in this State six years next preceding his election, and the last year thereof in the district for which he may be chosen." Section 35 sets the number of representatives at 100 and the number of senators at thirty-eight.

Suffrage and Elections, section 150, provides that using money or property to influence an election disqualifies a person from serving in the legislature and holding other public office. Other reasons for disqualification include, under Revenue and Taxation, section 173, receiving a personal profit on public funds; under Corporations, section 197, accepting free or reduced-rate passes (for example, on a railroad); and, under General Provisions, section 239, presenting or accepting a challenge to duel.

The Legislative Department, section 36, as amended in 1979, directs the legislature to meet "on the first Tuesday after the first Monday in January in odd-numbered years for a period not to exceed ten legislative days for the purposes of electing legislative leaders, adopting rules of procedure and the organizing of committees." It then adjourns "until the first Tuesday after the first Monday in January of the following even-numbered years," when it convenes "in regular session at the seat of government...." Attempts to reestablish annual regular sessions of the legislature, as provided for in Kentucky's first two constitutions, were defeated by the voters in 1967, 1969, and 1973. Section 37 defines a quorum as "[n]ot less than a majority of the members of each House of the General Assembly...." Sections 38 and 39, respectively, allow each house to judge the qualifications and elections of its members and to determine its procedural rules, punish a member for disorderly behavior, expel a member with the concurrence of two-thirds, and "punish for contempt any person who refuses to attend as a witness" or bring evidence before the general assembly. Section 43 exempts legislators from arrest "during their attendance on the sessions of their respective Houses, and in going to and returning from the same...." except in cases of treason, felony, and breach of the peace.

Section 46 addresses the passage of bills, which must be "reported by a committee and printed for the use of the members"; "read at length on three different days in each House," although the second and third reading can be dispensed with by a majority of all the members elected to the particular house; and approved on final passage by "the votes of at least two-fifths of the members elected to each House, and a majority of the members voting...." Pursuant to section 47, bills for raising revenue must originate in the house of representatives. Section 56 mandates that each bill passed be signed by the presiding officer of each house in open session and that "the Clerk of the latter House shall immediately present [the signed bill] to the Governor for his signature and approval." Section 57 requires a member with a personal or private interest in a matter before the legislature to "disclose the fact to the House of which he is a member, and . . . not vote thereon upon pain of expulsion."

The Executive Department, section 69, vests the commonwealth's supreme executive power in "a Chief Magistrate, who shall be styled the 'Governor of the Commonwealth of Kentucky.'" **Section 70,** as amended in 1992, provides that the governor and lieutenant governor are to be elected jointly "by the casting by each voter of a single vote applicable to both offices" for a term of four years. According to **section 71,** as amended in 1992, the governor is ineligible "for the succeeding four years after the expiration of any second consecutive term for which he shall have been elected." **Section 72,** as amended in 1992, specifies that the governor and lieutenant governor must be thirty years old and "citizens and residents of Kentucky for at least six years next preceding their election." The lieutenant governor's duties include those prescribed by law and delegated by the governor; however, unlike the vice president under the U.S. Constitution and most lieutenant governors under state constitutions, Kentucky's lieutenant governor does not preside over the upper house of the legislature. The disqualifications for legislators noted earlier also apply to the governor and lieutenant governor.

Section 75 designates the governor the commander in chief of the commonwealth's army, navy, and militia "except when they shall be called into the service of the United States"; however, he or she "shall not command personally in the field, unless advised so to do by a resolution of the General Assembly." Although in several cases the Kentucky supreme court has held that the governor's reasons for calling out the militia could not be questioned in court, in practice this power is circumscribed because state units of the National Guard are part of the U.S. military reserves and, according to **Militia, section 221,** the "organization, equipment and discipline of the militia" must conform "as nearly as practicable to the regulations for the government of the armies of the United States."

Section 76 authorizes the governor to fill vacancies by appointment, and **section 77** grants him or her power "to remit fines and forfeitures, commute sentences, grant reprieves and pardons," although expressly denying the power to remit fees. The governor's formal powers have remained basically unchanged since the first constitution, but the 1891 document requires the governor to file a public statement giving the reasons for granting a pardon. In *Commonwealth ex rel. Meredith v. Hall* (1939), the Kentucky court of appeals declared that the governor could attach conditions to a pardon, as long as they were not illegal, immoral, or impossible, and could revoke a pardon if the conditions were not met. Pursuant to **section 78,** the governor may "require information in writing from the officers of the Executive Department upon any subject" relating to their duties.

Section 79 directs the governor to "from time to time, give to the General Assembly information of the state of the Commonwealth . . . ," and **section 80** authorizes the office holder to convene the legislature "on extraordinary occasions" and adjourn it if the two houses cannot agree on a time for adjournment. **Section 81** states: "He shall take care that the laws be faithfully executed," a charge that mirrors language in the U.S. Constitution, article II, section 3, with respect to the president.

Sections 84 and **85,** as amended in 1992, provide for the lieutenant governor to assume the governor's duties if the governor, respectively, "be impeached and removed from office, die, refuse to qualify, resign" or is unable to discharge official duties. **Section 87,** as amended in 1992, specifies that the president of the senate is next in line of succession; however, if there is no president of the senate, the attorney general is to administer the government until a president is chosen by the senate. Before the 1992 amendment, the lieutenant governor served as president of the senate and assumed the duties of the governor when he or she was out of the state.

Section 88 provides that bills passed by both houses of the legislature be presented to the governor, who may approve or veto them, although the legislature can override the veto by a vote of a majority of the members elected to each house. If the governor vetoes a bill, it must be returned "with his objections." In *Arnett v. Meredith* (1938), the Kentucky supreme court invalidated a gubernatorial veto because it was not accompanied by the required veto message. Section 88 also gives the governor the power to "disapprove any part or parts of appropriation bills embracing distinct items."

Section 91, as amended in 1992, enumerates other elected constitutional state officers: "[a] Treasurer, Auditor of Public Accounts, Commissioner of Agriculture, Labor and Statistics, Secretary of State, and Attorney-General...." In *Commonwealth ex rel. Hancock v. Paxton* (1974), the Kentucky court of appeals confirmed a holding in a 1940 case that the legislature could restrict or add to the traditional duties of the attorney general as long as the office was not thereby rendered ineffective.

Judicial Branch

The Judicial Department, section 109, as amended in 1974, declares: "The judicial power of the Commonwealth shall be vested exclusively in one Court of Justice which shall be divided into a Supreme Court, a Court of Appeals, a trial court of general jurisdiction known as the Circuit Court and a trial court of limited jurisdiction known as the District Court. The court shall constitute a unified judicial system for operation and administration." Kentucky's prior constitutions allowed the legislature to create other courts as it deemed necessary, resulting in a variety of trial courts and inefficiency at the appellate court level.

Section 110, as amended in 1976, stipulates: "**(1)** The Supreme Court shall consist of the Chief Justice of the Commonwealth and six associate Justices." **Section 110(5)(a)** directs the justices to elect from among themselves a chief justice, who serves for a four-year term and, according to **section 110(5)(b),** is the "executive head of the Court of Justice." **Section 110(2)(a)** limits the supreme court's jurisdiction to appeals, "except it shall have the power to issue all writs necessary...." **Section 110(2)(b)** also expressly requires the supreme court to review directly cases in which the death penalty, life imprisonment, or imprisonment for more than twenty years is imposed. Pursuant to **section 110(3),** a majority of the justices constitute a quorum. There is no provision for the supreme court to issue advisory opinions, and in *In re Constitutionality of House Bill No. 222* (1936), the Kentucky supreme court held that without such an express provision it had no authority to issue an advisory opinion. The constitutions of a handful of states, including Colorado, Massachusetts, and Florida, however, do contain provisions authorizing the state's highest court to issue advisory opinions.

Section 117, as amended in 1976, states: "Justices of the Supreme Court and judges of the Court of Appeals, Circuit and District Court shall be elected from their respective districts or circuits on a nonpartisan basis as provided by law." **Section 119,** as amended in 1976, sets the terms for supreme court justices and court of appeals judges at eight years; the term for district court judges is four years. **Section 121,** as amended in 1976, outlines procedures for involuntary retirement and removal of justices and judges. In *Nicholson v. Judicial Retirement and Removal Comm.* (1978), the Kentucky supreme court ruled that because the purpose of section 121 was to improve the administration of justice in the state, it was proper to correct deficiencies by taking the least severe action necessary to remedy the situation.

Section 122, as amended in 1976, requires that a justice or a judge be a U.S. citizen, "licensed to practice law in the courts of this Commonwealth," and "a resident of [the] Commonwealth and of the district from which he is elected for two years next preceding his taking office." In addition, supreme court justices and court of appeals and circuit court judges must have been "licensed attorney[s] for at least eight years."

Impeachments, section 66, grants the house of representatives "the sole power of impeachment." **Section 67** directs that impeachments be tried in the senate; moreover, "the concurrence of two-thirds of the Senators present" is necessary for conviction. Pursuant to **section 68,** the "Governor and all civil officers" may be impeached "for any misdemeanors in office." Punishment for conviction on impeachment is removal and disqualification from office, but a person convicted is subject to further punishment under law.

Impeachment

Municipalities, section 156b, added by amendment in 1994, authorizes the legislature to "provide by general law that cities may exercise any power and perform any function within their boundaries that is in furtherance of a public purpose of a city and not in conflict with a constitutional provision or statute." **Section 160,** as amended in 1986 and with certain exceptions and restrictions, states: "The Mayor or Chief Executive, Police Judges, members of legislative boards or councils of towns and cities shall be elected by the qualified voters thereof...." Before 1986 mayors, chief executive officers, and fiscal officers of larger cities were expressly prohibited from succeeding themselves after one term.

Local Government

Revenue and Taxation, section 170, as amended most recently in 1990, allows cities to exempt factories from taxes for five years. **Section 172** requires that property be assessed at "fair cash value" and that assessors be punished for willful error, and **section 175** declares: "The power to tax property shall not be surrendered or suspended by any

Taxation and Finance

contract or grant to which the Commonwealth shall be a party." **Section 180,** as amended in 1996, no longer permits the legislature to allow local governments to "levy a poll [voting tax] not exceeding one dollar and fifty cents per head."

Legislative Department, section 49, states: "The General Assembly may contract debts to meet casual deficits or failures in the revenue" not to exceed $500,000. **Section 171** provides that "[t]he General Assembly shall provide by law an annual tax, which, with other resources, shall be sufficient to defray the estimated expenses of the Commonwealth for each fiscal year."

Education

Section 183 mandates: "The General Assembly shall, by appropriate legislation, provide for an efficient system of common schools throughout the State." **Section 187** originally stated: "In distributing the school fund no distinction shall be made on account of race or color, *and separate schools for white and colored children shall be maintained.*" The phrase in italics was removed by amendment in 1996; however, it had been rendered void by the ruling of the U.S. Supreme Court in *Brown v. Board of Education of Topeka* (1954), which held that school segregation on the basis of race violates the equal protection of the laws guaranteed by the Fourteenth Amendment (1868) to the U.S. Constitution.

Health and Welfare

General Provisions, section 243, mandates that the legislature shall, "by law, fix the minimum ages at which children may be employed in places dangerous to life and health, or injurious to morals; and shall provide adequate penalties for violations of such law." **Section 244a,** added in 1935, directs the general assembly to "prescribe such laws as may be necessary for the granting and paying of old persons an annuity or pension."

Amendment Procedures

Mode of Revision, section 256, as amended in 1979, provides: "Amendments to this Constitution may be proposed by either House of the General Assembly at a regular session...." If agreed to by three-fifths of the members elected to each house, they are to be submitted to the voters for ratification at the "next general election for members of the House of Representatives." If a majority of those voting on the amendment vote for it, it becomes a part of the constitution. **Section 257** instructs the secretary of state to publish the proposed amendment and the time of the vote "at least ninety days before vote is to be taken...."

Sections 258 through **263** prescribe procedures for calling a constitutional convention. **Section 258** provides that if a majority of the members of each house of the legislature concur in one session and a succeeding session in calling a convention, then the matter is put to the voters. If they approve by a majority vote, with at least one-fourth of the number of qualified voters who voted in the last general election voting, the legislature must enact a law at its next regular session to call a convention. **Sections 261** and **262** authorize the legislature to provide procedures for the election of delegates to the convention and for their compensation. Attempts to call a constitutional convention have been defeated four times by Kentucky voters: in 1931, 1947, 1959 (the state supreme court in *Chenault v. Carter* [1960] sustained the legislature's authority to call a "limited" constitutional convention), and 1976, when the proposed convention was defeated by a vote of 254,934 to 165,311.

Louisiana was admitted to the Union on April 30, 1812, as the eighteenth state. Baton Rouge is the capital of the "Pelican State," which encompasses 51,843 square miles and is bordered by Arkansas on the north, Mississippi on the east, the Gulf of Mexico on the south, and Texas on the west. Louisiana ranks twenty-first among the states with a population of approximately 4.3 million residents. Wholesale and retail trade, tourism, and manufacturing are among the state's principal industries; its chief crops include soybeans, sugarcane, rice, corn, and cotton.

General Information

Government: The governor and lieutenant governor are elected separately to four-year terms and are limited to two consecutive terms. The legislature consists of thirty-nine senators and 105 members of the house of representatives, all elected for four-year terms. Since January 8, 1996, senators and representatives have been limited to three consecutive terms. The state supreme court is composed of a chief justice and six associate justices elected to ten-year terms.

Dates of Constitutions: 1812, 1845, 1852, 1861, 1864, 1868, 1879, 1898, 1913, 1921, and 1974

Constitutional History

The Spanish explorer Hernando de Soto crossed the Mississippi River in 1542, but it was Robert Cavelier, sieur de La Salle, who claimed the Mississippi Valley for France in 1682, naming the territory Louisiana after the French king Louis XIV. La Salle's attempts to found a colony there failed, but in 1698 Pierre le Moyne, Sieur d'Iberville, led 200 French settlers to colonize the lower Mississippi Valley. After New Orleans was established in 1718, colonization efforts intensified.

Having sided with France during the French and Indian War (1754–63), Spain was forced to cede the Florida territory to the British victors but in 1762 gained Louisiana from France in partial compensation. Four years later a Spanish administrator arrived in New Orleans with eighty soldiers, only to be ordered out summarily by the superior council, the city's governing body.

Spain reasserted its authority with twenty-four ships and 2,000 troops in 1769 and introduced Spanish law. A *cabildo* (town council) replaced the superior council in New Orleans, and Louisiana was divided into twenty-one parishes under the administration of the bishop of Santiago, Cuba. From Canada came the Acadians, French-speaking refugees whose descendants would later be called Cajuns. During the Revolutionary War, Spain fought against England and recovered its Florida colony.

Napoleon's rise to power in Europe resulted in Spain's ceding Louisiana to France in 1800. Thomas Jefferson had warned, "The day France takes possession of New Orleans ... we must marry ourselves to the British fleet and nation," and as president he promoted the purchase of Louisiana for $15 million from Napoleon in 1803. On October 31, 1803, Congress passed an act enabling the president to take possession of this territory. A subsequent act, which became effective on March 26, 1804, created two territories, Louisiana and Orleans, and provided for their temporary government.

To prepare the Territory of Orleans for statehood, a new legal code combining elements of Spanish and French law with the new Code Napoleon was promulgated in 1808. On February 20, 1811, an act of Congress to "enable the territory of Orleans to form a constitution and state government" in preparation for statehood stipulated that laws need only be published in English and French and that the right of trial by jury and the principle of habeas corpus must be observed.

The state's first constitution was drafted by a convention that met in New Orleans in November 1811. Drafted in French with a "duly authenticated English translation" even though an express provision made English the official language, it went into effect on April 30, 1812, when the territory of Orleans was formally admitted to the Union as the state of Louisiana.

Pressure by promoters of Jacksonian popular government led to Louisiana's second constitution. Ratified on November 5, 1845, it created an elective governorship, removed property requirements for voting, and mandated voter approval of the document. The Whig Party faction countered in 1852 with a constitution that based legislative apportionment on adult white males and slaves, who could not vote, thus effectively restoring power to the slave owners.

Modifications to the 1852 constitution made in 1861 by a secessionist convention were mostly cosmetic, reflecting the state's assimilation into the Confederacy. At the end of the Civil War, the military commandant of the Gulf region called a Reconstructionist convention, which drafted the 1864 constitution. It restored some provisions of the 1845 document while introducing a progressive income tax and universal education.

In August 1868, after white extremists fired on a group of marching blacks, a new constitution was adopted by the voters in an effort to restore civil order. Its aim was to undermine the establishment's political power by strengthening the rights of freedmen and carpetbaggers, Northerners who had moved into the former Confederate states after the Civil War. This sixth constitution was the first of Louisiana's constitutions to include a bill of rights. Another constitution was promulgated in 1879, after the state's readmission to the Union. Reflecting the counter-Reconstructionist movement, it sought to limit the legislature's power and concentrate power in the executive branch.

In an effort to quell agrarian unrest and stem the growing political power of the Populist and Republican Parties, a convention meeting in New Orleans framed the state's eighth constitution in 1898. Among the additions was article 197, which restricted voter eligibility to only those males whose fathers or grandfathers had voted before 1876. A 1913 constitution made few major changes to the 1898 document.

A tenth constitution, drafted in 1921 in response to the reform movement following World War I, severely restricted the discretionary authority of the state government. As a result, by 1972 the document included more than 500 amendments and more than 250,000 words, some 246,500 words more than the U.S. Constitution. A constitutional convention that assembled in Baton Rouge on January 5, 1973, included among its 105 delegates ten women and twelve blacks. Their draft was approved by the people at a special election on April 20, 1974, and the constitution, as provided by article XIV, section 35, became effective at midnight on December 31, 1974.

The Constitution

Louisiana's French heritage has made it the only state in the Union that relies on a civil code of laws rather than on common law and statutory law as in the other forty-nine states. However, the relationship between state law, including constitutional law, and federal law is the same in Louisiana as in all the other states.

Only Georgia's 1982 constitution is more recent than Louisiana's 1974 document, which was simplified, made more consistent technically than its 1921 predecessor, and shortened to approximately 30,000 words. As of January 1, 1998, however, the 1974 constitution has been amended seventy-nine times and increased by more than 24,000 words.

The structure of government created by the constitution is fairly typical, consisting of a governor as the state's chief executive officer and eight other constitutionally named officials elected statewide, including a lieutenant governor; a bicameral legislature, all the members of which are elected for four years; and an elected judiciary. But compared with many other state constitutions, the 1974 document contains more detailed provisions and more restrictions on the legislature. An amendment to prohibit the legislature from diverting the proceeds of a gasoline tax to any other use except highway construction was approved by the voters in 1989.

The preamble to the Louisiana constitution reads: "We, the people of Louisiana, grateful to Almighty God for the civil, political, economic, and religious liberties we enjoy, and desiring to protect individual rights to life, liberty, and property; afford opportunity for the fullest development of the individual; assure equality of rights; promote the health, safety, education, and welfare of the people; maintain a representative and orderly government; ensure domestic tranquility; provide for the common defense; and secure the blessings of freedom and justice to ourselves and our posterity, do ordain and establish this constitution."

Preamble

Article I, Declaration of Rights, section 1, declares: "All government, of right, originates with the people, is founded on their will alone, and is instituted to protect the rights of the individual and for the good of the whole. Its only legitimate ends are to secure justice for all, preserve peace, protect the rights, and promote the happiness and general welfare of the people. The rights enumerated in this Article are inalienable by the state and shall be preserved inviolate by the state." **Section 2** affirms: "No person shall be deprived of life, liberty, or property, except by due process of law."

Fundamental Rights

Section 3 guarantees equal protection of the laws and prohibits discrimination "because of race or religious ideas, beliefs, or affiliations" and arbitrary, capricious, or unreasonable laws that "discriminate against a person because of birth, age, sex, culture, physical condition, or political ideas or affiliations"; in addition, "[s]lavery and involuntary servitude are prohibited, except in the latter case as punishment for crime." In *Succession of Brown* (1980), the Louisiana supreme court held that a provision of the Louisiana civil code that denied the inheritance of an illegitimate child was unconstitutional because it discriminated on the basis of birth status.

Section 4, as amended in 1989, through **section 11,** respectively, provide for the right to property, the right to privacy, freedom from intrusion, freedom of expression, freedom of religion, the right of assembly and petition, the right to vote, and the right to bear arms. **Section 5** protects against "unreasonable searches, seizures, or invasions of privacy." In *State v. Culotta* (1976), the Louisiana supreme court concluded that in order for a search warrant to be valid, the informant and the information on which the warrant is based must meet the constitutional standard for reliability. **Section 12** guarantees: "In access to public areas, accommodations, and facilities, every person shall be free from discrimination based on race, religion, or national ancestry and from arbitrary, capricious, or unreasonable discrimination based on age, sex, or physical condition." In *Bonomo v. Louisiana Downs, Inc.* (1976), the Louisiana courts of appeals, second circuit, declared that discrimination on a basis other than race, religion, or national ancestry may be constitutionally valid as long as the reasons for such laws and their application are not arbitrary, capricious, or unreasonable.

Sections 13 through **18** deal with rights of the accused. **Section 17** requires a jury trial in all cases in which the punishment may be confinement for more than six months. In *Duncan v. Louisiana* (1968), the U.S. Supreme Court had found that article VII, section 41, of the 1921 Louisiana constitution denying a jury trial in all cases except where the punishment involved hard labor was unconstitutional under the Sixth Amendment (1791) and Fourteenth Amendment (1868) to the U.S. Constitution. **Section 19** further provides that "[n]o person shall be subjected to imprisonment or forfeiture of rights or property without the right of judicial review based on a complete record of all evidence upon which the judgment is based."

Section 20 prohibits any law that would subject a person to euthanasia, torture, or cruel, excessive, or unusual punishment; **section 21** prohibits the suspension of the writ of habeas corpus; **section 22** guarantees access to all courts; and **section 23** prohibits bills of attainder, ex post facto laws, and laws impairing the obligation of contracts. **Section 24** declares: "The enumeration in this constitution of certain rights shall not deny or disparage other rights retained by the individual citizens of the state."

Division of Powers

Article II, Distribution of Powers, section 1, provides: "The powers of government of the state are divided into three separate branches: legislative, executive, and judicial." **Section 2** adds: "Except as otherwise provided by this constitution, no one of these branches, nor any person holding office in one of them, shall exercise power belonging to either of the others."

Legislative Branch

Article III, Legislative Branch, section 1(A), states in part: "The legislative power of the state is vested in a legislature, consisting of a Senate and a House of Representatives. The Senate shall be composed of one senator elected from each senatorial district. The House of Representatives shall be composed of one representative elected from each representative district." Pursuant to **section 1(B)**, "The legislature is a continuous body during the term for which its members are elected; however, a bill or resolution not finally passed in any session shall be withdrawn from the files of the legislature."

Section 2, as amended in 1989, 1992, and 1993, provides that "(A)(1) [t]he legislature shall meet annually in regular session for a limited number of legislative days in the state capital." Under **section 2(A)(2),** regular sessions held "in odd-numbered years shall be general in nature," and, under **section 2(A)(3),** those held "in even-numbered years ... shall be restricted to the consideration of legislation which provides for the enactment of a general appropriations bill" and other enumerated financial measures. In *Hainkel v.*

Henry (1975), the court declared that the action of a legislative committee on a day when neither house was in session did not constitute a legislative day under the constitution. According to **section 2(B)**, the governor or a majority of the members of each house may convene the legislature in extraordinary session. **Section 2(D)** directs the legislature to meet in an organizational session "at ten o'clock in the morning on the day the members are required to take office"; the primary purpose of this session, which may not exceed three days, is "judging the qualifications and elections of the members, taking the oath of office, organizing the two houses, and selecting officers."

Section 4, as amended in 1995, outlines legislators' qualifications and terms. **Section 4(A)** requires candidates for the legislature to be eighteen years old, state residents for two years, and residents of their legislative districts for one year, although, pursuant to **section 4(B)**, an exception is made in the case of reapportionment. **Section 4(C)** sets the term of office of all legislators at four years, and **section 4(D)** provides that vacancies are filled by election. **Section 4(E)** limits legislators' terms to three consecutive terms, effective January 8, 1996.

Section 7(A) permits each house to judge the qualifications and elections of its members and determine its own rules of procedure and choose its own officers, while **section 8** exempts legislators from arrest during attendance at and en route to or from legislative sessions and committee meetings, except in cases of felony. **Section 9** directs the legislature to "enact a code of ethics prohibiting conflict between public duty and private interests of members...." **Section 10(A)** defines a quorum for transacting business as "[n]ot less than a majority of the elected members of each house."

Section 15 addresses the passage of bills. **Section 15(A)** provides in part: "The legislature shall enact no law except by a bill introduced during that session, and propose no constitutional amendment except by a joint resolution introduced during that session, which shall be processed as a bill. Every bill, except the general appropriation bill and bills for the enactment, rearrangement, codification, or revision of a system of laws, shall be confined to one object." According to **section 15(C)**, amendments must be germane, and **section 15(D)** requires that "[e]ach bill shall be read at least by title on three separate days ... [and no] bill shall be considered for final passage unless a committee has held a public hearing and reported on the bill." **Section 15(G)** stipulates that to become law a bill must receive "the favorable vote of at least a majority of the members elected to each house." In essence, laws must be passed by an absolute majority of all the members of each house rather than by a simple majority of those present and voting, as provided in New Mexico's constitution, for example.

Section 18, as amended in 1989, provides that "**(A)** ... [a] bill, except a joint resolution, shall become law if the governor signs it or if he fails to sign or veto it within ten days after delivery...." Under **section 18(B)**, a veto may be overridden "by two-thirds of the elected members of each house."

Article IV, Executive Branch, section 1(A), mandates: "The executive branch shall consist of the governor, lieutenant governor, secretary of state, attorney general, treasurer,

Executive Branch

commissioner of agriculture, commissioner of insurance, superintendent of education, commissioner of elections, and all other executive offices, agencies, and instrumentalities of the state." **Section 1(B)** limits the number of executive departments, apart from the offices of the governor and lieutenant governor, to "not more than twenty." According to **section 1(C)**, "Reallocation of the functions, powers, and duties of all departments [and other executive branch entities], except those functions, powers, duties, and responsibilities allocated by this constitution, shall be as provided by law."

Section 2 requires that a candidate for statewide elective office be twenty-five years old, "an elector," and a U.S. citizen and state resident for five years. In addition, the attorney general "shall have been admitted to the practice of law in the state for at least the five years preceding his election." **Section 3,** as amended in 1986, prescribes, under **section 3(A),** a term of four years for elected executive officials, and **section 3(B)** bars a governor from being reelected after two consecutive terms in office.

Section 5(A) designates the governor "the chief executive officer of the state." **Sections 5(B)** through **5(I),** respectively, detail the governor's duties including reporting on "the affairs of state, including its complete financial condition" at the beginning of each regular session of the legislature; requesting reports and information from the heads of the executive departments; submitting an operating budget to the legislature; granting pardons, commutations, and reprieves; endorsing bills; exercising the item veto; making appointments, subject to senate confirmation; and removing appointees, except in the case of a fixed-term appointment. In *Humphrey's Executors v. United States* (1935), the U.S. Supreme Court held that such a restriction on the governor's removal power was similar to the president's under the U.S. Constitution. **Section 5(J)** designates the governor commander in chief of the state's armed forces except when they are in the service of the federal government.

Section 6 provides that the lieutenant governor, who is elected separately, serves "ex officio as a member of each committee, board, and commission on which the governor serves"; furthermore, the office holder "shall exercise the powers delegated to him by the governor and shall have other powers and perform other duties in the executive branch authorized by this constitution or provided by law." **Sections 7** through **12** briefly summarize the duties of the other statewide elected officers in the executive branch, beginning with the secretary of state and including the attorney general, treasurer, and commissioners of agriculture, insurance, and elections. **Section 18** sets forth procedures for determining an executive official's inability to continue to perform the duties of office.

Judicial Branch

Article V, Judicial Branch, section 1, vests the state's judicial power in "a supreme court, courts of appeal, district courts, and other courts authorized by this Article." According to **section 3,** "The supreme court shall be composed of a chief justice and six associate justices, four of whom must concur to render judgment [and the] term of a supreme court judge shall be ten years." **Section 4** directs that "[t]he state shall be divided into at least six supreme court districts, and at least one judge shall be elected from each." **Section 22,** as amended in 1983, mandates in part: "**(A)** ... Except as otherwise provided in this Section, all judges shall be elected. Election shall be at the regular congressional election. **(B)** A newly-created judgeship or a vacancy ... shall be filled by special election called by the governor...." Until the vacancy is filled, the supreme court shall appoint a person meeting the qualifications for the office, other than domicile, to serve at its pleasure."

Section 5, as amended in 1982 and 1987, establishes the supreme court's jurisdiction. **Section 5(A)** grants it "general supervisory jurisdiction over all other courts [and authorizes it to] establish procedural and administrative rules not in conflict with law and ... [to] assign a sitting or retired judge to any court." **Section 5(B)** grants it exclusive original jurisdiction of disciplinary proceedings against members of the bar. **Section 5(C)** extends the supreme court's review to both facts and the law in civil cases but only to questions of law in criminal cases. **Section 5(D)** confers appellate jurisdiction as provided by the constitution and in cases where a law or an ordinance has been declared unconstitutional and when the death penalty has been imposed. In addition, pursuant to **section 5(E)**, the supreme court has exclusive appellate jurisdiction in certain criminal cases where the order of appeal was filed before July 1, 1982.

Section 6 provides: "The judge oldest in point of service on the supreme court shall be chief justice. He is the chief administrative officer of the judicial system of the state, subject to rules adopted by the court." **Section 24** requires that judges of the supreme court and certain other courts "shall have been admitted to the practice of law in this state for at least five years prior to his election, and shall have been domiciled in the respective district, circuit, or parish for the two years preceding election"; moreover, judges are prohibited from practicing law. **Section 25** creates a judiciary commission to recommend to the supreme court such action as censure, suspension, or involuntary retirement of judges for willful misconduct relating to their official duties and other serious derelictions of duty.

Section 27 states: "In each parish a sheriff shall be elected for a term of four years. He shall be the chief law enforcement officer in the parish, except as otherwise provided by this constitution.... [However,] [t]his Section shall not apply to Orleans Parish."

Article X, Public Officials and Employees, part III, section 24, provides: "**(A)** ... A state or district official, whether elected or appointed, shall be liable to impeachment for commission or conviction, during his term of office of a felony or for malfeasance or gross misconduct while in such office." **Section 24(B)** stipulates that "[i]mpeachment shall be by the House of Representatives and trial by the Senate...." Conviction requires a two-thirds vote of the elected senators and results in immediate removal from office, although the person is liable to "other action, prosecution, or punishment authorized by law."

Impeachment

Article X, Public Officials and Employees, part III, section 26, directs the legislature to provide "by general law for the recall by election of any state, district, parochial, ward, or municipal official except judges of the courts of record," specifying that "[t]he sole issue at a recall election shall be whether the official shall be recalled."

Direct Democracy

Article VI, Local Government, part I, section 2, authorizes the legislature to provide "by general law for the incorporation, consolidation, merger, and government of

Local Government

municipalities." **Section 5** states: "Subject to and not inconsistent with this constitution, any local governmental subdivision may draft, adopt, or amend a home rule charter in accordance with this Section. The governing authority of a local governmental subdivision may appoint a commission to prepare and propose a charter or an alternate charter, or it may call an election to elect such a commission."

Taxation and Finance

Article VII, Revenue and Finance, part I, section 6, as amended in 1993, addresses the state debt, with **section 6(D)** noting, "The legislature, by law enacted by two-thirds of the elected members of each house, may propose a statewide public referendum to authorize incurrence of debt for any purpose for which the legislature is not herein authorized to incur debt." **Section 10,** as amended in 1990 and 1993, limits, under **section 10(E),** "[a]ppropriations by the legislature from the state general fund and dedicated funds for any fiscal year," except for certain severance tax allocations and royalty allocations, to "the official forecast in effect at the time the appropriations are made." **Section 10(F)** authorizes the legislature to "establish a procedure to determine if appropriations will exceed the official forecast and an adequate method for adjusting appropriations in order to eliminate a projected deficit," and **section 10(G)** states: "If a deficit exists in any fund at the end of a fiscal year, that deficit shall be eliminated no later than the end of the next fiscal year."

Education

Article VIII, Education, Preamble, begins: "The goal of the public educational system is to provide learning environments and experiences, at all stages of human development, that are humane, just, and designed to promote excellence in order that every individual may be afforded an equal opportunity to develop his full potential." **Section 4** states: "Upon application by a private elementary, secondary, or proprietary school with a sustained curriculum or specialized course of study of quality at least equal to that prescribed for similar public schools, the State Board of Elementary and Secondary Education shall approve the private school. A certificate issued by an approved private school shall carry the same privileges as one issued by a state public school."

Environment

Article IX, Natural Resources, section 1, declares: "The natural resources of the state, including air and water, and the healthful, scenic, historic, and esthetic quality of the environment shall be protected, conserved, and replenished insofar as possible and consistent with the health, safety, and welfare of the people. The legislature shall enact laws to implement this policy."

Amendment Procedures

Article XIII, Constitutional Revision, section 1(A), provides that an amendment may be proposed by a joint resolution at a regular session of the legislature but must "be prefiled, at least ten days before the beginning of the session" or by a joint resolution at an extraordinary session "if it is within the objects of the call of the session." If two-thirds of the members approve the resolution, it is sent to the secretary of state to be published. Pursuant to **section 1(C),** the proposed amendment must then be ratified by a majority of the electors voting on it and becomes effective twenty days after its adoption is proclaimed by the governor, unless it provides otherwise. **Section 2** authorizes two-thirds of the members of each house to call a convention to revise the constitution or propose a new constitution; any proposal must be ratified by a majority of the electors voting on it.

On March 15, 1820, Maine became the twenty-third state of the United States. Augusta is the capital of the "Pine Tree State," which encompasses 35,387 square miles and is bordered by the Canadian provinces of Quebec on the north and New Brunswick on the east, the Atlantic Ocean on the south, and New Hampshire on the west. Maine ranks thirty-ninth among the states in population, with approximately 1.2 million residents. Its principal industries include manufacturing, agriculture, and fishing; among its chief crops are potatoes, apples, hay, and blueberries.

Government: The governor is elected for a four-year term and is limited to two consecutive terms. There is no position of lieutenant governor. The legislature consists of thirty-five senators and 151 members of the house of representatives, all elected for two-year terms and limited to four consecutive terms; the officers of both houses are limited to three consecutive terms. The state's highest court, called the supreme judicial court, consists of a chief justice and six justices appointed by the governor with the consent of the senate for seven-year terms.

Date of Constitution: 1820

The earliest inhabitants of the glacier-raked land that would become the state of Maine probably hunted caribou there more than ten thousand years ago. It is believed that Leif Ericson and his crew of some thirty Vikings may have explored the region five hundred years before Giovanni Caboto (John Cabot), exploring for England, sailed the waters near Maine around 1498. When Europeans reached the New World, Maine was inhabited by Algonkian peoples, including the Abnaki, Penobscot, and Passamaquaddy.

In 1602 Bartholomew Gosnold, a former officer under the command of Sir Walter Raleigh, landed on the coast of Maine. On November 8, 1603, Henry IV of France issued a charter to Pierre du Gast, Sieur de Monts, that covered the land between the fortieth and forty-sixth parallels in the New World, which he designated as *la Cadie* (Acadia). The following year the French attempted to establish a permanent settlement on Passamaquaddy Bay, but a severe winter forced them to move to Nova Scotia. James I of England by charter in 1607 granted the Virginia Companies of London and Plymouth the right to establish a colony between the forty-first and forty-fifth parallels, which includes the lower half of Maine.

In 1621 the earl of Stirling, Sir William Alexander, received a patent from the English Crown for "a tract of the maine land of New England, beginning at St. Croix, and from thence extending along the sea-coast to Pemaquid and the river Kennebeck," a charter that Charles II would later revoke. An overlapping English grant was made "for the province of Maine" to Sir Ferdinando Gorges and Captain John Mason the following year. In 1628 Pilgrims from the Plymouth colony established several fur trading posts in the Maine region.

The French began building Catholic missions and converting the region's local inhabitants in the 1640s, but in 1652 the Massachusetts legislature declared the Maine territory a part of the Bay Colony and annexed it as a province. In 1677 Massachusetts purchased the Maine estate from Gorges for £1,250 (the equivalent of about $6,000 then). During the Revolutionary War, the Continental Congress divided Massachusetts into three separate districts; one of these, called the District of Maine, played an active role in the war. Later Maine was hard hit economically by the Embargo Act of 1807, which curtailed trading with the British, and the Embargo Act of 1813, during the War of 1812 with the United Kingdom. The latter embargo pushed all of Massachusetts to the verge of rebellion and Mainers to the brink of secession from Massachusetts.

In 1815 William King, a wealthy merchant and shipbuilder from Bath and a leader in the Massachusetts Democratic-Republican Party, organized a movement for separation from the Bay State, and the Massachusetts legislature agreed to hold a referendum on the question on May 20, 1816. Only six percent of Maine's 270,000 population cast votes in the referendum, which favored separation by nearly two to one. The legislature authorized a convention to draft a constitution for Maine on the condition that another referendum approve separation by at least a five-to-four margin.

The second referendum failed to get the necessary majority support for separation, but the issue was revived by King three years later, and a third referendum, requiring a 1,500-vote margin for approval, resulted in a 17,091 to 7,132 victory for the separationists. A constitution was drafted by a convention that met in Portland in October 1819 and was ratified by the voters on December 6. The document went into effect on March 15, 1820, when Maine was admitted to the Union.

The Constitution

In addition to the 1780 Massachusetts constitution, the framers of the 1820 Maine document considered the constitutions of Connecticut, Delaware, Indiana, Kentucky, and New Hampshire in their deliberations. When it became necessary a half century later to revise the constitution, Maine followed New York by using a commission appointed by the legislature, rather than a constitutional convention, to propose significant amendments. Eight of the commission's seventeen proposed revisions, which included confirming the election of senators by a plurality of the vote and authorizing the chief justice to codify the constitution by incorporating amendments, were approved by the legislature and then by voters on September 13, 1875. The most recent recodification of Maine's constitution by the chief justice occurred in 1993.

Maine's constitution is less than half the average length of state constitutions, containing only some 13,500 words. As of January 1, 1998, the document has been amended 167 times; an additional amendment to article VI, Judicial Power, section 6, requires action by the legislature to become effective and is still pending. An unusual feature of the constitution is the provision at the end stating that article X, Additional Provisions, sections 1, 2, and 5, "shall hereafter be omitted in any printed copies thereof prefixed to the laws of the State; but that this shall not impair the validity of acts under those sections...."

Preamble

The preamble to the 1820 Maine constitution reads in part: "We the people of Maine, in order to establish justice, insure tranquility, provide for our mutual defense, promote our common welfare, and secure to ourselves and our posterity the blessings of liberty, acknowledging with grateful hearts the goodness of the Sovereign Ruler of the Universe ... do ordain and establish the following Constitution for the government of the same."

Fundamental Rights

Article I, Declaration of Rights, section 1, proclaims: "All people are born equally free and independent, and have certain natural, inherent and unalienable rights, among which are those of enjoying and defending life and liberty, acquiring, possessing and protecting property, and of pursuing and obtaining safety and happiness." **Section 2** states that "[a]ll power is inherent in the people; all free governments are founded in their authority and instituted for their benefit; they have therefore an unalienable and indefeasible right to institute government, and to alter, reform, or totally change the same, when their safety and happiness require it."

Section 3 guarantees religious freedom, the equality of all sects, and the right of religious societies to elect "their public teachers" and prohibits religious tests "as a qualification for any office or trust, under this State." **Section 4** provides for freedom of speech and publication, that truth may be given as evidence in libel cases and that the jury in such cases "shall have a right to determine, at their discretion, the law and the fact." **Section 5** prohibits unreasonable searches and seizures.

Section 6 extends rights to the accused in criminal prosecutions, including the right to counsel, a copy of the "nature and cause of the accusation" against him or her, and confrontation by witnesses. This section also guarantees "a speedy, public and impartial trial, and, except in trials by martial law or impeachment, by a jury in the vicinity"; furthermore, "the accused shall not be compelled to furnish or give evidence against himself or herself, nor be deprived of life, liberty, property or privileges, but by judgment of that person's peers or the law of the land." **Section 6-A** states: "No person shall be deprived of life, liberty, or property without due process of law, nor be denied the equal protection of the laws, nor be denied the enjoyment of that person's civil rights or be discriminated against in the exercise thereof." In *Mathieu v. Bath Iron Works* (1995), the Maine supreme judicial court held that retroactive economic legislation meets the due process requirement if it is enacted to further a legitimate legislative purpose by rational means, in this case promoting efficiency and cost savings in workers compensation procedures.

Section 7 requires "a presentment or indictment of a grand jury" for major offenses; moreover, the legislature must "provide by law a suitable and impartial mode of selecting juries, and their usual number and unanimity, in indictments and convictions, shall be held indispensable." Under **section 8**, "No person, for the same offense, shall be twice put in jeopardy of life or limb." **Section 9** prohibits "sanguinary laws," excessive bail, and cruel and unusual punishment; **section 10**, however, disallows bail for capital offenses and the suspension of the writ of habeas corpus, "unless when in cases of rebellion or invasion. . . ."

Section 11 prohibits bills of attainder, ex post facto laws, and laws impairing the obligation of contracts. **Section 12** defines treason and establishes standards of proof of treason in terms similar to those used in the U.S. Constitution. **Section 13** proscribes the suspension of laws "but by the Legislature or its authority." Under **section 14,** corporal punishment is prohibited in the military, "except such as are employed in the army or navy, or in the militia when in actual service in time of war or public danger." **Sections 15** through **20**, respectively, guarantee the right to petition the government for the redress of grievances; guarantee the right to bear arms, stating that "this right shall never be questioned"; prohibit standing armies; limit the quartering of soldiers in private homes; guarantee the right of redress for injuries; and guarantee trial by juries in civil suits "except in cases where it has heretofore been otherwise practiced."

Section 21 provides that "[p]rivate property shall not be taken for public uses without just compensation; nor unless public exigencies require it." According to **section 22,** "No tax or duty shall be imposed without the consent of the people or of their representatives in the Legislature." **Section 24** states: "The enumeration of certain rights shall not impair nor deny others retained by the people."

Section 23 prohibits titles of nobility and the creation of any office "the appointment to which shall be for a longer time than during good behavior." In contrast, the Mississippi constitution provides that "[n]o person shall be elected or appointed to office ... for life or during good behavior" but for a specified period.

Division of Powers

Article III, Distribution of Powers, section 1, proclaims: "The powers of this government shall be divided into 3 distinct departments, the legislative, executive and judicial." According to **section 2,** "No person or persons, belonging to one of these departments, shall exercise any of the powers properly belonging to either of the others, except in the cases herein expressly directed or permitted." In *National Hearing Aid Centers, Inc. v. Smith* (1977), the Maine supreme judicial court upheld the general rule under the separation of powers doctrine that as long as an act is constitutional, courts should not substitute their view of policy for the legislature's "no matter how much the court might have preferred some other procedure."

Legislative Branch

Article IV, part first, House of Representatives, section 1, declares: "The legislative power shall be vested in 2 distinct branches, a House of Representatives, and a Senate, each to have a negative on the other, and both to be styled the Legislature of Maine...."

Section 2 states in part that the house of representatives is to consist of 151 members "to be elected by the qualified electors, and to hold their office 2 years from the day next preceding the first Wednesday in December following the general election." **Section 4** specifies that a house member must be at least twenty-one years old, a citizen of the United States for five years, a resident of the state for one year, and a resident of the district for the three months preceding the election and throughout the term.

Section 5 directs: "The meetings within this State for the choice of Representatives shall be warned in due course of law by qualified officials of the several towns and cities 7 days at least before the election, and the election officials of the various towns and cities shall preside impartially at such meetings, receive the votes of all the qualified electors, sort, count and declare them in open meeting...." According to **section 6,** "Whenever the seat of a member shall be vacated by death, resignation, or otherwise the vacancy may be filled by a new election." **Section 7** provides that house members elect their speaker, clerk and other officers. Since December 2, 1992, Maine law has limited the speaker, party floor leaders, and assistant floor leaders in the house to three consecutive two-year terms in those offices.

Article IV, part second, Senate, section 1, stipulates that the senate will consist of "an odd number of Senators, not less than 31 nor more than 35, elected at the same time and for the same term as Representatives by the qualified electors of the districts into which the State shall be from time to time divided." Currently there are thirty-five senators. **Section 3** instructs that "[t]he meetings within this State for the election of Senators shall be notified, held and regulated and the votes received, sorted, counted, declared and recorded, in the same manner as those for Representatives." According to **section 6,** senators must be twenty-five years old, and "in all other respects their qualifications shall be the same as those of the Representatives." **Section 8** allows senators to choose their president, secretary, and other officers. Since December 2, 1992, Maine law has limited the president, party floor leaders, and assistant floor leaders in the senate to three consecutive two-year terms in office.

Article IV, part third, Legislative Power, section 1, states in part: "The Legislature, with the exceptions hereinafter stated, shall have full power to make and establish all reasonable laws and regulations for the defense and benefit of the people of this State, not repugnant to this Constitution, nor to that of the United States." According to **section 1-A,** "A Legislature which is required to apportion the districts of the House of Representatives[,] the Senate . . . or both [every tenth year], shall establish, within the first 3 calendar days after the convening of that Legislature, a commission to develop in accordance with the requirements of this Constitution, a plan for apportioning the House of Representatives, the Senate, or both."

Section 3 allows each house to be the judge of the elections and qualifications of its own members; "a majority shall constitute a quorum to do business; but a smaller number may adjourn from day to day, and may compel the attendance of absent members. . . ." **Section 4** grants each house the power to "determine the rules of its proceedings, punish its members for disorderly behavior, and, with the concurrence of 2/3, expel a member, but not for a 2nd time for the same offense." Under **section 6,** the legislature has the power to punish persons who are not legislators for improper behavior such as obstructing its proceedings. **Section 8** exempts members from arrest "during their attendance at, going to, and returning from each session of the Legislature. . . ." **Sections 10** and **11** establish limits on the appointment of legislators to certain offices and disqualifications for membership in the legislature.

Section 9 specifies that bills, orders, and resolutions may originate in either house, although revenue bills must originate in the house of representatives. **Section 2** provides that each bill passed by both houses goes to the governor for signature. If the governor does not approve the bill, it is returned with objections to the house in which it originated. And if two-thirds of each house approves it, it takes effect "as if it had been signed by the Governor. . . ." The governor has ten days, "Sundays excepted," in which to sign or veto a bill, "unless the Legislature by their adjournment prevent its return, in which case it shall have such force and effect, unless returned within 3 days after the next meeting of the same Legislature which enacted the bill or resolution. . . ." If there is no such meeting, "the bill or resolution shall not be a law." **Section 2-A,** added by amendment in 1995, gives the governor the item veto power of dollar amounts appearing in appropriations or allocation provisions. **Section 13** states: "The Legislature shall, from time to time, provide, as far as practicable, by general laws, for all matters usually appertaining to special or private legislation." Pursuant to **section 16**, acts passed by the legislature generally take effect in ninety days.

Executive Branch

Article V, part first, Executive Power, section 1, vests the supreme executive power of the state in the governor. **Section 2** states: "The Governor shall be elected by the qualified electors, and shall hold the office for 4 years.... The person who has served 2 consecutive popular elective 4-year terms of office as Governor shall be ineligible to succeed himself or herself." **Section 4** specifies that the governor must be thirty years old, a citizen of the United States for at least fifteen years, and a resident of the state for five years before the election and during the term. **Section 5** disqualifies any "person holding any office or place under the United States, this State, or any other power...."

Section 7 designates the governor as the "commander in chief of the army and navy of the State, and of the militia, except when the same are called into the actual service of the United States." **Section 8** authorizes the governor to "nominate, and, subject to confirmation [by a joint legislative committee and the Senate], appoint all judicial officers, except judges of probate and justices of the peace...." The confirmation procedure includes recommendation by a joint committee of both houses of the legislature, which may be rejected by two-thirds vote in the senate. Section 8 continues: "All statutes enacted to carry out the purposes of [the confirmation procedure] shall require the affirmative vote of ⅔ of the members of each House present and voting." Both the governor and president of the senate can call the senate into session for the purpose of voting on confirmation of appointments.

Section 9 directs the governor "from time to time [to] give the Legislature information of the condition of the State, and recommend to their consideration such measures, as the Governor may judge expedient." Pursuant to **section 10**, the chief executive may require information from "any military officer, or any officer in the executive department, upon any subject relating to the duties of their respective offices."

Section 11 empowers the governor to "remit after conviction all forfeitures and penalties, and to grant reprieves, commutations and pardons, except in cases of impeachment, upon such conditions, and with such restrictions and limitations as may be deemed proper, subject to such regulations as may be provided by law.... Such power to grant reprieves, commutations and pardons shall include offenses of juvenile delinquency." **Section 12** enjoins the governor to "take care that the laws be faithfully executed." According to **section 13**, the governor "may, on extraordinary occasions, convene the Legislature...."

Section 14 provides: "Whenever the office of Governor shall become vacant because of the death, resignation or removal of a Governor in office, or any other cause, the President of the Senate shall assume the office of Governor until another Governor shall be duly qualified." **Section 15** outlines procedures in the event of the governor's temporary mental or physical disability.

Article V, part second, Secretary, section 1, states that the secretary of state is to be chosen "biennially at the first session of the Legislature, by joint ballot of the Senators and Representatives in convention." **Article V, part Third, Treasurer, section 1,** provides similarly for the election of the treasurer, and **article IX, General Provisions, section 11,** authorizes identical procedures for the election of the attorney general. In *Withee v. Lane & Libby Fisheries Co.* (1921), the Maine supreme judicial court found that the attorney general is a constitutional officer and is clothed with all the common law powers and duties pertaining to that office to the extent that they have not been restricted by statute.

Judicial Branch

Like the constitutions of several other states, including Connecticut and Massachusetts, the Maine constitution has minimal judicial provisions. These consist of only six sections, the last of which was repealed according to a 1967 amendment that was to take effect "at such time as the Legislature by proper enactment shall establish a different Probate Court system with full-time judges." The jurisdiction of the state's highest court is not expressly set forth in the article on the judiciary itself.

Article VI, Judicial Power, section 1, declares: "The judicial power of this State shall be vested in a Supreme Judicial Court, and such other courts as the Legislature shall from time to time establish." Pursuant to **section 3,** "The Justices of the Supreme Judicial Court shall be obliged to give their opinion upon important questions of law, and upon solemn occasions, when required by the Governor, Senate or House of Representatives."

Section 4 specifies that all judicial officers are appointed by the governor for a term of seven years, "provided, however, that a judicial officer whose term of office has expired or who has reached mandatory retirement age, as provided by statute, may continue to hold office until the expiration of an additional period not to exceed 6 months or until the successor to the judicial officer is appointed, whichever occurs first in time." According to **section 5,** "No Justice of the Supreme Judicial Court or any other court shall hold office under the United States or any other state, nor under this State, except as justice of the peace or as a member of the Judicial Council."

Article IV, part first, House of Representatives, section 3, and **part second, Senate, section 2,** state in identical language the court's jurisdiction: "The Supreme Judicial Court shall have original jurisdiction to hear any challenge to an apportionment law enacted by the Legislature, as registered by any citizen or group thereof. If any challenge is sustained, the [court] shall make the apportionment."

Impeachment

Article IX, General Provisions, section 5, states: "Every person holding any civil office under this State, may be removed by impeachment, for misdemeanor in office; and every person holding any office, may be removed by the Governor on the address of both branches of the Legislature. But before such address shall pass either House, the causes of removal shall be stated and entered on the journal of the House in which it originated, and a copy thereof served on the person in office, that the person may be admitted to a hearing in that person's own defense."

Article IV, part first, House of Representatives, section 8, grants the house of representatives the sole power of impeachment, while **part second, Senate, section 7,** gives the senate the sole power to try all impeachments. Conviction, which requires the concurrence of two-thirds of the members present, results only in removal from office and disqualification from holding other state offices, although **section 7** states that "the party, whether convicted or acquitted, shall nevertheless be liable to indictment, trial, judgment and punishment according to law."

Direct Democracy

Article IV, part first, House of Representatives, section 1, provides in part that "the people reserve to themselves power to propose laws and to enact or reject the same at the polls independent of the Legislature, and also reserve power at their own option to approve or reject at the polls any Act, bill, resolve or resolution passed by the joint action of both branches of the legislature...." Maine is one of thirty-three states with some type of constitutionally mandated direct democracy procedures (initiative, referendum, or recall at the state level). As in the Arizona constitution, these procedures are set forth at the beginning of the provisions regarding the legislative branch.

Part third, Legislative Power, section 17, provides for a "people's veto" over "[a]cts, bills, resolves or resolutions, or part or parts thereof," and **sections 18** through **22** outline the direct initiative of legislation. In *Wagner v. Secretary of State* (1995), the Maine supreme judicial court declared that providing the right of initiative must be liberally construed to facilitate rather than handicap the people's exercise of their sovereign power to legislate.

Local Government

Article VIII, part second, Municipal Home Rule, section 1, declares that "[t]he inhabitants of any municipality shall have the power to alter and amend their charters on all matters, not prohibited by Constitution or general law, which are local and municipal in character. The Legislature shall prescribe the procedure by which the municipality may so act." **Section 2** provides: "For the purposes of fostering, encouraging and assisting the physical location, settlement and resettlement of industrial and manufacturing enterprises within the physical boundaries of any municipality, the registered voters of the municipality may, by majority vote, authorize the issuance of notes or bonds in the name of the municipality...."

Taxation and Finance

Article IX, General Provisions, section 8, states in part: "All taxes upon real and personal estate, assessed by authority of this State, shall be apportioned and assessed equally according to the just value thereof." **Section 14** mandates: "The credit of the State shall not be directly or indirectly loaned in any case [except as provided]. The Legislature shall not create any debt or debts, liability or liabilities, on behalf of the State, which shall singly, or in the aggregate, with previous debts and liabilities hereafter incurred at any one time, exceed $2,000,000, except to suppress insurrection, to repel invasion, or for purposes of war, and except for temporary loans to be paid out of money raised by taxation during the fiscal year in which they are made...."

Article VIII, part first, Education, section 1, states in part: "A general diffusion of the advantages of education being essential to the preservation of the rights and liberties of the people; to promote this important object, the Legislature are authorized, and it shall be their duty to require, the several towns to make suitable provision, at their own expense, for the support and maintenance of public schools; and it shall further be their duty to encourage and suitably endow, from time to time, as the circumstances of the people may authorize, all academies, colleges and seminaries of learning within the State; provided, that no donation, grant or endowment shall at any time be made by the Legislature to any literary institution . . . , unless [the legislature is given power] to alter, limit or restrain any of the powers vested in any such literary institution. . . ."

Article X, Additional Provisions, section 4, outlines the constitutional amendment procedures: "The Legislature, whenever ⅔ of both Houses shall deem it necessary, may propose amendments to this Constitution; and when any amendments shall be so agreed upon, a resolution shall be passed and sent to the selectmen of the several towns, and the assessors of the several plantations, empowering and directing them to notify the inhabitants . . . to give in their votes on the question, whether such amendment shall be made; and if it shall appear that a majority of the inhabitants voting on the question are in favor of such amendment, it shall be come a part of this Constitution." In *Opinion of the Justices* (1970), the Maine supreme judicial court declared that in the absence of an explicit constitutional provision requiring the governor's signature on a proposed amendment, such a signature is not required because the proposal is generally approved by the legislature by joint resolution.

Article IV, part third, Legislative Power, section 15, authorizes the legislature "by a ⅔ concurrent vote of both branches" to call a constitutional convention.

Article X, Additional Provisions, section 6, provides that the chief justice of the supreme judicial court "shall arrange the Constitution, as amended, under appropriate titles and in proper articles, parts and sections, omitting all sections, clauses and words not in force and making no other changes in the provisions or language thereof, and shall submit the same to the Legislature. . . ." This procedure is to be carried out every ten years, and once the legislature approves the arrangement, "the Constitution, with the amendments made thereto . . . shall be the supreme law of the State." This approach eliminates the difficulty of understanding an old constitutional document that has been changed by numerous amendments simply appended to the original text, as is the case with the Massachusetts constitution.

MARYLAND

Maryland became the seventh state of the United States on April 28, 1788. The capital of the "Old Line State" or the "Free State" is Annapolis. Some 12,407 square miles in area, Maryland is bordered by Pennsylvania on the north, Delaware and the Atlantic Ocean on the east, the Potomac River and Virginia on the south, and Virginia and West Virginia on the west. Washington, D.C., the nation's capital, is built on land that was formerly a part of Maryland. With approximately 5 million inhabitants, Maryland ranks nineteenth among the states in population. Its principal industries include manufacturing, biotechnology and information technology, services, and tourism; among the state's chief crops are greenhouse and nursery products, soybeans, and corn.

General Information

Government: The governor and lieutenant governor are elected jointly for four-year terms, and both are limited to two consecutive terms. The legislature, called the general assembly, consists of forty-seven senators and 141 members of the house of delegates, all of whom are elected for four-year terms. The highest state court, the court of appeals, consists of a chief judge and six additional judges nominated by a judicial nominating commission and appointed by the governor with the advice and consent of the senate; after one year they stand for election for ten-year terms.

Dates of Constitutions: 1776, 1851, 1864, and 1867

Constitutional History

Before the Italian explorer Giovanni da Verrazano sailed into the Chesapeake Bay in the early sixteenth century, the land that would become the state of Maryland was inhabited by Nanticoke, Piscataway, and Susquehannock peoples. In 1526 Spanish explorers dubbed the bay Santa Maria. It was navigated in 1608 by an English expedition led by Captain John Smith, and William Claiborne, a Virginia settler, built a fort on Kent Island in 1631. The following year, on June 20, 1632, Charles I of England granted a charter to Cecilius Calvert, Lord Baltimore, to found a new colony in America. Lord Baltimore named the colony Maryland after the wife of the English monarch, Henrietta Maria, who was called Queen Mary.

On February 27, 1634, two hundred colonists sailed into the Chesapeake Bay in two ships, the *Ark* and the *Dove*. Although the Maryland colony was established principally as a haven for Roman Catholics, the Calverts nevertheless tried to accommodate various religious sects. But an Act of Toleration passed by the Maryland colonial assembly in 1649 led to confrontations between colonists of differing religions and denominations. In 1689, when the Protestants William and Mary assumed the throne of England, the Calvert family was stripped of its power. In 1715 the then-Lord Baltimore renounced Catholicism, and George I restored the family's fortunes. The original charter continued in effect until Maryland's independence from Great Britain in 1776.

In 1767 the Britons Charles Mason and Jeremiah Dixon completed their survey establishing the boundary separating Pennsylvania from Maryland and Delaware, which became known as the Mason-Dixon line. Anticipating a revolution and ultimate independence from Britain, Maryland joined several other colonies in creating its own provincial convention, which first met on June 22, 1774. A second convention, having seized authority for running the government, convened in Annapolis from August 14 to November 11, 1776, to form a new permanent government. The convention adopted a declaration of rights reflecting the representative, or Whig, theory of government, which called for elected representatives to use their own best judgment, as opposed to the agent theory, in which representatives were merely conduits for their constituents' wishes. The convention also adopted a state constitution creating a weak governor who lacked veto power and was elected by the legislature and whose actions were further circumscribed by a legislative council also chosen by the legislature.

Maryland was spared much of the ravages of the Revolutionary War. During the War of 1812, however, Fort McHenry in Baltimore sustained a twenty-five-hour British bombardment that inspired Francis Scott Key to write the poem "The Star Spangled Banner." Continual efforts to reform the 1776 constitution were thwarted by the legislature, but a convention was finally assembled in Annapolis on November 4, 1850. The product of its deliberations was ratified by the voters on June 4, 1851, and became effective that July 4. To increase popular control over the legislature, the electoral college scheme for choosing senators, a provision of the earlier constitution, was abandoned in favor of election by the people, and legislators' terms were shortened from six to four years. The governor was now popularly elected also, as were other statewide executive officers, creating a plural, or divided, executive branch still reflected in most state constitutions today.

During the Civil War, "Unconditional Unionists" led a movement to draft a new constitution, and a convention meeting in Annapolis produced a document that was at first narrowly rejected. After absentee ballots of Marylanders serving in the Union Army were allowed, the state court of appeals ruled that the new constitution had been approved by 375 votes. It went into effect on November 1, 1864. The restoration of voting rights to Confederate sympathizers after the war significantly changed the composition of the electorate, and a new convention was convened in Annapolis on May 8, 1867. The resulting constitution, which contained sweeping changes, was approved by the voters on September 18 by a margin of 47,152 to 23,036 and went into effect on October 5 of that year.

The 1867 Maryland constitution is a relatively long document with some 41,349 words and, as of January 1, 1998, at least 212 amendments. Its nineteenth-century character is clearly evident, and it contains a number of provisions that do not rise to the level of supreme laws. Article XI-C, for example, is entitled Off-Street Parking, and article XI-G addresses City of Baltimore—Residential Rehabilitation and Commercial Financing Loans. A more modern constitution was drafted by a blue-ribbon convention, but this "magnificent failure," as it was called, was rejected at the polls in 1968.

The Maryland constitution, like the constitutions of a number of other states including North Carolina, contains passages whose language derives directly from the English Magna Carta of 1215. Article II, section 18, a unique provision, directs the governor to examine the treasurer and comptroller of the state under oath at least semiannually, and article III, section 24, reflecting the influence of the British Parliament, authorizes the lower house of the legislature to constitute "the grand inquest of the State," with powers to commit a person to jail for any crime.

The preamble to the 1867 constitution of Maryland constitutes the first paragraph of its Declaration of Rights. The statement reads: "We, the People of the State of Maryland, grateful to Almighty God for our civil and religious liberty, and taking into our serious

The Constitution

Preamble

consideration the best means of establishing a good Constitution in this State for the sure foundation and more permanent security thereof, declare [the articles of the Declaration of Rights follow]."

Fundamental Rights

In *Barron v. Baltimore* (1833), the U.S. Supreme Court held that the Bill of Rights of the U.S. Constitution could be enforced only against the federal government. Thus, during the early legal history of the United States, the burden of protecting American civil liberties was placed on the state courts under state bills or declarations of rights.

Declaration of Rights, article 1, asserts that "all Government of right originates from the People, is founded in compact only, and instituted solely for the good of the whole; and they have, at all times, the inalienable right to alter, reform or abolish their Form of Government in such manner as they may deem expedient." According to **article 2,** "The Constitution of the United States, and the Laws made, or which shall be made, in pursuance thereof, and all Treaties made, or which shall be made, under the authority of the United States, are, and shall be the Supreme Law of the State; and the Judges of this State, and all the People of this State, are, and shall be bound thereby; anything in the Constitution or Law of this State to the contrary notwithstanding." **Article 3** provides: "The powers not delegated to the United States by the Constitution thereof, nor prohibited by it to the States, are reserved to the States respectively, or to the people thereof." The language of articles 2 and 3 echoes that in the U.S. Constitution.

Article 4 grants to the people of Maryland "the sole and exclusive right of regulating the internal government and police thereof, as a free, sovereign and independent State." **Article 5,** as amended in 1992, affirms: "**(a)** The Inhabitants of Maryland are entitled to the Common Law of England, and the trial by Jury, according to the course of that Law, and to the benefit of such of the English statutes as existed on the Fourth day of July, seventeen hundred and seventy-six...." **Article 6** notes that "all persons invested with the Legislative or Executive powers of Government are the Trustees of the Public, and, as such, accountable for their conduct...." **Article 7,** as amended in 1972, guarantees the right of free elections and of suffrage, and **sections 12** and **13** ensure the right to peaceably petition for the redress of grievances.

Article 14 mandates that "no aid, charge, tax, burthen [burden] or fees ought to be rated or levied, under any pretense, without the consent of the Legislature." According to **article 15,** as amended in 1915 and 1960, "the levying of taxes by the poll is grievous and oppressive, and ought to be prohibited." **Articles 16** through **18,** respectively, recommend avoidance of "sanguinary Laws" and prohibit any "Law to inflict cruel and unusual pains and penalties"; bar retrospective laws; and proscribe laws "to attaint particular persons of treason or felony." **Article 21** provides for the rights of the accused. **Article 24,** as amended in 1978, reflects the words of Magna Carta: "[N]o man ought to be taken or imprisoned or disseized of his freehold, liberties or privileges, or outlawed, or exiled, or, in any manner, destroyed, or deprived of his life, liberty or property, but by the judgment of his peers, or by the Law of the land."

Article 36 guarantees religious freedom but states in part: "... nor shall any person, otherwise competent, be deemed incompetent as a witness, or juror, on account of his religious belief, provided, he believes in the existence of God...." In *Schowgurow v. Maryland* (1965), the Maryland court of appeals ruled this provision unconstitutional with respect to jurors who convicted a Buddhist of homicide.

Article 40 guarantees freedom of speech and the press. **Article 46**, as amended in 1972 and 1978, mandates: "Equality of rights under the law shall not be abridged or denied because of sex." **Article 47**, added in 1994, provides rights to victims of crime, which include being "treated by agents of the State with dignity, respect, and sensitivity during all phases of the criminal justice process." Rights relating to compensation for the taking of private property and limiting imprisonment for debt are included in **article III, Legislative Department, sections 6(a)(2)** and **38**, respectively.

Declaration of Rights, article 8, provides that "the Legislative, Executive and Judicial powers of Government ought to be forever separate and distinct from each other; and no person exercising the functions of one of said Departments shall assume or discharge the duties of any other." In *Attorney General v. Waldron* (1981), the Maryland court of appeals ruled that a law prohibiting retired judges who received a state pension from practicing law for a fee violated this article as well as the state and federal guarantees of equal protection.

Maryland's constitution is one of only a few state constitutions that place the provisions concerning the legislative branch (article III) after those relating to the executive branch (article II).

Article III, Legislative Department, section 1, constitutes the legislature as "two distinct branches," a senate and a house of delegates, which together form the general assembly. **Section 2,** as amended in 1901, 1922, 1956, 1970, and 1972, provides: "The membership of the Senate shall consist of forty-seven (47) Senators. The membership of the House of Delegates shall consist of one hundred forty-one (141) Delegates." **Section 7,** as amended in 1956, specifies: "The election for Senators and Delegates shall take place ... [in 1958] and in every fourth year thereafter."

Section 9, as amended in 1974 and 1978, states in part: "A person is eligible to serve as a Senator or Delegate, who on the date of his election, **(1)** is a citizen of the State of Maryland, **(2)** has resided therein for at least one year next preceding that date, and **(3)** ... has resided in ... [the] district [he or she has chosen to represent] for six months next preceding that date.... A person is eligible to serve as a Senator, if he has attained the age of twenty-five years, or as a Delegate, if he has attained the age of twenty-one years, on the date of his election." **Sections 10, 11,** and **12** set forth disqualifications for members of the legislature.

Section 17 states: "No Senator or Delegate, after qualifying as such, notwithstanding he may thereafter resign, shall during the whole period of time, for which he was elected, be eligible to any office, which shall have been created, or the salary, or profits of which shall have

Division of Powers

Legislative Branch

been increased, during such term." According to **section 18,** "No Senator or Delegate shall be liable in any civil action, or criminal prosecution, whatever, for words spoken in debate."

Section 19, as amended in 1978, directs: "Each House shall be judge of the qualifications and elections of its members, as prescribed by the Constitution and the Laws of the State, and shall appoint its own officers, determine the rules of its own proceedings, punish a member for disorderly or disrespectful behaviour and with the consent of two-thirds of its whole number of members elected, expel a member; but no member shall be expelled a second time for the same offence." Regarding quorums, **section 20** provides: "A majority of the whole number of members elected to each House shall constitute a quorum for the transaction of business; but a smaller number may adjourn from day to day, and compel the attendance of absent members...."

Section 23 grants each house the power to "punish by imprisonment, during the session of the General Assembly, any person, not a member, for disrespectful, or disorderly behaviour in its presence, or for obstructing any of its proceedings, or any of its officers in the execution of their duties; provided, such imprisonment shall not, at any one time, exceed ten days." In addition, **section 24** provides in part: "The House of Delegates may inquire ... into all complaints, grievances and offenses, as the grand inquest of the State, and may commit any person, for any crime, to the public jail, there to remain, until discharged by due course of Law." It is rare for a state constitution to bestow such nonlegislative power on a legislative body.

Section 27, as amended in 1913, 1956, 1964, 1970, 1972, and 1988, sets forth procedures for legislation: "**(a)** Any bill may originate in either House of the General Assembly and be altered, amended or rejected by the other. No bill shall originate in either House during the last thirty-five calendar days of a regular session, unless [agreed to by] two-thirds of the members elected thereto.... A bill may not become a law until it is read on three different days of the session in each House, unless two-thirds of the members elected [determine otherwise], ... and no bill shall be read a third time until it shall have been actually engrossed or printed for a third reading." **Section 28,** as amended in 1972, further provides: "No bill ... shall become a Law unless it be passed in each House by a majority of the whole number of members elected.... [Joint resolutions] shall be passed in the same manner." **Section 29** specifies in part that "every Law enacted by the General Assembly shall embrace but one subject, and that shall be described in its title...."

Section 30, as amended in 1974, requires in part: "Every bill, when passed by the General Assembly, and sealed with the Great Seal, shall be presented by the presiding officer of the House in which it originated to the Governor for his approval.... Within 30 days after presentment, if the Governor approves the bill, he shall sign the same in the presence of the presiding officers and Chief Clerks of the Senate and House of Delegates." The constitutions of most other states do not require the governor to sign bills in the presence of any other official. **Section 31,** as amended in 1974, provides that laws take effect on the first day of June following the session at which they were passed, "unless it be otherwise expressly declared therein or provided for in this Constitution."

Section 33 enumerates a number of issues, such as extending the time for the collection of taxes and granting divorces, that may not be the subject of local and special laws. **Section 52,** as amended eleven times between 1916 and 1990, calls for a balanced budget: "**(5a)** The Budget and the Budget Bill as submitted by the Governor to the General Assembly shall have a figure for the total of all proposed appropriations and a figure for the total of all estimated revenues available to pay the appropriations, and the figure for the total proposed appropriations shall not exceed the figure for the total estimated revenues." Maryland's constitution also contains a "necessary and proper" clause, similar to the one found in the U.S. Constitution. According to **section 56,** "The General Assembly shall have power to pass all such Laws as may be necessary and proper for carrying into execution the powers vested, by this Constitution, in any Department, or office of the Government, and the duties imposed upon them thereby." This clause is unusual in state constitutions because of the predominant theory that state constitutions are limitations on the state's inherent power to govern, not a grant of specific powers.

Article II, Executive Department, section 1, as amended in 1948, 1964, and 1970, vests the state's executive power in a governor, "whose term of office shall commence on the third Wednesday of January next ensuing his election, and continue for four years, and until his successor shall have qualified; and a person who has served two consecutive popular elective terms ... shall be ineligible to succeed himself ... for the term immediately following the second [term]."

Executive Branch

Section 1A, as amended in 1970 and 1976, states in part: "There shall be a Lieutenant Governor, who shall have only the duties delegated to him by the Governor.... No person who is ineligible under this Constitution to be elected Governor shall be eligible to hold the office of Lieutenant Governor." **Section 1B,** as amended in 1970, provides in part: "Each candidate ... for Governor ... shall at the time of filing for said office designate a candidate for Lieutenant Governor ... [and they] shall be ... considered for nomination jointly with each other." **Section 5,** as amended in 1970, specifies: "A person to be eligible for the office of Governor or Lieutenant Governor must have attained the age of thirty years, and must have been a resident and registered voter of the State for five years next immediately preceding his election."

Section 6, as amended in 1960 and 1970, provides: "**(a)** If the Governor-elect is disqualified, resigns, or dies, the Lieutenant Governor-elect shall become Governor for the full term." **Section 6(b)** notes that the lieutenant governor serves as acting governor when the governor becomes temporarily unable to perform the duties of office; and **section 6(d)** stipulates that when a vacancy occurs in the office of governor, the lieutenant governor succeeds to the remainder of the term.

Section 8 designates the governor as "the Commander-in-Chief of the land and naval forces of the State," with the authority to "call out the militia to repel invasions, suppress insurrections, and enforce the execution of the Laws; but ... not [to] take the command in person, without the consent of the Legislature." Under **section 9,** "He shall take care that the Laws are faithfully executed." **Section 10** directs: "He shall nominate, and, by and with the advice and consent of the Senate, appoint all civil and military officers of the State, whose appointment, or election, is not otherwise herein provided for, unless a different mode of appointment be prescribed by the Law creating the office." **Section 16** authorizes the governor to "convene the Legislature, or the Senate alone, on extraordinary occasions...."

Section 17, as amended in 1891, 1950, 1960, 1974, and 1988, empowers the governor to veto a bill that has passed the legislature, but the veto may be overridden by "three-fifths of the members elected" to each house. The governor has six days in which to veto a bill; otherwise it "shall be a law in like manner as if he signed it ... ; [and he or she] shall have power to disapprove of any item or items of any Bills making appropriations of money embracing distinct items," which may be overridden by the legislature in the same manner as for other bills.

Section 18 gives the governor direct oversight responsibilities for the financial operations of the government: "It shall be the duty of the Governor, semiannually (and oftener, if he deem it expedient) to examine under oath the Treasurer and Comptroller of the State on all matters pertaining to their respective offices; and inspect and review their Bank and other Account Books." In addition, **section 19** directs that the governor shall, "from time to time, inform the Legislature of the condition of the State and recommend to their consideration such measures as he may judge necessary and expedient."

Section 20 provides that the governor "shall have power to grant reprieves and pardons, except in cases of impeachment, and in cases, in which he is prohibited by other Articles of this Constitution; and to remit fines and forfeitures for offenses against the State...."

Section 22, as amended in 1954, allows the governor to appoint a secretary of state, whereas most other state constitutions provide for an elected official in this position: "A Secretary of State shall be appointed by the Governor, by and with the advice and consent of the Senate, who shall continue in office, unless sooner removed by the Governor, till the end of the official term of the Governor...." **Section 24**, as amended in 1970, prescribes procedures by which the governor may reorganize the executive branch.

Judicial Branch

Article IV, Judiciary Department, part I, section 1, as amended in 1966, 1970, 1978, and 1980, declares: "The Judicial power of this State is vested in a Court of Appeals, such intermediate courts of appeal as the General Assembly may create by law, Circuit Courts, Orphans' Courts, and a District Court...." **Section 1A**, as amended in 1978, states: "The several Courts existing in this State at the time of the adoption of this Constitution, shall, until superseded under its provisions, continue with like powers and jurisdiction, and in the exercise thereof, both at Law and in Equity, in all respects, as if this Constitution had not been adopted...."

Section 2, as amended in 1966 and 1970, requires that judges of all these courts be citizens of the state of Maryland, qualified voters, residents of the state for at least five years, and residents of their jurisdiction for at least six months. They must be at least thirty years of age at the time of their election or appointment and "shall be selected from those who have been admitted to practice law in this State, and who are most distinguished for integrity, wisdom and sound legal knowledge." In *Kadan v. Board of Supervisors of Elections of Baltimore County* (1974), the Maryland court of appeals held that **part V, Orphans' Court, section 40**, which prescribes that judges of the orphans' court need only be "citizens of the State and residents of their jurisdiction for the twelve months preceeding [their election]," was a more specific provision than part I, section 2, which requires that all judges must have been admitted to the practice of law, and therefore that section 40, the specific provision, prevailed over section 2, the general provision, nullifying the "practice of law" requirement for orphans' court judges.

Part I, section 4, provides: "Any Judge shall be removed from office by the Governor, on conviction in a Court of Law, of incompetency, of wilful neglect of duty, misbehavior in office, or any other crime, or on impeachment ... ; or on the address of the General Assembly, two-thirds of each House concurring in such address...." **Section 4A**, as amended in 1966, 1970, 1978, 1980, and 1996, creates a commission on judicial disabilities, whose powers, enumerated in **section 4B(a)(2)**, as amended in 1966, 1970, 1974, 1980, and 1996, include "the power to issue a reprimand and the power to recommend to the Court of Appeals the removal, censure, or other appropriate disciplining of a judge or, in an appropriate case, retirement."

Section 5A, as amended in 1976, provides that if a vacancy occurs on an appellate court "**(b)** ... the Governor shall appoint, by and with the advice and consent of the Senate, a [qualified] person.... **(c)** [That person must stand for election] at the next general election following the expiration of one year from the date" the vacancy occurred and every ten years thereafter. **Section 5A(f)** mandates: "An appellate court judge shall retire when he attains his seventieth birthday."

Part II, section 14, as amended in 1945, 1956, 1960, 1976, 1978, and 1994, provides in part: "The Court of Appeals shall be composed of seven judges.... One of the Judges of the Court of Appeals shall be designated by the Governor as the Chief Judge." Five judges constitute a quorum. Moreover, "five judges shall sit in each case unless the Court [increases the number]. The concurrence of a majority of those sitting shall be sufficient for the decision of any cause, and an equal division of those sitting [affirms] the decision appealed from...."

Section 17, as amended in 1940 and 1956, states: "There shall be a Clerk of the Court of Appeals, who shall be appointed by and shall hold his office at the pleasure of said Court of Appeals." **Section 18**, as amended in 1944, 1966, 1970, 1978, and 1980, provides: "**(a)** The Court of Appeals from time to time shall adopt rules and regulations concerning the practice and procedure in and the administration of the appellate courts and in the other courts of this State, which shall have the force of law until rescinded, changed or modified by the Court of Appeals or otherwise by law. **(b)** The Chief Judge of the Court of Appeals shall be the administrative head of the Judicial system of the State. He shall from time to time require, from each of the judges of [certain other courts] reports as to the judicial work and business of each of the judges and their respective courts...."

Article II, Executive Department, section 6(g), as amended in 1960 and 1970, adds: "The Court of Appeals shall have original and exclusive jurisdiction to adjudicate disputes" relating to certain questions of succession to the office of governor.

Impeachment

Article III, Legislative Department, section 26, directs: "The House of Delegates shall have the sole power of impeachment.... All impeachments shall be tried by the Senate ...; but no person shall be convicted without the concurrence of two-thirds of all the Senators elected." Article II, Executive Department, section 7, as amended in 1960 and 1970, also notes that the legislature "may provide by law, not inconsistent with Section 26 of Article III ..., for the impeachment of the Governor and Lieutenant Governor."

Direct Democracy

Article XVI, The Referendum, section 1, added in 1915, declares: "(a) The people reserve to themselves power known as The Referendum, by petition to have submitted to the registered voters of the State, to approve or reject at the polls, any Act, or part of any Act of the General Assembly, if approved by the Governor, or if passed ... over the veto of the Governor...."

Local Government

Article XI-A, Local Legislation, section 1A, provides in part that a county may adopt a charter for local government, which must be submitted to the voters, and "if a majority of the votes cast ... are in favor of its adoption, the charter shall become effective on the thirtieth day after the election or such later date as shall be specified in the charter."

Education

Article VIII, Education, reads in its entirety: "**Section 1.** The General Assembly, at its First Session after the adoption of this Constitution, shall by Law establish throughout the State a thorough and efficient System of Free Public Schools; and shall provide by taxation, or otherwise, for their maintenance. **Section 2.** The System of Public Schools, as now constituted, shall remain in force until the end of the said First Session of the General Assembly, and shall then expire; except so far as adopted, or continued by the General Assembly. **Section 3.** The School Fund of the State shall be kept inviolate, and appropriated only to the purposes of Education."

Amendment Procedures

Article XIV, Amendments to the Constitution, section 1, as amended in 1944, 1972, and 1978, states in part: "The General Assembly may propose Amendments to this Constitution ... by three-fifths of all the members elected to each of the two Houses...." The proposed amendments are to be submitted "to the qualified voters of the State for adoption" at the next general election, and "if it shall appear to the Governor that a majority of the votes cast ... were cast in favor thereof, the Governor shall, by his proclamation, declare the said amendment ... to have been adopted ... as part of the Constitution."

Section 2, as amended in 1956, adds: "It shall be the duty of the General Assembly to provide by Law for taking, at the general election to be held in [1970] and every twenty years thereafter, the sense of the People in regard to calling a Convention for altering this Constitution." If a majority of the voters vote for a convention, the legislature is to provide for it.

On February 6, 1788, the Commonwealth of Massachusetts became the sixth state of the United States. Boston is the capital of the "Bay State," which encompasses some 10,555 square miles and is bordered by Vermont and New Hampshire on the north, the Atlantic Ocean on the east, Rhode Island and Connecticut on the south, and New York on the west. Massachusetts ranks thirteenth among the states in population with approximately 6 million residents. Its principal industries include services, trade, and manufacturing; among its chief crops are cranberries and greenhouse and nursery vegetables.

MASSACHUSETTS

Government: The governor and lieutenant governor are elected on a single ticket for a four-year term. The legislature, called the general court, consists of forty senators and 160 members of the house of representatives, each of whom is elected for a two-year term. The supreme judicial court is made up of seven justices, including a chief justice, appointed by the governor from a list submitted by a judicial nominating commission with the advice and consent of an executive advisory council.

General Information

Date of Constitution: 1780

Before the arrival of Europeans in the seventeenth century, the territory that would become the state of Massachusetts was inhabited by the Massachuset, Pennacook, and Nipmuc peoples, among others. The Pilgrims, members of a Christian sect from England called Puritans who established the Plymouth colony on Massachusetts Bay in 1620, are traditionally considered the founders of English colonial America. Before disembarking from their ship, the *Mayflower,* the colonists drew up an agreement stating in part: "[We] combine ourselves together into a civil Body Politick, for our better Ordering and Preservation...." Signers of this Mayflower Compact included Miles Standish and John Alden.

Constitutional History

In 1629 the English monarch Charles I granted to the Massachusetts Bay Company a charter that, together with the Cambridge Agreement of August 26, 1629, formed the basis of the constitution of the Massachusetts colony. It created the positions of governor, deputy governor, and assistants, as well as a legislative body called the general court, which included the freemen of the company. The general court, the charter stated, could be assembled "from tyme to tyme, to make, ordeine, and establish all Manner of wholesome and reasonable Orders, Lawes, Statutes, and Ordin[a]nces ... not contrary to the Lawes of this our Realme of England."

Following the outbreak of civil war in England in 1641, Massachusetts declared itself neutral, formed an alliance for defense called the United Colonies of New England, and by 1649 was characterizing itself as an independent commonwealth. In 1660, however, it acknowledged the restored authority of the English Crown.

In 1661 the Massachusetts general court, the legislature, adopted the Declaration of Liberties, which implied that the laws of England did not reach to America. One hundred seven years later, reacting to the Stamp Act, Samuel Adams in 1768 argued in a letter to the British government that Parliament could not pass acts contrary to fundamental laws, such as Magna Carta, that were embodied in the British constitution. This theory—that an elected legislature does not have the power to change a nation's supreme laws—would become a basic tenet of American constitutional law.

To protest a British tax on imported tea, colonists disguised as Native Americans boarded ships in Boston Harbor on December 16, 1773, and threw chests of tea overboard, an incident that became known as the Boston Tea Party. This and other disturbances in Massachusetts led the British Parliament to retaliate by passing coercive "intolerable acts," which in turn fanned the flames of rebellion in the American colonies. The most odious of these, the Boston Port Act, banned all trade through the port of Boston. But if any single incident in the early struggle between Great Britain and its American colonies triggered the process of modern constitutional development, it was "the shot heard round the world" fired at British troops by the American colonists in Lexington, Massachusetts, on the morning of April 19, 1775.

Once the American Revolution began in earnest, the thirteen British colonies transformed themselves into individual states. A constitution for the new state of Massachusetts was drafted by a committee appointed by the legislature in 1777. Among other provisions the proposed constitution denied voting rights to "negroes, Indians, and molottoes" and granted excessive appointive powers to the governor and the senate. After vigorous debate in town meetings it was rejected by the people by a five-to-one margin.

A second constitutional convention assembled in Cambridge on September 1, 1779. The draft constitution produced by this convention was approved by the voters and became effective on October 25, 1780. Unlike the first proposal, the second contained a declaration, or bill, of rights. John Adams, the foremost authority on constitutional law in his day and the principal drafter of the constitution, was responsible for the entire declaration of rights except for the article on religious freedom. Although Massachusetts was the last of the original thirteen states to adopt a written constitution, it was the first to submit a constitution to the electorate for approval. The 1780 constitution of Massachusetts is the oldest written constitution still in effect in the world, older even than the U.S. Constitution (1789), although it has been amended 117 times.

The Constitution

The 1780 Massachusetts constitution follows the commonwealth pattern of state constitutions that arose in New England. Rooted in the traditions of the early Puritans and the principles of the American revolutionaries, such constitutions express a philosophy of organization for civil society through the institutions of republican government. The first wave of state constitutions adopted around the time of the Declaration of Independence—including, for example, Pennsylvania's 1776 constitution—relied on frequent elections rather than institutional checks and balances to ensure responsible government. But with its provisions for a bicameral legislature, gubernatorial veto power that could be overridden by a two-thirds vote of the legislature, and life tenure for judges, Massachusetts's 1780 constitution prefigured the U.S. Constitution.

In many ways the Massachusetts constitution, like the U.S. Constitution, is a model constitutional document. However, its 117 amendments approved as of January 1, 1998, are not integrated into the original text, making it difficult for the average citizen to read and understand. A convention that met from 1917 to 1919 produced a rearrangement of the original document, corrected technical errors, and incorporated existing amendments into the body of the constitution. Although this revised constitution was approved by the voters in November 1919, the supreme judicial court of Massachusetts in *Opinions of the Justices* (1920) and *Loring v. Young* (1921) declared that only the original text and individual amendments were legally controlling.

The preamble to the 1780 constitution of Massachusetts begins: "The end of the institution, maintenance and administration of government, is to secure the existence of the body-politic, to protect it, and to furnish the individuals who compose it, with the power of enjoying in safety and tranquility their natural rights, and the blessings of life...."

Part the first, A Declaration of the Rights of the Inhabitants of the Commonwealth of Massachusetts, article I, as amended in 1976, proclaims: "All people are born free and equal and have certain natural, essential and inalienable rights; among which may be reckoned the right of enjoying and defending their lives and liberties; that of acquiring, possessing and protecting property; in fine [conclusion], that of seeking and obtaining their safety and happiness. Equality under law shall not be denied or abridged because of sex, race, color, creed or national origin." A 1980 amendment prohibits discrimination against disabled persons.

Article II states in part: "It is the right as well as the Duty of all men in society, publickly, and at stated seasons to worship the SUPREME BEING, the great Creator and preserver of the Universe." Several amendments deal with religion. One added in 1917 proclaims: "No law shall be passed prohibiting the free exercise of religion ..."; another, added in 1918, excludes "religion, religious practices or religious institutions" as subjects for the initiative and referendum process. **Article III,** which was replaced in its entirety by amendment in 1833 and then was affected by the 1917 and 1918 amendments, refers among other things to "piety, religion and morality."

Article IV secures the right of self-government for the people, while **article V** acknowledges that all power resides in the people and that government officers "are at all times accountable to them." **Article VII** declares: "Government is instituted for the Common good; for the protection, safety, prosperity and happiness of the people; and not for profit, honor, or private interest of any one man, family or Class of men...."

Article VIII invests the people with the right "at such periods and in such manner as they shall establish by their frame of government" to remove public officers and replace them through regular elections and appointments. **Article IX** asserts: "All elections ought to be free; and all the inhabitants of this Commonwealth, having qualification as they shall establish by their frame of government, have an equal right to elect officers, and to be elected, for public employments." In *Batchelder v. Allied Stores International, Inc.* (1983), the Massachusetts supreme judicial court for Essex held that article IX guaranteed a candidate's right to solicit signatures in the mall area of a large, private shopping center to support nomination to public office.

Articles X through **XV** provide recourse to the laws for "every subject of the Commonwealth" and rights for those accused of crimes, including security from unreasonable searches and seizures. **Articles XVI** through **XIX,** as amended, cover liberty of the press, the right to keep and bear arms, moral qualifications for office, and the right to instruct representatives and petition the legislature, among other issues. In *Nantucket Conservation Foundation, Inc. v. Russell Management, Inc.* (1980), the Massachusetts supreme judicial court for Nantucket confirmed that articles I, X, and XII of the Massachusetts Declaration of Rights were comparable to the U.S. Constitution's due process clause as set forth in *Pinnick v. Cleary* (1971).

Division of Powers

Part the first, article XXX, reads: "In the government of this Commonwealth, the legislative department shall never exercise the executive and judicial powers, or either of them: The executive shall never exercise the legislative and judicial powers, or either of them: The judicial shall never exercise the legislative and executive powers, or either of them: to the end it may be a government of laws and not of men."

Legislative Branch

Part the second, The Frame of Government, declares: "The people, inhabiting the territory formerly called the Province of Massachusetts Bay, do hereby solemnly and mutually agree with each other, to form themselves into a free, sovereign, and independent body-politic, or State, by the name of The Commonwealth of Massachusetts."

Chapter I, The Legislative Power, section I, The General Court, article I, mandates: "The department of legislation shall be formed by two branches, a Senate and a House of Representatives: each of which shall have a negative on the other [i.e., both branches must concur on legislative proposals]." **Article II,** as twice amended in 1918, authorizes the governor to veto a bill or resolution, but such veto may be overridden by a two-thirds vote of each house. Pursuant to an amendment in 1968, the last paragraph of article II now reads: "And in order to prevent unnecessary delays, if any bill or resolve shall not be returned by the governor within ten days after it shall have been presented, the same shall have the force of law." Under **amendment XC,** adopted in 1968, the governor has a similar power to veto individual items in appropriations bills.

Article III, as amended in 1918, declares: "The General Court shall forever have full power and authority to erect and constitute judicatories [courts of justice] and courts of record, or other Courts...." **Article IV,** also amended in 1918, grants the general court authority "from time to time, to make, ordain, and establish all manner of wholesome and reasonable orders, laws, statutes and ordinances ... as they judge to be for the good and welfare of this Commonwealth ... ," which are "not repugnant or contrary to this Constitution...."

Section II, Senate, article I, as amended in 1964, prescribes two-year terms of office for senators. According to an amendment in 1974, the senate consists of forty members, one from each senatorial district. **Article V,** as amended in 1970, confirms the qualifications originally set forth in this article, requiring a senator to "have been an inhabitant of this commonwealth five years at least immediately preceding his election, and at the time of his election [to be] an inhabitant of the district for which he is chosen."

Article VI provides that the "Senate shall have power to adjourn themselves, provided such adjournments do not exceed two days time"; but an amendment in 1974 allows the general court to take recesses of not more than thirty days. **Article VII** authorizes the senate to "choose its own President, appoint its own officers, and determine it own rules of proceedings." **Article IX,** which provides the basis for a quorum in the senate, was changed by amendment in 1891 and now reads: "A majority of the members of each branch of the general court shall constitute a quorum for the transaction of business...." The senate is extended, under **section III, House of Representatives, article XI,** "the same powers [and presumably privileges] in the like cases" as the house with respect to judging the qualifications of its own members, choosing its own officers, providing for its own rules, punishing members and others of improper behavior, and immunity from arrest.

Section III, House of Representatives, article I, announces: "THERE shall be in the Legislature of this Commonwealth a representation of the people ... elected, and founded upon the principle of equality." **Article II** has been amended so extensively that only one sentence remains of the original language: "And the House of Representatives shall have power from time to time to impose fines upon such towns as shall neglect to choose and return members to the same, agreeably to this Constitution." **Article III,** as amended in 1857, 1930, 1970, and 1974, sets the number of members of the house of representatives at 160 and requires that every representative "for one year at least immediately preceding his election, shall have been an inhabitant of the district for which he is chosen and shall cease to represent such district when he shall cease to be an inhabitant of the Commonwealth."

Article VII requires that "[a]ll money-bills shall originate in the House of Representatives"; however, "the Senate may propose or concur with amendments, as on other bills." **Article IX,** as amended in 1857 and 1891, defines a quorum as a majority of the members of the house. **Article X** empowers the house of representatives to "be the judge of the returns, elections, and qualifications of its own members"; "chuse their own Speaker; appoint their own officers, and settle the rules and orders of proceeding in their own House"; and punish their own members for "disorderly, or contemptuous behavior" and others for improper actions against the legislative body, its members, or witnesses. In *Paisner v. Atty. Gen.* (1983), the Massachusetts supreme judicial court for Suffolk ruled that although the legislature had chosen to enact a law in order to regulate its internal proceedings, a law adopted by popular initiative could not change the legislature's rules. Article x also extends broad immunity to a house member "during his going unto, returning from, or his attending the General Assembly." **Article XI** in its second paragraph states: "And the Senate and the House of Representatives may try, and determine, all cases where their rights and privileges are concerned...."

Chapter II, Executive Power, section I, Governor, article I, declares: "There shall be a supreme executive Magistrate, who shall be stiled, THE GOVERNOR OF THE COMMONWEALTH OF MASSACHUSETTS; and whose title shall be—HIS EXCELLENCY." According to **article II,** as amended in 1964, the governor is elected "quadrennially," and by amendment in 1966 the governor and lieutenant governor "shall be grouped on the official ballot for use at state elections according to the parties they represent, and the voters cast a single vote for any such group." Originally, no person was eligible for governor unless "at the time of his election, he shall have been an inhabitant of this Commonwealth for seven years next preceding; and unless he shall at the same time, be seized in

Executive Branch

his own right, of a freehold within the Commonwealth of the value of one thousand Pounds; and unless he shall declare himself to be of, the christian religion." The second and third requirements were deleted by amendment in 1892 and 1821, respectively.

Section III, Council . . . , article I, as amended in 1855, creates a council of eight members, besides the lieutenant governor, "for advising the Governor in the executive part of the government." **Section I, Governor, article IV,** states in part: ". . . the Governor, with the said Counsellors, or five of them at least, shall, and may, from time to time, hold and keep a Council, for the ordering and directing the affairs of the Commonwealth, agreeably to the Constitution and the laws of the land." The use of an advisory council, rare among the states, reflects the British government structure of a monarch and a privy council, which can make decisions and issue orders in certain matters without Parliament's formally adopting a law. The British used this model of a chief executive and an advisory council in their colonial administrations worldwide. According to **section III, Council . . . , article V,** the "resolutions and advice of the Council shall be recorded in a register, and signed by the members present. . . ." An amendment in 1964 provides that "councillors, senators, and representative shall be elected biennially. . . ."

Section I, Governor, article V, as amended in 1831, authorizes the governor to adjourn the legislature upon request and call it into session; and **article VI** provides that when the two houses of the legislature disagree on adjournment, "the Governor, with advice of the Council, shall have a right to adjourn or prorogue the General Court, not exceeding ninety days, as he shall determine the public good shall require." According to **article VII,** which was completely rewritten in 1918, the governor is the commander in chief of the state's military forces, but the legislature "shall provide by law for the recruitment, equipment, organization, training and discipline of the military and naval forces . . . [and may authorize the governor to] prescribe from time to time the organization of the military and naval forces and make regulations for their government."

Article VIII, as rewritten in 1964, specifies the governor's powers in granting pardons: "The power of pardoning offenses, except such as persons may be convicted of before the senate by an impeachment of the house, shall be in the governor, by and with the advice of council, provided, that if the offense is a felony the general court [the legislature] shall have power to prescribe the terms and conditions upon which a pardon may be granted." **Article IX,** as amended in 1855 and 1918, grants the governor the authority "by and with the advice and Consent of the Council" to nominate and appoint all "judicial officers, the Solicitor-General, [and] Coroners."

Section II, Lieutenant Governor, article I, as amended, provides in part: "There shall be quadrennially elected a Lieutenant Governor of the Commonwealth of Massachusetts, whose title shall be, His Honor." The lieutenant governor must have the same qualifications as the governor. "The Governor, and in his absence the Lieutenant Governor," states **article II,** "shall be President of the Council, but shall have no vote in Council: And the Lieutenant Governor shall always be a member of the Council except when the chair of the Governor shall be vacant." **Article III** authorizes the lieutenant governor to perform all the duties of the governor if the incumbent has died, is absent from the commonwealth, or is otherwise unable to perform them. According to **article IV,** as amended in 1918, the order of secession after the lieutenant governor is "the secretary of state, attorney-general, treasurer . . . , and auditor."

Judicial Branch

Chapter III, Judiciary Power, article I, as amended in 1972, states in part: "All judicial officers, duly appointed, commissioned and sworn, shall hold their offices during good behavior [unless otherwise specified in the constitution]; provided, nevertheless, the governor, with the consent of the council, may remove them upon address of both houses of the legislature." The governor and council may also force their retirement, and at age seventy they must retire. In *Apkin v. Treasurer & Receiver General* (1988), the Massachusetts supreme judicial court for Suffolk acknowledged that the state adheres to the principle that an independent and competent judiciary can best be achieved and maintained by appointment, rather than election, of judges.

Article II, as amended in 1964, provides: "Each branch of the legislature, as well as the governor and council shall have authority to require the opinions of the justices of the supreme judicial court, upon important questions of law, and upon solemn occasions." The constitution of Massachusetts, unlike the U.S. Constitution but like the state constitutions of Colorado, Florida, Maine, Michigan, New Hampshire, Rhode Island, and South Dakota, expressly authorizes the judicial branch to give advisory opinions. In *In re Municipal Suffrage to Women* (1894), Oliver Wendell Holmes, then a justice of the Massachusetts supreme judicial court, dissented from the court's answer to a question posed by the lower house of the legislature, stating that, because the constitution did not forbid it, the legislature might condition the validity of an act extending suffrage to women on the outcome of a popular referendum on the proposed law.

Articles III, IV, and **V,** respectively, deal with justices of the peace, probate court, and domestic relations.

Impeachment

Chapter I, The Legislative Power, section III, House of Representatives, article VI, provides: "The House of Representatives shall be the Grand Inquest of this Commonwealth; and all impeachments made by them, shall be heard and tried by the Senate." **Section II, Senate, article VIII,** invests the senate "with full authority to hear and determine all impeachments made by the House of Representatives, against any officer or officers of the Commonwealth, for misconduct and mal-administration in their offices. . . . Their judgement, however shall not extend further than to removal from office and disqualification [from any other office] under this Commonwealth; But the party . . . shall be, nevertheless, liable to . . . [further] punishment, according to the laws of the land.—"

Direct Democracy

Amendment XLVII, adopted in 1918 and amended in 1944, reserves for the people of Massachusetts the right to vote in referendums to approve or reject laws enacted by the legislature. It also adds the popular initiative as another means of submitting "constitutional amendments and laws to the people for approval or rejection."

Local Government

Amendment II, adopted in 1821, empowers the legislature to charter cities. **Amendment LXXXIX**, adopted in 1966, states in part: "No town of fewer than twelve thousand inhabitants shall adopt a city form of government, and no town of fewer than six thousand inhabitants shall adopt a form of government providing for a town meeting limited to such inhabitants of the town as may be elected to meet, deliberate, act and vote in the exercise of the corporate powers of the town." The concepts of townships, town meetings, and annually elected administrative officers called selectmen were patterned on the traditions of the manor villages that the early Puritan settlers had known in England.

Taxation and Finance

Part the second, The Frame of Government, chapter I, section I, article IV, as amended in 1912 and 1915, gives the legislature the power to levy an income tax and, as amended in 1972 and 1978, authorizes it to establish classes of real property for tax purposes. **Amendment CVII**, adopted in 1978, requires a balanced budget, equalizing "all the proposed expenditures ... for the fiscal year" and "all the taxes, revenues, loans and other means by which such expenditures shall be defrayed."

Education

Part the second, The Frame of Government, chapter V, The University of Cambridge, and the Encouragement of Literature &c, provides for Harvard College (now Harvard University) and directs the legislature to "cherish the interests of literature and the sciences, and all seminaries of them." An amendment in 1978 provides: "No student shall be assigned to or denied admittance to a public school on the basis of race, color, national origin or creed." After a 1965 report identified a number of racially imbalanced public schools, the resulting busing of students sparked violent demonstrations by opponents.

Environment

Amendment XCVII, adopted in 1972, asserts that "[t]he people shall have the right to clean air and water, freedom from excessive and unnecessary noise, and the natural, scenic, historic, and esthetic qualities of their environment; and the protection of the people in their right to the conservation, development, and utilization of the agricultural, mineral, forest, water, air and other natural resources is herby declared to be a public purpose. **Amendment LI**, adopted in 1918 as the first state constitutional provision protecting historic buildings, declares: "The preservation and maintenance of ancient landmarks and other property of historical or antiquarian interest is a public use...."

Amendment Procedures

Part the second, The Frame of Government, chapter VI, ... Provision for a Future Revisal of the Constitution, article X, was replaced in 1918 and altered by **amendment LXXXI** in 1950. Massachusetts now may amend its constitution through either a legislative measure or popular initiative. A legislator's amendment is referred to the next legislative session by a vote in a joint session of "a majority of all the members elected," while an amendment proposed by popular initiative is referred by an "affirmative vote of not less than one-fourth of all the members elected." If in the next legislative session a proposed amendment again receives the same votes of approval as before, it is presented to the people. An amendment introduced by a legislator is ratified if a majority of the voters approve it, and a popularly initiated amendment is ratified "if approved ... by voters equal in number to at least thirty percent of the total number of ballots cast at such state election and also by a majority of the voters voting on such amendment."

Michigan became the twenty-sixth state of the United States on January 26, 1837. Lansing is the capital of the "Wolverine State." Michigan, which consists of an upper and a lower section and encompasses some 96,705 square miles, is bordered by Lake Superior and the Canadian province of Ontario on the north; Lake Huron and Lake Erie on the east; Ohio and Indiana on the south; and Lake Michigan and Wisconsin on the west. With approximately 9.5 million inhabitants, Michigan ranks eighth among the states in population. Its principal industries include manufacturing, services, tourism, agriculture, and mining; its chief crops are corn, wheat, and soybeans.

Government: The governor and lieutenant governor are elected jointly for four-year terms and are limited to two terms. The legislature consists of thirty-eight senators elected for four-year terms and limited to eight years in office and 110 members of the house of representatives elected for two-year terms and limited to six years in office. The supreme court is composed of a chief justice and six additional justices elected for eight-year terms.

Dates of Constitutions: 1837, 1850, 1908, and 1964

The Ojibwa (Chippewa), Ottawa, and Huron were among the peoples living in the region that would become the state of Michigan (the name is derived from *majigan,* an Ojibwa word for "clearing") when the French explorer Étienne Brulé landed at what is now Sault Sainte Marie around 1620. The French established a mission there in 1666, and a formal claim to the territory made by Simon Daumont, sieur de St. Lusson, in 1671 led to its becoming a part of French Canada. In 1679 Robert Cavelier, sieur de La Salle, built a fort at the mouth of the St. Joseph River on Lake Michigan, and on July 24, 1701, Antoine de la Mothe Cadillac established a flourishing trading post on the present site of Detroit.

After defeating France in the French and Indian War in 1763, Great Britain gradually took control of the area. The Quebec Act of 1774 made Detroit a center for Britain's development of the province of Quebec. By the terms of the 1783 Treaty of Paris, which ended the Revolutionary War, the British were to leave Michigan territory but did not do so until July 11, 1796. The Northwest Ordinance passed by Congress in 1787 created a frame of government for the Territories of Michigan, Ohio, Illinois, Indiana, and Wisconsin, although Michigan did not send a representative to the territorial legislature in Cincinnati until 1799.

After Ohio became a state in 1803, for two years Michigan was administered as part of the Indiana Territory. On January 11, 1805, an act was approved making Michigan a separate territory, with Detroit as its capital, but Michiganders did not elect a delegate to Congress until 1819. The opening of the Erie Canal in 1825 provided a water route that facilitated the flow of new settlers into the territory. A petition for statehood was sent to Congress in 1834, but two issues had to be resolved first: a boundary dispute with Ohio and slavery. Michigan wished to be admitted as a free state but had to wait until a slave state was admitted (Arkansas gained statehood in 1836).

A constitutional convention met in Detroit from May 11 to June 29, 1835, nevertheless, and its efforts were ratified at the polls on November 2. The document built on the Northwest Ordinance, elaborating on the fundamental rights provisions and devoting a whole article to education. Because the convention refused to acknowledge Ohio's claim to disputed territory, Congress again refused to grant statehood. Another convention adopted an Ordinance of Assent on December 15, 1836, acceding to Congress's demand. Michigan was promptly admitted as a state of the Union on January 26, 1837, and its first constitution became effective on that date. This document soon came under criticism, however, for not being in tune with the changing conditions of state government.

In the summer of 1850 a convention met in Lansing, and a second constitution, embodying the wave of radicalism fostered by Jacksonian democracy that was sweeping through many other states, was ratified by the people on November 5. Attempts at constitutional revisions were defeated at the polls in 1868 and 1873. In October 1907 another convention met in Lansing, bent on implementing progressive reforms in the wake of President Theodore Roosevelt's landslide victory. A separate bill of rights was restored, but the complete document, which was ratified convincingly at the polls in 1908, was weighed down with needlessly detailed language.

A constitutional convention meeting in Lansing from October 3, 1961, to August 1, 1962, produced a fourth constitution, which was ratified by the electorate on April 1, 1963, and went into effect on January 1, 1964. Although the convention was still dominated by white males, for the first time in Michigan history women (eleven) and blacks (fourteen) participated in writing the document.

The Constitution

After World War II several states rewrote their constitutions. The first round of these new constitutions included Missouri's and New Jersey's in 1945, and the second round began with Michigan's in 1964. Relatively average in length containing approximately 25,000 words, the new Michigan constitution was primarily concerned with apportionment, a result of the U.S. Supreme Court's decision in *Baker v. Carr* (1962), which upheld suits for malapportionment by state legislatures. The delegates also focused on strengthening the governor's role and making the executive branch more efficient. The judicial branch received a new court of appeals, and the office of justice of the peace was eliminated.

Overall, the 1964 Michigan constitution reflects the Progressive Era in its expansion of civil rights, the inclusion of an antidiscrimination clause, and the dominant role of the federal courts in protecting civil rights. The earlier constitution's language regarding search and seizure was carried over into the new document on the theory that if it no longer passed constitutional muster, the federal courts could provide guidance in applying it. A new provision calling for a referendum on revising the constitution every sixteen years will help update it, should the need arise. As of January 1, 1998, the Michigan constitution has been amended only twenty-two times.

Preamble

The preamble to the 1964 Michigan constitution reads: "We, the people of the State of Michigan, grateful to Almighty God for the blessings of freedom, and earnestly desiring to secure these blessings undiminished to ourselves and our posterity, do ordain and establish this constitution."

Fundamental Rights

Article I, Declaration of Rights, section 1, proclaims: "All political power is inherent in the people. Government is instituted for their equal benefit, security and protection." **Section 2** affirms that "[n]o person shall be denied the equal protection of the laws; nor shall any person be denied the enjoyment of his civil or political rights or be discriminated against in the exercise thereof because of religion, race, color or national origin. The legislature shall implement this section by appropriate legislation." **Sections 3, 4, 5,** and **6,** respectively, guarantee to each person the right to peaceably assemble and petition the government for redress of grievances; the "liberty to worship God according to the dictates of [one's] own conscience ..."; the freedom to "speak, write, express and publish ... views on all subjects ..."; and the "right to keep and bear arms for the defense of himself and the state."

Section 7 strictly subordinates the military "in all cases and at all times ... to the civil power." **Sections 8, 9,** and **10,** respectively, limit the quartering of soldiers in private homes; prohibit slavery and involuntary servitude "unless for the punishment of crime"; and proscribe bills of attainder, ex post facto laws, and laws impairing the obligation of contracts. **Section 11** prohibits unreasonable searches and seizures but "shall not be construed to bar from evidence in any criminal proceeding any narcotic drug, firearm, bomb, explosive or any other dangerous weapon, seized by a peace officer outside the curtilage of any dwelling house in this state." In several cases, including *Lucas v. People of the State of Michigan* (1970), the U.S. Court of Appeals held that the last sentence of section 11 violated the Fourth Amendment (1791) to the U.S. Constitution.

Section 12 limits suspension of the writ of habeas corpus. According to **section 13,** "A suitor in any court of this state has the right to prosecute or defend his suit, either in his own proper person or by an attorney," and **section 14** guarantees the right to trial by jury. **Section 15,** as amended in 1978, prohibits double jeopardy and guarantees bail except in certain cases, while **section 16** bars excessive bail, excessive fines, cruel and unusual punishment, and unreasonable detention of witnesses. Under **section 17,** "No person shall be compelled in any criminal case to be a witness against himself, nor be deprived of life, liberty or property, without due process of law. The right of all individuals, firms, corporations and voluntary associations to fair and just treatment in the course of legislative and executive investigations and hearings shall not be infringed." This last sentence is unusual in state constitutions.

Section 18 prohibits challenges to a witness's competence on the basis of religious beliefs; **section 19** guarantees that the truth of an utterance may be given in prosecutions for libel; and **section 20** extends rights to the accused in criminal prosecutions. Under **section 21,** imprisonment for debt is prohibited "except in cases of fraud or breach of trust." **Section 22** defines treason and the evidence necessary to convict in terms similar to those in the U.S. Constitution. According to **section 23,** "The enumeration in this constitution of certain rights shall not be construed to deny or disparage others retained by the people." **Section 24,** added by amendment in 1988, provides rights for victims of crime, including the right to "timely disposition of the case following arrest of the accused"; reasonable protection from the accused; notification of court proceedings; attendence at the trial; conference with the prosecution; and restitution.

Article III, General Government, section 2, declares: "The powers of government are divided into three branches; legislative, executive and judicial. No person exercising powers of one branch shall exercise powers properly belonging to another branch except

Division of Powers

as expressly provided in this constitution." In *Farmington v. Scott* (1965), the Michigan supreme court found that where the legislature has enacted a law stating that a discretionary writ "shall" be issued, such language "merely authorizes rather than commands relief" and therefore is not an invasion of the judicial function by the legislature.

Legislative Branch

Article IV, Legislative Branch, section 1, vests the legislative power of the state in a senate and a house of representatives. **Section 2** specifies that "[t]he senate shall consist of 38 members to be elected from single member districts at the same election as the governor for four-year terms concurrent with the term of office of the governor," while **section 3** states in part that "[t]he house of representatives shall consist of 110 members elected for two-year terms from single member districts apportioned on a basis of population as provided in this article." Section 3 continues: "The districts shall consist of compact and convenient territory contiguous by land." **Section 6** creates a commission on legislative apportionment.

Section 7 stipulates that legislators must be citizens of the United States, at least twenty-one years old, and residents of their districts; furthermore, "[t]he removal of his domicile from the district shall be deemed a vacation of the office. No person who has been convicted of . . . a felony involving a breach of public trust shall be eligible for . . . the legislature." **Sections 8, 9,** and **10** place further restrictions on eligibility of legislators and prohibit them or any state officer from being "interested directly or indirectly in any contract with the state or any political subdivision thereof which shall cause a substantial conflict of interest." **Section 54** limits house members to three terms and senators to two terms.

Section 11 states: "Except as provided by law, senators and representatives shall be privileged from civil arrest and civil process during sessions of the legislature and for five days next before the commencement and after the termination thereof. They shall not be questioned in any other place for any speech in either house." According to **section 14,** "A majority of the members elected to and serving in each house shall constitute a quorum to do business. A smaller number . . . may adjourn from day to day, and may compel the attendance of absent members. . . ." **Section 15** provides for a bipartisan legislative council "consisting of legislators appointed in the manner prescribed by law . . . which shall maintain bill drafting, research and other services for the members . . . , [and which] shall periodically examine and recommend to the legislature revision of the various laws of the state." The Montana constitution also expressly authorizes a legislative council but does not detail its functions.

Section 16 mandates that each house, "except as otherwise provided in this constitution," may choose its own officers and determine its own procedural rules "but shall not adopt any rule that will prevent a majority of the members elected thereto and serving therein from discharging a committee from the further consideration of any measure." Each house is to be the judge of the qualifications, election, and returns of its members and may, by a two-thirds vote, expel a member. **Section 17** authorizes each house to establish committees and requires that on "all actions on bills and resolutions in each committee, names and votes of members shall be recorded ... [and the] vote shall be available for public inspection."

Section 22 provides that "[a]ll legislation shall be by bill and may originate in either house." The U.S. Constitution and the constitutions of some states, including Indiana, require that appropriations or money bills originate in the house of representatives. **Section 24** specifies: "No law shall embrace more than one object, which shall be expressed in its title. No bill shall be altered or amended on its passage ... so as to change its original purpose as determined by its total content and not alone by its title." Under **section 25,** "No law shall be revised, altered or amended by reference to its title only. The section or sections of the act altered or amended shall be re-enacted and published at length."

Section 26 directs the legislature not to pass any bill unless "it has been printed or reproduced and in the possession of each house for at least five days. Every bill shall be read three times in each house ... [and no] bill shall become a law without the concurrence of a majority of the members elected to and serving in each house." According to **section 27,** "No act shall take effect until the expiration of 90 days from the end of the session at which it was passed, [except by] a two-thirds vote of the members elected to and serving in each house."

Section 29 prohibits the legislature from passing a "local or special act in any case where a general act can be made applicable. ..." **Section 30** states: "The assent of two-thirds of the members elected to and serving in each house ... shall be required for the appropriation of public money or property for local or private purposes." The constitutions of several other states, including New York, contain similar language. **Section 31** notes that one of the general appropriations bills must contain an itemized statement of estimated revenue for the ensuing fiscal period, "the total of which shall not be less than the total of all appropriations ... in the general appropriation bills as passed."

Section 33 requires in part: "Every bill passed by the legislature shall be presented to the governor ... [who] shall have 14 days measured in hours and minutes from the time of presentation in which to consider it." If the governor approves it, he or she signs it and files it with the secretary of state. If not, it is returned to the originating house, "with his objections," and "two-thirds of the members elected to and serving in" each house may override the veto. A bill not signed by the governor and not returned becomes law after fourteen days as if it had been signed. **Section 34** provides: "Any bill passed by the legislature and approved by the governor, except a bill appropriating money, may provide that it will not become law unless approved by a majority of the electors voting thereon [in a referendum]."

Article V, Executive Branch, section 1, states simply: "The executive power is vested in the governor." According to **section 21,** "The governor, lieutenant governor, secretary of state and attorney general shall be elected for four-year terms ... ," and **section 30** stipulates that "[n]o person shall be elected more than two times to each office of the executive branch of government." **Section 21** requires that "[t]he lieutenant governor, secretary of

Executive Branch

state and attorney general shall be nominated by party conventions in a manner prescribed by law. In the general election one vote shall be cast jointly for the candidates for governor and lieutenant governor nominated by the same party." As stipulated in **section 22,** the governor and lieutenant governor must be at least thirty years old and registered voters of the state for four years.

Section 2 states in part: "All executive and administrative offices, agencies and instrumentalities of the executive branch … [with some exceptions] shall be allocated by law among and within not more than 20 principal departments." The governor may make changes in the organization, but if they "require the force of law" the legislature has an opportunity to disapprove the changes. The Illinois constitution contains a similar reorganization provision.

Section 3 specifies that each principal department is to be headed by a single executive, including a secretary of state, a state treasurer, and an attorney general. Heads of departments generally "shall be appointed by the governor by and with the advice and consent of the senate and … shall serve at the pleasure of the governor." **Section 6** notes: "Appointment by and with the advice and consent of the senate … means appointment subject to disapproval by a majority vote of the members elected to and serving in the senate … , [and any] appointment not disapproved within [60 days] shall stand confirmed."

Section 8 mandates in part: "Each principal department shall be under the supervision of the governor unless otherwise provided by this constitution. The governor shall take care that the laws be faithfully executed." According to **section 10,** the governor may "inquire into the condition and administration of any public office and the acts of any public officer … [and] may remove or suspend from office for gross neglect of duty or for corrupt conduct in office, or for any other misfeasance or malfeasance therein, any … state officer, except legislative or judicial, and shall report the reasons for such removal or suspension to the legislature."

Section 12 states: "The governor shall be commander-in-chief of the armed forces and may call them out to execute the laws, suppress insurrection and repel invasion." **Section 14** empowers the governor to grant reprieves, commutations, and pardons, except in cases of impeachment, "upon such conditions and limitations as he may direct, subject to procedures and regulations prescribed by law … [and to] inform the legislature annually of [his or her actions], stating reasons therefor." Under **section 15,** the governor is authorized to convene the legislature "on extraordinary occasions."

Section 17 directs the governor to "communicate by message to the legislature at the beginning of each session" and at other times information about the affairs of the state and to recommend any necessary or desirable measures. **Section 18** requires in part: "The governor shall submit to the legislature at a time fixed by law, a budget for the ensuing fiscal period setting forth in detail … the proposed expenditures and estimated revenue of the state. Proposed expenditures from any fund shall not exceed the estimated revenue thereof." **Section 19** gives the governor power to veto items in appropriations bills. **Section 20** states, however: "No appropriation shall be a mandate to spend. The governor, with the approval of the appropriating committees of the house and senate, shall reduce expenditures authorized by appropriations whenever it appears that actual revenues for a fiscal period will fall below the revenue estimates on which appropriations for that period were based."

Section 25 outlines the lieutenant governor's duties: "The lieutenant governor shall be president of the senate, but shall have no vote, unless they be equally divided. He may perform duties requested of him by the governor, but no power vested in the governor shall be delegated." **Section 26** provides that in the event of the governor's conviction on impeachment, removal from office, resignation, or death, "the lieutenant governor, the elected secretary of state, the elected attorney general and such other persons designated by law shall in that order be governor for the remainder of the governor's term." If the governor-elect dies, the lieutenant governor-elect becomes governor; and if the governor becomes temporarily unable to perform the duties of office because of absence from the state or disability, the lieutenant governor becomes acting governor.

Article VI, Judicial Branch, section 1, declares: "The judicial power of the state is vested exclusively in one court of justice which shall be divided into one supreme court, one court of appeals, one trial court of general jurisdiction known as the circuit court, one probate court, and courts of limited jurisdiction that the legislature may establish by a two-thirds vote of the members elected to and serving in each house." The constitutions of a number of states, including Iowa and Pennsylvania, for example, contain language that permits the legislature to create additional courts, but rarely is a supermajority required to do so. **Section 2** specifies in part that the supreme court is to consist of seven justices elected "at non-partisan elections as provided by law" for eight-year terms staggered so that "not more than two terms of office shall expire at the same time."

Section 3 mandates that the supreme court is to elect one of its members as chief justice and appoint an administrator of the courts and other assistants. **Section 4** outlines the court's authority: "The supreme court shall have general superintending control over all courts; power to issue, hear and determine prerogative and remedial writs; and appellate jurisdiction as provided by rules of the supreme court. The supreme court shall not have the power to remove a judge." In reviewing an opinion of the Michigan supreme court, the U.S. Supreme Court held in *Michigan v. Long* (1983) that where a state court cites both state and federal authority for its opinion, the Supreme Court will assume that the decision is based on the federal authority unless the opinion contains "a plain statement . . . that the federal cases are being used only for the purpose of guidance and do not themselves compel the result . . . reached."

Section 5 authorizes the supreme court to "establish, modify, amend and simplify the practice and procedure in all courts of this state. The distinctions between law and equity proceedings shall, as far as practicable, be abolished. The office of master in chancery is prohibited." The Delaware constitution expressly continues the distinction between equity and law courts.

Section 19 requires that all justices and judges be licensed to practice law in the state; none may be elected or appointed after the age of seventy. **Section 20** specifies that if "a justice or judge removes his domicile beyond the limits of the territory from which he was elected or appointed, he shall have vacated his office." **Section 21** disallows any justice or judge from running for any elective office other than a judicial position during his or her term and for one year afterward.

Article III, General Government, section 8, states that "[e]ither house of the legislature or the governor may request the opinion of the supreme court on important questions of law upon solemn occasions as to the constitutionality of legislation after it has been enacted into law but before its effective date." Seven other states—Colorado, Florida, Maine, Massachusetts, New Hampshire, Rhode Island, and South Dakota—have similar provisions permitting advisory opinions by the state's highest court, although the U.S. Constitution does not.

Impeachment

Article XI, Public Officers and Employment, section 7, gives the house of representatives "the sole power of impeaching civil officers for corrupt conduct in office or for crimes or misdemeanors, but a majority of the members elected thereto and serving therein shall be necessary to direct an impeachment. When an impeachment is directed, the house of representatives shall elect three of its members to prosecute the impeachment." The impeachment is tried in the senate, and "[n]o person shall be convicted without the concurrence of two-thirds of the senators elected and serving." Conviction results only in removal from office, "but the person convicted shall be liable to punishment according to law."

Direct Democracy

Article II, Elections, section 8, directs that "[l]aws shall be enacted to provide for the recall of all elective officers except judges of courts of record upon petition of electors equal in number to 25 percent of the number of persons voting in the last preceding election for the office of governor in the electoral district of the officer sought to be recalled." **Section 9** provides in part: "The people reserve to themselves the power to propose laws and to enact and reject laws, called the initiative, and the power to approve or reject laws enacted by the legislature, called the referendum. The power of initiative extends only to laws which the legislature may enact under this constitution. The power of referendum does not extend to acts making appropriations for state institutions or to meet deficiencies in state funds...."

Local Government

Article VII, Local Government, section 1, states that "[e]ach organized county shall be a body corporate with powers and immunities provided by law." **Section 2** provides in part: "Any county may frame, adopt, amend or repeal a county charter in a manner and with powers and limitations to be provided by general law, which shall among other things provide for the election of a charter commission."

Education

Article VIII, Education, section 1, declares: "Religion, morality and knowledge being necessary to good government and the happiness of mankind, schools and the means of education shall forever be encouraged." **Section 2** directs in part: "The legislature shall maintain and support a system of free public elementary and secondary schools as defined by law. Every school district shall provide for the education of its pupils without discrimination as to religion, creed, race, color or national origin."

Section 3 provides that the state board of education "shall serve as the general planning and coordinating body for all public education, including higher education...." In *The Regents of the University of Michigan v. State* (1975), the Michigan supreme court held, after reviewing comments at the 1962 constitutional convention, that the board's role was advisory in nature and that it therefore could not veto a proposed program of the university.

Article IX, Finance and Taxation, section 1, authorizes the legislature to "impose taxes sufficient with other resources to pay the expenses of state government." **Section 2** declares: "The power of taxation shall never be surrendered, suspended or contracted away." Under **section 4,** "Property owned and occupied by non-profit religious or educational organizations and used exclusively for religious or educational purposes, as defined by law, shall be exempt from real and personal property taxes." **Section 28,** added in 1978, provides that "[n]o expenses of state government shall be incurred in any fiscal year which exceed the sum of the revenue limit established [herein] plus federal aid and any surplus from a previous fiscal year."

Taxation and Finance

Article XII, Amendment and Revision, section 1, states that amendments may be proposed in either house of the legislature, "[if] agreed to by two-thirds of the members elected to and serving in each house...." A proposed amendment must be submitted within sixty days to the voters at the next general election or special election; "[i]f a majority of the electors voting on a proposed amendment approve the same, it shall become part of the constitution ... at the end of 45 days after the date of the election...."

Amendment Procedures

Section 2 provides for amendment by petition and vote of the electorate. According to **section 3,** "At the general election to be held in the year 1978, and in each 16th year thereafter and at such times as may be provided by law, the question of a general revision of the constitution shall be submitted to the electors of the state." A convention to revise the constitution will be held if a majority of the voters voting on the question approve the proposal.

MINNESOTA

On May 11, 1858, Minnesota became the thirty-second state of the United States. The capital of the "North Star State" is St. Paul. Some 86,943 square miles in area, Minnesota is bordered by the Canadian provinces of Manitoba and Ontario on the north, Lake Superior and Wisconsin on the east, Iowa on the south, and South Dakota and North Dakota on the west. Minnesota ranks twentieth among the states in population with approximately 4.6 million residents. The state's principal industries include agribusiness, forest products, and mining; corn, soybeans, and sugar beets are among its chief crops.

General Information

Government: The governor and lieutenant governor are elected jointly for four-year terms. The legislature consists of sixty-seven senators elected for four-year terms and 134 members of the house of representatives elected for two-year terms. The supreme court comprises a chief judge and six additional judges elected for six-year terms.

Date of Constitution: 1858

Constitutional History

When French explorers entered the upper Mississippi River valley in 1654, the Dakota Sioux and the Ojibwa, or Chippewa, peoples inhabited the region that would become the state of Minnesota (the name derives from a Sioux word meaning "cloudy water"). A quarter century later, in 1679, the French explorer Daniel Greysolon, sieur Du Luth, claimed the region for France. The French established a small fort on Lake Peppin in 1727 and another at Lake of the Woods in 1732.

Under the treaty ending the French and Indian War in 1763, the portion of Minnesota territory east of the Mississippi River was ceded to Great Britain and the portion west of the river was ceded to Spain. Jonathan Carver of Massachusetts made his way from Prairie du Chien, in the Wisconsin territory, to the Minnesota River in 1766. At the end of the Revolutionary War in 1783, the eastern part of the Minnesota territory became a part of the United States; the western part was acquired by the United States under the terms of the Louisiana Purchase in 1803.

The first American outpost, Fort Snelling, was established in 1819, and by an act of March 3, 1849, Congress granted Minnesota formal territorial status. Under the protection of the U.S. Army, lumbering and mining became important industries in the territory. By the terms of four major treaties between 1854 and 1866, additional land in the north was purchased from the Ojibwas, who had driven the Sioux out nearly a hundred years earlier. Frustrated over the loss of their lands, the Sioux killed 486 Minnesota settlers in 1862 during the great Sioux uprising.

By 1856 the territory's population exceeded 100,000, and on February 26 of the next year Congress passed enabling legislation to make statehood a viable goal. A constitutional convention that met in St. Paul from July 13 to August 29, 1857, was divided into two political parties, the Democrats and the Republicans. Neither party's delegates would sign the other's draft constitution, so two slightly different constitutions were ratified by the voters on October 13, 1857. The dual Minnesota constitutions went into effect when the territory was admitted as a state of the Union on May 11, 1858. Until the "restructuring" of the Minnesota constitution in 1974, two versions of the state's supreme law existed, although the differences were minor and had little if any significant effect on constitutional matters.

At approximately 23,700 words, the Minnesota constitution is a little shorter than the average length of state constitutions, and as of January 1, 1998, it has been amended 115 times. The structure of government created by the document is typical of most other state constitutions: it provides for a bicameral legislature; a governor and a lieutenant governor, jointly elected, along with four other statewide elected officials in the executive branch; and a judiciary subject to voter approval.

Between 1950 and 1970 forty-five states took steps to modernize their constitutions. Minnesota followed in 1971, when state law authorized the creation of the bipartisan Minnesota Constitutional Study Commission, consisting of twelve state legislators, eight citizen members, a supreme court justice, and a former governor. A major goal of the commission was to "put the constitution in language that the average citizen could understand." To accomplish this, obsolete provisions were removed (the document was shortened by one-third), the constitution itself was reorganized, and the number of articles was reduced by one-third, from twenty-one to fourteen. A recommendation to relax the requirements for passage of amendments, however, was defeated by the voters in 1974.

The preamble to the restructured Minnesota constitution proclaims: "We, the people of the state of Minnesota, grateful to God for our civil and religious liberty, and desiring to perpetuate its blessings and secure the same to ourselves and our posterity, do ordain and establish this Constitution."

Preamble

Article I, Bill of Rights, section 1, declares: "Government is instituted for the security, benefit and protection of the people, in whom all political power is inherent, together with the right to alter, modify or reform government whenever required by the public good." According to **section 2,** "No member of this state shall be disenfranchised or deprived of any of the rights or privileges secured to any citizen thereof, unless by the law of the land or the judgment of his peers. There shall be neither slavery nor involuntary servitude in the state otherwise than as punishment for a crime of which the party has been convicted." **Section 3** affirms that "the liberty of the press shall forever remain inviolate, and all persons may freely speak, write and publish their sentiments on all subjects, being responsible for the abuse of such right." In *Near v. Minnesota* (1931), the U.S. Supreme Court held that a Minnesota statute acted as a prior restraint on publication and therefore was in violation of liberty of the press and that the proper remedy for such abuses is punishment after publication.

Fundamental Rights

Sections 4 through **6,** respectively, guarantee the right to trial by jury, prohibit excessive bail or unusual punishments, and extend rights to the accused in criminal proceedings. **Section 7** guarantees due process and bail and prohibits double jeopardy, self-incrimination, and the suspension of habeas corpus "unless the public safety requires it in case of rebellion or invasion." **Section 8** entitles every person to remedies for injuries or wrongs, and **section 9** defines treason in terms similar to those used in the U.S. Constitution. **Sections 10** through **12,** respectively, prohibit unreasonable searches and seizures; bills of attainder, ex post facto laws, and laws impairing the obligation of contracts; and imprisonment for debt.

Section 13 provides that "[p]rivate property shall not be taken, destroyed or damaged for public use without just compensation therefor, first paid or secured." **Section 14** subordinates the military to civil power and prohibits standing armies in times of peace. **Section 15** declares: "All lands within the state are allodial [held without feudal obligations] and feudal tenures of every description with all their incidents are prohibited. Leases and grants of agricultural lands for a longer period than 21 years reserving rent or service of any kind shall be void."

Section 16 states in part: "The enumeration of rights in this constitution shall not deny or impair others retained by and inherent in the people. The right of every man to worship God according to the dictates of his own conscience shall never be infringed...." **Section 17** proscribes religious tests and property ownership as qualifications for holding public office or being eligible to vote and adds: "nor shall any person be rendered incompetent to give evidence in any court of law or equity in consequence of his opinion upon the subject of religion." The prohibition of religious tests is the general rule in state constitutions; however, the constitutions of several states, including Maryland and South Carolina, are exceptions to the rule.

Division of Powers

Article III, Distribution of the Powers of Government, section 1, declares: "The powers of government shall be divided into three distinct departments: legislative, executive and judicial. No person or persons belonging to or constituting one of these departments shall exercise any of the powers properly belonging to either of the others except in the instances expressly provided in this constitution." According to *Spirit of Laws* (1748), book 11, by Charles-Louis de Secondat, baron de La Brède et de Montesquieu, governments should be separated into three departments that act in harmony through a system of checks and balances. While the U.S. Constitution is a true example of Montesquieu's separation of powers theory, in state constitutions, especially the earlier ones, the separation tends to be more formal than real, with greater power being vested in the legislative branch.

Legislative Branch

Article IV, Legislative Department, section 1, states: "The legislature consists of the senate and house of representatives." **Section 2** notes that the number of legislators is to be prescribed by law and that "[t]he representation in both houses shall be apportioned equally throughout the different sections of the state in proportion to the population thereof." Currently, the Minnesota legislature has sixty-seven senators and 134 members of the house of representatives. According to **section 3,** "At its first session after [the U.S. census], the legislature shall have power to prescribe the bounds of congressional and legislative districts. Senators shall be chosen by single districts of convenient contiguous territory. No representative district shall be divided in the formation of a senate district. The senate districts shall be numbered in a regular series."

Section 4 provides in part: "Representatives shall be chosen for a term of two years, except to fill a vacancy. Senators shall be chosen for a term of four years, except to fill a vacancy and except there shall be an entire new election of all the senators at the first election of representatives after each new legislative apportionment provided for in this article." **Section 5** prohibits a legislator from holding any other U.S. or state office "except that of postmaster or notary public." **Section 6** requires that legislators be "qualified voters of the state," residents of the state for one year, and residents of their district for six months. Section 6 also provides that each house may judge the election returns and eligibility of its members and that "[t]he legislature shall prescribe by law the manner for taking evidence in cases of contested seats in either house."

Section 7 allows each house to "determine the rules of its proceedings, sit upon its own adjournment, punish its members for disorderly behavior, and with the concurrence of two-thirds expel a member; but no member shall be expelled a second time for the same offense." **Section 10** exempts legislators from arrest except for treason, felony, and breach of the peace "during the session of their respective houses and in going to or returning from the same. For any speech or debate in either house they shall not be questioned in any other place." Under **section 25**, each house may "punish by imprisonment for not more than 24 hours any person not a member who is guilty of any disorderly or con-temptuous behavior in its presence."

Section 11 notes: "Two or more members of either house may dissent and protest against any act or resolution which they think injurious to the public or to any individual and have the reason of their dissent entered in the journal." **Section 13** defines a quorum as a majority of each house, although "a smaller number may adjourn from day to day and compel the attendance of absent members. . . ." **Section 16** requires that in "all elections by the legislature members shall vote viva voce and their votes shall be entered in the journal." **Section 17** mandates: "No law shall embrace more than one subject, which shall be expressed in its title." In *Van Bergen v. State of Minn.* (1995), the U.S. Court of Appeals explained that this clause functions to provide notice to citizens and legislators of inter-ests likely to be affected by a bill and to ensure that the title does not cloak unrelated measures, thus preventing such provisions from being enacted *sub rosa*. In *Julius v. Callahan* (1895), however, the Minnesota supreme court found that the legislature in proposing amendments to the state constitution is not performing an ordinary legisla-tive function and therefore that the constitutional requirement that the subject be expressed in the title does not apply.

Section 18 requires that revenue bills originate in the house of representatives, although the senate "may propose and concur with the amendments as on other bills." **Section 19** states: "Every bill shall be reported on three different days in each house, unless, in case of urgency, two-thirds of the house where the bill is pending deem it expedient to dispense with this rule." The constitutions of many states use the phrase "shall be read in each house on three separate days" instead of "reported on three different days in each house." **Section 20** requires bills passed by the legislature to "be enrolled and signed by the presiding officer of each house." **Section 21** prohibits passage of bills "upon the day prescribed for adjournment," and **section 22** stipulates that laws be passed "by a majority of all the members elected to each house. . . ." The constitutions of some states, including New Jersey, however, require only a majority of those members present and voting.

Section 23 provides that all bills passed by the legislature must be presented to the governor. If the governor approves a bill, "he shall sign it, deposit it in the office of the secretary of state and notify the house in which it originated of that fact." For a vetoed bill, including items in appropriations bills, the governor returns the measure directly to the house in which it originated "with his objections." If two-thirds of both houses approve the bill, it becomes law and is deposited in the secretary of state's office. Section 23 also allows the governor only three days, not counting Sundays, to act on bills except bills passed during the last three days of the legislative session; in this case, if a bill "is not signed and deposited within 14 days after adjournment [it] does not become a law." Section 24 specifies that other legislative actions such as orders, resolutions, and votes "requiring the concurrence of the two houses except such as relate to the business or adjournment of the legislature" are also subject to veto by the governor.

Executive Branch

Article V, Executive Department, section 1, provides: "The executive department consists of a governor, lieutenant governor, secretary of state, auditor, treasurer and attorney general, who shall be chosen by the electors of the state." It adds that "[t]he governor and lieutenant governor shall be chosen jointly by a single vote applying to both offices in a manner prescribed by law." In *Clarke v. Growe* (1990), the Minnesota supreme court determined that after a gubernatorial candidate withdrew from an election, the joint candidate for the position of lieutenant governor was not entitled to keep her name on the ballot. According to section 2, the term of office for the governor and lieutenant governor is "four years and until a successor is chosen and qualified." Both must be at least twenty-five years old, "bona fide" state residents for one year, and citizens of the United States. Section 5 specifies that in the case of a vacancy "from any cause whatever" in the governor's office, the lieutenant governor serves as governor; moreover, "[t]he legislature may provide by law for the case of the removal, death, resignation, or inability both of the governor and lieutenant governor to discharge the duties of governor...."

Section 3 outlines the governor's powers and duties, beginning: "The governor shall communicate by message to each session of the legislature information touching the state and country. He is commander-in-chief of the military and naval forces and may call them out to execute the laws, suppress insurrection and repel invasion. He may require the opinion in writing of the principal officer in each of the executive departments upon any subject relating to his duties." With the advice and consent of the senate, the governor also appoints notary publics and other officers and "commissioners to take the acknowledgment of deeds and other instruments in writing to be used in the state." In addition, the governor "shall take care that the laws be faithfully executed" and "shall fill any vacancy that may occur in the offices of secretary of state, treasurer, auditor, attorney general and the other state and district offices hereafter created by law...." Section 7 creates a board of pardons, consisting of the governor, attorney general, and chief justice of the supreme court, whose "powers and duties shall be defined and regulated by law." In conjunction with the board, the governor may grant reprieves and pardons "after conviction for an offense against the state except in cases of impeachment."

Section 4 directs that the "term of office of the secretary of state, treasurer, attorney general and state auditor is four years ... [and that] the duties ... of the executive officers shall be prescribed by law." In *State ex rel. Mattson v. Kiedrowski* (1986), the Minnesota supreme court held that although the constitution states that the duties "shall be prescribed by law," the legislature could not "transfer inherent or core functions of executive officers to appointed officials."

Article VI, Judiciary, section 1, as amended in 1982, declares: "The judicial power of the state is vested in a supreme court, a court of appeals, if established by the legislature, a district court and such other courts, judicial officers and commissioners with jurisdiction inferior to the district court as the legislature may establish." **Section 2,** as amended in 1982, states in part: "The supreme court consists of one chief judge [**article V, section 7,** refers to the position as 'chief justice of the supreme court'] and not less than six nor more than eight associate judges as the legislature may establish." The supreme court's jurisdiction encompasses "original jurisdiction in such remedial cases as are prescribed by law, and appellate jurisdiction in all cases" but expressly prohibits trial by jury. In *State v. M.A.P.* (1979), the Minnesota supreme court declared that even where appellate review might be precluded as not timely under statutory provisions, case law, or rules of civil appellate procedure, it could accept jurisdiction in those situations if the interests of justice so warrant. Section 2 also instructs the supreme court to appoint "to serve at its pleasure a clerk, a reporter, a state law librarian and other necessary employees."

Section 5, amended in 1982, states in part: "Judges of the supreme court, the court of appeals and the district court shall be learned in the law." "Learned in the law" is a legal term that means having a law degree and, generally, having been admitted to the bar as proof. Most states, however, specify the number of years a person must have been a member of the state bar to be eligible for the supreme court; Alaska, however, simply requires that members be licensed to practice law in the state, although additional qualifications may be specified by statute. "The qualifications of all other judges and judicial officers," section 5 continues, "shall be prescribed by law."

Section 6, as amended in 1982, prohibits judges from holding "any office under the United States except a commission in a reserve component of the military forces of the United States [or] any other office under this state." **Section 7** sets judges' terms of office as "six years and until their successors are qualified." Judges are elected "by the voters from the area which they are to serve in the manner provided by law." **Section 8** indicates that in case of a vacancy in the office of a judge, the governor appoints "a qualified person" to fill the vacancy until the next general election, when a successor is elected for a six-year term.

Section 9 authorizes the legislature to "provide by law for retirement of all judges and for the extension of the term of any judge who becomes eligible for retirement within three years after expiration of the term for which he is selected." The legislature is also directed to "provide for the retirement, removal or other discipline of any judge who is disabled, incompetent or guilty of conduct prejudicial to the administration of justice."

Impeachment

Article VIII, Impeachment and Removal from Office, section 1, declares: "The house of representatives has the sole power of impeachment through a concurrence of a majority of all its members." Other states require the concurrence of two-thirds of the members present, as does Mississippi, or two-thirds of all the members, as does Vermont. Section 1 continues: "All impeachments shall be tried by the senate ... [and no] person shall be convicted without the concurrence of two-thirds of the senators present." Although this is the same requirement found in the U.S. Constitution, some other state constitutions, such as Delaware's, require the concurrence of two-thirds of all the senators, not just of those present. **Section 2,** as amended in 1982, provides: "The governor, secretary of state, treasurer, auditor, attorney general and the judges of the supreme court, court of appeals and district courts may be impeached for corrupt conduct in office or for crimes and misdemeanors...." Conviction, however, results only in removal from office and disqualification from other offices; the person impeached is not immune from further prosecution under the law.

Direct Democracy

To Provide for Recall of Elected State Officials, an amendment adopted in 1996, makes the governor, lieutenant governor, secretary of state, auditor, treasurer, attorney general, members of the state legislature, and judges of the supreme court, court of appeals, and district courts subject to recall from office by the voters. The grounds for recall of the judges are to be established by the supreme court, and the grounds for recall of other officers include "serious malfeasance or nonfeasance during the term of office in the performance of official duties or conviction during the term of office of a serious crime."

Local Government

Article XII, Special Legislation; Local Government, section 1, prohibits the enactment of a local or special law in certain enumerated cases, including remitting fines, penalties, or forfeitures and changing the names of persons, places, lakes, or rivers. **Section 2** requires that "[e]very law which upon its effective date applies to a single local government unit or to a group of such units in a single county or a number of contiguous counties is a special law and shall name the unit or, in the latter case, the counties to which it applies." **Section 4** provides in part: "Any local government unit when authorized by law may adopt a home rule charter for its government. A charter shall become effective if approved by such majority of the voters of the local government unit as the legislature prescribes by general law."

Taxation and Finance

Article X, Taxation, section 1, asserts in part: "The power of taxation shall never be surrendered, suspended or contracted away. Taxes shall be uniform upon the same class of subjects and shall be levied and collected for public purposes, but public burying grounds, public school houses, public hospitals, academies, colleges, universities, all seminaries of learning, all churches, church property, houses of worship, institutions of purely public charity, and public property used exclusively for any public purpose, shall be exempt from taxation except as provided in this section."

Section 2 encourages forestation and reforestation of private and public lands by authorizing the legislature to enact laws "fixing in advance a definite and limited annual tax on the lands for a term of years and imposing a yield tax on the timber and other forest products at or after the end of the term." **Section 5** authorizes the legislature to "tax aircraft using the airspace overlying the state on a more onerous basis than other personal property."

Article XI, Appropriations and Finances, section 1, mandates: "No money shall be paid out of the treasury of this state except in pursuance on an appropriation by law." **Section 2** provides that "[t]he credit of the state shall not be given or loaned in aid of any individual, association or corporation except as hereinafter provided."

Article IX, Amendments to the Constitution, section 1, provides: "A majority of the members elected to each house of the legislature may propose amendments to this constitution. Proposed amendments shall be published with the laws passed at the same session and submitted to the people for their approval or rejection [by a majority of all the electors voting] at a general election." In *Lyons v. Spaeth* (1945), the Minnesota supreme court stated that "[t]he purpose of constitutional construction [interpretation], as applied to a constitutional provision, is to discover its meaning and to ascertain and give effect to the intent of its framers and the people who adopted it."

Amendment Procedures

Section 2 describes the calling of a constitutional convention: "Two-thirds of the members elected to each house ... may submit to the electors at the next general election the question of calling a convention to revise this constitution. If a majority of all the electors voting at the election vote for a convention, the legislature at its next session, shall provide by law for calling the convention." **Section 3** requires that "three-fifths of all the electors voting on the question" vote to ratify the convention's proposal before "it becomes a new constitution of the state of Minnesota." New York, West Virginia, and most other states do not impose a supermajority requirement for approval of amendments or revisions proposed by a constitutional convention.

MISSISSIPPI

Mississippi was admitted to the Union on December 10, 1817, as the twentieth state. Jackson is the capital of the "Magnolia State," which encompasses some 48,434 square miles and is bordered by Tennessee on the north, Alabama on the east, the Gulf of Mexico and Louisiana on the south, and Louisiana and Arkansas on the west. Mississippi ranks thirty-first among the states with a population of approximately 2.7 million residents. Manufacturing, government, and wholesale and retail trade are among the state's principal economic activities; its chief crops include cotton, rice, and soybeans.

General Information

Government: The governor and lieutenant governor are elected separately for four-year terms and are limited to two terms. The legislature consists of fifty-two senators and 122 members of the house of representatives, all of whom are elected for four-year terms. The supreme court is composed of nine judges elected for eight-year terms.

Dates of Constitutions: 1817, 1832, 1869, and 1890

Constitutional History

Chickasaw, Choctaw, and Natchez peoples lived in the territory that would become the state of Mississippi when the Spaniard Panfilo de Narvaez began exploring it in 1528. The region took its name from *Mississippi* (meaning "large river"), which is what the Chippewas, also known as the Ojibwas, called the now-famous waterway. Although another Spaniard, Hernando de Soto, explored the region in 1540, Spain made no formal claims to these lands. The grant of Carolina to Sir Robert Heath by Charles I of England in 1629 included part of the Mississippi territory, and a second Carolina charter granted by Charles II in 1663 added more of the territory.

In 1682 Robert Cavelier, sieur de La Salle, led an expedition in the Mississippi River valley and claimed it for France. Seventeen years later the French built Fort Maurepas on the Bay of Biloxi. In 1704, to promote settlement of the region, poor young Frenchwomen called "casket girls" were imported to become wives of the settlers, and in 1717 Louis xv chartered the Mississippi Company to encourage exploitation of the area's resources. Under the treaty ending the French and Indian War in 1763, however, the territory was ceded to Great Britain.

During the American Revolution, the Mississippi region, then a part of British West Florida, remained loyal to the Crown, attracting many loyalist settlers. The 1783 treaty ending that war confirmed Spain's conquest of West Florida but left undefined the limits of the Mississippi territory, which Britain had extended to the Yazoo River. By an act dated April 7, 1798, Congress officially assumed jurisdiction of the Mississippi territory partly because of the vacuum of authority there and partly to expedite settlement of claims resulting from the Yazoo land fraud scheme sanctioned by the Georgia legislature in 1795. Georgia's claim to the extremely fertile Yazoo delta in what is now northwestern Mississippi had fueled abortive attempts by land speculators to settle the area.

The 1798 act was modeled on the Northwest Ordinance of 1787 but allowed slavery. An act of Congress on May 10, 1800, established a government for the Mississippi Territory and provided for Georgia's cession of western lands to the new territory.

By 1810 the western part of the Mississippi Territory had a population of around 40,000, and a movement began to acquire statehood. But the residents of the eastern part did not want to be included in a single large state. An act dated March 1, 1817, was passed by Congress to enable the "people of the western part of the Mississippi Territory to form a constitution and state government and for the admission of such state to the Union." The same year Congress carved the Territory of Alabama out of the eastern portion of the Mississippi Territory. A convention controlled by the wealthy residents of Natchez in the southwestern part of the territory met between July 7 and August 15 and produced a conservative constitution that was not submitted to the voters for ratification. The first Mississippi constitution went into effect when the state was admitted to the Union on December 10, 1817.

Pressure from adherents of Jacksonian democracy resulted in a second constitutional convention, held in Jackson in 1832. The new document provided that all public officials, including judges, were to be elected, office holders were to have definite terms of office (no one could serve for life or simply during "good behavior"), and property ownership was no longer necessary to vote or hold office. The Missouri Compromise of 1820, which provided for new states to be equally apportioned between free (nonslave) and slave, and the admission of California as a free state led to a third convention, called in 1851. Although the convention produced no new constitutional document, for the first time the secession of slave states from the Union was openly debated.

In 1861, like other southern states, Mississippi held a convention that passed an ordinance of secession and amended its constitution to conform to the new government of the Confederacy. Following the Civil War, another convention met in August 1865 to rescind the ordinance of secession and amend the 1832 constitution to abolish slavery and disqualify Confederate activists from participating in the new state government. However, the legislature's failure to ratify the Thirteenth Amendment (1865) and Fourteenth Amendment (1868) of the U.S. Constitution precluded the state's return to the Union.

A Reconstructionist constitution drafted by a "black and tan" convention of freedmen and carpetbaggers in 1868 was rejected by the voters on June 28. After some slight changes, it was approved and became effective on February 18, 1869, the date of Mississippi's readmission to the Union. This document contained authorization for public education; a provision requiring separate but equal schools for black and white children was discussed at the convention but was not adopted then (it was included in the 1890 constitution). The Republican Reconstruction government was toppled in 1875, and a new constitution drafted by a convention that met in Jackson from August 12 to November 1, 1890, was promulgated in November without having been submitted to the voters for approval.

Mississippi's 1890 constitution was part of a movement by the state's pre–Civil War establishment to recapture the institutions of state government and circumscribe the recent enfranchisement of former slaves. For example, the document contained a provision for an "understanding" test on the provisions of the constitution, which was used by white registrars to fail blacks and thus prevent them from voting. In *Williams v. Mississippi* (1898), the U.S. Supreme Court upheld the "understanding" test provision, thus diminishing civil rights for blacks in the United States for the next half century. Mississippi's 1890 constitution also states: "Separate schools shall be maintained for children of the white and colored races." This provision and similar ones in the constitutions of other states were ruled repugnant to the U.S. Constitution by the U.S. Supreme Court in *Brown v. Board of Education of Topeka* (1954).

The 1890 constitution is a relatively short document of approximately 24,000 words

The Constitution

and, as of January 1, 1998, has been amended 119 times. It creates a fairly typical structure of government—a plural executive branch, including a secretary of state, treasurer, and auditor of accounts elected statewide in addition to the governor and lieutenant governor; a bicameral legislature; and an elected judiciary—but the document is out of touch with the realities of the state's governing processes. One commentator claims that virtually every bill passed by the legislature is enacted in violation of one or more provisions of the constitution, thus demeaning the concept of constitutional government.

Preamble

The preamble to the 1890 Mississippi constitution reads: "We, the people of Mississippi in convention assembled, grateful to Almighty God, and invoking his blessing on our work, do ordain and establish this constitution."

Fundamental Rights

Article 3, Bill of Rights, section 5, proclaims: "All political power is vested in, and derived from, the people; all government of right originates with the people, is founded upon their will only, and is instituted solely for the good [of] the whole." **Section 6** declares: "The people of this state have the inherent, sole, and exclusive right to regulate the internal government and police thereof, and to alter and abolish their constitution and form of government whenever they deem it necessary to their safety and happiness; Provided, Such change be not repugnant to the constitution of the United States."

Section 7 provides: "The right to withdraw from the Federal Union on account of any real or supposed grievance, shall never be assumed by this state, nor shall any law be passed in derogation of the paramount allegiance of the citizens of this state to the government of the United States." This provision was included in the 1869 constitution and is obviously the result of post–Civil War Reconstructionist influence. **Section 8** states that "[a]ll persons, resident in this state, citizens of the United States, are hereby declared citizens of the state of Mississippi." **Section 9** subordinates the military to civil power, and **section 10** defines treason and requirements for conviction in language similar to that in the U.S. Constitution.

Sections 11 and **12**, respectively, affirm the right to peaceably assemble and petition the government and the right to keep and bear arms. **Section 13** provides that "[t]he freedom of speech and of the press shall be held sacred"; in prosecutions for libel, "if it appear to the jury that the matter charged as libelous is true, and was published with good motives and for justifiable ends, the party [accused] shall be acquitted." In *Ferguson v. Watkins* (1984), the Mississippi supreme court held that doctors who issued an ultimatum to the board of trustees of a hospital regarding a controversial emergency room administrator became public figures and therefore, to successfully sue for libel, the doctors had to prove actual malice by a newspaper writer who criticized them.

Section 14 guarantees due process of law; **section 15** forbids slavery, except as punishment for a crime; and **section 16** prohibits ex post facto laws and laws impairing contracts. **Section 17** guarantees compensation for the taking of private property for public use; moreover, "… the question whether the contemplated use be public shall be a judicial question" regardless of any "legislative assertion that the use is public." **Section 18** bars religious tests for office and confirms religious freedom, although further providing: "The rights hereby secured shall not be construed to justify acts of licentiousness injurious to morals or dangerous to the peace and safety of the state, or to exclude the Holy Bible from use in any public school of this state."

Section 20 stipulates that "[n]o person shall be elected or appointed to office in this state for life or during good behavior, but the term of all officers shall be for some specified period." **Section 21** limits the conditions under which the writ of habeas corpus may be suspended; **section 22** prohibits double jeopardy; and **section 23** bars unreasonable searches and seizures. According to **section 24,** "All courts shall be open; and every person for an injury done him in his lands, goods, person, or reputation, shall have remedy by the due course of law...." In general, however, states may not be sued because of the doctrine of sovereign immunity, and in *Monaco v. Mississippi* (1934), the U.S. Supreme Court ruled that the Eleventh Amendment (1798) of the U.S. Constitution prevented a state of the Union from being sued by a foreign state (in this case the Principality of Monaco) without its consent.

Section 25 mandates: "No person shall be debarred from prosecuting or defending any civil cause for or against him or herself, before any tribunal in the state, by him or herself, or counsel, or both." This language, using both masculine and feminine pronouns, was included in the original 1817 constitution.

Sections 26 through **29** provide for rights of the accused, and **section 30** prohibits imprisonment for debt. Pursuant to **section 31,** "The right of trial by jury shall remain inviolate, but the legislature may, by enactment, provide that in all civil suits tried in the circuit and chancery court, nine or more jurors may agree on the verdict and return it as the verdict of the jury." In *Gilliard v. Mississippi* (1983), the U.S. Supreme Court denied a petition by a black defendant sentenced to death by an all-white jury from which black members had been intentionally removed by the prosecution's peremptory challenges, holding that the states may be considered laboratories for constitutional development, and, therefore "... defendants in Mississippi and numerous other States have no legal remedy for what a majority of this court agrees may well be a constitutional defect in the jury selection process." Justice Thurgood Marshall, joined by Justice William Brennan, dissented from this ruling.

Section 32 provides: "The enumeration of rights in this constitution shall not be construed to deny and impair others retained by, and inherent in, the people."

Article 1, Distribution of Powers, section 1, declares: "The powers of the government of the state of Mississippi shall be divided into three distinct departments, and each of them confided to a separate magistracy, to-wit: those which are legislative to one, those which are judicial to another, and those which are executive to another." **Section 2** restricts persons who are part of one of these departments from exercising "any power properly belonging to either of the others"; moreover, "[t]he acceptance of an office in either of said departments shall, of itself, and at once, vacate any and all offices held by the person so accepting

Division of Powers

in either of the other departments." In *Alexander v. State* (1983), the Mississippi supreme court held that a statute creating positions for legislators on a commission on budget and accounting violated the separation of powers doctrine as expressed in article 1.

Legislative Branch

Article 4, Legislative Department, section 33, vests the state's legislative power "in a legislature which shall consist of a senate and a house of representatives." **Section 34** specifies that members of the house of representatives are chosen "every four years by the qualified electors of the several counties and representative districts." Similarly, **section 35** specifies that senators are chosen "every four years by the qualified electors of the several districts." **Section 36,** as amended in 1912 and 1968, calls for one 125-day regular session every four years and ninety-day sessions for the other three years; however, by joint resolution "by a two-thirds (⅔) vote of those present and voting in each house," the legislature may extend a session "for a period of thirty (30) days...."

Section 38 permits each house to elect its own officers and judge the qualifications and election of its own members. Pursuant to **section 39,** "The senate shall choose a president pro tempore to act in the absence or disability of its presiding officer [the lieutenant governor]." **Section 41,** as amended in 1987, requires a member of the house of representatives to be twenty-one years old, "a qualified elector of the state," and "a resident citizen of the state for (4) four years and within the district such person seeks to serve for (2) two years, immediately preceding his election." **Section 42** requires a senator to be twenty-five years old, a "qualified elector of the state" for four years, and "an actual resident of the district or territory he may be chosen to represent for two years before his election." **Section 44,** as amended in 1992, and **section 45** set forth additional qualifications for and restrictions on legislators.

Section 48 exempts legislators from arrest during legislative sessions and for fifteen days before and after each session "in all cases, except treason, felony, theft, or breach of the peace." The U.S. Constitution and most other state constitutions do not include theft among the exceptions to privilege from arrest.

Section 54 defines a quorum as "[a] majority of each house," although a lesser number may adjourn from day to day and compel attendance. **Section 55** allows each house to determine its own rules, punish members for disorderly behavior, and, "with the concurrence of two-thirds of the members present, expel a member...." According to **section 58,** each house may punish, "by fine and imprisonment, any person not a member who shall be guilty of disrespect to the house by any disorderly or contemptuous behavior in its presence...."

Sections 59 through **75** address the passage of bills. **Section 59** provides: "Bills may originate in either house, and be amended or rejected in the other; and every bill shall be read by its title on three (3) different days in each house, unless two-thirds (⅔) of the house where the same is pending shall dispense with the rules; and every bill shall be read in full immediately before the vote on its final passage upon the demand of any member; and every bill, having passed both houses, shall be signed by the President of the Senate and the Speaker of the House...." Pursuant to **section 65**, "All votes on the final passage of any measure shall be subject to reconsideration for at least one whole legislative day, and no motion to reconsider such vote shall be disposed of adversely on the day on which the original vote was taken, except on the last day of the session."

Section 66 prohibits laws "granting a donation or gratuity in favor of any person or object," except those enacted "by the concurrence of two-thirds of the members elect of each branch of the legislature," and also prohibits such laws for a sectarian purpose or use. **Section 70** provides that revenue bills and any bills "providing for assessments of property for taxation" require a vote "of at least three-fifths of the members of each house present and voting."

Section 72, as amended in 1970, requires that bills that pass both houses of the legislature be presented to the governor for signature. However, **section 60** states in part that "orders, votes, and resolutions of both houses, affecting the prerogatives and duties thereof, or relating to adjournment, to amendments to the Constitution, to the investigation of public officers and the like," do not require the governor's signature. Section 72 continues: "If [the governor] approve [the bill], he shall sign it; but if he does not approve, he shall return it, with his objections, to the House in which it originated...." The governor's veto may be overridden by "two-thirds (⅔) of [each] House." **Section 73** grants the governor the power to "veto parts of any appropriation bill...."

Article 5, Executive, section 116, as amended in 1986, provides: "The chief executive power of this state shall be vested in a Governor who shall hold his office for four (4) years." The governor may succeed himself or herself but is limited to only two terms. **Section 117** requires that the governor be thirty years old, a citizen of the United States for twenty years, and a state resident for "five years next preceding the day of his election."

Executive Branch

Section 119 designates the governor the commander in chief of the state's army, navy, and militia, "except when they shall be called into the service of the United States." **Sections 120** and **121**, respectively, authorize the governor to "require information in writing from the officers in the executive departments of the state on any subject relating to the duties of their respective offices" and "convene the legislature in extraordinary session whenever, in his judgment, the public interest requires it." Pursuant to **section 53**, "For reasonable cause, which shall not be sufficient grounds of impeachment, the governor shall, on joint address of two-thirds of each branch of the legislature, remove from office the judges of the Supreme and inferior courts...."

Section 122 requires the governor to "from time to time, give the legislature information of the state of the government, and recommend for consideration such measures as may be deemed necessary and expedient." **Section 123** mandates: "The governor shall see that the laws are faithfully executed." **Section 124** empowers the incumbent "to grant reprieves and pardons [in all criminal and penal cases, except treason and impeachment], to remit fines, and in cases of forfeiture, to stay the collection until the end of the next session of the legislature, and by and with the consent of the senate to remit forfeitures." According to **section 125**, "The governor shall have the power, and it is hereby made his duty, to suspend alleged defaulting state and county treasurers, and defaulting tax-collectors, pending the investigation of their respective accounts...."

Section 128, as amended in 1992, provides for a lieutenant governor "who shall be elected at the same time, in the same manner, and for the same term, and who shall possess the same qualifications as required of the Governor," although they are elected on separate tickets. The lieutenant governor may succeed himself or herself in office, although "no person who has been elected to the office of Lieutenant Governor for two successive terms shall be eligible to hold that office until one term has intervened." **Section 129** designates the lieutenant governor to serve as president of the senate; as such, "[i]n committee of the whole he may debate all questions, and where there is an equal division in the senate, or on a joint vote of both houses, he shall give the casting vote."

Section 131, as amended in 1992, outlines the order of succession to the governorship. If the governor's office becomes vacant, "by death or otherwise, the Lieutenant Governor shall possess the powers and discharge the duties of the office." For temporary periods—for example, when the governor is absent from the state—the lieutenant governor acts as governor. Next in line of succession are the president pro tempore of the senate and the speaker of the house.

Sections 133 and **134,** as amended in 1986, enumerate other executive officers who are elected statewide, including the secretary of state, treasurer, and auditor of accounts.

Judicial Branch

Article 6, Judiciary, section 144, declares: "The judicial power of the state shall be vested in a Supreme Court and such other courts as are provided for in this constitution." **Section 145B,** as amended in 1950 and 1952, provides that "[t]he supreme court shall consist of nine judges, ... any five of whom when convened, shall constitute a quorum."

Section 149, as amended in 1916, sets the term for supreme court judges at eight years and directs the legislature to ensure "that the offices of not more than a majority of the judges ... shall become vacant at any one time...." The judges are elected from three supreme court districts. In *Magnolia Bar Ass'n, Inc. v. Lee* (1992), the U.S. District Court ruled that dividing the state into three east-west supreme court voting districts did not dilute black votes and thus did not violate the Voting Rights Act of 1965, even though it split the majority black population in the western part of the state among predominantly majority white districts. **Section 150** requires that a supreme court judge be thirty years old "at the time of his appointment, and ... a practicing attorney and a citizen of the state for five years immediately preceding such appointment."

Section 146, as amended in 1984, establishes the supreme court's jurisdiction: "The Supreme Court shall have such jurisdiction as properly belongs to a court of appeals and shall exercise no jurisdiction on matters other than those specifically provided by this Constitution or by general law. The Legislature may by general law provide for the Supreme Court to have original and appellate jurisdiction as to any appeal directly from an administrative agency charged by law with the responsibility for approval or disapproval of rates sought to be charged the public by any public utility." Pursuant to **section 147,** "No judgment or decree in any chancery or circuit court rendered in a civil cause shall be reversed or annulled on the ground of want of jurisdiction to render said judgment or decrees from any error or mistake as to whether the cause in which it was rendered was of equity or common-law jurisdiction; but if the Supreme Court shall find error in the proceedings other than as to jurisdiction, and it shall be necessary to remand the case, the Supreme Court may remand it to that court which, in its opinion, can best determine the controversy."

Section 149A, as amended in 1916, provides: "The Supreme Court shall have power, under such rules and regulations as it may adopt to sit in two divisions of three judges each, any two of whom when convened shall form a quorum; each division shall have full power to hear and adjudge all cases that may be assigned to it by the court." In cases where a judge certifies that a division's decision is in conflict with court precedents, the matter is to be considered by the full court.

Section 152, as amended in 1992, authorizes the legislature to "divide the state into an appropriate number of circuit court districts and chancery court districts" and "by statute, establish certain criteria by which the number of judges in each district shall be determined, such criteria to be based on population, the number of cases filed and other appropriate data." According to **section 162,** "All cases that may be brought in the chancery court whereof the circuit court has exclusive jurisdiction shall be transferred to the circuit court."

Section 173 provides: "There shall be an attorney-general elected at the same time and in the same manner as the governor is elected, whose term of office shall be four years.... The qualification for the attorney-general shall be the same as herein pre-scribed for judges of the circuit and chancery courts." **Section 177** grants the governor the power to fill vacancies in the office of judge or chancellor [in the chancery court], and **section 177A,** added by amendment in 1979, creates a commission on judicial per-formance, which can make recommendations to the supreme court for the removal, suspension, censure, reprimand, and retirement of judges.

Article 4, Legislative Department, section 49, states: "The house of representatives shall have the sole power of impeachment; but two-thirds of all the members present must concur therein. All impeachments shall be tried by the senate...." Under **section 52,** "... no person shall be convicted without concurrence of two-thirds of all the senators present." **Section 50** notes that "[t]he governor and all other civil officers of this state, shall be liable to impeachment for treason, bribery, or any high crime or misdemeanor in office." According to **section 51,** conviction on impeachment results only in "removal from office and disqualification to hold any office" in the state; however, "the party con-victed shall, nevertheless, be subject to ... punishment according to law."

Impeachment

Article 15, Amendments to the Constitution, provides for direct democracy procedures only with respect to "preparing and enacting constitutional amendments by initiative."

Direct Democracy

Education

Article 8, Education, section 201, as amended in 1934, 1960, and 1987, mandates: "The Legislature shall, by general law, provide for the establishment, maintenance and support of free public schools upon such conditions and limitations as the Legislature may prescribe." Pursuant to section 206, as amended in 1904, "There shall be a state common-school fund, to be taken from the General Fund in the State Treasury, which shall be used for the maintenance and support of the common schools. Any county or separate school district may levy an additional tax, as prescribed by general law, to maintain its schools. The state common-school fund shall be distributed among the several counties and separate school districts in proportion to the number of educable children in each...."

Environment

Article 11, Levees, section 227, provides: "A levee system shall be maintained in the state as provided in this article." Section 228 states: "The division heretofore made by the legislature of the alluvial land of the state into two levee districts—viz., the Yazoo-Mississippi Delta Levee District and the Mississippi Levee District, as shown by the laws creating the same, and the amendments thereto—is hereby recognized, and said districts shall so remain until changed by law; but the legislature may hereafter add to either of said districts any other alluvial land in the state."

Amendment Procedures

Article 15, Amendments to the Constitution, section 273, as amended in 1992, provides in part: "(1) Amendments to this constitution may be proposed by the Legislature or by initiative of the people." Section 273(2) outlines the procedure: "Whenever two thirds (⅔) of each house of the Legislature, which two thirds (⅔) shall consist of not less than a majority of the members elected to each house, shall deem any change, alteration, or amendment necessary to this Constitution, such proposed amendment ... shall be read and passed by two-thirds (⅔) vote of each house.... [After public notice] if it shall appear that a majority of the qualified electors voting directly for or against the same shall have voted for the proposed change ... then it shall be inserted as part of the Constitution by proclamation of the Secretary of State...."

Section 273(3) begins: "The people reserve unto themselves the power to propose and enact constitutional amendments by initiative." If at least twelve percent of the voters who voted for all the candidates for governor in the last election sign a petition for a proposed amendment within a twelve-month period, it is placed on the ballot at the next general election. However, the number of signatures from any one congressional district that may be used to obtain the required twelve percent is limited. Section 273(5) stipulates that certain parts of the constitution, including the bill of rights, may not be amended by initiative. According to section 273(6), a constitutional initiative may be adopted "by a majority vote of each house of the Legislature" or may be amended or rejected by the legislature; in any case the original initiative and any proposed amendment adopted by the legislature are submitted to the voters for approval. Section 273(7) provides: "An initiative or legislative alternative must receive a majority of the votes thereon and not less than forty percent (40%) of the total votes cast at the election," and the proposal "receiving the highest number of affirmative votes shall prevail."

Missouri became the twenty-fourth state of the United States on August 10, 1821. Jefferson City is the capital of the "Show Me State." Some 69,709 square miles in area, Missouri is bordered by Iowa on the north; Illinois, Kentucky, and Tennessee on the east; Arkansas on the south; and Oklahoma and Kansas on the west. Missouri ranks sixteenth among the states in population with approximately 5.3 million inhabitants. The state's principal industries include agriculture, manufacturing, and aerospace; its chief crops are soybeans, corn, wheat, and hay.

Government: The governor and lieutenant governor are elected separately for four-year terms, and the governor is limited to two terms. The legislature, called the general assembly, consists of thirty-four senators elected for four-year terms, half elected every two years, and 163 members of the house of representatives elected for two-year terms. Legislators are limited to serving eight years in each house and a total of sixteen years in both houses combined. The supreme court consists of a chief justice and six additional judges who are initially appointed by the governor from a list submitted by a judicial nominating commission; they must stand for election after one year in office and afterward serve for twelve-year terms.

Dates of Constitutions: 1821, 1865, 1875, and 1945

Algonquin Sauk, Osage, Iowa, Missouri, and Kansa peoples, among others, inhabited the region that would become the state of Missouri when the Spanish explorer Hernando de Soto led an expedition there in 1541. France, however, was first to become interested in the territory, and by 1724 Etienne Véniard de Bourgmond had established Fort Orleans near a village of Missouri people; the following year he returned to France with a delegation of them. French trappers and lead miners built the first permanent settlement, Ste. Genevieve, in 1735.

Although France's power waned in Europe and America after its 1763 defeat by Great Britain in the French and Indian War, a village was established in Missouri territory in 1764 in honor of the medieval French king Louis IX, known as St. Louis. Its founder, Pierre Liguest Laclède, was well acquainted with the works of John Locke and Jean-Jacques Rousseau, two philosophers who would greatly influence constitutionalism in the United States and France. Spain tried to fill the void left by France, but few Spanish settlers came to Missouri, although by 1776 St. Louis had become the capital of Upper Louisiana.

A 1795 agreement between Spain and the United States opened the Mississippi River to trade with Americans, and immigration increased. By treaty in 1800, Spain ceded its rights to the Louisiana Territory to France, which in turn sold them to the United States in 1803. President Thomas Jefferson commissioned Meriwether Lewis and William Clark to explore the new territory, and they proceeded from St. Louis up the Missouri River in 1804. Both Lewis and Clark later served as territorial governors of Missouri.

When Louisiana became a state in 1812, most of what remained of the Louisiana Purchase was renamed the Missouri Territory. On April 29, 1816, Congress authorized the inhabitants to elect members of a legislative council (formerly they had been selected by the federal government). With the admission of Illinois as a state in 1818, Missouri sought enabling legislation from Congress to draft a constitution and apply for statehood. The

General Information

Constitutional History

legislation was approved on March 6, 1820, and a convention was assembled in St. Louis on June 12. A provision in the draft document regarding slavery delayed admission and led to the Missouri Compromise, by which Congress agreed to admit new states individually on the basis of whether they were free (nonslave) or slave states.

By resolution on March 2, 1821, Congress made it a condition of Missouri's admission as a slave state that the portion of the slavery provision in the state's draft constitution denying free blacks the right to settle there, which might be an unconstitutional denial of U.S. citizenship rights, never be implemented. After Missouri agreed in the Solemn Public Act on June 26, 1821, admission was granted on August 10, 1821, and the state's first constitution took effect on that date. The growth of the state's economy led to a constitutional convention in Jefferson City in 1845, but the document it produced was narrowly rejected at the polls.

In 1865 a state form of Reconstruction was implemented in a new constitution, which provided for popular ratification of amendments. This document was approved by the voters on June 6 and went into effect on July 4, 1865. Another constitution, which introduced the concept of home rule for local governments, was drafted by a convention meeting in Jefferson City in 1875. It was ratified at the polls on October 30 and went into effect on November 30, 1875. A year-long convention that assembled in Jefferson City on September 21, 1943, produced Missouri's current constitution, which was approved by the voters on February 27, 1945, and became effective on March 30 of that year.

The Constitution

Beginning a wave of post–World War II state constitutions, which includes the 1948 New Jersey constitution and the 1964 Michigan constitution, the 1945 Missouri constitution is relatively long, with approximately 42,000 words and ninety amendments as of January 1, 1998. The innovative document, since often copied, introduced the "Missouri Plan" of nonpolitical judicial selection.

The Missouri constitution is typical of many current state constitutions in that it provides for a plural, or divided, executive branch that includes three statewide elected officials as well as the governor and lieutenant governor. Unlike the constitutions of most other states that specify gubernatorial term limits, however, the Missouri constitution strictly limits the governor to two terms, not just two consecutive terms. The legislative branch article also contains a section, adopted in 1992, requiring term limits for members of Congress to become effective "when at least one-half of the states enact [similar] term limits"; until then the section asks that the term limits be observed voluntarily.

Preamble

The preamble to the 1945 Missouri constitution reads: "We, the people of Missouri, with profound reverence for the Supreme Ruler of the Universe, and grateful for His goodness, do establish this Constitution for the better government of the state." Most preambles include the word *ordain* as well as *establish*.

Fundamental Rights

Article I, Bill of Rights, begins: *"In order to assert our rights, acknowledge our duties, and proclaim the principles on which our government is founded, we declare:* **Section 1.** That all political power is vested in and derived from the people; that all government of right originates from the people, is founded upon their will only, and is instituted solely for the good of the whole." **Section 2** declares: "... [A]ll constitutional government is intended to promote the general welfare of the people. . . ." **Section 3** states that "the people of this state have the inherent, sole and exclusive right to regulate the internal government and police thereof, and to alter and abolish their constitution and form of government whenever they may deem it necessary to their safety and happiness, provided such change be not repugnant to the Constitution of the United States." In *Missouri v. Holland* (1920), the U.S. Supreme Court held that a treaty between the United States and the United Kingdom on behalf of Canada gave Congress authority under the "necessary and proper" clause of the U.S. Constitution to enact legislation that otherwise might be deemed to interfere with the powers reserved to the states by the Tenth Amendment (1791) to the U.S. Constitution.

Section 4 proclaims: ". . . [A]ll proposed amendments to the Constitution of the United States qualifying or affecting the individual liberties of the people or which in any wise may impair the right of local self-government belonging to the people of this state, should be submitted to conventions of the people." **Section 5** guarantees freedom of religion, conscience, and belief, although "this section shall not be construed to excuse acts of licentiousness, nor to justify practices inconsistent with good order, peace or safety of the state, or with the rights of others." According to **section 6**, religious support is voluntary; however, "if any person shall voluntarily make a contract for any such object, he shall be held to the performance of the same." **Section 7** prohibits public aid for religious purposes.

Sections 8 and **9**, respectively, guarantee freedom of speech, "no matter by what means communicated," and "the right peaceably to assemble . . . and to apply to those invested with the powers of government for redress of grievances. . . ." **Section 10** states that "no person shall be deprived of life, liberty or property without due process of law." **Section 11** prohibits imprisonment for debt, "except for nonpayment of fines and penalties imposed by law." The constitutions of a number of other states, including Illinois, make exception for fraud. Pursuant to **section 12**, "[T]he privilege of the writ of habeas corpus shall never be suspended." **Section 13** prohibits ex post facto laws, laws impairing contracts, and "any irrevocable grant of special privileges or immunities."

Section 14 affirms that "the courts of justice shall be open to every person . . ."; **section 15** prohibits unreasonable searches and seizures; and **section 16** provides for grand juries "to investigate and return indictments for all character and grades of crime . . ."; furthermore, "the power of grand juries to inquire into the willful misconduct in office of public officers, and to find indictments in connection therewith, shall never be suspended." **Section 17** provides for indictments and information in criminal cases. **Sections 18(a)** and **18(b)**, respectively, provide for rights of the accused and depositions in felony cases; **section 19** prohibits self-incrimination and double jeopardy; **section 20** guarantees bail "except for capital offenses, when the proof is evident or the presumption great"; and **section 21** prohibits excessive bail, excessive fines, and cruel and unusual punishment.

Section 22(a) states in part that "the right of trial by jury as heretofore enjoyed shall remain inviolate; provided that a jury for the trial of criminal and civil cases in courts

not of record may consist of less than twelve citizens as may be prescribed by law...."
And **section 22(b)** declares: "No citizen shall be disqualified from jury service because
of sex, but the court shall excuse any woman who requests exemption therefrom before
being sworn as a juror." **Section 23** guarantees the right to bear arms but not to carry
concealed weapons; **section 24** subordinates the military to civil power and limits the
quartering of soldiers in private homes; and **section 25** provides that "all elections shall
be free and open; and no power, civil or military, shall at any time interfere to prevent
the free exercise of the right of suffrage."

Sections 27 and **28**, respectively, provide for state eminent domain rights and the right
to compensation for the taking of private property. **Section 29** states that "employees
shall have the right to organize and to bargain collectively through representatives of
their own choosing." **Section 30** defines treason, prohibits a person from being "attainted
of treason or felony" and corruption of blood, and guarantees that estates of suicides
will "descend or vest as in cases of natural death." **Section 31** prohibits the fixing of fines
or punishments by any administrative agencies. **Section 32**, adopted in 1992, provides
rights for victims of crime.

Division of Powers

Article II, The Distribution of Powers, section 1, declares: "The powers of government shall
be divided into three distinct departments—the legislative, executive and judicial—each
of which shall be confided to a separate magistracy, and no person, or collection of
persons, charged with the exercise of powers properly belonging to one of those
departments, shall exercise any power properly belonging to either of the others, except
in the instances in this constitution expressly directed or permitted." In *Americans
United v. Rogers* (1976), the Missouri supreme court declared that "[j]udicial deference
[to the legislature] is not indicative of the avoidance of a duty but to the contrary is
the performance thereof with an appreciation that judicial interference with the legislative process should occur only when there is an unavoidable and legally compelling
reason to do so."

Legislative Branch

Article III, Legislative Department, section 1, proclaims: "The legislative power shall be
vested in a senate and house of representatives to be styled 'The General Assembly of
the State of Missouri.'" **Section 2,** as amended in 1966 and 1982, specifies that "[t]he
house of representatives shall consist of one hundred sixty-three members elected at
each general election ... ," while **section 5,** as amended in 1966, provides in part: "The
Senate shall consist of thirty-four members elected by the qualified voters of the respective districts for four years."

Section 11 states in part that "the whole number of representatives and the senators
from the districts having even numbers, who shall compose the first class" are elected
at the first election in 1946; two years later all the representatives and the remainder of
the senators, "who shall compose the second class," are elected, "and so on at each
succeeding general election." **Section 8,** adopted in 1992, sets term limits for state legislators: "No one shall be elected or appointed to serve more than eight years total in any
one house of the General Assembly nor more than sixteen years total in both houses...."

Section 4 requires that representatives be at least twenty-four years old, "qualified voter[s]" of the state for two years, and residents of their county or district for one year. **Section 6** requires that senators be at least thirty years old, "qualified voter[s]" of the state for three years, and residents of their district for one year. Pursuant to **section 12**, "No person holding any lucrative office or employment under the United States, this state or any municipality thereof shall hold the office of senator or representative." **Section 13** states: "If any senator or representative remove his residence from the district or county for which he was elected, his office shall thereby be vacated."

Section 18 empowers each house to appoint its own officers; be sole judge of the qualifications, election, and returns of its members; and establish its own rules, "except as herein provided." In addition, each house "may arrest and punish ... any person not a member ... [for] disorderly or contemptuous behavior ... ; may punish its members for disorderly conduct; and, with the concurrence of two-thirds of all members elect, may expel a member [although] no member shall be expelled a second time for the same cause." **Section 19** exempts legislators from arrest during legislative sessions and for "the fifteen days next before the commencement and after the termination of each session," except in cases of treason, felony, or breach of the peace; moreover, "they shall not be questioned for any speech or debate in either house in any other place." **Section 20**, as amended in 1970 and 1988, defines a quorum as "[a] majority of the elected members of each house," although "a smaller number may adjourn from day to day, and may compel the attendance of absent members...."

Section 21 states in part: "No law shall be passed except by bill, and no bill shall be so amended in its passage through either house as to change its original purpose. Bills may originate in either house and may be amended or rejected by the other. Every bill shall be read by title on three different days in each house." According to **section 22**, as amended in 1970 and 1988, "Every bill shall be referred to a committee of the house in which it is pending." By a vote of one-third of the members of each house, however, a bill can be moved out of committee for consideration. **Section 23** requires, with certain exceptions, that bills not "contain more than one subject which shall be clearly expressed in its title"; and **section 24** requires bills to be "printed and copies distributed among the members...." **Section 25** provides that bills generally must be introduced before the sixty-first day of a legislative session.

Section 27 states that final passage of a bill requires that "a vote by yeas and nays be taken and a majority of the members elected to each house be recorded as voting favorably." **Section 29**, as amended in 1970, provides that in general no bill except an appropriations bill takes effect "until ninety days after the adjournment of the session in either odd-numbered or even-numbered years at which it was enacted." Pursuant to **section 30**, bills passed must be signed "by the presiding officer of each house in open session." And **section 31**, as amended in 1986, mandates: "Every [passed] bill ... shall be presented to and considered by the governor," who has fifteen days in which to return it "endorsed" or "accompanied by his objections" to the house in which it originated. The governor's veto may be overridden by "two-thirds of the elected members" in each house.

Section 39, as amended in 1978, 1984, 1986, and 1994, enumerates certain limitations on the legislature's power. **Sections 40(1)** through **40(29)** list subjects regarding which the legislature may not pass local or special laws, and **section 40(30)** prohibits a local or special law "where a general law can be made applicable," noting that such a determination is a judicial question.

Section 45(a), added in 1992, provides: "**(1)** No United States Senator from Missouri shall serve more than two terms in the United States Senate, and no United States Representative from Missouri shall serve more than four terms in the United States House of Representatives.... The provisions of this subsection (1) shall become effective whenever at least one-half of the states enact [similar] term limits.... **(2)** The people of Missouri declare that ... their intention is that federal officials elected from Missouri will continue voluntarily to observe the wishes of the people as stated in this section...."

Executive Branch

Article IV, Executive Department, section 1, vests the state's supreme executive power in the governor, who, according to **section 2**, "shall take care that the laws are distributed and faithfully executed, and shall be a conservator of the peace." The constitutions of most states tend to follow the language of the U.S. Constitution and simply direct that the governor, like the president, "shall take care that the laws be faithfully executed."

Section 17, as amended in 1970, stipulates: "The governor, lieutenant governor, secretary of state, state treasurer and attorney general shall be elected at the presidential elections for terms of four years each.... No person shall be elected governor or treasurer more than twice...." **Section 3** requires the governor to be thirty years old, a U.S. citizen for fifteen years, and a state resident for ten years before the election. **Section 10** provides that the lieutenant governor must have the same qualifications as the governor, although they are elected on separate tickets, and serve as ex officio president of the senate; as such, "[i]n [the] committee of the whole he may debate all questions, and shall cast the deciding vote on equal division in the senate and on joint vote of both houses."

Section 17, as amended in 1970, also specifies: "The heads of all the executive departments shall be appointed by the governor, by and with the advice and consent of the senate. All appointive officers may be removed by the governor and shall possess the qualifications required by this constitution or by law." According to **section 4**, "The governor shall fill all vacancies in public offices unless otherwise provided by law, and his appointees shall serve until their successors are duly elected or appointed and qualified." **Section 5** provides in part: "The governor shall commission all officers unless otherwise provided by law."

Section 6 mandates: "The governor shall be the commander in chief of the militia, except when it is called into the service of the United States, and may call out the militia to execute the laws, suppress actual and prevent threatened insurrection, and repel invasion." **Section 7** empowers the governor to "grant reprieves, commutations and pardons, after conviction, for all offenses except treason and cases of impeachment, upon such conditions and with such restrictions and limitations as he may deem proper, subject to provisions of law as to the manner of applying for pardons"; however, "[t]he power to pardon shall not include the power to parole."

Section 8 requires that joint resolutions of the legislature, except those dealing with adjournment, joint sessions, and amendment of the constitution, be approved by the governor. (This power is in addition to the veto power conferred by **article III, section 32.**) **Section 9** directs that "[t]he governor shall, at the commencement of each session of the general assembly, at the close of his term of office, and at such other times as he may deem necessary, give to the general assembly information as to the state of the government, and shall recommend to its consideration such measures as he shall deem necessary and expedient."

Section 24 requires that the governor submit to the legislature "within thirty days after it convenes in each regular session … a budget for the ensuing appropriation period … together with his recommendations of any laws necessary to provide revenues sufficient to meet the expenditures." Pursuant to **section 26,** "The governor may object to one or more items or portions of items of appropriation of money in any bill presented to him, while approving other portions of the bill." The constitutions of many states, including Illinois, Montana, and Mississippi, for example, restrict the item veto to appropriations bills.

Section 11(a), adopted in 1968, states: "If the governor-elect dies before taking office, the lieutenant governor-elect shall take the term of the governor-elect. On the death, conviction or impeachment, or resignation of the governor, the lieutenant governor shall become governor for the remainder of the term." **Section 11(b),** adopted in 1968, provides for the lieutenant governor and others in the line of succession to become acting governor in the event of the governor's temporary inability to perform the duties of office.

Article V, Judicial Department, section 1, as amended in 1970 and 1976, declares: "The judicial power of the state shall be vested in a supreme court, a court of appeals consisting of districts as prescribed by law, and circuit courts." **Section 2,** as amended in 1884 and 1890, designates the supreme court "the highest court in the state." It is made up of seven judges, "who shall hold their sessions in Jefferson City at times fixed by the court." According to **section 19,** as amended in 1976, "Judges of the supreme court and of the court of appeals shall be selected for terms of twelve years...."

Judicial Branch

Section 21, as amended in 1976, provides in part that supreme court and court of appeals judges must be U.S. citizens for fifteen years, "qualified voters of the state" for nine years, and thirty years old. In addition, "[e]very supreme, appellate, circuit, and associate court judge shall be licensed to practice law in this state."

Section 8, as amended in 1970 and 1976, directs: "The judges of the supreme court shall elect from their number a chief justice to preside over the court en banc.... The terms of the chief justice and chief judges shall be fixed by the courts over which they preside. The chief justice of the supreme court shall be the chief administrative officer of the judicial system and, subject to the supervisory authority of the supreme court, shall supervise the administration of the courts of this state."

Section 3, as amended in 1970, 1976, and 1982, delineates the supreme court's jurisdiction: "The supreme court shall have exclusive appellate jurisdiction in all cases involving the validity of a treaty or statute of the United States, or of a statute or provision of the constitution of this state, the construction of the revenue laws of this state, the title to any state office and in all cases where the punishment imposed is death. The court of appeals shall have general appellate jurisdiction in all cases except those within the exclusive jurisdiction of the supreme court." **Section 5,** as amended in 1976, provides: "The supreme court may establish rules relating to practice, procedure and pleading for all courts and administrative tribunals, which shall have the force and effect of law. The rules shall not change substantive rights, or the law relating to evidence, the oral examination of witnesses, juries, the right of trial by jury, or the right of appeal.... Any rule may be annulled or amended in whole or in part by a law limited to that purpose."

Section 24.1, as amended in 1976, creates a "commission on retirement, removal, and discipline ... , [which] shall receive and investigate all requests and suggestions for retirement for disability, and all complaints concerning misconduct of all judges...." **Section 24.2** states: "Upon the recommendation of an affirmative vote of at least four members of the commission, the supreme court en banc shall retire from office any judge ... who is found to be unable to discharge the duties of his office...." Pursuant to **section 24.3,** the supreme court, if it concurs with the commission's recommendation, "shall remove, suspend, discipline or reprimand any judge of any court...." **Section 25(a),** as amended in 1976, provides that "[w]henever a vacancy shall occur [on the] supreme court [or the] court of appeals ... , the governor shall fill such vacancy by appointing one of three persons possessing the qualifications for such office, who shall be nominated ... by a nonpartisan judicial commission...."

Section 26, as amended in 1976, stipulates: "**1.** All judges other than municipal judges shall retire at the age of seventy years, except as provided in the schedule to this article, under a retirement plan provided by law."

Impeachment

Article VII, Public Officers, section 1, states: "All elective executive officials of the state, and judges of the supreme court, courts of appeals and circuit courts shall be liable to impeachment for crimes, misconduct, habitual drunkenness, willful neglect of duty, corruption in office, incompetency, or any offense involving moral turpitude or oppression in office." This list of grounds for impeachment is one of the most extensive found in state constitutions.

Section 2 directs: "The house of representatives shall have the sole power of impeachment. All impeachments shall be tried before the supreme court, except that the governor or a member of the supreme court shall be tried by a special commission of seven eminent jurists to be elected by the senate.... [N]o person shall be convicted without the concurrence of five-sevenths of the court or special commission." The constitutions of most states provide that impeachments are tried in the senate rather than the supreme court and that conviction requires a two-thirds majority.

Section 3 notes that a judgment of impeachment results only in removal but does not prevent further punishment under the law, and **section 4** states: "Except as provided in this constitution, all officers not subject to impeachment shall be subject to removal from office in the manner and for the causes provided by law."

Article III, Legislative Department, sections 49 through **53,** prescribe procedures for popular initiative and referendum. In *State ex rel. Voss v. Davis* (1967), the Missouri supreme court reasoned that initiative and referendum provisions in the state constitution should be liberally construed in favor of the people's right to determine all proper questions by free and open elections.

Direct Democracy

Article VI, Local Government, section 19, as adopted in 1920 and amended in 1971, states in part: "Any city having more than five thousand inhabitants or any other incorporated city as may be provided by law may frame and adopt a charter for its own government." **Section 19(a),** adopted in 1971, provides: "Any city which adopts or has adopted a charter for its own government, shall have all powers which the general assembly . . . has authority to confer . . . [and such] a city shall, in addition to its home rule powers, have all powers conferred by law."

Local Government

Article X, Taxation, section 1, mandates: "The taxing power may be exercised by the general assembly for state purposes, and by counties and other political subdivisions under power granted to them by the general assembly for county, municipal and other corporate purposes." **Section 23,** adopted in 1980, provides in part: "Notwithstanding other provisions of this constitution or other law, any taxpayer of the state, county, or other political subdivision shall have standing to bring suit in a circuit court of proper venue . . . and, if the suit is sustained, [the plaintiff] shall receive from the applicable unit of government his costs, including reasonable attorneys' fees incurred in maintaining such suit."

Taxation and Finance

Article IX, Education, section 1, as amended in 1976, declares: "**(a)** A general diffusion of knowledge and intelligence being essential to the preservation of the rights and liberties of the people, the general assembly shall establish and maintain free public schools for the gratuitous instruction of all persons in this state within ages not in excess of twenty-one years as prescribed by law. **(b)** Specific schools for any contiguous territory may be established by law. Adult education may be provided from funds other than ordinary school revenues." In *Missouri ex rel. Gaines v. Canada* (1938), some sixteen years before *Brown v. Board of Education of Topeka* (1954), the U.S. Supreme Court found that Missouri's offer to pay for a black resident to attend an out-of-state law school rather than accommodate him at the state university law school violated the guarantee of equal protection under the Fourteenth Amendment (1868) of the U.S. Constitution.

Education

Health and Welfare

Article IV, Executive Department, section 37, as amended in 1972, provides: "The health and general welfare of the people are matters of primary public concern; and to secure them there shall be established a department of social services in charge of a director appointed by the governor, by and with the advice and consent of the senate, charged with promoting improved health and other social services to the citizens of the state as provided by law, and the general assembly may grant power with respect thereto to counties, cities or other political subdivisions of the state."

Amendment Procedures

Article XII, Amending the Constitution, section 2(a), states: "Constitutional amendments may be proposed at any time by a majority of the members-elect of each house of the general assembly, the vote to be taken by yeas and nays and entered on the journal." Pursuant to **section 2(b),** "All amendments proposed by the general assembly or by the initiative shall be submitted to the electors for their approval … at the next general election, or at a special election called by the governor.… If a majority of the votes cast thereon is in favor of any amendment, the same shall take effect at the end of thirty days after the election.…"

Section 3(a) provides: "At the general election on the first Tuesday following the first Monday in November 1962, and every twenty years thereafter, the secretary of state shall … submit to the electors … the question 'Shall there be a convention to revise and amend the constitution?'" The governor must call a convention "if a majority of the votes cast thereon is for the affirmative." **Section 3(c)** directs that a constitution or constitutional amendments proposed by the convention be submitted to the voters "at a special election not less than sixty days nor more than six months after the adjournment of the convention. Upon [their] approval … the same shall take effect at the end of thirty days after the election.…"

On November 8, 1889, Montana became the forty-first state of the United States. The capital of the "Treasure State," which encompasses some 147,046 square miles, is Helena. Montana is bordered by the Canadian provinces of British Columbia, Alberta, and Saskatchewan on the north, North Dakota and South Dakota on the east, Wyoming on the south, and Idaho on the west. With approximately 870,000 inhabitants, Montana ranks forty-fourth among the states in population. Its principal industries include agriculture, timber, and mining; among its chief crops are wheat, barley, and sugar beets.

Government: The governor and lieutenant governor are elected jointly for four-year terms and are limited to holding office for eight years in any sixteen-year period. The legislature consists of fifty senators elected for four-year terms, half elected every two years, and 100 members of the house of representatives elected for two-year terms; all are eligible to serve for only eight years in any sixteen-year period. The supreme court includes a chief justice and six additional justices elected for eight-year terms.

Dates of Constitutions: 1889 and 1973

General Information

Constitutional History

The Cheyenne, Blackfoot, and Crow peoples, among others, inhabited the land that would become the state of Montana when the sons of Pierre Gaultier de Varennes, sieur de La Vérendrye, first saw the "Shining Mountains" of what was most likely the Big Horn mountain range in 1743. The Vérendrye family tried to claim the region for France, but its 1763 defeat in the French and Indian War left the Montana territory claimed by both Spain and Great Britain. Because no nation was rushing to settle the region, the local inhabitants were disturbed only by occasional Canadian trappers and traders.

Britain's defeat in the Revolutionary War moved its borders north to Canada. Spain was then alone in claiming the Montana ("mountainous" in Spanish) territory, which it eventually ceded to France in 1800. Under the terms of the Louisiana Purchase of 1803, the United States acquired the rights to the Montana region. Commissioned by President Thomas Jefferson to explore the nation's new western frontier, Meriwether Lewis and William Clark led an expedition through Montana in the summer of 1805. In November 1807 Manuel Lisa established a trading post where the Yellowstone and Little Big Horn Rivers meet, and two years later another post was built near the present-day town of Thompson Falls.

By treaty in 1846 the Montana-Canada border was officially demarcated, and two years later Congress included Montana in the newly organized Oregon Territory. The administration of this vast region fell to the Washington Territory in 1853, the Nebraska Territory in 1854, and the Idaho Territory in 1863. On May 26, 1864, an act of Congress was approved "to provide a temporary Government for the Territory of Montana," and the following year Virginia City became its capital. The territorial legislature adjourned its first session without providing for further meetings, but a constitutional convention was called in 1866 to organize a new government. The 1870 census reflected a population of only some 20,000 people—too few for Montana to acquire statehood.

Discoveries of gold, silver, and copper spurred an increase in settlers, as did the federal government's effort to contain the indigenous peoples after the defeat of General George Custer at the Battle of the Little Big Horn in June 1876 and the opening of the Northern

Pacific Railroad line along the territory's eastern border in 1881. In 1884 another constitutional convention produced a document that was sent to Congress with a petition for statehood. Congress rejected the proposed constitution on a technicality, but its real objection was to the document's preferred tax treatment of railroad and mining interests.

A federal act approved on February 22, 1889, "to enable the people of North Dakota, South Dakota, Montana and Washington to form constitutions and State governments and to be admitted to the Union" resulted in a convention that met in Helena from July 4 to August 17 of that year. Its constitution, approved at the polls on October 1, became effective when Montana was admitted to the Union on November 8, 1889.

Montana's second and current constitution was produced by a convention that assembled in Helena on January 17, 1972. It was ratified in a special election held on June 22 of that year and went into effect on July 1, 1973.

The Constitution

Only Georgia's 1983 constitution and Louisiana's 1975 constitution are more recent than Montana's 1973 constitution, which at 13,200 words is half the length of Georgia's document and one-fourth the length of Louisiana's. Montana's constitution is also the least amended of the three, with only twenty-one amendments as of January 1, 1998.

The constitution contains a number of innovations, especially in its fundamental rights provisions—for example, making human dignity inviolable; giving citizens the right to participate in the operation of public agencies, examine public documents, and observe the deliberations of public bodies; confirming adult rights for persons eighteen years old; and extending fundamental rights to those who are not yet adults. The constitution also provides extensive rights to persons accused of crimes and even to those convicted of crimes.

Although the 1973 Montana constitution was drafted well after the more modern state constitutions of New Jersey, Alaska, and Hawaii, it avoids making the governor as dominant in the executive branch by retaining five additional executive officers, including the lieutenant governor, who are elected statewide. Among its several innovative provisions is a rare term-limit stipulation that restricts elected executive officials and legislators to serving only eight years out of any sixteen-year period. Variations on this type of limitation can be found in the Wyoming, Indiana, and Oregon constitutions.

Preamble

The preamble to the 1973 Montana constitution proclaims: "We the people of Montana grateful to God for the quiet beauty of our state, the grandeur of our mountains, the vastness of our rolling plains, and desiring to improve the quality of life, equality of opportunity and to secure the blessings of liberty for this and future generations do ordain and establish this constitution."

Fundamental Rights

Article II, Declaration of Rights, section 1, declares: "All political power is vested in and derived from the people. All government of right originates with the people, is founded upon their will only, and is instituted solely for the good of the whole." **Section 2** confirms the right of the people to "alter or abolish the constitution," and **section 3** guarantees "certain inalienable rights" while requiring that "[i]n enjoying these rights, all persons recognize corresponding responsibilities." According to **section 4**, "The dignity of the human being is inviolable. No person shall be denied the equal protection of the laws. Neither the state nor any person, firm, corporation, or institution shall discriminate against any person in the exercise of his civil or political rights on account of race, color, sex, culture, social origin or condition, or political or religious ideas." In *Ham v. Holy Rosary Hosp.* (1974), the Montana supreme court held that a Catholic hospital's refusal to allow its facilities to be used for voluntary sterilization constituted private conduct and not state action even though the hospital was supported by public funds, was regulated by the state, and had a tax-exempt status.

Sections 5, 6, and **7,** respectively, guarantee freedom of religion, freedom of assembly, and freedom of speech, expression, and the press, including expressly permitting the truth of an utterance as a defense in cases of libel or slander. **Section 8** notes: "The public has the right to expect governmental agencies to afford such reasonable opportunity for citizen participation in the operation of the agencies prior to the final decision as may be provided by law." According to **section 9,** "No person shall be deprived of the right to examine documents or to observe the deliberations of all public bodies or agencies of state government and its subdivisions, except in cases in which the demand of individual privacy clearly exceeds the merits of public disclosure." These last two sections, which attempt to expand the rights of private citizens vis-à-vis the state government, are rare in state constitutions.

Section 10 mandates: "The right of individual privacy is essential to the well-being of a free society and shall not be infringed without the showing of a compelling state interest." **Section 11** prohibits unreasonable searches and seizures in language similar to that found in the U.S. Constitution, and **section 12** guarantees to any person the right to bear arms "in defense of his own home, person, and property, or in aid of the civil power," noting, however, that "nothing herein contained shall be held to permit the carrying of concealed weapons." **Section 13** states: "All elections shall be free and open, and no power, civil or military, shall at any time interfere to prevent the free exercise of the right of suffrage." The constitutions of several other states, including Missouri, contain similar language.

Section 14 provides that "[a] person 18 years of age or older is an adult for all purposes, except that the legislature or the people by initiative may establish the legal age for purchasing, consuming, or possessing alcoholic beverages." **Section 15** states: "The rights of persons under 18 years of age shall include, but not be limited to, all the fundamental rights of this Article unless specifically precluded by laws which enhance the protection of such persons." These two provisions are rare fundamental rights accorded by state constitutions.

Section 16 guarantees the right of a speedy legal remedy "for every injury of person, property, or character"; moreover, "[n]o person shall be deprived of this full legal redress for injury incurred in employment for which another person may be liable except as to fellow employees and his immediate employer who hired him if such immediate employer provides coverage under the Workmen's Compensation Laws of this state. Right and justice shall be administered without sale, denial, or delay."

Section 17 states: "No person shall be deprived of life, liberty, or property without due process of law." Section 18 voids immunity for the state and its subdivisions and entities from suits "for injury to a person or property," unless provided by the legislature "by a ⅔ vote of each house." Section 19 declares: "The privilege of the writ of habeas corpus shall never be suspended." The constitutions of most other states permit suspension in times of rebellion or invasion.

Section 20 prescribes the methods of initiating criminal proceedings; section 21 guarantees the right to bail except "for capital offenses, when the proof is evident or the presumption great"; section 22 prohibits excessive bail, fines, "or cruel and unusual punishments"; and section 23 states in part: "No person shall be imprisoned for the purpose of securing his testimony in any criminal proceeding longer than may be necessary in order to take his deposition." This provision is also rare among state constitutions. Sections 24, 25, and 26, respectively, extend rights to those accused of crimes, prohibit self-incrimination and double jeopardy, and guarantee the right of trial by jury. Section 27 prohibits imprisonment for debt, except "where there is strong presumption of fraud." Section 28 provides: "Laws for the punishment of crime shall be founded on the principles of prevention and reformation. Full rights are restored by termination of state supervision for any offense against the state." This allowance is relatively rare, although Indiana's constitution also refers to "principles of reformation" as the basis of the state's penal code.

Section 29 guarantees compensation for the taking of or damage to private property for public use; section 30 defines treason and confirms that the "estates of suicides shall descend or vest as in cases of natural death"; and section 31 prohibits ex post facto laws and laws impairing the obligation of contracts. Section 32 subordinates the military to civil power. According to section 33, "No armed person or persons or armed body of men shall be brought into this state for the preservation of the peace, or the suppression of domestic violence, except upon the application of the legislature, or of the governor when the legislature cannot be convened." Section 34 guarantees rights not otherwise contained in the constitution, and section 35 provides: "The people declare that Montana servicemen, servicewomen, and veterans may be given special considerations determined by the legislature."

Division of Powers

Article III, General Government, section 1, states: "The power of the government of this state is divided into three distinct branches—legislative, executive, and judicial. No person or persons charged with the exercise of power properly belonging to one branch shall exercise any power properly belonging to either of the others, except as in this constitution expressly directed or permitted."

Legislative Branch

Article V, The Legislature, section 1, declares: "The legislative power is vested in a legislature consisting of a senate and a house of representatives. The people reserve to themselves the powers of initiative and referendum." Section 2 stipulates: "The size of the legislature shall be provided by law, but the senate shall not have more than 50 or fewer than 40 members and the house shall not have more than 100 or fewer than 80 members." Currently both houses have the maximum number of members.

Section 3 provides that members of the house of representatives serve two-year terms and members of the senate four-year terms, with one-half elected every two years. Legislators are limited under **article IV, Suffrage and Elections, section 8,** to serving eight years in any sixteen-year period. A candidate for the legislature, according to **article V, The Legislature, section 4,** must be a state resident for one year; moreover, "[f]or six months next preceding the general election, he shall be a resident of the county if it contains one or more districts or of the district if it contains all or parts of more than one county." Under **section 9,** "No member of the legislature shall, during the term for which he shall have been elected, be appointed to any civil office under the state; and no member of congress, or other person holding an office (except notary public, or [in] the militia) under the United States or this state, shall be a member of the legislature during his continuance in office."

Section 10(1) allows each house to judge the election and qualifications of its members, noting that each "may by law vest in the courts the power to try and determine contested elections"; to choose its officers and make its own rules; and with the concurrence of two-thirds of its members to expel or punish a member "for good cause." **Section 10(2)** defines a quorum as a majority of each house, although "[a] smaller number may adjourn from day to day and compel attendance of absent members." **Section 10(3)** mandates that all sessions of the legislature and legislative committees, all committee meetings, and all hearings be open to the public; and **section 10(4)** authorizes the legislature to establish a legislative council, other interim committees, and a "legislative post-audit committee which shall supervise post-auditing duties provided by law."

Section 11 addresses the passage of bills, providing in part: "**(1)** A law shall be passed by bill which shall not be so altered or amended on its passage through the legislature as to change its original purpose. No bill shall become law except by a vote of the majority of all members present and voting. **(2)** Every vote of each member … on each substantive question … , in any committee, or in [the] committee of the whole shall be recorded and made public. On final passage, the vote shall be taken by ayes and noes and the names entered on the journal. **(3)** Each bill, except general appropriation bills and bills for the codification and general revision of the laws, shall contain only one subject, clearly expressed in its title." If a subject is not expressed in the title, that portion of the act is void. **Section 11(6)** states: "A law may be challenged on the ground of noncompliance with this section only within two years after its effective date."

Section 12 restricts the legislature from passing a special or local act "when a general act is, or can be made, applicable." In *Grossman v. State Department of Natural Resources* (1984), the Montana supreme court held that a law funding projects in only some of the state's political subdivisions was a special or local law but that it was constitutional because the legislature could not have achieved its purpose by a general law.

Article VI, The Executive, section 1, addresses the state's executive officers: "**(1)** The executive branch includes a governor, lieutenant governor, secretary of state, attorney general, superintendent of public instruction, and auditor. **(2)** Each holds office for a term of four years which begins on the first Monday of January next succeeding

Executive Branch

election, and until a successor is elected and qualified. **(3)** Each shall reside at the seat of government, there keep the public records of his office, and perform such other duties as are provided in this constitution and by law."

Section 2(2) requires that "[e]ach candidate for governor shall file jointly with a candidate for lieutenant governor in primary elections, or so otherwise comply with nomination procedures provided by law that [these two offices] are voted upon together in primary and general elections." **Section 3** states that candidates for any elected executive office must be twenty-five years old, citizens of the United States, and state residents for two years. Additional qualifications are set forth for the position of attorney general and may be required by law for the superintendent of public instruction. A candidate for a statewide executive position, according to **article IV, Suffrage and Elections, section 8,** cannot be certified if he or she has already served "8 or more years in any 16-year period."

Article VI, The Executive, section 4(1) declares: "The executive power is vested in the governor who shall see that the laws are faithfully executed. He shall have such other duties as are provided in this constitution and by law." **Section 4(2)** specifies that the lieutenant governor's duties include those provided by law and "those delegated to him by the governor"; however, "[n]o power specifically vested in the governor by this constitution may be delegated to the lieutenant governor." **Sections 4(3), 4(4),** and **4(5),** respectively, require the secretary of state to "maintain the official records of the executive branch and of the acts of the legislature …"; define the attorney general as "the legal officer of the state"; and direct that the superintendent of public instruction and auditor "shall have such duties as are provided by law."

Section 7 limits the executive branch to twenty principal departments. According to **section 8,** these departments are under the supervision of the governor, who appoints the heads of each department not otherwise provided for in the constitution; these appointees are subject to confirmation by the senate and "hold office until the end of the governor's term unless sooner removed by the governor." **Section 9** directs the governor, at the beginning of each legislative session and at other times, to give the legislature information and recommend measures he or she considers necessary; in addition, "[t]he governor shall submit to the legislature at a time fixed by law, a budget for the ensuing fiscal period setting forth in detail … the proposed expenditures and estimated revenue…."

Section 10(1) mandates: "Each bill passed by the legislature, except bills proposing amendments to the Montana constitution, bills ratifying proposed amendments to the United States constitution, resolutions, and initiative and referendum measures, shall be submitted to the governor for his signature. If he does not sign or veto the bill within 10 days … , it shall become law. The governor shall return a vetoed bill to the legislature with a statement of his reasons therefor." **Section 10(2)** allows the governor to return a bill to the legislature with recommendations for amendment; if the legislature passes the amended bill, it is returned to the governor for reconsideration. The Illinois constitution has a similar provision that allows the governor and the legislature to function in concert rather than by confrontation.

Section 10(3) provides that the governor's veto of a bill may be overridden by a vote of "two-thirds of the members of each house present." The constitutions of some states, such as Hawaii, require two-thirds of the elected members to override a veto, while Delaware requires three-fifths of the elected members. **Section 10(4)(a)** states: "If the legislature is not in session when the governor vetoes a bill approved by two-thirds of the members present, he shall return the bill with his reasons therefor to the secretary of state," who polls the members by mail; "[i]f two-thirds or more of the members of each house vote to override the veto, the bill shall become law." The legislature may also choose to reconvene to reconsider a vetoed bill. **Section 10(5)** allows "[t]he governor to veto items in appropriations bills; in such cases "the procedure shall be the same as upon veto of an entire bill."

Sections 11, 12, and **13**, respectively, authorize the governor to convene a special session of the legislature whenever he or she considers it in the public interest; "grant reprieves, commutations and pardons, restore citizenship, and suspend and remit fines and forfeitures subject to procedures provided by law"; and serve as commander in chief of the state's militia. **Section 15** directs the governor to "require information in writing, under oath when required, from the officers of the executive branch upon any subject relating to the duties of their respective offices." The governor may also require such information from "officers and managers of state institutions" and may appoint an investigative committee "to report to him upon the condition of any executive office or state institution."

Section 14(1) provides that the lieutenant governor-elect becomes governor if the governor-elect is disqualified or dies and becomes acting governor if the governor-elect fails to assume office for any other reason. Pursuant to **sections 14(2)** and **14(3)**, the lieutenant governor becomes acting governor if the governor so requests in writing, is absent from the state for more than forty-five consecutive days, or becomes disabled. **Sections 14(4)** and **14(5)** provide procedures for determining if the governor is unable to perform his or her duties, in which case the lieutenant governor becomes acting governor. **Section 14(6)** states that if the office becomes vacant "by reason of death, resignation, or disqualification, the lieutenant governor shall become governor for the remainder of the term...."

Article VII, The Judiciary, section 1, vests the state's judicial power in "one supreme court, district courts, justice courts, and such other courts as may be provided by law." **Section 3(1)** states in part: "The supreme court consists of one chief justice and four justices, but the legislature may increase the number of justices from four to six." The Montana supreme court currently has seven members. Section 3(1) continues: "A majority shall join in and pronounce decisions, which must be in writing." In *Kaiser v. Whitehall* (1986), the Montana supreme court concluded that its decisions are binding even if only three justices sign the majority opinion, with one justice specially concurring and three justices dissenting. **Section 3(2)** directs that "[a] district judge shall be substituted for the chief justice or a justice in the event of disqualification or disability...."

Section 2(1) establishes the supreme court's jurisdiction: "The supreme court has appellate jurisdiction and may issue, hear, and determine writs appropriate thereto. It has

Judicial Branch

original jurisdiction to issue, hear, and determine writs of habeas corpus and such other writs as may be provided by law." In *Montana v. Jackson* (1983), the U.S. Supreme Court, having reviewed the state court's decision to determine if it was based on adequate and independent state grounds and therefore beyond reversal at the federal level, held that it could vacate, continue, or remand such a case for clarification by the state court. **Section 2(2)** provides that the supreme court has "general supervisory control over all other courts." **Section 2(3)** authorizes the court to make "rules governing appellate procedure, practice and procedure for all other courts, admission to the bar and the conduct of its members"; however, these rules of procedure are "subject to disapproval by the legislature in either of the two sessions following promulgation."

Section 7(2) specifies the length of judges' terms: "Terms of office shall be eight years for supreme court justices, six years for district court judges, four years for justices of the peace, and as provided by law for other judges." **Section 8(1)** states: "Supreme court justices and district court judges shall be elected by the qualified electors as provided by law." **Section 8(2)** provides in part: "For any vacancy in the office of supreme court justice or district court judge, the governor shall appoint a replacement from nominees selected in the manner provided by law"; furthermore, "[a]ppointments made under this subsection shall be subject to confirmation by the senate.... The appointee shall serve until the election for the office as provided by law and until a successor is elected and qualified."

Section 9(1) requires that a candidate for supreme court justice or district court judge be a U.S. citizen, a state resident for two years, and "admitted to the practice of law in Montana for at least five years prior to the date of appointment or election." **Section 9(3)** prohibits supreme court justices and district court judges from practicing law during their term of office, holding any other paying job, or holding office in a political party. According to **section 9(4)**, "Supreme court justices shall reside within the state." **Section 10** provides: "Any holder of a judicial position forfeits that position by either filing for an elective public office other than a judicial position or absenting himself from the state for more than 60 consecutive days."

Section 11(1) instructs the legislature to create a judicial standards commission, which, under **section 11(2)**, is empowered to "investigate complaints, and make rules implementing this section" and subpoena witnesses and documents. Pursuant to **section 11(3)**, on the commission's recommendation the supreme court may "**(a)** [r]etire any justice or judge for disability ..., or **(b)** [c]ensure, suspend, or remove any justice or judge for willful misconduct in office, willful and persistent failure to perform his duties, violations of cannons of judicial ethics adopted by the supreme court ..., or habitual intemperance."

Impeachment

Article V, The Legislature, section 13(1), states: "The governor, executive officers, heads of state departments, judicial officers, and such other officers as may be provided by law are subject to impeachment, and upon conviction shall be removed from office. Other proceedings for removal from public office for cause may be provided by law." **Section 13(2)** directs that "the legislature shall provide for the manner, procedure, and causes for impeachment and may select the senate as tribunal." The constitutions of most states expressly designate the senate as the trier of impeachment charges, mirroring the procedures in the U.S. Constitution. These are derived from the British Parliament, where impeachment charges are brought in the House of Commons (lower house) and tried in the House of Lords (upper house). **Section 13(3)** provides: "Impeachment shall be brought only by a two-thirds vote of the house. The tribunal hearing the charges shall convict only by a vote of two-thirds or more of its members." **Section 13(4)** notes that conviction extends only to removal from office but does not exempt "prosecution according to law."

Article III, General Government, sections 4 and **5**, contain provisions for popular initiatives to enact laws "on all matters except appropriations of money and local or special laws" and for popular referendums on "any act of the legislature except an appropriation of money." A 1977 act provides for the recall of elected and appointed officials. Under **article XI, Local Government, section 8**, "The legislature shall extend the initiative and referendum powers reserved to the people by the constitution to the qualified electors of each governmental unit." **Article XIV, Constitutional Revision, section 2**, prescribes procedures for a constitutional convention by popular initiative.

Direct Democracy

Article XI, Local Government, section 5(1), authorizes the legislature to provide "procedures permitting a local government unit or combination of units to frame, adopt, amend, revise, or abandon a self-government charter with the approval of a majority of those voting on the question. The procedures shall not require approval of a charter by a legislative body."

Local Government

Article VIII, Revenue and Finance, section 1, asserts: "Taxes shall be levied by general laws for public purposes." **Section 9**, which provides for a balanced budget, states: "Appropriations by the legislature shall not exceed anticipated revenues."

Taxation and Finance

Article IX, Environment and Natural Resources, section 1(1), declares: "The state and each person shall maintain and improve a clean and healthful environment in Montana for present and future generations." **Section 3(1)** states that "[a]ll existing rights to the use of any waters for any useful or beneficial purpose are hereby recognized and confirmed." **Section 4** directs the legislature to "provide for the identification, acquisition, restoration, enhancement, preservation, and administration of scenic, historic, archeologic, scientific, cultural, and recreational areas, sites, records and objects, and for their use and enjoyment by the people."

Environment

Article I, Compact with the United States, states that "[a]ll provisions of the enabling act of Congress (approved February 22, 1889, 25 Stat. 676), as amended and of Ordinance No. 1, appended to the Constitution of the State of Montana and approved February 22, 1889, including the agreement and declaration that all lands owned or held by any Indian or Indian tribes shall remain under the absolute jurisdiction and control of the congress of the United States, continue in full force and effect until revoked by the consent of the United States and the people of Montana."

Compact with the United States

Article XIV, Constitutional Revision, section 1, states: "The legislature, by an affirmative vote of two-thirds of all the members, whether one or more bodies, may at any time submit to the qualified electors the question of whether there shall be an unlimited convention to revise, alter, or amend this constitution." This language, unlike that in many other state constitutions, specifically authorizes a convention called under its provisions to have "unlimited" or full authority to change the constitution. Section 2 allows voters to petition the secretary of state to let the electorate decide at the next general election whether a convention should be held. "The petition shall be signed by at least ten percent of the qualified electors of the state," notes section 2(1). "That number shall include at least ten percent of the qualified electors in each of two-fifths of the legislative districts." Section 3 stipulates that the question of whether to call a constitutional convention must be submitted to the people every twenty years.

Section 8 provides that amendments may also be proposed "by an affirmative roll call vote of two-thirds of all the members [of the legislature], whether one or more bodies ..., [which] shall be submitted to the qualified electors at the next general election"; if approved by "a majority of the electors voting thereon," an amendment becomes effective "on the first day of July after certification of the election returns unless the amendment provides otherwise."

Section 9 prescribes procedures for amendment by popular initiative. Under section 9(1), "Petitions including the full text of the proposed amendment shall be signed by at least ten percent of the qualified electors of the state. That number shall include at least ten percent of the qualified electors in each of two-fifths of the legislative districts." The petition is then to be filed with the secretary of state and, if certified, published twice each month for two months preceding the next regular statewide election. If approved by a majority of voters, adds section 9(3), the amendment "shall become a part of the constitution effective the first day of July following its approval, unless the amendment provides otherwise."

Nebraska became the thirty-seventh state of the United States on March 1, 1867. Lincoln is the capital of the "Cornhusker State." Some 77,358 square miles in area, Nebraska is bordered by South Dakota on the north, Iowa and Missouri on the east, Kansas on the south, and Colorado and Wyoming on the west. Nebraska ranks thirty-seventh among the states in population with approximately 1.6 million inhabitants. The state's principal industries include agriculture and manufacturing; its chief crops include corn, sorghum, and soybeans.

Government: The governor and lieutenant governor are elected jointly for four-year terms, and the governor is limited to two consecutive terms. The unicameral legislature consists of forty-nine members elected for four-year terms, one-half every two years. The supreme court consists of a chief justice and six additional judges initially appointed by the governor from a list prepared by a judicial nominating commission; they stand for election after an initial term of three years and every six years thereafter.

Dates of Constitutions: 1867 and 1875

The region that would become the state of Nebraska was first inhabited some ten thousand years ago by paleo-Indians. They were followed by the Woodland people, who lived there between A.D. 400 and 600. When the first Europeans arrived, the Omaha, Oto, and Pawnee peoples were living in the area. Nebraska's name is derived from *niboathka* (broad river), the name given by the Omaha people to the Platte River.

On August 13, 1720, members of a Spanish expedition along the South Platte River were attacked and beaten by the Pawnees. Two decades later, in 1739, Pierre and Paul Mallet, French traders, crossed the Nebraska region on a trek to Santa Fe, New Mexico. But only a few Europeans ventured into Nebraska territory when it was administered by the Spanish and then the French from New Orleans. In 1803, under the terms of the Louisiana Purchase, the United States received the Nebraska territory from France, and the following year President Thomas Jefferson commissioned Meriwether Lewis and William Clark to explore the nation's newly acquired territory. The Lewis and Clark expedition followed the Missouri River, skirting Nebraska.

In the wake of this famed expedition, several fur trading posts were built along the Missouri River. The first permanent settlement in Nebraska was a post established in 1810 and named Bellevue, just south of the present-day site of Omaha. The explorer Zebulon Pike had traversed Nebraska in 1806 and pronounced it "barren of soil, parched and dried up for eight months of the year." In 1820 Major Stephen H. Long led a scientific expedition through Nebraska and remarked that it was "almost wholly unfit for cultivation, and of course uninhabitable."

After Missouri became a state in 1821, Nebraska, which had been administered as part of the Missouri Territory since 1812, was left on its own by the U.S. government. By 1841, however, wagon trains were regularly passing through the region, and in 1844 a proposal was made to Congress to provide for the governance of Nebraska. But it was not until ten years later that Congress formally organized the Nebraska Territory under the terms of the Kansas-Nebraska Act of May 30, 1854.

In March 1860, with a civil war looming, Nebraska voters rejected a proposal to call a constitutional convention. Four years later, even as the war still raged, Republicans dominating Congress sought new western states to increase their voting majority, and an act was approved on April 19, 1864, "to enable the People of Nebraska to form a Constitution and State Government, and for the Admission of such State into the Union...." A second proposal for a constitutional convention, however, was also rejected by the voters, apparently out of fear of an increase in taxation if Nebraska became a state.

At the urging of the territorial governor, Alvin Saunders, the legislature drew up a constitution that was ratified by a narrow margin in a questionable election on June 21, 1866. The constitution, which went into effect when statehood was granted on March 1, 1867, was only a basic outline for a government with limitations on public spending. That year the state capital was moved from Omaha to Lancaster, which was renamed Lincoln in honor of the assassinated president.

An 1871 scandal led to the impeachment of the governor and fueled the demand for a new and better constitution. A convention meeting in Lincoln in June 1871 produced a document based on the recently adopted Illinois constitution. This effort was rejected at the polls, but the 1867 constitution's lack of checks and balances and inadequate accountability for state officers resulted in a new convention held in Lincoln from May 11 through June 12, 1875. The convention's proposal was ratified by the voters on October 12 and went into effect on November 1, 1875.

The Constitution

The 1875 Nebraska constitution, which contains 20,000 words, is a relatively short document that has been amended 199 times as of January 1, 1998.

Under an amendment initiated by the voters in 1934, Nebraska changed its legislative form and became unique—the only one of the fifty states to have a unicameral legislature. Although Benjamin Franklin had been a proponent of unicameral legislatures, and the constitutions of many nations, including Bulgaria, China, and Turkey, create unicameral legislative bodies, the idea of a bicameral legislature, such as the British Parliament's House of Commons and House of Lords, has been ingrained in the American political psyche since before the framing of the U.S. Constitution in 1787. The British Parliament evolved to accommodate the disparate policies of the aristocracy and the commoners, while in the United States bicameralism provided a way to accommodate the sovereignty of the people and the semisovereignty of the individual states in a federal republic. In state governments, which have only one class of citizens and no semisovereign subdivisions (counties are not sovereign or semisovereign entities), a bicameral legislature is a matter more of form than of function.

Preamble

The preamble to the 1875 Nebraska constitution reads: "We, the people, grateful to Almighty God for our freedom, do ordain and establish the following declaration of rights and frame of government, as the Constitution of the State of Nebraska."

Fundamental Rights

Article I, Bill of Rights, section 1, as amended by initiative in 1988, declares: "All persons are by nature free and independent, and have certain inherent and inalienable rights; among these are life, liberty, the pursuit of happiness, and the right to keep and bear arms for security or defense of self, family, home, and others, and for lawful common defense, hunting, recreational use, and all other lawful purposes, and such rights shall not be denied or infringed by the state or any subdivision thereof." Similarly, the North

Dakota constitution mentions the right to bear arms in the first section of its fundamental rights provision. Section 1 continues: "To secure these rights, and the protection of property, governments are instituted among people, deriving their just powers from the consent of the governed."

Section 2 prohibits slavery and involuntary servitude except as "punishment of crime," and **section 3** states: "No person shall be deprived of life, liberty, or property, without due process of law." In *Olsen v. Nebraska* (1941), the U.S. Supreme Court held that a statute limiting the fees charged by employment agencies did not violate the Fourteenth Amendment (1868) of the U.S. Constitution, but the Nebraska state court on remand in *Boomer v. Olsen* (1943) found that the statute did violate the due process clause of section 3.

Section 4 provides in part: "All persons have a natural and indefeasible right to worship Almighty God according to the dictates of their own consciences." **Section 5** guarantees the right to "freely speak, write and publish on all subjects" and makes truth a defense to libel. **Section 6,** as amended in 1920, guarantees the right to trial by jury, and **section 7** prohibits unreasonable searches and seizures. **Section 8** proscribes suspension of the writ of habeas corpus, "unless, in case of rebellion or invasion, the public safety requires it, and then only in such manner as shall be prescribed by law." According to **section 9,** which states in part as amended in 1978: "All persons shall be bailable by sufficient sureties, except for treason, sexual offenses involving penetration by force or against the will of the victim, and murder, where the proof is evident or the presumption great." Section 9 also prohibits excessive bail, excessive fines, and cruel and unusual punishment.

Sections 10, 11, and **12,** respectively, require, with certain exceptions, presentment or indictment for criminal charges; guarantee certain rights to those accused of crime, including the right "to appear and defend in person or by counsel, to demand the nature and cause of accusation, ... and [to] a speedy public trial by an impartial jury of the county or district in which the offense is alleged to have been committed"; and prohibit self-incrimination and double jeopardy. **Section 13,** as amended in 1996, provides in part: "All courts shall be open, and every person, for any injury done him or her in his or her lands, goods, person, or reputation, shall have a remedy by due course of law and justice administered without denial or delay...." Under **section 14,** treason is defined in terms similar to those in the U.S. Constitution. **Section 15** requires that "[a]ll penalties shall be proportioned to the nature of the offense" and prohibits corruption of the blood, forfeiture of estate, or transportation "out of the state for any offense committed within the state." **Section 16** prohibits bills of attainder, ex post facto laws, and laws that impair the obligation of contracts or make "any irrevocable grant of special privileges or immunities."

Sections 17 through **22,** respectively, subordinate the military to civil power; limit the quartering of soldiers in private homes; guarantee the right to peaceably assemble and petition the government; prohibit imprisonment "for debt in any civil action on mesne [intermediate] or final process, unless in cases of fraud"; guarantee just compensation for taking or damaging private property; and declare that "[a]ll elections shall be free...." In *Doak v. Milbauer* (1984), however, the Nebraska supreme court determined that a person may be imprisoned for failure to comply with a court order for child support, since the obligation is not a debt.

Section 25, as amended in 1920, states: "There shall be no discrimination between citizens of the United States in respect to the acquisition, ownership, possession, enjoyment or descent of property. The right of aliens in respect to the acquisition, enjoyment and descent of property may be regulated by law." **Section 26** guarantees that rights not enumerated are retained by the people.

Section 28, added in 1996, extends rights to victims of crime, including the right to "**(1)** ... be informed of all criminal court proceedings; ... be present at trial unless the trial court finds sequestration necessary for a fair trial for the defendant; and ... be informed of, be present at, and make an oral or written statement at sentencing, parole, pardon, commutation and conditional release proceedings."

Division of Powers

Article II, Distribution of Powers, section 1, declares: "The powers of the government of this state are divided into three distinct departments, the legislative, executive and judicial, and no person or collection of persons being one of these departments, shall exercise any power properly belonging to either of the others, except as hereinafter expressly directed or permitted." With respect to the legislature's delegation of rule-making power to the executive branch, the Nebraska supreme court in *State ex rel. Douglas v. Sporhase* (1981) described executive rule making as allowing the executive or administrative agency to determine the existence of facts under which the law will become operative.

Legislative Branch

Article III, Legislative Power, section 1, as amended in 1912 and 1934, proclaims in part: "Commencing with the regular session of the Legislature to be held in January, nineteen hundred and thirty-seven, the legislative authority of the state shall be vested in a Legislature consisting of one chamber." **Section 6,** as amended in 1920, 1934, and 1970, sets the legislature at no more than fifty and no fewer than thirty members. It currently has forty-nine members. **Section 7,** which was amended nine times between 1886 and 1988, provides in part:"At the general election to be held in November 1964, one-half the members of the Legislature, or as nearly thereto as may be practicable, shall be elected for a term of four years and the remainder for a term of two years, and thereafter all members shall be elected for a term of four years...."

Section 8, as amended in 1972 and 1992, specifies: "No person shall be eligible to the office of member of the Legislature unless on the date of the general election at which he is elected, or on the date of his appointment he is a registered voter, has attained the age of twenty-one years and has resided within the district from which he is elected for the term of one year next before his election, unless he shall have been absent on the public business of the United States or of this State. And no person elected as aforesaid shall hold his office after he shall have removed from such district." This section was amended by initiative in 1994 to include term limits, but in *Duggan v. Beerman*

(1996), the Nebraska supreme court found that term limits on federal elected officials violated the U.S. Constitution and that terms limits on state officials were also void because that portion of the amendment was, in fact, not severable from the portion relating to federal officials.

Section 9, as amended in 1972, provides: "No person holding office under the authority of the United States, or any lucrative office under the authority of this state, shall be eligible to, or have a seat in the Legislature. No person elected or appointed to the Legislature shall receive any civil appointment to a state office while holding membership in the Legislature...."

Section 10, as amended in 1934, 1970, and 1974, states in part: "A majority of the members elected to the Legislature shall constitute a quorum; the Legislature shall determine the rules of its proceedings and be the judge of the election, returns, and qualifications of its members, shall choose its own officers, including a Speaker to preside when the Lieutenant Governor shall be absent, incapacitated, or shall act as Governor." Continues section 10: "No member shall be expelled except by a vote of two-thirds of all members elected ... , and no member shall be twice expelled for the same offense. The Legislature may punish by imprisonment any person not a member thereof who shall be guilty of disrespect to the Legislature by disorderly or contemptuous behavior in its presence, but no such imprisonment shall extend beyond twenty-four hours at one time, unless the person shall persist in such ... behavior."

Section 13, as amended in 1912, 1920, and 1972, states in part: "No bill shall be passed by the Legislature unless by the assent of a majority of all members elected and the yeas and nays on the question of final passage of any bill shall be entered upon the journal." **Section 14**, as amended in 1920, 1934, and 1996, provides in part: "Every bill and resolution shall be read by title when introduced, and a printed copy thereof provided for the use of each member.... No vote upon the final passage of any bill shall be taken until five legislative days after its introduction nor until it has been on file for final reading and passage for at least one legislative day." Section 14 continues: "No bill shall contain more than one subject, and the subject shall be clearly expressed in the title.... The Lieutenant Governor, or the Speaker if acting as presiding officer, shall sign, in the presence of the Legislature while it is in session and capable of transacting business, all bills and resolutions passed by the Legislature." **Section 27**, as amended in 1972, stipulates: "No act shall take effect until three calendar months after the adjournment of the session at which it passed, unless in case of emergency, to be expressed in the ... act, the Legislature shall, by a vote of two-thirds of all the members elected otherwise direct...."

Section 15 directs that legislators, "in all cases except treason, felony or breach of the peace, shall be privileged from arrest during the session ... , and for fifteen days next before [and after]." **Section 16** requires that no legislator or state officer "shall have a conflict of interest, as defined by the Legislature, directly in any contract, with the state or any county or municipality thereof...." According to **section 26**, "No member of the Legislature shall be liable in any civil or criminal action whatever for words spoken in debate."

Section 18, as amended in 1964, prohibits the legislature from passing local or special laws in a number of cases including granting divorces, changing the names of persons or places, and changing the law of descent.

<table>
<tr><td>Executive Branch</td><td>

Article IV, Executive, section 1, which was amended eight times between 1920 and 1970, specifies in part: "The executive officers of the state shall be the Governor, Lieutenant Governor, Secretary of State, Auditor of Public Accounts, Treasurer, Attorney General, and the heads of such other executive departments as set forth herein or as may be established by law." In *State ex rel. Spire v. Conway* (1991), the Nebraska supreme court implied that the executive branch of the state government is the residual branch—that is, any function not obviously a part of the legislature or judiciary must be by default an executive function. Section 1 stipulates that the executive officers are to be elected for four-year terms, the governor and lieutenant governor are to be elected jointly, and the governor is ineligible for more than two consecutive terms. Continues section 1: "The heads of all executive departments established by law, other than those to be elected . . . , shall be appointed by the Governor, with the consent of a majority of all members elected to the Legislature, but officers so appointed may be removed by the Governor." The governor is granted other appointive powers in **sections 10, 11,** and **12.**

</td></tr>
</table>

Section 2, as amended in 1920, 1962, and 1966, requires: "No person shall be eligible to the office of Governor, or Lieutenant Governor, who shall not have attained the age of thirty years, and who shall not have been for five years next preceding his election a resident and citizen of this state and a citizen of the United States."

Section 6, as amended in 1920, mandates: "The supreme executive power shall be vested in the Governor, who shall take care that the laws be faithfully executed and the affairs of the state efficiently and economically administered." **Section 7,** as amended in 1920, 1964, and 1972, states: "The Governor may, at the commencement of each session, and at the close of his term and whenever the Legislature may require, give by message to the Legislature information of the condition of the state, and shall recommend such measures as he shall deem expedient. At a time fixed by law, he shall present, by message, a complete itemized budget . . . and a budget bill to be introduced by the Speaker of the Legislature. . . ." **Section 8** provides: "The Governor may, on extraordinary occasions, convene the Legislature by proclamation, stating therein the purpose for which they are convened, and the Legislature shall enter upon no business except that for which they were called together."

Section 13, as amended in 1920 and 1968, notes in part: "The Governor, Attorney General and Secretary of State, sitting as a board, shall have power to remit fines and forfeitures and to grant respites, reprieves, pardons, or commutations in all cases of conviction for offenses against the laws of the state, except treason and cases of impeachment. The Board of Parole may advise [them] . . . but such advice shall not be binding on them." **Section 14** declares: "The Governor shall be commander-in-chief of the military and naval forces of the state (except when they shall be called into the service of the United States) and may call out the same to execute the laws, suppress insurrection, and repel invasion."

Section 15, as amended in 1972, 1974, and 1976, directs in part: "Every bill passed by the Legislature, before it becomes a law, shall be presented to the Governor. If he approves he shall sign it, and thereupon it shall become a law, but if he does not approve or reduce any item or items of appropriations, he shall return it with his objections to the Legislature...." If "three-fifths of the members elected agree," it shall become a law without the governor's signature. The constitutions of most states, like the U.S. Constitution, require a two-thirds vote in both houses of the legislature—a more stringent criterion—to override a veto. Section 15 continues: "Any bill which shall not be returned by the Governor within five days (Sundays excepted) after it shall have been presented to him, shall become a law ... as if he had signed it; unless the Legislature by their adjournment prevent its return; in which case it shall be filed, with his objections, in the office of the Secretary of State...."

Section 16, as amended in 1970 and 1972, directs in part: "In case of the conviction of the Governor on impeachment, his removal from office, his resignation or his death, the Lieutenant Governor, the Speaker of the Legislature and such other persons designated by law shall in that order be Governor for the remainder of the Governor's term." The order of succession is similar in the case of the death of the governor-elect.

Article V, Judicial, section 1, as amended in 1920, 1970, and 1990, declares: "The judicial power of the state shall be vested in a Supreme Court, an appellate court, district courts, county courts ... and such other courts inferior to the Supreme Court as may be created by law. In accordance with rules established by the Supreme Court and not in conflict with other provisions of this Constitution and laws governing such matters, general administrative authority over all courts in this state shall be vested in the Supreme Court and shall be exercised by the Chief Justice. The Chief Justice shall be the executive head of the courts and may appoint an administrative director thereof."

Judicial Branch

Section 2, as amended in 1908, 1920, 1968, 1970, and 1990, provides in part: "The Supreme Court shall consist of seven judges, one of whom shall be the Chief Justice. A majority of the judges shall be necessary to constitute a quorum. A majority of the members sitting shall have authority to pronounce a decision except in cases involving the constitutionality of an act of the Legislature [which requires] the concurrence of five judges." Regarding the court's purview, section 2 continues: "The Supreme Court shall have jurisdiction in all cases relating to the revenue, civil cases in which the state is a party, mandamus, quo warranto, habeas corpus, election contests involving state officers other than members of the Legislature, and such appellate jurisdiction as may be provided by law.... The judges of the Supreme Court, sitting without division, shall hear and determine all cases involving the constitutionality of a statute and all appeals involving capital cases and may review any decision rendered by a division of the court." Under **article I, Bill of Rights, section 23,** as amended in 1972 and 1990, "In all capital cases, appeal directly to the Supreme Court shall be as a matter of right and shall operate ... until further order of the Supreme Court. In all other cases, criminal or civil, an aggrieved party shall be entitled to one appeal to the appellate court created pursuant to Article v, section 1, of this Constitution or to the Supreme Court...."

Article V, section 5, as amended in 1908, 1912, 1920, 1962, and 1970, provides in part: "The Legislature shall divide the state into six contiguous and compact districts of approximately equal population, which shall be numbered from one to six, which shall be known as the Supreme Court judicial districts." Tennessee's constitution divides that state into divisions and further stipulates that no more than two members of the supreme court may be from any one district. Mississippi also has similar districts.

Section 21, as amended in 1920, 1962, and 1972, states in part: "(1) In the case of any vacancy in the Supreme Court or in [other courts] ... , such vacancy shall be filled by the Governor from a list of at least two nominees presented to him by the appropriate judicial nominating commission.... (3) At the next general election following the expiration of three years from the date of appointment ... and every six years thereafter as long as such judge retains office, each Justice or Judge of the Supreme Court or [other courts] ... shall have his right to remain in office subject to approval or rejection by the electorate in such manner as the Legislature shall provide.... (4) There shall be a judicial nominating commission for the Chief Justice of the Supreme Court and one for each judicial district of the Supreme Court."

Section 28, adopted in 1966 and amended in 1980, requires the legislature to provide for a judicial qualifications commission. Section 30, adopted in 1966 and amended in 1980 and 1984, states in part: "(1) A Justice or Judge of the Supreme Court or judge of any court of this state may be reprimanded, disciplined, censured, suspended without pay for a definite period of time, not to exceed six months, or removed from office for (a) willful misconduct in office, (b) willful disregard of or failure to perform his or her duties, (c) habitual intemperance, (d) conviction of a crime involving moral turpitude, (e) disbarment as a member of the legal profession licensed to practice law in the State of Nebraska, or (f) conduct prejudicial to the administration of justice that brings the judicial office into disrepute, or he or she may be retired for physical or mental disability seriously interfering with the performance of his or her duties if such disability is determined to be permanent or reasonably likely to become permanent." Section 30(1) continues: "Any citizen of the State of Nebraska may request the Commission on Judicial Qualifications to consider the qualifications of any Justice or Judge of the Supreme Court or other judge...."

Impeachment

Article IV, Executive, section 5, proclaims: "All civil officers of this state shall be liable to impeachment for any misdemeanor in office."

Article III, Legislative Power, section 17, as amended in 1972 and 1986, mandates that the legislature has "the sole power of impeachment, but a majority of the members elected must concur therein.... [A] notice of an impeachment of any officer, other than a Judge of the Supreme Court, shall be forthwith served upon the Chief Justice, by the Clerk of the Legislature, who shall thereupon call a session of the Supreme Court ... to try the impeachment.... The case against the impeached civil officer ... shall be managed by two senators, appointed by the Legislature.... No person shall be convicted without the concurrence of two-thirds of the members of the Court of impeachment that clear and convincing evidence exists indicating that such person is guilty of one or more impeachable offenses, but judgment in cases of impeachment shall not extend further than removal from office and disqualification to hold and enjoy any office of honor, profit, or trust, in this State, but the party impeached ... , shall nevertheless be liable to ... [further] punishment according to law."

Article III, Legislative Power, section 1, as amended in 1912 and 1934, provides in part: "The people reserve for themselves ... the power to propose laws, and amendments to the constitution, and to enact or reject the same at the polls, independent of the Legislature, and also reserve power at their own option to approve or reject at the polls any act, item, section, or part of any act passed by the Legislature." The first power is that of the initiative, the second that of the referendum.

Direct Democracy

Article XI, Municipal Corporations, section 2, provides in part: "Any city having population of more than five thousand (5000) inhabitants may frame a charter for its own government consistent with ... the ... constitution and laws of this state."

Local Government

Article VIII, Revenue, section 1, as amended eleven times between 1920 and 1992, indicates in part: "The necessary revenue of the state and its governmental subdivisions shall be raised by taxation in such manner as the Legislature may direct. ... **(1)** Taxes shall be levied by valuation uniformly and proportionately upon all real property and franchises as defined by the Legislature except as otherwise provided in or permitted by this Constitution."

Taxation and Finance

Article XIII, State, County, and Municipal Indebtedness, section 1, as amended in 1968, 1970, and 1982, authorizes the state to contract debts to meet "casual deficits, or failures in the revenue" not to exceed $100,000, except in certain extreme circumstances.

Article VII, Education, section 1, which was amended five times between 1940 and 1972, directs the legislature to "provide for the free instruction in the common schools of this state of all persons between the ages of five and twenty-one years. The Legislature may provide for the education of other persons in educational institutions owned and controlled by the state or a political subdivision thereof." **Section 2,** as amended in 1972, specifies: "The State Department of Education shall be comprised of a State Board of Education and a Commissioner of Education. The State Department of Education shall have general supervision and administration of the school system of the state and of such other activities as the Legislature may direct."

Education

Article I, Bill of Rights, section 27, added in 1920, mandates: "The English language is hereby declared to be the official language of this state, and all official proceedings, records and publications shall be in such language, and the common school branches shall be taught in said language in public, private, denominational and parochial schools." In *Meyer v. Nebraska* (1923), the U.S. Supreme Court held that a Nebraska statute prohibiting the teaching of any subject in any language other than English violated the "liberty" protection guaranteed by the Fourteenth Amendment (1868) of the U.S. Constitution.

Official Language

Amendment Procedures

Article XVI, Amendments, section 1, as amended in 1920, 1952, and 1968, states in part: "The Legislature may propose amendments to this Constitution. If the same be agreed to by three-fifths of the members elected to the Legislature, such proposed amendments shall be ... published once each week for three consecutive weeks, in at least one newspaper in each county, ... immediately preceding the next election of members of the Legislature or a special election called by the vote of four-fifths of the members elected to the Legislature for the purpose of submitting such proposed amendments to the electors." If a majority of the electors vote for the amendment, "it shall become a part of this Constitution, provided the votes cast in favor of such amendment shall not be less than thirty-five per cent of the total votes cast at such election."

Section 2, as amended in 1952, provides in part: "When three-fifths of the members elected to the Legislature deem it necessary to call a convention to revise, amend, or change this constitution, they shall recommend to the electors to vote at the next election of members ... for or against a convention." The legislature is directed to provide for a convention if a majority voting on the proposition vote for it and if the favorable votes are more than thirty-five percent of the total votes cast at the election. The convention's proposals must be "adopted by a majority of those voting [on them]" at an election.

Article III, Legislative Power, section 1, grants the people the right to propose constitutional amendments by popular initiative.

On October 31, 1864, Nevada became the thirty-sixth state of the United States. Its capital is Carson City. Known variously as the "Sagebrush State," the "Battle Born State," and the "Silver State," Nevada encompasses some 110,567 square miles and is bordered by Oregon and Idaho on the north, Utah and Arizona on the east, and California on the south and west. With approximately 1.5 million inhabitants, Nevada ranks thirty-eighth among the states in population. Its principal industries include gaming, tourism, and mining; among its chief crops are hay, alfalfa seed, and potatoes.

Government: The governor and lieutenant governor are elected separately for four-year terms and are limited to two terms. The legislature consists of twenty-one senators elected for four-year terms and forty-two members of the assembly elected for two-year terms, all of whom are limited to twelve years in office. The supreme court consists of a chief justice and four associate justices elected for six-year terms.

Date of Constitution: 1864

By A.D. 1000 the agricultural villages of the Anasazi ("the ancient ones" in the Navajo language) had expanded into the Virgin River valley of the southwestern region that is now the state of Nevada. The land was later inhabited by the Shoshone, Paiute, Bannock, and Washoe peoples. In 1775 or 1776 a Spanish missionary, Father Francisco Garcés, and his party, en route from New Mexico to California territory, are said to have stopped at a spring and meadow near the present-day site of Las Vegas. The future state would take its name from the Sierra Nevadas (*nevada* is Spanish for "snowy").

Jedediah Smith and Peter S. Ogden, trappers for the Rocky Mountain and Hudson Bay Companies, respectively, blazed trails in the central and northern Nevada territory in 1826 and 1828. The Old Spanish Trail across southern Nevada soon became a regular route, and between 1843 and 1845, while the area was still under Spanish administration, U.S. General John C. Frémont, an explorer and mapmaker, led two expeditions through Nevada. In 1846 heavy snows blocked passage through the Sierra Nevadas, trapping the Donner wagon train as it headed west, resulting in forty deaths.

The Nevada territory was part of the vast southwest region ceded to the United States by Mexico under the terms of the 1848 Treaty of Guadalupe Hidalgo, which ended the Mexican War. About this time members of the Church of Jesus Christ of Latter-day Saints, the Mormons, arrived in Nevada, and in 1851 they established a permanent settlement called Mormon Station, later renamed Genoa. A part of the Mormon state of Deseret, it was administered from Mormon headquarters in Salt Lake City, Utah, and grew quickly. In 1854 the Utah government created an independent Carson County out of the Nevada territory around Carson Valley and accorded it a representative in the Utah legislature.

In 1859 the Comstock Lode, the richest mineral region in the United States, was discovered just thirty miles north of Genoa. One result was that the residents of Carson Valley called their own constitutional convention and elected a governor and legislature for the proposed state of Carson Valley. After a number of boundary changes, President James Buchanan, toward the end of his administration, approved a bill on March 2, 1861, "to organize the Territory of Nevada." Abraham Lincoln, Buchanan's successor as president, appointed a governor for the territory, who took with him a territorial secretary named Orion Clemens. Accompanying Clemens to his new post was his younger brother Samuel Clemens, who would later write under the name of Mark Twain.

The road to statehood for Nevada, as for California, was smooth and quick. In 1863, just two years after Nevada acquired territorial status, a constitutional convention that included eight lawyers, four miners, and five merchants met. On the national level an anti-slavery amendment to the U.S. Constitution was an important issue, but in Nevada the taxation of mines was more crucial. The proposed constitution, which provided for federal taxation of the mines because they were located on federal lands, was rejected at the polls.

A second convention meeting in Carson City in July 1864 proposed a new constitution, minus the taxation provision, that was approved at the polls in September of that year. To speed up admission, the text was telegraphed to Washington, D.C., at great expense. The Nevada constitution went into effect on October 31, 1864, when statehood was proclaimed by President Lincoln. Additional land, taken from the territories of Utah and Arizona in 1866 and 1867, however, was added to Nevada after it became a state.

The Constitution

Nevada's constitution is relatively short, containing some 20,770 words, and as of January 1, 1998, has been amended 117 times since 1864, including six amendments approved by the voters but nullified by the state's supreme court. Nevada went from a territory to a state in only three years, and the framers of its constitution relied heavily on the constitutions of California and New York. Still, the Nevada constitution may be classed as a frame-of-government type—that is, a businesslike document for a nondiverse group of people—typical of most of the less populous states in the western United States.

During the Progressive Era, the Nevada constitution was amended to include direct democracy provisions such as the initiative, referendum, and recall. Other significant amendments include a two-term limitation on the governorship in 1970 and a return to equality of representation in legislative apportionment, also in 1970, to conform to the requirements of the U.S. Constitution. In 1996 a provision was added to limit campaign contributions, but attempts to create an intermediate appeals process in the judicial system were turned down by the voters in 1980, 1992, and 1996.

Preamble

The preamble to the 1864 Nevada constitution is preceded by two preliminary statements: an introductory clause entitled "[Preliminary Action]," which begins, "WHEREAS, The Act of Congress Approved March Twenty First A.D. [1864] 'To enable the People of the Territory of Nevada to form a Constitution and State Government ... '"; and an ordinance, in two nearly identical sections, that addresses slavery and involuntary servitude, toleration of religion, and land within the state belonging to the United States. The preamble itself reads: "We the people of the State of Nevada Grateful to Almighty God for our freedom in order to secure its blessings, insure domestic tranquility, and form a more perfect Government, do establish this CONSTITUTION."

Fundamental Rights

Article 1, Declaration of Rights, section 1, declares: "All men are by Nature free and equal and have certain inalienable rights among which are those of enjoying and defending life and liberty; Acquiring, Possessing and Protecting property and pursuing and obtaining safety and happiness[.]" **Section 2** asserts: "All political power is inherent in the people[.] Government is instituted for the protection, security and benefit of the people; and they have the right to alter or reform the same whenever the public good may require it. But the Paramount Allegiance of every citizen is due to the Federal Government in the exercise of all its Constitutional powers as the same have been or may be defined by the Supreme Court of the United States...." Section 2 also authorizes the federal government's use of armed force in the event that Nevada attempts to secede from the Union.

Section 3 guarantees the right of trial by jury; **section 4** ensures the "free exercise and enjoyment of religious profession and worship ..."; and **section 5** limits the suspension of the writ of habeas corpus. **Section 6** states: "Excessive bail shall not be required, nor excessive fines imposed, nor shall cruel or unusual punishments be inflicted, nor shall witnesses be unreasonably detained." The U.S. Constitution and the constitutions of most states prohibit cruel *and* unusual punishment, but some states, including Nevada and California, use *or* instead of *and.*

Section 7 guarantees bail except in certain cases of "Capital Offenses or murders." **Section 8,** as amended in 1912 and 1996, extends rights to those accused of crimes, including the right to "appear and defend themselves in person and with counsel, as in civil actions." In *Miller v. State* (1970), the Nevada supreme court held that notwithstanding the use of the word *and* in section 8, the defendant was not entitled to have his case presented in court by both himself and counsel but must chose one way or the other. Section 8 also prohibits self-incrimination and double jeopardy.

Section 9 guarantees: "Every citizen may freely speak, write and publish his sentiments on all subjects being responsible for the abuse of that right...." Under **section 10,** "The people shall have the right freely to assemble together to consult for the common good, to instruct their representatives and to petition the Legislature for redress of Grievances." **Section 11,** as amended in 1982, guarantees the right to bear arms and subordinates the military to civil power, and **section 12** limits the quartering of soldiers in private homes. **Section 13** notes: "Representation shall be apportioned according to population."

Section 14 provides: "The privilege of the debtor to enjoy the necessary comforts of life shall be recognized by wholesome laws, exempting a reasonable amount of property from seizure or sale for payment of any debts or liabilities hereafter contracted; And there shall be no imprisonment for debt, except in cases of fraud, libel, or slander, and no person shall be imprisoned for a Militia fine in time of Peace." **Section 15** states: "No bill of attainder, ex-post-facto law, or law impairing the obligation of contracts shall ever be passed." **Sections 17** through **20,** respectively, prohibit slavery and involuntary servitude, "unless for the punishment of crimes"; proscribe unreasonable searches and seizures; define treason in terms similar to those used in the U.S. Constitution; and guarantee that the enumerated rights "shall not be construed to impair or deny others retained by the people."

Article 3, Distribution of Powers, section 1, as amended in 1996, states in part: "1. The powers of the Government of the State of Nevada shall be divided into three separate departments,—the Legislative,—the Executive and the Judicial; and no persons charged with the exercise of powers properly belonging to one of these departments shall

Division of Powers

exercise any functions, appertaining to either of the others, except in the cases expressly directed or permitted in this constitution." In *Goldberg v. Eighth Judicial District Court* (1977), the Nevada supreme court ruled that a statute requiring the meetings of all public bodies, including judicial bodies, to be open and public was an unconstitutional infringement on the inherent powers of the judiciary and a violation of the separation of powers doctrine. **Section 1** also provides: "**(2)** If the legislature authorizes the adoption of regulations by an executive agency which bind persons outside the agency, the legislature may provide by law for [legislative oversight of such regulations]."

Legislative Branch

Article 4, Legislative Department, section 1, declares: "The Legislative authority of this State shall be vested in a Senate and Assembly which shall be designated 'The Legislature of the State of Nevada....'" **Section 3,** as amended in 1996, provides: "**1.** The members of the Assembly shall be chosen biennially by the qualified electors of their respective districts.... **2.** No person may be elected or appointed as a member of the Assembly who has served in that office ... 12 years or more, from any district of this state." **Section 4,** as amended in 1996, instructs: "**1.** Senators shall be chosen ... by the qualified electors of their respective districts, and their term of Office shall be four Years.... **2.** No person may be elected or appointed as a Senator who has served in that office ... 12 years or more, from any district of this state."

Section 5, as amended in 1950 and 1970, requires: "Senators and members of the assembly shall be duly qualified electors in the respective counties and districts which they represent, and the number of senators shall not be less than one-third nor more than one-half of that of the members of the assembly. It shall be the mandatory duty of the legislature at its first session after the taking of the decennial census ... , to fix by law the number of senators and assemblymen...." Currently there are twenty-one senators. **Section 6** gives each house the power to judge "the qualifications, elections and returns of its own members, choose its own officers (except the President of the Senate), determine the rules of its proceedings and ... punish its members for disorderly conduct, and with the concurrence of two thirds of all the members elected, expel a member." **Section 7** prescribes: "Either House, during the session, may punish, by imprisonment, any person not a member, who shall have been guilty of disrespect to the House by disorderly or contemptuous behavior in its presence; but such imprisonment shall not extend beyond the final adjournment of the session." According to **section 11,** "Members of the Legislature shall be privileged from arrest on civil process during the session of the Legislature, and for fifteen days next before the commencement of each session."

Section 8 specifies: "No Senator or member of Assembly shall, during the term for which he shall have been elected, nor for one year thereafter be appointed to any civil office of profit under this State which shall have been created, or the emoluments of which shall have been increased during such term, except such office as may be filled by elections by the people." **Section 9** states: "No person holding any lucrative office under the Government of the United States or any other power, shall be eligible to any civil office of Profit under this State; Provided, that Post-Masters whose compensation does not exceed Five Hundred dollars per annum, or commissioners of deeds, shall not be deemed as holding a lucrative office." According to **section 10,** a conviction for embezzlement of public funds or bribery to obtain an office also disqualifies a person from any state office.

Section 12, as amended in 1922 and 1944, is a unique provision, directing: "In the case of the death or resignation of any member of the legislature ... , the county commissioners of the county from which such member was elected shall appoint a person of the same political party ... to fill such vacancy; *provided,* that this section shall apply only in cases where no biennial election or any regular election at which county officers are to [be] elected takes place between the time of such death or resignation and the next succeeding session of the legislature."

Section 13 mandates: "A majority of all the members elected to each House shall constitute a quorum to transact business, but a smaller number may adjourn, from day to day [and] compel the attendance of absent members...." **Section 15** states in part: "The doors of each House shall be kept open during its session, and neither [house] shall, without the consent of the other, adjourn for more than three days nor to any other place than that in which they may be holding their sessions."

Section 16 provides: "Any bill may originate in either House ... , and all bills passed by one may be amended in the other." The U.S. Constitution and the constitutions of a number of states, including New Hampshire and Wyoming, for example, specify that revenue or money bills originate in the lower house. **Section 17** requires that each law "shall embrace but one subject, and matter, properly connected therewith, which subject shall be briefly expressed in the title; and no law shall be revised or amended by reference to its title only; but, in such case, the act as revised or section as amended, shall be reenacted and published at length."

Section 18, as amended in 1976 and 1996, stipulates: "**1.** Every bill, except [uncontested bills], must be read by sections on three several days, in each House, unless in case of emergency, two thirds of the House where such bill is pending shall deem it expedient to dispense with this rule. The reading of a bill by sections, on its final passage, shall in no case be dispensed with.... [Generally,] a majority of all the members elected to each house is necessary to pass every bill or joint resolution, [which] shall be signed by the presiding officers of the respective Houses and by the Secretary of the Senate and Clerk of the Assembly." The constitutions of a number of other states including Oregon and Washington, for example, require measures passed by the legislature to be signed only by the presiding officers of each house. Section 18 continues: "**2.** Except as otherwise provided in subsection 3, an affirmative vote of not fewer than two-thirds of the members elected to each house is necessary to pass a bill or joint resolution which creates, generates, or increases any public revenue in any form, including but not limited to taxes, fees, assessments and rates, or changes in the computation bases for [them]. **3.** A majority of all of the members elected to each house may refer any measure which ... increases any revenue ... to the people ... at the next general election, [which] shall become effective ... only if it has been approved by a majority of the votes cast...."

Section 20, as amended in 1889 and 1926, prohibits the passage of local or special laws in certain cases such as "the punishment of crimes and misdemeanors" and "regulating the practice of courts of justice." **Section 21** provides: "In all cases enumerated in the preceding section and in all other cases where a general law can be made applicable, all laws shall be general and of uniform operation throughout the State."

Section 35 specifies: "Every bill which may have passed the Legislature, shall, before it becomes a law be presented to the Governor. If he approve it, he shall sign it, but if not he shall return it with his objections, to the House in which it originated...." The governor's veto may be overridden by a vote of two-thirds of the members elected to each House. Section 35 continues: "If any bill shall not be returned within five days ... (Sunday excepted) ... the same shall be a law, in like manner as if he had signed it, unless the Legislature by its final adjournment, prevent such return...." In such a case, the bill will become law "unless the Governor within ten days next after the adjournment (Sundays excepted) shall file such bill with his objections thereto, in the office of the Secretary of State, who shall lay the same before the Legislature at its next Session...."

Executive Branch

Article 5, Executive Department, section 1, declares: "The supreme executive power of this State, shall be vested in a Chief Magistrate who shall be Governor of the State of Nevada." **Section 2** provides in part: "The Governor shall be elected by the qualified electors at the time and places of voting for members of the Legislature, and shall hold his office for Four Years...." Under **section 3,** as amended in 1970, "No person shall be eligible to the office of Governor, who is not a qualified elector, and who, at the time of such election, has not attained the age of twenty five years; and who shall not have been a citizen resident of this State for two years next preceding the election; nor shall any person be elected to the office of Governor more than twice...." **Section 12** stipulates: "No person shall, while holding any office under the United States Government hold the office of Governor, except as herein expressly provided."

Section 5 authorizes the governor to serve as commander in chief of the state military forces "except when they shall be called into the service of the United States." Under **section 6,** "He shall transact all executive business with the Officers of the Government Civil and Military; and may require information in writing, from the Officers of the Executive Department, upon any subject relating to the duties of their respective Offices." **Section 7** states that the governor "shall see that the laws are faithfully executed." **Section 8** grants the governor the power to fill certain vacancies "by granting a commission which shall expire at the next election and qualification of the person elected to such Office."

Section 9 advises: "The Governor may on extraordinary occasions, convene the Legislature by Proclamation ... ," and **section 10** notes: "He shall communicate by Message to the Legislature at every regular Session the condition of the State and recommend such measures as he may deem expedient[.]" **Section 11** authorizes the governor "to adjourn the Legislature to such time as he may think proper" in case of a disagreement between the houses on adjournment.

Section 13 grants the governor "the power to suspend the collection of fines and forfeitures and grant reprieves for a period not exceeding sixty days dating from the time of conviction, for all offenses, except in cases of impeachment." In cases of treason the legislature makes the final determination of what action may be taken. "The Governor," continues the section, "shall communicate to the Legislature, at the beginning of every session" his disposition of such matters. According to **section 14,** as amended in 1950 and 1982, the "governor, justices of the supreme court, and attorney general, or a major part of them, of whom the governor shall be one, may ... remit fines and forfeitures, commute punishments [with some exceptions], and grant pardons, after convictions in all cases, except treason and impeachments...." In *Pinana v. State* (1960), the Nevada supreme court declared that a pardon is distinguishable from a parole and that the latter is not a constitutional right but is bestowed by legislative grace.

Section 17 states in part: "A Lieutenant Governor shall be elected at the same time and places and in the same manner as the Governor," although they are elected on separate tickets, "and his term of Office, and his eligibility, shall also be the same." Moreover, "[h]e shall be President of the Senate, but shall only have a casting vote therein." Following the lieutenant governor in the line of succession is the president pro tempore of the senate. **Section 18** instructs in part: "In case of the impeachment of the Governor, or his removal from Office, death, inability to discharge the duties of the said Office, resignation or absence from the State, the powers and duties of the Office devolve upon the Lieutenant Governor for the residue of the term, or until the disability shall cease." **Section 19,** as amended in 1954 and 1996, provides for the election of "**1.** [a] secretary of state, a treasurer, a controller, and an attorney general...." These officers also serve four years and are limited to two terms.

Article 6, Judicial Department, section 1, as amended in 1976, declares: "The Judicial power of this State shall be vested in a court system, comprising a Supreme Court, District Courts, and Justices of the Peace. The Legislature may also establish, as part of the system, Courts for municipal purposes only in incorporated cities and towns." **Section 2,** as amended in 1976, states in part: "**1.** The supreme court consists of the chief justice and two or more associate justices, as may be provided by law." There are currently four associate justices on the supreme court in addition to the chief justice. Section 2 also notes that "the legislature shall provide for the arrangement of [the] terms [of the associate justices] so that an equal number of terms, as nearly as may be, expire every 2 years."

Section 3 provides: "The Justices of the Supreme Court, shall be elected by the qualified electors of the State at the general election, and shall hold office for the term of Six Years.... They shall meet as soon as practicable after their election and qualification, and at their first meeting shall determine by lot, the term of Office each shall fill, and the Justice drawing the shortest term shall be Chief Justice...." After the first chief justice's term expires, the justice with the next shortest term becomes chief justice, and finally the most senior member assumes the position.

Section 4, as amended in 1920, 1976, and 1978, sets forth in part: "The supreme court shall have appellate jurisdiction in all civil cases arising in district courts, and also on

Judicial Branch

questions of law alone in all criminal cases in which the offense charged is within the original jurisdiction of the district courts. The court shall also have power to issue writs of *mandamus, certiorari*, prohibition, *quo warranto*, and *habeas corpus* and also all writs necessary or proper to the complete exercise of its appellate jurisdiction."

Section 11, as amended in 1950, states: "The justices of the supreme court and the district judges shall be ineligible to any office, other than a judicial office, during the term for which they shall have been elected or appointed; and all elections or appointments of any such judges by the people, legislature, or otherwise, during said period, to any office other than judicial, shall be void."

Section 19, as added in 1976, provides in part: "**1.** The chief justice is the administrative head of the court system." **Section 20**, as added in 1976, directs: "**1.** When a vacancy occurs before the expiration of any term of office in the supreme court or among the district judges, the governor shall appoint a justice or judge from among three nominees selected ... by the commission on judicial selection. **2.** The term of office of any justice or judge so appointed expires on the first Monday of January following the next general election."

Section 21, added in 1976 and amended in 1994, creates a commission on judicial discipline and states in part: "**1.** A justice of the supreme court, a district judge, a justice of the peace or a municipal judge may, in addition [to impeachment], be censured, retired, removed or otherwise disciplined by the commission.... A justice or judge may appeal from the action of the commission to the supreme court, which may reverse such action or take any alternative action provided in this subsection."

Impeachment

Article 7, Impeachment and Removal from Office, section 1, declares: "The Assembly shall have the sole power of impeaching," by a majority of the members elected. Impeachments are to be tried in the senate, and a conviction requires "the concurrence of two thirds of the senators elected." According to **section 2**, all state and judicial officers, "except Justices of the Peace shall be liable to impeachment...." **Section 3** provides for the removal of judicial officers by "the vote of two thirds of the Members elected to each branch of the Legislature...."

Direct Democracy

Article 19, Initiative and Referendum, section 1, added in 1904 and amended in 1962 and 1988, describes procedures whereby "10 percent or more of the number of voters who voted at the last general election" can require a referendum on "any statute or resolution or any part thereof enacted by the legislature...." **Section 2**, added in 1912 and amended in 1958, 1962, 1972, and 1988, allows the same percentage of voters, "in not less than 75 percent of the counties," to petition for the enactment of or amendments to legislation and amendments to the constitution. **Article 2, Right of Suffrage, section 9**, added in 1921 and amended in 1970 and 1996, provides procedures for recalling public officers.

Local Government

Article 4, Legislative Department, section 25, mandates: "The Legislature shall establish a system of County and Township Government which shall be uniform throughout the State." **Section 26** directs: "The Legislature shall provide by law, for the election of a

Board of County Commissioners in each County, and such County Commissioners shall jointly and individually perform such duties as may be prescribed by law."

Article 9, Finance and State Debt, section 2, as amended in 1956, 1974, and 1996, sets forth in part: "**1.** The legislature shall provide by law for an annual tax sufficient to defray the estimated expenses of the state for each fiscal year; and whenever the expenses of any year exceed the income, the legislature shall provide for levying a tax sufficient, with other sources of income, to pay the deficiency, as well as the estimated expenses of such ensuing year or two years." **Article 19, section 6,** added in 1972, also requires appropriations, whether authorized by the legislature or popular initiative, to be paid for by a sufficient tax.

Article 10, Taxation, section 1, which was amended eleven times between 1902 and 1990, states in part: "**1.** The legislature shall provide by law for a uniform and equal rate of assessment and taxation, and shall prescribe such regulations as shall secure a just valuation for taxation of all property, real, personal and possessory, except mines and mining claims...." In *Crandall v. Nevada* (1868), the U.S. Supreme Court held that a capitation tax of one dollar per person leaving the state by any railroad, stage coach, or other vehicle levied by Nevada was an unconstitutional infringement on the rights of U.S. citizens.

Article 11, Education, section 1, as amended in 1956, declares: "The legislature shall encourage by all suitable means the promotion of intellectual, literary, scientific, mining, mechanical, agriculture, and moral improvements, and also provide for a superintendent of public instruction and by law prescribe the manner of appointment, term of office and the duties thereof."

Article 16, Amendments, section 1, as amended in 1972, provides in part: "**1.** Any amendment or amendments to this Constitution may be proposed in the Senate or Assembly; and if the same shall be agreed to by a Majority of all the members elected to each of the two houses, such proposed amendment or amendments shall be entered on their respective journals ... and referred to the Legislature then next to be chosen, and shall be published.... [And if such] shall be agreed to by a majority of all the members elected to each house [of the succeeding legislature], then it shall be the duty of the Legislature to submit [such] to the people ...; and if the people shall approve ... by a majority of the electors qualified to vote for members of the Legislature voting thereon [such] shall ... become a part of the Constitution." In *State ex rel. Stevenson v. Tufly* (1887), the Nevada supreme court declared that an amendment to article 16, sections 1 and 2, ratified by the people in 1886, was ineffective because no entry had been made on the journal of either house of the legislature.

Section 2 adds that the "Legislature by a vote of two-thirds of the Members elected to each house" may recommend to the voters that a convention for revising the constitution be called. If "a majority of the electors voting at such election [vote for it], the Legislature shall, at its next session provide" for such a convention.

Article 19, Initiative and Referendum, section 2, provides procedures for amendment of the constitution by popular initiative.

NEW HAMPSHIRE

New Hampshire was admitted to the Union on June 21, 1788, as the ninth state. Concord is the capital of the "Granite State," which encompasses 9,351 square miles and is bordered by the Canadian province of Quebec on the north, Maine and the Atlantic Ocean on the east, Massachusetts on the south, and Vermont on the west. New Hampshire ranks forty-second among the states with a population of approximately 1.1 million inhabitants. Tourism, manufacturing, and agriculture are among the state's principal industries; its chief crops include dairy products, nursery and greenhouse products, vegetables, and fruit.

General Information

Government: The governor is elected for a two-year term. There is no lieutenant governor. The legislature, called the general court, consists of twenty-four senators and 400 members of the house of representatives, all elected for two-year terms. The supreme court includes a chief justice and four additional justices appointed by the governor and confirmed by an executive council; the justices hold office until the age of seventy.

Dates of Constitutions: 1776 and 1784

Constitutional History

When the Europeans arrived at the beginning of the seventeenth century, some three thousand Algonkians, the most numerous of which were the Pennacooks, were living in the area that would become the state of New Hampshire. In 1603 English merchants hired Martin Pring to explore the mouth of the Piscataque River near the present site of Portsmouth. Two years later, on July 15, 1605, the French explorer Samuel de Champlain arrived at Piscataque Bay. Captain John Smith sailed along the New Hampshire coast in 1614.

In 1620 the English king James I granted to the Council of New England in Plymouth, Massachusetts, a charter for a large expanse of land, which by 1622 had been subdivided into a number of smaller tracts. The territory including Vermont and New Hampshire was awarded jointly to Sir Ferdinando Gorges and Captain John Mason.

In 1623 Mason engaged a Scotsman, David Thompson, to establish a settlement on the Piscataque River, and six years later he and Gorges divided their lands, with Mason taking the area west of the Piscataque. Mason called his colony New Hampshire, after the English county of Hampshire. The title to the lands of New Hampshire, however, became clouded by a number of new grants and Mason's death in 1635. As a result of religious disputes among Anglicans, Puritans, and Quakers, the administration of New Hampshire was turned over to Massachusetts, which annexed the territory in 1641, and for the next forty years New Hampshire was governed from Boston.

In 1679 Charles II of England separated New Hampshire from Massachusetts, opening the door for the heirs of Gorges and Mason to renew their claims to proprietorship over the colony. A succession of colonial governors had to contend with the competing interests of the Crown, the settlers, and the heirs. By the time the American independence movement had begun, New Hampshirites had developed a good deal of resistance to British rule. New Hampshire became the first colony to declare its independence, six months before the signing of the Declaration of Independence, and it was the first to adopt its own constitution after the Continental Congress recommended that independent colonies do so on December 21, 1775.

The 911-word document was adopted by the state's fifth provincial congress meeting in Exeter on January 5, 1776, thus becoming the world's first written constitution for an independent state. It denounced royal government and created a bicameral legislature—a lower chamber called the house of representatives or assembly, elected by adult male taxpayers, and an upper chamber consisting of a twelve-member council, chosen by the lower chamber—but no chief executive or governor. A judicial system was established by legislative enactment.

A committee of safety, a type of collegial executive body used by a number of the thirteen colonies after declaring their independence from Great Britain, continued to operate with broad executive powers. But the lack of an elected executive branch, together with ambiguous methods for apportionment, no guarantee of individual rights, and no process for amending the constitution, resulted in the convening of the world's first constitutional convention in Concord in June 1778. As an independent body that was not a part of a legislature, the convention broke new ground by framing a constitution and submitting it to the people for approval, a process that has since become the standard the world over for drafting and adopting constitutions for popular sovereignties. The New Hampshire assembly had put the question of calling a constitutional convention to the towns, and the representatives elected in 1778 were instructed to vote for the convention.

Because a two-thirds vote of the people—a high proportion—was required for adoption of the convention's document, its first two proposals—in 1779 and 1781—were rejected. Three years later, a third proposal was approved and went into effect on June 2, 1784. This constitution, as amended, is the state's current constitution.

The 1784 New Hampshire constitution bears a strong resemblance to the 1780 Massachusetts constitution. It is only one-fourth the length of the older document, however, containing just some 9,200 words, and is the shortest of any state constitution except that of Vermont. Extensively revised in 1792, the 1784 constitution has been amended 143 times as of January 1, 1998.

The constitution expressly vests executive power solely in the governor, who is elected for two years. New Hampshire and Vermont are the only states in which the governor is not elected for a four-year term. But the constitution also creates, as does the Massachusetts document, a council of five members that has the power to act in some ways like a parliamentary cabinet and check the governor's actions. The council and both houses of the legislature are also elected every two years. Similar to the constitutions of several states, including Massachusetts and Maine, the New Hampshire constitution devotes only a few provisions specifically to the judicial branch of government.

The document contains one provision not found in any other state constitution. **Article 101** specifies: "This form of government shall be enrolled on parchment, and deposited in the secretary's office, and be a part of the laws of the land and printed copies thereof shall be prefixed to the books containing the laws of this state, in all future editions thereof."

The 1784 New Hampshire constitution has no preamble.

Part first, Bill of Rights, article 1, proclaims: "All men are born equally free and independent; therefore, all government of right originates from the people, is founded in

The Constitution

Preamble

Fundamental Rights

consent, and instituted for the general good." **Article 2,** as amended in 1974, declares: "All men have certain natural, essential, and inherent rights—among which are, the enjoying and defending life and liberty; acquiring, possessing, and protecting, property; and, in a word, of seeking and obtaining happiness. Equality of rights under the law shall not be denied or abridged by this state on account of race, creed, color, sex or national origin." In 1870 Marilla Ricker, New Hampshire's first female attorney, became the first woman in the country to attempt to vote (she was unsuccessful); her bid for the governorship in 1910 was also thwarted when the secretary of state refused to put her name on the ballot even though she met all the constitutional eligibility requirements.

Article 2-a, added in 1982, guarantees the right to bear arms, and **article 3** avers: "When men enter into a state of society, they surrender up some of their natural rights to that society, in order to ensure the protection of others; and, without such an equivalent, the surrender is void." This language reflects the influence of *The Social Contract* (1762) of Jean-Jacques Rousseau. **Article 4** provides: "Among the natural rights, some are, in their very nature unalienable, because no equivalent can be given or received for them. Of this kind are the Rights of Conscience." **Article 5** concerns religious freedom. In *Cox v. New Hampshire* (1941), the U.S. Supreme Court held that a state requirement that a license be obtained for a public parade by Jehovah's Witnesses did not infringe freedom of worship or any other freedom guaranteed by the U.S. Constitution.

Article 7 acknowledges the right of state sovereignty to the extent that it "is not, or may not hereafter be, by [the people] expressly delegated to the United States of America in congress assembled." **Article 8,** as amended in 1976, confirms the accountability of government officials and the public's right to government information. According to **article 10,** "The doctrine of nonresistance against arbitrary power, and oppression, is absurd, slavish, and destructive of the good and happiness of mankind." **Article 12,** amended in 1964 to remove reference to buying one's way out of military service, provides in part: "Every member of the community ... is therefore bound to contribute his share [of expense] and ... personal service when necessary." **Article 13,** also amended in 1964, acknowledges the rights of conscientious objectors and is unusual among state constitutions.

Article 14 guarantees to every citizen "a certain remedy, by having recourse to the laws, for all injuries he may receive in his person, property, or character," and that remedy is free, complete, and prompt. **Article 15,** as amended in 1966 and 1984, provides for rights of those accused of crimes; **article 16** prohibits double jeopardy and mandates a jury trial in cases involving capital punishment; and **article 17,** as amended in 1792 and 1978, requires that criminal prosecutions be tried "in the vicinity where [the crime] happened...." **Article 18,** as amended in 1792, sets forth in part: "All penalties ought to be proportioned to the nature of the offense.... The true design of all punishments being to reform, not to exterminate mankind." The constitutions of several other states, including Illinois, also contain language emphasizing reform as the object of punishment.

Article 19, as amended in 1792, prohibits unreasonable searches and seizures; **article 20,** as last amended in 1988, sets criteria for jury trials in civil cases; and **article 21** states: "In order to reap the fullest advantage of the inestimable privilege of the trial by jury, great care ought to be taken, that none but qualified persons should be appointed to serve; and such ought to be fully compensated for their travel, time and attendance." **Articles 22** through **28**, respectively, guarantee freedom of speech and the press, prohibit retrospective laws, confirm the need for a well-regulated militia, require the consent of the legislature for standing armies, subordinate the military to civil power, limit the quartering of soldiers in private homes, and prohibit taxation that is not authorized by the people either directly or indirectly.

Article 28-a, added in 1984, prohibits the mandating of "any new, expanded or modified programs or responsibilities to any political subdivision ... unless such programs or responsibilities are fully funded by the state" or are approved by the local legislature. **Article 29** proscribes suspension of the laws or their execution, except by the legislature.

Article 30 states: "The freedom of deliberation, speech, and debate, in either house of the legislature, is so essential to the rights of the people, that it cannot be the foundation of any action, complaint, or prosecution, in any other court or place whatsoever." **Article 31**, as amended in 1792, indicates: "The legislature shall assemble for the redress of public grievances and for making such laws as the public good may require."

Article 32 guarantees the right of assembly and petition for redress of wrongs; and **article 33** prohibits excessive bail, fines, and "cruel or unusual punishment." Unlike the U.S. Constitution and most state constitutions, the New Hampshire state constitution uses *or* instead of *and* in this phrase, as does the California constitution. **Article 34** limits the application of martial law, and **articles 36** and **36-a**, the latter added in 1984, address pensions and the use of retirement funds. **Article 38** provides in part: "A frequent recurrence to the fundamental principles of the constitution, and a constant adherence to justice, moderation, temperance, industry, frugality, and all the social virtues, are indispensably necessary to preserve the blessings of liberty and good government...."

Part first, Bill of Rights, article 37, declares: "In the government of this state, the three essential powers thereof, to wit, the legislative, executive, and judicial, ought to be kept as separate from, and independent of, each other, as the nature of a free government will admit, or as is consistent with that chain of connection that binds the whole fabric of the constitution in one indissoluble bond of union and amity."

Division of Powers

Part second, Form of Government, article 1, proclaims: "The people inhabiting the territory formerly called the province of New Hampshire, do hereby solemnly and mutually agree with each other, to form themselves into a free, sovereign and independent body-politic, or state, by the name of THE STATE OF NEW HAMPSHIRE."

Legislative Branch

Article 2 reads: "The supreme legislative power, within this state, shall be vested in the senate and house of representatives, each of which shall have a negative on the other." **Article 3**, as amended four times between 1877 and 1984, states: "The senate and house ... shall be styled THE GENERAL COURT OF NEW HAMPSHIRE." **Article 4**, as amended in

1966, provides in part: "The general court (except as ... provided by Article 72-a of Part 2 [relating to the judicial branch]) shall forever have full power and authority to erect and constitute judicatories and courts of record, or other courts...." Pursuant to **article 5,** as amended in 1792, 1877, and 1942, "And farther, full power and authority are hereby given and granted to the said general court, from time to time, to make, ordain, and establish, all manner of wholesome and reasonable orders, laws, statutes, ordinances, directions, and instructions, either with penalties, or without, so as the same be not repugnant or contrary to this constitution...." This language reflects the influence of the 1629 constitution of the Massachusetts Bay Colony.

Article 5-a, added in 1942, provides for the continuity of state government in the case of enemy attack; **article 7,** dating from 1792, prohibits legislators from taking a fee or acting as counsel "[i]n any cause before either branch of the legislature"; and **article 8,** also added in 1792, states: "The doors of the galleries, of each house of the legislature, shall be kept open to all persons who behave decently, except when the welfare of the state, in the opinion of either branch, shall require secrecy."

Article 9, as amended in 1877, 1942, and 1964, specifies in part: "The whole number of representatives to be chosen from the towns, wards, places, and representative districts thereof established hereunder, shall be not less than three hundred seventy-five or more than four hundred." The New Hampshire house of representatives currently has 400 members—more than any other state. **Article 12,** as amended in 1877, states: "The members of the house of representatives shall be chosen biennially, in the month of November, and shall be the second branch of the legislature." **Article 14,** as amended in 1852, 1877, 1956, and 1964, provides: "Every member of the house of representatives shall be chosen by ballot; and, for two years, at least, next preceding his election shall have been an inhabitant of this state; shall be, at the time of his election, an inhabitant of the town, ward, place, or district he may be chosen to represent and shall cease to represent [such jurisdiction] immediately on his ceasing to be qualified as aforesaid."

Article 18 requires money bills to originate in the house; **article 19,** as amended in 1948 and 1966, grants the house the power to adjourn by itself; and **article 20** states: "A majority of the members of the house of representatives shall be a quorum for doing business: But when less than two-thirds of the representatives elected shall be present, the assent of two-thirds of those members shall be necessary to render their acts and proceedings valid." **Article 22,** as amended in 1792, provides: "The house of representatives shall choose their own speaker, appoint their own officers, and settle rules of proceedings in their own house ... and shall be judge of the returns, elections, and qualifications, of its members.... [The house shall have the authority to] punish, by imprisonment, every person who shall be guilty of disrespect to the house...."

Article 25, as amended in 1792, 1877, 1889, and 1974, stipulates that the senate is to consist of twenty-four members. **Article 27,** as amended in 1792 and 1877, directs: "The freeholders and other inhabitants of each [senatorial] district, qualified as in this constitution provided shall biennially give in their votes for a senator, at some meeting holden in the month of November." **Article 29,** as amended in 1852, 1877, and 1976, sets forth in part: "[N]o person shall be capable of being elected a senator, who is not of the age of thirty years, and who shall not have been an inhabitant of this state for seven years immediately preceding his election, and at the time thereof he shall be an inhabitant of the district for which he shall be chosen." As with members of the house, if a senator moves from the jurisdiction from which he or she was elected, the position will be declared vacant. No comparable age requirement for representatives is expressly stated in the constitution. **Article 30,** as amended in 1958 and 1976, defines an inhabitant as a person domiciled within the state, town, or ward.

Article 32, as amended in 1792, 1889, 1958, 1974, and 1976, requires in part: "The meetings for the choice of governor, council and senators, shall be warned by warrant from the selectmen, and governed by a moderator, who shall, in the presence of the selectmen (whose duty it shall be to attend) in open meeting, receive the votes of all the inhabitants...."

Article 35 instructs: "The senate shall be final judges of the elections, returns, and qualifications, of their own members...." **Article 36,** as amended in 1792, 1948, and 1966, provides that the senate, like the house, "shall have power to adjourn themselves...." **Article 37,** as amended in 1792 and 1877, sets forth: "The senate shall appoint their president and other officers, and determine their own rules of proceedings: And not less than thirteen members of the senate shall make a quorum for doing business; and when less than sixteen senators shall be present, the assent of ten, at least, shall be necessary to render their acts and proceedings valid." In contrast, the constitutions of most states define a quorum as merely a majority of the members elected to a legislative house.

Article 21 provides: "No member of the house of representatives, or senate shall be arrested, or held to bail, on mesne [intermediate or intervening] process, during his going to, returning from, or attendance upon, the court." **Article 23,** as amended in 1792, states that the senate, governor, and council have the same power to punish misconduct as granted to the house of representatives under article 22, "provided, that no imprisonment by either, for any offense, exceeds ten days." **Article 24,** as amended in 1792 and 1966, mandates: "The journals of the proceedings, and all public acts of both houses ... shall be printed and published immediately after every adjournment or prorogation.... And any member of the senate, or house of representatives, shall have a right ... to have his protest, or dissent, with the reasons, against any vote, resolve, or bill passed, entered on the journal."

Part second, Form of Government, article 41, as amended in 1792 and 1966, declares: "There shall be a supreme executive magistrate, who shall be styled the Governor of the State of New Hampshire, and whose title shall be His Excellency. The executive power of the state is vested in the governor." The 1792 amendment substituted *Governor* for *President;* an early draft of the U.S. Constitution also required the president to be addressed as "His Excellency." Article 41 continues: "The governor shall be responsible for the faithful execution of the laws. He may, by appropriate court action

Executive Branch

or proceeding brought in the name of the state, enforce compliance with any constitutional or legislative mandate, or restrain violation of any constitutional or legislative power, duty, or right, by any officer, department or agency of the state. This authority shall not be construed to authorize any action or proceedings against the legislative or judicial branches."

Article 42, which was amended six times between 1792 and 1982, directs: "The governor shall be chosen biennially in the month of November . . . ," making New Hampshire one of only two states in which the governor is not elected for a four-year term of office. Article 42 concludes: "And no person shall be eligible to this office, unless at the time of his election, he shall have been an inhabitant of this state for 7 years next preceding, and unless he shall be of the age of 30 years."

Article 43, as amended in 1792, 1889, 1974, and 1980, states: "In cases of disagreement between the two houses [of the legislature], with regard to the time or place of adjournment or prorogation, the governor, with advice of council, shall have a right to adjourn or prorogue the general court. . . ." According to **article 44,** added in 1792, "Every bill which shall have passed both houses of the general court, shall, before it becomes a law, be presented to the governor, if he approves, he shall sign it, but if not, he shall return it, with his objections, to that house in which it shall have originated. . . ." The governor's veto may be overridden if the bill is "approved by two-thirds" of both houses. In *Washburn v. Thomas* (1992), the New Hampshire supreme court, after considering the sentiments of the framers, comparable provisions on which the constitution was based, and the history of the actions of the legislature, decided that the two-thirds approval necessary for overriding a veto meant two-thirds of the members present, not two-thirds of all the members of the legislature. Article 44 continues: "If any bill shall not be returned by the governor within five days (Sundays excepted) after it shall have been presented to him, the same shall be a law . . . , unless the legislature, by their adjournment, prevent its return. . . ." Under **article 45,** added in 1792, resolves are treated in the same manner as bills.

Article 46, as amended in 1792, 1877, and 1976, states: "All judicial officers, the attorney general, and all officers of the navy, and general and field officers of the militia, shall be nominated and appointed by the governor and council; and every such nomination shall be made at least three days prior to such appointment; and no appointment shall take place, unless a majority of the council agree thereto." **Article 47,** added in 1792, provides in part: "The governor and council shall have a negative on each other, both in the nominations and appointments." **Article 50,** as amended in 1792, authorizes the governor, "with advice of council," to prorogue the legislature; **article 51,** as amended in 1792 and 1968, designates the governor "commander-in-chief of all the military forces of the state"; and **article 52,** as amended in 1792, provides in part: "The power of pardoning offenses, except [conviction on impeachment], shall be in the governor, by and with the advice of council . . . [after conviction]."

Article 49, which was amended five times between 1972 and 1984, sets forth in part: "In the event of the death, resignation, removal from office, failure to qualify, physical or mental incapacity, absence from the state, or other incapacity of the governor, the president of the senate, for the time being, shall act as governor until the vacancy is filled or the incapacity is removed.... Whenever a vacancy for the duration or remainder of the governor's term of office occurs before the commencement of the last year of such term, a special election for governor shall take place to fill the vacancy, as provided by law." New Hampshire is one of eight states that do not have a lieutenant governor who can serve as acting governor or succeed to the governorship in the event the governor becomes unable to perform the duties of office.

Article 60, as amended in 1792, 1877, 1889, and 1984, states: "There shall be biennially elected, by ballot, five councilors, for advising the governor in the executive part of government. The freeholders and other inhabitants in each county, qualified to vote for senators, shall some time in the month of November, give in their votes for one councilor...." **Article 62,** added in 1792, provides in part: "[T]he governor shall have full power and authority to convene the council, from time to time, at his discretion; and, with them, or the majority of them, may and shall, from time to time hold a council, for ordering and directing the affairs of the state, according to the laws of the land."

Article 67, as amended in 1950, directs: "The secretary and treasurer shall be chosen by joint ballot of the senators and representatives assembled in one room." This is one of the few instances in which a state constitution provides for a joint session of the houses of the legislature. Some national constitutions, including the constitution of Australia but not that of the United States, provide expressly for joint sessions of the two houses to act on certain measures. **Article 68,** as amended in 1792, stipulates: "The records of the state shall be kept in the office of the secretary, and he shall attend the governor and council, the senate and representatives, in person, or by deputy, as they may require."

Part second, Form of Government, article 72-a, added in 1966, declares: "The judicial power of the state shall be vested in the supreme court, a trial court of general jurisdiction known as the superior court, and such lower courts as the legislature may establish...." The supreme court consists of a chief justice and four additional justices appointed by the governor and confirmed by a majority of the five-member council in the executive branch. **Article 73,** as amended in 1792 and 1966, directs that "all judicial officers duly appointed, commissioned and sworn, shall hold their offices during good behavior except those for whom a different provision is made in this constitution. The governor with consent of the council may remove any commissioned officer ... [but] no officer shall be so removed unless he shall have had an opportunity to be heard in his defense by a joint committee of both houses of the legislature." The mandatory retirement age is seventy.

Article 73-a, added in 1978, provides that the chief justice of the supreme court is to be the administrative head of the courts. "He shall, with the concurrence of a majority of the supreme court justices, make rules governing the administration of all courts ... and the practice and procedure to be followed in all such courts. The rules so promulgated shall have the force and effect of law." **Article 74,** as amended in 1792 and 1958,

Judicial Branch

states: "Each branch of the legislature as well as the governor and council shall have authority to require the opinions of the justices of the supreme court upon important questions of law and upon solemn occasions."

Impeachment

Part second, Form of Government, article 17, states: "The house of representatives shall be the grand inquest of the state; and all impeachments made by them, shall be heard and tried by the senate." **Article 38,** as amended in 1792, provides in part: "The senate shall be a court, with full power and authority to hear, try, and determine, all impeachments made by the house of representatives against any officer or officers of the state, for bribery, corruption, malpractice or maladministration, in office...." Adds **article 39,** "Their judgment, however, shall not extend further than removal from office, disqualification to hold or enjoy any place of honor, trust, or profit, under this state, but the party so convicted, shall nevertheless be liable to indictment, trial, judgment, and punishment, according to the laws of the land." **Article 63,** as amended in 1792, expressly includes members of the council among those who may be impeached.

Local Government

Part first, Bill of Rights, article 39, added in 1966, indicates: "No law changing the charter or form of government of a particular city or town shall be enacted by the legislature except to become effective upon the approval of the voters of such city or town upon a referendum to be provided for in said law. The legislature may by general law authorize cities and towns to adopt or amend their charters or forms of government in any way which is not in conflict with general law, provided that such charters or amendments shall become effective only upon the approval of the voters of each such city or town on a referendum."

Taxation and Finance

Part second, Form of Government, article 6, as amended in 1903, directs: "The public charges of government, or any part thereof, may be raised by taxation upon polls, estates, and other classes of property, including franchises and property when passing by will or inheritance; and there shall be a valuation of the estates within the state taken anew once in every five years, at least, and as much oftener as the general court shall order." In *Austin v. New Hampshire* (1975), the U.S. Supreme Court determined that a New Hampshire commuter tax that treated unequally citizens of the taxing state and nonresident taxpayers violates the privileges and immunities clause of the U.S. Constitution.

Education

Part second, Form of Government, article 83, as amended in 1877 and 1903, notes in part: "Knowledge and learning, generally diffused through a community, being essential to the preservation of a free government; and spreading the opportunities and advantages of education through the various parts of the country, being highly conducive to promote this end; it shall be the duty of the legislators and magistrates, in all future periods of this government, to cherish the interest of literature and the sciences...."

Amendment Procedures

Part second, Form of Government, article 100, added in 1792 and amended in 1964 and 1980, sets forth in part: "Amendments to this constitution may be proposed by the general court or by a constitutional convention selected as herein provided. **(a)** The senate and house of representatives, voting separately, may propose amendments by a three-fifths vote of the entire membership of each house at any session. **(b)** The general court, by an affirmative vote of a majority of all members of both houses voting separately, may at any time submit the question 'Shall there be a convention to amend or revise the constitution?' to the qualified voters of the state." If the question is not submitted for a period of ten years, the secretary of state must submit it. Article 100(b) continues: "If a majority of the qualified voters voting on the question" approve it, "delegates shall be chosen at the next regular general election...."

Article 100(c) states: "The constitutional convention may propose amendments by a three-fifths vote of the entire membership of the convention.... Each constitutional amendment proposed [by either method] shall be submitted to the voters ... at the next biennial November election and shall become a part of the Constitution only after approval by two-thirds of the qualified voters present and voting...."

NEW JERSEY

New Jersey became the third state of the United States on December 18, 1787. Trenton is the capital of the "Garden State," which ranks ninth in population with approximately 8 million residents. Some 8,722 square miles in area, New Jersey is bordered by New York on the north, the Atlantic Ocean on the east, the Delaware Bay on the south, and the Delaware River and Pennsylvania on the west. New Jersey's principal industries include services, trade, and manufacturing; among its chief crops are nursery and hothouse plants, hay, corn, and soybeans.

General Information

Government: The governor is elected for a four-year term and is limited to two consecutive terms. There is no lieutenant governor. The legislature consists of forty senators and an eighty-member general assembly. The terms for senators follow a pattern of two four-year terms followed by one two-year term; the members of the general assembly serve two-year terms. The supreme court includes a chief justice and six associate justices appointed by the governor with the advice and consent of the senate; the justices' initial term is for seven years, and they may be reappointed and serve until age seventy.

Dates of Constitutions: 1776, 1844, and 1948

Constitutional History

In 1524, sailing under the French flag, the Genoese navigator Giovanni da Verrazano scouted the coast of present-day New Jersey. Nearly a century later, in 1609, the English explorer Henry Hudson came ashore at Sandy Hook on the northern New Jersey coast. The Dutch followed, and in 1629 Michael Pauw of Amsterdam was granted land where Jersey City stands today. Swedish settlers arrived soon after and acquired land from the indigenous Lenni-Lenape people in the southern region of New Jersey.

The Dutch took over the Swedish-controlled territory in 1655, only to lose New Jersey and all their North American possessions in a war with England in 1664. Even before the war, Charles II of England, recently reinstated to the throne, gave the title to most of the Dutch territory to his brother, the duke of York, who had only to oust the Dutch to take possession of it. The duke in turn conveyed a large part of the land to John Lord Berkeley and Sir George Carteret in the same year, 1664. In liquidating the Dutch holdings, these two adventurers issued concessions for the Province of New Caesarea or New-Jersey in 1665.

Settlers in New Jersey, named for England's island of Jersey, Sir George's home, were guaranteed a general assembly so that they could participate in governing, as well as freedom of trade and conscience. But the governing of New Jersey did not go smoothly because of religious conflicts between the early settlers—Puritans, who had fled from England rather than be forced to worship under the Church of England, and Quakers, members of the Society of Friends. To accommodate these factions New Jersey was divided into eastern and western sections. The Quaker leader William Penn was one of the purchasers of the Province of West-New Jersey in 1676, and under his influence a charter for the province was promulgated on March 3, 1676. In 1682 he also acquired an interest in East New Jersey. A document entitled the Fundamental Constitutions for the Province of East-New Jersey, drafted in 1681, was never put into effect.

In 1702 East and West New Jersey were reunified as a royal English colony, and Queen Anne of England issued a declaration on November 16 of that year creating a royal government for the colony. The 1702 declaration and a clarifying document issued in 1712 served as the basis for New Jersey's government until July 2, 1776, when a revolutionary type of constitution was adopted.

After the American Revolution began in 1775, supporters of independence from Great Britain in the Second Continental Congress sought to persuade reluctant states, including Pennsylvania and New Jersey, to join the cause. On May 10, 1776, they pushed through a resolution directing states in which the colonial government no longer functioned to create governments of their own. Although New Jersey's government was still in operation, on May 8 Jerseymen elected a revolutionary provincial congress, which, while not established as a constitutional convention, nevertheless proceeded to select a ten-man committee to draft a state constitution. The drafting was spearheaded by Jonathan Dickinson Sergeant, who sought help from John Adams. With nearly half the delegates absent, the constitutional document was adopted by a vote of twenty-six to nine.

New Jersey's 1776 constitution, the fourth new state constitution written that year, was never submitted to the voters for ratification. The document's validity was challenged on this ground, but in 1828 the New Jersey supreme court ruled that "not withstanding these considerations [that the document had been drafted by delegates not elected as a constitutional convention and not ratified at the polls], it has by general consent been received, and used ever since as the legitimate constitution of the state." The opinion continues: "Without looking, therefore, into the spuriousness of its origin, we must receive and treat it as such, until the people shall think proper to lay it aside and establish a better in its place."

By 1844 New Jersey's constitution of 1776 had become outmoded. Like Pennsylvania's constitution and others among the first wave of state constitutions, it relied on frequent elections rather than institutional checks and balances to ensure responsible government. In addition, the legislative branch elected the governor annually and appointed all state officials including judges. Other states had revised their constitutions in light of the evolution of constitutional theory as embodied in the U.S. Constitution, and New Jersey determined to do so also. A constitutional convention called by the legislature met in Trenton from May 14 to June 29, 1844, and drafted a second constitution for the state, which was ratified by the voters on August 13 and became effective on September 2, 1844.

The new frame of government outlined by the 1844 constitution, which was relatively brief, strengthened the executive branch. The governor was elected for three years and had veto power, although this could be overridden by a majority vote of the legislature, and judges were appointed by the executive branch. Eventually it became clear that even these changes did not invest the executive branch with sufficient power, and by 1913 Governor Woodrow Wilson was advising the legislature that the state had outgrown this document. A movement to modernize the constitution began in earnest in 1940, and a convention met in New Brunswick from June 12 to September 10, 1947. The document was ratified in November by the electorate and went into effect on January 1, 1948.

The 1948 New Jersey constitution reflects the general trend in state constitutions away from domination by the legislative branch toward a structural separation of powers. A model for the 1959 Alaska constitution, it strengthened the governor's power by extending the term of office from three to four years, permitting two consecutive terms,

The Constitution

limiting the number of executive departments, and investing the governor with removal, directive, and investigative power. One innovation is the "conditional veto" power granted to the governor, which allows the executive to change parts of proposed legislation and resubmit it for the legislature's approval. This precedent appears to have helped rather than hindered cooperation between the legislative and executive branches. In addition, the new constitution strengthens the judicial branch by making the chief justice of the supreme court the head of the judicial system and allowing the incumbent an administrative office, along the lines of the administrative office for the federal courts. As of January 1, 1998, New Jersey's 1948 constitution of 17,800 words has been amended forty-eight times.

Preamble

No specific preamble is included in the 1948 New Jersey constitution, but following a paragraph on the constitutional convention that drafted it, the document declares: "We, the people of the State of New Jersey grateful to Almighty God for the civil and religious liberty which He hath so long permitted us to enjoy, and looking to Him for a blessing upon our endeavors to secure and transmit the same unimpaired to succeeding generations, do ordain and establish this Constitution."

Fundamental Rights

Article I, Rights and Privileges, paragraph 1, proclaims: "All persons are by nature free and independent, and have certain natural and unalienable rights, among which are those of enjoying and defending life and liberty, of acquiring, possessing, and protecting property, and of pursuing and obtaining safety and happiness." In the draft of the 1948 constitution the second word in this paragraph was *men*, but New Jersey's first woman attorney, Mary Philbrook, was instrumental in changing it to *persons*. The New Jersey supreme court in *Peper v. Princeton* (1978) interpreted the phrase *[a]ll persons* to guarantee equal employment and property rights for women. In *Right to Choose v. Byrne* (1982), the New Jersey supreme court held, on the basis of paragraph 1, that a woman's right to choose to protect her health by terminating pregnancy outweighed the state's interest in protecting the potential life of a child. Further in the constitution, **article X, General Provisions, paragraph 4,** states: "Wherever in this Constitution the term 'person,' 'persons,' 'people' or any personal pronoun is used, the same shall be taken to include both sexes."

Article I, Rights and Privileges, paragraph 2, as amended in 1994, affirms in **paragraph 2(a)** that all power is inherent in the people. **Paragraphs 3** and **4** address freedom of religion, and **paragraph 5** provides: "No person shall be denied the enjoyment of any civil or military right, nor be discriminated against in the exercise of any civil or military right, nor be segregated in the militia or in the public schools, because of religious principles, race, color, ancestry or national origin." **Paragraphs 6** and **7** set forth the rights of free speech and publication and the guarantee against unreasonable searches and seizures. **Paragraphs 8** through **12** cover rights of the accused. **Paragraph 15** mandates the subordination of the military to civil authority. **Paragraph 18** extends the rights to peaceably assemble and to petition the government for redress of grievances.

Paragraph 19 addresses the issue of collective bargaining: "Persons in private employment shall have the right to organize and bargain collectively. Persons in public employment shall have the right to organize, present to and make known to the State ... their grievances and proposals through representatives of their own choosing." **Paragraph 20,** like the Fifth Amendment (1791) of the U.S. Constitution, prohibits the taking of private property for public use without just compensation. **Paragraph 22,** added by amendment in 1991, extends rights to victims of crime.

Article IV, Legislative, section VII.3, provides: "The Legislature shall not pass any bill of attainder, ex post facto law, or law impairing the obligation of contracts, or depriving a party of any remedy for enforcing a contract which existed when the contract was made."

Article III, Distribution of the Powers of Government, paragraph 1, states: "The powers of government shall be divided among three distinct branches, the legislative, executive, and judicial. No person or persons belonging to or constituting one branch shall exercise any of the powers properly belonging to either of the others, except as expressly provided in this Constitution." This statement regarding separation of powers is like that found in most state constitutions. In *State v. Leonardis* (1977), however, the New Jersey supreme court held that this language is not absolute and does not preclude cooperation between the branches. Whether these powers can be kept strictly separate was the subject of the U.S. Supreme Court ruling in *Springer v. Government of the Philippine Islands* (1928). Writing in dissent, Justice Oliver Wendell Holmes noted that "however we may disguise it by veiling words we do not and cannot carry out the distinction between the legislative and executive branches with mathematical precision and divide the branches into watertight compartments...."

Division of Powers

Article IV, Legislative, section I, paragraph 1, states: "The legislative power shall be vested in a Senate and General Assembly." **Paragraph 2,** as amended in 1966, specifies that a senator must be thirty years old and "a citizen and resident of the State for four years, and of the district for which he shall be elected one year, next before his election." A member of the general assembly must be twenty-one years old, a citizen of the state for two years, and a resident of the district one year preceding the election. Senators and members must otherwise be eligible voters.

Legislative Branch

Paragraph 3, as amended in 1968 and applicable to the legislature in 1970, requires that "[e]ach Legislature shall be constituted for a term of 2 years beginning at noon on the second Tuesday in January in each even numbered year." **Paragraph 4** specifies: "Special sessions of the Legislature shall be called by the Governor upon petition of a majority of all the members of each house, and may be called by the Governor whenever in his opinion the public interest shall require."

Section II, as amended in 1966, requires in **paragraph 1** that the senate "be composed of forty senators apportioned among Senate districts" on the basis of the U.S. census and elected for four-year terms. However, as stated in **paragraph 2,** "each Senator, to be elected for a term beginning in January of the second year following the year in which the decennial census of the United States is taken, shall be elected for a term of two years." According to **paragraph 3,** "The General Assembly shall be composed of eighty members," each senate district constitutes an assembly district, and two members of the general assembly are elected for two-year terms from each assembly district.

Section III, as amended in 1966, prescribes the procedures for apportioning the senate and assembly districts based on the U.S. census, using an apportionment committee consisting of, according to **paragraph 1,** "ten members, five to be appointed by the chairman of the State committee of each of the two political parties whose candidates for Governor receive the largest number of votes at the most recent gubernatorial election."

Section IV, paragraph 2, authorizes each house of the legislature to be "the judge of elections, returns and qualifications of its own members" and requires "a majority of all its members" for a quorum. **Paragraph 3** provides that each house may choose its own officers, determine its own rules, and punish its members for disorderly behavior. **Paragraph 6** mandates that "[a]ll bills and joint resolutions shall be read three times in each house before final passage" and that "[n]o bill or joint resolution shall pass, unless there shall be a majority of all members of each body personally present and agreeing thereto...." **Paragraph 9** provides that legislators are privileged from arrest during attendance at and travel to and from their respective chambers, except in the case of treason or high misdemeanor. Members of Congress and most other state legislatures are granted immunity except in cases of "treason, felony or breach of the peace."

Section VI, paragraph 1, requires that bills raising revenue originate in the general assembly, although the senate may propose amendments. Pursuant to a 1961 amendment, **paragraph 4** also empowers the legislature to act in emergency situations resulting from disasters.

Section VII, paragraph 1, states: "No divorce shall be granted by the Legislature." **Paragraph 2** addresses the powers of the legislature with respect to gambling, certain private organizations, state lotteries, and horse racing. **Paragraph 4** requires that "every law shall embrace but one object, and that shall be expressed in the title." Other state constitutions also limit bills to a single subject, but the New Jersey constitution provides a rationale for this requirement: "To avoid improper influences which may result from intermixing in one and the same act such things as have no proper relation to each other...." **Paragraph 5** prohibits reviving or amending a law by its title only; **paragraph 7** disallows a general law embracing "any provision of a private, special or local character"; and **paragraphs 8, 9, and 10** deal with private, special, and local laws.

Executive Branch

Article V, Executive, section I, paragraph 1, declares: "The executive power shall be vested in a Governor." Such absolute language—some other state constitutions say that "supreme executive power is vested in a governor"—indicates that the framers intended the governor to have full executive authority and not to have to share such authority with other constitutional executive officials.

Paragraph 2 stipulates: "The Governor shall not be less than thirty years of age" and shall have been a citizen of the United States for at least twenty years and a resident of the state for "seven years next before his election...." The governor's term of office is four years, and after two consecutive terms an office holder is barred from a third term until four years later. According to **paragraph 6,** "[T]he functions, powers, duties and emoluments of the office shall devolve upon the President of the Senate, for the time being" should there be a vacancy in the office of the governor or should the governor be unable to discharge his or her duties. The speaker of the general assembly is next in line.

Paragraph 11 mandates that the governor "take care that the laws be faithfully executed..." and authorizes the executive "to enforce compliance with any constitutional or legislative mandate...." **Paragraph 12** requires the governor to "communicate to the Legislature, by message at the opening of each regular session ... the condition of the State" and "recommend such measures as he may deem desirable."

Paragraph 14, as amended in 1968, 1981, and 1983, specifies in **paragraph 14(a)** that a bill passed by both houses of the legislature must be presented to the governor "before the close of the calendar day next following the date of the session at which such final action was taken." Legislation will become law if, according to **paragraph 14(b),** "the Governor approves and signs it"; "does not return it to the house of origin, with a statement of his objections, before the expiration of the period allowed for his consideration"; or "upon reconsideration of a bill objected to by the Governor, two-thirds of all the members of each house agree to pass the bill." **Paragraph 15** states in part: "If any bill presented to the Governor shall contain one or more items of appropriation of money, he may object in whole or in part to any such item or items while approving the other portions of the bill."

Section II, paragraph 1, empowers the governor to "grant pardons and reprieves in all cases other than impeachment and treason...." **Section III, paragraph 2,** avoids expressly making the governor the commander in chief of the state armed forces but directs the incumbent to "nominate and appoint all general and flag officers of the militia, with the advice and consent of the Senate." According to **section IV, paragraph 2,** "Each principal department shall be under the supervision of the Governor ... [the heads of which] shall be nominated and appointed by the Governor, with the advice and consent of the Senate, to serve at the pleasure of the Governor during his term of office...."

Article VI, Judicial, section I, as amended in 1978, states: "The judicial power shall be vested in a Supreme Court, a Superior Court, and other courts of limited jurisdiction. The other courts and their jurisdiction may from time to time be established, altered or abolished by law."

Judicial Branch

Section II, paragraph 1, provides in part: "The Supreme Court shall consist of a Chief Justice and six Associate Justices. Five members of the court shall constitute a quorum." According to **paragraph 2,** "The Supreme Court shall exercise appellate jurisdiction in the last resort in all cases provided in this Constitution." **Paragraph 3** empowers the supreme court to "make rules governing the administration of all courts in the State and, subject to the law, the practice and procedures in all such courts." In *Winterberry v. Salisbury* (1950), the New Jersey supreme court interpreted the phrase *subject to the law* to mean that the court could issue procedural rules, while substantive rules could be made by legislation. However, in *Busik v. Levine* (1973), the same court had to admit that "it is simplistic to assume that all law is divided neatly between 'substance' and 'procedure.'" Paragraph 3 also gives the supreme court "jurisdiction over the admission to the practice of law and the discipline of persons admitted."

Section III, paragraph 1, as amended in 1978, creates a superior court, which, according to **paragraph 2,** has "original general jurisdiction throughout the state in all cases." **Paragraph 3,** as amended in 1983, provides in part that "the Superior Court shall be divided into an Appellate Division, a Law Division, and a Chancery Division, which shall include a family part." **Paragraph 4** states: "Subject to rules of the Supreme Court, the Law Division and the Chancery Division shall each exercise the powers and functions of the other division when the ends of justice so require, and legal and equitable relief shall be granted in any cause so that all matters in controversy between parties may be completely determined." Although in many states the distinction between law courts and equity or chancery courts has all but disappeared, the New Jersey constitution, like Mississippi's, still recognizes this historic difference that developed in the English court system centuries ago; however, by merging legal and equitable relief the constitution in fact blurs the distinction.

Section V, paragraph 1, as amended in 1978, states that appeals may be taken to the supreme court: "**(a)** In causes determined by the Appellate Division of the Superior Court involving a question arising under the Constitution of the United States or this State; **(b)** In causes where there is a dissent in the Appellate Division ... ; **(c)** In capital causes; **(d)** On certification by the Supreme Court to the Superior Court and, where provided by rules of the Supreme Court, to inferior courts; and **(e)** In such causes as may be provided by law." **Paragraph 2,** also amended in 1978, permits appeals from the law and chancery divisions of the superior court to the appellate division.

Section VI, paragraph 1, as amended in 1978 and 1983, provides in part that the governor "shall nominate and appoint, with the advice and consent of the Senate, the Chief Justice and associate justices of the Supreme Court, the Judges of the Superior Court, and the judges of the inferior courts with jurisdiction extending to more than one municipality. . . ." **Paragraph 2,** as amended in 1978, requires that "[t]he justices of the Supreme Court and the judges of the Superior Court shall each prior to his appointment have been admitted to the practice of law in this State for at least ten years." According to **paragraph 3,** as amended in 1978 and 1983, "The Justices of the Supreme Court and the Judges of the Superior Court shall hold their offices for initial terms of 7 years and upon reappointment shall hold their offices during good behavior . . ."; furthermore, "such justices and judges shall be retired upon attaining the age of 70 years."

Section VII, paragraph 1, makes the chief justice of the supreme court the administrative head of all the state courts with the power to appoint an administrative director to serve at his or her pleasure. **Paragraph 2** empowers the chief justice to "assign Judges of the Superior Court to the Divisions and Parts of the Superior Court, and ... from time to time transfer Judges from one assignment to another, as need appears."

Article VII, Public Officers and Employees, section III, provides: "1. The Governor and all other State officers, while in office and for two years thereafter, shall be liable to impeachment for misdemeanor.... 2. The General Assembly shall have sole power of impeachment by vote of a majority of all the members. All impeachments shall be tried by the Senate.... No person shall be convicted without the concurrence of two-thirds of all the members of the Senate.... 3. Judgment ... shall not extend further than to removal from office, and to disqualification [from any other state office]; but the person convicted shall nevertheless be liable to ... [further] punishment according to law."

Impeachment

Article I, Rights and Privileges, paragraph 2(b), states in part: "The people reserve unto themselves the power to recall, after at least one year of service, any elected official in this State or representing this State in the United States Congress. The Legislature shall enact laws to provide for such recall elections."

Direct Democracy

Because the New Jersey constitution does not contain provisions allocating power to local governments, the state supreme court has ruled in *City of Trenton v. New Jersey* (1923) that local governments are therefore subject to the whims of the state legislature. However, article IV, Legislative, section VII, paragraph 11, states in part: "The provisions of this Constitution and of any law concerning municipal corporations formed for local government, or concerning counties, shall be liberally construed in their favor."

Local Government

Article VIII, Taxation and Finance, section I, paragraph 1, as amended in 1963, addresses property taxes. Paragraph 1(a) requires that "[p]roperty shall be assessed for taxation under general laws and by uniform rules." According to paragraph 1(b), the legislature shall enact laws to assess land greater than five acres in area that has been used for two successive years preceding the tax year at the value of agricultural or horticultural land. Paragraph 2 states in part: "Exemption from taxation may be granted only by general laws." Paragraph 7, added in 1976 and amended in 1984, provides that any personal income taxes must go to reduce or offset property taxes but that no personal income tax shall "be levied on payments received under the federal Social Security Act, the federal Railroad Retirement Act, or any federal law which substantially reenacts the provisions of either of those laws." The Utah constitution expressly authorizes a personal income tax to be applied to support the public school system.

Taxation and Finance

Section II, paragraph 2, added in 1996, provides in part that no law appropriating money for a fiscal period "shall exceed the total amount of revenue on hand and anticipated ... during such fiscal period...." Paragraph 6, added in 1996, creates a special account "equivalent to 4% of the revenue annually derived from the tax imposed pursuant to the 'Corporation Business Tax Act (1945),'" to be dedicated to paying for "the remediation of discharges of hazardous substances...."

Article VIII, Taxation and Finance, section IV, paragraph 1, states: "The Legislature shall provide for the maintenance and support of a thorough and efficient system of free public schools for the instruction of all children in the State between the ages of five and eighteen years." In *San Antonio Independent School District v. Rodriguez* (1973), the

Education

U.S. Supreme Court rejected a challenge to a system of school financing in Texas similar to New Jersey's, which is based largely on local property taxes, saying that it did not violate the equal protection clause of the Fourteenth Amendment (1868) of the U.S. Constitution. But just thirteen days later the New Jersey supreme court in *Cahill v. Robinson* (1973) held that its financing method violated the "thorough and efficient system of free public schools" mandated by the New Jersey constitution. In the two decades following the *Robinson* decision, courts in ten other states found that their school financing systems were unconstitutional.

Amendment Procedures

Article IX, Amendments, paragraph 1, states in part: "Any specific amendment or amendments to this Constitution may be proposed in the Senate or General Assembly." Furthermore, "[i]f the proposed amendment or amendments . . . shall be agreed to by three-fifths of all the members" of each house of the legislature, they are to be submitted to the people. Amendments that receive only a majority vote are referred to the legislature the following legislative year, and if they are again agreed to by a majority vote of all the members of both houses, they are submitted to the people. **Paragraph 6** provides: "If the proposed amendment or amendments or any of them shall be approved by a majority of the legally qualified voters of the State voting thereon, the same shall become part of the Constitution on the thirtieth day after the election, unless otherwise provided in the amendment or amendments."

On January 6, 1912, New Mexico became the forty-seventh state of the United States. The capital of the "Land of Enchantment" is Santa Fe. New Mexico, which encompasses some 121,598 square miles, is bordered by Colorado on the north, Oklahoma and Texas on the east, Texas and Mexico on the south, and Arizona on the west. With approximately 1.7 million inhabitants, New Mexico ranks thirty-sixth among the states in population. Its principal economic activities include government, services, and trade; its chief crops are hay, onions, pecans, and chilis.

General Information

Government: The governor and lieutenant governor are elected jointly for four-year terms and are limited to two consecutive terms. The legislature consists of forty-two senators elected for four-year terms and seventy members of the house of representatives elected for two-year terms. The supreme court includes a chief justice and four additional justices appointed by the governor from a list prepared by a judges nominating commission; they must be elected at the next general election and stand for retention every eight years.

Date of Constitution: 1912

Constitutional History

Between 12,000 and 10,000 B.C. the Sandia people inhabited the land that would become the state of New Mexico. They were succeeded by the Mogollon and Anasazi civilizations, who in turn were followed by the Pueblo, Navajo, and Apache peoples. Having heard tales of wealthy cities north of Mexico from Alvar Nuñez Cabeza de Vaca and others, the Spanish explorer Francisco Vásquez de Coronado, accompanied by a Franciscan priest, crossed New Mexico territory in 1540 in search of the fabled Seven Cities of Cíbola and their wealth. He found, instead, only the poor pueblos of the Zuñi. A half century later, in 1598–99, however, an expedition of Spanish soldiers and settlers established a settlement near the current site of Española, the second oldest European settlement in the United States.

There is evidence that in 1610, just three years after the founding of Jamestown by the English on the East Coast, Don Pedro de Peralta, the royal governor of Mexico, himself established Santa Fe. A revolt by the Pueblos in 1680 forced the Spanish to evacuate Santa Fe, but they reoccupied it twelve years later. During the eighteenth century Spain continued to promote settlement of the region, a goal aided by discovery of copper deposits at Santa Rita in 1804. After Mexico gained its independence from Spain in 1821, the New Mexico territory fell under its jurisdiction and remained so for twenty-five years.

The admission of Texas to the Union toward the end of 1845, disputes over boundaries, and American citizens' unpaid claims against Mexico led to war between these two successors to the European colonial powers. On August 18, 1846, U.S. General Stephen Kearny's troops seized Santa Fe. Claiming the entire Southwest for the United States, Kearny drafted a provisional constitution and appointed a governor. The desire for statehood resulted in the convoking of a constitutional convention and the drafting of a document that was sent to Congress in 1850. But Congress ignored the proposed constitution and created the New Mexico Territory by an act dated September 9, 1850. Another proposed constitution, called the "Tom-Cat constitution" in honor of Thomas

Catron, a politician who owned vast amounts of land in the territory, was soundly rejected at the polls on October 7, 1890.

Finally, an act of Congress dated June 20, 1910, authorized both New Mexico and Arizona to "form a constitution and state government and be admitted to the Union...." A constitutional convention met in Santa Fe from October 3 through November 21, 1910, and its efforts were overwhelmingly approved by the voters on January 21, 1911. However, President William Howard Taft objected to a provision calling for the popular recall of judges, and Congress found the amendment procedures too stringent. The constitution was resubmitted with the provision for recalling judges deleted and a less difficult amendment procedure that was printed on blue paper and became known as the "blue ballot amendment." The amended document was adopted by the voters in November 1911. Both Congress and the president having been mollified, New Mexico was admitted as a state on January 6, 1912, and its constitution became effective on that date.

The Constitution

The 1912 New Mexico constitution has been characterized as "flawed and cumbersome," reflecting a distrust of democratic institutions and overburdened with details. Changing the names of some state institutions and increasing compensation for state officials, for example, require constitutional amendments. Yet this product of a continual struggle between American and Spanish cultures and legal doctrines has provided a basis for stability and growth in the state. Through a series of 134 amendments adopted as of January 1, 1998, the 1912 document, which at 27,200 words is of relatively average length, has been modernized in a piecemeal fashion. In 1969 the efforts of a constitutional convention to create a concise, well-integrated document were rejected by the voters, as occurred in Maryland a year earlier.

New Mexico's constitution is not unique. Like the constitutions of many other states, it creates a plural, or divided, executive branch with five officers elected statewide in addition to the governor and lieutenant governor. Judges are elected, and the supreme court has a constitutionally guaranteed supervisory role in the judiciary system. The document includes provisions for popular referendums on legislation and municipal home rule but does not set term limits for legislators. Like the citizens of several other states, including Maryland and New York, for example, the people of New Mexico seem to be satisfied, for the time being anyway, with their makeshift constitution.

Preamble

The preamble to the 1911 New Mexico constitution proclaims: "We, the people of New Mexico, grateful to Almighty God for the blessings of liberty, in order to secure the advantages of a state government, do ordain and establish this constitution."

Article I, Name and Boundaries, states the name of the state and describes its boundaries.

Fundamental Rights

Article II, Bill of Rights, section 1, declares: "The State of New Mexico is an inseparable part of the federal union, and the constitution of the United States is the supreme law of the land." **Section 2** states: "All political power is vested in and derived from the people: all government of right originates with the people, is founded upon their will and is instituted solely for their good." **Section 3** provides that "[t]he people of the state have the sole and exclusive right to govern themselves as a free, sovereign and independent state."

Section 4 affirms: "All persons are born equally free, and have certain natural, inherent and inalienable rights, among which are the rights of enjoying and defending life and liberty, of acquiring, possessing and protecting property, and of seeking and obtaining safety and happiness." **Section 5** mandates that "[t]he rights, privileges and immunities, civil, political and religious guaranteed to the people of New Mexico by the Treaty of Guadalupe Hidalgo shall be preserved inviolate." This treaty ending the Mexican War, made public on July 4, 1848, confirmed the acquisition of New Mexico and California by the United States and recognized the Rio Grande as the southern boundary of Texas.

Section 6, as amended in 1971 and 1986, guarantees, with some limitations, the right to bear arms "for lawful hunting and recreational use and for other lawful purposes...." **Section 7** limits the suspension of the writ of habeas corpus; **section 8** guarantees free elections; and **section 9** subordinates the military to civil power and limits the quartering of soldiers in private homes. **Section 10** prohibits unreasonable searches and seizures in language similar to that in the U.S. Constitution. In *State v. Sutton* (1991), the New Mexico court of appeals held that the defendant's contention that section 10 provided greater protection than the Fourth Amendment (1791) of the U.S Constitution could not be considered because it was neither briefed nor argued before the court and that mere reference to the state provision was not sufficient. **Section 11** states: "Every man shall be free to worship God according to the dictates of his own conscience, and no person shall ever be molested or denied any civil or political right or privilege on account of his religious opinion or mode of religious worship. No person shall be required to attend any place of worship or support any religious sect or denomination; nor shall any preference be given by law to any religious denomination or mode of worship." **Article XX, Miscellaneous, section 13,** declares: "The use of wines solely for sacramental purposes under church authority at any place within the state shall never be prohibited."

Article II, Bill of Rights, section 12, asserts: "The right of trial by jury as it has heretofore existed shall be secured to all and remain inviolate. In all cases triable in courts inferior to the district court the jury may consist of six. The legislature may provide that verdicts in civil cases may be rendered by less than a unanimous vote of the jury." **Section 13,** as amended in 1980 and 1988, guarantees bail "except for capital offenses when the proof is evident or the presumption great...." Bail may also be denied "by the district court for a period of sixty days after the incarceration of the defendant by an order entered within seven days after the incarceration, in the following instances: **A.** the defendant is accused of a felony and has previously been convicted of two or more felonies ... [and] **B.** the defendant is accused of a felony involving the use of a deadly weapon and has a prior felony conviction, within the state."

Section 14, as amended in 1925, 1980, and 1994, provides for indictment and information, grand juries, and rights of the accused, including "the right to appear and defend himself in person, and by counsel; to demand the nature and cause of the accusation; to be confronted with the witnesses against him; to have the charge and testimony interpreted to him in a language he understands; to have compulsory process to compel the attendance of witnesses in his behalf, and a speedy public trial by an impartial jury of the county or district in which the offense is alleged to have been committed." **Section 15** prohibits self-incrimination and double jeopardy.

Section 16 defines treason in terms similar to those used in the U.S. Constitution. **Section 17** states in part: "Every person may freely speak, write and publish his sentiments on all subjects, being responsible for the abuse of that right; and no law shall ... restrain or abridge the liberty of speech or of the press." Section 17 also calls for an acquittal on a charge of libel "if it shall appear to the jury that the matter charged as libelous is true and was published with good motives and for justifiable ends." And **section 18,** as amended in 1973, provides: "No person shall be deprived of life, liberty or property without due process of law; nor shall any person be denied equal protection of the laws. Equality of rights under law shall not be denied on account of the sex of any person."

Section 19 prohibits ex post facto laws, bills of attainder, and laws impairing the obligation of contracts; **section 20** states that "[p]rivate property shall not be taken or damaged for public use without just compensation"; and **section 21** prohibits "imprisonment for debt in any civil action." **Section 22,** as amended in 1921, mandates: "Until otherwise provided by law no alien, ineligible to citizenship under the laws of the United States, or corporation, copartnership or association, a majority of the stock or interest in which is owned or held by such aliens, shall acquire title, leasehold or other interest in or to real estate in New Mexico."

Section 23 provides that "[t]he enumeration in this constitution of certain rights shall not be construed to deny, impair or disparage others retained by the people." **Section 24,** added in 1992, establishes rights for victims of crime, including "**(1)** the right to be treated with fairness and respect for the victim's dignity and privacy throughout the criminal justice process; ... **(3)** the right to be reasonably protected from the accused ... ; **(4)** the right to notification of court proceedings; ... [and] **(9)** the right to information about the conviction, sentencing, imprisonment, escape or release of the accused...."

Division of Powers

Article III, Distribution of Powers, section 1, as amended in 1986, provides in part: "The powers of the government of this state are divided into three distinct departments, the legislative, executive and judicial, and no person or collection of persons charged with the exercise of powers properly belonging to one of these departments, shall exercise any powers properly belonging to either of the others...." However, the legislature is expressly authorized to establish "by statute, a body with statewide jurisdiction other than the courts ... for the determination of rights and liabilities ... [which] arise from transactions or occurrences involving personal injury sustained in the course of employment by an employee."

Legislative Branch

Article IV, Legislative Department, section 1, declares: "The legislative power shall be vested in a senate and house of representatives which shall be designated the legislature of the state of New Mexico, and shall hold its sessions at the seat of government." **Section 2,** as amended in 1960, states in part: "In addition to the powers herein enumerated, the legislature shall have all powers necessary to the legislature of a free state, including the power to enact reasonable and appropriate laws to guarantee the continuity and effective operation of state and local government by providing emergency procedure for use only during periods of disaster emergency."

Section 3, as amended in 1976, requires: "**A.** Senators shall not be less than twenty-five years of age and representatives not less than twenty-one years of age at the time of their election. If any senator or representative permanently removes his residence from or maintains no residence in the district from which he was elected, then he shall be deemed to have resigned. . . . No person shall be eligible to serve in the legislature who, at the time of qualifying, holds any office of trust or profit with the state, county or national governments, except notaries public and officers of the militia who receive no salary." **Section 3B** specifies that "[t]he senate shall be composed of no more than forty-two members elected from single-member districts," while **section 3C** specifies that "[t]he house of representatives shall be composed of no more than seventy members elected from single-member districts." Currently the legislature has the maximum number of members. According to **section 4,** as amended in 1953 and 1960, senators are elected for staggered four-year terms of office and representatives for two-year terms.

Section 7 allows each house to judge the election and qualifications of its members and defines a quorum as "[a] majority of either house," although "a less number may effect a temporary organization, adjourn from day to day and compel the attendance of absent members." **Section 8** directs: "The senate shall be called to order in the hall of the senate by the lieutenant governor. The senate shall elect a president pro tempore who shall preside in the absence of the lieutenant governor and shall serve until the next session of the legislature. The house of representatives shall be called to order in the hall of said house by the secretary of state. He shall preside until the election of a speaker. . . ."

Section 11 empowers each house to establish its own procedural rules, "punish its members or others for contempt or disorderly behavior in its presence[,] and protect its members against violence. . . ." By a two-thirds vote of its members, each house may "expel a member, but not a second time for the same act." Such punishment does not preclude criminal prosecution. Pursuant to **section 13,** legislators are exempt from arrest while attending or on their way to and from legislative sessions, except in cases of treason, felony, and breach of the peace; in addition, they may not be "questioned in any other place for any speech or debate or for any vote cast in either house."

Section 15 directs that laws are to be passed by bill: "No law shall be passed except by bill, and no bill shall be so altered or amended on its passage through either house as to change its original purpose. . . . Any bill may originate in either house. No bill, except bills to provide for the public peace, health and safety, and the codification or revision of laws, shall become a law unless it has been printed, and read three different times in each house, not more than two of which readings shall be on the same day, and the third of which shall be in full." **Section 16** provides that "[t]he subject of every bill shall be clearly expressed in its title, and no bill embracing more than one subject shall be passed except general appropriation bills and bills for the codification or revision of the laws. . . ."

Section 17 requires that bills be passed by "a vote of a majority of the members present in each house" and that on final passage "a vote be taken by yeas and nays, and entered on the journal." **Section 20** states in part: "Immediately after the passage of any bill or resolution, it shall be enrolled and engrossed, and read publicly in full in each house, and thereupon shall be signed by the presiding officers of each house in open session. . . ." **Section 22,** as amended in 1953, provides in part: "Every bill passed by the legislature shall, before it becomes a law, be presented to the governor for approval. If he approves, he shall sign it, and deposit it with the secretary of state; otherwise, he shall return it to the house in which it originated, with his objections. . . ." The governor's veto may be overridden by a vote of "two-thirds of the members present and voting in each house." Section 22 continues: "Any bill not returned by the governor within three days, Sundays excepted, . . . shall become a law, whether signed by him or not, unless the legislature by adjournment prevent such return. . . ." Section 22 also extends to the governor the power to veto "items in any bill appropriating money. . . ." In *State ex rel. Sego v. Kirkpatrick* (1974), the New Mexico supreme court found, partly on the basis of the constitutional convention's record of its proceedings, that while the governor's item veto power was not limited to appropriations bills, it was held to be only a negative power and could not be used to "create legislation inconsistent with that enacted by the legislature."

Section 23 stipulates that "[l]aws shall go into effect ninety days after the adjournment of the legislature enacting them, except general appropriation laws, which shall go into effect immediately upon their passage and approval." **Section 24** prohibits the legislature from passing local or special laws in certain enumerated cases, including "regulating county, precinct or district affairs; . . . the rate of interest on money, [and] the punishment for crimes and misdemeanors. . . ." Other types of laws prohibited include, under **section 25,** "legalizing the unauthorized or invalid act of any officer . . ."; under **section 26,** ". . . [granting any] exclusive right, franchise, privilege or immunity . . ."; and under **section 29,** "authorizing indebtedness . . . which does not provide for levying a tax sufficient to pay the interest, and for the payment at maturity of the principal."

Executive Branch

Article V, Executive Department, section 1, as amended in 1914, 1959, 1962, 1970, and 1986, provides in part: "The executive department shall consist of a governor, lieutenant governor, secretary of state, state auditor, state treasurer, attorney general and commissioner of public lands, who shall, unless otherwise provided in the constitution . . . be elected for terms of four years. . . . The governor and lieutenant governor shall be elected jointly. . . . Such officers shall, after having served two terms in a state office, be ineligible to hold that state office until one full term has intervened." **Section 3** specifies that to be eligible to these offices a person must be a U.S. citizen, thirty years old, and a state resident "for the five years next preceding his election. . . ."

Section 4 vests the state's supreme executive power in the governor, "who shall take care that the laws be faithfully executed." The governor acts as commander in chief of the state's military forces, except when they are in the service of the country, and may call them out to "preserve the public peace, execute the laws, suppress insurrection and repel invasion." **Section 5,** as amended in 1988, authorizes the governor to "nominate and, by and with the consent of the senate, appoint all officers whose appointment or election is not otherwise provided for and may remove any officer appointed by him unless otherwise provided by law." And **section 6** allows the governor, "[s]ubject to such regulations as may be prescribed by law," to grant reprieves and pardons "after conviction for all offenses except treason and in cases of impeachment."

Section 7, as amended in 1948, addresses the succession to the governorship: "If at the time fixed for the beginning of the term of the governor, the governor-elect shall have died, the lieutenant governor-elect shall become governor." The lieutenant governor-elect "shall act as governor" in other cases where the governor-elect cannot take office at the beginning of his or her term. Section 7 continues: "If after the governor-elect has qualified [for office] a vacancy occurs ... the lieutenant governor shall succeed to that office.... In case the governor is absent from the state, or is for any reason unable to perform his duties, the lieutenant governor shall act as governor...." **Section 8** designates the lieutenant governor as president of the senate, but he or she may vote "only when the senate is equally divided."

Article VI, Judicial Department, section 1, as amended in 1965 and 1966, declares: "The judicial power of the state shall be vested in the senate when sitting as a court of impeachment, a supreme court, a court of appeals, district courts; probate courts, magistrate courts and such other courts inferior to the district courts as may be established by law from time to time in any district, county or municipality of the state."

Judicial Branch

Sections 2 and 3 outline the supreme court's jurisdiction. **Section 2,** as amended in 1965, provides: "Appeals from a judgment of a district court imposing a sentence of death or life imprisonment shall be taken directly to the supreme court. In all other cases, criminal and civil, the supreme court shall exercise appellate jurisdiction as may be provided by law; provided that an aggrieved party shall have an absolute right to one appeal." **Section 3** states in part: "The supreme court shall have original jurisdiction in quo warranto and mandamus against all state officers, boards and commissions, and shall have a superintending control over all inferior courts; it shall also have power to issue writs of mandamus, error, prohibition, habeas corpus, certiorari, injunction and all other writs necessary or proper for the complete exercise of its jurisdiction and to hear and determine the same."

Section 4, as amended in 1988, specifies that the supreme court consists of "at least five justices who shall be chosen as provided in this constitution," one of whom is selected as chief justice "as provided by law." **Section 33,** added in 1988 and as amended in 1994, provides in part: "**A.** Each justice of the supreme court, judge of the court of appeals, district judge or metropolitan court judge shall have been elected to that position in a partisan election prior to being eligible for a nonpartisan retention election. Thereafter, each said justice or judge shall be subject to retention or rejection on a nonpartisan ballot. Retention of the judicial office shall require at least fifty-seven percent of the vote cast on the question of retention or rejection. **B.** Each justice of the supreme court or judge of the court of appeals shall be subject to retention or rejection in like manner at the general election every eighth year." **Sections 34** and **35,** also added in 1988 (section 34 as amended in 1994), authorize the governor to fill a vacancy on the supreme court or court of appeals from names on a list prepared by a judicial nominating commission. Appointees serve until the next general election.

Section 8, as amended in 1988, requires that supreme court justices be thirty-five years old, practicing attorneys for ten years, and state residents for three years. The section specifies: "The actual practice of law shall include a lawyer's service upon the bench of any court of this state."

Section 18, as amended in 1966, provides for the disqualification of judges: "No justice, judge or magistrate of any court shall, except by consent of all parties, sit in any cause in which either of the parties are related to him by affinity or consanguinity within the degree of first cousin, or in which he was counsel, or in the trial of which he presided in any inferior court, or in which he has an interest." According to **section 19,** as amended in 1988, "No justice of the supreme court [or other judge], while serving, shall be nominated, appointed or elected to any other office in this state except a judicial office."

Section 5 stipulates that "[a] majority of the justices of the supreme court shall be necessary to constitute a quorum for the transaction of business, and a majority of the justices must concur in any judgment of the court." **Section 6** provides that if a supreme court justice has an interest in a case or is absent or incapacitated, "the remaining justices of the court may, in their discretion, call in any district judge of the state to act as a justice of the court." **Section 9** authorizes the supreme court to "appoint and remove at pleasure its reporter, bailiff, clerk and such other officers and assistants as may be prescribed by law."

Section 32, added in 1967 and amended in 1978, creates a judicial standards commission, stating in part: "In accordance with this section, any justice, judge or magistrate of any court may be disciplined or removed for willful misconduct in office, persistent failure or inability to perform a judge's duties, or habitual intemperance, or he may be retired for disability seriously interfering with the performance of his duties which is, or is likely to become, of a permanent character."

Impeachment

Article IV, Legislative Department, section 35, vests "the sole power of impeachment" in the house of representatives, further stipulating that "a concurrence of a majority of all the members elected shall be necessary to the proper exercise thereof. All impeachments shall be tried by the senate.... No person shall be convicted without the concurrence of two-thirds of the senators elected." **Section 36** states in part: "All state officers and judges of the district court shall be liable to impeachment for crimes, misdemeanors and malfeasance in office, but judgment in such cases shall not extend further than removal from office and disqualification to hold any office of honor, trust or profit, or to vote under the laws of this state." Disenfranchisement as a punishment for conviction on impeachment is unusual in state constitutions; more typical is the section's subsequent express provision that officers and judges "whether convicted or aquitted" are still liable to criminal and civil penalties applicable under the law.

Article IV, Legislative Department, section 1, provides in part: "The people reserve the power to disapprove, suspend and annul any law enacted by the legislature, except general appropriation laws; laws providing for the preservation of the public peace, health or safety; for the payment of the public debt or interest thereon . . . ; for the maintenance of public schools or state institutions[;] and local or special laws." In *Otto v. Buck* (1956), the New Mexico supreme court ruled that for the "public peace, health or safety" exception to be applicable, no immediate crisis was necessary but that the statute only need bear a valid relationship to some permissible objective for the exercise of the state's police power. **Article X, County and Municipal Corporations, section 9,** as amended in 1996, states in part: "**A.** An elected official of a county is subject to recall by the voters of the county."

Direct Democracy

Article VIII, Taxation and Revenue, section 1, as amended in 1914 and 1971 (a 1997 proposed amendment has not yet been ratified at the polls), states: "Taxes levied upon tangible property shall be in proportion to the value thereof, and taxes shall be equal and uniform upon subjects of taxation of the same class. Different methods may be provided by law to determine value of different kinds of property, but the percentage of value against which tax rates are assessed shall not exceed thirty-three and one-third percent."

Taxation and Finance

Article IX, State, County and Municipal Indebtedness, section 7, specifies: "The state may borrow money not exceeding the sum . . . $200,000 . . . to meet casual deficits or failure in revenue, or for necessary expenses. The state may also contract debts to suppress insurrection and to provide for the public defense."

Article X, County and Municipal Corporations, section 6, added in 1970, provides: "**D.** A municipality which adopts a charter may exercise all legislative powers and perform all functions not expressly denied by general law or charter. This grant of powers shall not include the power to enact private or civil laws governing civil relationships except as incident to the exercise of an independent municipal power, nor shall it include the power to provide for a penalty greater than the penalty provided for a petty misdemeanor."

Local Government

Article XII, Education, section 1, mandates: "A uniform system of free public schools sufficient for the education of, and open to, all the children of school age in the state shall be established and maintained." **Section 8** authorizes the legislature to "provide for the training of teachers in the normal schools or otherwise so that they may become proficient in both the English and Spanish languages, to qualify them to teach Spanish-speaking pupils and students in the public schools and educational institutions of the state. . . ." In *Lopez Tijerina v. Henry* (1969), the U.S. District Court held that the 1848 Treaty of Guadalupe Hidalgo ending the Mexican War did not contemplate administration of public schools or confer the right to have Spanish language and culture preserved in public schools.

Education

Article XXI, Compact with the United States, contains sections on religious toleration (as amended in 1953), control of unappropriated Indian lands, assumption of territorial debt, public schools, suffrage (as amended in 1912), the state capital, and reclamation

Compact with the United States

projects, among others. The preamble to the compact begins: "In compliance with the requirements of the act of congress, entitled, 'An Act to enable the people of New Mexico to form a constitution and state government . . . and be admitted into the union on an equal footing with the original states,' approved [June 20, 1910]. . . ." Several other states, including North Dakota, South Dakota, and Washington, have compacts with the federal government as part of their constitutions.

Amendment Procedures

Article XIX, Amendments, section 1, as amended in 1911 and 1996, states in part: "An amendment or amendments to this constitution may be proposed in either house of the legislature at a regular session . . . if a majority of all members elected to each of the two houses voting separately votes in favor thereof. . . ." Amendments may also be proposed by an independent commission "established by law for that purpose" and submitted to the legislature for review. The secretary of state must then publish the proposed amendments in English and Spanish newspapers, and these "shall be voted upon at the next regular election held after that adjournment of the legislature or at a special election to be held not less than six months after the adjournment of that legislature. . . ." Such amendments become a part of the constitution if "ratified by a majority of the electors voting [thereon]."

Section 2, as amended in 1911 and 1996, provides in part: "Whenever the legislature, by a two-thirds vote of the members elected to each house, deems it necessary . . . they shall submit the question of calling [a constitutional] convention to the electors at the next general election, and if a majority of all the electors voting on such questions at said election . . . votes in favor of calling a convention . . . the legislature shall . . . provide for [it] by law. . . ." If a majority of the electors voting favor the convention's proposal, it is adopted and becomes effective "thirty days after the certification of the election returns unless otherwise provided by the convention."

New York became the eleventh state of the United States on July 26, 1788. Albany is the capital of the "Empire State." Some 54,471 square miles in area, it is bordered by the Canadian provinces of Ontario and Quebec on the north; Vermont, Massachusetts, and Connecticut on the east; Long Island Sound, New Jersey, and Pennsylvania on the south; and Lake Erie, Lake Ontario, and the St. Lawrence River on the west. New York ranks third among the states in population with approximately 18 million residents. Its principal industries include manufacturing, finance, and communications; among its chief crops are fruits, onions, and potatoes.

General Information

Government: The governor and lieutenant governor are elected on a single ballot for four-year terms. The legislature consists of sixty-one senators and 150 members of the assembly, all elected for identical two-year terms. The court of appeals, the highest state court, includes a chief judge and six associate judges appointed by the governor, with the advice and consent of the senate, to fourteen-year terms.

Dates of Constitutions: 1777, 1822, 1847, and 1895

Constitutional History

Ancestors of the Iroquois and the Algonquins flourished in the region that would become the state of New York for well over five thousand years before the arrival of Europeans. In 1524 Giovanni da Verrazano, exploring for France, anchored off Staten Island. In 1609 the English explorer Henry Hudson sailed the *Half Moon* up the river that now bears his name to the present site of Albany, and Samuel de Champlain discovered the lake named for him.

The Dutchman Adriaen Block sailed past Manhattan and around Long Island in 1614, and the Dutch settlers who followed founded the colony of New Amsterdam, which later would become New York City. The Dutch West India Company, organized in 1621, purchased Manhattan Island from the local Native Americans five years later for 60 guilders—the equivalent of approximately $200 today. The government of The Netherlands in 1629 bestowed grants of "freedoms, privileges, and exemptions" on a few members of the Dutch West India Company, thus ensuring its control of most of the land along the Hudson River. In 1640 a Charter of Freedoms and Exemptions was issued, offering 200 acres of land to anyone who brought over five adult immigrants and promising self-government.

After being restored to the English throne in 1660, Charles II in 1664 gave his brother, the duke of York, a huge grant of land in North America that included all of the present-day state of New York. The duke, with only four medium-sized war ships and without firing a shot, forced Peter Stuyvesant, the Dutch governor of New Amsterdam, to surrender. A legislative assembly was created in 1683 with the duke's permission, and it adopted a charter, borrowing language from Magna Carta, to protect the colonists' liberty, property, and right of participation in the government.

During the eighteenth century, New York law relied heavily on English common law and even the statutory law of the British Parliament, which altered the common law, at least as it existed up to 1691. This allowed New York lawyers to avoid having to make reference to later colonial acts by Great Britain that attempted to dilute the colonists' constitutional rights and inspired colonial political leaders to demand rights predicated on the rights of British subjects.

With the outbreak of the American Revolution, a state constitutional convention was assembled on July 10, 1776. The constitution adopted by this convention on April 20, 1777, was never submitted to the people for approval. This document differed from the constitutions adopted just a year earlier by states such as Pennsylvania and New Jersey in that it recognized the need for checks on the legislature in addition to annual elections and thus included provisions for the executive veto and an upper house. In 1801 the New York legislature called a constitutional convention that adopted amendments to reapportion the legislature, clarify the appointment powers of the legislative and executive branches, and provide a formal method of amendment.

A convention held in Albany in 1821 completely rewrote the 1777 document. This second constitution, which eliminated impractical provisions and provided for popular referendums on amendments, was approved by the voters in 1822. A third constitution, framed by a convention meeting in 1846, was the result of a general reform movement that saw the creation of a labor party and temperance, women's rights, and antislavery organizations. It took effect on January 1, 1847, after being ratified by the electorate.

In 1886 the people of New York voted overwhelmingly for a new constitutional convention under the provision of the 1847 constitution requiring such a vote every twenty years. A partisan split between the legislature and the governor postponed action until 1892, when legislation was passed providing for another constitutional convention, held in Albany from May 8 to September 29, 1894. A new constitution was approved at the polls on November 6 and went into effect on January 1, 1895. Major constitutional revisions were proposed by a constitutional convention in 1938, and the people ratified six of nine proposed changes, which took effect on January 1, 1939.

The Constitution

The 1895 New York constitution is one of twenty-six state constitutions, excluding the Confederate and Reconstruction documents, that were promulgated between 1861 and 1897. The document and state court interpretations give the citizens of New York broader protections for civil liberties and individual rights than the U.S. Constitution and its construction by the U.S. Supreme Court. Under the New York constitution, for example, an accused person's right to counsel is one of the most effective in the nation, surpassing the protection of the Sixth Amendment (1791) of the U.S. Constitution. Moreover, the constitution provides protection for the environment as well as care for the needy.

New York's constitution, however, is wordy. Nearly 52,000 words long, it is surpassed in length by only a few, mostly southern, state constitutions. As of January 1, 1998, the 1895 document has been amended 216 times, making it the fifth most amended current state constitution. In addition, it contains a residue of policy problems, including fragmentation of executive power resulting primarily from an elected attorney general and a mandated unified court system that is not truly unified.

New York is one of fourteen states that require the question of whether to call a constitutional convention to be submitted periodically to the people. The constitution mandated such a referendum in 1997, but the voters vetoed this once-in-every-twenty-years opportunity to completely revise their supreme state law.

Preamble

The preamble to the 1895 New York constitution reads: "WE THE PEOPLE of the State of New York, grateful to Almighty God for our Freedom, in order to secure its blessings, DO ESTABLISH THIS CONSTITUTION."

Article I, Bill of Rights, section 1, as amended in 1959, declares: "No member of this state shall be disfranchised, or deprived of any of the rights or privileges secured to any citizen thereof, unless by the law of the land, or the judgment of his peers . . ."; the only stated exception is that the legislature may prohibit primary elections where there is no contest for the nomination. The first part of section 1 has been compared with paragraph 39 of Magna Carta. And in *People v. Priest* (1912), the New York court of appeals found that the phrase "the law of the land" was not materially different from the phrase "due process of law" as used in the U.S. Constitution.

Section 2, as amended in 1938, guarantees trial by jury. **Section 3** affirms freedom of worship and religious liberty. With respect to religious liberty, in *In re Kempf's Will* (1937), the New York court of appeals held that a provision of a will requiring a legatee to be brought up according to the Roman Catholic religion was not a denial of religious freedom. **Section 4,** as amended in 1938, prohibits the suspension of the writ of habeas corpus, "unless, in the case of rebellion or invasion, the public safety requires it"; **section 5** prohibits excessive bail, fines, cruel and unusual punishment, and detention of witnesses; and **section 6,** as amended in 1938, 1949, 1959, and 1973, allows indictment by a grand jury in cases such as infamous crimes or crimes punishable by the death penalty, except for impeachment and certain military proceedings.

Section 7, as amended in 1938, 1963, and 1964, states in part: "**(a)** Private property shall not be taken for public use without just compensation." **Section 8** guarantees freedom of speech and the press and provides for criminal prosecutions for libel. And **section 9,** as amended five times between 1939 and 1984, guarantees the right to assemble and petition the government and addresses divorce, lotteries, pool selling and gambling, pari-mutuel betting on horse racing, and games of chance, bingo, and lotto.

Section 11, added by amendment in 1938, declares: "No person shall be denied the equal protection of the laws of this state or any subdivision thereof. No person shall, because of race, color, creed or religion, be subjected to any discrimination in his civil rights by any other person or by any firm, corporation, or institution, or by the state, or any agency or subdivision of the state." **Section 12,** as amended in 1938, provides for security against unreasonable searches, seizures, and interceptions of telephone and telegraph communications. In *People v. Class* (1986), the New York court of appeals ruled that even though the U.S. Supreme Court had held that a police officer's nonconsensual search of an automobile stopped for a traffic violation did not violate the Fourth Amendment (1791) of the U.S. Constitution, the search did violate this section of the New York constitution. **Section 14,** as amended in 1938, continues in force parts of the common law and colonial legislation of the New York Colony in force as of 1775, certain state resolutions and a convention in force as of 1777, and subsequent state legislation not otherwise "repugnant to this constitution. . . ."

Sections 16, 17, and **18,** all as amended in 1938, assert, respectively, that "[t]he right of action now existing to recover damages for injuries resulting in death, shall never be abrogated . . ."; that "[l]abor of human beings is not a commodity nor an article of commerce and shall never be so considered or construed ...";￼ and that "[n]othing contained in this constitution shall be construed to limit the power of the legislature to enact laws for the protection of the lives, health, or safety of employees...." Two New York court cases reflect an important battle between the federal government and the states over the power to legislate economic philosophy. In *Lochner v. New York* (1905), the U.S. Supreme Court struck down a state law limiting employees' working hours as interference with the right of contract and, therefore, a violation of the Fourteenth Amendment (1868) of the U.S. Constitution. And in *Nebbia v. New York* (1934), just two years after the retirement of Justice Oliver Wendell Holmes, who had consistently dissented from rulings based on *Lochner*, the U.S. Supreme Court, by a five-to-four majority, found that a state law fixing the price of milk did not violate the Fourteenth Amendment, marking the beginning of the court's deference to economic experimentation by other branches of state and federal government.

Division of Powers

The 1895 New York constitution contains no formal expression of the principle of the separation of government powers, but the major government institutions are divided into the legislature, executive, and judiciary. In *County of Oneida v. Berle* (1980), the New York court of appeals, while declaring that the principle of separation of powers should not lead to a "captious, doctrinaire and inelastic classification of government functions," nevertheless found that the governor's refusal to spend appropriated funds "consititued a usurpation of the legislative function" and was therefore unconstitutional.

Legislative Branch

Article III, Legislature, section 1, provides: "The legislative power of this state shall be vested in the senate and assembly." In *People ex rel. Simon v. Bradley* (1913), the New York court of appeals declared that the people, in framing the constitution, had committed to the legislature the whole lawmaking power of the state, except as expressly or implicitly withheld in that document, and hence that plenary power in the legislature for all purposes of civil government is the rule. And in *Levin v. Whalen* (1976), the New York court of appeals held that this section prohibited the legislature from delegating its lawmaking functions to other bodies.

Section 2, as amended in 1937, specifies that "[t]he senate shall consist of fifty members, except as hereinafter provided ... [and] [t]he assembly shall consist of one hundred and fifty members." Members of both bodies are elected for two years. **Section 4,** as amended in 1945, however, permits additional senators based on new apportionments. Currently there are sixty-one senators. **Section 5,** as amended in 1945, mandates: "The members of the assembly shall be chosen by single districts and shall be apportioned by the legislature at each regular session at which the senate districts are readjusted or altered, and by the same law, among the several counties of the state, ... according to the number of their respective inhabitants, excluding aliens." **Section 7,** added in 1938 and amended in 1943, requires that legislators be U.S. citizens, state residents for five years, and residents "of [their] assembly or senate district for twelve months immediately preceding [their] election."

Section 9, as amended in 1963, allows each house to determine its own procedural rules; judge the election, returns, and qualifications of its members; and choose its own officers, noting that "the senate shall choose a temporary president and the assembly shall choose a speaker." Section 9 also specifies: "A majority of each house shall constitute a quorum to do business." However, **section 23**, as amended in 1938, provides that during final passage of a bill "three-fifths of the members elected to either house" are necessary to constitute a quorum. **Section 11** states: "For any speech or debate in either house of the legislature, the members shall not be questioned in any other place."

Sections 12 through **16**, as amended in 1938, and **section 17**, as amended in 1938 and 1964, concern the passage of bills. Unlike the constitutions of Massachusetts and many other states requiring that money bills originate in the lower house of the legislature, **section 12** asserts: "Any bill may originate in either house of the legislature, and all bills passed by one house may be amended by the other." For a bill to become law, **section 14** provides that, except in emergency situations, it must be printed and on the legislators' desks "in its final form, at least three calendar legislative days prior to its final passage . . . ," assented to by "a majority of the members elected to each branch of the legislature," and not amended on its last reading. **Section 20**, however, requires the assent of "two-thirds of the members elected to each branch of the legislature" for bills "appropriating the public moneys or property for local or private purposes." The New York courts have held that under this section the legislature may grant underwater land rights to private land owners by a two-thirds vote of the members of each house. And in *People v. Allen* (1870), the courts held that a local purpose is one in which the people of a particular locality directly and mainly benefit from an appropriation of public money. Although New York's constitution permits private bills, **section 17** contains a list of cases in which private bills may not be passed.

Section 22, as amended in 1938 and 1959, mandates: "Every law which imposes, continues or revives a tax shall distinctly state the tax and the object to which it is to be applied. . . ." **Section 23** stipulates that "[o]n the final passage, in either house of the legislature, of any act which imposes, continues or revives a tax, or creates a debt or charge, or makes, continues or revives any appropriation . . . , the question shall be taken by yeas and nays, which shall be duly entered upon the journals, and three-fifths of all the members elected to either house shall, in all such cases, be necessary to constitute a quorum therein."

Article IV, Executive, section 1, as amended in 1938 and 1953, provides: "The executive power shall be vested in the governor, who shall hold his office for four years; the lieutenant governor shall be chosen at the same time, and for the same term. . . . They shall be chosen jointly, by the casting by each voter of a single vote applicable to both offices. . . ." **Section 2** requires that the governor and lieutenant governor be U.S. citizens, thirty years old, and state residents for five years "next preceding [their] election. . . ."

Section 3, as amended in 1938, 1953, and 1963, outlines the governor's power and duties. The governor serves as commander in chief of the state's military and naval forces and has the power to "convene the legislature, or the senate only, on extraordinary occasions . . ."; to "communicate by message to the legislature at every session of the condition of the state, and recommend such matters to it as he shall judge expedient . . ."; to "expedite all such measures as may be resolved upon by the legislature, and . . . take care that the laws are faithfully executed." **Section 4** empowers the governor to grant "reprieves, commutations and pardons after conviction, for all offenses except treason and cases of impeachment . . . subject to such regulations as may be provided by law. . . ."

Section 5, as amended in 1938 and 1963, provides that "in case of the removal of the governor from office or of his death or resignation, the lieutenant-governor shall become governor for the remainder of the term." If the governor-elect dies or declines to serve, the lieutenant governor becomes governor for the full term; and if the governor "is impeached, is absent from the state or is otherwise unable to discharge the powers and duties of his office," the lieutenant governor acts temporarily as governor. **Section 6,** as amended in 1938, 1945, 1953, and 1963, states that the lieutenant governor must "possess the same qualifications . . . for office as the governor" and that he or she "shall be the president of the senate but shall have only a casting vote therein."

Section 7 grants the governor the power to veto legislation, including items in appropriations bills, although such veto may be overridden by "two-thirds of the members elected" to each house. In *Four Maple Drive Realty Corp. v. Abrams* (1956), the New York supreme court's appellate division pronounced that the governor performs a legislative function when approving or vetoing legislation.

Article V, Officers and Civil Departments, section 1, as amended in 1938, 1953, and 1955, provides that "[t]he comptroller and attorney-general shall be chosen at the same general election as the governor and hold office for the same term. . . ." The attorney general's independent status has been criticized as frustrating the state's criminal policy and creating confusion with respect to authority in the executive branch, because the constitution expressly charges the governor, not the attorney general, with seeing that the laws be faithfully executed. The other states are divided over whether the attorney general should be elected, as in Arizona, or appointed by the governor, as in New Jersey. **Section 2,** as amended in 1938, 1943, 1951, and 1961, states in part: "There shall be not more than twenty civil departments in the state government, including those referred to in this constitution."

Judicial Branch

Article VI, Judiciary, was totally revised in 1961. **Section 1** mandates: "a. There shall be a unified court system for the state. The state-wide courts shall consist of the court of appeals, the supreme court including the appellate divisions thereof, the court of claims, the county court, the surrogate's court and the family court . . . ; [and] **b.** [in addition to these courts the] courts or court of civil and criminal jurisdiction of the city of New York, and such other courts as the legislature may determine shall be courts of record."

Section 2, as amended in 1977, in **section 2a** states in part: "The court of appeals is continued. It shall consist of the chief judge and the six . . . associate judges now in office . . . [and the] official terms of the chief judge and the six associate judges shall be fourteen years." According to **section 2b,** if the workload of the court of appeals requires it, the governor may designate up to four justices of the supreme court to serve as associate judges of the court of appeals.

Section 2c, added in 1977, creates a commission on judicial nomination "to evaluate the qualifications of candidates for appointment to the court of appeals and to prepare a written report and recommend to the governor those persons who by their character, temperament, professional aptitude and experience are well qualified to hold such judicial office." **Section 2e,** also added in 1977, directs the governor to "appoint, with the advice and consent of the senate, from among those recommended by the judicial nominating commission, a person to fill the office of chief judge or associate judge ... whenever a vacancy occurs in the court of appeals; provided ... [the nominee] is a resident of the state and has been admitted to the practice of law in this state for at least ten years." And, according to **section 20,** as amended in 1977, "**a.** No person, other than one who holds such office at the effective date of this article, may assume the office of judge of the court of appeals, justice of the supreme court, or judge of the court of claims unless he has been admitted to practice law in this state at least ten years...."

Section 3a delineates the jurisdiction of the court of appeals as "the review of questions of law except where the judgment is of death, or where the appellate division, on reversing or modifying a final ... or interlocutory order in a special proceeding, finds new facts...." **Section 3b** enumerates other instances, including criminal cases "or otherwise as the legislature may from time to time provide" and certain civil cases and proceedings.

Section 4a divides the state into four judicial departments: "The first ... shall consist of the counties within the first judicial district of the state ... , [t]he second ... of the counties within the second, ninth, tenth and eleventh judicial districts ... , [t]he third ... of the counties within the third, fourth and sixth judicial districts ... , [and the] fourth ... of the counties within the fifth, seventh and eighth.... Once every ten years the legislature may alter the boundaries of the judicial departments, but without changing the number thereof." A twelfth judicial district consisting of the county of the Bronx was created in 1983. **Section 4b** creates appellate divisions of the supreme court, assigning seven justices in each of the first two departments and five justices in each of the other departments.

Section 7a grants the supreme court "general original jurisdiction in law and equity and the appellate jurisdiction herein provided." The supreme court is also given in New York City "exclusive jurisdiction over crimes prosecuted by indictment ... ," with some exceptions. **Sections 9** through **17,** as amended variously, deal with other courts, including the court of claims, county courts, surrogate's courts, family court, New York City courts, district courts, and town, village, and city courts.

Section 22, as amended in 1977, creates a commission on judicial conduct, and **section 23** provides that "[j]udges of the court of appeals and justices of the supreme court may be removed by concurrent resolution of both houses of the legislature, if two-thirds of all the members elected to each house concur therein." **Section 25,** as amended in 1966, requires a judge or justice to retire "on the last day of December in the year in which he reaches the age of seventy."

Section 28, as amended in 1977, provides that "[t]he chief judge of the court of appeals shall be the chief judge of the state of New York and shall be the chief judicial officer of the unified court system." It also establishes an administrative board of the courts "which shall consist of the chief judge of the court of appeals as chairman and the presiding justice of the appellate division of the supreme court of each judicial department." With the advice and consent of this board, the chief judge "shall appoint a chief administrator of the courts who shall serve at his pleasure."

Impeachment

Article VI, Judiciary, section 24, gives the assembly, the lower house of the legislature, the power to impeach judicial officers by "a vote of a majority of all members elected thereto" and specifies that the court for impeachment trials consists of "the president of the senate, the senators, or the major part of them, and the judges of the court of appeals, or the major part of them." Section 24 also provides that during an impeachment trial of the governor or lieutenant governor "neither the lieutenant-governor nor the temporary president of the senate shall act as a member of the court." Conviction requires the vote of "two-thirds of the members present" and results in "removal from office, or removal from office and disqualification to hold and enjoy any public office of honor, trust, or profit under this state...." The party impeached, however, is also liable to indictment and punishment "according to law." In addition to New York, Idaho, North Carolina, and Wisconsin place impeachment provisions in the article on the judiciary.

Local Government

Article IX, Local Governments, section 1, added in 1963, declares: "Effective local self-government and intergovernmental cooperation are purposes of the people of the state." There follows a list of "rights, powers, privileges and immunities in addition to those granted by other provisions of this constitution." Section 2 provides for local government home rule.

Taxation and Finance

Article XVI, Taxation, added in 1938, declares in section 1: "The power of taxation shall never be surrendered, suspended or contracted away, except as to securities issued for public purposes pursuant to law...." Section 2 states in part: "The legislature shall provide for the supervision, review and equalization of assessments for the purposes of taxation. Assessments shall in no case exceed full value."

Article VII, State Finances, section 2, added in 1938 and amended in 1965 and 1995, requires the governor annually to "submit to the legislature a budget containing a complete plan of expenditures proposed to be made before the close of the ensuing fiscal year and all moneys and revenues estimated to be available therefor ..." and mandates a balanced budget. In *Wein v. State of New York* (1976), the New York court of appeals upheld state appropriations funded by short-term borrowing "in the form of revenue or tax anticipation notes" for New York City to avert a financial crisis, saying that, although the line in the constitution between permitted and unpermitted borrowing is a narrow one, short-term borrowing is expressly and unconditionally authorized by section 9.

Section 3, added in 1938, provides that the governor, when submitting the budget, "shall submit a bill or bills containing all the proposed appropriations and reappropriations...."

Section 4, added in 1938, states in part: "The legislature may not alter an appropriation bill submitted by the governor except to strike out or reduce items therein, but it may add thereto items of appropriation provided that such additions are stated separately and distinctly from the original items of the bill and refer each to a single object or purpose. Such an appropriation bill shall when passed by both houses be a law immediately without further action by the governor...."

Article XI, Education, as amended in 1938 and 1962, declares in **section 1**: "The legislature shall provide for the maintenance and support of a system of free common schools, wherein all the children of this state may be educated." Although the courts in Kentucky, New Jersey, and Washington have invalidated their school finance programs described in similar language, New York, like Colorado, Michigan, and Ohio, has upheld the state's school finance programs. **Section 2** deals with the University of the State of New York.

Article XVII, Social Welfare, section 1, added in 1938, mandates: "The aid, care and support of the needy are public concerns and shall be provided by the state and by such of its subdivisions, and in such manner and by such means, as the legislature may from time to time determine."

Article XVIII, Housing, added in 1938, states in **section 1,** as amended in 1965: "Subject to the provisions of this article, the legislature may provide in such manner, by such means and upon such terms and conditions as it may prescribe for low rent housing and nursing home accommodations for persons of low income as defined by law, or for [rehabilitating substandard and unsanitary areas]...."

Article XIV, Conservation, section 1, as amended twelve times between 1938 and 1995, begins: "The lands of the state, now owned or hereafter acquired, constituting the forest preserve as now fixed by law, shall be forever kept as wild forest lands. They shall not be leased, sold, or exchanged, or be taken by any corporation, public or private, nor shall the timber thereon be sold, removed or destroyed." Section 1 further states: "Nothing herein contained shall prevent the state from constructing, completing and maintaining any highway heretofore specifically authorized by constitutional amendment...." **Section 4,** added in 1969, declares in part: "The policy of the state shall be to conserve and protect its natural resources and scenic beauty and encourage the development and improvement of its agricultural lands for the production of food and other agricultural products."

Article XIX, Amendments to Constitution, section 1, as amended in 1938 and 1941, provides that amendments to the constitution may be proposed in either the senate or the assembly, after which they are "referred to the attorney-general," who renders an opinion to the legislature as to their effect on other provisions of the constitution. The proposed amendments, if approved "by a majority of the members elected to each of the two houses," are referred to the "next regular session convening after the succeeding general election of members of the assembly," and if again approved by a majority of the legislators, they are submitted to the people. Amendments approved "by a majority of the electors voting thereon" become a part of the constitution on January 1 of the next year.

Education

Health and Welfare

Environment

Amendment Procedures

Section 2, as amended in 1938, states in part: "At the general election to be held in the year nineteen hundred and fifty-seven, and every twentieth year thereafter, and also at such times as the legislature may by law provide, the question 'Shall there be a convention to revise the constitution and amend the same?' shall be submitted to and decided by the electors of the state...." If answered in the affirmative, delegates are elected and must "convene at the capitol on the first Tuesday of April next ensuing after their election...." Six weeks after the adjournment of the convention, any amendments are to be submitted to the people. Required voter approval and the effective date of the amendments are the same as outlined in section 1.

On November 21, 1789, North Carolina became the twelfth state of the United States. The capital of the "Tar Heel State" or the "Old North State" is Raleigh. Some 53,821 square miles in area, North Carolina is bordered by Virginia on the north, the Atlantic Ocean on the east, South Carolina and Georgia on the south, and Tennessee on the west. With approximately 7.2 million inhabitants, North Carolina ranks eleventh among the states in population. Its principal industries include manufacturing, agriculture, and tourism; among its chief crops are tobacco, soybeans, corn, and cotton.

Government: The governor and lieutenant governor are elected separately for four-year terms and are limited to two consecutive terms. The legislature, called the general assembly, consists of fifty senators and 120 members of the house of representatives, all of whom are elected for two-year terms. The supreme court includes a chief justice and six associate justices elected for eight-year terms.

General Information

Dates of Constitutions: 1776, 1868, and 1971

Constitutional History

In 1524, when the Italian navigator Giovanni da Verrazano, exploring for France, arrived at the coast of what would become the state of North Carolina, it was inhabited by Algonquin, Sioux, and Iroquois peoples. Verrazano's enthusiastic report on the territory to the French king, Francis I, however, fell on deaf ears. Two years later a Spaniard, Lucas Vásquez de Ayllon, attempted to establish a Spanish colony there, but it succumbed to diseases bred in the marshy coast. On March 25, 1584, Walter Raleigh, soon to be knighted, was granted a patent of discovery by England, and in September of that year Raleigh's agents returned with high praise for Roanoke Island. The new land was called Virginia in honor of the Virgin Queen, Elizabeth I. In 1585 Raleigh established the Roanoke colony, which mysteriously disappeared in 1590 and became known as the "Lost Colony."

In 1629 Charles I of England gave a large grant of land to his attorney general, Sir Robert Heath, who named it Carolana in honor of the king. But civil strife in England prevented Heath from carrying out his plans to develop the territory. After the English civil war, Charles II, the restored monarch, reclaimed this grant. Through a charter of March 24, 1663, he rewarded eight of his most loyal supporters with lands "in the parts of America not yet cultivated or planted, and only inhabited by some barbarous people. . . ." In August of that year the "lords proprietors," as they were titled, issued a declaration of their intentions to develop the Carolina Colony, the lands south of Virginia extending into the territory of what is now Florida. Three counties were initially established: Albemarle, Clarendon, and Craven.

In 1669 John Locke, later noted for his work *Two Treatises of Government* (1690), drafted the Fundamental Constitutions for the governance of the Carolina Colony at the request of one of the proprietors. In 1691 Albemarle was renamed North Carolina, and in 1712 it was separated administratively from the Carolina Colony. The North Carolina territory was transferred to the British monarch George II and became a royal colony in 1729. With antiroyalist sentiment running high in the colony, a group of patriots disdainful of the British authorities reportedly met in Mecklenberg in 1775 and declared the colony's independence.

On April 12, 1776, North Carolina became the first of the colonies to instruct its delegates to the Continental Congress to vote for independence. Its first constitution, drafted and adopted by a "congress" that met in Halifax in November and December 1776, consisted of a relatively general and abstract declaration of rights followed by provisions establishing the frame of government.

With the beginning of the Civil War, on May 20, 1861, the North Carolina constitution was amended to conform to the state's secession from the Union and membership in the Confederacy, but after the war, on October 9, 1865, this amendment was formally repealed. Under the Reconstruction Acts passed by Congress, a constitutional convention met in Raleigh on January 14, 1868, and drafted a new constitution that was ratified by the voters in April. This document provided for universal suffrage for men and a poll tax as well as a property tax. A number of amendments to this constitution were proposed by a convention held in Raleigh and approved by the voters on November 6, 1876.

The present constitution of North Carolina was proposed by the legislature in 1969. Along with five amendments, it was approved by state voters in November 1970 and went into effect on July 1, 1971.

The Constitution

Unlike North Carolina's two previous constitutions, the 1971 document was conceived in an era of prosperity and civil calm. Carefully crafted by legal and political experts retained by the legislature rather than by a constitutional convention, it aimed to modernize the government without jettisoning the more salutary aspects of the past constitutions. A significant new provision, for example, authorizes the legislature to place limits on any future constitutional convention if such limits are approved by the voters. Other new provisions address the state's finances. Until an amendment was adopted in 1996, North Carolina was the only state whose constitution did not grant the governor the power to veto legislation.

North Carolina is one of three states, along with Illinois and Virginia, that adopted new constitutions effective in 1971. Containing only some 11,000 words, it is tied with Utah as the sixth shortest of all the state constitutions. As of January 1, 1998, it has been amended thirty times. The document creates the typical plural executive branch of government, a bicameral legislature, and an elected judiciary.

Preamble

The preamble to the 1971 North Carolina constitution reads: "We, the people of the State of North Carolina, grateful to Almighty God, the Sovereign Ruler of Nations, for the preservation of the American Union and the existence of our civil, political and religious liberties, and acknowledging our dependence upon Him for the continuance of those blessings to us and our posterity, do, for the more certain security thereof and for the better government of this State, ordain and establish this Constitution."

Fundamental Rights

Article I, Declaration of Rights, begins: "That the great, general, and essential principles of liberty and free government may be recognized and established, and that the relations of this State to the Union and government of the United States and those of the people of this State to the rest of the American people may be defined and affirmed, we do declare that. . . ." This language represents an amalgam of some of the expressions in the 1776 Revolution-era and the 1868 Reconstruction constitutions.

Section 1 declares: "We hold it to be self-evident that all persons are created equal; that they are endowed by their Creator with certain inalienable rights; that among these are life, liberty, the enjoyment of the fruits of their own labor, and the pursuit of happiness." The influence of the Declaration of Independence on this section is obvious. **Section 2** proclaims: "All political power is vested in and derived from the people; all government of right originates from the people, is founded upon their will only, and is instituted solely for the good of the whole."

Section 3 states: "The people of this State have the inherent, sole, and exclusive right of regulating the internal government and police thereof, and of altering or abolishing their Constitution and form of government ... in pursuance of law and consistently with the Constitution of the United States." **Section 4** declares: "This State shall ever remain a member of the American Union ... ," and **section 5** enjoins: "Every citizen of this state owes paramount allegiance to the Constitution and government of the United States...." In *South Dakota v. North Carolina* (1904), the U.S. Supreme Court declared that because the U.S. Constitution did not limit its judicial power over "controversies between two or more States," it had jurisdiction in a suit between two states that did not require a personal judgment against a state. According to **section 7**, "All power of suspending laws or the execution of laws by any authority, without the consent of the representatives of the people, is injurious to their rights and shall not be exercised." **Section 8** asserts: "The people of this State shall not be taxed or made subject to the payment of any impost or duty without the consent of themselves or their representatives...."

Sections 9 through **12**, respectively, mandate frequent elections; declare that "[a]ll elections shall be free"; prohibit property qualifications to vote or hold office; and guarantee the right of assembly and petition for the redress of grievances, with the caveat that "secret political societies are dangerous to the liberties of a free people and shall not be tolerated." **Sections 13** through **15**, respectively, guarantee religious liberty, freedom of speech and press, and the right "to the privilege of education." **Sections 16** and **17** prohibit ex post facto laws and slavery; section 17 also bars involuntary servitude "except as a punishment for crime."

Section 18 declares: "All courts shall be open; every person for an injury done him in his lands, goods, person, or reputation shall have remedy by due course of law; and right and justice shall be administered without favor, denial, or delay." Under **section 19**, "No person shall be taken, imprisoned, or disseized of his freehold, liberties, or privileges, or outlawed, or exiled, or in any manner deprived of his life, liberty, or property, but by the law of the land." (In comparison, paragraph 39 of Magna Carta, the charter of liberties forced on King John by the English barons in 1215, reads: "No freeman shall be taken or imprisoned, or disseised, or outlawed, or banished, or any ways destroyed ... unless by the lawful judgment of his peers, or by the law of the land.") Section 19 continues: "No person shall be denied the equal protection of the laws; nor shall any person be subjected to discrimination by the State because of race, color, religion, or national origin." **Section 20** prohibits general warrants; **section 21** guarantees a remedy for restraint of liberty and prohibits the suspension of the writ of habeas corpus; and **section 22** requires indictment, presentment, or impeachment to charge a person for criminal action, except in certain misdemeanor cases. **Sections 23** through **29**, respectively, address rights of the accused; the right to a jury trial in criminal cases; the right to a jury trial in civil cases; equality in selection for jury service; bail, fines, and punishments; imprisonment for debt; and treason, which is defined in terms similar to those used in the U.S. Constitution.

Section 30 guarantees the right to bear arms, prohibits standing armies in peacetime, and subordinates the military to civil power. **Sections 31** through **section 34**, respectively, prohibit the quartering of soldiers in private homes in peacetime without the consent of the owner; exclusive or separate emoluments or privileges; hereditary emoluments, privileges, or honors; and perpetuities and monopolies as "contrary to the genius of a free state." Notes **section 35**: "A frequent recurrence to fundamental principles is absolutely necessary to preserve the blessings of liberty." **Section 36** declares: "The enumeration of rights in this Article shall not be construed to impair or deny others retained by the people." An amendment approved by the voters in 1996 added **section 37**, which provides that victims of crime "shall be entitled to the following basic rights: **(a)** The right as prescribed by law to be informed of and to be present at court proceedings of the accused. **(b)** The right to be heard at sentencing of the accused in a manner prescribed by law, and at other times as prescribed by law or deemed appropriate by the court."

Division of Powers

Article I, Declaration of Rights, section 6, states: "The legislative, executive, and supreme judicial powers of the State government shall be forever separate and distinct from each other."

Legislative Branch

Article II, Legislative, section 1, vests the legislative power of the state in a general assembly, consisting of a senate and a house of representatives. **Section 2** specifies that "the Senate shall be composed of 50 Senators, biennially chosen by ballot." Under **section 4,** the house of representatives is composed of 120 representatives, "biennially chosen by ballot." North Carolina is one of twelve states in which the members of both houses of the legislature are elected for two-year terms. **Section 8** directs: "The election for members of the General Assembly shall be held for the respective districts in 1972 and every two years thereafter, at the places and on the day prescribed by law."

Section 6 stipulates: "Each Senator, at the time of his election, shall be not less than 25 years of age, shall be a qualified voter of the State, and shall have resided in the State as a citizen for two years and in the district for which he is chosen for one year immediately preceding his election." According to **section 7,** "Each Representative, at the time of his election, shall be a qualified voter of the State, and shall have resided in the district for which he is chosen for one year immediately preceding his election."

Section 14(1) states in part: "The Senate shall elect from its membership a President Pro Tempore, who shall become President of the Senate upon the failure of the Lieutenant Governor-elect to qualify, or upon succession by the Lieutenant Governor to the office of Governor, or upon the death, resignation, or removal from office of the President of the Senate, and who shall serve until the expiration of this term of office as Senator." In the case of the senate president's physical or mental incapacity or during an absence, **section 14(2)** authorizes the president pro tempore to preside. **Section 14(3)** provides for the senate to elect its other officers, while **section 15** authorizes the house of representatives to elect its speaker and other officers.

Section 20 specifies: "Each house shall be judge of the qualifications and elections of its own members, shall sit upon its own adjournment from day to day, and shall prepare bills to be enacted into laws. The two houses may jointly adjourn to any future day or other place. Either house may, of its own motion, adjourn for a period not in excess of three days." According to **section 22,** "All bills and resolutions of a legislative nature shall be read three times in each house before they become laws, and shall be signed by the presiding officer of both houses." The constitutions of a number of other states, including Oregon and South Carolina, have a similar signature requirement, although the U.S. Constitution and other state constitutions do not. **Section 23** requires: "No laws shall be enacted to raise money on the credit of the State … for the payment of any debt, or to impose any tax upon the people … or to allow the counties, cities, or towns to do so, unless the bill for the purpose shall have been read through several times in each house of the General Assembly … on three different days, and shall have been agreed to by each house respectively. …" As provided in **section 18,** "Any member of either house may dissent from and protest against any act or resolve which he may think injurious to the public or to any individual, and have the reasons of his dissent entered on the journal [of that house]."

Section 24(1) prohibits "any local, private, or special act or resolution" in certain cases, such as those "**(a)** [r]elating to health, sanitation, and the abatement of nuisances; **(b)** [c]hanging the names of cities, towns, and townships; … [and] **(l)** [g]iving effect to informal wills and deeds. …" **Section 24(4)** provides: "The General Assembly may enact general laws regulating the matters set out in this Section."

Conspicuously absent from the legislative provisions in the North Carolina constitution are any reference to the legislature's authority to determine its own rules of procedure, the definition of a quorum for doing business, the enumeration of privileges and immunities of legislators, and the power of the legislature to punish its members and others for improper behavior—provisions that are generally found in other state constitutions.

Article III, Executive, section 1, declares: "The executive power of the State shall be vested in the Governor." Terms for the governor and lieutenant governor, who are elected on separate tickets, are four years, as set out in **section 2(1):** "The Governor and Lieutenant Governor shall be elected by the qualified voters of the State in 1972 and every four years thereafter. …" **Section 2(2)** provides: "No person shall be eligible for election to the office of Governor or Lieutenant Governor unless, at the time of his election, he shall have attained the age of 30 years and shall have been a citizen of the United States for five years and a resident of this State for two years immediately preceding his election." Each is limited to "two consecutive terms of the same office."

Executive Branch

Section 5(2) mandates that the governor, among other responsibilities, "shall from time to time give the General Assembly information of the affairs of the State and recommend to their consideration such measures as he shall deem expedient." Under section 5(3), the governor is directed to "prepare and recommend to the General Assembly a comprehensive budget of the anticipated revenue and proposed expenditures of the State for the ensuing fiscal period." Once enacted, the budget "shall be administered by the Governor ... ," with this proviso: "The total expenditures of the State for the fiscal period covered by the budget shall not exceed the total of receipts during that fiscal period and the surplus remaining in the State Treasury at the beginning of the period."

Section 5(4) specifies that the governor "shall take care that the laws be faithfully executed, and section 5(5) indicates that the office holder "shall be Commander in Chief of the military forces of the State except when they shall be called into the service of the United States. Under section 5(6), "The Governor may grant reprieves, commutations, and pardons, after conviction, for all offenses (except in cases of impeachment), upon such conditions as he may think proper, subject to regulations prescribed by law relative to the manner of applying for pardons. The terms *reprieves, commutations,* and *pardons* [italics added] shall not include parole." This distinction has been expressly recognized by some state courts, including the Nevada supreme court. In section 5(7), the constitution additionally provides that the governor "may, on extraordinary occasions, by and with the advice of the Council of State, convene the General Assembly in extra session by its proclamation...."

Sections 5(8) and 5(9), respectively, empower the governor to "nominate and by and with the advice and consent of a majority of the Senators appoint all officers whose appointments are not otherwise provided for" and "require information in writing from the head of any administrative department or agency upon any subject relating to the duties of his office." Section 5(10) states: "The General Assembly shall prescribe the functions, powers, and duties of the administrative departments and agencies of the State and may alter them from time to time, but the Governor may make such changes in the allocation of offices and agencies and in the allocation of those functions, powers, and duties as he considers necessary for efficient administration. If those changes affect existing law, they shall be set forth in executive orders, which shall be submitted to the General Assembly ... , and shall have the force of law ... , unless specifically disapproved by resolution of either house ... or specifically modified by joint resolution of both houses...."

Section 6 relates in part: "The Lieutenant Governor shall be President of the Senate, but shall have no vote unless the Senate is equally divided. He shall perform such additional duties as the General Assembly or the Governor may assign to him." According to section 7(1), "A Secretary of State, an Auditor, a Treasurer, a Superintendent of Public Instruction, an Attorney General [and commissioners of agriculture, labor, and insurance] shall be elected ... every four years...." Section 7(7) requires that the attorney general be a person "duly authorized to practice law in the courts of this State." Section 8 adds: "The Council of State shall consist of the officers whose offices are established by this Article."

The constitutions of several other states, including Massachusetts, create an executive council, but the use of the term *council of state* is unique here, although it is common in many national constitutions such as those of Greece and Portugal.

Article IV, Judicial, section 1, places the judicial power of the state, "except as provided in Section 3 of this Article," in a court for the trial of impeachments and a general court of justice. "The General Assembly," continues section 1, "shall have no power to deprive the judicial department of any power or jurisdiction that rightfully pertains to it as a coordinate department of the government, nor shall it establish or authorize any courts other than as permitted by this Article." In *State v. Matthews* (1967), the North Carolina supreme court explained that the constitutional prohibition against the legislature's establishing or authorizing additional courts was added to ensure a unified judicial system. To carry out the provisions of this article the constitution does allow the general assembly in **section 15** to "provide for an administrative office of the courts."

Section 2 states: "The General Court of Justice shall constitute a unified judicial system for the purposes of jurisdiction, operation, and administration, and shall consist of an Appellate Division, a Superior Court Division, and a District Court Division." Under **section 3,** "The General Assembly may vest in administrative agencies established pursuant to law such judicial powers as may be reasonably necessary as an incident to the accomplishment of the purposes for which the agencies were created. Appeals from administrative agencies shall be to the General Court of Justice." **Section 5** provides that the appellate division "shall consist of the Supreme Court and the Court of Appeals."

Section 6 specifies in part: "**(1)** . . . The Supreme Court shall consist of a Chief Justice and six Associate Justices, but the General Assembly may increase the number of Associate Justices to not more than eight." Currently, the North Carolina supreme court has seven justices. Among other provisions **section 16** stipulates: "Justices of the Supreme Court, Judges of the Court of Appeals, and regular Judges of the Superior Court shall be elected by the qualified voters and shall hold office for terms of eight years and until their successors are elected and qualified." Notes **section 19,** "Unless otherwise provided in this Article, all vacancies occurring in the offices provided for by this Article shall be filled by appointment of the Governor, and the appointees shall hold their places until the next election for members of the General Assembly that is held more than 60 days after the vacancy occurs, when elections shall be held to fill the offices." Under **section 22,** "Only persons duly authorized to practice law in the courts of this State shall be eligible for election or appointment as a Justice of the Supreme Court, Judge of the Court of Appeals, Judge of the Superior Court, or Judge of [the] District Court."

Section 12(1) defines the supreme court's jurisdiction: "The Supreme Court shall have jurisdiction to review upon appeal any decision of the courts below, upon any matter of law or legal inference. The jurisdiction of the Supreme Court over 'issues of fact' and 'questions of fact' shall be the same exercised by it prior to the adoption of this Article, and the Court may issue any remedial writs necessary to give it general supervision and control over the proceedings of the other courts. The Supreme Court also has jurisdiction to review, when authorized by law, direct appeals from a final order or decision of the North Carolina Utilities Commission."

Sections 8 and 17, respectively, relate to the retirement and removal of justices. Section 8 states: "The General Assembly shall provide by general law for the retirement of Justices and Judges of the General Court of Justice, and may provide for the temporary recall of any retired Justice or Judge to serve on the court from which he was retired. The General Assembly shall also prescribe maximum age limits for service as a Justice or Judge." Section 17(1) provides: "Any Justice or Judge of the General Court of Justice may be removed from office for mental or physical incapacity by joint resolution of two-thirds of all the members of each house of the General Assembly. Any Justice or Judge against whom the General Assembly may be about to proceed shall receive notice thereof, accompanied by a copy of the causes alleged for his removal, at least 20 days before [action thereon]. Removal from office by the General Assembly for any other cause shall be by impeachment." Under section 17(2), "The General Assembly shall prescribe a procedure, in addition to impeachment and address set forth in this Section, for the removal of a Justice or Judge of the General Court of Justice for mental or physical incapacity interfering with the performance of his duties which is, or is likely to become, permanent, and for the censure and removal of a Justice or Judge ... for willful misconduct in office, willful and persistent failure to perform his duties, habitual intemperance, conviction of a crime involving moral turpitude, or conduct prejudicial to the administration of justice that brings the judicial office into disrepute." In *In re Peoples* (1978), the North Carolina supreme court concluded that the purpose of section 17(2) was to provide an alternative to the "cumbersome and antiquated" process of impeachment or address.

Impeachment

Article IV, Judicial, section 1, introduces the impeachment process by authorizing a court for the trial of impeachments as part of the general court system. In the Wyoming constitution, the senate's role as the venue for impeachments is similarly placed in the article on the judicial branch, although in other state constitutions this authority is more commonly found in the legislative article, in a separate section, or in a provision on public employees.

Section 4 states: "The State House of Representatives solely shall have the power of impeaching. The Court for the Trial of Impeachments shall be the Senate. When the Governor or Lieutenant Governor is impeached, the Chief Justice shall preside over the Court. A majority of the members shall be necessary to a quorum, and no person shall be convicted without the concurrence of two-thirds of the Senators present. Judgment upon conviction shall not extend beyond removal from and disqualification to hold office in this State, but the party shall be liable to indictment and punishment according to law."

Local Government

Article VII, Local Government, section 1, indicates in part: "The General Assembly shall provide for the organization and government and the fixing of boundaries of counties, cities and towns, and other governmental subdivisions, and, except as otherwise prohibited by this Constitution, may give such powers and duties to counties, cities and towns, and other governmental subdivisions as it may deem advisable."

Article V, Finance, section 1, declares: "No poll or capitation tax shall be levied by the General Assembly or by any county, city or town, or other taxing unit." **Section 2(1)** provides: "The power of taxation shall be exercised in a just and equitable manner, for public purposes only, and shall never be surrendered, suspended, or contracted away."

Article IX, Education, section 1, proclaims: "Religion, morality, and knowledge being necessary to good government and the happiness of mankind, schools, libraries, and the means of education shall forever be encouraged." Under **section 2(1),** "The General Assembly shall provide by taxation and otherwise for a general and uniform system of free public schools...." In *Sneed v. Greensboro City Bd. of Ed.* (1980), the North Carolina supreme court declared, in determining that section 2(1) did not preclude charging public school students incidental course and instructional fees, that it was incumbent on the court to interpret the constitution in accordance with the intent of the framers and the citizens who adopted it.

Article XI, Punishments, Corrections, and Charities, section 4, declares: "Beneficent provision for the poor, the unfortunate, and the orphan is one of the first duties of a civilized and a Christian state. Therefore the General Assembly shall provide for and define the duties of a board of public welfare."

Article XIII, Conventions, Constitutional Amendment and Revision, section 1, states in part: "No Convention of the People of this State shall ever be called unless by the concurrence of two-thirds of all the members of each house of the General Assembly, and unless the proposition 'Convention or No Convention' is first submitted to the qualified voters of the State at the time and in the manner prescribed by the General Assembly. If a majority of the votes cast upon the proposition are in favor of a Convention, it shall assemble on the day prescribed by the General Assembly." **Section 2** provides: "The people of this State reserve the power to amend this Constitution and to adopt a new or revised Constitution. This power may be exercised by either of the methods set out hereinafter in this Article, but in no other way."

Section 3 states: "A Convention of the People of this State may be called pursuant to Section 1 of this Article to propose a new or revised Constitution or to propose amendments to this Constitution. Every [proposal] adopted by a Convention shall be submitted to the qualified voters ... at the time and in the manner prescribed by the Convention. If a majority of the votes cast thereon are in favor of ratification of the [proposal], it ... shall become effective January first next after ratification ... unless ... [otherwise] prescribed by the Convention."

Section 4 prescribes that any proposal for a new or revised constitution or for an amendment or amendments "may be initiated by the General Assembly, but only if three fifths of all the members of each house shall adopt an act submitting the proposal to the qualified voters of the State for their ratification or rejection...." If a majority of the votes favor the proposals, they become effective "January first next after ratification by the voters unless a different effective date is prescribed in the act submitting the proposal or proposals to the qualified voters."

NORTH DAKOTA

North Dakota became the thirty-ninth state of the United States on November 2, 1889. Bismarck is the capital of the "Peace Garden State," which encompasses some 70,704 square miles. North Dakota is bordered by the Canadian provinces of Saskatchewan and Manitoba on the north, Minnesota on the east, South Dakota on the south, and Montana on the west. It ranks forty-seventh among the states in population with approximately 641,000 inhabitants. The state's principal industries include agriculture, mining, and tourism; among its chief crops are spring wheat, barley, and rye.

General Information

Government: The governor and lieutenant governor are elected jointly for four-year terms. The legislature, called the legislative assembly, consists of forty-nine senators and ninety-eight members of the house of representatives; all are elected for four-year terms, and one-half of the members of each house are elected every two years. The supreme court includes a chief justice and four additional justices elected for ten-year terms, one every two years.

Date of Constitution: 1889

Constitutional History

Although the harsh conditions of the Great Plains delayed settlement of the region until around A.D. 1200, the Ojibwa, Teton Sioux (Dakota), Mandan, and Hidatsa peoples eventually inhabited the territory that became North Dakota. One of the first Europeans there was the French fur trader Pierre Gaultier de Varennes, sieur de La Vérendrye, who arrived on December 3, 1738. Between 1797 and 1798 the English explorer David Thompson made contact with the Mandans and Hidatsas in central North Dakota, and in 1803 part of North Dakota was transferred to the United States under the terms of the Louisiana Purchase.

The expedition of Meriwether Lewis and William Clark, who were commissioned by President Thomas Jefferson to explore the newly acquired Louisiana Territory, arrived in North Dakota on October 13, 1804, and wintered on the Missouri River near the present site of Washburn. Until it became a separate territory in 1861, the Dakota region was administered successively as a part of the territories of Louisiana, Missouri, Michigan, Wisconsin, Iowa, Minnesota, and Nebraska.

Americans did not rush to settle the Dakota region, and in the early eighteenth century the earl of Selkirk attempted to establish in the Red River Valley a colony for refugees from eastern Canada. In 1818 a treaty between the United Kingdom and the United States fixed the borders between North Dakota and Canada, but it was not until 1851 that the first permanent American agricultural community was established by settlers from Minnesota. The future state of North Dakota would become home to many Scandinavian immigrants, especially Norwegians.

An act of Congress dated March 2, 1861, provided "a temporary Government for the Territory of Dakota" and created an "Office of Surveyor General therein." With the coming of the railroad to the Northwest and the containment of the Sioux on reservations five years after the defeat of General George Custer at the battle of the Little Big Horn in 1876, the number of settlers increased. In 1883 Bismarck was made the capital of the Dakota Territory. In 1880 territorial leaders, including Moses Armstrong, had asked Congress to divide the Dakota Territory into two parts, but Congress did not pass an omnibus act directed at the statehood aspirations of Montana, North and South Dakota, and Washington until 1889.

A constitutional convention met in Bismarck from July 4 to August 17, 1889, and its draft constitution, together with a proposition relating to alcoholic beverages, was approved at the polls on October 1. On November 2, 1889, President Benjamin Harrison signed the proclamation admitting the states of North and South Dakota to the Union, and the constitution of North Dakota went into effect on that date.

Six states—North Dakota, South Dakota, Idaho, Montana, Washington, and Wyoming— adopted constitutions in 1889, and of these only Montana has promulgated a new constitution since then. Relatively short in length, North Dakota's constitution has some 20,564 words and has been amended 137 times as of January 1, 1998, the most of any of the 1889 state constitutions still in effect today.

The North Dakota constitution is similar to those of most other states. Although executive power is expressly vested in a governor, the addition of twelve statewide elected officials besides the governor and lieutenant governor makes the executive branch, like that of most other states, plural, or divided, thus differing from the federal model. Unlike the legislature of its sister state, South Dakota, the members of North Dakota's bicameral legislature are not subject to term limits, but the final word on the election of members is given to the courts rather than left in the hands of the legislature, as is generally the rule in other states. The unified judicial branch consists of elected justices and judges.

The Constitution

The preamble to the 1889 North Dakota constitution reads: "We, the people of North Dakota, grateful to Almighty God for the blessings of civil and religious liberty, do ordain and establish this constitution."

Preamble

Article I, Declaration of Rights, section 1, proclaims: "All individuals are by nature equally free and independent and have certain inalienable rights, among which are those of enjoying and defending life and liberty; acquiring, possessing and protecting property and reputation; pursuing and obtaining safety and happiness; and to keep and bear arms for the defense of their person, family, property, and the state, and for lawful hunting, recreational, and other lawful purposes, which shall not be infringed." The constitutions of Kentucky and Nebraska also place the right to bear arms in the first section or article. **Section 2** states: "All political power is inherent in the people. Government is instituted for the protection, security and benefit of the people, and they have a right to alter or reform the same whenever the public good may require."

Fundamental Rights

Section 3 guarantees the free exercise of religion, "but the liberty of conscience ... shall not be so construed as to excuse acts of licentiousness, or justify practices inconsistent with the peace or safety of this state." **Section 4** provides in part that everyone may "freely write, speak and publish his opinions on all subjects, being responsible for the abuse of that privilege." **Section 5** guarantees the right to assemble in a peaceable manner and petition the government for redress of grievances, and **section 6** prohibits slavery and involuntary servitude, "unless for the punishment of crime." **Section 7** states: "Every citizen of this state shall be free to obtain employment wherever possible, and any person, corporation, or agent thereof, maliciously interfering or hindering in any way, any citizen from obtaining or enjoying employment already obtained, from any other corporation or person, shall be guilty of a misdemeanor."

Sections 8, 9, 10, and **11,** respectively, prohibit unreasonable searches and seizures; provide that "[a]ll courts shall be open, and every man for any injury done him in his lands, goods, person or reputation shall have remedy by due process of law …"; require generally that an indictment is necessary for prosecution of a felony; and guarantee bail, "unless for capital offenses when the proof is evident or the presumption great," and prohibit excessive bail, fines, and cruel or unusual punishment. The constitutions of several other states including California use *or* rather than *and* in referring to this prohibited type of punishment. **Section 12** guarantees, among other things, the right to "a speedy and public trial," and **section 13** ensures the right of trial by jury.

Section 14 limits the suspension of the writ of habeas corpus, and **section 15** prohibits imprisoning a person for debt "unless upon refusal to deliver up his estate for the benefit of creditors … ; or in cases of tort; or where there is strong presumption of fraud." **Sections 16** through **19,** respectively, guarantee compensation for private property taken or damaged for public use; define treason in terms similar to those used in the U.S. Constitution; prohibit bills of attainder, ex post facto laws, and laws impairing the obligation of contracts; and subordinate the military to civil power, prohibit standing armies in peacetime, and limit the quartering of soldiers in private homes.

Section 20 proclaims: "To guard against transgressions of the high powers which we have delegated, we declare that everything in this article is excepted out of the general powers of government and shall forever remain inviolate." According to **section 21,** "No special privileges or immunities shall ever be granted which may not be altered, revoked or repealed by the legislative assembly; nor shall any citizen or class of citizens be granted privileges or immunities which upon the same terms shall not be granted to all citizens." **Section 22** requires that "[a]ll laws of a general nature shall have a uniform operation." **Section 23** declares: "The state of North Dakota is an inseparable part of the American union and the Constitution of the United States is the supreme law of the land." According to **section 24,** "The provisions of this constitution are mandatory and prohibitory unless, by express words, they are declared to be otherwise."

Division of Powers

The North Dakota constitution, like those of several other states, including Hawaii and New York, does not expressly set forth the principle of the separation of powers of government. However, the structure of the government it creates reflects this principle, and **article XI, General Provisions, section 26,** provides in part: "The legislative, executive, and judicial branches are coequal branches of government."

Legislative Branch

Article IV, Legislative Branch, section 1, specifies that "[t]he senate must be composed of not less than forty nor more than fifty-four members, and the house of representatives must be composed of not less than eighty nor more than one hundred eight members. These houses are jointly designated as the legislative assembly of the state of North

Dakota." As a result of redistricting, the senate currently has forty-nine members and the house ninety-eight members. **Section 3,** as amended in 1997, directs the legislative assembly to establish by law a procedure "whereby one-half of the members of the senate and one-half of the members of the house of representatives, as nearly as is practicable, are elected biennially." **Section 4,** as amended in 1997, stipulates that representatives must be elected for four-year terms.

Section 5 requires that candidates for the legislative assembly be qualified voters in their district and state residents for one year before the election. **Section 6** restricts legislators from holding "any full-time appointive state office established by this constitution or designated by law." Furthermore, they may not be appointed to any full-time office that the legislative assembly has created or increased the compensation for during that term.

Section 7 provides in part: "Neither house may recess nor adjourn for more than three days without consent of the other house." **Section 8** instructs the house of representatives to "elect one of its members to act as presiding officer at the beginning of each organizational session." According to **section 9,** a person will be deemed guilty of bribery for making an "offer or promise to give his vote or influence, in favor of, or against any measure or proposition pending or proposed to be introduced into the legislative assembly" in exchange for a similar action by another member on another measure. The penalty for such bribery is expulsion from the legislature, loss of eligibility to serve in the legislature in the future, and any other penalty prescribed by law. **Section 10** mandates: "No member of the legislative assembly, expelled for corruption, and no person convicted of bribery, perjury or other infamous crime shall be eligible to [that body], or to any office in either branch thereof."

Section 12 defines a quorum as a majority of the members in each house and authorizes each legislative body to be the judge of its members' qualifications, although "election contests are subject to judicial review as provided by law." The constitutions of most other states provide that each house is to be the judge of the elections of its members. Section 12 continues: "Each house shall determine its rules of procedure, and may punish its members or other persons for contempt or disorderly behavior in its presence. With the concurrence of two-thirds of its elected members, either house may expel a member."

Section 13 outlines the procedure for enacting bills: "No bill may become law except by a recorded vote of a majority of the members elected to each house, and the lieutenant governor is considered a member-elect of the senate when the lieutenant governor votes. No law may be enacted except by a bill passed by both houses, and no bill may be amended on its passage ... in a manner which changes its general subject matter. No bill may embrace more than one subject, which must be expressed in its title; but a law violating this provision is invalid only to the extent the subject is not so expressed." Bills must be read on "two separate natural days" and may be read by title only unless one-fifth of the members present demand a full-length reading. Bills may not be amended, extended, or incorporated into other bills by reference to their titles only, "except in the case of definitions and procedural provisions," and all bills and resolutions passed are to be signed by the presiding officer of each house. "The legislative assembly," section 13 further provides, "shall enact all laws necessary to carry into effect the provisions of this constitution. Except as otherwise provided in this constitution, no local or special laws may be enacted...."

Section 14 requires all sessions of the legislative assembly, "including the committee of the whole and meetings of legislative committees," to be open and public. **Section 15** exempts legislators from arrest during attendance at legislative sessions and while traveling to or returning from the sessions, except in cases of felony. Furthermore, "members of the legislative assembly may not be questioned in any other place for any words used in any speech or debate in legislative proceedings."

Executive Branch

Article V, Executive Branch, as amended in 1996 and effective July 1, 1997, declares in **section 1:** "The executive power is vested in the governor, who shall reside in the state capital and shall hold the office for the term of four years beginning in the year 2000, and until a successor is elected and duly qualified." **Section 3** states that the governor and lieutenant governor must be elected on a joint ballot.

Section 2 provides that, in addition to the governor and lieutenant governor, the voters choose an agriculture commissioner, an attorney general, an auditor, an insurance commissioner, three public service commissioners, a secretary of state, a superintendent of public instruction, a tax commissioner, and a treasurer, whose "powers and duties ... must be prescribed by law." The legislature was additionally authorized to create a department of labor, which is also a statewide elective office. **Section 5** specifies that the terms of office of the elected state officials "are four years, except that terms of the public service commissioners are six years," with one elected every two years.

Section 4 requires that candidates for executive offices be qualified voters of the state, at least twenty-five years old "on the day of the election," and state residents for five years. Candidates for governor and lieutenant governor must be at least thirty years old "on the day of the election," and the attorney general must be licensed to practice law in North Dakota.

Section 7 declares: "The governor is the chief executive of the state." The governor's responsibilities are "to see that the state's business is well administered and that its laws are faithfully executed"; serve as commander in chief of the state's military forces, "except when they are called into the service of the United States"; prescribe the duties of the lieutenant governor "in addition to those prescribed in this article"; call special sessions of the legislative assembly; present information on the condition of the state and recommend legislation to every regular and special session of the legislative assembly; and "transact and supervise all necessary business of the state with the United States, the other states, and the officers and officials of this state." The governor is also authorized to "grant reprieves, commutations, and pardons" and may "delegate this [last] power in a manner provided by law." According to **section 8,** the governor may "fill a vacancy in any office by appointment if no other method is provided by this constitution or by law."

If senate confirmation is required and the senate is in recess or adjourned, "the governor shall make a temporary appointment to the office."

Section 9 requires that bills passed by the legislative assembly be presented to the governor for signature. "If the governor signs the bill, it becomes law. The governor may veto a bill … [and] may veto items in an appropriation bill. Portions of the bill not vetoed become law." To veto a bill or item, the governor "shall return [it], with a written statement of the governor's objections, to the house in which it originated. If … two-thirds of the members elected to [each house] pass a vetoed item or bill …, the vetoed item or bill becomes law." Also according to section 9, if the governor does not sign or veto a bill within three days, it becomes law without his or her signature if the legislature is in session. If the legislature is not in session, "a bill becomes law if the governor neither signs nor vetoes it within fifteen days, Saturdays and Sundays excepted, after its delivery to the governor."

Section 11 provides that the lieutenant governor succeeds to the office of governor when a vacancy occurs in that office. If the lieutenant governor is unable to serve, the secretary of state acts as governor "until the vacancy is filled or the disability removed." **Section 12** specifies that the lieutenant governor serves as president of the senate; "[i]f the senate is equally divided on a question, the lieutenant governor may vote on procedural matters and on substantive matters if the lieutenant governor's vote would be decisive." This section was amended specifically to include the phrase "substantive matters" after the North Dakota supreme court held in *State ex rel. Sanstead v. Freed* (1977) that the lieutenant governor's tie-breaking vote was limited to procedural matters because such a vote on substantive matters would interfere with the governor's veto power.

Section 10 defines bribery and prescribes punishment for a governor guilty of such an offense.

Article VI, Judicial Article, section 1, declares: "The judicial power of the state is vested in a unified judicial system consisting of a supreme court, a district court, and such other courts as may be provided by law." **Section 2** describes its jurisdiction: "The supreme court shall be the highest court of the state. It shall have appellate jurisdiction, and shall also have original jurisdiction with authority to issue, hear, and determine such original and remedial writs as may be necessary to properly exercise its jurisdiction." The supreme court consists of five justices, "one of whom shall be designated chief justice in the manner provided by law."

Judicial Branch

Section 3 directs that "[t]he supreme court shall have authority to promulgate rules of procedure, including appellate procedure, to be followed by all the courts of this state; and, unless otherwise provided by law, to promulgate rules and regulations for the admission to practice, conduct, disciplining, and disbarment of attorneys at law." The administrative head of the judicial system is the chief justice, who appoints a court administrator for the unified judicial system; "[u]nless otherwise provided by law, the powers, duties, qualifications, and terms of office of the court administrator, and other court officials, shall be as provided by rules of the court."

Section 4 states that a majority of the supreme court justices is required to constitute a quorum or render a decision. Declaring a legislative act unconstitutional, however, requires the concurrence of at least four of the five justices; in contrast, the Nebraska constitution requires five of the seven members of the state supreme court to declare a legislative act invalid. In *Cardiff v. Bismarck Public School District* (1978), the North Dakota supreme court declared that the rationale behind the rule of constitutional interpretation that requires looking first at the language selected by the drafters was that such language was the best indicator of the meaning intended and the meaning the voters believed they were ratifying. **Section 6** notes that "[a]ppeals shall be allowed from decisions of lower courts to the supreme court as may be provided by law."

Section 7 provides that supreme court justices are elected for ten-year terms, with one justice elected every two years. Justices are to hold office "until their successors are duly qualified, and shall receive compensation as provided by law, but the compensation of any justice shall not be diminished during his term of office." **Section 10** stipulates that "supreme court justices and district court judges shall be citizens of the United States and residents of this state, shall be learned in the law, and shall possess any additional qualifications prescribed by law." No justice or judge may practice law or hold public office, "elective or appointive, not judicial in nature." Furthermore, "[n]o duties shall be imposed by law on the supreme court or any of the justices thereof, except such as are judicial, nor shall any of the justices exercise any power of appointment except as herein provided."

Sections 12 and **12.1** direct the legislature to "provide for the retirement, discipline, and removal of judges [and justices of the supreme court]." Such removal procedures "may be used in addition to ... impeachment proceedings" and other constitutional removal procedures. **Section 13** establishes a judicial nominating committee, which creates a list of candidates for supreme court justices and district court judges. If any vacancy occurs, the governor may appoint one of these candidates or call a special election. Justices and judges so appointed serve until the next general election, "when the office shall be filled by election for the remainder of the term." In *State ex rel. Vogel v. Garass* (1978), the North Dakota supreme court upheld the governor's judicial appointment under this section without reference to a list of names from the nominating committee, rather than requiring a special election to fill the position, because the legislature had not created a nominating committee as required by the constitution.

Impeachment

Article XI, General Provisions, section 8, grants the house of representatives the sole power of impeachment, which requires the concurrence of a majority of the members. **Section 9** states in part that the senate tries all impeachments and that conviction requires the concurrence of two-thirds of the members. According to **section 10,** "The governor and other state and judicial officers, except county judges, justices of the peace and police magistrates, shall be liable to impeachment for habitual drunkenness, crimes, corrupt conduct, or malfeasance or misdemeanor in office. Conviction results only in removal from office and disqualification to hold future office, but "the person accused, whether convicted or acquitted, shall nevertheless be liable to ... [additional] punishment according to law."

Section 11 states: "All officers not liable to impeachment shall be subject to removal for misconduct, malfeasance, crime or misdemeanor in office, or for habitual drunkenness or gross incompetency in such manner as may be provided by law."

Article III, Powers Reserved to the People, section 1, declares: "While the legislative power of this state shall be vested in a legislative assembly consisting of a senate and a house of representatives, the people reserve the power to propose and enact laws by the initiative, including the call for a constitutional convention; to approve or reject legislative Acts, or parts thereof, by the referendum; to propose and adopt constitutional amendments by the initiative; and to recall certain elected officials. This article is self-executing and all of its provisions are mandatory. Laws may be enacted to facilitate and safeguard, but not to hamper, restrict, or impair these powers." **Direct Democracy**

Article VII, Political Subdivisions, section 1, declares: "The purpose of this article is to provide for maximum local self-government by all political subdivisions with a minimum duplication of functions." Section 2 states that "the legislative assembly shall provide by law for the establishment and the government of all political subdivisions. Each political subdivision shall have and exercise such powers as provided by law." Pursuant to section 6, "The legislative assembly shall provide by law for the establishment and exercise of home rule in counties and cities." **Local Government**

Article X, Finance and Public Debt, section 1, prohibits the legislative assembly from levying a tax on the assessed value of real or personal property in order to defray state expenses. Section 3 provides in part: "No tax shall be levied except in pursuance of law, and every law imposing a tax shall state distinctly the object of the same, to which only it shall be applied." In *State ex rel. Haig v. Hauge* (1917), the North Dakota supreme court liberally interpreted this provision to permit tax revenues expressly earmarked for "school purposes" to be paid into a teachers' pension fund. **Taxation and Finance**

Section 13, as amended in 1918, 1924, and 1980, requires a balanced budget: "No debt in excess of the limit named herein shall be incurred except for the purpose of repelling invasion, suppressing insurrection, defending the state in time of war or to provide for the public defense in case of threatened hostilities."

Article VIII, Education, section 1, mandates: "A high degree of intelligence, patriotism, integrity and morality on the part of every voter in a government by the people being necessary in order to insure the continuance of that government and the prosperity and happiness of the people, the legislative assembly shall make provision for the establishment and maintenance of a system of public schools which shall be open to all children of the state of North Dakota and free from sectarian control. This legislative requirement shall be irrevocable without the consent of the United States and the people of North Dakota." In *In the Interest of G.H.* (1974), the North Dakota supreme court determined that the state was obligated to educate a severely handicapped child even though the child's parents had left the state, because the residence of the child, not of the parents, determines the state's responsibility for education. **Education**

**Compact with the
United States**

Article XIII, Compact with the United States, provides, among other things, assurances for the toleration of religion and cedes to the United States jurisdiction over certain military reservations, "provided, legal process, civil and criminal, of this state, extends over those reservations in all cases in which exclusive jurisdiction is not vested in the United States." The constitutions of South Dakota, New Mexico, and Washington also contain similar articles incorporating a compact with the United States.

Amendment Procedures

Article IV, Legislative Branch, section 16, provides: "Any amendment to this constitution may be proposed in either house of the legislative assembly, and if agreed to upon a roll call by a majority of the members elected to each house, must be submitted to the electors and if a majority of the votes cast thereon are in the affirmative, the amendment is a part of this constitution."

Article III, Powers Reserved to the People, section 1, gives the state's citizens the right to use the initiative to call for a constitutional convention and "to propose and adopt constitutional amendments. . . ." **Sections 2** through **8** set out detailed procedures for circulating and approving initiatives. According to **section 9,** "A constitutional amendment may be proposed by initiative petition. If signed by electors equal in number to four percent of the resident population of the state at the last federal decennial census [compared with two percent for other North Dakota initiatives], the petition may be submitted to the secretary of state. All other provisions relating to initiative measures apply hereto."

On March 1, 1803, Ohio, the "Buckeye State," became the seventeenth state of the Union. Its capital is Columbus. Some 44,828 square miles in area, Ohio is bordered by Michigan and Lake Erie on the north, Pennsylvania and West Virginia on the east, West Virginia and Kentucky on the south, and Indiana on the west. With approximately 11.2 million inhabitants, Ohio ranks seventh among the states in population. Its principal industries include manufacturing, trade, and services; among its chief crops are corn, hay, winter wheat, and soybeans.

Government: The governor and lieutenant governor are elected jointly for four-year terms, and the governor is limited to two successive terms. The legislature, called the general assembly, consists of thirty-three senators elected for four-year terms, one-half every two years, and ninety-nine members of the house of representatives elected for two-year terms. Senators are limited to two successive terms, while representatives are limited to four. The supreme court includes a chief justice and six additional justices elected for six-year terms.

Dates of Constitutions: 1803 and 1851

The Wyandot, Miami, and Shawnee peoples, among others, inhabited the land that would become the state of Ohio when the French explorer Robert Cavelier, sieur de La Salle, is believed to have entered the Ohio River from Lake Erie in 1669. France laid claim to the territory, but by 1730 traders from the British colonies of Pennsylvania and Virginia were making incursions into it. In 1749 a French Canadian, Céleron de Bienville, buried lead markers throughout the territory to underscore France's claim.

In 1750, however, Virginia organized the Ohio Company and through it obtained large tracts of land in the region to sell to potential settlers. The conflict between France and Great Britain culminated in the French and Indian War, which ended in 1763 with Britain winning the rights to the Ohio region and later annexing it to Canada pursuant to the Quebec Act of 1774. During the American Revolution, however, George Rogers Clark of Virginia secured the area for the United States.

In 1787 Congress passed the Northwest Ordinance, which provided a territorial government for Ohio, and on April 7, 1788, the first permanent white settlement in Ohio was founded at Marietta. At the Battle of Fallen Timbers on August 20, 1794, U.S. troops commanded by General Anthony Wayne succeeded in decisively defeating the native peoples of Ohio. William Henry Harrison, who later became the ninth president of the United States, in 1799 was sent to Congress as the Ohio Territory's representative.

Although the Federalists argued for restraint in granting statehood, supporters of President Thomas Jefferson, whose purchase of the Louisiana Territory from France in 1803 spurred even more settlers to move west, pressed for the early admission of new states. On April 30, 1802, an act "to enable the people of the Eastern division of the territory northwest of the river Ohio to form a constitution and state government" was approved. On November 29, 1802, a constitutional convention meeting in Chillicothe produced a document that went into effect on March 1, 1803, when Ohio was admitted as a state of the Union.

By 1810 Ohio's population had grown to more than 230,000 inhabitants. The state's growing economy demanded a government more responsive than that provided in its first constitution, which also allowed excessive domination by the legislative branch over the other two branches. These two concerns led voters to approve a constitutional convention in 1849. The convention, which first met in Columbus in 1850, produced a document that was ratified at the polls on June 17, 1851, and went into effect on September 1 of that year.

The Constitution

Like a number of other states, including Maryland and New Mexico, Ohio has updated its constitution on an ad hoc basis rather than by wholesale revision, as other states such as Florida and New Jersey have done. In 1912 Ohioans approved thirty-four of forty-two amendments proposed by a convention meeting in Columbus from January 9 to August 26, and as of January 1, 1998, the 1851 document has been amended 158 times. Partly because of the inclusion of a number of provisions of less than constitutional stature, such as the establishment of a Vietnam conflict compensation fund, guarantees of loans for industrial development, and numerous bond issue provisions, the 1851 Ohio constitution is a little longer than average, containing some 36,900 words.

The Ohio constitution creates the typical state government structure of a plural executive branch, a bicameral legislature, and an elected judiciary. As one of the earliest midwestern states, Ohio and its constitutions, particularly the 1803 document, have influenced those of a number of later states, including the 1816 Indiana constitution.

Preamble

The preamble to the 1851 Ohio constitution reads: "We, the people of the State of Ohio, grateful to Almighty God for our freedom, to secure its blessings and promote our common welfare, do establish this Constitution."

Fundamental Rights

Article I, Bill of Rights, section 1, declares: "All men are, by nature, free and independent, and have certain inalienable rights, among which are those of enjoying and defending life and liberty, acquiring, possessing, and protecting property, and seeking and obtaining happiness and safety." **Section 2** states: "All political power is inherent in the people. Government is instituted for their equal protection and benefit, and they have the right to alter, reform, or abolish the same, whenever they may deem it necessary; and no special privileges or immunities shall ever be granted, that may not be altered, revoked, or repealed by the General Assembly."

Section 3 asserts the right to assemble and petition the legislature for the redress of grievances; **section 4** guarantees the right to bear arms, prohibits standing armies in peacetime, and subordinates the military to civil power; **section 5,** as amended in 1912, guarantees the right to trial by jury; and **section 6** prohibits slavery and "involuntary servitude, unless for the punishment of crime." **Section 7** states in part: "All men have a natural and indefeasible right to worship Almighty God according to the dictates of their own conscience. . . . Religion, morality, and knowledge, however, being essential to good government, it shall be the duty of the General Assembly to pass suitable laws, to protect every religious denomination in the peaceable enjoyment of its own mode of public worship, and to encourage schools and the means of instruction." In *Wolman v. Walter* (1977), the U.S. Supreme Court declared a three-part test for challenges to state aid for nonpublic schools: a statute must have a secular purpose, it must primarily neither advance nor inhibit religion, and it must not foster excessive government entanglement with religion.

Section 8 restricts the suspension of the writ of habeas corpus, "unless, in cases of rebellion or invasion, the public safety require it," and **section 9** guarantees bail "except for capital offenses where the proof is evident, or the presumption great." **Section 10**, as amended in 1921, provides: "Except in cases of impeachment, cases arising in the army and navy, or in the militia when in actual service in time of war or public danger, and cases involving offenses for which the penalty provided is less than imprisonment in the penitentiary, no person shall be held to answer for a capital, or otherwise infamous, crime, unless on presentment or indictment of a grand jury...." Section 10 also includes a list of rights of the accused. Rights for crime victims are ensured under **section 10a**, added in 1994.

Section 11 extends to citizens freedom of speech and the press and provides: "In all criminal prosecutions for libel, truth may be given in evidence to the jury, and if it shall appear to the jury, that the matter charged as libelous is true, and was published with good motives, and for justifiable ends, the party shall be acquitted." **Section 12** prohibits transportation out of the state "for any offense committed within the same"; furthermore, "no conviction shall work corruption of blood, or forfeiture of estate." **Section 13** limits the quartering of soldiers in private homes, and **section 14** proscribes unreasonable searches and seizures. In *Mapp v. Ohio* (1961), the U.S. Supreme Court, overruling a previous holding, mandated that the federal sanction against the use of evidence obtained by violating the unreasonable search and seizure provision of the Fourth Amendment (1791) of the U.S. Constitution would be enforced in the states through the due process of law clause of the Fourteenth Amendment (1868). **Section 15** prohibits imprisonment for debt "unless in cases of fraud."

Section 16, as amended in 1912, affirms: "All courts shall be open, and every person, for an injury done him in his land, goods, person, or reputation, shall have remedy by due course of law, and shall have justice administered without denial or delay. Suits may be brought against the state, in such courts and in such manner, as may be provided by law." **Section 17** prohibits hereditary emoluments, honors, and privileges, and **section 18** states that "[n]o power of suspending laws shall ever be exercised, except by the General Assembly." **Section 19** guarantees the inviolability of private property and compensation when it is taken for public use. **Section 19a**, added in 1912, provides: "The amount of damages recoverable by civil action in the courts for death caused by the wrongful act, neglect, or default of another, shall not be limited by law." **Section 20** guarantees to the people rights not specified and "all powers, not herein delegated...."

Like the U.S. Constitution and the constitutions of several other states, including Hawaii and New York, for example, the Ohio constitution does not expressly mention the separation of powers principle, but it is evidenced in the government structure created by the document.

Division of Powers

Article II, Legislative, section 1, as amended in 1953, declares: "The legislative power of the state shall be vested in a General Assembly consisting of a Senate and House of Representatives but the people reserve to themselves the power [of initiative and referendum.]" **Section 2,** added in 1992, provides: "Representatives shall be elected biennially by the electors of the respective house of representatives districts ... [and] [s]enators shall be elected by the electors of the respective senate districts.... All terms of senators which commence on the first day of January, 1969 shall be four years, and all terms which commence on the first day of January, 1971 shall be four years...." Section 2 also sets term limits for legislators: "No person shall hold the office of State Senator for a period of longer than two successive terms of four years. No person shall hold the office of State Representative for a period longer than four successive terms of two years."

Article XI, Apportionment, section 2, as amended in 1967, provides in part that the "whole population of the state ... shall be divided by the number 'ninety-nine' and the quotient shall be the ratio of representation in the House of Representatives for ten years next succeeding such apportionment"; in addition, "the whole population of the state ... shall be divided by the number 'thirty-three' and the quotient shall be the ratio of representation in the senate for ten years...." Currently the Ohio legislature has thirty-three senators and ninety-nine members of the house of representatives.

Article XV, Miscellaneous, section 4, as amended in 1953, stipulates: "No person shall be elected or appointed to any office in this state unless possessed of the qualifications of an elector." **Article II, Legislative, section 3,** as amended in 1967, requires that senators and representatives be residents "in their respective districts one year next preceding their election, unless they shall have been absent on the public business of the United States, or of this state."

Section 4, as amended in 1973, stipulates: "No member of the General Assembly shall, during the term for which he was elected, unless during such term he resigns therefrom, hold any [other] public office ... [although] this provision does not extend to officers of a political party, notaries public, or officers of the militia or of the United States armed forces." This language differs from the usual provisions of state constitutions by specifically mentioning political party officers, a topic about which the U.S. Constitution is also silent. Section 4 also restricts legislators from accepting, during their term and for up to one year afterward, an office that was created or whose salary was increased during their term. **Section 5** prohibits certain persons from serving as legislators, including those convicted of embezzling public funds.

Section 6, as amended in 1973, allows each house to judge the election and qualifications of its members and defines a quorum as "[a] majority of all the members elected to each house," although "a less number may adjourn from day to day, and compel the attendance of absent members...." In addition, each house may "punish its members for disorderly conduct and, with the concurrence of two-thirds of the members elected thereto, expel a member, but not a second time for the same cause." Section 6 continues: "Each house has all powers necessary to provide for its safety and the undisturbed transaction of its business, and to obtain, through committees or otherwise, information affecting legislative action under consideration or in contemplation, or with reference to any alleged breach of its privileges or misconduct of its members, and to that end to enforce the attendance and testimony of witnesses, and the production of books and papers." **Section 12** exempts legislators from arrest during and on their way to and from legislative sessions, except in cases of treason, felony, or breach of the peace; furthermore, "for any speech, or debate, in either house, they shall not be questioned elsewhere."

Section 7, as amended in 1973, mandates: "The mode of organizing each house of the General Assembly shall be prescribed by law. Each house, except as otherwise provided in this constitution, shall choose its own officers. The presiding officer in the Senate shall be designated as president of the Senate and the House of Representatives as speaker of the House of Representatives. Each house shall determine its own rules of proceeding." According to **section 10,** "Any member of either house shall have the right to protest against any act, or resolution thereof; and such protest, and the reasons therefor, shall, without alteration, commitment, or delay, be entered upon the journal." **Section 11,** an unusual provision amended in 1961, 1968, and 1973, authorizes: "A vacancy in [either house] for any cause ... shall be filled by election by the members of the [house], who are affiliated with the same political party as the person last elected ... to the seat...." Section 11 also contains additional requirements relating to the time during which the vacancy must have occurred and how long the seat may remain filled in this manner before the next general election.

Section 15, as amended in 1973, addresses the passage of bills: "**(A)** The General Assembly shall enact no law except by bill, and no bill shall be passed without the concurrence of a majority of the members elected to each house. Bills may originate in either house, but may be altered, amended, or rejected in the other.... **(C)** Every bill shall be considered by each house on three different days, unless two-thirds of the members elected to the house in which it is pending suspend this requirement.... No bill may be passed until the bill has been reproduced and distributed to members ... and every amendment been made available upon a member's request. **(D)** No bill shall contain more than one subject, which shall be clearly expressed in its title. **(E)** Every bill which has passed both houses ... shall be signed by the presiding officer of each house to certify that the procedural requirements for passage have been met and shall be presented forthwith to the governor for his approval." Pursuant to **section 15(F),** joint resolutions are similarly signed and then "filed with the secretary of state."

Section 16, as amended in 1973, discusses the governor's approval or veto of bills: "If the governor approves an act, he shall sign it, it becomes law and he shall file it with the secretary of state. If he does not approve it, he shall return it with his objections in writing, to the house in which it originated...." The governor's veto may be overridden by "three-fifths of the members elected" to each house. If the governor does not return a bill within ten days (Sundays excepted) of receiving it, it becomes law "in like manner as if he had signed it." The legislature by adjournment may prevent its return, in which case "it becomes law unless, within ten days after such adjournment, it is filed by [the governor], with his objections in writing, in the office of the secretary of state." Section 16 also grants the governor the power to "disapprove any item or items in any bill making an appropriation of money and the item or items, so disapproved, shall be void, unless repassed in the manner prescribed [for] a bill."

Section 26 mandates that "[a]ll laws, of a general nature, shall have a uniform operation throughout the state; nor, shall any act, except such as relates to public schools, be passed, to take effect upon the approval of any other authority than the General Assembly, except, as otherwise provided in this constitution." Section 28 restricts the legislature from passing retroactive laws and laws impairing the obligation of contracts, but in *State v. Morris* (1978), the Ohio supreme court found it permissible for the legislature to retroactively reduce criminal penalties. Section 32 prohibits the legislature from granting divorces or exercising judicial power. Sections 33 through 42 expressly authorize laws relating to, repectively, mechanics' and builders' liens; welfare of employees; workers' compensation; conservation of natural resources; the work day and work week hours for public work; removal of state officials, "including state officers, judges, and members of the General Assembly;" regulation of expert testimony; registration of land titles; prison labor; and the government's continuity in emergencies.

Executive Branch

Article III, Executive, section 1, as amended in 1885, declares: "The executive department shall consist of a governor, lieutenant governor, secretary of state, auditor of state, treasurer of state, and an attorney general, who shall be elected on the first Tuesday after the first Monday in November, by the electors of the state, and at the places of voting for members of the General Assembly."

Section 1a, added in 1976, provides in part: "In the general election for governor and lieutenant governor, one vote shall be cast jointly for the candidates nominated by the same political party or petition." Section 1b, added in 1979, delegates to the lieutenant governor "such duties in the executive department as are assigned to him by the governor and as are prescribed by law." Section 2, added in 1992, prescribes in part: "The [officers of the executive department, except the auditor] shall hold their offices for four years ... , [and t]he auditor of state shall hold his office for a term of two years.... No person shall hold the office of governor for a period longer than two successive terms of four years."

Section 5 vests the state's supreme executive power in the governor. According to section 6, the governor "may require information, in writing, from the officers in the executive department, upon any subject relating to the duties of their respective offices; and shall see that the laws are faithfully executed." Section 7 requires the office holder to "communicate at every session, by message, to the General Assembly, the condition of the state, and recommend such measures as [deemed] expedient." Section 20 directs officers of executive departments and state institutions "at least five days preceding each regular session of the General Assembly, [to] severally report to the governor, who shall transmit such reports, with his message to the General Assembly." Section 8, as amended in 1912, allows the governor "on extraordinary occasions" to convene the legislature "by proclamation...." According to **section 9,** "In case of disagreement between the two houses, in respect to the time of adjournment, he shall have the power to adjourn [them]." **Section 14** states: "No member of Congress, or other person holding office under the authority of this state, or of the United States, shall execute the office of governor, except as herein provided."

Section 10 designates the governor to serve as commander in chief of the state's military and naval forces "except when they shall be called into the service of the United States." Pursuant to **section 11,** as amended in 1996, "The Governor shall have power, after conviction, to grant reprieves, commutations, and pardons, for all crimes and offenses, except treason and cases of impeachment, upon such conditions as the Governor may think proper; subject, however, to such regulations, as to the manner of applying for commutations and pardons, as may be prescribed by law.... The Governor shall communicate to the general assembly, at every regular session, each case ... [and the action thereon], with his reasons therefor." In *State ex rel. Gordon v. Zangerle* (1940), the Ohio supreme court defined the terms *full pardon, partial pardon, conditional pardon, reprieve,* and *commutation.*

Section 18, as amended in 1970, empowers the governor to fill any vacancy in the office of auditor, treasurer, secretary of state, and attorney general "until the disability is removed, or a successor is elected and qualified." According to **section 21,** as amended in 1961, "When required by law, appointments to state office shall be subject to the advice and consent of the Senate." **Section 15,** as amended in 1976, provides in part: "**(A)** In the case of the death, conviction on impeachment, resignation, or removal of the governor, the lieutenant governor shall succeed to the office of governor. **(B)** When the governor is unable to discharge the duties of office by reason of disability, the lieutenant governor shall serve as governor until the governor's disability terminates."

Article IV, Judicial, section 1, as amended in 1968 and 1973, declares: "The judicial power of the state is vested in a supreme court, courts of appeals, courts of common pleas and divisions thereof, and such other courts inferior to the Supreme Court as may from time to time be established by law." **Section 2,** as amended in 1968 and 1994, states in part: "**(A)** The Supreme Court shall, until otherwise provided by law, consist of seven judges, who shall be known as the chief justice and justices.... A majority of the Supreme Court shall be necessary to constitute a quorum or to render a judgment."

Section 2(B)(1) grants the supreme court original jurisdiction in the following instances: "**(a)** Quo warranto; **(b)** Mandamus; **(c)** Habeas corpus; **(d)** Prohibition; **(e)** Procedendo; **(f)** In any cause on review as may be necessary to its complete determination; [and] **(g)** Admission to the practice of law, the discipline of persons so admitted, and all other matters relating to the practice of law." **Section 2(B)(2),** as amended in 1994, grants the supreme court appellate jurisdiction as follows: "**(a)** In appeals from the courts of appeals as a matter of right in the following: **(i)** Cases originating in the courts of appeals; [and] **(ii)** Cases involving questions arising under the constitution of the United States or of this state." Additional jurisdiction includes, under **section 2(B)(2)(c),** "direct appeals from the courts of common pleas or other courts of record inferior to the court of appeals as a matter of right in cases in which the death penalty has been imposed; under **section 2(B)(2)(d)**, "revisory jurisdiction of the proceedings of administrative officers or agencies as may be conferred by law"; and, under **section 2(B)(2)(e)**, "cases of public or great general interest...." **Article III, Executive, section 22**, as amended in 1976, gives the supreme court "original, exclusive, and final, jurisdiction to determine disability of the governor or governor-elect upon presentment to it of a joint resolution by the General Assembly...." And pursuant to **article XVI, Amendments, section 1,** as amended in 1974, "The Supreme Court shall have exclusive, original jurisdiction in all cases challenging the adoption or submission of a proposed constitutional amendment to the electors."

Article IV, Judicial, section 5, added in 1968 and amended in 1973, provides: "(A)(1) In addition to all other powers vested by this article in the Supreme Court, [it] shall have general superintendence over all courts in the state[, which] shall be exercised by the chief justice in accordance with rules promulgated by the Supreme Court. (2) The Supreme Court shall appoint an administrative director who shall assist the chief justice and who shall serve at the pleasure of the court."

Section 6, added in 1968 and amended in 1973, specifies in part: "(A)(1) The chief justice and the justices of the Supreme Court shall be elected by the electors of the state at large, for terms of not less than six years." **Section 6(B)** provides: "All votes for any judge, for any elective office, except a judicial office, under the authority of this state, given by the General Assembly, or the people shall be void...." And **section 6(C)** stipulates: "No person shall be elected or appointed to any judicial office if on or before the day when he shall assume the office and enter upon the discharge of its duties he shall have attained the age of seventy years." Pursuant to **section 13,** "In case the office of any judge shall become vacant, before the expiration of the regular term for which he was elected, the vacancy shall be filled by appointment by the governor, until a successor is elected and has qualified...."

Section [21]22, added in 1875, authorizes a supreme court commission, whose members "shall hold office for the term of three years from and after the first day of February, 1876, to dispose of such part of the business then on the dockets of the Supreme Court...." The commission's decisions "shall be ... enforced as the judgments of the Supreme Court ... , provided, that the term of any such commission shall not exceed two years, nor shall it be created oftener than once in ten years."

Section 17 allows for judges' removal from office "by concurrent resolution of both houses of the General Assembly, if two-thirds of the members, elected to each house, concur therein"; however, no such removal shall be made, except upon complaint, the substance of which shall be entered on the journal, nor, until the party charged shall have had notice thereof, and an opportunity to be heard."

Impeachment

Article II, Legislative, section 23, gives to the house of representatives "the sole power of impeachment," although "a majority of the members elected must concur therein."

Impeachments are tried by the senate, and "[n]o person shall be convicted without the concurrence of two-thirds of the senators." **Section 24** states: "The governor, judges, and all state officers, may be impeached for any misdemeanor in office; but judgment shall not extend further than removal from office, and disqualification to hold any office under the authority of this state." Impeachment, however, is no bar to further punishment according to law.

Article II, Legislative, section 1, as amended in 1953, provides in part that "the people reserve to themselves the power to propose to the General Assembly laws and amendments to the constitution, and to adopt or reject the same at the polls on a referendum vote as hereinafter provided. They also reserve the power to adopt or reject any law, section of any law or any item in any law appropriating money passed by the General Assembly, except as hereinafter provided; and independent of the General Assembly to propose amendments to the constitution and to adopt or reject the same at the polls. The limitations expressed in the constitution, on the power of the General Assembly to enact laws, shall be deemed limitations on the power of the people to enact laws."

Direct Democracy

Article X, County and Township Organizations, section 2, added in 1933, authorizes the legislature to "provide by general law for the election of such township officers as may be necessary." **Section 3,** as amended in 1957, states in part: "The people of any county may frame and adopt or amend a charter as provided in this article but the right of the initiative and referendum is reserved to the people of each county on all matters which such county may now or hereafter be authorized to control by legislative action." **Article XVIII, Municipal Corporations, section 7,** added in 1912, provides: "Any municipality may frame and adopt or amend a charter for its government and may, [within certain limits], exercise thereunder all powers of local self-government."

Local Government

Article XII, Finance and Taxation, section 2, added in 1990, mandates: "Land and improvements thereon shall be taxed by uniform rule according to value [with some enumerated exceptions]." Under its equal protection clause, the Fourteenth Amendment (1868) to the U.S. Constitution sets a nationwide standard for the uniformity of state taxes. In *Allied Stores of Ohio, Inc. v. Bowers* (1959), however, the U.S. Supreme Court, in an appeal from a decision of the Ohio supreme court, held that the federal constitutional standard did not require the state legislature to explicitly declare its purpose for unequal tax treatment to be constitutional as long as the treatment was not "invidious or palpably arbitrary."

Taxation and Finance

Section 4 specifies a balanced budget: "The General Assembly shall provide for raising revenue, sufficient to defray the expenses of the state, for each year, and also a sufficient sum to pay principal and interest as they become due on the state debt."

Article VI, Education, section 4, as amended in 1953, creates a board of education, which "shall be elected in such manner and for such terms as shall be provided by law...." The board appoints a superintendent of public instruction, whose powers and duties, as well as the board's, "shall be prescribed by law."

Education

Amendment Procedures

Article XVI, Amendments, section 1, as amended in 1974, provides: "Either branch of the General Assembly may propose amendments to this constitution; and, if the same shall be agreed to by three-fifths of the members elected to each house, such proposed amendments ... shall be ... submitted to the electors, for their approval or rejection." The ballot language "shall be prescribed by a majority of the Ohio ballot board...." And if "the majority of the electors voting on [the proposed amendments]" approve them, "the same shall become a part of the constitution...."

Section 2, as amended in 1912, directs that "[w]henever two-thirds of the members elected to each branch of the General Assembly shall think it necessary to call a convention, to revise, amend, or change this constitution," they may so recommend to the voters. If "a majority of all the electors, voting for and against the calling of a convention" approves it, the legislature must at its next session call for a convention. **Section 3,** as amended in 1912, states that the question of calling a convention must be presented to the voters every twenty years, the first time being in 1932, and that "no amendment of this constitution, agreed upon by any convention ... shall take effect, until the same shall have been submitted to the electors of the state, and adopted by a majority of those voting thereon."

Article II, Legislative, section 1a, specifies procedures for amending the constitution through popular initiative. "[T]he signatures of ten per centum of the electors," it states, "shall be required upon a petition to propose an amendment to the constitution." After the petition is filed with the secretary of state and certified, "the secretary of state shall submit for the approval or rejection of the electors, the proposed amendment, in the manner hereinafter provided, at the next succeeding regular or general election in any year occurring subsequent to ninety days after the filing of such peitition."

Oklahoma became the forty-sixth state of the United States on November 16, 1907. Oklahoma City is the capital of the "Sooner State." Some 69,903 square miles in area, Oklahoma is bordered by Colorado and Kansas on the north, Missouri and Arkansas on the east, Texas on the south, and New Mexico and Texas on the west. With approximately 3.3 million inhabitants, Oklahoma ranks twenty-seventh among the states in population. Its principal industries include manufacturing, mineral and energy exploration and production, and agriculture; among its chief crops are wheat, cotton, hay, and peanuts.

Government: The governor and lieutenant governor are elected separately for four-year terms, but the governor is limited to two successive terms. The legislature consists of forty-eight senators elected for four-year terms and 101 members of the house of representatives elected for two-year terms; they are limited to twelve years' total service in the legislature. The supreme court comprises a chief justice, a vice chief justice, and seven associate justices initially appointed by the governor from a list prepared by a judicial nominating commission; thereafter they are elected for six-year terms.

Date of Constitution: 1907

In 1541, when the first Europeans entered the region that would become the state of Oklahoma—a name derived from the Choctaw words *ukla* (person) and *huma* (red)—it was inhabited by scattered groups of Pawnee, Comanche, and Arapaho peoples, among others. The leader of the first expedition, Francisco Vásquez de Coronado, claimed the land for Spain; but in 1682 Robert Cavelier, sieur de La Salle, without visiting the territory, claimed it along with other lands as part of French Louisiana. France ceded the entire region to Spain in 1762, and in 1800 Spain transferred it back to France.

In 1803 France sold its vast North American holdings, including all of Oklahoma except the panhandle, to the United States as part of the Louisiana Purchase. Although fur trading with the indigenous peoples enhanced the potential for development in the Oklahoma region, the other parts of the Louisiana Territory attained statehood sooner.

In 1804 Congress assigned management of the portion of the Louisiana Territory above the thirty-third parallel, including Oklahoma, to the Administration for Indian Affairs. During the first part of the nineteenth century the Choctaws and many other Native Americans continued to migrate into Oklahoma. An 1819 treaty with Spanish Mexico settled the southern border of the Louisiana Territory. A decade later Cherokees, including Sequoya, the inventor of the Cherokee system of writing, moved into the region.

Beginning in 1834 the United States sought to carve out of Oklahoma a separate state or nation for the indigenous peoples. With this goal in mind a council meeting in Talequah in 1843 drafted a code of intertribal laws. As late as 1853 Congress considered creating a state named Neosho out of the Oklahoma territory, whose northern boundary was established by the Kansas-Nebraska Act a year later. During the Civil War, however, most of the Indian tribes sided with the Confederacy, thus eliminating any chance of a separate Native American state. In the 1870s the western portion of the territory was ceded back to the United States for the resettlement of indigenous peoples subdued by the U.S. military. However, many white settlers, called "boomers," encroached on the land.

The Dawes Act in 1887 established the reservation system for the Indians, and an act of Congress dated May 2, 1890, provided for "a temporary government of the Territory of Oklahoma...." At the time Oklahoma had more than 72,000 white settlers, including the "sooners," who were the first to make claims for the land as soon as the territory was officially opened for settlement. A statehood convention was held in Oklahoma City in 1891, but the roughly equal division of Native Americans and white settlers hampered the process of attaining statehood. The Choctaw, Creek, Chickasaw, and Cherokee nations had their own written constitutions and desired a separate state of their own. In 1905, together with the Seminoles, they drafted a constitution for the state of Sequoya.

Discoveries of oil, some on Indian reservations, persuaded Congress to create only one state from the Oklahoma Territory. A constitutional convention that met in Guthrie from November 20, 1906, to July 16, 1907, produced a document that was ratified by the voters on September 17; among other provisions, it prohibited alcoholic beverages. The constitution went into effect on November 16, 1907, when Oklahoma was admitted to the Union.

The Constitution

William Howard Taft, president and later chief justice of the United States, called the framers of the 1907 Oklahoma constitution a "zoological garden of cranks." President Theodore Roosevelt, also not one to mince words, decried it as "not fit for publication." One of the longer state constitutions, it contains approximately 68,800 words. As of January 1, 1998, it has been amended 152 times, although five of those amendments have been invalidated by the U.S. and Oklahoma supreme courts. The document has been criticized for its excessive length and, like the Maryland constitution, the inclusion of nonconstitutional details, such as a section on solid waste management.

Oklahoma's constitution creates a plural executive branch, which is typical of most state constitutions, but the governor's power to control this branch of the state government is particularly weak. The document also creates a bicameral legislature and an elected judiciary, which are typical of most other state constitutions. A constitutional revision commission's efforts to make significant changes in the Oklahoma document failed in 1990, when the state supreme court struck down two of three proposals because they did not meet the requirement that amendments be limited to a single subject.

Preamble

The preamble to the 1907 Oklahoma constitution reads: "Invoking the guidance of Almighty God, in order to secure and perpetuate the blessing of liberty; to secure just and rightful government; to promote our mutual welfare and happiness, we, the people of the State of Oklahoma, do ordain and establish this Constitution."

Fundamental Rights

Article I, Federal Relations, section 1, proclaims just before the bill of rights: "The State of Oklahoma is an inseparable part of the Federal Union, and the Constitution of the United States is the supreme law of the land." **Section 2** establishes that "[p]erfect toleration of religious sentiment shall be secured ..." and "[p]olygamous or plural marriages are forever prohibited." **Section 3** notes that the people "forever disclaim all right and title in or to any unappropriated public lands lying within the boundaries thereof, and to all lands lying within said limits owned or held by any Indian, tribe, or nation...."

Article II, Bill of Rights, section 1, declares: "All political power is inherent in the people; and government is instituted for their protection, security, and benefit, and to promote their general welfare; and they have the right to alter or reform the same whenever the public good may require it: Provided, such change be not repugnant to the Constitution of the United States." Under **section 2**, "All persons have the inherent right to life, liberty, the pursuit of happiness, and the enjoyment of the gains of their own industry." **Section 3** guarantees the right of peaceable assembly and petition for redress of grievances; **section 4** prohibits interference with the free exercise of the right of suffrage; and **section 5** prohibits the use of public money or property for religious purposes.

Section 6 provides: "The courts of justice of the State shall be open to every person, and speedy and certain remedy afforded for every wrong and for every injury to person, property, or reputation; and right and justice shall be administered without sale, denial, delay, or prejudice." **Section 7** underscores that "[n]o person shall be deprived of life, liberty, or property, without due process of law." In *McLaurin v. Oklahoma State Regents* (1950), the U.S. Supreme Court held that the University of Oklahoma's segregation of a black person in a graduate study program deprived him of his right to equal protection of the laws under the U.S. Constitution.

Section 8, as amended in 1989, guarantees bail except in certain cases including violent offenses; **section 9** prohibits excessive bail, fines, and "cruel or unusual punishments"; and **section 10** prohibits the suspension of the writ of habeas corpus. **Section 11,** added by initiative in 1914, directs: "Every person elected or appointed to any office or employment of trust or profit under the laws of the State … shall give personal attention to the duties of [such] office…. Drunkenness and the excessive use of intoxicating liquors while in office shall constitute sufficient cause for impeachment or removal therefrom." **Section 12A,** added in 1994, attempts to place term limits on candidates for Congress.

Section 13 prohibits imprisonment for debt, "except for the non-payment of fines and penalties imposed for the violation of law." **Sections 14** through **17,** respectively, subordinate the military to civil authorities and limit the quartering of soldiers in private homes; prohibit bills of attainder, ex post facto laws, laws impairing the obligation of contracts, corruption of blood, and forfeiture of estate; define treason in terms similar to those used in the U.S. Constitution; and require presentment, indictment, or information to charge a person with a felony or misdemeanor. **Section 18,** as amended in 1952, 1968, 1971, and 1996, addresses grand juries; **section 19,** as amended in 1990, deals with trial by jury; and **section 20,** as amended in 1961, provides rights for a person accused of a crime, including the right to "be informed of the nature and cause of the accusation against him and have a copy thereof, and be confronted with the witnesses against him…."

Sections 21 through **24,** respectively, prohibit self-incrimination and double jeopardy; guarantee liberty of speech and the press and direct that a true statement "written or published with good motives and for justifiable ends" requires an acquittal in a libel case; guarantee compensation for private property taken or damaged for public use, "except for private ways of necessity, or for drains and ditches across lands of others for agricultural, mining, or sanitary purposes …"; and provide for judicial determination in cases of condemnation of private property. **Section 25** authorizes the legislature to "pass laws defining contempts and regulating the proceedings and punishment in matters of contempt"; **section 26** guarantees the right to bear arms; and **section 27,** as amended in 1971, prohibits self-incrimination under state law as a basis for refusing to testify as a witness. In *Pate v. State* (1967), the Oklahoma criminal court of appeals held that this section does not conflict with the protection against self-incrimination established in section 21. **Section 29** prohibits transportation of a person out of state for any purpose "without his consent, except by due process of law."

Section 30 limits unreasonable searches and seizures; **section 31** authorizes the state to engage in any business for public purposes except "agriculture for any other than educational and scientific purposes and for the support of its penal, charitable, and educational institutions"; and **section 32** prohibits perpetuities and monopolies and the enforcement of the law of primogeniture or entailments. Adds **section 33:** "The enumeration in this Constitution of certain rights shall not be construed to deny, impair, or disparage others retained by the people." **Section 34,** added in 1996, provides rights for victims of crime.

Division of Powers

Article IV, Distribution of Powers, section 1, declares: "The powers of the government of the State of Oklahoma shall be divided into three separate departments: The Legislative, Executive, and Judicial; and except as provided in this Constitution, the Legislative, Executive, and Judicial departments of government shall be separate and distinct, and neither shall exercise the powers properly belonging to either of the others."

Legislative Branch

Article V, Legislative Department, section 1, vests the state's legislative authority in a legislature, "consisting of a Senate and a House of Representatives...." **Section 9A,** added in 1964, states in part: "Each senatorial district, whether single county or multi-county, shall be entitled to one senator, who shall hold office for four years...." The current number of senators is forty-eight. According to **section 10A,** added in 1964, "The House of Representatives shall consist of the number of Representatives as determined by the formula and procedure set forth herein." Representatives, who "shall hold office for two years," currently number 101. In *Reynolds v. State Election Board* (1964), the U.S. District Court held that portions of sections 9A and 10A were in conflict with the U.S. Constitution with respect to apportionment but that only those portions were therefore void, not the entire amendment adding these sections.

Section 17 requires that senators be at least twenty-five and representatives at least twenty-one years old when elected; they must be "qualified electors" in their county or district and must reside there during their term of office. **Section 17A,** added in 1990, mandates: "Any member of the Legislature who is elected to office after the effective date of this amendment [January 1, 1991] shall be eligible to serve no more than 12 years in the Oklahoma State Legislature. Years in Legislative office need not be consecutive...."

Section 18 prohibits any legislator from simultaneously serving as "an officer of the United States or State government" or being paid as such and prohibits convicted felons from running for the legislature. According to **section 19,** "A member of the Legislature expelled for corruption shall not thereafter be eligible to membership in either House.

Punishment for contempt or disorderly conduct, or for any other cause, shall not bar an indictment for the same offense." **Section 21,** as amended in 1948 and 1968, provides in part: "The Legislature shall enact laws to prohibit members of the Legislature from engaging in activities or having interests which conflict with the proper discharge of their duties and responsibilities." **Section 23** restricts legislators from holding certain other offices, and **section 24** requires that "[a] member of the Legislature, who has a personal or private interest in any measure or bill, proposed or pending before the Legislature, shall disclose the fact to the House of which he is a member, and shall not vote thereon."

Section 28 provides: "The Senate shall, at the beginning of each regular session and at such other times as may be necessary, elect one of its members President pro tempore, who shall preside over its deliberations in the absence or place of the Lieutenant Governor; and the Senate shall provide for all its standing committees and, by a majority vote, elect the members thereof." **Section 29** similarly directs: "The House of Representatives shall, at the beginning of each regular session and at such other times as may be necessary, elect one of its members Speaker." **Section 22** exempts legislators from arrest during or on their way to or from legislative sessions, "except for treason, felony, or breach of the peace"; furthermore, "for any speech or debate in either House, [they] shall not be questioned in any other place."

Section 30 authorizes each house to be the judge of the elections, returns, and qualifications of its members and to "determine the rules of its proceedings, punish its members for disorderly behavior, and with the concurrence of two-thirds, expel a member." **Section 31** provides that "[i]n all elections made by the Legislature, except for officers and employees thereof, the members thereof shall vote yea or nay, and each vote shall be entered upon the journal."

Section 36 states: "The authority of the Legislature shall extend to all rightful subjects of legislation, and any specific grant of authority in this Constitution, upon any subject whatsoever, shall not work a restriction, limitation, or exclusion of such authority upon the same or any other subject or subjects whatsoever." This language emphasizes that, in contrast to the U.S. Constitution, state constitutions are generally not considered express grants of specific powers but only limitations on the residual power of government inherent in the state. According to **section 32,** the legislature may not vote on any special or local law "until notice of the intended introduction of such bill or bills shall first have been published for four consecutive weeks in some weekly newspaper published or of general circulation in the city or county affected by such law...." **Section 46** prohibits certain types of local and special laws, including laws authorizing "[t]he creation, extension, or impairing of liens ... [and r]elating to cemeteries, graveyards, or public grounds not owned by the State." **Section 45** instructs the legislature to "pass such laws as are necessary for carrying into effect the provisions of this Constitution."

Section 33, as amended in 1992, provides in part in **section 33A** that "[a]ll bills for raising revenue shall originate in the House of Representatives." In *Anderson v. Ritterbusch* (1908), the Oklahoma supreme court cited William Blackstone's *Commentaries on the Laws of England* (1755–65) in discussing the justification for the U.S. Constitution's requirement that money bills originate in the lower house of Congress. The court went on to note that the House of Representatives was analogous to the British House of Commons, both of whose members are elected directly by the people, and that revenue bills could only be initiated in the House of Commons. Section 33A further provides that the Oklahoma senate may propose amendments to revenue bills. **Section 33B** prohibits the legislature from passing any revenue bill during the last five days of a session. **Section 33C** provides that revenue bills may be put to voters and approved by "a majority of the votes cast" at the next general election, or, under **section 33D**, they may also be approved by "three-fourths (¾) of the membership" of both houses.

Section 34 requires that "[e]very bill shall be read on three different days in each House, and no bill shall become a law unless, on its final passage, it be read at length, and no law shall be passed unless upon a vote of a majority of all the members elected to each House...." **Section 35** directs: "The presiding officer of each House shall, in the presence of the House over which he presides, sign all bills and joint resolutions passed by the Legislature, immediately after the same shall have been publicly read at length ... , but the reading at length may be dispensed with by a two-thirds vote of a quorum present...."

Executive Branch

Article VI, Executive Department in General, section 1, as amended in 1986 and 1988, declares: "**A.** The Executive authority of the state shall be vested in a Governor, Lieutenant Governor, Secretary of State, State Auditor and Inspector, Attorney General, State Treasurer, Superintendent of Public Instruction, Commissioner of Labor, Commissioner of Insurance and other officers provided by law and this Constitution.... **B.** The Secretary of State shall be appointed by the Governor by and with the consent of the Senate for a term of four (4) years...." Pursuant to **section 2,** "The Supreme Executive power shall be vested in a Chief Magistrate, who shall be styled 'The Governor of the State of Oklahoma.'" The governor and lieutenant governor are elected on separate tickets.

Section 3, as amended in 1942 and 1979, states: "No person shall be eligible to the first seven offices above except a citizen of the United States of the age of not less than thirty-one (31) years and who shall have been ten (10) years next preceding his or her election, or appointment, a qualified elector of the state." According to **section 4,** as amended in 1988, "The term of office [of the above officers] shall be four (4) years.... The said officers [except the secretary of state] shall be eligible to immediately succeed themselves. No person shall be elected Governor more than two times in succession."

Section 6 authorizes the governor to serve as commander in chief of the state militia, "except when in service of the United States, and [he] may call out the same to execute the laws, protect the public health, suppress insurrection, and repel invasion." **Section 7** grants the governor the power to "convoke the Legislature, or the Senate only, on extraordinary occasions." **Section 8** provides: "The Governor shall cause the laws of the State to be faithfully executed, and shall conduct in person or in such manner as may be prescribed by law, all intercourse and business of the State with other states and with the United States, and he shall be a conservator of the peace throughout the State." *Conservator of the peace* is an English legal term for an officer charged with preventing breaches of the peace and arresting violators; until the reign of Edward III (1327–77), such officers were elected, and thereafter they were appointed.

Section 9 states in part: "At every session of the Legislature, and immediately upon its organization, the Governor shall communicate by message, delivered to a joint session of the two Houses, upon the condition of the State; and shall recommend such matters to the Legislature as he shall judge expedient." **Section 10**, as amended in 1986 and 1994, creates a pardon and parole board and empowers the governor "to grant, after conviction and after favorable recommendation by a majority vote of the said Board, commutations, pardons and paroles for all offenses, except cases of impeachment, upon such conditions and with such restrictions and limitations as he may deem proper, subject to such regulations as may be prescribed by law."

Section 11 addresses the procedure by which a bill becomes law: "Every bill which shall have passed the [legislature], and every resolution requiring the assent of both [houses], shall, before it becomes a law, be presented to the Governor; if he approve, he shall sign it; if not, he shall return it with his objections to the house in which it shall have originated, [which] shall … proceed to reconsider it." The governor's veto may be overridden by a vote of "two-thirds of the members elected to" both houses. "If any bill or resolution shall not be returned by the Governor within five days (Sundays excepted) … the same shall be a law in like manner as if he had signed it, unless the Legislature shall, by their adjournment, prevent its return…." **Section 12** states in part: "Every bill passed by the Legislature, making appropriations of money embracing distinct items, shall, before it becomes a law, be presented to the Governor; if he disapproves the bill, or any item, or appropriation therein contained, he shall communicate such disapproval, with his reasons therefor, to the house in which the bill shall have originated, but all items not disapproved shall have the force and effect of law…." The governor's item veto may be overridden in the same manner as provided in section 11.

Section 15 notes that the lieutenant governor must have the same qualifications as the governor. He or she is to serve as president of the senate but "shall have only a casting vote therein, and also in joint vote of both houses." Section 15 further provides for the lieutenant governor to "act as Governor" under certain conditions, and **section 16** states that the office of governor will "devolve upon the Lieutenant Governor" under other circumstances.

Article VII, Judicial Department, sections 1 through **6**, were all added in 1967. **Section 1** declares in part: "The judicial power of this State shall be vested in the Senate, sitting as a Court of Impeachment, a Supreme Court, the Court of Criminal Appeals, the Court on the Judiciary, [other courts], and such intermediate appellate courts as may be provided by statute…." **Section 2** provides in part that "[t]he Supreme Court shall consist of nine Justices until the number shall be changed by statute and each Justice shall be from a separate district of the State." The justices are to serve six-year terms beginning "on the second Monday of January following their election"; justices appointed or elected to fill vacancies assume office "immediately upon qualifying for the office." Section 2 further stipulates that a justice must be thirty years old, a qualified

Judicial Branch

elector in the district for at least one year, and "a licensed practicing attorney [or] judge of a court of record, or both, in Oklahoma for five years preceding his election or appointment and shall continue to be a duly licensed attorney while in office...." The justices choose from among themselves a chief justice and a vice chief justice.

Section 3 provides in part: "From each of the Supreme Court districts and Court of Criminal Appeals districts, the voters thereof shall elect a Justice of the Supreme Court and a Judge of the Court of Criminal Appeals at a nonpartisan election, in a manner provided by statute. In the event of a vacancy the Governor shall, by appointment from said district, fill such vacancy until the next election...."

Section 4 states that "[t]he appellate jurisdiction of the Supreme Court shall be co-extensive with the State and shall extend to all cases at law and in equity; except that the Court of Criminal Appeals shall have exclusive appellate jurisdiction in criminal cases until otherwise provided by statute and in the event there is any conflict as to jurisdiction, the Supreme Court shall determine which court has jurisdiction and such determination shall be final." The supreme court's original jurisdiction extends "to a general superintending control over all inferior courts and all Agencies, Commissions and Boards created by law," an unusual provision in state constitutions. Section 4 continues: "The Supreme Court, Court of Criminal Appeals, in criminal matters[,] and all other appellate courts shall have power to issue, hear and determine writs of habeas corpus, mandamus, quo warranto, certiorari, prohibition and such other remedial writs as may be provided by law and may exercise such other and further jurisdiction as may be conferred by statute...."

Section 5 defines a quorum as a majority of the members, requires concurrence of a majority to decide questions, and notes that "[t]he jurisdiction, powers, duties and procedures of intermediate appellate courts shall be as provided by rules of the Supreme Court until otherwise provided by statute." Pursuant to **section 6**, "Except with reference to the Senate sitting as a Court of Impeachment and the Court on the Judiciary, general administrative authority over all courts ... is hereby vested in the Supreme Court and shall be exercised by the Chief Justice in accordance with its rules...."

Article VII-A, Court on the Judiciary, section 2, added in 1966, creates, like the Delaware constitution, a "court on the judiciary." Under **section 1**, in addition to other methods prescribed by the constitution and laws, all judges "shall be subject to removal from office, or to compulsory retirement from office, for causes herein specified, by proceedings in the Court on the Judiciary."

Impeachment

Article VIII, Impeachment and Removal from Office, section 1, as amended in 1966, provides in part that "[t]he governor and other elective state officers, including the Justices of the Supreme Court, shall be liable and subject to impeachment for wilful neglect of duty, corruption in office, habitual drunkenness, incompetency, or any offense involving moral turpitude committed while in office." **Section 3** states: "The House of Representatives shall present all impeachments" and designates the senate as a "court of impeachment." **Section 4** specifies that "no person shall be convicted without the concurrence of two-thirds of the Senators present." According to **section 5**, "Judgment of impeachment shall not extend beyond removal from office, but this shall not prevent punishment of any such officer on charges growing out of the same matter by the courts...."

Article V, Legislative Department, section 1, asserts in part that "the people reserve to themselves the power to propose laws and amendments to the Constitution and to enact or reject the same at the polls independent of the Legislature, and also reserve power at their own option to approve or reject at the polls any act of the Legislature."

Direct Democracy

Article XVIII, Municipal Corporations, section 3(a), states in part: "Any city containing a population of more than two thousand inhabitants may frame a charter for its own government ... by causing a board of freeholders, composed of two from each ward, ... to be elected by the qualified electors ... at any general or special election, whose duty it shall be, within ninety days after such election, to prepare and propose a charter for such city...."

Local Government

Article X, Revenue and Taxation, section 3, mandates: "Whenever the expenses of any fiscal year shall exceed the income, the Legislature may provide for levying a tax for the ensuing fiscal year, which, with other resources, shall be sufficient to pay the deficiency, as well as the estimated ordinary expenses of the State for the ensuing year."

Taxation and Finance

Article XXV, Social Security, section 1, added in 1936 and amended in 1941, declares: "In order to promote the general welfare of the people of the State of Oklahoma and for their protection, security, and benefit, the Legislature and the people by initiative petition are hereby authorized to provide by appropriate legislation for the relief and care of needy aged persons who are unable to provide for themselves [and others]...."

Health and Welfare

Article XXIV, Constitutional Amendments, section 1, as amended in 1952 and 1974, states in part that amendments may be proposed in either house of the legislature, "and if ... agreed to by a majority of all the members elected to each of the two (2) houses, such proposed amendment or amendments shall ... be ... referred by the Secretary of State to the people ... at the next regular general election, except when the Legislature, by a two-thirds (⅔) vote of each house, shall order a special election for that purpose." It is ratified if "a majority of all the electors voting" approve it. In *Austin, Nichols & Co. v. Okl. Cty. Bd., etc.* (1978), the Oklahoma supreme court held that the ballot title is a contemporaneous construction of an amendment that weighs heavily in determining its meaning.

Amendment Procedures

Section 2 provides: "No convention shall be called by the Legislature to propose alterations, revisions, or amendments to this Constitution, or to propose a new Constitution, unless the law providing for such convention shall first be approved by the people on a referendum vote at a regular or special election, ... and any [proposals] by such convention, shall be submitted to the electors ... and be approved by a majority of the electors voting thereon ...: Provided, That the question of such proposed convention shall be submitted to the people at least once in every twenty years." **Section 3** states that the people retain the right "to amend this Constitution by a vote upon an initiative petition...."

OREGON

On February 14, 1859, Oregon became the thirty-third state of the United States. The capital of the "Beaver State," which encompasses some 98,386 square miles, is Salem. Oregon is bordered by Washington on the north, Idaho on the east, Nevada and California on the south, and the Pacific Ocean on the west. With approximately 3.1 million inhabitants, Oregon ranks twenty-ninth among the states in population. Its principal industries include manufacturing, forestry, agriculture, and high technology; greenhouse plants, hay, wheat, and grass seed are among its chief crops.

General Information

Government: The governor is elected for a four-year term and may hold office for eight years out of any twelve-year period. There is no lieutenant governor position. The legislature, called the legislative assembly, consists of thirty senators elected for four-year terms, one-half every two years, and sixty members of the house of representatives elected for two-year terms. Legislators' length of service is limited to eight years in the senate, six years in the house, and twelve years total in both houses combined. The supreme court includes a chief justice and six additional justices elected for six-year terms.

Date of Constitution: 1859

Constitutional History

Oregon was first sighted by Europeans in 1543 when sailors on board the ship of the Spanish explorer Juan Cabrillo, who had died earlier in the voyage, spotted its coastline. In 1579 Sir Francis Drake, on his round-the-world voyage from England, sailed past the same coast. Two centuries later, in 1778, the British navigator Captain James Cook is believed to have landed there. And in 1785 Jean-François de Galaud, comte de La Pérouse, sailing for Louis XVI of France, explored the west coast of North America from Alaska to Monterey, California. At the time more than a hundred native peoples, including the Chinooks, Yakimas, Modocs, and Nez Percés, lived in the territory that would become the state of Oregon.

The first European settlement in the area—on Vancouver Island in 1789—was established by José Estavan Martínez, who also claimed all of the Northwest for Spain. On May 11, 1792, a Yankee sea captain, Robert Gray, sailed into the mouth of the Columbia River, named for his ship, and in 1803, as part of the Louisiana Purchase, the United States acquired rights to the Oregon territory from France.

On October 18, 1805, the expedition of Meriwether Lewis and William Clark, who had been commissioned by President Thomas Jefferson to explore the newly acquired Louisiana Purchase, reached Oregon. Americans began to take an interest in the area, and John Jacob Astor's Pacific Fur Trading Company built Fort Astoria near the mouth of the Columbia River in April 1811. Although the United States lost Oregon to the British during the War of 1812, treaties in 1819 and 1827 attempted to accommodate the interests of both Canadian and American fur traders.

Dr. Marcus Whitman, a medical doctor representing an ecumenical church group, founded a mission at Walla Walla in 1836, and three years later immigrants began arriving from Illinois. On May 2, 1843, a small group of American settlers in the Willamette River valley set up a provisional government supported by voluntary contributions. Although the Articles of Provisional Government of 1843, adopted on July 25, 1845, provided that "there shall be neither Slavery nor Involuntary Servitude in said territory ... ," racism was practiced against blacks and Asians during this period. The 1843 articles remained in effect until an act passed by Congress was approved on August 14, 1848, officially establishing the "Territorial Government of Oregon."

Wagon trains on their way west helped increase Oregon's population, and in 1853, when the Washington Territory was separated from Oregon, efforts to prepare for statehood began in earnest. A proposed constitution, crafted by a convention meeting in Salem from August 17 to September 18, 1857, was ratified by the voters on November 9 of that year. The document went into effect on February 14, 1859, the date that An Act for the Admission of Oregon into the Union was approved.

The Constitution

As originally drafted in 1857, nearly all the sections of the Oregon constitution were copied from the constitutions of older states, including those of Indiana, Maine, and Iowa. Although the document was said to be distinguished only by its conventionality and small-mindedness, it has influenced progressive state constitutional developments through its direct democracy provisions, first adopted by amendment in 1902. Moreover, in the past twenty years the state's supreme court has spearheaded a revival of the concept of state constitutionalism—reliance on the fundamental rights and guarantees found in the state's constitution in addition to provisions of the U.S. Constitution and federal case law.

Oregon's constitution, which is nearly average in length with approximately 26,000 words, has been amended 210 times as of January 1, 1998, and structurally is typical of other state constitutions (but it contains numerous spelling and punctuation errors, many acknowledged in the document itself). It creates a plural executive branch, albeit with only two statewide elected officials other than the governor; a bicameral legislature; and a separate judicial system, provided for by an original article of the constitution and an amended form of that article added beginning in 1910.

Preamble

The preamble to the 1859 Oregon constitution proclaims: "We the people of the State of Oregon to the end that Justice be established, order maintained, and liberty perpetuated, do ordain this Constitution."

Fundamental Rights

Article 1, Bill of Rights, section 1, affirms: "We declare that all men, when they form a social compact are equal in right: that all power is inherent in the people, and all free governments are founded on their authority, and instituted for their peace, safety, and happiness; and they have at all times a right to alter, reform, or abolish the government in such manner as they may think proper." **Section 2** provides: "All men shall be secure in the Natural right, to worship Almighty God according to the dictates of their own consciences." **Section 3** guarantees freedom of religious opinion and the rights of conscience, and **sections 4** through **6,** respectively, prohibit religious tests as a qualification for office, the use of public money for religion, and religious tests for witnesses or jurors.

Section 8 guarantees freedom of speech and the press. **Section 9** prohibits unreasonable searches and seizures in language similar to that used in the U.S. Constitution, and **section 10** states: "No court shall be secret, but justice shall be administered, openly and without purchase, completely and without delay, and every man shall have remedy by due course of law for injury done him in his person, property, or reputation." **Section 11,** as amended in 1932 and 1934, provides rights for those accused of crimes, and **section 12** prohibits double jeopardy and self-incrimination. In *State v. Haycraft* (1975), the Oregon court of appeals declared that a defendant who was tried and convicted in a circuit court and awaiting sentencing waived double jeopardy by failing to raise the previous conviction in another trial in a district court. **Section 13** stipulates: "No person arrested, or confined in jail, shall be treated with unnecessary rigor." The constitutions of several other states, including Indiana, contain similar language.

Section 14 allows bail for all offenses except murder and treason, and **section 16** prohibits excessive bail, fines, and cruel and unusual punishment. **Section 15,** as amended in 1996, states: "Laws for the punishment of crime shall be founded on these principles: protection of society, personal responsibility, accountability for one's actions and reformation." Previously section 15 read: "Laws for the punishment of crime shall be founded on the principles of reformation, and not vindictive justice." **Sections 17, 18,** and **19,** respectively, guarantee the right to jury trials in all civil cases, ensure compensation for the taking of private property for public use, and prohibit imprisonment for debt "except in case of fraud or absconding debtors."

Sections 20 through **29,** respectively, address equality of privileges and immunities of citizens; ex post facto laws; suspension of the operation of laws; habeas corpus; treason; corruption of blood and forfeiture of estate; the right of assembly; the right to bear arms and the subordination of military to civil power; quartering of soldiers; and titles of nobility and hereditary distinctions. **Section 39,** adopted in 1952, deals with the sale of liquor by the glass, and **section 41,** added by initiative in 1994, requires work and training for inmates of correctional institutions. **Section 42,** added by initiative in 1996, enumerates the rights of victims of crime.

Division of Powers

Article III, Distribution of Powers, section 1, declares: "The powers of the Government shall be divided into three separate departments, the Legislative, the Executive, including the administrative, and the Judicial; and no person charged with official duties under one of these departments, shall exercise any of the functions of another, except as in this Constitution expressly provided." **Section 2,** added in 1952, empowers the legislature to create "an agency to exercise budgetary control over all executive and administrative state officers, departments, boards, commissions and agencies of the State Government." **Section 3,** added in 1952, authorizes a joint legislative committee to exercise certain powers "during the interim between sessions of the Legislative Assembly...." This is an unusual provision in state constitutions but not in national constitutions such as Mexico's, for example.

Legislative Branch

Article IV, Legislative Department, section 1, replaced in 1968 and amended in 1986, sets forth in part: "**(1)** The legislative power of the state, except for the initiative and referendum powers reserved to the people, is vested in a Legislative Assembly, consisting of a Senate and a House of Representatives." **Section 2** specifies: "The Senate shall consist of sixteen, and the House of Representatives of thirty four members, [which may be increased]: Provided that the Senate shall never exceed thirty and the House of Representatives sixty members." The Oregon legislature currently has the maximum number of members. According to **section 4,** as amended in 1952 and 1960, "**(1)** The Senators shall be elected for the term of four years, and representatives for the term of two years.... **(2)** The Senators shall continue to be divided into two classes ... , so that one-half, as nearly as possible, of the number of Senators shall be elected biennially." **Article II, Suffrage and Elections, section 19,** adopted by initiative in 1992, restricts house members to six years and senators to eight years, or a total of twelve years in the legislature, "in his or her lifetime." **Section 20,** also added in 1992, attempts to place term limits on members of Congress from Oregon.

Article IV, Legislative Department, section 8, as amended in 1986, 1994, and 1995, requires: "**(1)** No person shall be a Senator or Representative who at the time of election is not a citizen of the United States; nor anyone who has not been for one year next preceding the election an inhabitant of the district from which the Senator or Representative may be chosen.... **(2)** Senators and Representatives shall be at least twenty-one years of age." **Sections 8(4)** through **8(7)** discuss legislators' disqualifications. Under **section 9,** "Senators and Representatives in all cases, except for treason, felony, or breaches of the peace, shall be privileged from arrest during the session of the Legislative Assembly, and in going to and returning from the same; and shall not be subject to any civil process during the session ... nor during the fifteen days next before the commencement thereof; nor shall a member for words uttered in debate in either house, be questioned in any other place."

Section 11 allows each house to choose its own officers; judge the election, qualifications, and returns of its own members; determine its procedural rules; and "sit upon its own adjournments ... [although] neither house shall without the concurrence of the other, adjourn for more than three days, nor to any other place than that in which it may be sitting." **Section 12** defines a quorum as two-thirds of the members of each house; however, "a smaller number may meet; adjourn from day to day, and compel the attendance of absent members...."

Section 15 provides that each house may punish its members "for disorderly behavior"; with the concurrence of two-thirds of the members, each house may expel a member "but not a second time for the same cause." **Section 16** authorizes the legislature to punish non-members by imprisonment, although "such imprisonment shall not at any time, exceed twenty four hours." According to **section 17,** "Each house shall have all powers necessary for a branch of the Legislative Department, of a free, and independent State." The constitutions of most states do not provide for such "necessary" powers on the theory that, unlike the national government, which derives its powers from a grant by the people of the states, state governments inherently have all residual powers necessary to govern.

Section 18 notes that "[b]ills may originate in either house, but may be amended, or rejected in the other; except that bills for raising revenue shall originate in the House of Representatives." The constitutions of Ohio, Tennessee, and a number of other states do not limit the introduction of money bills to the legislature's lower house, although the U.S. Constitution does. **Section 19,** as amended 1946, requires: "Every bill shall be read by title only on three several days, in each house, unless in case of emergency two-thirds of the house where such bill may be pending shall … deem it expedient to dispense with this rule; provided, however, on its final passage such bill shall be read section by section …" unless again dispensed with by a two-thirds vote. **Section 20**, as amended in 1952, mandates: "Every Act shall embrace but one subject, and matters properly connected therewith, which subject shall be expressed in the title." And, according to **section 21**, "Every act, and joint resolution shall be plainly worded, avoiding as far as practicable the use of technical terms."

Section 23 prohibits certain local and special laws, including laws for the "punishment of Crimes, and Misdemeanors" and granting divorces. **Section 25**, as amended in 1996, states: "**(1)** Except as otherwise provided in subsection (2) … a majority of all the members elected to each House shall be necessary to pass every bill or Joint resolution." But **section 33**, added by initiative in 1994, requires "a two-thirds vote of all the members elected to each house … to pass a bill that reduces a criminal sentence approved by the people under section 1 of this Article." Section 25 continues: "**(2)** Three-fifths of all members elected to each House shall be necessary to pass bills for raising revenue. **(3)** All bills, and Joint resolutions passed, shall be signed by the presiding officers of the respective houses."

Section 26 states: "Any member of either house, shall have the right to protest, and have his protest, with his reasons for dissent, entered on the journal." **Section 28** provides that "[n]o act shall take effect, until ninety days from the end of the session at which the same shall have been passed, except in case of emergency…."

Executive Branch

Article V, Executive Department, section 1, mandates: "The chief executive power of the State, shall be vested in a Governor, who shall hold his office for the term of four years; and no person shall be eligible to such office more than Eight, in any period of twelve years." **Section 2**, as amended in 1974, specifies that only persons who are U.S. citizens, at least thirty years old, and state residents for three years are eligible for the office of governor. According to **section 3**, "No member of Congress, or person holding any office under the United States, or under this State, or under any other power, shall fill the Office of Governor, except as may be otherwise provided in this Constitution."

Section 9 designates the governor to serve as commander in chief of the state's military and naval forces; in this role he or she may "call out such forces to execute the laws, to suppress insurrection, or to repel invasion." According to **section 10**, the governor "shall take care that the Laws be faithfully executed." **Sections 11, 12,** and **13**, respectively, direct the governor to "from time to time give to the Legislative Assembly information touching the condition of the State, and recommend such measures as he shall judge to be expedient"; "on extraordinary occasions convene the Legislative Assembly by proclamation …"; and "transact all necessary business with the officers of government, and … require information in writing from the offices of the Administrative, and Military Departments upon any subject relating to [their] offices." **Section 14**, as amended in 1916, empowers the governor to grant "reprieves, commutations, and pardons, after conviction, for all offenses except treason, subject to such regulations as may be provided by law." The constitutions of a number of states exempt cases of impeachment as well. **Section 16**, as amended in

1926, 1986, and 1994, authorizes the governor to fill certain vacancies by appointment. And, pursuant to **article VIII, Education and School Lands, section 1,** "The Governor shall be superintendent of public instruction, and his powers, and duties in that capacity shall be such as may be prescribed by law."

Article V, Executive Department, section 15b, added in 1916 and amended in 1938 and 1988, addresses the governor's approval or disapproval of bills: "**(1)** Every bill which shall have passed the Legislative Assembly shall, before it becomes a law, be presented to the Governor; if the Governor approve, the Governor shall sign it; but if not, the Governor shall return it with written objections to that house in which it shall have originated...." **Section 15b(2)** provides that if, after reconsideration of the bill, two-thirds of the members present again approve it, "it shall be sent ... to the other house ... and, if approved by two-thirds of the members present, it shall become a law." If a bill is not returned by the governor "within five days (Saturdays and Sundays excepted)," notes **section 15b(3),** it becomes law without the governor's signature, unless adjournment of the legislature prevents its return. In this case the governor has thirty days to file the bill with objections in the office of the secretary of state, who then presents it to the legislature at the next session. **Section 15a,** added in 1916 and amended in 1921, gives the governor power to veto "single items in appropriation bills, and any provision in new bills declaring an emergency, without thereby affecting any other provision of such bill."

Section 8a, added by initiative in 1972, provides that if the governor is removed from office or dies, resigns, or becomes disabled, the secretary of state or, if there is none, the state treasurer "shall become Governor until the disability be removed, or a Governor be elected at the next general biennial election." Next in line of succession are the president of the senate and the speaker of the house of representatives. Pursuant to **section 2,** the minimum age requirement for elected governors does not apply to those who succeed to the office under section 8a.

The Oregon constitution contains two articles numbered VII relating to the judicial branch: article VII (Amended), Judicial Department, followed by article VII (Original), The Judicial Department. The provisions of the amended article have the status of constitutional law, whereas the provisions of the original article have been given the status of statutory law pursuant to article VII (Amended), section 2.

Judicial Branch

Article VII (Amended), Judicial Department, section 1, added by initiative in 1910, declares: "The judicial power of the state shall be vested in one supreme court and in such other courts as may from time to time be created by law. The judges of the supreme and other courts shall be elected by the legal voters of the state or of their respective districts for a term of six years...."

Article VII (Original), The Judicial Department, section 2, specifies that "[t]he Supreme Court shall consist of Four Justices to be chosen in districts by the electors thereof, who shall be citizens of the United States, and who shall have resided in the State at least three years next preceding their election, and after their election to reside in their respective districts:—The number of Justices ... may be increased, but shall not exceed five until the white population of the State shall amount to One Hundred Thousand, and shall never exceed seven...." Currently the Oregon supreme court has seven members. **Section 3 (Original)** requires staggered terms for judges, and **section 5 (Original)** provides: "The Judge who has the shortest term to serve, or the oldest of several having such shortest term, and not holding by appointment shall be the Chief Justice."

Section 6 (Original) establishes the supreme court's jursdiction: "The Supreme Court shall have jurisdiction only to revise the final decisions of the Circuit Courts, and every cause shall be tried, and every decision shall be made by those Judges only, or a majority of them, who did not try the cause, or make the decision in the Circuit Court." In *Oregon v. Kennedy* (1982), the U.S. Supreme Court, in deciding whether there was sufficient reliance on federal law to review a decision by an Oregon court, stated that even "if the case admitted of more doubt as to whether federal and state grounds for decision were intermixed, the fact that the state court relied to the extent it did on federal grounds requires us to reach the merits."

Section 1a (Amended), added in 1960, sets forth in part: "Notwithstanding the provisions of section 1, Article VII (Amended) ... , a judge of any court shall retire from judicial office at the end of the calendar year in which he attains the age of 75 years. The Legislative Assembly or the people may by law: **(1)** Fix a lesser age for mandatory retirement not earlier than the end of the calendar year in which the judge attains the age of 70 years; **(2)** Provide for recalling retired judges to temporary active service on the court from which they are retired; and **(3)** Authorize or require the retirement of judges for physical or mental disability or any other cause rendering judges incapable of performing their judicial duties...."

Section 8 (Amended), added in 1968 and amended in 1976, provides in part: "**(1)** In the manner provided by law, and notwithstanding section 1 of this Article, a judge of any court may be removed or suspended from his judicial office by the Supreme Court, or censured by the Supreme Court, for: **(a)** Conviction ... of ... a felony or a crime of moral turpitude; or **(b)** Willful misconduct in a judicial office ... ; or **(c)** Willful or persistent failure to perform judicial duties; or **(d)** Generally incompetent performance of judicial duties; or **(e)** Willful violation of any rule of judicial conduct as shall be established by the Supreme Court; or **(f)** Habitual drunkenness or illegal use of narcotic or dangerous drugs."

Section 20 (Original) allows the governor to "remove from Office a Judge of the Supreme Court, or Prosecuting Attorney upon the Joint resolution of the Legislative Assembly, in which Two Thirds of the members elected to each house shall concur, for incompetency, Corruption, malfeasance, or delinquency in office, or other sufficient cause stated in such resolution."

Impeachment

Article VII (Amended), Judicial Department, section 6, added by initiative in 1910, provides: "Public officers shall not be impeached; but incompetency, corruption, malfeasance or delinquency in office may be tried in the same manner as criminal offenses, and judgment may be given of dismissal from office, and such further punishment as may have been prescribed by law." Oregon is the only state not to provide for some form of impeachment.

Article IV, Legislative Department, section 1, replaced in 1968 and amended in 1986, states in part: "**(2)(a)** The people reserve to themselves the initiative power, which is to propose laws and amendments to the Constitution and enact or reject them at an election independently of the Legislative Assembly.... **(3)(a)** The people reserve to themselves the referendum power, which is to approve or reject at an election any Act, or part thereof, of the Legislative Assembly that does not become effective earlier than 90 days after the end of the session at which the Act is passed." In *Pacific States Telephone and Telegraph Co. v. State of Oregon* (1912), the U.S. Supreme Court held that a challenge to a tax law, enacted by initiative, on the grounds that it destroyed the republican form of government in Oregon was a political question and therefore beyond its jurisdiction to decide.

Article VI, Administrative Department, section 10, added in 1958 and amended in 1960 and 1978, provides in part: "The Legislative Assembly shall provide by law a method whereby the legal voters of any county, by majority vote of such voters voting thereon ... , may adopt, amend, revise or repeal a county charter. A county charter may provide for the exercise by the county of authority over matters of county concern."

Article IX, Finance, section 2, mandates a balanced budget: "The Legislative Assembly shall provide for raising revenue sufficiently to defray the expenses of the State for each fiscal year, and also a sufficient sum to pay the interest on the State debt, if there be any." And **section 6** requires that "[w]henever the expenses, of any fiscal year, shall exceed the income, the Legislative Assembly shall provide for levying a tax, for the ensuing fiscal year, sufficient, with other sources of income, to pay the deficiency, as well as the estimated expense of the ensuing fiscal year."

Article XVII, Amendments and Revisions, section 1, added in 1906, states in part: "Any amendment or amendments to this Constitution may be proposed in either branch of the legislative assembly, and if the same shall be agreed to by a majority of all the members elected to each of the two houses, [it] shall ... be ... referred by the secretary of state to the people for their approval or rejection, at the next regular general election.... If a majority of the electors voting on any such amendment shall vote in favor thereof, it shall thereby become a part of this Constitution." Section 1 continues: "No convention shall be called to amend or propose amendments to this Constitution, or to propose a new Constitution, unless the law providing for such convention shall first be approved by the people on a referendum vote at a regular general election." Pursuant to **section 2,** added in 1960, a revision of the constitution may be "agreed to by at least two-thirds of all the members of each house ... and referred by the Secretary of State to the people for their approval or rejection ... [by a] majority of the votes cast in the election on the proposed revision...."

Article IV, Legislative Department, section 1(2)(c), added in 1968 and amended in 1986, provides: "An initiative amendment to the Constitution may be proposed only by a petition signed by a number of qualified voters equal to eight percent of the total number of votes cast for all candidates for Governor at the election at which a Governor was elected...."

PENNSYLVANIA

The Commonwealth of Pennsylvania became the second state of the United States on December 12, 1787. Harrisburg is the capital of the "Keystone State." Some 46,058 square miles in area, Pennsylvania is bordered by Lake Erie and New York on the north; New Jersey on the east; Delaware, Maryland, and Ohio on the south; and Ohio on the west. With approximately 12 million inhabitants, Pennsylvania ranks fifth among the states in population. Its principal industries include steel, biotechnology, apparel, and agriculture; among its chief crops are corn, hay, mushrooms, and apples.

General Information

Government: The governor and lieutenant governor are elected jointly and are eligible to succeed themselves for one term. The legislature, called the general assembly, consists of fifty senators elected for four-year terms and 203 members of the house of representatives elected for two-year terms. The supreme court includes a chief justice and six additional justices elected for ten-year terms.

Dates of Constitutions: 1776, 1790, 1839, 1874, and 1968 (the effective dates of the provisions varied)

Constitutional History

Before the arrival of Europeans in the seventeenth century, the territory that would become the state of Pennsylvania was the home of the Lenni-Lenape (also called the Delaware), Susquehannocks, Erie, and Seneca peoples. In 1626 Dutchmen from New Amsterdam, now New York, built Fort Nassau on the eastern shore of the Delaware River, and in 1638 colonists from Sweden and Finland began settling on the west bank of the river.

By the early 1650s Swedish and Finnish settlers were living near trading posts such as the one in Passyunk, on the site of present-day Philadelphia. To protect their fur trading interests, the Dutch seized the settlements in 1655. Nine years later, in 1664, troops of the duke of York, the future James II of England, took control of the area, and by the Treaty of Westminster in 1674 the Dutch ceded jurisdiction to England. As repayment of a loan to the Crown by Admiral William Penn, Charles II of England granted the deceased admiral's son, William Penn, proprietary title to the province of Pennsylvania in 1681.

A Quaker, William Penn promoted the settlement of the rich and strategic stretch of land in the middle of the English North American colonies. Desirous of establishing a model commonwealth, Penn emphasized written charters or constitutions as the basis for governing the province. On July 11, 1681, he issued the document entitled Concessions to the Province of Pennsylvania, ensuring rights to the settlers, and in 1682 he promulgated the Frame of Government of Pennsylvania as the new colony's constitution.

Unlike most other grantees of territory in the New World, Penn personally visited his province and sought to educate the colonists about the freedoms wrested from the monarchy. On April 2, 1683, he issued a Charter of Liberty that provided: "That the government of this province shall, according to the powers of patent, consist of the Governor and freemen of the said province, in form of a provincial Council and General Assembly, by whom laws shall be made, officers chosen and public affairs transacted. . . ." The author of *The Excellent Privilege of Liberty and Property; Being the Birthright of the Free Born Subjects of England* (1686), which would influence the development of democratic theory and practice in America, Penn promulgated a second Frame of Government in 1683, a third in 1696, and a final Charter of Privileges in 1701.

The first congress of representatives of the British colonies, convened in response to punitive laws enacted by Parliament after the Boston Tea Party, met on September 5, 1774, in Philadelphia because of the city's central location. When war broke out in Massachusetts in April 1775, a committee of public safety in Pennsylvania seized power from its conservative assembly and in the spring of that year issued a new constitution. After Benjamin Franklin and two other Pennsylvania delegates to the Second Continental Congress voted for independence from Great Britain on July 2, 1776, a constitutional convention, with Franklin presiding, began drafting a new document for Pennsylvania on July 15.

The 1776 Pennsylvania constitution, which became effective when adopted by the convention on September 28 without being submitted for popular approval, reflects the initial constitutional thinking of early Americans: it embodies the doctrine of separation of powers but lacks institutional checks and balances. In Pennsylvania and states such as New York, it soon became evident that pure republicanism, without protection from abuses of power, especially by the legislature, was not the best frame of government for a democracy. However, not until 1789 was a convention assembled to revise the document. The body met in Philadelphia and proclaimed the new constitution in effect on September 2, 1790, again without ratification by popular vote.

A third constitution was drafted by a convention that met from May 2, 1837, to February 22, 1838. Ratified by the electorate in October, it went into effect on January 1, 1839. A fourth constitution was approved by the voters on December 16, 1873, and became effective on January 1, 1874. The current constitution, popularly known as the "revised constitution" of 1968, was created in three stages. In 1966 the legislature proposed two amendments relating primarily to public officers and the oath of office, both approved by the voters in May. The following year the legislature proposed seven more amendments revising the articles on the legislative and executive branches, elections, corporations, and the amendment process, and these were approved at the polls on May 16, 1967. On the same day voters approved the calling of a limited constitutional convention to revise the provisions on legislative apportionment, finance and taxation, and the judicial branch. These proposals were ratified by the people on April 23, 1968, with the effective dates of the provisions varying according to a schedule included with the amendments.

Pennsylvania's 1776 constitution was a radical state document reflecting Thomas Paine's advice that a simple government was the best government. A unicameral legislature, for which some credit Benjamin Franklin, and a plural executive branch with a president chosen by the virtually unchecked legislature proved to be an untenable way to run a state government. Like many other states, Pennsylvania is still trying to find the proper mix of elements between the early experiments with legislature-dominated governments and the more balanced structure represented by the federal model and adopted most recently by Alaska, Hawaii, and New Jersey. Because state legislatures are generally considered the repository of government powers not delegated to the national government, legislators are reluctant to accept a lesser role in a state government with truly balanced branches.

The 1968 Pennsylvania constitution, with nearly 22,000 words and twenty-four amendments effective as of January 1, 1998, is neither radical nor conservative. It instead represents an attempt to meld the old with the new. The plural executive branch and

The Constitution

overall legislative dominance remain intact, but the unified judicial branch and local government provisions reflect a more modern trend in state constitutions.

Preamble

The preamble to the 1968 constitution of the Commonwealth of Pennsylvania reads: "We, the people of the Commonwealth of Pennsylvania, grateful to Almighty God for the blessings of civil and religious liberty, and humbly invoking His guidance, do ordain and establish this Constitution."

Fundamental Rights

Article I, Declaration of Rights, begins: "That the general, great and essential principles of liberty and free government may be recognized and unalterably established, WE DECLARE THAT—"

Section 1 proclaims: "All men are born equally free and independent, and have certain inherent and indefeasible rights, among which are those of enjoying and defending life and liberty, of acquiring, possessing and protecting property and reputation, and of pursuing their own happiness." **Section 2** states that "[a]ll power is inherent in the people, and all free governments are founded on their authority and instituted for their peace, safety and happiness. For the advancement of these ends they have at all times an inalienable and indefeasible right to alter, reform or abolish their government in such manner as they may think proper." Language similar to that of the last sentence appears in many state constitutions and expresses a philosophically important concept of modern constitutional democracy: a dynamic society cannot be bound to rigid, dogmatic rules that have outlived their usefulness.

Section 3 provides for freedom of religion. **Section 4** states: "No person who acknowledges the being of a God and a future state of rewards and punishments shall, on account of his religious sentiments, be disqualified to hold any office or place of trust or profit under this Commonwealth." The South Carolina constitution, in contrast, makes acknowledgment of "the Supreme Being" a requirement for eligibility for public office. Under **section 5,** "Elections shall be free and equal; and no power, civil or military, shall at any time interfere to prevent the free exercise of the right of suffrage." **Section 6,** as amended in 1971, mandates: "Trial by jury shall be as heretofore and the right thereof remain inviolate. The General Assembly may provide, however, by law, that a verdict may be rendered by not less than five-sixths of the jury in any civil case."

Section 7 states in part: "The printing press shall be free to every person who may undertake to examine the proceedings of the Legislature or any branch of government, and no law shall ever be made to restrain the right thereof. The free communication of thoughts and opinions is one of the invaluable rights of man, and every citizen may freely speak, write and print on any subject, being responsible for the abuse of that liberty." In *Western Pennsylvania Socialist Workers 1982 Campaign v. Connecticut General Life Insurance Company* (1986), the Pennsylvania supreme court held that neither this section nor sections 2 and 20 guarantee the right to conduct political activities on private property where the owner uniformly and effectively prohibits such use. Section 7 also bars "any prosecution for the publication of papers relating to the official conduct of officers or men in public capacity" and requires that "in all indictments for libels the jury shall have the right to determine the law and the facts, under the direction of the court...."

Section 8 prohibits unreasonable searches and seizures, and **section 9,** as amended in 1984 and 1995, provides rights for the accused in criminal prosecutions, including the right to "be heard by himself and his counsel," "compulsory process for obtaining witnesses in his favor," and "a speedy public trial by an impartial jury of the vicinage." **Section 10,** as amended in 1973, restricts the use of an information as a method of initiating a criminal indictment, prohibits double jeopardy, and guarantees just compensation for the taking of private property for public use. According to **section 11,** "All courts shall be open; and every man for an injury done him in his lands, goods, person or reputation shall have remedy by due course of law.... Suits may be brought against the Commonwealth in such manner, in such courts and in such cases as the Legislature may by law direct." **Section 12** states: "No power of suspending laws shall be exercised unless by the Legislature or by its authority." **Section 13** prohibits excessive bail and fines and "cruel punishments." **Section 14** guarantees bail in all cases except for "capital offenses when the proof is evident or presumption great" and restricts the suspension of the writ of habeas corpus to cases of "rebellion or invasion [when] the public safety may require it." As specified in **section 15,** "No commission shall issue creating special temporary criminal tribunals to try particular individuals or particular classes of cases."

Sections 16, 17, 18, and **19,** respectively, limit prison time for insolvent debtors and prohibit ex post facto laws and laws "impairing the obligations of contracts," attainder by the legislature for treason or felony, and attainder that "shall work corruption of blood...." **Section 20** guarantees the right to assemble in a peaceable manner and "to apply to those invested with the powers of government for redress of grievances...." **Section 21** guarantees the right to bear arms; **section 22** subordinates the military to civil power; **section 23** limits the quartering of troops in private homes; and **section 24** prohibits the granting of "any title of nobility."

Section 26 mandates: "Neither the Commonwealth nor any political subdivision thereof shall deny to any person the enjoyment of any civil right, nor discriminate against any person in the exercise of any civil right." **Section 28,** added in 1971, declares: "Equality of rights under the law shall not be denied or abridged in the Commonwealth of Pennsylvania because of the sex of the individual."

The Pennsylvania constitution, like the U.S. Constitution and the constitutions of a number of states, including New York and Hawaii, does not expressly acknowledge the principle of the separation of the powers of government. The structure of the government created by the document, however, contains three major divisions: legislative, executive, and judicial branches.

Division of Powers

Article II, The Legislature, section 1, proclaims: "The legislative power of this Commonwealth shall be vested in a General Assembly, which shall consist of a Senate and a House of Representatives." **Section 2** states in part that the voters shall elect members of the

Legislative Branch

general assembly "every second year." In case of a vacancy in either house, "the presiding officer thereof shall issue a writ of election to fill such vacancy for the remainder of the term." According to **section 3**, "Senators shall be elected for the term of four years and Representatives for the term of two years." **Section 16** divides the commonwealth into fifty senatorial and 203 representative districts, each of which elects one senator and one representative, respectively.

Section 5 requires that senators be at least twenty-five years old and representatives at least twenty-one years old; all must be citizens and residents of the state for four years and residents of their respective districts "one year next before their election (unless absent on the public business of the United States or of this State)" and during their terms of service. **Section 6** disqualifies from serving as legislators any persons "appointed to any civil office under this Commonwealth to which a salary, fee or perquisite is attached," members of Congress, and anyone holding a federal or state office "(except of attorney-at-law or in the National Guard or in a reserve component of the armed forces of the United States) ... to which a salary, fee or perquisite is attached...." **Section 7** adds that no one convicted of "embezzlement of public moneys, bribery, perjury or other infamous crime, shall be eligible to the General Assembly, or capable of holding any office of trust or profit in this Commonwealth."

Section 9 states: "The Senate shall, at the beginning and close of each regular session and at such other times as may be necessary, elect one of its members President pro tempore, who shall perform the duties of the Lieutenant Governor, in any case of absence or disability of that officer, and whenever the ... office ... shall be vacant. The House of Representatives shall elect one of its members as Speaker. Each House shall choose its other officers, and shall judge of the election and qualifications of its members." **Section 10** defines a quorum as a majority of each house, although "a smaller number may adjourn from day to day and compel the attendance of absent members." **Section 11** allows each house to determine its own rules, punish its members "for contempt or disorderly behavior in its presence," enforce obedience to its process, protect its members against "violence or offers of bribes or private solicitation," expel a member by a two-thirds vote (although not twice for the same offense), and have "all other powers necessary for the Legislature of a free State." Section 11 continues: "A member expelled for corruption shall not thereafter be eligible to either House, and punishment for contempt or disorderly behavior shall not bar an indictment for the same offense." **Section 15** exempts legislators from arrest during attendance at and travel to and from their respective chambers, except for "treason, felony, violation of their oath of office, and breach or surety of the peace."

Article III, Legislation, A, Procedure, section 1, mandates: "No law shall be passed except by bill, and no bill shall be so altered or amended, on its passage ... as to change its original purpose." In *Scudder v. Smith* (1938), the Pennsylvania supreme court concluded that a joint resolution passed by the legislature violated this language and could not therefore be considered a law. **Section 2** requires that "[n]o bill shall be considered unless referred to a committee, printed for the use of the members and returned therefrom." According to **section 3**, no bill, except appropriations or codifying bills, may contain more than one subject, "which shall be clearly expressed in its title." **Section 4** states: "Every bill shall be considered on three different days in each House. All amendments made thereto shall be printed for the use of the members before the final vote is taken . . . and . . . upon written request . . . by at least 25% of the members elected to [a particular house], any bill shall be read at length in that House. No bill shall become a law, unless . . . a majority of the members elected to each House is recorded . . . as voting in its favor."

Section 7 prohibits local and special bills "unless notice of the intention to apply therefor shall have been published in the locality . . . at least 30 days prior to the introduction . . . of such bill." **Section 8** states that bills passed must be signed by the presiding officers of each house "in the presence of the House over which he presides," and **section 9** provides that, in addition to bills, "[e]very order, resolution or vote, to which the concurrence of both Houses may be necessary, except on the question of adjournment, shall be presented to the Governor [for approval]." The governor's veto, as with bills, may be overridden if the measure is repassed "by two-thirds of both Houses. . . ." **Section 10** stipulates that revenue bills originate in the house of representatives, although the senate may propose amendments to these. Pursuant to **section 11,** "The general appropriation bill shall embrace nothing but appropriations for the executive, legislative and judicial departments . . . , for the public debt and for public schools." **Section 13** requires: "A member who has a personal or private interest in any measure or bill . . . shall disclose the fact to the House of which he is a member, and shall not vote thereon." The constitutions of a number of other states have similar provisions.

Article III, Legislation, E, Restrictions on Legislative Power, prohibits certain laws and certain delegations of legislative power, as well as certain local and special laws. **Section 28** proscribes "changing the permanent location of the Capital of the State" unless approved by the electors, and **section 29** prohibits with certain exceptions appropriating funds "to any persons or communities for "charitable, educational or benevolent purposes" or to any "denominational and sectarian institution, corporation or association. . . ."

Article IV, The Executive, section 1, declares: "The Executive Department of this Commonwealth shall consist of a Governor, Lieutenant Governor, Attorney General, Auditor General, State Treasurer, and Superintendent of Public Instruction and such other officers as the General Assembly may from time to time prescribe." This is one of the clearest expressions of the plural executive concept in any state constitution. Rather than vesting all executive power in a single executive officer, the governor, as in the more modern constitutions of Alaska and Hawaii, the Pennsylvania constitution expressly authorizes the legislature to create more statewide positions to share executive power with the governor and other constitutional executive officers. **Section 2** states in part: "The supreme executive power shall be vested in the Governor, who shall take care that the laws be faithfully executed. . . ." **Section 3** provides that the governor's term is four years and that the incumbent may "succeed himself for one additional term."

Section 4 directs that the lieutenant governor be elected on a joint ballot with the governor and serve as president of the senate. In this role, "he may vote in case of a tie

Executive Branch

on any question except the final passage of a bill or joint resolution, the adoption of a conference report or the concurrence in amendments made by the House of Representatives." **Section 4.1**, added in 1978, provides for the election of an attorney general "on the day the general election is held for the Auditor General and State Treasurer." The attorney general, who may not serve continuously for more than two successive terms, "shall be the chief law officer of the Commonwealth and shall exercise such powers and perform such duties as may be imposed by law."

Section 5 requires that candidates for governor, lieutenant governor, and attorney general be U.S. citizens, at least thirty years old, and residents of the commonwealth for seven years "unless ... absent on the public business...." The attorney general, furthermore, must be "a member of the bar of the Supreme Court of Pennsylvania." The constitutions of most states require bar membership as a prerequisite for being attorney general, and some states, such as Florida, prescribe a minimun number of years of bar membership. According to **section 6**, "No member of Congress or person holding any office (except of attorney-at-law or in the National Guard or in a reserve component of the armed forces ...) under the United States or this Commonwealth shall exercise the office of Governor, Lieutenant Governor or Attorney General."

Section 7 authorizes the governor to act as commander in chief of the commonwealth's military forces, "except when they shall be called into actual service of the United States." **Section 8** empowers the governor, "subject to the consent of two-thirds or a majority of the members elected to the Senate as is specified by law," to appoint a secretary of education and other officers and to fill vacancies in appointive offices "by nominating to the Senate a proper person to fill the vacancy within 90 days of the first day of the vacancy and not thereafter."

Section 9 extends to the governor the power of the pardon, with certain exceptions and limitations. In *Commonwealth v. Gaito* (1980), the Pennsylvania supreme court declared that the governor's power to commute sentences on the recommendation of the board of pardons is exclusive and courts may not impinge in any way on the exercise of this power. **Section 10** authorizes the governor to "require information in writing from the officers of the Executive Department, upon any subject relating to the duties of their respective offices." According to **section 11**, the governor "shall from time to time, give to the General Assembly information of the state of the Commonwealth, and recommend to their consideration such measures as he may judge expedient." **Section 12** allows the governor to convene the general assembly "on extraordinary occasions."

Section 13 provides that "[i]n the case of the death, conviction on impeachment, failure to qualify or resignation of the Governor, the Lieutenant Governor shall become Governor for the remainder of the term and in the case of the disability of the Governor, the powers, duties and emoluments of the office shall devolve upon the Lieutenant Governor until the disability is removed." **Section 14** authorizes the president pro tempore of the senate to replace the lieutenant governor in a similar manner under similar circumstances.

Section 15 directs that "[e]very bill which shall have passed both Houses shall be presented to the Governor; if he approves he shall sign it, but if he shall not approve he shall return it with his objections to the House in which it shall have originated. . . ." To override the veto, "two-thirds of all the members elected" to each house must agree to pass it again. Any bill not returned by the governor within ten days becomes law without a signature; if the legislature prevents its return by adjourning, the governor may file it with objections with the secretary of state. **Section 16** grants the governor the power "to disapprove of any item or items of any bill, making appropriations of money, embracing distinct items. . . ." The legislature may override such item vetoes in the same manner as prescribed for bills.

Section 18 provides for the election of the auditor general and state treasurer for four-year terms, but they are ineligible "to serve continuously for more than two successive terms [and the] "State Treasurer shall not be eligible to the office of Auditor General until four years after he has been State Treasurer." **Article VI, Public Officers, section 7,** provides that all civil officers hold their offices "on the condition that they behave themselves well while in office"; if convicted of "misbehavior . . . or of any infamous crime," they may be removed from office.

Article V, The Judiciary, section 1, declares: "The judicial power of the Commonwealth shall be vested in a unified judicial system consisting of the Supreme Court, the Superior Court, the Commonwealth Court, courts of common pleas, community courts, municipal and traffic courts in the City of Philadelphia, such other courts as may be provided by law and justices of the peace. All courts and justices of the peace and their jurisdiction shall be in this unified judicial system." **Section 2** states that the supreme court "**(a)** shall be the highest court of the Commonwealth and in this court shall be reposed the supreme judicial power of the Commonwealth; **(b)** shall consist of seven justices, one of whom shall be the Chief Justice; and **(c)** shall have such jurisdiction as shall be provided by law." **Section 9** provides that "[t]here shall be a right of appeal in all cases to a court of record from a court not of record; and there shall also be a right of appeal from a court of record or from an administrative agency to a court of record or to an appellate court, the selection of such court to be as provided by law; and there shall be such other rights of appeal as may be provided by law."

Section 10(a) states that the supreme court "shall exercise general supervisory and administrative authority over all the courts and justices of the peace. . . ." **Section 10(b)** directs the supreme court to appoint a court administrator and other necessary administrators and staff. In *Commonwealth v. Pennsylvania Labor Relations Bd.* (1978), the Pennsylvania supreme court ruled that by placing the court reporters of Philadelphia under the Public Employee Relations Act, the legislature did not unconstitutionally interfere with the independence of the courts. **Section 10(c)** provides that "[t]he Supreme Court [with certain limitations] shall have the power to prescribe general rules governing practice, procedure and the conduct of all courts . . . and for admission to the bar and to practice law . . ."; and **section 10(d)** designates "[t]he Chief Justice and president judges of all courts with seven or less judges [as] the justice or judge longest in

Judicial Branch

continuous service. . . ." **Section 12(a)** requires that all justices, judges, and justices of the peace be commonwealth citizens; furthermore, "[j]ustices and judges [in general] shall be members of the bar of the Supreme Court. Justices and judges of statewide courts, for a period of one year preceding their election or appointment and during their continuance in office, shall reside within the Commonwealth."

Section 13(a) provides for the election of judges: "Justices, judges and justices of the peace shall be elected at the municipal election next preceding the commencement of their respective terms of office by the electors of the Commonwealth or the respective districts in which they are to serve." According to **section 13(b)**, the governor, "with the advice and consent of two-thirds of the members elected to the Senate," appoints replacements for any vacancy in the office of a justice or a judge. The appointee serves until the next election if it is more than ten months after the vacancy occurred. **Section 14** creates a judicial qualifications commission to "recommend to the Governor not fewer than ten nor more than 20 of those qualified for each vacancy to be filled. . . ." **Section 15(a)** specifies: "The regular term of office of justices and judges shall be ten years. . . ." **Section 17(a)** states in part: "Justices and judges shall devote full time to their judicial duties, and shall not engage in the practice of law, hold office in a political party or political organization, or [public office]," except in the U.S. or state armed forces. **Section 18** creates a judicial inquiry and review board that has authority to suspend, remove, or discipline any justice or judge under the procedures prescribed in this section.

Impeachment

Article VI, Public Officers, section 4, vests the house of representatives with the sole power of impeachment. **Section 5** directs that "[a]ll impeachments shall be tried by the Senate" but that no one can be convicted "without the concurrence of two-thirds of the members present." The Oklahoma constitution also requires concurrence of only two-thirds of the senators present, but the constitutions of many states require concurrence of two-thirds of the total members of the senate.

Local Government

Article IX, Local Government, section 1, states: "The General Assembly shall provide by general law for local government within the Commonwealth. Such general law shall be uniform as to all classes of local government regarding procedural matters." Under **section 2,** "Municipalities shall have the right and power to frame and adopt home rule charters. Adoption, amendment or repeal of a home rule charter shall be by referendum."

Taxation and Finance

Article VIII, Taxation and Finance, section 1, proclaims: "All taxes shall be uniform, upon the same class of subjects, within the territorial limits of the authority levying the tax, and shall be levied and collected under general laws." **Section 7** provides in part: "**(a)** No debt shall be incurred by or on behalf of the Commonwealth except by law and in accordance with the provisions of this section. **(1)** Debt may be incurred without limit to suppress insurrection, rehabilitate areas affected by man-made or natural disaster . . . ; [and] **(2)** The Governor, State Treasurer and Auditor General, acting jointly, may **(i)** issue tax anticipation notes having a maturity within the fiscal year of issue and payable exclusively from revenues received in the same fiscal year, and **(ii)** incur debt for the purpose of refunding other debt, if such refunding debt matures within the term of the original debt."

Section 12, added in 1968, requires: "Annually, at the times set by law, the Governor shall submit to the General Assembly: (a) a balanced operating budget for the ensuing fiscal year setting forth in detail (i) proposed expenditures classified by department or agency and by program and (ii) estimated revenues from all sources. If estimated revenues and available surplus are less than proposed expenditures, the Governor shall recommend specific additional sources of revenue sufficient to pay the deficiency and the estimated revenue to be derived from each source...." And **section 13(a)**, added in 1968, provides: "Operating budget appropriations made by the General Assembly shall not exceed the actual and estimated revenues and surpluses available in the same fiscal year."

Article III, Legislation, section 14, mandates: "The General Assembly shall provide for the maintenance and support of a thorough and efficient system of public education to serve the needs of the Commonwealth." **Section 15** directs that "[n]o money raised for the support of the public schools ... shall be appropriated to or used for the support of any sectarian school."

Article III, Legislation, section 29, authorizes appropriations for, among others, "blind persons 21 years of age and upwards and for assistance to mothers having dependent children and to aged persons without adequate means of support...."

Article 1, Declaration of Rights, section 27, added in 1971, asserts: "The people have a right to clean air, pure water, and to the preservation of the natural, scenic, historic and esthetic values of the environment."

Article XI, Amendments, section 1, provides in part: "Amendments to this constitution may be proposed in the Senate or House of Representatives; and if the same shall be agreed to by a majority of the members elected to each House ... [they shall be] published three months before the next general election, in at least two newspapers in every county...." If they are agreed to during the next general assembly as well, they are again published and voted on at an election held at least three months later. If approved by a majority of the voters, they "shall become a part of the Constitution." No amendment, however, "shall be submitted oftener than once in five years."

Section 1 also provides procedures for amendments if "a major emergency threatens or is about to threaten the Commonwealth...." For such amendments, "at least two-thirds of the members elected to each House" must vote their approval and the measure must be submitted to the electorate within one month of its passage by the general assembly.

Education

Health and Welfare

Environment

Amendment Procedures

RHODE ISLAND

Rhode Island was admitted to the Union on May 29, 1790, as the thirteenth state. Providence is the capital of "Little Rhody" or the "Ocean State," which encompasses 1,545 square miles and is bordered by Massachusetts on the north and east, Rhode Island Sound on the south, and Connecticut on the west. Rhode Island ranks forty-third among the states with a population of approximately 1 million residents. Services and the manufacturing of costume jewelry, toys, machinery, and electronics are among the state's principal industries; its chief crops include nursery products, turf, and potatoes.

General Information

Government: The governor and lieutenant governor are elected at the same time although on separate tickets for four-year terms but may not serve more than two consecutive terms. The legislature, called the general assembly, consists of fifty senators and 100 members of the house of representatives, all elected for two-year terms. The supreme court is composed of a chief justice and four other justices appointed for life terms by the governor, with the advice and consent of both houses of the legislature, from a list prepared by a judicial nominating commission.

Dates of Constitutions: 1790 (1663 charter continued after statehood) and 1843

Constitutional History

The first European to sail along the Rhode Island coast was the Portuguese navigator Miguel Corte Real in 1511, followed by Giovanni da Verrazano, sailing for France, who explored the Narragansett Bay in 1524. The Dutch navigator Adriaen Block named a Narragansett Bay island *Roodt Eyland* (red island), and the name was soon applied to the mainland as well. These early European explorers found peaceful groups of Native Americans, all members of the Algonquin nation, living in the area.

Although William Blackstone may have been the first Englishman to settle near what is today Providence, the first permanent settlement in Rhode Island was founded by the English clergyman Roger Williams in 1636. A religious nonconformist, Williams led his followers out of Massachusetts, where they had suffered persecution because of their religious views, to settle in Providence Plantations. A Plantation Agreement at Providence, dated August 27–September 6, 1640, laid down the basic principles of political organization for the colonists, and in March 1641 a Frame of Government of Rhode Island was promulgated.

The Rhode Islanders had obtained "letters patent" in 1643 from England's earl of Warwick granting them title to the territory, but subsequent boundary disputes with Massachusetts led Charles II to issue a royal charter in 1663. Like the charters of other English colonies, including Massachusetts and Connecticut, it was suspended by England but reinstated after the Glorious Revolution of 1688–89.

Under the Munificent Charter, as Rhode Island's 1663 charter has been called, the colonists possessed more religious freedom than did subjects of the Crown in England. The major feature of Rhode Island's colonial government was the supremacy of the general assembly, which had extensive powers of appointment. The assembly's authority was checked by the overiding authority of the king, his privy council, and Parliament; the charter's requirement that any statutes enacted could not be repugnant to the laws of England; and frequent elections of public officials by all freemen (semiannual elections of deputies and annual elections of the governor and his assistants).

Rhode Island settled its boundary disputes, first with Connecticut and then with Massachusetts, before the American Revolution. On May 29, 1790, it ratified the U.S. Constitution by two votes, the last of the original thirteen colonies to do so, and attained statehood. Having enjoyed many aspects of self-government under its Munificent Charter, Rhode Islanders kept the document as their first state constitution.

A failed movement in the 1820s to scrap the pre-independence constitution and draft a new state constitution may have presaged the uprising of small freeholders, led by Thomas Wilson Dorr and called Dorr's Rebellion, that began in 1841. A "people's convention," called independently of the general assembly and consisting of disenfranchised citizens, drafted a constitutional document—radical for its time—that provided for, among other things, universal suffrage. It received a significant majority of the popular vote.

In response, the state government functioning under the charter quickly assembled a constitutional convention of its own, referred to by some as the "landholders convention." The document drafted by this convention, called the "freemen's constitution," expanded the franchise but did not provide universal suffrage. It was defeated by a narrow margin when submitted to the voters. Dorr, a leader of the people's convention, was elected governor by the "Dorrites," but the incumbent governor refused to leave office, claiming that the people's convention had not been legally authorized and branding support for the new constitution insurrectionary.

One of Dorr's followers, Martin Luther, moved to Massachusetts to bring an action in federal court claiming that Rhode Island's incumbent government was depriving the state of the republican government guaranteed by the U.S. Constitution. In *Luther v. Borden* (1849), the U.S. Supreme Court refused to decide whether the 1841 constitution was legitimate, stating that the question was a political one that could be settled only by the other branches of government. Afterward President John Tyler pronounced the charter government Rhode Island's legitimate government but urged both sides to settle their differences reasonably.

In the meantime, however, the entrenched state government, conceding that some changes were in order, had produced a second "freemen's constitution," which was approved by the voters in November 1842. The new Rhode Island constitution went into effect on May 3, 1843. A constitutional convention held a century and a half later, in 1986, revised and modernized the 1843 document.

The Constitution

The Rhode Island constitution, a relatively short document containing approximately 19,000 words, has been amended only fifty-nine times as of January 1, 1998. As a result of the 1986 updating of the 1843 constitution, the document is integrated with all amendments up to 1986. In this respect it differs from the Massachusetts constitution, for example, in which all amendments since 1780 are simply appended, leaving to individual readers the chore of integrating the changes into the original document. Nevertheless, the Rhode Island constitution is not particularly well organized; for example, the qualifications and lengths of terms of elected officials such as the governor and legislators are not included in the articles that deal specifically with the executive and legislative branches.

Although the Rhode Island constitution reflects some modernizing changes made in 1986, such as the addition of rights for women, the disabled, and victims of crime, it continues to allocate greater power to the legislature rather than create truly coequal branches of government. The governor must share executive power with other statewide elected officials whose duties can be changed by the legislature. Moreover, while the court system is less under the thumb of the legislature, the supreme court's jurisdiction "may, from time to time, be prescribed by law."

Preamble

The preamble to the 1843 Rhode Island constitution reads: "WE, the people of the State of Rhode Island and Providence Plantations, grateful to Almighty God for the civil and religious liberty which He hath so long permitted us to enjoy, and looking to Him for a blessing upon our endeavors to secure and to transmit the same, unimpaired, to succeeding generations, do ordain and establish this Constitution of government."

Fundamental Rights

Article I, Declaration of Certain Constitutional Rights and Principles, begins: "In order effectually to secure the religious and political freedom established by our venerated ancestors, and to preserve the same for our posterity, we do declare that the essential and unquestionable rights and principles hereinafter mentioned shall be established, maintained, and preserved, and shall be of paramount obligation in all legislative, judicial and executive proceedings." **Section 1** proclaims: "In the words of the Father of his Country, we declare that 'the basis of our political systems is the right of the people to make and alter their constitutions of government; but that the constitution which at any time exists, till changed by an explicit and authentic act of the whole people, is sacredly obligatory upon all.'"

Section 2 affirms: "All free governments are instituted for the protection, safety, and happiness of the people.... No person shall be deprived of life, liberty or property without due process of law, nor shall any person be denied protection of the laws. No otherwise qualified person shall, solely by reason of race, gender or handicap be subject to discrimination...." However, the section ends with this disclaimer regarding abortion: "Nothing in this section shall be construed to grant or secure any right relating to abortion or the funding thereof." **Section 3** provides for freedom of religion, and **section 4** prohibits slavery.

Section 5 declares: "Every person within this state ought to find a certain remedy, by having recourse to the laws, for all injuries or wrongs which may be received in one's person, property, or character. Every person ought to obtain right and justice freely, and without purchase, completely and without denial; promptly and without delay; conformably to the laws." The U.S. Bill of Rights (1791) contains no comparable guarantee, but some other state constitutions, including those of Connecticut and New York, include this right of recourse to the laws for redress of injuries. In *Henry v. Cherry & Webb* (1909), the Rhode Island supreme court found that section 5 did not provide authority for recognizing a right of privacy.

Section 6 guarantees protection against unreasonable searches and seizures, and **sections 7** through **15** extend rights to the accused. **Section 14,** for example, provides: "Every person being presumed innocent, until pronounced guilty by law, no act of severity which is not necessary to secure an accused person shall be permitted." Because not all constitutional rights are, or need be, written, the U.S. Constitution and most other state constitutions, unlike the Rhode Island document, do not expressly recognize the judicial principle of the presumption of innocence; nevertheless, this principle is enforced by the courts as if it were specifically included in federal and other state constitutions.

Section 16, in language similar to that in the Fifth Amendment (1791) to the U.S. Constitution, states in part: "Private property shall not be taken for public uses, without just compensation." However, the state's powers "to regulate and control the use of land and waters in furtherance of the preservation, regeneration, and restoration of the natural environment" is not "deemed to be a public use of private property." **Sections 17** through **22,** respectively, address the people's enjoyment and free exercise of "all the rights of fishery, and the privileges of the shore … "; subordinate the military to civil authority; prohibit quartering soldiers "in any house in time of peace, without the consent of the owner [or] in time of war, but in manner to be prescribed by law"; guarantee freedom of the press; allow peaceable assembly, petition for redress of grievances, and freedom of speech; and guarantee the people's right "to keep and bear arms."

Section 23 provides in part that victims of crime "shall, as a matter of right, be treated by agents of the state with dignity, respect and sensitivity during all phases of the criminal justice process." They are entitled to "financial compensation for any injury or loss caused by the perpetrator of the crime, and … other compensation as the state may provide." In addition, "[b]efore sentencing, a victim shall have the right to address the court regarding the impact which the perpetrator's conduct has had upon the victim."

Section 24 concludes: "The enumeration of the foregoing rights shall not be construed to impair or deny others retained by the people. The rights guaranteed by this Constitution are not dependent on those guaranteed by the Constitution of the United States."

Article V, Of the Distribution of Powers, divides "[t]he powers of the government … into three departments: the legislative, executive and judicial."

Division of Powers

Article VI, Of the Legislative Power, section 1, proclaims: "This Constitution shall be the supreme law of the state, and any law inconsistent therewith shall be void. The general assembly shall pass all laws necessary to carry this Constitution into effect." The second sentence is similar to the "necessary and proper" clause of the U.S. Constitution. In *In re Opinion to the Governor* (1935), the Rhode Island supreme court reversed an earlier opinion holding that this section implies that the legislature, on its own, is entitled to call a constitutional convention even though the constitution contains no such express authorization. And in *Forte Bros. v. State DOT* (1988), the court declared that since the time of the 1663 charter the general assembly's power has been plenary and can be limited only by the state and federal constitutions. **Section 2** states in part: "The legislative power, under this Constitution, shall be vested in two houses, the one to be called the senate, the other the house of representatives; and both together the general assembly. The concurrence of the two houses shall be necessary to the enactment of laws."

Legislative Branch

Article VII, Of the House of Representatives, section 1, as amended in 1994, stipulates that "[t]here shall be one hundred members of the house of representatives, provided, however, that commencing in 2003 there shall be seventy-five members of the house of representatives." **Article VIII, Of the Senate, section 1,** as amended in 1994, specifies: "The senate shall consist of the lieutenant governor and fifty members from the senatorial districts in the state, provided, however, that commencing in 2003 the senate shall consist of thirty-eight members from the senatorial districts in the state." According to **article IV, Of Elections and Campaign Finance, section 1,** as amended in 1992, senators and representatives "shall be elected . . . biennially in even numbered years, and shall severally hold their offices for two (2) years."

Article III, Of Qualifications for Office, sets forth the constitution's only qualifications for holding office, beginning with **section 1:** "No person shall hold any civil office unless that person be a qualified elector for such office." **Article II, Of Suffrage, section 1,** enfranchises "every citizen of the United States of the age of eighteen years or over who has had residence and home in this state for thirty days preceding the time of voting, who has resided thirty days in the town or city from which such citizen desires to vote, and whose name shall be registered at least thirty days next preceding the time of voting provided by law. . . ." Exceptions include anyone "who has been lawfully adjudicated to be non compos mentis" and certain felons.

Article VI, Of the Legislative Power, section 5, exempts legislators "from arrest and their estates from attachment in any civil action, during the session of the general assembly, and two days before [and after]. . . ."; furthermore, "[f]or any speech in debate in either house, no member shall be questioned in any other place." In *Holmes v. Farmer* (1984), the Rhode Island supreme court held that the "speech in debate" privilege applied even if meetings of legislators took place outside the statehouse and were not formal committee meetings.

Section 3 provides for the compensation of legislators, as well as health benefits, travel expenses, and pension benefits. **Section 4** prohibits legislators from taking a fee or being "of counsel in any case pending before either house of the general assembly. . . ."; punishment is "forfeiture of seat."

Section 6, allows each house to judge the elections and qualifications of its members and defines a quorum as a "majority," while **section 7** authorizes each house to "determine its rules of proceeding, punish contempts, punish its members for disorderly behavior, and, with the concurrence of two-thirds, expel a member. . . ."

Article VII, Of the House of Representatives, section 2, directs the house of representatives to elect a speaker, clerks, and other officers and specifies that "[t]he senior member from the City of Newport, if any be present, shall preside in the organization of the house." **Article VIII, Of the Senate, section 2,** as amended in 1994, states: "The lieutenant governor shall preside in the senate and in grand committee until 2003. Commencing in 2003, the senate shall elect its president, who shall preside in the senate and in grand committee, as well as its secretary and other officers from among its members and shall elect its clerks. The senior member from the city of Newport, if any be present, shall preside in the organization of the senate." **Section 3** provides for the election of an officer to preside in the senate in the absence of the lieutenant governor.

Article VI, Of the Legislative Power, section 11, requires concurrence of two-thirds of the members of each house for bills "appropriating the public money or property for local or private purposes." The New York constitution has a similar requirement. **Sections 12** through **14,** respectively, direct the legislature to provide by law for "making new valuations of property, for the assessment of taxes ..."; "the continuance in office of any officers ... until other persons are qualified to take their places"; and "the creation and control of corporations...." **Section 15** outlaws lotteries, with some exceptions. **Section 16** prohibits the legislature from incurring "state debts to an amount exceeding fifty thousand dollars," but **section 17** permits the state to borrow "in any fiscal year, in anticipation of receipts from taxes" up to "twenty percent of the receipts from taxes during the next prior fiscal year...." **Sections 18** through **21** enumerate other legislative powers. **Section 22** restricts the types of gambling permitted in the state.

Article IX, Of the Executive Power, section 1, as amended in 1992, vests the state's chief executive power in the governor, who "together with a lieutenant governor, shall be elected by the people," although on separate tickets. **Article IV, Of Elections and Campaign Finance, section 1,** as amended in 1992, mandates: "The governor, lieutenant governor, secretary of state, attorney-general, and general treasurer shall be elected on the Tuesday after the first Monday in November, quadrennially commencing AD 1994, and every four (4) years thereafter.... No person shall serve consecutively ... for more than two (2) full terms, excluding any partial term of less than two (2) years previously served."

Article III, Of Qualifications for Office, section 1, contains the only constitutional qualifications for holding any public office: "No person shall hold any civil office unless that person be a qualified elector of such office." The same provision applies to legislators.

Article IX, Of the Executive Power, section 2, directs the governor to "take care that the laws be faithfully executed." **Sections 3, 4,** and **5,** respectively, empower the governor to serve as "captain general and commander in chief" of the state's military and naval forces; grant reprieves, except in cases of impeachment, "until the end of the next session of the general assembly"; and fill vacancies in office "not otherwise provided for by this Constitution or by law, until the same shall be filled by the general assembly, or by the people." In *In re Advisory Opinion to Governor* (1997), the Rhode Island supreme court concluded that the governor's power to fill any vacancy was not mandatory. **Sections 6** and **7** authorize the governor to adjourn the legislature, if the two houses disagree on a time or place, and to convene it "on extraordinary occasions."

Section 13 grants to the governor, "by and with the advice and consent of the senate ... the pardoning power, except in cases of impeachment, to the same extent as such power is now exercised by the general assembly." **Section 15** directs the governor to "prepare and present to the general assembly an annual, consolidated operating and capital improvement state budget," although **section 16,** added by amendment in 1992, prohibits appropriations in excess of "ninety-eight percent (98%) of the estimated state general revenues for such fiscal year from all sources...."

Section 14 requires that "[e]very bill, resolution, or vote [with some exceptions] which shall have passed both houses of the general assembly shall be presented to the governor." If the governor does not approve it, it is returned with written objections to the house in which it originated. The governor's veto may be overridden by "three-fifths of the members present and voting in that house." This is a smaller majority for overriding a gubernatorial veto than required by the U.S. Constitution and most other state constitutions. New Mexico, for example, calls for two-thirds of the members present and voting in each house, while New York specifies two-thirds of the members elected to each house.

Section 12 states: "The duties and powers of the secretary, attorney-general and general treasurer shall be the same under this Constitution as are now established, or as from time to time may be prescribed by law."

Section 9, as amended in 1992, provides that if the office of governor becomes vacant "by reason of death, resignation, impeachment or inability to serve," the lieutenant governor succeeds to the office, exercising "the powers and authority appertaining thereto, until a governor is qualified to act, or until the office is filled at the next election." **Section 10,** also amended in 1992, designates the speaker of the house of representatives to serve as governor if the offices of both governor and lieutenant governor are vacant.

Judicial Branch

In the Rhode Island constitution, as in the constitutions of Massachusetts and Connecticut, the article dealing with the judiciary is relatively short.

Article X, Of the Judicial Power, section 1, declares: "The judicial power of this state shall be vested in one supreme court, and in such inferior courts as the general assembly may, from time to time, ordain and establish." As established by statute, the supreme court consists of "a chief justice and (4) associate justices."

Section 4, as amended in 1994, provides that supreme court justices are nominated by the governor from a list prepared by "an independent non-partisan judicial nominating commission" and appointed "by and with the advice and consent of the senate, and by and with the separate advice and consent of the house of representatives." **Section 5,** as amended in 1944, stipulates that "[j]ustices of the supreme court shall hold office during good behavior." **Section 6** prohibits reducing the compensation of supreme court justices while in office.

Section 2 defines a quorum as "[a] majority of its judges" and delineates the supreme court's jurisdiction: "The supreme court shall have final revisory and appellate jurisdiction upon all questions of law and equity. It shall have power to issue prerogative writs, and shall also have such other jurisdiction as may, from time to time, be prescribed by law.... The inferior courts shall have such jurisdiction as may, from time to time, be prescribed by law." In addition, **section 3** requires the supreme court justices to "give their written opinion upon any question of law whenever requested by the governor or by either house of the general assembly."

Article XI, Of Impeachments, section 1, as amended in 1994, grants the house of representatives "the sole power of impeachment." Impeachment requires a resolution "signed by one-quarter (¼) of the members," and impeachment of a governor requires "[a] vote of two-thirds (⅔) of the members." **Section 2** empowers the senate to try all impeachments, specifying concurrence of "two-thirds of the members elected" for conviction. According to **section 3,** the governor and all other executive and judicial officers are "liable to impeachment."

Article IV, Of Elections and Campaign Finance, section 1, provides in part: "The governor, lieutenant governor, secretary of state, attorney-general, and general treasurer shall be ... subject to recall as provided for herein.... Recall is authorized in the case of a general officer who has been indicted or informed against for a felony, convicted of a misdemeanor, or against whom a finding of probable cause of violation of the code of ethics has been made by the ethics commission. Recall shall not, however, be instituted at any time during the first six (6) months or the last year of an individual's term of office." Recall petition applications must be signed by "duly qualified electors equal to three percent (3%) of the total number of votes cast in the last preceding general election for that office." If the recall petition is signed by fifteen percent of those same voters within a ninety-day period, a special recall election is scheduled on the question of removing the office holder.

Article XIII, Home Rule for Cities and Towns, section 1, states: "It is the intention of this article to grant and confirm to the people of every city and town in this state the right of self-government in all local matters." Pursuant to **section 2,** "Every city and town shall have the power at any time to adopt a charter, amend its charter, enact and amend local laws relating to its property, affairs and government not inconsistent with this Constitution and laws enacted by the general assembly...." **Section 3** adds this proviso: "Notwithstanding anything contained in this article, every city and town shall have a legislative body composed of one or two branches elected by vote of its qualified electors."

Article VI, Of the Legislative Power, section 16, requires a balanced budget: "The general assembly shall have no powers, without the express consent of the people, to incur state debts to an amount exceeding fifty thousand dollars, except in time of war, or in case of insurrection or invasion; nor shall it in any case, without such consent, pledge the faith of the state for the payment of the obligations of others."

Article XII, Of Education, section 1, mandates: "The diffusion of knowledge, as well as of virtue among the people, being essential to the preservation of their rights and liberties, it shall be the duty of the general assembly to promote public schools and public libraries, and to adopt all means which it may deem necessary and proper to secure to the people the advantages and opportunities of education and public library services." In *City of Pawtucket v. Sundlun* (1995), the Rhode Island supreme court held that this section confers no fundamental and constitutional right to education, nor does it guarantee an "equal, adequate, and meaningful education."

Amendment Procedures

Article XIV, Constitutional Amendments and Revisions, section 1, states: "The general assembly may propose amendments to the Constitution of the state by a roll call vote of a majority of the members elected to each house." Proposed amendments are to be published and "submitted to the electors at the next general election"; if approved by "a majority of the electors voting thereon," they become a part of the constitution.

Section 2 authorizes the legislature "by a vote of a majority of the members elected to each house" to submit to the voters at any general election the question: "'Shall there be a convention to amend or revise the Constitution?'" If ten years pass without the question being submitted for a vote, "the secretary of state shall submit it at the next general election" thereafter. A bipartisan commission may be created to "assemble information on constitutional questions for the electors." The number of convention delegates must be the same as the number of members of the house of representatives, and any amendments or revisions adopted by the convention must be approved by "a majority of those voting thereon."

South Carolina became the eighth state of the United States on May 23, 1788. Columbia is the capital of the "Palmetto State," which ranks twenty-sixth among the states in population with approximately 3.7 million inhabitants. Some 32,008 square miles in area, South Carolina is bordered by North Carolina on the north, the Atlantic Ocean on the east and south, and Georgia on the south and west. The state's principal industries include tourism, agriculture, and manufacturing; its chief crops include tobacco, soybeans, and cotton.

Government: The governor and lieutenant governor are elected separately for four-year terms, and the governor is limited to two successive terms. The legislature, called the general assembly, consists of forty-six senators elected for four-year terms and 124 members of the house of representatives elected for two-year terms. The supreme court includes a chief justice and four associate justices elected jointly by the two branches of the legislature for ten-year terms.

Dates of Constitutions: 1776, 1778, 1790, 1861, 1865, 1868, and 1896

As early as 9000 B.C. humans were living in the region that would become the state of South Carolina, and by 1000 B.C. the inhabitants were farming and building mounds in the area. The complex Mississippian culture expanded eastward into the Carolina territory between A.D. 700 and 900. By the time the Spanish slaver Francisco Gordillo began cruising the Carolina coast in 1521 in search of stock for his trade, many indigenous peoples, including the Cherokees and Catawbas, inhabited the land.

In 1524 Giovanni da Verrazano, sailing under the French flag, explored the Carolina coast, and in 1525 a Spaniard, Pedro de Quexos, discovered Hilton Head Island. A Spanish settlement on Winyah Bay established the following year was abandoned after only a few months, however. Some forty years later a more permanent Spanish settlement was started on Hilton Head Island. The Carolina region was still relatively unsettled by Europeans when in 1629 Charles I of England granted much of the territory to his attorney general, Sir Robert Heath. Heath named the land Carolana in honor of Charles I, but the civil conflict between the king and Parliament thwarted his plans for development there.

Because of Heath's failure to develop the area, Charles II granted the same territory to eight "Lords Proprietors of Carolina" under a charter issued on March 24, 1663. One of the proprietors, Lord Shaftesbury, helped stimulate interest in the undertaking by having his secretary and physician, John Locke—later noted for his work *Two Treatises of Government* (1690)—draft the Fundamental Constitutions for the governance of the Carolina Colony in 1669. Although the document was never put into effect, some of its provisions, such as trial by jury and a prohibition against double jeopardy, found their way into the laws of South Carolina.

In 1693 the Carolina Colony was granted authority to initiate legislation subject to the veto of the proprietors. In 1712 the colony was split into northern and southern provinces, each with its own governor. The English Crown purchased the South Carolina territory from the proprietors in 1729, and in 1730 it became a royal colony of Great Britain. Originally content with their lot, South Carolinians became increasingly disgruntled after 1763, particularly because of taxes levied by Parliament on the North American colonies. In 1773, in retaliation, they attempted a limited boycott of imported

British goods, and in September 1774 five delegates from South Carolina were sent to the first Continental Congress in Philadelphia.

In January 1775 the colony organized its own provincial congress, and on June 4 a safety council was appointed to manage the affairs of government. The British royal government collapsed on September 15, and on March 26, 1776, the provincial congress adopted a hastily improvised constitution, which was not submitted to the voters for ratification. A second constitution, promulgated by the state's legislature on March 19, 1778, did not go into effect until November of that year. In addition to creating a more systematic structure of government, the new document severed the state's avowed association with the Anglican Church and adopted the principle of the separation of church and state.

A convention meeting in Columbia adopted a third constitution on June 3, 1790, again without seeking voter approval, and this constitution remained in force for seventy-one years. A convention called by the legislature in 1861 passed an ordinance of secession from the Union on April 8 of that year and amended the constitution to reflect the state's inclusion in the Confederacy. In September 1865 another convention repealed the ordinance and unilaterally adopted a new constitution. A convention meeting in Charleston pursuant to the Reconstruction Acts of Congress drafted a new document that was approved by the voters in April 1868.

South Carolina's seventh and current constitution was drafted by a convention that met in Columbia from September 10 to December 4, 1895. Again the convention promulgated the document, which went into force on January 1, 1896, without submitting it to the people for ratification.

The Constitution

The 1896 South Carolina constitution is similar to other state constitutions adopted in the latter part of the nineteenth century, particularly those of southern states, in that it diffuses power among a number of officials. For example, in addition to the governor, eight other executive branch officers are elected in the state as a whole. The constitution shows its age most strikingly in the retention of language prohibiting interracial marriage, despite the fact that the U.S. Supreme Court in 1967 abrogated it, and in its requirement that a person "who denies the existence of the Supreme Being" is ineligible for the office of governor or any other officer "under this Constitution." However, the provisions for a unified court system and a relatively independent judicial system (except for the archaic feature requiring members of the supreme court to be elected by the legislature for ten-year terms) reflect modern constitutional trends.

Relatively short in length, with approximately 22,500 words, the South Carolina constitution has been amended some 474 times as of January 1, 1998. Before 1981 approximately two-thirds of the amendments were of a local, rather than a statewide, nature. Since 1981 all the amendments have related to statewide concerns. Uniquely, the amendment provisions in the constitution require the legislature to vote on proposed amendments again after they have been approved by the voters.

Preamble

The untitled preamble to the 1896 South Carolina constitution reads: "We, the people of the state of South Carolina, in Convention assembled, grateful to God for our liberties, do ordain and establish this Constitution for the preservation and perpetuation of the same."

Article I, Declaration of Rights, section 1, declares: "All political power is vested in and derived from the people only, therefore, they have the right at all times to modify their form of government." **Section 2** states: "The General Assembly shall make no law respecting an establishment of religion or prohibiting the free exercise thereof, or abridging the freedom of speech or of the press; or the right of the people peaceably to assemble and to petition the government or any department thereof for a redress of grievances." Under **section 3,** "The privileges and immunities of citizens of this State and of the United States under this Constitution shall not be abridged, nor shall any person be deprived of life, liberty, or property without due process of law, nor shall any person be denied the equal protection of the laws." The "privileges and immunities of citizens" language, although found in the U.S. Constitution, is rare in state constitutions.

Section 4 prohibits bills of attainder, ex post facto laws, and laws impairing "the obligation of contracts," among other things. **Section 5** mandates: "All elections shall be free and open, and every inhabitant of this State possessing the qualifications provided for in this Constitution shall have an equal right to elect officers and be elected to fill public office." **Section 6,** an unusual provision, states: "Temporary absence from the State shall not forfeit a residence once obtained."

Section 7 limits the power to suspend the laws to the legislature or pursuant to its authority. **Section 9** provides: "All courts shall be public, and every person shall have speedy remedy therein for wrongs sustained." **Section 10** prohibits unreasonable searches and seizures, and **section 11** mandates in part: "No person may be held to answer for any crime the jurisdiction over which is not within the magistrate's court, unless on a presentment or indictment of a grand jury of the county where the crime has been committed, except in cases arising in the land or naval forces or in the militia when in actual service in time of war or public danger." **Section 12** prohibits double jeopardy.

Section 13 states: "Except as otherwise provided in this Constitution, private property shall not be taken for private use without the consent of the owner, nor for public use without just compensation being first made therefor." In *Moore v. Sumter County Council* (1990), the South Carolina supreme court held that a plaintiff who sought judicial relief for a taking of property must first exhaust all administrative remedies.

Section 14 guarantees "a speedy and public trial by an impartial jury" and the right "to be fully informed of the nature and cause of the accusation; to be confronted with the witnesses against [the accused]; to have compulsory process for obtaining witnesses in [favor of the accused], and to be fully heard in his defense by himself or by his counsel or by both." **Section 15** guarantees the right to bail, except in cases of "capital offenses or offenses punishable by life imprisonment"; prohibits excessive bail, excessive fines, cruel, corporal, or unusual punishment; and proscribes the unreasonable detention of witnesses.

Section 16 provides that in libel cases "the truth of the alleged libel may be given in evidence, and the jury shall be the judges of the law and facts." **Section 17** defines treason and the requirement for conviction of treason in language similar to that found in the U.S. Constitution. **Section 18** limits the suspension of the writ of habeas corpus; **section 19** prohibits imprisonment for debt "except in cases of fraud"; and **section 20** guarantees the right to bear arms, requires the consent of the legislature to maintain an army in peacetime, subordinates the military to civil authority, and restricts the quartering of soldiers in private homes.

Section 22 mandates: "No person shall be finally bound by a judicial or quasi-judicial decision of an administrative agency affecting private rights except on due notice and an opportunity to be heard; nor shall he be subject to the same person for both prosecution and adjudication; nor shall he be deprived of liberty or property unless by a mode of procedure prescribed by the General Assembly, and he shall have in all such instances the right to judicial review." An express manifesto ensuring fair treatment by administrative agencies of the government, such as this, is rare in state constitutions.

Section 23 states: "The provisions of the Constitution shall be taken, deemed, and construed to be mandatory and prohibitory, and not merely directory, except where expressly made directory or permissory by its own terms." In this provision the framers are basically saying that the constitution means what it says.

Article III, Legislative Department, section 33, declares: "The marriage of a white person with a negro or mulatto, or person who shall have one-eighth or more of negro blood, shall be unlawful and void." In *Loving v. Virginia* (1967), the U.S. Supreme Court found that state laws prohibiting marriage on the grounds of race violated the equal protection and due process clauses of the Fourteenth Amendment (1868) of the U.S. Constitution. Section 33 continues: "No unmarried woman shall legally consent to sexual intercourse who shall not have attained the age of fourteen years." It is unusual to find such statutory rape language in a constitution.

Division of Powers

Article I, Declaration of Rights, section 8, proclaims: "In the government of this State, the legislative, executive, and judicial powers of the government shall be forever separate and distinct from each other, and no person or persons exercising the functions of one of said departments shall assume or discharge the duties of any other." Most other state constitutions acknowledge that in a republican form of government, the functions of the three traditional branches of government may overlap to some degree. The governor's veto role in the legislative function, for example, is recognized as an exception to the separation of powers principle through typical language such as "except as otherwise provided in this constitution."

Legislative Branch

Article III, Legislative Department, section 1, declares: "The legislative power of this State shall be vested in two distinct branches, the one to be styled the Senate and the other the House of Representatives, and both together the General Assembly of the State of South Carolina." **Section 1A,** as amended in 1971, states: "The General Assembly ought frequently to assemble for the redress of grievances and for making new laws, as the common good may require."

Section 2 provides: "The House of Representatives shall be composed of members chosen by ballot every second year by citizens of this State, qualified as in this Constitution is provided." **Section 3** specifies in part: "The House of Representatives shall consist of one hundred and twenty-four members, to be apportioned among the several Counties according to the number of inhabitants contained in each. Each County shall constitute one election district. An enumeration of the inhabitants for this purpose shall be made in the year Nineteen hundred and One, and shall be made in the course of every tenth year thereafter, in such manner as shall be by law directed. . . ." **Section 5** stipulates: "No apportionment of Representatives shall take effect until the general election which shall succeed such apportionment."

Section 6 states: "The Senate shall be composed of one member from each County, to be elected for the term of four years by the qualified electors in each County, in the same manner in which members of the House of Representatives are chosen." Currently there are forty-six senators. **Section 7** directs: "No person shall be eligible for a seat in the Senate or House of Representatives who, at the time of his election, is not a duly qualified elector under this Constitution in the Senatorial District in regard to any particular seat as may be designated by the General Assembly, as to the Senate, and in the county, as to the House, in which he may be chosen." Senators must be at least twenty-five years old and representatives at least twenty-one years old. **Section 24** stipulates in part: "No person is eligible to a seat in the General Assembly while he holds any office or position of profit or trust under this State, the United States of America, or any of them, or under any other power, except officers in the militia, members of lawfully and regularly organized fire departments, constables, and notaries public."

Section 11 provides: "Each house shall judge of the election returns and qualifications of its own members, and a majority of each house shall constitute a quorum to do business; but a smaller number may adjourn from day to day, and may compel the attendance of absent members. . . ." Pursuant to **section 12,** "Each house shall choose its own officers, determine its rules of procedure, punish its members for disorderly behavior, and, with the concurrence of two-thirds, expel a member, but not a second time for the same cause." **Section 27** states: "Officers [of the legislature] shall be removed for incapacity, misconduct or neglect of duty, in such manner as may be provided by law, when no mode of trial or removal is provided in this Constitution."

Section 13 notes that each house may punish nonmembers for "disorderly or contemptuous behavior," threats made against members, and assault against members or witnesses. **Section 14** provides: "The members of both houses shall be protected in their persons and estates during their attendance on, going to and returning from the General Assembly, and ten days previous to the sitting and ten days after. . . ." An exception is made for "treason, felony, or breach of the peace."

Section 15 requires: "Bills for raising revenue shall originate in the House of Representatives, but may be altered, amended or rejected by the Senate. . . ." **Section 17** mandates: "Every Act or Resolution having the force of law shall relate to but one subject, and that shall be expressed in the title." **Section 18** directs: "No Bill or Joint Resolution shall have the force of law until it shall have been read three times and on three several days in each house, has had the Great Seal of the State affixed to it, and has been signed by the President of the Senate and the Speaker of the House of Representatives...." **Section 22** provides in part: "Any member of either house shall have liberty to dissent from and protest against any Act or resolution which he may think injurious to the public or to an individual...."

Section 28, as amended in 1981, directs the general assembly to "enact such laws as will exempt real and personal property of a debtor from attachment, levy and sale under any mesne [intermediate] or final process issued by any court or bankruptcy proceeding." Under **section 30,** "The General Assembly shall never grant extra compensation, fee or allowance to any public officer, agent, servant or contractor after service rendered, or contract made, nor authorize payment or part payment of any claim under any contract not authorized by law; but appropriations may be made for expenditures in repelling invasion, preventing or suppressing insurrection."

Section 31 mandates: "Lands belonging to or under the control of the State shall never be donated, directly or indirectly, to private corporations or individuals, or to railroad companies. Nor shall such lands be sold to corporations, or associations, for a less price than that for which it can be sold to individuals. This, however, shall not prevent the General Assembly from granting a right of way, not exceeding one hundred and fifty feet in width, as a mere easement to railroads across State land, nor to interfere with the discretion of the General Assembly in confirming the title to lands claimed to belong to the State, but used or possessed by other parties under adverse claim." **Section 35** directs: "It shall be the duty of the General Assembly to enact laws limiting the number of acres of land which any alien or any corporation controlled by aliens may own within this State."

Section 34 prohibits the legislature from enacting "local or special laws" concerning certain subjects, including changing the name of persons or places and authorizing the "adoption or legitimation" of children. **Section 34(IX)** provides: "In all other cases, where a general law can be made applicable, no special law shall be enacted ..." except in the case of compensation paid to county officers and the fees they collect.

Executive Branch

Article IV, Executive Department, section 1, declares: "The supreme executive authority of this State shall be vested in a Chief Magistrate, who shall be styled The Governor of the State of South Carolina." In *Stanley v. Darlington County School Dist.* (1995), the U.S. District Court held that the governor, as chief magistrate of the state with the duties to faithfully execute the laws of the state, was the proper defendant in a suit seeking injunctive relief from alleged segregation of schools. **Section 2** mandates: "No person shall be eligible to the office of Governor who denies the existence of the Supreme Being...." The governor must be thirty years old by the election and must have been a U.S. citizen and a citizen and resident of the state for five years before the election. Section 2 continues: "No person while Governor shall hold any office or other commission (except in the militia) under the authority of this State, or of any other power."

Section 3 states: "The Governor shall be elected by the qualified voters of the State at the regular election every other even-numbered year after 1970. No person shall be elected Governor for more than two successive terms." **Section 8** provides: "A Lieutenant Governor shall be chosen at the same time, in the same manner, continue in office for the same period, and be possessed of the same qualifications as the Governor," although they are elected on separate tickets. Pursuant to **section 10,** "The Lieutenant Governor shall be President of the Senate, *ex officio*, and while presiding in the Senate, shall have no vote, unless the Senate be equally divided." **Section 9** directs in part: "The Senate shall ... choose a President *Pro Tempore* to act in the absence of the Lieutenant Governor."

Sections 6, 11, and **12** address the issue of succession. **Section 6** states: "If the Governor-elect dies or declines to serve, the Lieutenant Governor-elect shall become Governor for a full term. If the Governor-elect fails to take the oath of office at the commencement of his term, the Lieutenant Governor shall act as Governor until the oath is administered." **Section 11** provides: "In the case of the removal of the Governor from office by impeachment, death, resignation, disqualification, disability, or removal from the State, the Lieutenant Governor shall be Governor. In case the Governor is impeached, the Lieutenant Governor shall act in his stead and have his powers until judgment [is] pronounced. In the case of the temporary disability of the Governor and in the event of the temporary absence of the Governor from the State, the Lieutenant Governor shall have full authority to act in an emergency." **Section 12** provides procedures for determining when the governor is unable to discharge his or her duties.

Section 13 declares that the governor "shall be Commander-in-Chief of the organized and unorganized militia of the State." **Section 14** provides: "With respect to clemency, the Governor shall have the power only to grant reprieves and to commute a sentence of death to that of life imprisonment. The granting of all other clemency shall be regulated and provided for by law." **Section 15** mandates: "The Governor shall take care that the laws be faithfully executed. To this end, the Attorney General shall assist and represent the Governor, but such power shall not be construed to authorize any action or proceeding against the General Assembly or the Supreme Court." This express requirement that the attorney general "assist and represent the Governor" is intended to avoid the difficulties that some other states, particularly New York, have had in coordinating the efforts of the governor and an elected attorney general in seeing that the laws are faithfully executed. In *State ex rel. McLeod v. McLeod* (1978), the South Carolina supreme court declared that section 15 did not preclude a complaint by the attorney general challenging the constitutionality of a statue passed by the general assembly.

Section 17 states: "All State officers, agencies, and institutions within the Executive Branch shall, when required by the Governor, give him information in writing upon any subject relating to the duties and functions of their respective offices, agencies, and institutions, including itemized accounts of receipts and disbursements." **Section 18** requires that the governor "shall, from time to time, give to the General Assembly information on the condition of the State and recommend for its consideration such measures as he shall deem necessary or expedient." **Section 19** provides in part: "The

Governor may on extraordinary occasions convene the General Assembly in extra session." **Section 20** states: "The Governor shall reside at the Capital of the State except in case of epidemics, natural disasters, or the emergencies of war; but during the sittings of the General Assembly he shall reside where its sessions are held."

Section 21 sets forth in part: "Every bill or joint resolution which shall have passed the General Assembly, except on a question of adjournment, shall, before it becomes a law, be presented to the Governor, and if he approves he shall sign it; if not, he shall return it, with his objections, to the house in which it originated...." The governor's veto may be overridden if "two-thirds of [each] house shall agree to pass" the bill again. Section 21 also grants the governor the power of the item veto with respect to "any bill appropriating money," which may be overridden in the same manner as any other bill. Section 21 continues: "If a bill or joint resolution shall not be returned by the Governor within five days after it shall have been presented to him, Sundays excepted, it shall have the same force and effect as if he had signed it, unless the General Assembly, by adjournment, prevents return, in which case it shall have such force and effect unless returned within two days after the next meeting."

Article VI, Officers, section 7, enumerates other elected state officers: "There shall be elected by the qualified voters of the State a Secretary of State, an Attorney General, a Treasurer, a Superintendent of Education, Comptroller General, Commissioner of Agriculture, and an Adjutant General who shall hold their respective offices for a term of four years, coterminous with that of the Governor. The duties ... of such offices shall be prescribed by law...."

Judicial Branch

Article V, The Judicial Department, section 1, declares: "The judicial power shall be vested in a unified judicial system, which shall include a Supreme Court, a Court of Appeals, a Circuit Court, and such other courts of uniform jurisdiction as may be provided for by general law." **Section 2** states: "The Supreme Court shall consist of a Chief Justice and four Associate Justices, any three of whom shall constitute a quorum for the transaction of business. The Chief Justice shall preside, and in his absence the senior Associate Justice. In all cases decided by the Supreme Court, the concurrence of three of the Justices shall be necessary for a reversal of the judgment below."

Section 3 provides in part: "The members of the Supreme Court shall be elected by a joint public vote of the General Assembly for a term of ten years ... and shall be classified so that the term of one of them shall expire every two years." **Section 4** states in part: "The Chief Justice of the Supreme Court shall be the administrative head of the unified judicial system. He shall appoint an administrator of the courts and such assistants as he deems necessary.... The Chief Justice shall set the terms of any court and shall have the power to assign any judge to sit in any court within the unified judicial system." Section 4 continues: "The Supreme Court shall make rules governing the administration of all the courts of the State. Subject to the statutory law, the Supreme Court shall make rules governing the practice and procedure in all such courts. The Supreme Court shall have jurisdiction over the admission to the practice of law and discipline of persons admitted." **Section 4A** provides: "All rules and amendments to rules governing practice and procedure in all courts of this State promulgated by the Supreme Court must be submitted ... to the Judiciary Committee of each House of the General Assembly during a regular session, but not later than the first day of February.... Such rules or amendments shall become effective ninety calendar days after submission unless disapproved by concurrent resolution of the General Assembly, with the concurrence of three-fifths of the members of each House present and voting."

Section 5 sets forth: "The Supreme Court shall have power to issue writs or orders of injunction, *mandamus*, *quo warranto*, prohibition, *certiorari*, *habeas corpus*, and other original and remedial writs. The Court shall have appellate jurisdiction only in cases of equity, and in such appeals they shall review the findings of fact as well as the law, except in cases where the facts are settled by a jury and the verdict not set aside. The Supreme Court shall constitute a court for the correction of errors at law under such regulations as the General Assembly may prescribe." **Sections 7** through **10** provide for a court of appeals, whose members are elected by the legislature for six-year terms.

Section 15 states: "No person shall be eligible to the office of Chief Justice, Associate Justice of the Supreme Court, judge of the Court of Appeals, or judge of the Circuit Court who is not at the time of his election a citizen of the United States and of this State, and has not attained the age of twenty-six years, has not been a licensed attorney at law for at least five years, and has not been a resident of this State for five years next preceding his election." **Section 17** grants the supreme court the power, after a hearing, "to remove or retire any judge ... upon a finding of disability seriously interfering with the performance of his duties...." **Section 19** provides in part: "The General Assembly shall specify the grounds for disqualification of Justices and Judges to sit on certain cases."

Article XV, Impeachment, section 1, states in part: "The House of Representatives alone shall have the power of impeachment in cases of serious crimes or serious misconduct in office by officials elected on a statewide basis, state judges, and such other state officers as may be designated by law. The affirmative vote of two-thirds of all members elected shall be required for an impeachment." **Section 2** provides in part: "All impeachments shall be tried by the Senate ... [and no] person shall be convicted except by a vote of two-thirds of all members elected." Conviction is limited to removal from office, and it does not bar "criminal prosecution and punishment according to law."

Article VIII, Local Government, section 7, states in part: "The General Assembly shall provide by general law for the structure, organization, powers, duties, functions, and the responsibilities of counties, including the power to tax different areas at different rates ... related to the nature and level of governmental services provided." **Section 11** authorizes the assembly to "provide by general law two or more optional procedures by which incorporated municipalities may select a charter commission for framing, publishing and adopting a municipal charter and making amendments thereto. Any municipality so eligible shall have the power to frame and amend a municipal charter setting forth its governmental structure and organization, powers, duties, functions, and responsibilities."

Impeachment

Local Government

Taxation and Finance

Article III, Legislative Department, section 29, provides that "[a]ll taxes upon property, real and personal, shall be laid upon the actual value of the property taxed, as the same shall be ascertained by an assessment made for the purpose of laying such tax."

Article X, Finance, Taxation and Bonded Debt, section 7(a), directs the general assembly to "provide by law for a budget process to insure that annual expenditures of State government may not exceed annual State revenue."

Education

Article XI, Public Education, section 1, directs in part: "There shall be a State Board of Education composed of one member from each of the judicial circuits of the State. The members shall be elected by the legislative delegations of the several counties within each circuit for terms and with such powers and duties as may be provided by law.... One additional member shall be appointed by the Governor." The members' terms and the powers and duties of the board are to be specified by law.

Health and Welfare/ Environment

Article XII, Functions of Government, section 1, declares: "The health, welfare, and safety of the lives and property of the people of this State and the conservation of its natural resources are matters of public concern. The General Assembly shall provide appropriate agencies to function in these areas of public concern and determine the activities, powers, and duties of such agencies."

Amendment Procedures

Article XVI, Amendment and Revision of the Constitution, section 1, provides in part: "Any amendment or amendments to this Constitution may be proposed in the Senate or House of Representatives.... If it is agreed to by two-thirds of the members elected to each House ... [the amendment] must be submitted to the qualified electors of the State at the next general election for Representatives. If a majority of the electors qualified to vote for [the legislature] voting on the question vote in favor of [it] and a majority of each branch of the next General Assembly ... ratify [it], [it becomes] part of the Constitution."

Section 3 permits the legislature, by a vote of "two-thirds of the members elected to each branch ... to call a Convention to revise, amend or change this Constitution...." The question is then put to the voters, and "if a majority of all the electors voting" vote for it, "the General Assembly shall, at its next session, provide by law for calling the same...."

On November 2, 1889, South Dakota became the fortieth state of the United States. Its capital is Pierre. The "Coyote State" or the "Mount Rushmore State" encompasses some 77,121 square miles and is bordered by North Dakota on the north, Minnesota and Iowa on the east, Nebraska on the south, and Wyoming and Montana on the west. With approximately 730,000 inhabitants, South Dakota ranks forty-fifth among the states in population. Its principal industries include agriculture, services, and manufacturing; corn, oats, wheat, and sunflowers are among its chief crops.

Government: The governor and lieutenant governor are elected jointly for four-year terms and are limited to two consecutive terms. The legislature consists of thirty-five senators and seventy members of the house of representatives, all elected for two-year terms and limited to four consecutive terms in each house. The supreme court includes a chief justice and four associate justices initially appointed by the governor for three years; they must stand for election after the first three years and every eighth year afterward.

Date of Constitution: 1889

On March 30, 1743, when the two sons of the French explorer Pierre Gaultier de Varennes, sieur de La Vérendrye, buried an inscribed lead marker noting their arrival near the site of Pierre in what would become the state of South Dakota, the inhabitants of the region included the Mandan, Hidatsa, and Sioux, or Dakota, peoples. French Canadians began entering the territory, and between 1804 and 1806 the expedition of the American explorers Meriwether Lewis and William Clark crossed the territory both on its way west and on its return. The fur trade became of economic importance to the new nation, and to protect its economic and strategic interests the U.S. government employed a special agent, Manuel Lisa, to keep the indigenous peoples from assisting the British during the War of 1812.

Fort Pierre, the first permanent settlement in South Dakota, was built by French Canadians in 1817, but when the fur trading boom ended in 1855, it was sold to the U.S. Army. Neighboring Minnesota became a state in 1854, and Nebraska followed suit in 1858, but the Dakota region's sparse population delayed efforts to set up a provisional government there. On March 2, 1861, however, President James Buchanan, in one of his last acts in office, approved a bill "to provide a temporary Government for the Territory of Dakota...."

Yankton became the capital of the Dakota Territory in 1862, and on April 29, 1868, the Fort Laramie Treaty created a reservation for Native Americans out of South Dakota lands west of the Missouri River. After Montana and Wyoming achieved territorial status in 1864 and 1868, respectively, the Dakota Territory was reduced to a more manageable size. The discovery of gold in the Black Hills on July 30, 1874, attracted many immigrants, increasing the nonindigenous population to around 10,000 by the spring of 1876.

In 1883 a draft constitution and petition for statehood on behalf of the southern portion of the remaining Dakota Territory was submitted to Congress, but it died in committee, as did another petition in 1885. Fearing the addition of four new senators aligned with the Republican Party, Democrats, who then controlled Congress, delayed statehood for both South and North Dakota. The Republicans returned to power in the 1889 session and passed an enabling act on February 22. On November 2, 1889, President Benjamin Harrison signed a proclamation admitting both South and North Dakota as states of the Union.

A convention meeting in Sioux Falls drafted a constitution on July 4, 1889. It was ratified by the voters on October 1 and went into effect on November 2, 1889, when South Dakota became a state.

The Constitution

The 1889 South Dakota constitution is a little under average length, containing approximately 25,000 words, and as of January 1, 1998, has been amended 103 times. The governor, lieutenant governor, and five other executive officers elected statewide are limited to two consecutive terms. South Dakota is one of twelve states that elect members of both houses of the legislature for two-year terms. Legislators are limited to four consecutive terms, and a constitutional provision attempts to limit the terms of the state's congressional delegation also. The justices and judges of the unified judicial system are initially appointed and then must stand for election to be retained in office.

In 1898, through an amendment allowing for popular initiative, South Dakota became the first state to adopt some procedures for direct democracy. Such provisions allow citizens to propose and approve laws outside the traditional legislative process of representative democracy and include popular initiative of new laws and constitutional amendments, the referendum for approval or rejection of laws enacted by the legislature, and recall of state officials. Within twenty years of South Dakota's amendment, approximately a dozen states had followed its example, and today thirty-three state constitutions contain some form of direct democracy procedures. In 1972 the South Dakota constitution was amended to allow constitutional changes by initiative, in addition to the right of initiative for statutory laws, and in 1998 an amendment authorizing local government initiatives was to be voted on by the people.

Preamble

The preamble to the 1889 South Dakota constitution reads: "*We, the people of South Dakota*, grateful to Almighty God for our civil and religious liberties, in order to form a more perfect and independent government, establish justice, insure tranquillity, provide for the common defense, promote the general welfare and preserve to ourselves and to our posterity the blessings of liberty, do ordain and establish this Constitution for the state of South Dakota." In 1976 a proposed amendment to the preamble to add the phrase "In order to provide for the health, safety and welfare of the people, maintain a representative and orderly government, eliminate poverty and inequality, assure legal, social and economic opportunity ..." was defeated by a vote of 183,458 to 75,174.

Fundamental Rights

In almost all state constitutions, the fundamental rights article precedes the articles concerning the three major branches of government. In the South Dakota constitution, however, it follows these.

Article VI, Bill of Rights, section 1, declares: "All men are born equally free and independent, and have certain inherent rights, among which are those of enjoying and defending life and liberty, or acquiring and protecting property and the pursuit of happiness. To secure these rights governments are instituted among men, deriving their just powers from the consent of the governed." This language is similar to that found in the Declaration of Independence. **Section 2** states: "No person shall be deprived of life, liberty or property without due process of law. The right of persons to work shall not be denied or abridged on account of membership or nonmembership in any labor union, or labor organization." A number of states have "right to work" laws, which in effect limit the power of organized labor to control the labor market, but this policy is generally not included in state constitutions.

Section 3 asserts the right to worship "according to the dictates of conscience"; however, "the liberty of conscience hereby secured shall not be so construed as to excuse licentiousness, the invasion of the rights of others, or justify practices inconsistent with the peace or safety of the state." **Section 4** secures the right of petition and of peaceable assembly; and **section 5** guarantees freedom of speech, noting that in "all trials for libel ... the truth, when published with good motives and for justifiable ends, shall be a sufficient defense." According to **section 6,** "The right of trial by jury shall remain inviolate and shall extend to all cases at law ... , but the Legislature may provide for a jury of less [than] twelve in any court not a court of record and for the decision of civil cases by three-fourths of the jury in any court."

Section 7 guarantees a person accused of crime certain rights, including "the right to defend in person and by counsel; to demand the nature and cause of the accusation against him ... and to a speedy public trial....." **Section 8** guarantees bail for persons accused of crimes "except for capital offenses when proof is evident or presumption great" and proscribes the suspension of the writ of habeas corpus "unless, when in case of rebellion or invasion, the public safety may require it." **Section 9** prohibits self-incrimination and double jeopardy. According to **section 10,** "No person shall be held for a criminal offense unless on the presentment or indictment of a grand jury, or information of the public prosecutor, except in cases of impeachment, in cases cognizable by county courts, by justices of the peace, and in cases arising in the army and navy, or in the militia when in actual service in time of war or public danger: provided, that the grand jury may be modified or abolished by law." **Section 11** prohibits unreasonable searches and seizures in language similar to that in the U.S. Constitution. In *State v. Wilson* (1982), however, the South Dakota supreme court held that "the fruit of the poison tree" doctrine (the concept that evidence illegally obtained is not admissible in court) did not require the exclusion of evidence obtained independent of an illegal search.

Section 12 prohibits ex post facto laws and laws impairing the obligation of contracts. **Section 13** guarantees just compensation for the taking of private property for public use or damage to such property, adding that "[n]o benefit which may accrue to the owner as the result of an improvement made by any private corporation shall be considered in fixing the compensation for property taken or damaged." **Sections 14** and **15,** respectively, prohibit distinctions between aliens and citizens with respect to property laws and imprisonment for "debt arising out of ... a contract." **Sections 16** through **24,** respectively, address subordination of military to civil power and the quartering of soldiers in homes; consent to and uniformity of taxation; equality of privileges granted to citizens;

free and equal elections; open courts and guarantee of a legal remedy for injuries; the suspension of laws by the legislature only; barring of attainder for treason and felony; excessive bail, fines, and cruel punishment; and the right to bear arms. **Section 25** defines treason in terms similar to those used in the U.S. Constitution.

Section 26 affirms that "[a]ll political power is inherent in the people ... ," who may "alter or reform their forms of government"; furthermore, "South Dakota is an inseparable part of the American Union and the Constitution of the United States is the supreme law of the land." **Section 27** declares: "The blessings of a free government can only be maintained by a firm adherence to justice, moderation, temperance, frugality and virtue and by frequent recurrence to fundamental principles."

Division of Powers

Article II, Division of the Powers of Government, states: "The powers of the government of the state are divided into three distinct departments, the legislative, executive and judicial; and the powers and duties of each are prescribed by this Constitution." In *Application of Nelson* (1968), the South Dakota supreme court held that the inclusion of a circuit judge on a mediation board "with quasi-judicial powers" violated the separation of powers provisions of the state's constitution.

Legislative Branch

Article III, Legislative Department, section 1, provides in part: "The legislative power of the state shall be vested in a Legislature which shall consist of a senate and house of representatives." Section 1 also declares the people's right to implement procedures for direct democracy. **Section 2** states that "the number of members of the house of representatives shall not be less than fifty nor more than seventy-five and the number of members of the senate shall not be less than twenty-five nor more than thirty-five." Currently the legislature has thirty-five senators and seventy representatives. **Section 6** provides in part: "The terms of office of members of the Legislature shall be two years; ... [n]o person may serve more than four consecutive terms or a total of eight consecutive years in the senate [or the house of representatives]. However, this restriction does not apply to partial terms to which a legislator may be appointed or to Legislative service before January 1, 1993." Section 6 also limits legislative sessions to forty days in odd-numbered years and thirty-five in even-numbered years.

Section 3 requires that, among other qualifications, a legislator must be a "qualified elector" of his or her district, a citizen of the United States, at least twenty-five years old, and a state resident for two years. **Section 4** states: "No person who has been, or hereafter shall be, convicted of bribery, perjury, or other infamous crime, nor any person who has been, or may be collector or holder of public moneys, who shall not have accounted for and paid over, according to law, all such moneys due from him, shall be eligible to the Legislature...."

Section 9 allows each house to judge the election and qualifications of its members; defines a quorum as "[a] majority of the members of each house," noting that "a smaller number may adjourn from day-to-day, and may compel the attendance of absent members in such a manner and under such penalty as each house may provide"; determine its own rules;

and choose its own officers and employees and "fix the pay thereof, except as otherwise provided in this Constitution." **Section 11** exempts legislators from arrest during and while traveling to and from legislative sessions "in all cases except treason, felony or breach of the peace"; moreover, "for words used in any speech or debate in either house, they shall not be questioned in any other place." **Section 12** provides in part: "No member of the Legislature shall, during the term for which he was elected, be appointed or elected to any civil office in the state which shall have been created, or the emoluments of which shall have been increased during [such] term...."

Section 17 mandates: "Every bill shall be read twice, by number and title once when introduced, and once upon final passage, but one reading at length may be demanded at any time before final passage." The constitutions of most other states require three readings. **Section 18** requires the vote of a majority of the members of each house of the legislature for a bill to be passed. **Section 19** provides: "The presiding officer of each house shall, in the presence of the house over which he presides, sign all bills and joint resolutions passed by the Legislature, after their titles have been publicly read immediately before signing...."

Section 20 states that bills may originate in either the senate or the house of representatives and that either house may amend bills passed by the other. **Section 21** limits each law to one subject, "which shall be expressed in its title." In *State v. Morgan* (1891), the South Dakota supreme court described the evils of legislation embracing more than one subject; and in *South Dakota Association of Tobacco and Candy Distributors v. State by and through Department of Revenue* (1979), the court described the diversity of subjects in one bill as having "no common basis except, perhaps, their separate inability to receive a favorable vote on their own merits."

Section 22 provides that "[n]o act shall take effect until ninety days after the adjournment of the session at which it passed, unless in case of emergency, (to be expressed in the preamble or body of the act) the Legislature shall by a vote of two-thirds of all the members elected of each house, otherwise direct." **Section 23** prohibits private and special laws in certain cases, such as granting divorces and authorizing people to keep ferries across streams wholly within the state, and directs: "In all other cases where a general law can be applicable no special law shall be enacted."

Article XXI, Miscellaneous, section 2, allows the legislature "by two-thirds vote of each branch thereof ... [to] fix the salary of any or all constitutional officers including members of the Legislature ... [and] determine the effective date thereof...." In general, state constitutions prohibit legislators from benefiting from pay raises during their own term in office, as does the Twenty-seventh Amendment (1992) to the U.S. Constitution.

Article III, Legislative Department, section 32, amended in 1992, mandates for the state's congressional delegation: "Commencing with the 1992 election, no person may be elected to more than two consecutive terms in the United States senate or more than six consecutive terms in the United States house of representatives." However, the U.S.

Supreme Court in *U.S. Term Limits, Inc. v. Thornton* (1995) invalidated a similar provision in the Arkansas constitution, explaining that state-imposed restrictions on congressional offices violate the concept that the people, not the states, have the right to choose representatives.

Executive Branch

Article IV, Executive Department, section 1, mandates: "The executive power of the state is vested in the Governor." **Section 2** requires that the governor and lieutenant governor be citizens of the United States and state residents for two years. They are jointly elected for four-year terms at "a general election held in a non-presidential election year"; in addition, "[c]ommencing with the 1974 general election, no person shall be elected to more than two consecutive terms as Governor or as lieutenant governor."

Section 3 outlines the governor's powers and duties, beginning: "The Governor shall be responsible for the faithful execution of the law. He may, by appropriate action or proceeding brought in the name of the state, enforce compliance with any constitutional or legislative mandate, or restrain violation of any constitutional or legislative power, duty or right by any officer, department or agency of the state or any of its civil divisions. This authority shall not authorize any action or proceedings against the Legislature." The governor serves as commander in chief of the state's military forces, except when in the service of the United States, and "may call them out to execute the laws, to preserve order, to suppress insurrection or to repel invasion." The governor also commissions all state officers and may require "information, in writing or otherwise, from the officers of any administrative department, office or agency upon any subject relating to the respective offices." Section 3 continues: "The Governor shall at the beginning of each session, and may at other times, give the Legislature information concerning the affairs of the state and recommend the measures he considers necessary." The governor may convene special sessions of the legislature or of either house and fill vacancies in offices by appointment. Except in impeachment cases, the governor may grant pardons and reprieves and suspend fines.

Article III, Legislative Department, section 10, directs the governor also to "make appointments to fill such vacancies as may occur in either house of the Legislature."

Article IV, Executive Department, section 4, provides in part: "Whenever the Legislature is in session, any bill presented to the Governor ... shall become law when the Governor signs the bill or fails to veto the bill within five days of presentation. A vetoed bill shall be returned by the Governor to the Legislature together with his objections...." The veto may be overridden by two-thirds of the members of each house. The governor has fifteen days to veto a bill if "the legislature has adjourned or recessed within five days from presentation" and may "strike any items of any bill passed by the Legislature making appropriations...." An item veto may be overridden in the same manner "as is prescribed for the passage of bills over the executive veto." Section 4 also states that "[b]ills with errors in style or form may be returned to the Legislature by the Governor with specific recommendations for change." Such alterations may be approved by the legislature by a majority vote of the members of each house.

Section 5 describes the lieutenant governor's role: "The lieutenant governor shall be president of the senate but shall have no vote unless the senators be equally divided. The lieutenant governor shall perform the duties and exercise the powers that may be delegated to him by the Governor." The constitutions of a number of other states, including Florida and Utah, permit the lieutenant governor's duties to be defined by law as well as by the governor. **Section 6** provides that the lieutenant governor becomes governor in the case of the governor's "death, resignation, failure to qualify, conviction after impeachment or permanent disability." The lieutenant governor also performs the duties of the governor during the governor's "continuous absence from the state, or other temporary disability."

Section 7 establishes additional elected statewide officials—an attorney general, a secretary of state, an auditor, a treasurer, and a commissioner of school and public lands—who are elected for four-year terms and limited to two consecutive terms in office. **Section 8** limits the principal executive departments, not including those of statewide elected officials, to no more than twenty-five and authorizes the governor to reorganize executive offices, requiring that the legislature be given an opportunity to "disapprove [such reorganization] by a resolution concurred in by a majority of all the members of either house." According to **section 9**, "Each principal department shall be under the supervision of the Governor and, unless otherwise provided in this Constitution or by law, shall be headed by a single executive ... , [who], unless provided otherwise by the Constitution, shall be nominated and, by and with the advice and consent of the senate, appointed by the Governor ..." to hold office as long as the governor does, "unless sooner removed by the Governor."

Article V, Judicial Department, section 1, vests the state's judicial power in "a unified judicial system consisting of a Supreme Court, circuit courts of general jurisdiction and courts of limited jurisdiction as established by the Legislature." **Section 2** states: "The Supreme Court is the highest court of the state. It consists of a chief justice and four associate justices. Upon request by the Supreme Court the Legislature may increase the number of justices to seven. All justices shall be selected from compact districts established by the Legislature, and each district shall have one justice."

Judicial Branch

Section 6 requires that supreme court justices, circuit court judges, and "persons presiding over courts of limited jurisdiction" be citizens of the United States, state residents, and voting residents of their district, circuit, or jurisdiction. "No Supreme Court justice," it adds, "shall be deemed to have lost his voting residence in a district by reason of his removal to the seat of government in the discharge of his official duties." Supreme court justices and circuit court judges must be licensed to practice law in South Dakota.

Section 7 provides in part that vacancies on South Dakota's supreme court and its circuit courts are filled by appointment by the governor from a list of people nominated by a judicial qualifications commission. The appointment of a supreme court justice "shall be subject to approval or rejection ... on a nonpolitical ballot at the first general election following the expiration of three years from the date of his appointment." Afterward, each Supreme Court justice "shall be subject to approval or rejection in like manner every eighth year."

Section 8 provides that the chief justice be selected from among the supreme court justices "for a term and in a manner to be provided by law," noting that he or she may resign from the office without resigning from the court. **Section 11** states in part: "The chief justice is the administrative head of the unified judicial system."

Section 5 outlines the court's jurisdiction: "The Supreme Court shall have such appellate jurisdiction as may be provided by the Legislature, and the Supreme Court or any justice thereof may issue any original or remedial writ which shall then be heard and determined by that court. The Governor has authority to require opinions of the Supreme Court upon important questions of law involved in the exercise of his executive power and upon solemn occasions." And, according to **section 12**, "The Supreme Court shall have general superintending powers over all courts and may make rules of practice and procedure and rules governing the administration of all courts. The Supreme Court by rule shall govern terms of courts, admission to the bar, and discipline of members of the bar. These rules may be changed by the Legislature."

Impeachment

Article XVI, Impeachment and Removal from Office, section 1, delegates to the house of representatives "the sole power of impeachment." Impeachment requires the concurrence of a majority of all members. **Section 2** provides in part: "All impeachments shall be tried by the senate.... No person shall be convicted without the concurrence of two-thirds of the members elected."

Direct Democracy

Article III, Legislative Department, section 1, provides in part: "[T]he people expressly reserve to themselves the right to propose measures, which shall be submitted to a vote of the electors of the state, and also the right to require that any laws which the Legislature may have enacted shall be submitted to a vote of the electors of the state before going into effect, except such laws as may be necessary for the immediate preservation of the public peace, health or safety, support of the state government and its existing public institutions. Not more than five per cent of the qualified electors of the state shall be required to invoke either the initiative or the referendum."

Local Government

Article IX, Local Government, section 1, grants to the legislature "plenary powers to organize and classify units of local government, except that any proposed change in county boundaries shall be submitted to the voters of each affected county at an election and be approved by a majority of those voting thereon in each county." **Section 2** states in part: "Any county or city or combinations thereof may provide for the adoption or amendment of a [home rule] charter.... Powers and functions of home rule units shall be construed liberally."

Taxation and Finance

Article XI, Revenue and Finance, section 1, states in part: "The legislature shall provide for an annual tax, sufficient to defray the estimated ordinary expenses of the state for each year, not to exceed in any one year two mills on each dollar of the assessed valuation of all taxable property in the state, to be ascertained by the last assessment made for state and county purposes. And whenever it shall appear that such ordinary expenses shall exceed the income of the state for such year, the Legislature shall provide for levying a tax for the ensuing year, sufficient, with other sources of income, to pay the deficiency of the preceding year, together with the estimated expenses of such ensuing year."

Article VIII, Education and School Lands, section 1, acknowledging that "[t]he stability of a republican form of government [depends] on the morality and intelligence of the people," directs the legislature "to establish and maintain a general and uniform system of public schools wherein tuition shall be without charge, and equally open to all; and to adopt all suitable means to secure to the people the advantages and opportunities of education."

Education

Article XXII, Compact with the United States, begins: "The following article shall be irrevocable without the consent of the United States and the people of the state of South Dakota expressed by their legislative assembly: **First.** The perfect toleration of religious sentiment shall be secured, and that no inhabitant of this state shall ever be molested in person or property on account of his or her mode of religious worship. **Second.** That we, the people inhabiting the state of South Dakota, do agree and declare that we forever disclaim all right and title to the unappropriated public lands lying within the boundary of South Dakota, and to all lands lying within said limits owned or held by any Indian or Indian tribes...."

Compact with the United States

Article XXIII, Amendments and Revisions of the Constitution, section 1, as amended in 1972, provides in part: "Amendments to this Constitution may be proposed by initiative or by a majority vote of all members of each house of the Legislature. An amendment proposed by initiative shall require a petition signed by qualified voters equal in number to at least ten percent of the total votes cast for Governor in the last gubernatorial election. The petition containing the text of the proposed amendment and the names and addresses of its sponsors shall be filed at least one year before the next general election at which the proposed amendment is submitted to the voters."

Amendment Procedures

Section 2, as amended in 1972, states: "A convention to revise this Constitution may be called by a three-fourths vote of all the members of each house ... [or the calling] may be initiated and submitted to the voters in the same manner as an amendment. If a majority of the voters voting thereon approve the calling of a convention, the Legislature shall provide for the holding thereof.... Proposed amendments or revisions approved by a majority of all the members of the convention shall be submitted to the electorate at a special election in a manner to be determined by the convention."

Section 3, as amended in 1972, provides: "Any constitutional amendment or revision must be submitted to the voters and shall become a part of the Constitution only when approved by a majority of the votes cast thereon. The Legislature may provide for the withdrawal by its sponsors of an initiated amendment at any time prior to its submission to the voters."

TENNESSEE

Tennessee became the sixteenth state of the United States on June 1, 1796. Nashville is the capital of the "Volunteer State." Some 42,146 square miles in area, Tennessee shares with Missouri the distinction of bordering the greatest number of states (eight): Kentucky and Virginia on the north; North Carolina on the east; Georgia, Alabama, and Mississippi on the south; and Arkansas and Missouri on the west. With approximately 5.3 million inhabitants, Tennessee ranks seventeenth among the states in population. Its principal industries include manufacturing, trade, and services; its chief crops are tobacco, cotton, and soybeans.

General Information

Government: The governor is elected for a four-year term and is limited to two consecutive terms. There is no lieutenant governor. The legislature, called the general assembly, consists of thirty-three senators elected for four-year terms (one-half every two years) and ninety-nine members of the house of representatives elected for two-year terms. The supreme court is composed of a chief justice and four additional judges elected for eight-year terms.

Dates of Constitutions: 1796, 1835, and 1870

Constitutional History

The Creek and Yuchi peoples had long lived in the region that would become the state of Tennessee when, in 1540, Spanish marauders attacked their villages, and the Cherokees would settle there in the early eighteenth century. In 1673 Virginia traders hired James Needham to explore the eastern Tennessee territory, but he was killed by the local inhabitants. In 1682 Robert Cavelier, sieur de La Salle, claimed the region for France and built Fort Prud'homme.

The British emerged as the dominant regional power as a result of a treaty with the Cherokees in 1730, negotiated by Sir Alexander Cuming, and France's transfer of its rights in Tennessee following the French and Indian War (1754–63). In 1772 a group of farms on the Nolichucky River called the Watauga Settlement formed the Watauga Association to provide a basic framework of government. Three years later the Wataugans revised their constitution to provide for a thirteen-member committee of safety with authority to exercise military power. Also in 1775, through the Treaty of Sycamore Shoals, land speculators of the Transylvania Company purchased 20 million acres, including parts of Tennessee and Kentucky, from the Cherokees.

In 1776, at the request of the Watauga settlers, North Carolina annexed the Tennessee territory. After the American Revolution, with settlements now extending to the Cumberland River, the settlers proclaimed themselves a separate state and promulgated a constitution for the state of Franklin. Congress, however, refused to grant the self-proclaimed admission to the Union.

Following ratification of the U.S. Constitution, North Carolina ceded its western lands to the United States, and on May 26, 1790, President George Washington signed the Act for the Government of the Territory of the United States, South of the River Ohio. The population of the territory increased rapidly, and in preparation for statehood a constitutional convention was assembled on January 11, 1796, in Knoxville, then the territorial capital. The 1796 Tennessee constitution, which Thomas Jefferson declared the "least imperfect and most republican" of its time, was adopted by the convention but not submitted to the people for approval. It went into effect when Tennessee was admitted to the Union on June 1, 1796.

Jefferson's admiration notwithstanding, the 1796 document had a number of defects, including the lack of a provision for an independent judicial branch, and these led to a new convention that met in Nashville from May 19 to August 30, 1834. The convention's efforts were ratified at the polls on March 5 and 6, 1835. The new document expressly included the principle of the separation of powers and established the judiciary as an independent branch of government.

During the Civil War, Tennessee quickly fell to Union troops, and on March 3, 1862, President Abraham Lincoln appointed Andrew Johnson, later his running mate and successor as president, to be military governor of the state. Troop engagements late in the war caused a constitutional convention in Nashville to be postponed until January 8, 1865. Eager to reestablish civil government in Tennessee, the convention of mostly federal soldiers drafted two amendments, one aimed at abolishing slavery and involuntary servitude, the other a schedule that contained several substantive constitutional changes. A select pro-Union electorate approved the proposal at the polls by a vote of 21,104 to 40.

In January 1870 another constitutional convention was called in Nashville. Its avowed purpose was to restore majority rule, which had been infringed by the 1865 changes to the constitution restricting suffrage. The convention, called the greatest intellectual body ever assembled in the state for any purpose, finished its work in February 1870, and the new constitution was approved by the voters on March 26, 1870. It went into effect on May 5 of that year.

The Constitution

The 1870 Tennessee constitution remained unamended until 1953, and as of January 1, 1998, has been altered only thirty-two times, the fewest number of amendments for any state constitution in effect for such a long period of time. In 1953 the extreme difficulty of the amendment process was eased somewhat; legislative pay, which had been frozen since 1870 at $4 per each day of a session, was raised; and the governor's term was extended from two to four years. An overhaul of the judicial branch, however, was defeated by the voters in 1978, leaving the attorney general's position under the judiciary. The governor is the only statewide elected official; other executive officers, including the secretary of state, treasurer, and comptroller, are chosen by the legislature.

Tennessee served as a focal point for the great reapportionment undertaking in the states set in motion by the U.S. Supreme Court's 1962 decision in *Baker v. Carr*. The Tennessee legislature had not reapportioned the voting districts as required by the state's constitution, despite years of changes in the population of those districts. The U.S. Supreme Court, holding that the federal courts have jurisdiction over state reapportionment, remanded the case to the district court for further proceedings, which ultimately resulted in the "one man, one vote" rule announced in *Reynolds v. Sims* (1964) and enforced in similar cases throughout the states under the U.S. Constitution's equal protection clause and Fourteenth Amendment (1868).

Preamble

The preamble to the 1870 Tennessee constitution reads in part: "Whereas, The people of the state, in the mode provided . . . , have called [a] convention, and elected delegates to represent them therein; now therefore, We, the delegates and representatives of the people of the state of Tennessee, duly elected, and in convention assembled, . . . have ordained and established the following Constitution and form of government for this state, which we recommend to the people of Tennessee for their ratification...."

Fundamental Rights

Article I, Declaration of Rights, section 1, declares that "all power is inherent in the people, and all free governments are founded on their authority, and instituted for their peace, safety, and happiness; for the advancement of those ends they have at all times, an unalienable and indefeasible right to alter, reform, or abolish the government in such manner as they may think proper." **Section 2** states that "government being instituted for the common benefit, the doctrine of nonresistance against arbitrary power and oppression is absurd, slavish, and destructive of the good and happiness of mankind." The constitution of New Hampshire contains similar language.

Section 3 provides in part: "[A]ll men have a natural and indefeasible right to worship Almighty God according to the dictates of their own conscience...." **Section 4** mandates that "no political or religious test, other than an oath to support the Constitution of the United States and of this state, shall ever be required as a qualification to any office or public trust under this state." Under **section 5,** "The elections shall be free and equal, and the right of suffrage, as hereinafter declared, shall never be denied to any person entitled thereto, except upon a conviction by a jury of some infamous crime...." **Section 6** guarantees the right of trial by jury; **section 7** prohibits unreasonable searches and seizures; and **section 8** declares that "no man shall be taken or imprisoned, or disseized of his freehold, liberties or privileges, or outlawed, or exiled, or in any manner destroyed or deprived of his life, liberty or property, but by the judgment of his peers, or the law of the land." This last sentence is based on language in Magna Carta, the 1215 English constitutional document.

Section 9 guarantees certain rights to the accused in criminal prosecutions. **Sections 10** through **13,** respectively, prohibit double jeopardy, ex post facto laws, corruption of the blood or forfeiture of estate, and "unnecessary rigor" in the treatment of persons "arrested and confined in jail." **Section 14** requires "presentment, indictment or impeachment" for criminal charges; **section 15** guarantees bail "unless for capital offences, when the proof is evident, or the presumption great"; **section 16** prohibits excessive bail and fines and "cruel and unusual punishments"; and **section 17** directs in part that "all courts shall be open; and every man, for an injury done him in his lands, goods, person or reputation, shall have remedy by due course of law...."

Section 18 states: "The Legislature shall pass no law authorizing imprisonment for debt in civil cases." **Section 19** guarantees freedom of the press and communication of thoughts and opinions; **section 20** prohibits "retrospective law, or law impairing the obligations of contracts"; **section 21** ensures just compensation for the taking of private property or use of personal services; **section 23** affirms the right of peaceable assembly; **section 24,** among other things, subordinates the military to civil authority; and **section 25** limits the use of martial and military law. **Section 26** guarantees the right to bear arms but notes that "the Legislature shall have power, by law, to regulate the wearing of arms with a view to prevent crime." **Section 28** states that "no citizen of this state [shall] be compelled to bear arms, provided he will pay an equivalent, to be ascertained by law."

Section 29 provides in part: "[A]n equal participation in the free navigation of the Mississippi is one of the inherent rights of the citizens of this state...." Section 30 prohibits "hereditary emoluments, privileges, or honors," and section 31 defines the boundaries of the state. Section 32 requires "the erection of safe and comfortable prisons"; section 33 prohibits slavery and involuntary servitude, "except as a punishment for crime"; and, to emphasize the extent of these prohibitions, section 34 mandates: "The General Assembly shall make no law recognizing the right of property in man."

Article II, Distribution of Powers, section 1, declares: "The powers of the Government shall be divided into three distinct departments: legislative, executive, and judicial." Section 2 notes: "No person or persons belonging to one of these departments shall exercise any of the powers properly belonging to either of the others, except in the cases herein directed or permitted." Courts generally hold that the separation of powers doctrine expressed here precludes the delegation of the legislature's lawmaking power. However, in *Metropolitan Development and Housing Agency v. Leech* (1979), the Tennessee supreme court found that the legislature may delegate the power to implement law but not the power to say what the law is.

Division of Powers

The Tennessee constitution's provisions covering the legislative branch do not constitute a separate article but are contained in article II.

Legislative Branch

Article II, Legislative Department, section 3, specifies: "The legislative authority of this state shall be vested in a General Assembly, which shall consist of a Senate and House of Representatives, both dependent on the people." Representatives serve two-year terms, and senators serve four-year terms. The speaker of the senate and the speaker of the house of representatives, however, hold office for two years or until their successors are elected and qualified, "provided however, that in the first general election ... senators elected in districts designated by even numbers shall be elected for four years [and the others shall be elected for two years]...."

Section 5 provides: "The number of representatives shall be ninety-nine ..."; and section 6 states: "The number of senators shall ... not exceed one-third the number of representatives." Currently there are thirty-three senators. Section 9 requires that a representative "be a citizen of the United States, of the age of twenty-one years, and shall have been a citizen of this state for three years, and a resident in the county he represents one year, immediately preceding the election." Section 10 requires that a senator "be a citizen of the United States, of the age of thirty years, and shall have resided three years in this state, and one year in the county or district, immediately preceding the election." Section 10 also prohibits a legislator from holding other offices "except [that] of trustee of a literary institution."

Section 11 directs: "The Senate and House of Representatives, when assembled, shall each choose a speaker and its other officers; be judges of the qualifications and election of its members, and sit upon its own adjournments from day to day. Not less than two-thirds of all the members to which each House shall be entitled shall constitute a quorum to do business; but a smaller number may adjourn from day to day, and may be authorized, by law, to compel the attendance of absent members." The constitutions of most other states require only a majority of the members elected to make up a quorum. **Section 12** provides: "Each House may determine the rules of its proceedings, punish its members for disorderly behavior, and, with the concurrence of two-thirds, expel a member, but not a second time for the same offense; and shall have all other powers necessary for a branch of the Legislature of a free state."

Section 13 states that "[s]enators and representatives shall, in all cases, except treason, felony, or breach of the peace, be privileged from arrest during the session of the General Assembly, and in going to and returning from the same; and for any speech or debate in either House, they shall not be questioned in any other place." **Section 14** provides: "Each House may punish, by imprisonment, during its session, any person not a member, who shall be guilty of disrespect to the House, by any disorderly or any contemptuous behavior in its presence." **Section 22** orders: "The doors of each House and of committees of the whole shall be kept open, unless when the business shall be such as ought to be kept secret."

Section 17 addresses the passage of legislation: "Bills may originate in either House; but may be amended, altered or rejected by the other. No bill shall become law which embraces more than one subject, that subject to be expressed in the title. All acts which repeal, revive or amend former laws, shall recite in their caption, or otherwise, the title or substance of the law repealed, revived or amended." **Section 18** stipulates: "A bill shall become law when it has been considered and passed on three different days in each House and on third and final consideration has received the assent of a majority of all the members to which each House is entitled under this Constitution, when the respective speakers have signed the bill ... , and when the bill has been approved by the governor or otherwise passed under the provisions of this Constitution." According to **section 19,** "After a bill has been rejected, no bill containing the same substance shall be passed into a law during the same session." **Section 27** allows "[a]ny member of either House of the General Assembly ... liberty to dissent from and protest against, any act or resolve which he may think injurious to the public or to any individual, and to have the reasons for his dissent entered on the journals."

Executive Branch

Article III, Executive Department, section 1, declares: "The supreme executive power of this state shall be vested in a governor." **Section 3** requires that the governor "shall be at least thirty years of age, shall be a citizen of the United States, and shall have been a citizen of this state seven years next before his election." **Section 4** provides that the governor "shall be elected to hold office for four years and until a successor is elected and qualified" and shall be ineligible for election "to more than two terms consecutively, including an election to a partial term." Under **section 13,** "No member of Congress, or person holding any office under the United States, or this state, shall execute the office of governor."

Section 5 mandates that the governor "shall be commander-in-chief of the Army and Navy of this state, and of the Militia, except when they shall be called into the service of the United States. But the Militia shall not be called into service except in case of rebellion or invasion, and then only when the General Assembly shall declare, by law, that the public safety requires it." **Section 6** gives to the governor "power to grant reprieves and pardons, after conviction, except in cases of impeachment." **Sections 8** through **11**, respectively, provide that the governor may require written information from the officers in the executive department on subjects relating to their respective offices; convene the general assembly on extraordinary occasions by proclamation; see that the laws are faithfully executed; and periodically give to the general assembly information as to the state of the government and recommend certain measures for its consideration.

Section 12 stipulates in part: "In case of the removal of the governor from office, or of his death, or resignation, the powers and duties of the office shall devolve on the speaker of the Senate." The speaker of the house of representatives is next in the line of succession. **Section 14** directs: "When any officer, the right of whose appointment is by this Constitution vested in the General Assembly, shall, during the recess [of the legislature], die, or the office, by the expiration of the term, or by other means, become vacant, the governor shall have the power to fill such vacancy [temporarily]...."

Section 17 indicates: "A secretary of state shall be appointed by joint vote of the General Assembly [for] the term of four years, [and] he shall keep a fair register of all the official acts and proceedings of the governor ... [and] such other duties as shall be enjoined by law." In addition, **article VII, State and County Officers, section 3,** provides: "There shall be a treasurer or treasurers and a comptroller of the treasury appointed for the state, by the joint vote of both Houses of the General Assembly who shall hold their offices for two years." The attorney general for the state is appointed by the supreme court.

Article III, Executive Department, section 18, states in part: "Every bill which may pass both Houses of the General Assembly shall, before it becomes a law, be presented to the governor for his signature. If he approve, he shall sign it, and the same shall become a law; but if he refuse to sign it, he shall return it with his objections thereto, in writing, to the House in which it originated." The governor's veto may be overridden if a majority of the members of both the house and the senate approve the bill. Section 18 continues: "If the governor shall fail to return any bill with his objections in writing within ten calendar days (Sundays excepted) after it shall have been presented to him, the same shall become a law without his signature. If the General Assembly ... prevents [its] return ... the bill shall become a law, unless ... filed by [the governor] ... in the office of the secretary of state within said ten-day period." Every joint resolution or order, except those regarding adjournment and proposals of specific amendments to the constitution, is presented to the governor for signature; if vetoed, the veto may be overridden as in the case of a bill. The governor "may reduce or disapprove the sum of money appropriated by any one or more items or parts of items in any bill appropriating money ... ," and the governor's veto in such cases may also be overridden in the same manner as in the case of bills.

Article VI, Judicial Department, section 1, vests judicial power "in one Supreme Court and in such Circuit, Chancery and other Inferior Courts as the Legislature shall from time to time, ordain and establish; in the judges thereof, and in justices of the peace." In *Tennessee v. Davis* (1879), the U.S. Supreme Court ruled that Congress has the power

Judicial Branch

to enact legislation that allows for the removal of a criminal case involving a federal officer from the courts of any state to prevent the obstruction of the actions of federal functionaries. Section 1 continues: "The Legislature may also vest such jurisdiction in Corporation Courts as may be deemed necessary."

Section 2 specifies that "[t]he Supreme Court shall consist of five judges, of whom not more than two shall reside in any one of the grand divisions of the state." The constitutions of a number of states, including Nebraska, also divide the state into districts for the selection of supreme court members. "The judges shall designate one of their own number who shall preside as chief justice," section 2 continues. "The concurrence of three of the judges shall in every case be necessary to a decision. The jurisdiction of this court shall be appellate only, under such restrictions and regulations as may from time to time be prescribed by law; but it may possess such other jurisdiction as is now conferred by law. . . ." **Section 3** states: "The Judges of the Supreme Court shall be elected by the qualified voters of the state. The Legislature shall have power to prescribe such rules as may be necessary to carry out the provisions of section two of this article. Every judge of the Supreme Court shall be thirty-five years of age, and shall before his election, have been a resident of the state for five years. His term of service shall be eight years."

Section 5 provides in part: "An attorney general and reporter for the state, shall be appointed by the judges of the Supreme Court and shall hold his office for a term of eight years." **Section 11** mandates in part: "No judge of the Supreme or Inferior Courts shall preside on the trial of any cause in the event of which he may be interested, or where either of the parties shall be connected with him by affinity or consanguinity, within such degrees as may be prescribed by law, or in which he may have been of counsel, or in which he may have presided in any Inferior Court, except by consent of all the parties."

Section 6 states in part: "Judges and attorneys for the state may be removed from office by a concurrent vote of both Houses of the General Assembly, each House voting separately; but two-thirds of the members to which each House may be entitled must concur in such vote. . . . The judge or attorney for the state, against whom the Legislature may be about to proceed, shall receive notice thereof accompanied with a copy of the causes alleged for his removal, at least ten days before the day on which either House . . . shall act thereupon."

Impeachment

Article V, Impeachments, section 1, declares: "The House of Representatives shall have the sole power of impeachment." According to **section 2,** "All impeachments shall be tried by the Senate. . . . No person shall be convicted without the concurrence of two-thirds of the senators sworn to try the officer impeached." **Section 3** directs that the house of representatives "shall elect from their own body three members, whose duty it shall be to prosecute impeachments. No impeachment shall be tried until the Legislature shall have adjourned *sine die*, when the Senate shall proceed to try such impeachment."

Section 4 provides in part: "The governor, judges of the Supreme Court, judges of the inferior courts, chancellors, attorneys for the state, treasurer, comptroller, and secretary of state, shall be liable to impeachment ... [for] any crime in their official capacity which may require disqualification but judgment shall only extend to removal from office, and disqualification to fill any office thereafter. The party shall, nevertheless, be liable to ... [other] punishment according to law."

Article VII, State and County Officers, section 1, states in part: "The General Assembly may provide alternate forms of county government including the right to charter and the manner by which a referendum may be called. The new form of government shall replace the existing form if approved by a majority of the voters in the referendum."

Article II, Legislative Department, section 24, added in 1978, provides in part: "Expenditures for any fiscal year shall not exceed the state's revenues and reserves, including the proceeds of any debt obligation, for that year. No debt obligation, except as shall be repaid within the fiscal year of issuance, shall be authorized for the current operation of any state service or program...." **Section 28** sets forth in part: "[A]ll property real, personal or mixed shall be subject to taxation, but the Legislature may except such as may be held by the state, by counties, cities or towns, and used exclusively for public or corporation purposes, and such as may be held and used for purposes purely religious, charitable, scientific, literary or educational, and shall except ... the entire amount of money deposited in an individual's personal or family checking or savings accounts." In *Tusculum College v. State Board of Equalization* (1980), the Tennessee supreme court found that the leasing of property by a charity with the rent going to charitable purposes does not qualify for the charitable tax exemption provided in this section.

Article XI, Miscellaneous Provisions, section 3, states: "Any amendment or amendments to this Constitution may be proposed in the Senate or House of Representatives...." If approved by a majority of the members of both houses, the proposed amendment is referred to the next general assembly. If approved by two-thirds of the members of both houses, it is then submitted to the people at the next general election for governor. Any amendment ratified by a majority of the citizens voting for governor "shall become a part of this Constitution."

Section 3 continues in part: "The Legislature shall have the right by law to submit to the people, at any general election, the question of calling a convention to alter, reform, or abolish this Constitution" or any part thereof. If a majority of the voters voting approve of calling a convention, the delegates are to be chosen at the general election. A proposal drafted by the convention "shall become effective ... [if] approved and ratified by a majority of the qualified voters voting separately on such change or amendment at an election to be held in such manner and on such date as may be fixed by the convention. No such convention shall be held oftener than once in six years."

Article II, Legislative Department, section 32, provides: "No convention or General Assembly of this state shall act upon any amendment of the Constitution of the United States proposed by Congress to the several states; unless such [body] shall have been elected after such amendment is submitted."

TEXAS

Texas became the twenty-eighth state of the United States on December 29, 1845. The capital of the "Lone Star State" is Austin. The second largest state in size, with some 268,601 square miles, Texas is bordered by Oklahoma on the north, Arkansas on the northeast, Louisiana and the Gulf of Mexico on the east, Mexico on the southwest, and New Mexico on the west. Texas ranks second among the states in population with approximately 19 million residents. Its major industries include trade, oil and gas extraction, and manufacturing; its chief crops are cotton, grains, vegetables, and fruits.

General Information

Government: The governor and lieutenant governor are elected separately for four-year terms. The legislature consists of thirty-one senators elected for four-year terms (one-half every two years) and 150 members of the house of representatives elected for two-year terms. The supreme court is composed of a chief justice and eight additional justices, all of whom are elected for six-year terms.

Dates of Constitutions: 1845, 1861, 1866, 1869, and 1876

Constitutional History

The great expanse of land that would become the state of Texas was originally inhabited by paleo-Americans who possibly belonged to a Caucasoid race. A thousand years before Christopher Columbus, the Tonkawas and Hasinai, descendants of Asian invaders who crossed the Bering land bridge more than twenty thousand years earlier, settled in the region. Their term *tayshas* (allies or friends) was written in Spanish as *tejas* and later became the name Texas. The first European in Texas was Alonzo Alvarez de Piñeda, who sailed into the mouth of the Rio Grande in 1519 while searching for a passage to the Pacific.

Six years after being shipwrecked on the Texas coast, Alvar Nuñez Abeza de Vaca returned to Mexico in 1535 with rumors of "gold, antimony, and iron" to the north. Spurred on by the Spanish successes in Peru and Mexico, in 1541 Francisco Vásquez de Coronado led an expedition northward through desolate territory, reaching a small and valueless Zuñi pueblo on the upper Rio Grande on July 7. In the wake of a number of unsuccessful expeditions, Spain abandoned any attempts to colonize the Texas plain for the next century and a half.

In 1685 Robert Cavelier, sieur de La Salle, and his French expedition landed on the Texas coast, where he built a wooden stockade that he named Fort St. Louis. The French incursion renewed Spain's interest in the Texas territory, but by 1730 it had established only a few missions and three small settlements: San Antonio, Goliad, and Nacogdoches. The Texas territory became a province of the Republic of Mexico when it won its independence from Spain in 1821. Mexico adopted a national constitution in 1824, and in 1827 a separate constitution was drafted for the combined Mexican province of Coahuila and Texas.

American adventurers known as filibusters (from the French *flibustier*, meaning "freebooter") soon began filtering into the Texas territory. At first Mexico encouraged American settlers by granting them colonization contracts, and an American colony grew up around Austin. However, the democratic newcomers chafed under the rigid Spanish law, derived from Roman law, and in 1826 Hayden Edwards attempted to establish an autonomous republic called Fredonia. Frightened by this turn of events, the Mexican government revoked Edwards's colonization contract.

Mexico reversed its immigration policy in 1830, and when an early American colonizer, Stephen Austin, proposed a regional constitution in 1833, he was arrested. In retaliation the American colonizers drafted a new provisional constitution for the autonomous state of Texas in November 1835. After Americans known as "Volunteers for Texas," led by Sam Houston, Jim Bowie, and others, seized San Antonio, the Mexican army attacked. Americans declared Texas independent on March 2, 1836, and four days later the massacre at the Alamo mission occurred.

In March 1836, the Americans held a convention in the town of Washington on the Brazos River and adopted a new constitution incorporating elements from the U.S. Constitution and state constitutions and making Texas an independent unitary republic. Continual fighting with Mexico led Texans to request annexation by the United States as a prelude to statehood. The area was annexed on March 1, 1845, and Texans ratified the state's first constitution on October 13. Texas was admitted to the Union on December 29.

Just sixteen years later, on February 1, 1861, a "people's convention" held in Austin passed an ordinance of secession from the Union that was ratified by popular vote; however, the constitutional changes adopted were not presented to the voters. After the Civil War, a new constitution drafted by a convention in Austin was approved by the people on June 25, 1866. Although the document failed to approve the Thirteenth Amendment (1865) to the U.S. Constitution, abolishing slavery, blacks were guaranteed personal safety and protection of their property. A convention required by the Reconstruction Acts of Congress met in Austin in 1868 and produced a fourth state constitution, which voters approved in December 1869.

The current Texas constitution was drafted by a convention meeting in Austin from September 6 to November 24, 1875. Ratified at the polls, the new constitution went into effect on February 15, 1876.

The Constitution

Texas's 1876 constitution is typical of southern state constitutions, which evolved in response to changes after the Civil War. For example, Texas adopted its 1866 constitution in order to rejoin the Union, its 1869 document to appease radical Republican Reconstructionists, and its current constitution in 1876 to restore white supremacy and the Democratic Party's control over a limited state government. The framers looked to the 1875 Missouri and the 1873 Pennsylvania constitutions for guidance.

Southern state constitutions such as Texas's serve two purposes: they formally acknowledge the supremacy of the U.S. Constitution, and they attempt to diffuse the power of the state as a means of moderating conflicts between the established pre–Civil War oligarchy and other political factions typically found in southern states. Such documents are not highly venerated and must be frequently amended—the Texas constitution has some 377 amendments as of January 1, 1998—because the power of government authorities is so fragmented and circumscribed. In a light turnout on November 4, 1975, however, voters rejected by a margin of 73 to 27 percent a proposed revision of the constitution consisting of eight amendments, which, among other things, would have reduced the number of articles from seventeen to eleven and the number of words from 80,800 to 17,700.

Preamble

The short preamble reads: "Humbly invoking the blessings of Almighty God, the people of the State of Texas, do ordain and establish this constitution."

Fundamental Rights

Article 1, Bill of Rights, begins: "That the general, great and essential principles of liberty and free government may be recognized and established, we declare: **Section 1.** ... Texas is a free and independent State, subject only to the Constitution of the United States, and the maintenance of our free institutions and the perpetuity of the Union depend upon the preservation of the right of local self-government, unimpaired to all the States." **Section 2** declares, in part, that "[a]ll political power is inherent in the people" and that "Texas stands pledged to the preservation of the republican form of government...." In *Brown v. City of Galveston* (1903), the Texas supreme court, in reference to section 2, commented that "it does not mean that political power is inherent in a part of the people of the state, but in the body, who have a right to control by proper legislation the entire State and all its parts."

Section 3a, which was added in 1972, mandates: "Equality under the law shall not be denied or abridged because of sex, race, color, creed, or national origin." **Sections 4, 5,** and **6,** respectively, prohibit religious tests for public office, disqualification of witnesses "for want of any religious belief," and "preference ... by law to any religious society or mode of worship." **Section 7** bars appropriations for sectarian purposes.

Sections 8 and **9** guarantee freedom of speech and the press and prohibit unreasonable searches and seizures. **Sections 10** through **15** outline rights of the accused. **Section 15a,** added in 1956, provides in part: "No person shall be committed as a person of unsound mind except on competent medical or psychiatric testimony." **Section 19** reads: "No citizen of the State shall be deprived of life, liberty, property, privileges or immunities, or in any manner disfranchised, except by the due course of the law of the land." The phrase *due course of law,* like *due process of law,* is equivalent to *law of the land* as derived from the English Magna Carta of 1215. **Sections 23** and **24** cover the right to bear arms and the subordination of the military to civil authority. Under the constitution's **article 16, General Provisions, section 47,** "any person who conscientiously scruples to bear arms, shall not be compelled to do so, but shall pay an equivalent for personal service."

Article I, Bill of Rights, section 27, addresses the right to assemble and petition for the redress of grievances. **Section 29** proclaims: "To guard against transgressions of the high powers herein delegated, we declare that everything in this 'Bill of Rights' is excepted out of the general powers of government, and shall forever remain inviolate, and all laws to the contrary thereto, or to the following provisions shall be void." While obviously intended to emphasize the importance of the fundamental rights expressed in the constitution, section 29 may appear to be superfluous language, but in *Traveler's Ins. Co. v. Marshall* (1934) the Texas supreme court used section 29 to underscore the more restrictive nature of a provision of the state constitution when compared with the same provision of the federal constitution.

Section 30, added in 1989, extends rights to victims of crime.

Division of Powers

Article 2, The Powers of Government, section 1, divides the government's powers "into three distinct departments": the legislative, executive, and judicial. The separation of powers in the Texas constitution is derived from both Anglo-American and Mexican influences; the concept appeared in both the 1824 Mexican constitution and the 1827 constitution of Coahuila and Texas. The use of the term *departments* has been carried over from the Texas constitution of 1836, written before statehood.

Article 3, Legislative Department, section 1, vests legislative power in a senate and a house of representatives, "which together shall be styled 'The Legislature of the State of Texas.'" **Section 2** sets the senate membership at thirty-one, which "shall never be increased above this number." The number of house members was initially ninety-three but limited to 150, the current number. **Section 3,** as amended in 1966, requires senators to "be chosen by the qualified electors for a term of four years" with one-half elected every two years; and **section 4** specifies two-year terms for representatives. According to **sections 6** and **7,** members of the legislature must be citizens of the United States and qualified electors. A senator must have been a resident of the state for five years preceding the election and for "the last year thereof a resident of the district for which he shall be chosen"; a representative must have been resident in the state two years preceding the election and for "the last year thereof a resident of the district for which he shall be chosen."

Section 5, as amended in 1930, provides: "The legislature shall meet every two years at such time as may be provided by law and at other times when convened by the Governor." In *Walker v. Baker* (1946), the Texas supreme court, by a five-to-four margin, held that the legislature could not convene itself in a special session. Section 5 also states that the first thirty days of a regular session "shall be devoted to the introduction of bills and resolutions, acting on emergency appropriations," confirming recess appointments, and emergency matters submitted by the governor.

Section 9, as amended in 1984, authorizes the senate to elect a president pro tempore to act as presiding officer in the absence of the lieutenant governor and the house to elect a speaker from among its members. **Section 10** defines a quorum as two-thirds of each house. Some states, including Oregon, also require a supermajority for a quorum, while others, like Louisiana, require only a majority of the members.

Sections 29 through **41,** under the general heading Proceedings, detail the passage of legislation. Only bills may result in laws. A bill may originate in either house, except for those raising revenue, which must come from the house, and may be amended, altered, or rejected by the other house. A bill must be read on three days in each house. Once defeated, no bill containing the same substance may be passed into law during the same session. A bill is considered only after it has been first referred to a committee and reported on. With regard to revenue bills originating in the house, the Texas supreme court declared in *Smith v. Davis* (1968) that this language does not extend to bills for other purposes that incidentally create revenue.

Section 23a, which requires an appropriation to pay the claims of the John Tarleton Agricultural College, was added in 1946 without designation as to article or section number, for reasons that are unclear today. Article 3 covers a wide range of other topics, from bond issues and student loans to assistance for local fire departments.

Article 4, Executive Department, section 1, as amended in 1995, states: "The Executive Department of the State shall consist of a Governor, who shall be the Chief Executive Officer of the State, a Lieutenant Governor, Secretary of State, Comptroller of Public Accounts, Commissioner of the General Land Office, and Attorney General." An unnumbered "Temporary Provision," which was inserted after section 1 and which expired on September 1, 1997, provided for the transition of the power and duties of the office of treasurer, which was abolished on September 1, 1996. **Section 2** requires that "[a]ll the above officers of the Executive Department (except the Secretary of State) shall be elected by the qualified voters of the State at the time and places of election of the members of the legislature."

Section 3 prescribes the procedures for handling the election returns of the executive officers. According to **section 3a,** added in 1948, in the event that the candidate for governor with the highest number of votes dies, "the person having the highest number of votes for lieutenant governor shall act as Governor until the next general election." **Section 4,** as amended in 1972, requires the governor to be "at least thirty years of age, a citizen of the United States," and a resident of the state "at least five years immediately preceding his election" for a term of four years.

Section 7 designates the governor as "Commander-in-Chief of the military forces of the state, except when they are called into actual service of the United States." **Section 8** authorizes the governor to convene the legislature "on extraordinary occasions." Under **section 14,** the governor has the power to veto legislation, or "items of appropriation," but the veto may be overridden by a vote of "two-thirds of the members present" in the house in which the bill originated and "by two-thirds of the members" of the other house. **Section 15** requires that "[e]very order, resolution or vote" in which both houses concur, except in the case of questions of adjournment, "shall be presented to the Governor," who may veto it. The legislature may override the veto in the same manner as for a bill.

Section 11, as amended in 1936, 1983, and 1989, gives the governor the power, except in cases of treason and impeachment, to grant reprieves, commutations, and pardons after conviction based on the recommendation of a board of parole and pardons. In *Ex parte Miers* (1933), the Texas court of criminal appeals suggested that where the governor's power was limited to clemency after conviction, the legislature may be free to exercise this power at other times—for example, in passing laws to provide immunity from prosecution for witnesses. The governor is authorized to grant clemency in the case of treason "[w]ith the advice and consent of the Legislature."

Section 16 mandates that there be "a Lieutenant Governor, who shall be chosen at every election for Governor, by the same electors, in the same manner, continue in office for the same time, and possess the same qualifications. The electors shall distinguish for whom they vote as governor and for whom as Lieutenant Governor." Like Texas, eighteen states permit the governor and lieutenant governor to run on separate tickets, which may result in their being of different political parties. Other states, such as Alaska and Maryland, for example, require them to run on the same ticket. The lieutenant governor of Texas is designated to "exercise the powers and authority appertaining to the office of the Governor" in the event of the "death, resignation, removal from office, inability or refusal of the Governor to serve, or ... his impeachment or absence from the State."

Sections 21 and **22,** as amended in 1936 and 1954 and in 1936, 1954, and 1972, respectively, outline the duties of the secretary of state, who is appointed by the governor with the advice and consent of the senate, and those of the elected attorney general. **Section 23,** as amended in 1936, 1954, 1972, and 1995, covers the comptroller of public accounts, the commissioner of the general land office, and other elected state officers authorized by statute.

Article 5, Judicial Department, section 1, as amended in 1891, 1977, and 1980, declares: "The judicial power of this State shall be vested in one Supreme Court, in one Court of Criminal Appeals, in Courts of Appeal, in District Courts, in County Courts, in Courts of Justices of the Peace, and in such other courts as may be provided by law." An analogous section of Florida's constitution promotes a unified court system with its statement, "No other courts may be established by the state...." The Texas legislature, however, is expressly given the power to "establish such other courts as it may deem necessary...."

Section 2, as amended in 1891, 1945, and 1980, provides that the "Supreme Court shall consist of the Chief Justice and eight Justices, any five of whom shall constitute a quorum, and the concurrence of five shall be necessary to a decision of a case...." Justices must be licensed to practice law in the state at the time of election, must be citizens of the United States and of Texas, must be not less than thirty-five years of age, and must have been "a practicing lawyer, or a lawyer and judge of a court of record together at least ten years." The justices are elected for six-year terms, three every two years. The governor is authorized to fill vacancies until the next general election.

Section 3, as amended in 1891, 1930, and 1980, defines the state supreme court's jurisdiction as "final, except in criminal law matters." **Section 4,** as amended in 1891, 1966, and 1977, creates a court of criminal appeals, consisting of eight judges and one presiding judge elected for six-year terms, whose "determinations shall be final, in all criminal cases of whatever grade...." The neighboring state of Oklahoma also has a separate court of last resort in criminal cases. **Sections 6** and **7,** as amended three times each between 1891 and 1985, divide the state into courts of appeals districts and judicial districts.

Section 1a, added in 1948 and amended in 1965, 1970, 1977, and 1984, addresses retirement, censure, removal, and compensation of justices and judges and replaces the state judicial qualifications commission with a state commission on judicial conduct. By an affirmative vote of at least six of the commission's eleven members, it may recommend retirement, censure, suspension, or removal of any "Justice or Judge of the courts established by this Constitution or created by the Legislature" pursuant to section 1. As outlined by the Texas supreme court in *Matter of Carrillo* (1976), judges may be removed in four ways: by impeachment; by action of the supreme court on recommendation of the judicial qualifications commission; by the governor if directed to do so by two-thirds of each house of the legislature; and, in the case of district court judges only, by the supreme court's action on charges filed by lawyers practicing before the judge whose removal is being sought.

Impeachment

Article 15, Impeachment, section 1, states: "The power of impeachment shall be vested in the House of Representatives." **Section 2,** as amended in 1995, specifies: "Impeachment of the Governor, Lieutenant Governor, Attorney General, Commissioner of the General Land Office, Comptroller and the Judges of the Supreme Court, Court of Appeals and District Court shall be tried by the Senate." According to **section 3,** impeachment is sustained by a two-thirds vote of the senators present. **Section 4** limits the results of impeachment to removal from office and disqualification from holding public office, although the person convicted is subject to prosecution under the law.

Local Government

Article 9, Counties, section 1, gives the legislature the power, with some limits, "to create counties for the convenience of the people." **Article 11, Municipal Corporations, section 5,** as amended in 1909, 1912, and 1991, authorizes cities with more than 5,000 inhabitants to "adopt or amend their charters" by a majority vote of the qualified voters in that city.

Taxation and Finance

Article 8, Taxation and Revenue, section 1(a), as amended in 1978 and 1987, declares: "Taxation shall be equal and uniform." **Section 10** denies the legislature the "power to release the inhabitants of, or property in, any county, city or town from payment of taxes levied for State or county purposes, unless in case of great public calamity ... [and] by the vote of two-thirds of each House of the Legislature."

Article 3, Legislative Department, section 49, as amended in 1992, requires a balanced budget: "**(a)** No debt shall be created by or on behalf of the State, except: **(1)** to supply casual deficiencies of revenue, not to exceed in the aggregate at any one time two hundred thousand dollars; **(2)** to repel invasion, suppress insurrection, or defend the State in war ..." or as otherwise authorized by the constitution through special elections in which the voters approve the creation of limited state debt.

Education

Article 7, Education, The Public Free Schools, section 1, proclaims: "A general diffusion of knowledge being essential to the preservation of the liberties and rights of the people, it shall be the duty of the legislature of the State to establish and make suitable provision for the support and maintenance of an efficient system of public free schools." The Texas supreme court cited this section in its opinion in *Edgewood Independent School District v. Kirby* (1989), which declared that the Texas school financing system was unconstitutional. The supreme courts of other states, including Kentucky, New Jersey, and Washington, have invalidated school finance programs under education articles.

Section 10 mandates the establishment of the University of Texas, stating in part: "The legislature shall as soon as practicable establish, organize and provide for the maintenance, support and direction of a University of the first class...."

Health and Welfare

Article 3, Legislative Department, section 51-a, added in 1945 and amended seven times between 1954 and 1982, in part authorizes the legislature to provide "for assistance grants to needy dependent children and the caretakers of such children, needy persons who are totally and permanently disabled because of a mental or physical handicap, needy aged persons and needy blind persons."

Article 8, Taxation and Revenue, section 1(d)1, added in 1978 and amended in 1995, directs the legislature to promote the preservation of open-space land by providing "by general law for taxation of open-space land devoted to farm, ranch, or wildlife management purposes...." **Section 1(f)**, added in 1977, authorizes the legislature to "provide for the preservation of cultural, historical, or natural resources by: (1) granting exemptions or other relief from state ad valorem taxes on appropriate property ... and (2) authorizing political subdivisions to grant exemptions from ad valorem taxes on appropriate property...."

Article 16, section 22, authorizes the legislature "to pass such fence laws ... as may be needed to meet the wants of the people," while **section 39** gives it power "from time to time, [to] make appropriations for preserving and perpetuating memorials of the history of Texas, by means of monuments, statues, paintings and documents of historical value."

Article 17, Mode of Amending the Constitution of This State, section 1, as amended in 1972, authorizes the legislature "by a vote of two-thirds of all the members elected to each House" to "propose amendments revising the Constitution, to be voted on by the qualified electors ... [and the] date of the elections shall be specified by the Legislature." Provision is made for public notice of proposed amendments and the dates of the elections. An amendment "shall become a part of" the constitution if "it appears from the returns that a majority of the votes cast have been in favor of [the] amendment."

Section 2, added in 1972, directed the legislature to establish a constitutional revision commission to recommend changes to the legislature by November 1, 1973. The members of the legislature were then to convene as a constitutional convention to adopt a new state constitution by a two-thirds vote and submit it to the voters. The constitutional convention that was convened to act on the commission's proposals adjourned on July 30, 1974, after failing to approve any changes to the constitution. The legislature subsequently approved a simplified version, which the voters rejected on November 4, 1975.

UTAH

Utah was admitted to the Union on January 4, 1896, as the forty-fifth state. Salt Lake City is the capital of the "Beehive State," which encompasses 84,904 square miles and is bordered by Idaho and Wyoming on the north, Colorado on the east, Arizona on the south, and Nevada on the west. Utah ranks thirty-fourth among the states with a population of approximately 2 million inhabitants. Services, trade, manufacturing, and government are among the state's chief sources of economic activity; its chief crops include hay, corn, wheat, barley, and apples.

General Information

Government: The governor and lieutenant governor are elected jointly for four-year terms and are limited by statute to twelve consecutive years in office. The legislature consists of twenty-nine senators elected for four-year terms, one-half every two years, and seventy-five members of the house of representatives elected for two-year terms, all of whom are similarly restricted by statute to serving twelve consecutive years. The supreme court comprises a chief justice and four additional justices initially appointed by the governor from a list submitted by a judicial nominating commission with the consent of the senate; they must stand for election after the first three years and every ten years thereafter.

Constitutional History

Date of Constitution: 1896

Ute, Southern Paiute, and Navajo peoples inhabited the land that would become the state of Utah when the Franciscans Silvestre Velez de Escalante and Francisco Atanasio Domínguez passed through the region in 1776 searching for an overland route from New Mexico to California. According to Escalante, the peoples of the Utah and Colorado region spoke dialects of the same language and were commonly known as Yutas. The word *Utah* has been traced to the White Mountain Apache word *yuttahih* (one who lives on the mountain tops), referring to the Navajos.

Trappers such as Kit Carson from Taos, New Mexico, and Jim Bridger from St. Louis, Missouri, began entering the Utah territory in the first quarter of the nineteenth century, and in 1824 Bridger discovered the Great Salt Lake, which he at first believed to be part of the Pacific Ocean. Between 1843 and 1845 Captain John C. Frémont led U.S. Army expeditions through the area. And beginning in 1845, because of persecution in Illinois, the leaders of the Church of Jesus Christ of Latter-day Saints, or Mormons, undertook a migration to the Great Basin, which includes the western part of Utah. Calling the region Deseret, the Land of the Honey Bee, the Mormons formed a government with a constitution in 1849.

Under the terms of the Treaty of Guadalupe Hidalgo, which ended the Mexican War in 1848, the United States had acquired title to the entire Southwest from Mexico, and by an act dated September 9, 1850, Congress established the Utah Territory, which also contained parts of Colorado, Nevada, and Wyoming. In 1852 polygamy was declared an official tenet of the Mormon religion, leading the federal government to replace Brigham Young, the Mormon leader, as governor five years later. A petition to Congress for statehood, accompanied by a draft constitution, was turned down in 1860.

Congress enacted legislation prohibiting polygamy and revoking the Mormon Church's corporate status in 1862 and later disenfranchised some 12,000 polygamists. A constitution drafted in 1872 in support of Utah's admission as a state was also rejected by Congress. In 1890 the president of the Mormon Church, Wilford Woodruff, rescinded the doctrine of plural marriages, and an act enabling "the people of Utah to form a constitution and State government, and to be admitted into the Union on an equal footing with the original States" was approved on July 16, 1894. A convention meeting in Salt Lake City from March 4 to May 8, 1895, drafted a new constitution, which was ratified at the polls on November 5, 1895. It went into effect on January 4, 1896, when Utah became a state.

The 1896 Utah constitution, which contains approximately 11,000 words, is a relatively short document and, as of January 1, 1998, has been amended ninety times. The constitution creates a typical state government with a plural or divided executive branch, although the document expressly invests the governor with "[t]he executive power of the state" rather than "supreme executive power" as in most other constitutions of this type. Also typical of a number of state constitutions is the stipulation that the supreme court justices and other judges are initially appointed by the governor with the approval of the senate but then must stand for election to be retained in office.

Article XII, Corporations, section 20, an unusual provision added to the constitution in 1993, declares: "It is the policy of the state that a free market system shall govern trade and commerce in this state to promote the dispersion of economic and political power and the welfare of the people." Whether this policy actually accomplishes its objectives remains to be seen.

The preamble to the 1896 Utah constitution reads: "Grateful to Almighty God for life and liberty, we, the people of Utah, in order to secure and perpetuate the principles of free government, do ordain and establish this CONSTITUTION."

Preamble

Article I, Declaration of Rights, section 1, proclaims: "All men have the inherent and inalienable right to enjoy and defend their lives and liberties; to acquire, possess and protect property; to worship according to the dictates of their consciences; to assemble peaceably, protest against wrongs, and petition for redress of grievances; to communicate freely their thoughts and opinions, being responsible for the abuse of that right." **Section 2** affirms that "[a]ll political power is inherent in the people; and all free governments are founded on their authority for their equal protection and benefit, and they have the right to alter or reform their government as the public welfare may require." According to **section 3,** "The State of Utah is an inseparable part of the Federal Union and the Constitution of the United States is the supreme law of the land."

Fundamental Rights

Section 4 declares: "The rights of conscience shall never be infringed. The State shall make no law respecting an establishment of religion or prohibiting the free exercise thereof...." **Section 5** limits the suspension of the writ of habeas corpus; **section 6,** as amended in 1985, guarantees the right to bear arms, with certain limitations; and **section 7** states: "No person shall be deprived of life, liberty or property, without due process of law."

Section 8, as amended in 1973 and 1989, guarantees bail to those accused of a crime, except, among others, "**(1)** ... **(a)** persons charged with a capital offense when there is substantial evidence to support the charge; or **(b)** persons charged with a felony while on probation or parole . . . ; or **(c)** persons charged with any other crime, designated by statute as one for which bail may be denied, if there is substantial evidence to support the charge and the court finds by clear and convincing evidence that the person would constitute a substantial danger to any other person or to the community or is likely to flee the jurisdiction of the court. . . ." **Section 9** prohibits excessive bail, excessive fines, and cruel and unusual punishment, noting that "[p]ersons arrested or imprisoned shall not be treated with unnecessary rigor."

Section 10, as amended in 1997, declares: "In capital cases the right of trial by jury shall remain inviolate. In capital cases the jury shall consist of twelve persons, and in all other felony cases, the jury shall consist of no fewer than eight persons. . . . In criminal cases the verdict shall be unanimous. In civil cases three-fourths of the jurors may find a verdict. . . ." **Section 11** provides in part: "All courts shall be open, and every person, for an injury done to him in his person, property or reputation, shall have remedy by due course of law, which shall be administered without denial or unnecessary delay. . . ." **Section 12,** as amended in 1995, extends rights to those accused of a crime, stating in part: "Nothing in this constitution shall preclude the use of reliable hearsay evidence as defined by statute or rule in whole or in part at any preliminary examination to determine probable cause or at any pretrial proceeding with respect to release of the defendant if appropriate discovery is allowed as defined by statute or rule." This amount of procedural detail is rare in fundamental rights sections of state constitutions. In *American Fork City v. Crosgrove* (1985), the Utah supreme court decided that the language in section 12 protecting the accused from self-incrimination was not violated by requiring the defendant to submit to a breathalyzer test.

Section 13, as amended in 1949, authorizes prosecution by information rather than by indictment under certain circumstances. **Sections 14, 15,** and **16,** respectively, prohibit unreasonable searches and seizures; guarantee freedom of speech and the press; and forbid imprisonment for debt, "except in the cases of absconding debtors." **Section 17** guarantees free elections, providing that "[s]oldiers, in time of war, may vote at their post of duty, in or out of the State, under regulations to be prescribed by law." **Section 18** prohibits bills of attainder, ex post facto laws, and laws impairing the obligation of contracts; **section 19** defines treason in language similar to that used in the U.S. Constitution; and **section 20** subordinates the military to civil power and limits the quartering of soldiers in private homes.

Sections 21, 22, and **23,** respectively, forbid slavery, except as punishment for a crime; require just compensation for private property "taken or damaged for public use"; and prohibit laws granting "irrevocably any franchise, privilege or immunity." Pursuant to **section 24,** "All laws of a general nature shall have uniform operation"; and under **section 25,** "This enumeration of rights [in the constitution] shall not be construed to impair or deny others retained by the people." **Section 26** states: "The provisions of this Constitution are mandatory and prohibitory, unless by express words they are declared to be otherwise." The South Carolina constitution includes a similar provision. **Section 27**

emphasizes that "[f]requent recurrence to fundamental principles is essential to the security of individual rights and the perpetuity of free government."

Section 28, added in 1995, sets forth rights for victims of crime, including "**(b)** [u]pon request, to be informed of, be present at, and to be heard at important criminal justice hearings related to the victim, either in person or through a lawful representative, once a criminal information or indictment charging a crime has been publicly filed in court...."

Article IV, Elections and Rights of Suffrage, section 1, guarantees: "The rights of citizens ... to vote and hold office shall not be abridged on account of sex. Both male and female citizens ... shall enjoy equally all civil, political, and religious rights and privileges." In *Stanton v. Stanton* (1975), the U.S. Supreme Court held that a Utah law prescribing a lower age of majority for females than males with respect to child-support responsibilities was discriminatory.

Article III, Ordinance, provides in part: "The following ordinance shall be irrevocable without the consent of the United States and the people of this State: **First:**—Perfect toleration of religious sentiment is guaranteed. No inhabitant of this State shall ever be molested in person or property on account of his or her mode of religious worship; but polygamous or plural marriages are forever prohibited."

Article V, Distribution of Powers, section 1, divides "[t]he powers of the government of the State of Utah ... into three distinct departments, the Legislative, the Executive, and the Judicial"; furthermore, "no person charged with the exercise of powers properly belonging to one of these departments, shall exercise any functions appertaining to either of the others, except in the cases herein expressly directed or permitted."

Division of Powers

Article VI, Legislative Department, section 1, as amended in 1900, states in part: "The Legislative power of the State shall be vested: **1.** In a Senate and House of Representatives which shall be designated the Legislature of the State of Utah." **Section 3,** as amended in 1972 and 1993, provides: "**(1)** The members of the House of Representatives shall be chosen biennially on even-numbered years.... **(2)** Their term of office shall be two years, from the first day of January next after their election." According to **section 4,** as amended in 1972 and 1993, "**(1)** The senators shall be chosen by the qualified voters of the respective senatorial districts, at the same times and places as members of the House of Representatives. **(2)** Their term of office shall be four years from the first day of January next after their election. **(3)** As nearly one-half as may be practicable shall be elected in each biennium as the Legislature shall determine by law with each apportionment." Currently, as prescribed by statute, there are twenty-nine senators and seventy-five representatives in the legislature. A 1994 statute limits representatives and senators to twelve consecutive years in office.

Legislative Branch

Section 5, as amended in 1972 and 1983, requires that senators and representatives be, "as of the last date provided by law for filing for the office," U.S. citizens, at least twenty-five years old, qualified voters in their district, state residents for three years, and district residents for six months; furthermore, they may not continue to serve in office if they move from their district. Pursuant to **section 6,** "No person holding any public office of profit or trust under authority of the United States, or of this State, shall be a member of the Legislature, [except for] appointments in the State militia, and the offices of notary public, justice of the peace, United States commissioner, and postmaster of the fourth class...." **Section 7** prohibits a legislator from holding an office that was created or that had a salary increase during the term for which he or she was elected.

Section 8 exempts legislators from arrest "during each session of the Legislature, for fifteen days next preceding each session, and in returning therefrom" except in cases of treason, felony, and breach of the peace; furthermore, "for words used in any speech or debate in either house, they shall not be questioned in any other place." **Section 10** allows each house to judge the election and qualifications of its members, punish them for disorderly conduct, and "with the concurrence of two-thirds of all the members elected" expel a member "for cause." **Section 11** defines a quorum as "[a] majority of the members of each house," although "a smaller number may adjourn from day to day, and may compel the attendance of absent members in such manner and under such penalties as each house may prescribe." According to **section 12,** each house may "determine the rules of its proceedings and choose its own officers and employees."

Section 22, as amended in 1900, 1972, and 1983, provides: "Every bill shall be read by title three separate times in each house except in cases where two-thirds of the house where such bill is pending suspend this requirement. Except general appropriation bills and bills for the codification and general revision of laws, no bill shall be passed containing more than one subject, which shall be clearly expressed in its title.... No bill or joint resolution shall be passed except with the assent of the majority of all the members elected to each house...." **Section 24,** as amended in 1972, specifies that "[t]he presiding officer of each house, not later than five days following adjournment, shall sign all bills and joint resolutions passed by the Legislature, certifying to their accuracy and authenticity as enacted by the Legislature." And pursuant to **section 25,** as amended in 1972, "All acts shall be officially published, and no act shall take effect until sixty days after the adjournment of the session at which it passed, unless the Legislature by a vote of two-thirds of all the members elected to each house, shall otherwise direct."

Section 26, as amended in 1972, stipulates that "[n]o private or special law shall be enacted where a general law can be applicable." **Section 28** prohibits the legislature from delegating "to any special commission, private corporation or association, any power to make, supervise or interfere with any municipal improvement, money, property or effects, whether held in trust or otherwise, to levy taxes, to select a capitol site, or to perform any municipal functions."

Executive Branch

Article VII, Executive Department, section 1, as amended in 1981 and 1993, enumerates the state's executive officers and describes their terms: "**(1)** The elective constitutional officers of the Executive Department shall consist of Governor, Lieutenant Governor, State Auditor, State Treasurer, and Attorney General. **(2)** Each officer shall: **(a)** hold office for four years beginning on the first Monday of January next after their election; **(b)** during their terms of office reside within the State; and **(c)** perform such duties as are prescribed by this Constitution and as provided by statute." All are limited by a 1994 statute to twelve consecutive years in their positions. Pursuant to **section 2**, as amended in 1981 and 1993, "**(2)** In the election the names of the candidates for Governor and Lieutenant Governor for each political party shall appear together on the ballot and the votes cast for a candidate for Governor shall be considered as also cast for the candidate for Lieutenant Governor." **Section 14,** as amended in 1981, directs the lieutenant governor to "**(1)** serve on all boards and commissions in lieu of the Governor whenever so designated by the Governor; **(2)** perform such duties as may be delegated by the Governor; and **(3)** perform other duties as may be provided by statute."

Section 3, as amended in 1981 and 1993, requires: "**(1)** To be eligible for the office of Governor or Lieutenant Governor a person shall be 30 years of age or older at the time of election.... **(4)** No person is eligible to any of the offices provided for in Section 1 unless at the time of election that person is a qualified voter and has been a resident citizen of the State for five years next preceding the election."

Section 5, as amended in 1981 and 1993, states: "**(1)** The executive power of the State shall vest in the Governor who shall see that the laws are faithfully executed." Generally, state constitutions that create a plural, or divided, executive branch vest the governor with "supreme" executive power, denoting that he or she shares executive power with other officers. Section 5 outlines the governor's duties: "**(2)** The Governor shall transact all executive business with the officers of the government, civil and military, and ... require information in writing from the officers of the Executive Department, and from [others], [as well as] appoint a committee to investigate and report on ... the condition of any executive office or State Institution [when the legislature is not in session]. **(3)** The Governor shall communicate by message the condition of the State to the Legislature at every annual general session and recommend such measures as may be deemed expedient. **(4)** The Governor may appoint legal counsel to advise the Governor."

Section 4, as amended in 1981, designates the governor to serve as commander in chief of the state's military forces, "except when they shall be called into the service of the United States," and empowers him or her to call out the militia "to execute the laws, to suppress insurrection, or to repel invasion." **Section 9** authorizes the governor to fill vacancies in "any State or district office." **Section 10,** as amended in 1981, states in part: "The Governor shall nominate, and by and with consent of the Senate, appoint all State and district officers whose offices are established by this Constitution, or which may be created by law, and whose appointment or election is not otherwise provided for." **Section 12,** as amended in 1981 and 1993, creates, under **section 12(2)(a),** a board of pardons and parole and allows the governor, under **section 12(3)(a),** to "grant respites or reprieves in all cases of convictions for offenses against the state except treason or conviction on impeachment"; however, "[t]hese respites or reprieves may not extend beyond the next session of the board [at which time] the board shall continue or determine the respite or reprieve, commute the punishment, or pardon the offense...."

Section 6 authorizes the governor on "extraordinary occasions" to convene the legislature "by proclamation...." Section 8, as amended in 1981 and 1993, mandates: "(1) Each bill passed by the Legislature, before it becomes a law, shall be presented to the Governor. If the bill is approved, the Governor shall sign it, and thereupon it becomes a law. If the bill is disapproved, it shall be returned with the Governor's objections to the house in which it originated." The governor's veto may be overridden by a "vote of two-thirds of the members elected to each house." According to section 8(2), "If any bill is not returned by the Governor within ten days ..., Sunday and the day it was received excepted, it shall become a law without a signature." Under section 8(3), the governor may "disapprove any item of appropriation contained in any bill while approving other portions of the bill"; this veto may be overridden as in the case of the veto of an entire bill. Under section 8(4), the legislature may reconvene to consider vetoes by the governor after the "adjournment sine die of any session...."

Section 11, as amended in 1981, addresses the issue of succession: "In case of the death of the Governor, impeachment, removal from office, resignation, or disability to discharge the duties of the office, or in case of a Governor-elect who fails to take office, the powers and duties of the Governor shall devolve upon the Lieutenant Governor until the disability ceases or until the next general election."

Judicial Branch

Article VIII, Judicial Department, was completely revised in 1985; thus, dates are given only for subsequent amendments. Section 1 declares: "The judicial power of the state shall be vested in a Supreme Court, in a trial court of general jurisdiction known as the district court, and in such other courts as the Legislature by statute may establish. The Supreme Court, the district court, and [others] designated by statute shall be courts of record." Pursuant to section 2, "The Supreme Court shall ... consist of at least five justices. The number of justices may be changed by statute, but no change shall have the effect of removing a justice from office." The Utah supreme court currently has five members. Section 2 continues: "The Supreme Court by rule may sit and render final judgment either en banc or in divisions. The court shall not declare any law unconstitutional ..., except on the concurrence of a majority of all [the] justices." In *State v. Young* (1995), the Utah supreme court upheld the process of jury selection in capital cases whereby jurors are excluded when their strong opposition to the death penalty might preclude their imposing it after a conviction, although it has been argued that such exclusion may unconstitutionally result in a jury more prone to convict the accused.

Section 3 establishes the supreme court's jurisdiction: "The Supreme Court shall have original jurisdiction to issue all extraordinary writs and to answer questions of state law certified by a court of the United States. [It] shall have appellate jurisdiction over all other matters to be exercised as provided by statute, and power to issue all writs and orders necessary for the exercise of [its] jurisdiction or the complete determination of any cause." Section 4 provides: "The Supreme Court shall adopt rules of procedure and evidence to be used in the courts of the state and shall by rule manage the appellate process. The Legislature may amend the rules of procedure and evidence ... upon a vote of two-thirds of all the members of both houses.... The Supreme Court by rule shall govern the practice of law, including admission to practice law and the conduct and discipline of persons admitted to practice law."

Section 7 requires that supreme court justices be at least thirty years old, U.S. citizens, state residents for five years, and "admitted to practice law in Utah." **Section 8,** as amended in 1993, addresses the filling of court vacancies: "**(1)** When a vacancy occurs in a court of record, the governor shall fill [it] by appointment from a list of at least three nominees certified ... by the Judicial Nominating Commission having authority over the vacancy.... **(3)** The Senate shall consider and render a decision on each judicial appointment within 60 days of the date of appointment ... , [and it] shall be effective upon approval of a majority of all members of the Senate. **(4)** Selection of judges shall be based solely upon consideration of fitness for office without regard to any partisan political considerations." The Delaware constitution, on the other hand, requires a political party balance among justices of the supreme court.

Section 9 mandates: "Each appointee to a court of record shall be subject to an unopposed retention election at the first general election held more than three years after appointment. Following initial voter approval, each Supreme Court justice every tenth year ... shall be subject to an unopposed retention election at the corresponding general election, [which] shall be held on a nonpartisan ballot...." **Section 12,** as amended in 1993, creates a judicial council, "which shall adopt rules for the administration of the courts"; while **section 13** creates a judicial conduct commission, which may "order the reprimand, censure, suspension, removal, or involuntary retirement of any justice or judge...." **Section 15** states that "[t]he Legislature may provide standards for the mandatory retirement of justices and judges from office."

Article VI, Legislative Department, section 17, grants the house of representatives "the sole power of impeachment" but stipulates that impeachment requires the vote of "two-thirds of all the members elected." Pursuant to **section 18,** "All impeachments shall be tried by the Senate ... , [and no] person shall be convicted without the concurrence of two-thirds of the senators elected." **Section 19** provides in part: "The Governor and other State and Judicial officers, except justices of the peace, shall be liable to impeachment for high crimes, misdemeanors, or malfeasance in office...." Conviction results only in removal from office and disqualification from any state office but does not prevent a person from being "liable to ... punishment according to law." **Section 20** states that "[n]o person shall be tried on impeachment, unless he shall have been served with a copy of the articles thereof, at least ten days before the trial...."

Article VI, Legislative Department, section 1, as amended in 1900, provides in part: "The Legislative power of the state shall be vested: ... **2.** In the people of the State of Utah, as hereinafter stated: The legal voters or such fractional part thereof ... may initiate any desired legislation and cause the same to be submitted to a vote of the people for approval or rejection, or may require any law passed by the Legislature (except those laws passed by a two-thirds vote of the members elected to each house of the Legislature) to be submitted to the voters of the State before such law shall take effect." Section 1 also provides for popular initiative of and referendums on laws for subdivisions of the state.

Local Government

Article XI, **Counties, Cities, and Towns, section 5,** as amended in 1933, states: "Corporations for municipal purposes shall not be created by special laws. The legislature by general laws shall provide for the incorporation, organization and classification of cities and towns in proportion to population, which laws may be altered, amended or repealed. Any incorporated city or town may frame and adopt a charter for its own government...."

Taxation and Finance

Article XIII, **Revenue and Taxation, section 9,** as amended in 1997, prohibits the legislature from making any appropriation or authorizing any expenditure "if the expenditure of the State, during any fiscal year, shall exceed the total tax then provided for by law ... , unless [it] provides for levying a sufficient tax to pay the appropriation or expenditure within the current fiscal year."

Education

Article X, **Education, section 1,** as amended in 1987, mandates: "The Legislature shall provide for the establishment and maintenance of the state's education systems including: **(a)** a public education system, which shall be open to all children of the state; and **(b)** a higher education system. Both systems shall be free from sectarian control." **Section 3,** as amended in 1987, provides in part: "The general control and supervision of the public education system shall be vested in a State Board of Education. The membership of the board shall be established and elected as provided by statute."

Health and Welfare

Article XVI, **Labor, section 1,** asserts that "[t]he rights of labor shall have just protection through laws calculated to promote industrial welfare of the State." **Section 3,** as amended in 1980, directs the legislature to prohibit, among other things, "**(1)** [t]he employment of children under the age of fourteen years, in underground mines...."

Amendment Procedures

Article XXIII, **Amendment and Revision, section 1,** as amended in 1971, provides: "Any ... amendments to this Constitution may be proposed in either house of the Legislature, and if two-thirds of all the members elected to each of the two houses, shall vote in favor thereof ... , [they] shall be submitted to the electors of the state for their approval or rejection...." They become a part of the constitution "if a majority of the electors voting thereon shall approve the same."

Section 2 specifies: "Whenever two-thirds of the members, elected to each branch of the Legislature, shall deem it necessary to call a convention to revise or amend this Constitution, they shall recommend to the electors to vote, at the next general election, for or against a convention.... [I]f a majority of all the electors, voting at such an election, shall vote for a convention, the Legislature, at its next session, shall provide by law for calling the same...." **Section 3** requires that any new constitution or amendments be approved by a majority of the electors voting.

Vermont became the fourteenth state of the United States on March 4, 1791. Montpelier is the capital of the "Green Mountain State." Some 9,615 square miles in area, Vermont is bordered by the Canadian province of Quebec on the north, New Hampshire on the east, Massachusetts on the south, and New York on the west. Vermont ranks forty-ninth among the states in population with approximately 585,000 residents. The state's principal industries include manufacturing, tourism, and agriculture; its chief crops include dairy products, apples, and maple syrup.

Government: The governor and lieutenant governor are elected separately for two-year terms. The legislature, called the general assembly, consists of thirty senators and 150 members of the house of representatives, all elected for two-year terms. The supreme court comprises a chief justice and four associate justices appointed by the governor from a list of nominees presented by a judicial nominating body with the advice and consent of the senate; they initially serve for six years and then, unless removed by the general assembly, for subsequent six-year terms until age seventy.

Dates of Constitutions: 1777, 1786, and 1793

Despite some contradictory evidence and theories, it is generally agreed that Frenchmen led by Samuel de Champlain in 1609 were the first Europeans to view the *verd mont* (green mountains) in the region that would become the state of Vermont. On the New York side of Lake Champlain these early explorers drove off a party of Iroquois, angering that tribe and setting the stage for later alliances: the French and the Algonquins, century-old rivals of the Iroquois, against the English and the Iroquois. In 1666 the French established Forte Sainte Anne on Lake Champlain, and in 1690 the Dutch built a temporary outpost in the southeastern part of the territory now known as Vermont.

As part of a settlement over a border dispute with Connecticut in 1715, the British colony of Massachusetts acquired rights to what was vaguely described as "Equivalent Lands" in the area named *Verd Mont* by the early French explorers. To establish its authority in the new territory, Massachusetts built Fort Drummer in 1724 near present-day Brattleboro. Seven years later the colony of New Hampshire, on the authority of its colonial charter, began granting title to land near the present site of Bennington.

Soon after the Treaty of Paris, which ended the French and Indian War in 1763, the British Crown issued a decree reorganizing its American territories and appearing to confirm New York's claim to the *Verd Mont* territory under its 1662 grant of land from the duke of York. In 1770 the established settlers, led by Ethan Allen, formed a self-protection force against newcomers claiming land under the authority of New York. Known as the Green Mountain Boys, they captured Fort Ticonderoga at the head of Lake Champlain in 1775, an important early victory in the Revolutionary War.

The outbreak of the war scuttled an attempt by the entrenched settlers in April 1775 to obtain a new charter from Great Britain. Statehood became their goal, and a constitutional convention assembled in July 1777 in Windsor. A Philadelphian, Dr. Thomas Young, who desired a social as well as a political revolution, sent the convention a copy of the radical Pennsylvania constitution of 1776 and proposed the name Vermont for

VERMONT

General Information

Constitutional History

the new state. The convention adopted the name and a constitution, but Massachusetts, New York, and New Hampshire refused to recognize the document, and it was challenged by delegates to the Continental Congress.

The 1777 constitution, the first state constitution to prohibit slavery, was not submitted to the people for ratification, but it was affirmed by the legislature at its sessions in 1779 and 1782 and declared to be a part of state law. An unusual provision, section XLIV, stated: "In order that the freedom of the Commonwealth may be preserved inviolate, forever, there shall be chosen, by ballot, by the freemen of this State ... [in 1785 and] in seven years thereafter, thirteen persons ... whose duty it shall be to enquire whether the constitution has been preserved inviolate, in every part [etc.]." This council of censors, reminiscent of Plato's nocturnal council established by the constitution for a fictitious Greek colony on Crete and described in his work *The Laws* (350–340 B.C.) was given the power to "send for persons, papers and records ... , order impeachments, and recommend to the legislature the repealing of laws as appear to them to have been enacted contrary to the principles of the constitution."

The council of censors was also charged with proposing amendments to the constitution, and the first council recommended adoption of a new constitution drawn up by a convention held in Manchester in June 1786. The second council's proposals resulted in a convention in Windsor that adopted a third constitution for Vermont on July 9, 1793. No provision was made in this constitution for a council of censors, and the 1793 constitution, as amended, remains in effect today.

The Constitution

The 1793 Vermont constitution is the third oldest state constitution still in force (the oldest is the 1780 Massachusetts document and the second oldest is the 1784 New Hampshire document). Vermont's constitution is the shortest of the current state constitutions, containing only 8,300 words, but it is still twice as long as the U.S. Constitution. And, whereas Massachusetts's constitution has been amended 117 times and New Hampshire's 143 times, Vermont's, as of January 1, 1998, has been amended only fifty-two times in more than two hundred years. This is still nearly twice the number of times the U.S. Constitution has been amended.

Vermont and New Hampshire are the only two states whose constitutions require biennial elections for governor, and Vermont is one of only twelve states requiring biennial elections for members of both the upper and lower houses of the legislature. The structure of the 1793 document is similar to the Massachusetts and New Hampshire constitutions in that it consists of only two major divisions: chapter I, a declaration of rights; and chapter II, a plan of government. The document, although modernized in some respects from the 1786 version, still reflects early religious influence, as in chapter I, article 3rd, for example, which recommends that "christians ought to observe the sabbath or the Lord's day, and keep up some sort of religious worship...."

Preamble

The 1793 Vermont constitution has no preamble.

Fundamental Rights

Chapter I, A Declaration of the Rights of the Inhabitants of the State of Vermont, article 1st, as amended in 1924 and 1994, proclaims: "That all persons are born equally free and independent, and have certain natural, inherent, and unalienable rights, amongst which are the enjoying and defending life and liberty, acquiring, possessing and protecting property, and pursuing and obtaining happiness and safety; therefore no person born in this country, or brought from over sea, ought to be holden by law, to serve any person as a servant, slave or apprentice, after arriving to the age of twenty-one years, unless bound by the person's own consent...." By an amendment in 1994, which was incorporated into the constitution as **chapter II, Plan or Frame of Government, section 76,** the justices of the Vermont supreme court were authorized to revise the constitution to make the language "gender inclusive." No further reference will be made to this general amendment with respect to specific provisions.

Article 2nd provides: "That private property ought to be subservient to public uses when necessity requires it, nevertheless, whenever any person's property is taken for the use of the public, the owner ought to receive an equivalent in money." This language has the same purpose as "nor shall private property be taken for public use without just compensation" in the Fifth Amendment (1791) to the U.S. Constitution.

Article 3rd establishes freedom of religion but also states: "Nevertheless, every sect or denomination of christians ought to observe the sabbath or Lord's day, and keep up some sort of religious worship, which to them shall seem most agreeable to the revealed will of God." **Article 4th** guarantees a remedy at law for all, and **article 5th** declares: "That the people of this State by their legal representatives, have the sole, inherent, and exclusive right of governing and regulating the internal police of the same."

Article 6th mandates that all officers of the government are servants of the people; **article 7th** declares that government is for the people and they have a right to reform or alter it; and **article 8th** states: "That all elections ought to be free and without corruption, and that all voters, having a sufficient, evident, common interest with, and attachment to the community, have a right to elect officers, and be elected into office, agreeably to the regulations made in this constitution." **Article 9th** in part describes citizen rights and duties, exempting conscientious objectors from having to bear arms.

Article 10th, as amended in 1974, enumerates the rights of persons accused of a crime, while **article 11th** regulates searches and seizures. In ruling on a possible violation of article 11th, the Vermont supreme court in *Slate v. Jewett* (1985) decried the attorneys' failure to adequately address the state constitutional issue, quoting the Oregon justice Hans Linde's 1981 comment: "A lawyer today representing someone who claims some constitutional protection and who does not argue that the state constitution provides that protection is skating on the edge of malpractice."

Chapter II, Plan or Frame of Government, Judiciary Department, section 28, as amended in 1974, declares: "The Courts of Justice shall be open for the trial of all causes proper for their cognizance; and justice shall be therein impartially administered, without corruption or unnecessary delay." In *State v. Hall* (1985), the Vermont supreme court decided that the reversal of a conviction required a showing that the defendant suffered a substantial prejudice as a result of a seventeen-month delay in the state's appellate process. **Sections 40** and **41** prohibit excessive bail, imprisonment for debt, and the suspension of the writ of habeas corpus.

Chapter I, A Declaration of the Rights of the Inhabitants of the State of Vermont, article 12th, provides: "That when any issue in fact, proper for the cognizance of a jury is joined in a court of law, the parties have a right to a trial by jury, which ought to be held sacred." In *State v. Becker* (1972), which involved entitlement to a jury trial in the case of a minor offense, the Vermont supreme court, citing an earlier case, held that a rule of constitutional construction contrary to long established practice will not be indulged in lightly. **Articles 13th** through **17th,** respectively, relate to freedom of speech and the press; immunity for words spoken in legislative debate (in other constitutions this right is generally found in the section dealing with the legislative branch); restrictions on the suspension of laws; the right to bear arms and the subordination of military power to civil authority; and restrictions on martial law. With respect to freedom of speech and the press, the Vermont supreme court held in *Shields v. Gerhart* (1995) that article 13th was self-executing and therefore would support a private action against the state.

Article 18th contains fundamental principles and virtues necessary to preserve liberty, including "a firm adherence to justice, moderation, temperance, industry, and frugality...." **Article 19th** ensures the right to emigrate; **article 20th** guarantees the right to assemble, instruct representatives, and petition for the redress of grievances; and **article 21st** prohibits the transportation of persons out of the state for trial for "any offence committed within the [state]."

Division of Powers

Chapter II, Plan or Frame of Government, Delegation and Distribution of Powers, section 5, declares: "The Legislative, Executive, and Judiciary departments, shall be separate and distinct, so that neither exercise the powers properly belonging to the others." **Sections 1** through **3,** as amended in 1836, provide: "The Commonwealth or State of Vermont shall be governed by a Governor (or Lieutenant-Governor), a Senate and a House of Representatives, in manner and form following: 2. The Supreme Legislative power shall be exercised by a Senate and a House of Representatives. 3. The Supreme Executive power shall be exercised by a Governor, or in the Governor's absence, a Lieutenant-Governor." **Section 4,** as amended in 1974, vests the state's judicial power in "a unified judicial system which shall be composed of a Supreme Court, a Superior Court, and such other subordinate courts as the General Assembly may from time to time ordain and establish."

Legislative Branch

Chapter II, Plan or Frame of Government, Legislative Department, section 6, as amended in 1836 and 1913, mandates in part: "The Senate and House of Representatives shall be styled, *The General Assembly of the State of Vermont.*" **Section 13,** as amended in 1924, 1974, and 1986, stipulates that the house of representatives be composed of 150 members and that voters "shall elect one or two Representatives from [each representative district], the number from each district to be established by the General Assembly." Pursuant to **section 18,** as amended in 1836, 1850, and 1974, "The Senate shall be composed of thirty Senators ... [and the] voters of each senatorial district ... shall elect one or more Senators from that district, the number from each district to be established by the General Assembly...." In *In re Reapportionment of Towns of Hartland, Windsor and West Windsor* (1993), the Vermont supreme court held that in redistricting, county lines must, if necessary, yield to the higher priority of equal representation by population.

Section 46, as amended in 1870, 1913, and 1974, provides: "The term of office of Senators and Representatives shall be two years, commencing on the first Wednesday next after the first Monday of January following their election." **Section 15,** as amended in 1974, requires both representatives and senators to be state residents for two years, "the last year of which shall be in the legislative district for which the person is elected."

Section 14, as amended in 1836, authorizes members of the house of representatives to, among other things, "choose their Speaker, their Clerk and other necessary officers; ... judge of the elections and qualifications of their own members; ... expel members ..., [and] impeach state criminals." A majority of the representatives elected constitute a quorum, except in the case of "raising a State tax," when "two-thirds of the members elected shall be present."

Section 19, as amended in 1836, outlines similar powers of the senate: "The Senate shall have the like powers to decide on the election and qualifications of, and to expel any of, its members, make its own rules, and appoint its own officers, as ... the House of Representatives. A majority shall constitute a quorum." Section 19 also designates the lieutenant governor to serve as president of the senate, "except when exercising the office of Governor ..., in which [case or if the office is vacant] the Senate shall appoint one of its own members to be President of the Senate, *pro tempore*"; moreover, "[t]he President of the Senate shall have casting vote, but no other."

Section 6 provides: "Each [house] shall have and exercise the like powers in all acts of legislation; and no bill, resolution, or other thing, which shall have been passed by the one, shall have the effect of, or be declared to be, a law, without the concurrence of the other. *Provided,* That all Revenue bills shall originate in the House of Representatives...." If the two houses disagree with respect to adjournment, the governor may adjourn them. The two houses are empowered to "prepare bills and enact them into laws, redress grievances, grant charters of incorporation ... , [and] constitute towns, boroughs, cities and counties"; moreover, "they shall have all other powers necessary for the Legislature of a free and sovereign State; but they shall have no power to add to, alter, abolish, or infringe any part of this Constitution."

Section 11, as amended in 1836 and 1913, addresses the passage of bills: "Every bill which shall have passed the Senate and House of Representatives shall, before it becomes a law, be presented to the Governor." If the governor disapproves a bill, he or she "shall return it, with objections in writing, to the House in which it shall have originated...." The governor's veto may be overridden by a vote of "two-thirds of the members present" of each house. Bills not signed and not returned become law, "unless the two Houses by their adjournment, within three days after the presentation of such bill shall prevent its return...."

Section 8 notes: "The doors of the House in which the General Assembly of this Commonwealth shall sit, shall be open for the admission of all persons who behave decently, except only when the welfare of the State may require them to be shut."

Executive Branch

Chapter II, Plan or Frame of Government, Executive Department, section 43, as amended in 1836, 1850, 1870, 1883, and 1913, mandates: "The Governor, Lieutenant-Governor, Treasurer, Secretary of State, Auditor of Accounts, Senators, [and other officials] shall be elected biennially on the first Tuesday next after the first Monday of November, beginning in A.D. 1914." **Section 49,** as amended in 1850 and 1870, specifies that the term of the first three officials begins "when they shall be chosen and qualified, and shall continue for the term of two years...." According to **section 23,** candidates for governor and lieutenant governor "shall have resided in [the] State four years next preceding the day of election." They are elected on separate tickets.

Section 20, as amended in 1836, empowers the governor and, in his or her absence, the lieutenant governor to "commission all officers, and also to appoint officers" unless precluded by law or the constitution; "supply every vacancy in any office, occasioned by death or otherwise, until the office can be filled in the manner directed by law or [the] Constitution"; and "grant pardons and remit fines ... , except in [the case of] treason in which the Governor shall have power to grant reprieves, but not to pardon, until after the end of the next session of the General Assembly; and except in cases of impeachment...." The governor is authorized to "correspond with other States; transact business with officers of government, civil and military, and prepare such business as may appear necessary, to lay before the General Assembly." The governor is further enjoined to "take care that the laws be faithfully executed" and "expedite the execution of such measures as may be resolved upon by the General Assembly." Section 20 also designates the governor to serve as "Captain-General and Commander-in-Chief of the forces of the State, but shall not command in person, in time of war, or insurrection" except for such time as authorized by the senate. Rhode Island also uses both the terms *Captain General* and *Commander-in-Chief* to describe the governor's position as the head of the state's military forces. **Section 21,** as amended in 1836, is a unique provision authorizing the governor to "have a Secretary of Civil and Military Affairs, to be appointed during [his or her] pleasure, whose services the Governor may at all times command...." Hawaii's constitution authorizes the appointment of an administrative director to serve at the governor's pleasure. **Section 24,** as amended in 1850, directs the legislature to "provide by general law what officer shall as act as Governor whenever there shall be a vacancy in both the offices of Governor and Lieutenant-Governor...."

Judicial Branch

Chapter II, Plan or Frame of Government, Judiciary Department, section 29, as amended in 1974, specifies that "[t]he Supreme Court shall consist of the Chief Justice of the State and four associate justices of the Supreme Court." **Section 32,** as amended in 1974, provides: "The Governor, with the advice and consent of the Senate, shall fill a vacancy in the office of the Chief justice of the State, associate justice of the Supreme Court or judge ... [with some exceptions] from a list of nominees presented by a judicial nominating body...." Pursuant to **section 33,** as amended in 1974, the governor may make interim appointments when the senate is not in session, although the senate must later consent to the appointments.

Section 34, as amended in 1974, sets the justices' terms: "The justices of the Supreme court and judges of all subordinate courts, except Assistant Judges and Judges of Probate, shall hold office for terms of six-years.... At the end of the initial six-year term and ... of each six year term thereafter, [they] may give notice ... of a desire to continue in office." They will be continued in office for six more years "unless a majority of the members of the General Assembly voting on the question vote against continuation in office." **Section 35,** as amended in 1974, stipulates: "All justices of the Supreme Court and judges of all subordinate courts shall be retired at the end of the calendar year in which they attain seventy years of age.... The chief justice may from time to time appoint retired justices or judges to special assignments as permitted under the rules of the Supreme Court."

Section 30, as amended in 1974, establishes the supreme court's jurisdiction, beginning: "The Supreme Court shall exercise appellate jurisdiction in all cases, criminal and civil, under such terms and conditions as it shall specify in rules not inconsistent with law." However, **section 37,** as amended in 1974, states in part: "Any rule adopted by the Supreme Court may be revised by the General Assembly." Contrary to the separation of powers principle, this language gives the legislature the power to influence the court's rules of procedure, which in turn can affect substantive rights of parties before the court. Section 30 continues: "The Supreme Court shall have original jurisdiction only as provided by law, but it shall have the power to issue all writs necessary or appropriate in aid of its appellate jurisdiction [and] shall have administrative control of all the courts of the state, and disciplinary authority concerning all judicial officers and attorneys at law in the State." With or without this language, however, a state's highest court would assume that it possessed inherent authority over the members of the state bar. In *In re Steady* (1994), the Vermont supreme court found that even after judges leave the bench, the court still has authority to discipline them for conduct during their judicial tenure. **Section 31,** as amended in 1974, directs that "[a]ll other courts ... shall have ... jurisdiction as provided by law."

Chapter II, Plan or Frame of Government, section 57, as amended in 1836 and 1870, states: "The House of Representatives shall have the power to order impeachments, which shall in all cases be by a vote of two-thirds of its members." **Section 58,** as amended in 1836, notes that "[e]very officer of State, whether judicial or executive, shall be liable to be impeached by the House of Representatives, either when in office or after resignation or removal for maladministration." The senate is to try impeachments, and "no person shall be convicted, without the concurrence of two-thirds of the members present." The penalty for conviction is limited to "removal from office and disqualification to hold or enjoy any [state] office...." but does not exclude other punishment in accordance with the law.

Impeachment

Chapter I, A Declaration of the Rights of the Inhabitants of the State of Vermont, article 9th, states in part: "... and previous to any law being made to raise a tax, the purpose for which it is to be raised ought to appear evident to the Legislature to be of more service to community than the money would be if not collected."

Taxation and Finance

Education   **Chapter II, Plan or Frame of Government, section 68,** as amended in 1954, 1964, and 1994, provides in part: "Laws for the encouragement of virtue and prevention of vice and immorality ought to be constantly kept in force, and duly executed; and a competent number of schools ought to be maintained in each town unless the general assembly permits other provisions for the convenient instruction of youth." In *Vermont Educational Buildings Financing Agency v. Mann* (1968), the Vermont supreme court said that this provision imposed a duty on the general assembly in regard to education that is universally accepted as a public purpose.

Amendment Procedures   **Chapter II, Plan or Frame of Government, section 72,** as amended in 1870 and 1974, provides: "At the biennial session of the General Assembly of this State which convenes in A.D. 1975, and at the biennial session convening every fourth year thereafter, the Senate by a vote of two-thirds of its members, may propose amendments to this Constitution, with the concurrence of a majority of the members of the House of Representatives...." A proposed amendment is "referred to the next biennial session of the General Assembly"; if at that session a majority of legislators approve it, the legislature submits it directly to the voters. If "approved by a majority of the voters voting thereon," it becomes a part of the constitution. Before a public vote, the governor must give public notice of the proposed amendment, and the legislature is directed to provide the voting method.

Section 75, added in 1913, authorizes the supreme court justices to revise chapter II of the constitution (the frame of government chapter), but not chapter I (the declaration of rights portion), "by incorporating into [chapter II] all amendments of the Constitution that are now or may be then in force and excluding therefrom all sections, clauses, and words not in force and rearrang[ing] and renumbering the sections thereof...." Maine's constitution authorizes the chief justice to "arrange the constitution, as amended," at least every ten years; such updating of the constitution, however, must be approved by the legislature.

The Commonwealth of Virginia became the tenth state of the United States on June 25, 1788. Richmond is the capital of the "Old Dominion," as it was dubbed by Charles II of England. Some 42,777 square miles in area, Virginia is bordered by West Virginia and Maryland on the north, the Chesapeake Bay and the Atlantic Ocean on the east, North Carolina and Tennessee on the south, and Kentucky and West Virginia on the west. Virginia ranks twelfth among the states in population with approximately 6.6 million residents. The state's principal industries include services, trade, manufacturing, and agriculture; among its chief crops are soybeans, tobacco, and corn.

General Information

Government: The governor and the lieutenant governor are elected separately for four-year terms, but the governor may not serve a second consecutive term. The legislature, called the general assembly, consists of forty senators elected for four-year terms and 100 members of the house of delegates elected for two-year terms. The supreme court includes a chief justice and six justices elected by the legislature for twelve-year terms.

Constitutions: 1776, 1830, 1851, 1869, 1902, and 1971

Constitutional History

The first permanent English settlement in what would become the United States was established on Jamestown Island on May 14, 1607. At that time the territory that later became Virginia was inhabited by the Cherokee and Susquehanna peoples and Algonquin members of the Powhatan Confederacy. The Virginia Colony's 1606 charter granted settlers the same "liberties, franchises, and immunities" as other subjects of the English Crown. By 1619 the colonists had created the first representative legislature in the Americas.

A key colony during the Revolutionary War, which ended in 1783 with the British surrender at Yorktown, Virginia also played a significant role in the constitutional development of the nation. In 1776 a Virginia native, Thomas Jefferson, drafted the Declaration of Independence, and another Virginian, George Mason, drafted the state's first constitution, which included a declaration of rights—the first bill of rights guaranteeing individual rights and freedoms of any state. Virginia's call in 1786 for a conference on trade problems among the states under the 1781 Articles of Confederation led to a national convention in Philadelphia that drafted the world's first written national constitution the following year. The "Virginia Plan" for a bicameral national legislature, with a lower house representing the people and an upper house representing the states, provided the basis for agreement by the framers of the revolutionary document.

Thomas Jefferson had criticized the 1776 Virginia state constitution for its restricted suffrage, malapportioned legislature, and failure to effectuate a true separation of powers, and in 1829 a convention was assembled to reconsider it. Among the distinguished delegates were two past U.S. presidents, James Madison—the "Father of the Constitution"—and James Monroe; a future president, John Tyler; and John Marshall, chief justice of the United States. The growing western part of the state, populated primarily by residents who did not own slaves, pushed for reforms—extending the qualifications for suffrage, apportionment of seats in the legislature on the basis of the white male population only (without counting slaves), and popular election of the governor. Delegates from the eastern, slave-holding counties defeated the reforms, and the resulting constitution with few changes was approved by the voters and became effective in 1830.

By 1840 the western counties had attained a population advantage, and another constitutional convention was called in 1850. The product of that convention was ratified in 1851 and provided that a majority of the seats in the legislature's lower house were to go to westerners, extended sufrage to white males over twenty-one years old, and authorized popular election of the governor.

Another constitutional convention in 1861 voted for secession from the Union, but its proposed new constitution was defeated at the polls. During the Civil War, Richmond became the capital of the Confederacy. A constitution adopted in 1864 by a convention of delegates from Union-occupied territory, excluding the new state of West Virginia and never ratified by the electorate, is considered of dubious legality. A new constitution approved by President Ulysses S. Grant and Congress went into effect in 1869; for the first time a method of amending the constitution was included.

The citizens of Virginia approved another constitution in 1902, one that greatly restricted the ability to register to vote and created a state corporation commission in response to the growing power of the railroads operating in Virginia.

In 1968 the legislature authorized the governor to appoint a commission on constitutional revision. In addition to commenting that a constitution "embodies fundamental law ... [and] not a code of laws and ... unnecessary detail," the commission recommended giving more power to local governments, strengthening the education provisions, and adding an article on conservation. The new constitution was approved by the voters and became effective on July 1, 1971.

The Constitution

The current constitutions of Illinois, North Carolina, and Virginia all went into effect on July 1, 1971, and among all the states only Georgia, Louisiana, and Montana have adopted new constitutions since then. The Virginia constitution creates a plural executive branch, with only one statewide official—the attorney general—elected in addition to the governor and lieutenant governor. The legislature is bicameral, and judges are elected by the legislature as in Rhode Island and South Carolina. A relatively short state constitution with only 18,500 words, it has been amended thirty-one times as of January 1, 1998.

Virginia's constitution is basically a conservative document. The desire to maintain a link with the state's historic past is reflected in the traditional language of the bill of rights and the continued restrictions on the use of legislative powers, selection of judges by the legislature, and retention of limitations on borrowing. Little innovation is exhibited— for example, there are no direct democracy procedures, such as initiative, referendum, and recall, or new individual rights, such as the right of privacy, although rights for victims of crime were added by amendment in 1997.

Fundamental Rights

Article I, Bill of Rights, section 1, proclaims: "That all men are by nature equally free and independent and have certain inherent rights...." **Section 2** adds that "all power is vested in, and consequently derived from, the people, [and] that magistrates are their trustees and servants, and at all times [are] amenable to them." In *Staples v. Gilmer* (1945), the Virginia supreme court declared that the people, not the legislature, are possessed with ultimate sovereignty and are the source of all state authority.

Sections **3** and **4**, respectively, declare that "government is, or ought to be, instituted for the common benefit, protection, and security of the people …" and that no exclusive emoluments or hereditary offices will be allowed. **Section 5** states in part that members of the government "should, at fixed periods, be reduced to a private station, return into that body from which they were originally taken, and the vacancies be supplied by regular elections…." **Section 6** mandates free elections and the consent of the people or their representatives for the taking of "their property for public uses."

Section 7 prohibits the suspension of laws without the consent of the legislature. **Section 8** extends rights to those facing criminal prosecution, while **section 8-A**, added in 1997, provides rights for victims of crime. **Sections 9** and **10**, respectively, address excessive bail, cruel and unusual punishment, the suspension of habeas corpus, bills of attainder, and ex post facto laws; and prohibit search and seizure by general warrant. **Section 11** guarantees due process of law, prohibits laws impairing the obligation of contracts, the taking of private property without compensation, and "governmental discrimination upon the basis of religious conviction, race, color, sex, or national origin …, except that the mere separation of the sexes shall not be considered discrimination." In *Shaheed v. Winston* (1995), the U.S. District Court ruled that this antidiscrimination clause is no broader than the right to equal protection under the U.S Constitution. Section 11 also states that jury trials in civil cases "ought to be held sacred."

Section 12 guarantees freedom of the press as well as the right of peaceable assembly and petition; **section 13** ensures the right to bear arms and subordinates the military to civilian authority; **section 14** mandates a uniform, or unitary, government; and **section 15** outlines the qualities necessary for the preservation of free government. **Section 16** guarantees the free exercise of religion and prohibits laws requiring "any religious test whatever." As stated in **section 17**, "The rights enumerated in this Bill of Rights shall not be construed to limit other rights of the people not therein expressed."

Division of Powers

Article I, Bill of Rights, section 5, states in part: "[T]he legislative, executive, and judicial departments of the Commonwealth should be separate and distinct…." According to **article III, Division of Powers, section 1,** "The legislative, executive, and judicial departments shall be separate and distinct, so that none exercise the powers properly belonging to the others, nor any person exercise the power of more than one of them at the same time; provided, however, administrative agencies may be created by the General Assembly with such authority and duties as the General Assembly may prescribe. Provisions may be made for judicial review of any finding, order, or judgment of such administrative agencies." In *Prentis v. Atlantic Coast Line* (1908), the U.S. Court of Appeals declared that so far as the federal constitution is concerned, a state may, by constitutional provision, unite legislative and judicial powers in the same body. In 1816, however, Thomas Jefferson had warned that what "has destroyed liberty and the rights of man in every government … [is] generalizing and contracting all cares and powers into one body…." Unlike Virginia, the U.S. Constitution and the constitutions of some states, including Hawaii and New York, do not expressly mandate the separation of government powers.

Article 4, Legislature, section 1, declares: "The legislative power of the Commonwealth shall be vested in a General Assembly, which shall consist of a Senate and House of Delegates." In *Standard Drug Co. v. General Electric* (1960), the Virginia supreme court held under the prior state constitution that a statute delegating legislative powers to private persons violates the provision that legislative power is vested in a general assembly.

Section 2 states: "The Senate shall consist of not more than forty and not less than thirty-three members, who shall be elected quadrennially by the voters of the several senatorial districts...." Under **section 3,** "The House of Delegates shall consist of not more than one hundred and not less than ninety members, who shall be elected biennially by the voters of the several house districts...." Currently there are forty senators and 100 members of the house of delegates. **Section 4** requires that members of the senate and house of delegates be at least twenty-one years old and residents of the districts they seek to represent, as well as otherwise qualified to vote for members of the general assembly.

Section 7 provides that the house of delegates chooses its own speaker and that the senate chooses a president pro tempore to act in the absence of the lieutenant governor (the senate's constitutional president); each house is also directed to "select its officers and settle its rules of procedure." According to **section 8,** "A majority of the members elected to each house shall constitute a quorum to do business, but a smaller number may adjourn from day to day and shall have power to compel ... attendance...." **Section 9** grants members of the legislature immunity "from arrest during the sessions," except in cases of "treason, felony, or breach of the peace." They are also not subject to arrest "under any civil process during the sessions" or fifteen days before and after any session, and they may not be questioned anywhere else "for any speech or debate in either house."

Section 11, as amended in 1980, states that only bills may be enacted into laws and that "[a] bill may originate in either house, may be approved or rejected by the other, or may be amended by either, with the concurrence of the other." To become law a bill must be considered by and reported on by a committee of each house; printed by the house in which it originated; and read by its title or have its title printed in the daily calendar on three days in each house. "[U]pon its final passage a vote [must be] taken [on the bill] in each house, the name of each member voting for and against recorded in the journal, and a majority of those voting in each house, which majority shall include at least two-fifths of the members elected to that house, recorded in the affirmative."

Section 12 prohibits any law embracing "more than one object, which shall be expressed in its title." When interpreting such language, courts generally hold that the sufficiency of a title must be resolved in favor of the legislature. **Section 13,** as amended in 1980, mandates that, with some exceptions, laws take effect on the first day of July following the adjournment of the legislative session in which it is enacted. Pursuant to **section 14,** as amended in 1995, "The authority of the General Assembly shall extend to all subjects of legislation not herein forbidden or restricted...." Unlike the U.S. Constitution, state constitutions act as a limit on the inherent powers of government retained by the states, as acknowledged in the Tenth Amendment (1791) to the U.S. Constitution.

Article V, Executive, section 1, declares: "The chief executive power of the Common-wealth shall be vested in a Governor. He shall hold office for a term commencing upon his inauguration on the Saturday after the second Wednesday in January, next suc-ceeding his election, and ending in the fourth year thereafter immediately upon the inauguration of his successor. He shall be ineligible to the same office for the term next succeeding that for which he was elected, and to any other office during his term of service." Section 2 requires that the governor be elected by a plurality of votes; in the event that two persons receive the same number of votes or the election is contested, "a majority of the total membership of the General Assembly" chooses between the can-didates. Section 3 states: "No person except a citizen of the United States shall be eligible to the office of Governor." The office holder must be at least thirty years old and a resident of and a registered voter in Virginia for five years preceding the election.

Sections 5, 6, 7, and 12 set forth the powers and duties of the governor, which include convening and informing the state legislature "at every regular session" of "the condi-tion of the Commonwealth" and recommending measures to it; approving or vetoing bills passed by the legislature; taking "care that the laws be faithfully executed," being commander in chief of the state's armed forces, conducting "all intercourse with other and foreign states," and filling vacancies not otherwise provided for by the constitution; and granting reprieves and pardons, except when the prosecution has been carried out by the legislature. As in most other states, the governor has express power to veto "any item or items of an appropriation bill." Section 8 authorizes the governor to require, "under oath, from any officer of any executive or administrative department, office, or agency, or any public institution" information in writing relating to their activities and may inspect their records. The governor may also require the written opinion of the attorney general on questions of law affecting the governor's official duties.

Section 13 declares: "A Lieutenant Governor shall be elected at the same time and for the same term as the Governor…," although they are elected on separate tickets. The candidate must possess the same qualifications as the governor, but there is no term limit to the office. Pursuant to section 14, the lieutenant governor "shall be President of the Senate but shall have no vote except in case of an equal division." Section 16 provides in part: "When the Governor-elect is disqualified, resigns, or dies following his election but prior to taking office, the Lieutenant Governor-elect shall succeed to the office of Governor for the full term." But if the governor-elect fails to take office for any other reason, the lieutenant governor becomes acting governor. The incumbent also becomes acting governor if the chief executive is unable to discharge the duties of office. "In the case of the removal of the Governor from office or in the case of his disqualification, death, or resignation, the Lieutenant Governor shall become Governor." Section 15 creates the position of an elected attorney general.

Article 6, Judiciary, section 1, as amended in 1997, vests judicial power in a supreme court and "such other courts of original or appellate jurisdiction subordinate to the Supreme Court as the General Assembly may from time to time establish." The supreme court is granted "original jurisdiction in cases of habeas corpus, mandamus, and prohibition, in matters of judicial censure, retirement, and removal [of judges for disability or unfitness], and to answer questions of state law certified by a court of the United States or the highest appellate court of any other state." Section 1 also confers on the supreme court appellate jurisdiction in cases involving "the constitutionality of a law under this Constitution or the Constitution of the United States and in cases involving the life or liberty of any person." Added by the 1997 amendment was this language: "The General Assembly may allow the Commonwealth the right to appeal in all cases, including those involving the life or liberty of a person, provided such appeal would not otherwise violate this Constitution or the Constitution of the United States." Section 1 further provides that "[s]ubject to the foregoing limitations, the General Assembly shall have the power to determine the original and appellate jurisdiction of the courts of the Commonwealth."

Section 2 calls for a minimum of seven and a maximum of eleven supreme court justices, the number to be determined by a majority of three-fifths of the members of each house of the legislature at two successive regular sessions. Currently the Virginia supreme court consists of seven members including the chief justice. "No decision," adds section 2, "shall become the judgment of the Court, however, except on the concurrence of at least three justices, and no law shall be declared unconstitutional under either this Constitution or the Constitution of the United States except on the concurrence of at least a majority of all justices of the Supreme Court."

Section 7 provides that the supreme court justices are chosen by a majority of the members elected to each house of the legislature and serve twelve-year terms. Other judges are similarly chosen for eight-year terms. **Sections 3** and **4**, respectively, prescribe that the chief justice is to be selected "from among the justices in a manner provided by law" and that the chief justice is the administrative head of the state judicial system.

Section 10 calls for legislature to create a judicial inquiry and review commission "consisting of members of the judiciary, the bar, and the public" to investigate charges brought that would require the retirement, censure, or removal of a judge. If the charges are "well-founded," the commission may file a complaint with the supreme court. **Section 12,** as amended in 1976, prohibits a judge from making "any appointment of any local governmental official elected by the voters except to fill a vacancy" pending a general election.

Impeachment

Article IV, Legislature, section 17, sets forth the procedures for impeachment of the governor, lieutenant governor, attorney general, judges, members of state corporation commissions, and all officers appointed by the governor or elected by the legislature for malfeasance, corruption, neglect of duty, or other high crime or misdemeanor. Impeachment is to be conducted by the lower house and prosecuted before the senate, which may convict by "the concurrence of two-thirds of the senators present."

Local Government

Article VII, Local Government, section 2, authorizes the legislature to provide by general law or special act that any county, city, town, or other unit of government may exercise any of its powers or perform any of its functions and may participate in the financing thereof jointly or in cooperation with the commonwealth or any other unit of government within or without the commonwealth. **Section 4** requires the voters of each county and city to elect a treasurer, a sheriff, an attorney for the commonwealth, a clerk of the court, and a commissioner of revenue.

Article X, Taxation and Finance, section 1, as amended in 1990, states: "All property, except as hereinafter provided, shall be taxed." The state legislature is granted authority to define and classify taxable subjects and to "determine upon what subjects State taxes, and upon what subjects local taxes, may be levied." **Section 8** limits the amount of tax or revenue to an amount "required for the necessary expenses of the government, or to pay the indebtedness of the Commonwealth." In *DKM Richmond Assoc. v. City of Richmond* (1995), the Virginia supreme court found that exemption from taxation is the exception and any doubt is to be resolved against the one claiming the exemption.

Section 7, as amended in 1986, directs: "Other than as may be provided for in the debt provision of this Constitution, the Governor, subject to criteria as may be established by the General Assembly, shall insure that no expenses of the Commonwealth be incurred which exceed total revenues on hand and anticipated during a period not to exceed … two years and six months…."

Article VIII, Education, section 1, requires the legislature to provide "a system of free public elementary and secondary schools for all children of school age throughout the Commonwealth, and [to] seek to ensure that an educational program of high quality is established and continually maintained." **Section 8,** as amended in 1990, authorizes the payment of various state revenue into a "literary fund" for public school purposes.

Article XI, Conservation, section 1, states that it is the policy of the commonwealth "to conserve, develop, and utilize its natural resources, its public lands, and its historical sites and buildings." This policy ensures protection of the "atmosphere, lands, and waters from pollution, impairment, or destruction, for the benefit, enjoyment, and general welfare of the people of the Commonwealth." **Section 3** adds that Virginia's natural oyster beds "shall not be leased, rented, or sold" but instead held in trust for the citizens.

Article XII, Future Changes, section 1, provides that an amendment may be proposed in either house of the legislature. If the proposed amendment is agreed to by a majority of each of the two houses, it is referred to the first regular session held after the next general election of the house of delegates. If it is agreed to at the regular session or the next special session by a majority of all the members elected to each house, it is submitted to the voters. If approved by a majority of those voting, the amendment becomes a part of the constitution. **Section 2** prescribes an alternative method for revision or amendment by convention if two-thirds of the elected members of the legislature vote to call such a convention.

Taxation and Finance

Education

Environment

Amendment Procedures

WASHINGTON

Washington became the forty-second state of the United States on November 11, 1889. The capital of the "Evergreen State" is Olympia. Some 71,302 square miles in area, Washington is bordered by the Canadian province of British Columbia on the north, Idaho on the east, Oregon on the south, and the Pacific Ocean on the west. Washington ranks fifteenth among the states in population with approximately 5.4 million inhabitants. The state's principal industries include forestry, aerospace, manufacturing, and agriculture; its chief crops include apples, potatoes, hay, and forest products.

General Information

Government: The governor and lieutenant governor are elected separately for four-year terms and are limited to eight of fourteen years. The legislature consists of forty-nine senators elected for four-year terms, one-half every two years, and ninety-eight members of the house of representatives elected for two-year terms. The supreme court is composed of a chief justice and eight additional judges elected for six-year terms.

Date of Constitution: 1889

Constitutional History

In 1579, nine years before leading the English naval forces to victory over the Spanish Armada, the navigator Sir Francis Drake sailed north along the Pacific coast within sight of the coastline beyond the Columbia River. That same year Juan de Fuca, a Greek sailing for Spain, also passed this way. But Europeans did not set foot in what would become the state of Washington until two centuries later, when Bruno Heceta landed at Pointe Grenville in 1775 and claimed the region for Spain. At that time the land was already inhabited by, among other peoples, the Nez Percé, Spokan, Walla Walla, and Puyallup.

An expedition led by Captain James Cook landed in the Washington territory in 1778, and in 1787 Captain Charles Barkley, after naming the strait between Washington and Vancouver Island for Juan de Fuca, claimed the area for Great Britain. The British naval captain George Vancouver, after exploring Puget Sound in 1792, renewed his country's claim to the region, which he called New Georgia. During the eighteenth century the Washington territory had figured prominently in the search for a northwestern water route to the Pacific Ocean from the east, but in the first few decades of the nineteenth century the lure of the region came from the profitable fur trade.

Following the purchase of the Louisiana Territory from France in 1803, President Thomas Jefferson commissioned Meriwether Lewis and William Clark to explore the nation's new acquisition. Their expedition followed the Snake River into the Washington territory and on to the Pacific coast. Competition between Britain and the United States in the fur trade led to an 1818 agreement that the two nations would jointly occupy the northwestern territory, including Washington, for ten years, and in 1827 the agreement was extended indefinitely. But the growing American population south of the Columbia River, in what would become the state of Oregon, led to the establishment of a provisional government by the American settlers there, and a treaty signed on June 15, 1846, established a border between the United States and Canada.

All of the Pacific Northwest was first organized by Congress as a single, large territory, but on August 14, 1848, the Oregon Territory, which included Washington, was created from it. As the population of the southern portion grew, a separate Washington Territory was carved out pursuant to the terms of an act of March 2, 1853. The prospect of future statehood improved as the indigenous peoples were subdued, gold was discovered in the eastern region of the territory, Oregon became a state in 1859, and a separate Idaho Territory was created by Congress in 1863.

In 1872, four years after the final settlement of the boundary between the United States and Canada at the forty-ninth parallel, a convention drafted a constitution for the state of Washington. However, Congress did not act until February 22, 1889, when it passed, as part of an "omnibus" plan, an enabling act that provided for the admission of the states of North and South Dakota, Montana, and Washington. A second constitutional convention met in Olympia in July and August 1889. The document produced by this convention was approved by the voters on October 1, but separate provisions on women's suffrage and the prohibition of alcohol were not approved. On November 11, 1889, President Benjamin Harrison proclaimed Washington's admission into the Union, and the state's constitution went into effect on the same day.

The framers of the 1889 Washington constitution had to grapple with a fundamental change in the concept of liberty as it had been developed by natural law scholars. Historically, liberty meant personal or individual freedom, but with the rise of powerful economic interests, state and federal courts began focusing instead on the liberty of contractual rights as a means of supporting laissez-faire economic policies. Because this new concept of liberty could slow social progress and infringe on individual rights and because the Washington Territory had a history of government corruption, the framers removed some traditional powers from the legislature and instituted a system of democratic checks on all three branches of government.

Washington's constitution is average in length, containing some 29,400 words, and has been amended ninety-one times as of January 1, 1998. The structure of government created by the current document is typical, consisting of a plural executive branch (with six statewide elected officials in addition to the governor and lieutenant governor), a bicameral legislature, and elected judges. A pioneer in grafting direct democracy procedures onto the traditional representative form of government, Washington, along with such states as Oregon and New Jersey, has also led the recent movement toward broadening individual rights under state constitutional guarantees beyond those declared by the U.S. Supreme Court under the U.S. Constitution.

The Constitution

The preamble to the 1889 Washington constitution reads: "We, the people of the State of Washington, grateful to the Supreme Ruler of the Universe for our liberties, do ordain this constitution."

Preamble

Article I, Declaration of Rights, section 1, declares: "All political power is inherent in the people, and governments derive their just powers from the consent of the governed, and are established to protect and maintain individual rights." **Section 2** proclaims: "The Constitution of the United States is the supreme law of the land." According to **section 3,** "No person shall be deprived of life, liberty, or property, without due process of law." **Section 4** guarantees the right of petition and the right of peaceful assembly "for the common good," while **section 5** guarantees freedom of speech and the press, as long as such liberty is not abused. In *State v. Coe* (1984), the Washington supreme court ruled that in a case

Fundamental Rights

involving freedom of speech and of the press, questions of constitutionality should be examined with respect first to the state constitution and only secondarily to the national constitution because state courts have a duty to independently interpret and apply their state constitutions under the United States's federal system of government.

Section 6 prescribes the mode of administering oaths and affirmations, and **section 7** guarantees privacy in one's private affairs and home, except under "authority of law." Pursuant to **sections 8** and **12**, the legislature is prohibited from granting irrevocable and special privileges or immunities. **Section 9** protects a person from testifying against himself or herself and from double jeopardy, and **section 10** provides: "Justice in all cases shall be administered openly and without unnecessary delay." **Section 11**, as amended in 1904, 1958, and 1993, establishes religious freedom, although "the liberty of conscience hereby secured shall not be so construed as to excuse acts of licentiousness or justify practices inconsistent with the peace and safety of the state."

Section 13 prohibits the suspension of the writ of habeas corpus "unless in case of rebellion or invasion the public safety requires it." **Section 14** proscribes excessive bail or fines and "cruel punishment." **Section 15** provides: "No conviction shall work corruption of blood, nor forfeiture of estate." As amended in 1920, **section 16** states in part: "Private property shall not be taken for private use, except for private ways of necessity, and for drains, flumes, or ditches on or across the lands of others for agricultural, domestic, or sanitary purposes. No private property shall be taken or damaged for public or private use without just compensation having been first made, or paid into court for the owner...."

Sections 17 through **20**, respectively, prohibit imprisonment for debt, except in cases of "absconding debtors"; subordinate the military to civil power; guarantee free and equal elections; and authorize bail, "except for capital offenses when the proof is evident, or the presumption great." In *Foster v. Sunnyside Valley Irr. Dist.* (1984), the Washington supreme court acknowledged the strict scrutiny test for any departure from the "one man, one vote" rule enunciated by the U.S. Supreme Court. **Section 21** guarantees the right of trial by jury, and **section 22**, as amended in 1922, provides rights for those accused of crimes, including the right to appear and defend themselves in person or by counsel and to know the nature of the accusation.

Section 23 prohibits any bills of attainder, ex post facto laws, and laws impairing the obligation of contracts. The right to bear arms is guaranteed in **section 24**, although "nothing in this section shall be construed as authorizing individuals or corporations to organize, maintain or employ an armed body of men." **Sections 25** through **28**, respectively, permit prosecution by indictment or information, require a superior judge to convene a grand jury, define treason in terms similar to those used in the U.S. Constitution, and prohibit "hereditary emoluments, privileges, or powers."

Section 29 asserts: "The provisions of this Constitution are mandatory, unless by express words they are declared to be otherwise," and **section 30** guarantees that rights not enumerated are reserved to the people. **Section 31** prohibits a standing army in peacetime. **Section 32** declares: "A frequent recurrence to fundamental principles is essential to the security of individual right and the perpetuity of free government." Added in 1989, **section 35** provides rights for victims of crime. **Article XXXI, section 1,** added in 1972, states: "Equality of rights and responsibility under the law shall not be denied or abridged on account of sex."

Like the U.S. Constitution and a number of other state constitutions, the Washington constitution does not expressly declare the separation of powers doctrine, although it is evident in the government structure created by the document.

Division of Powers

Article II, Legislative Department, section 1, as amended in 1912 and 1981, begins: "The legislative authority of the state of Washington shall be vested in the legislature, consisting of a senate and house of representatives, which shall be called the legislature of the state of Washington...." **Section 2** stipulates: "The house of representatives shall be composed of not less than sixty-three nor more than ninety-nine members. The number of senators shall not be more than one-half nor less than one-third of the number of members of the house of representatives." The first Washington legislature, as specified by this section, comprised seventy members of the house and thirty-five senators. Currently there are ninety-eight members of the house of representatives and forty-nine senators.

Legislative Branch

Section 5 provides that the term for members of the house of representatives is two years. Senators' terms, according to **section 6,** are four years, "one-half of their number retiring every two years." **Section 7** states that an eligible candidate must be a citizen of the United States and a qualified voter in his or her district, and **section 14** restricts a member of Congress or a person holding any U.S. civil or military office from simultaneously serving as a state legislator.

Section 8 allows each house to judge the election, returns, and qualifications of its members and defines a quorum as a majority of each house, although "a smaller number may adjourn from day to day and may compel the attendance of absent members...." Under **section 9,** each may determine its own procedural rules and punishment for contempt and disorderly behavior, including expulsion of a member with the concurrence of two-thirds of the members elected. **Section 10** permits legislators to elect their own officers and also provides that "when the lieutenant governor shall not attend as president, or shall act as governor, the senate shall choose a temporary president. When presiding, the lieutenant governor shall have the deciding vote in case of an equal division of the senate." **Section 16** exempts legislators from arrest except in cases of treason, felony, and breach of the peace; moreover, "they shall not be subject to any civil process during the session of the legislature, nor for fifteen days next before the commencement of each session." **Section 17** allows further immunity from "any civil action or criminal prosecution whatever, for words spoken in debate."

Section 19 limits each bill to one subject, which must be expressed in the title. **Section 20** provides that "[a]ny bill may originate in either house of the legislature, and a bill passed by one house may be amended in the other." In contrast, the U.S. Constitution and the constitutions of some states, including New Hampshire and Wyoming, require that bills raising revenue originate in the lower house. Pursuant to **section 36**, "No bill shall be considered in either house unless the time of its introduction shall have been at least ten days before the final adjournment of the legislature, unless ... otherwise direct[ed] by a vote of two-thirds of all the members elected to each house...."

Section 22 mandates that no bill may become a law unless "on its final passage the vote be taken by yeas and nays, the names of members voting for and against the same be entered on the journal of each house, and a majority of the members elected to each house be recorded thereon as voting in its favor." **Section 32** further stipulates that bills be signed "by the presiding officer of each of the two houses in open session, and under such rules as the legislature shall prescribe." According to **section 41**, added in 1952 and amended in 1981, "No act, law, or bill subject to referendum shall take effect until ninety days after the adjournment of the session at which it was enacted. No act, law or bill approved by a majority of the electors voting thereon [in general] shall be amended or repealed by the legislature within a period of two years following such enactment...."

Section 24, as amended in 1972, prohibits the legislature from granting any divorce; furthermore, lotteries may be approved only by "the affirmative vote of sixty percent of the members of each house of the legislature...." **Section 28** proscribes private and special laws in certain cases, including "**1.** ... changing the names of persons, or constituting one person the heir at law of another" and "**3.** ... authorizing persons to keep ferries wholly within this state."

Executive Branch

Article III, The Executive, section 1, provides that the executive department comprises a governor, a lieutenant governor, a secretary of state, a treasurer, an auditor, an attorney general, a superintendent of public instruction, and a commissioner of public lands, "who shall be severally chosen by the qualified electors of the state at the same time and place of voting as for the members of the legislature." **Section 2** declares: "The supreme executive power of this state shall be vested in a governor, who shall hold his office for a term of four years...." Under a 1992 statute, the governor and lieutenant governor, who are elected on separate tickets, are limited to eight of fourteen years in office. According to **section 25**, as amended in 1956, qualified candidates for state office must be U.S. citizens and electors of the state. "The legislature," adds section 25, "may in its discretion abolish the offices of the lieutenant governor, auditor and commissioner of public lands."

Section 5 directs the governor to require information in writing from the state officers on any subject relating to their official duties and to "see that the laws are faithfully executed." According to **section 6**, the governor "shall communicate at every session by message to the legislature the condition of the affairs of the state, and recommend such measures as he shall deem expedient for their action." **Section 7** authorizes the chief executive, "on extraordinary occasions, [to] convene the legislature by proclamation ..."; **section 8** designates the governor "commander-in-chief of the military in the state except when they shall be called into the service of the United States"; and **section 9** provides:

"The pardoning power shall be vested in the governor under such regulations and restrictions as may be prescribed by law." **Section 11** also gives the governor the "power to remit fines and forfeitures, under such regulations as may be prescribed by law. . . ."

Section 13 authorizes the governor to fill certain vacancies by appointment. In *Biggs v. State Dept. of Retirement Systems* (1981), the Washington court of appeals found that the constitutional provision for filling vacancies in appointive office has no application to appointments made pursuant to specific statutory authority or within the governor's general grant of executive powers; and that where neither the state's case law nor minutes of the constitutional convention can resolve a question of constitutional interpretation, the court may look to similar provisions in other state constitutions for guidance.

Section 12, as amended in 1974, addresses the governor's veto powers. Every act passed by the legislature must be presented to the governor for signature. If the governor does not approve the bill, it is returned to the house in which it originated. If two-thirds of the members of each house override the governor's veto, it becomes a law. "If any bill shall not be returned by the governor within five days, Sundays excepted," continues section 12, ". . . it shall become a law without his signature, unless the general adjournment shall prevent its return, in which case it shall become a law unless the governor, within twenty days next after the adjournment, Sundays excepted, shall file such bill with his objections thereto, in the office of secretary of state, who shall lay the same before the legislature at its next session. . . ." This section grants the governor the authority to "object to one or more sections or appropriation items while approving other portions. . . ." In an unusual provision, section 12 also allows the legislature to reconvene to reconsider a vetoed bill upon the petition of a "two-thirds majority or more of the membership of each house."

Section 10, as amended in 1910, states that in the event of the governor's removal, resignation, death, or disability, the duties of the office are assumed by the lieutenant governor. If both the offices of the governor and lieutenant governor are vacant, the secretary of state shall assume the governor's duties. According to **section 16,** the lieutenant governor is also the presiding officer of the senate and "shall discharge such other duties as may be prescribed by law."

Article IV, The Judiciary, section 1, declares: "The judicial power of the state shall be vested in a supreme court, superior courts, justices of the peace, and such inferior courts as the legislature may provide." **Section 2** stipulates that "[t]he supreme court shall consist of five judges, a majority of whom shall be necessary to form a quorum, and pronounce a decision . . . ," although the legislature does have the power to increase the number of supreme court judges and provide for separate departments of the court. Nine judges currently serve on the Washington supreme court.

Judicial Branch

Section 3, as amended in 1995, provides that supreme court judges are to be elected in the general state election "at the times and places at which state officers are elected, unless some other time be provided by the legislature." At the first election for supreme court justices, they are classified by lot, "so that two shall hold their office for the term of three years, two for the term of five years, and one for the term of seven years." The supreme court judges choose from among themselves a chief justice who serves for a four-year term and presides at sessions of the supreme court. In subsequent elections the term of judges is six years. Section 3 continues: "If a vacancy occurs in the office of a judge of the supreme court the governor shall only appoint a person to ensure the number of judges as specified by the legislature, to hold the office until the election and qualification of a judge to fill the vacancy...."

Section 17 provides that supreme court and superior court judges must be members of the Washington state bar, and, according to **section 15,** they are ineligible to hold any other judicial or public office during their term. **Section 19** mandates: "No judge of a court of record shall practice law in any court of this state during his continuance in office." **Section 3(a),** added in 1952, states that judges of the supreme court and superior courts must retire "at the end of the calendar year in which [they attain] the age of seventy-five years." The legislature can lower the age for mandatory retirement, but it cannot be earlier "than the end of the calendar year in which any such judge attains the age of seventy years...."

Section 4 states that the supreme court has original jurisdiction in habeas corpus, quo warranto, and mandamus with respect to all state officers, and appellate jurisdiction in all actions and proceedings. However, its appellate jurisdiction does not extend to "civil actions at law for the recovery of money or personal property when the original amount in controversy, or the value of the property does not exceed ... ($200) unless the action involves the legality of a tax, impost, assessment, toll, municipal fine, or the validity of a statute."

Section 9 provides that all judges, the attorney general, and prosecuting attorneys may be removed from office by joint resolution of the legislature, approved by three-fourths of the members of each house, for "incompetency, corruption, malfeasance, or delinquency in office, or other sufficient cause stated in such resolution." **Section 31,** added in 1980 and amended in 1986 and 1989, creates a commission on judicial conduct to act "**(1)** ... as an independent agency of the judicial branch...." **Section 31(5)** states in part that on the commission's recommendation "the supreme court may suspend, remove, or retire a judge or justice."

Impeachment

Article V, Impeachment, section 1, mandates in part: "The house of representatives shall have the sole power of impeachment. The concurrence of a majority of all the members shall be necessary to an impeachment." The senate tries all impeachments, and convictions require the concurrence of two-thirds of the senators. **Section 2** provides that "[t]he governor and other state and judicial officers, except judges and justices of courts not of record, shall be liable to impeachment for high crimes or misdemeanors, or malfeasance in office, but judgment in such cases shall extend only to removal from office and disqualification to hold any office of honor, trust or profit, in the state." Whether convicted or exonerated, the officer is liable to further punishment "according to law."

Section 3 states that all officers not liable to impeachment may be removed "for misconduct or malfeasance in office, in such manner as may be provided by law."

Article II, Legislative Department, section 1, as amended in 1912, 1962, and 1981, declares in part: "[T]he people reserve to themselves the power to propose bills, laws, and to enact or reject the same at the polls, independent of the legislature, and also reserve power, at their own option, to approve or reject at the polls any act, item, section, or part of any bill, act, or law passed by the legislature." **Article I, Declaration of Rights, section 33,** added in 1912, provides in part: "Every elective public officer of the state of Washington ... [except] judges of courts of record is subject to recall and discharge by the legal voters of the state, or of the political subdivision of the state, from which he was elected whenever a petition demanding his recall, reciting that such officer has committed some act or acts of malfeasance or misfeasance while in office, or who has violated his oath of office...." In *Cudihee v. Phelps* (1913), the Washington supreme court held that the question of the truth of the charges on which the recall of a public official was based was a political rather than a judicial question.

Article XI, County, City, and Township Organization, section 4, as amended in 1948, directs the legislature to "establish a system of county government, which shall be uniform throughout the state except as hereinafter provided, and by general laws shall provide for township organization, under which any county may organize whenever a majority of the qualified electors of such county voting at a general election shall so determine."

Article VII, Revenue and Taxation, section 1, as amended in 1930 and 1988, declares in part: "The power of taxation shall never be suspended, surrendered or contracted away. All taxes shall be uniform upon the same class of property within the territorial limits of the authority levying the tax and shall be levied and collected for public purposes only." **Section 10,** added in 1966, gives the legislature the power, "by appropriate legislation, to grant to retired property owners relief from the property tax on the real property occupied as a residence by those owners...."

Article IX, Education, section 1, proclaims: "It is the paramount duty of the state to make ample provision for the education of all children residing within its borders, without distinction or preference on account of race, color, caste, or sex." **Section 2** directs the legislature to provide for "a general and uniform system of public schools"; furthermore, "the entire revenue derived from the common school fund and the state tax for common schools shall be exclusively applied to the support of the common schools."

Article XXVI, Compact with the United States, states in part: "**First.** That perfect toleration of religious sentiment shall be secured and that no inhabitant of this state shall ever be molested in person or property on account of his or her mode of religious worship. **Second.** That the people inhabiting this state do agree and declare that they forever disclaim all right and title to the unappropriated public lands lying with the boundaries of this state, and to all lands lying within said limits owned or held by any Indian or Indian tribes...."

Direct Democracy

Local Government

Taxation and Finance

Education

Compact with the United States

Amendment Procedures   **Article XXIII, Amendments, section 1,** as amended in 1962, provides that amendments to the state constitution may be proposed in either house of the legislature. If two-thirds of the members of each house approve the proposal, it is submitted to the voters at the next general election. And if a majority of voters approve and ratify the proposal, "the same shall become part of this Constitution, and proclamation thereof shall be made by the governor. . . ."

Section 2 addresses the issue of calling a convention: "Whenever two-thirds of the members elected to each branch of the legislature shall deem it necessary to call a convention to revise or amend this Constitution, they shall recommend to the electors to vote at the next general election, for or against a convention, and if a majority of all the electors voting at said election shall have voted for a convention, the legislature shall at the next session, provide by law for calling the same. . . ." **Section 3** requires that any constitution adopted by such convention "shall have no validity until it has been submitted to and adopted by the people."

On June 20, 1863, West Virginia became the thirty-fifth state of the United States. Charleston is the capital of the "Mountain State," which encompasses some 24,231 square miles. West Virginia, which has a northern and an eastern panhandle, is bordered by Ohio, Pennsylvania, and Maryland on the north; Maryland and Virginia on the east; Virginia on the south; and Kentucky and Ohio on the west. With approximately 1.8 million residents, it ranks thirty-fifth among the states in population. West Virginia's principal industries include manufacturing, services, and mining; apples, peaches, hay, and tobacco are among its chief crops.

Government: The governor is elected for a four-year term but is limited to two consecutive terms. There is no position of lieutenant governor. The legislature consists of thirty-four senators elected for four-year terms, one-half of whom are elected every two years, and 100 members of the house of delegates elected for two-year terms. The supreme court of appeals includes a chief justice and four associate justices elected for twelve-year terms.

Dates of Constitutions: 1863 and 1872

General Information

Constitutional History

The concept of a separate state comprising the territory of western Virginia predates the Declaration of Independence, but the idea did not become a reality until 1863. Until then, West Virginia's history was bound up with Virginia's and its citizens were governed by the Virginia constitutions of 1776, 1830, and 1851. In 1773 the committee on plantation affairs and the privy council in London were nearly persuaded by the Grand Ohio or Walpole Company, an Anglo-Pennsylvania business enterprise, to create a fourteenth British colony—to be called Vandalia—from the western territory of the Virginia Colony. In fact, George III's approval of the scheme was pending when the Revolutionary War broke out in 1775.

Following the formation of the United States, the population of the western portion of the Old Dominion grew more rapidly than that of the eastern portion, creating a demand for greater representation in the state legislature. The 1830 Virginia constitution, however, failed to make meaningful reforms demanded by the westerners. By 1840 the population of the trans-Allegheny region had exceeded that of the eastern region. A constitutional convention known as the "reform convention" met in 1850 and produced a new document, adopted the following year, that allotted the west the bulk of the seats in the lower house of the legislature while the east retained control of the upper house. However, the document's taxation provisions greatly favored the Tidewater aristocrats over the mountaineers.

Western Virginians, few of whom were large landowners or slaveholders, were economically and socially as well as geographically distinct from the easterners. When Virginia started moving toward secession from the Union in 1861, citizens in a number of the western counties began to explore the possibility of forming a separate state. A convention held in Wheeling on May 13 simply made another convention contingent on approval of secession by the entire commonwealth, which occurred on May 23. Another convention then met in Wheeling between June 11 and 15 and called for the formation of the state of Kanawha (the Kanawha River is a major waterway in the area).

Thirty-nine western counties voted overwhelmingly for separation from the Commonwealth of Virginia, and a constitutional convention assembled on November 26, 1861. The constitution that emerged was based in many respects on the Virginia document, but one important change had to do with the apportionment of both houses of the legislature, which was to be based on the white population, as the westerners had argued for in the Virginia legislature. Another change was that the governor was to be elected for two years and eligible for reelection (Virginia's governor served four years and was ineligible for succeeding terms). The court system created, however, was similar to Virginia's.

On New Year's Eve 1862, President Abraham Lincoln signed an act for the admission of West Virginia as a state of the Union. Its constitution, however, had to be revised to accommodate an amendment in Congress sponsored by Virginia's Union senator, Waitman Willey, which granted freedom for slaves of various age categories within the jurisdiction of the potential new state. On March 12, 1863, the revised constitution was overwhelmingly approved by the voters and went into effect on June 20, 1863, when West Virginia officially joined the Union.

The 1863 constitution did not last long. The legislature's call for a constitutional convention was narrowly approved by the voters in August 1871, and a constitutional convention assembled in Charleston on January 16, 1872. A major issue was the treatment of former members of the Confederate Army and Confederate sympathizers, who had been disqualified from participating in the state government. Although these disqualifications were eliminated by law, to drive home the point two sections were added to the new document: article III, section 11, which barred political tests for civil and political rights; and article VI, section 43, which declared that the legislature would never "authorize or establish a board or court of registration for voters." The new constitution was approved at the polls on August 22, 1872, and went into effect on the same day.

The Constitution

The 1872 West Virginia constitution and its 1863 predecessor both borrowed liberally from Virginia's constitutions, but differences reflect disputes between the eastern and western regions about particular provisions of Virginia's documents. Although the 1872 convention represented a conservative reaction to the Reconstruction period, it nevertheless perpetuated many of the progressive elements of the 1863 constitution.

The current West Virginia constitution has held up well in spite of serious attempts in 1897, 1903, 1929, and 1965 to overhaul it. In 1965 the legislature called for a referendum on assembling a constitutional convention, but the West Virginia supreme court of appeals, in *State ex rel. Smith v. Gore* (1965), voided the process, ruling that the apportionment of delegates violated article II, section 4. A number of reforms, enacted especially between 1968 and 1974 and including modernization of the state government and meaningful budget reform, have helped the constitution keep pace with the times. At approximately 26,000 words, the 1872 West Virginia constitution is a little shorter than the average length of state constitutions, and as of January 1, 1998, it has been amended sixty-seven times.

Preamble

The preamble to the 1872 West Virginia constitution, which was added by amendment in 1960, proclaims: "Since through Divine Providence we enjoy the blessings of civil, political and religious liberty, we, the people of West Virginia, in and through the provisions of this constitution, reaffirm our faith in and constant reliance upon

God and seek diligently to promote, preserve and perpetuate good government in the state of West Virginia for the common welfare, freedom and security of ourselves and our posterity."

Preceding the constitution's bill of rights are two articles that relate to West Virginia's unique origin, its creation from an existing state of the Confederacy. **Article I, Relations to the Government of the United States, section 1,** declares: "The state of West Virginia is, and shall remain, one of the United States of America. The constitution of the United States of America, and the laws and treaties made in pursuance thereof, shall be the supreme law of the land." A similar provision formally acknowledging the acceptance or supremacy of the U.S. Constitution, however, can be found in the constitutions of some other states, including Hawaii. In *Lance v. Board of Educ.* (1969), the West Virginia supreme court of appeals held that, pursuant to the clear and unambiguous language of section 1, a provision of the U.S. Constitution takes precedence over a provision of the state constitution.

Section 2 provides in part: "Among the powers so reserved to the states is the exclusive regulation of their own internal government and police; and it is the high and solemn duty of the several departments of government, created by this constitution, to guard and protect the people of this state from all encroachments upon the rights so reserved."

Article II, The State, section 1, lists the counties of the state. **Section 2** lodges the power of government in the citizens; **section 3** confers state citizenship on all persons "residing in this state, born, or naturalized in the United States, and subject to the jurisdiction thereof"; and **section 4** provides: "Every citizen shall be entitled to equal representation in the government, and, in all apportionments of representation, equality of numbers of those entitled thereto, shall as far as practicable, be preserved."

Article III, Bill of Rights, section 1, declares: "All men are, by nature, equally free and independent, and have certain inherent rights, of which, when they enter into a state of society, they cannot, by any compact, deprive or divest their posterity, namely: The enjoyment of life and liberty, with the means of acquiring and possessing property, and of pursuing and obtaining happiness and safety." **Section 2** states that "[a]ll power is vested in, and consequently derived from, the people. Magistrates are their trustees and servants, and at all times amenable to them."

Section 3 confirms that the people have a right to "reform, alter or abolish" any government found to be inadequate or contrary to their purposes. **Sections 4, 5,** and **6,** respectively, prohibit the suspension of the writ of habeas corpus, ex post facto laws, and laws impairing the obligation of contracts; prohibit excessive bail; and guarantee security against unreasonable searches and seizures, in language similar to the Fourth Amendment (1791) to the U.S. Constitution.

Section 7 states: "No law abridging the freedom of speech, or of the press, shall be passed; but the Legislature may, by suitable penalties, restrain the publication or sale of obscene books, papers, or pictures, and provide for the punishment of libel, and defamation of character, and for the recovery, in civil actions, by the aggrieved party, of suitable damages for such libel, or defamation." In *UMW v. Parsons* (1983), the West Virginia supreme court of appeals found that this section and article III, section 3, required the state to preserve its neutrality in political debates by providing a reasonable opportunity for the presentation of views contrasting with those expressed by the state in the media. **Section 8** authorizes truth as a defense against a charge of libel.

Section 9 provides in part: "Private property shall not be taken or damaged for public use, without just compensation...." **Section 10** mandates that "[n]o person shall be deprived of life, liberty, or property, without due process of law, and the judgment of his peers." **Section 11** proclaims in part: "Political tests, requiring persons, as a prerequisite to the enjoyment of their civil and political rights, to purge themselves by their own oaths, of past alleged offenses, are repugnant to the principles of free government, and are cruel and oppressive." No religious or political tests are required "to vote, serve as a juror, sue, plead, appeal, or pursue any profession or employment."

Sections 12 through **15**, respectively, provide for subordination of the military to civilian power, the right to trial by jury, rights of those accused of crimes, and religious freedom. **Section 15a**, added in 1984, states in part: "Public schools shall provide a designated brief time at the beginning of each school day for any student desiring to exercise [his or her] right to personal and private contemplation, meditation or prayer." **Sections 16** through **22**, respectively, address the right to public assembly; the right to open courts and speedy justice; prohibition of any "corruption of blood or forfeiture of estate" for persons convicted of crimes; prohibition of hereditary emoluments, honors, and privileges; preservation of free government; the right of women to serve on juries; and the right to keep and bear arms, the latter two added in 1956 and 1986, respectively.

Division of Powers

Article V, Division of Powers, section 1, declares: "The legislative, executive and judicial departments shall be separate and distinct, so that neither shall exercise the powers properly belonging to either of the others; nor shall any person exercise the powers of more than one of them at the same time, except that justices of the peace shall be eligible to the Legislature."

Legislative Branch

Article VI, The Legislature, section 1, vests the state's legislative power in a senate and house of delegates and notes: "The Style of their Acts shall be, 'Be it enacted by the Legislature of West Virginia.'" **Section 2** specifies: "The Senate shall be composed of twenty-four, and the House of Delegates of sixty-five, members subject to be increased according to the provisions hereinafter contained." Currently there are thirty-four senators from seventeen senatorial districts and 100 members of the house of delegates. **Section 3** provides that senators serve four-year terms and delegates two-year terms, with the senators' terms staggered: "The senators first elected, shall divide themselves into two classes ... the first to be designated by lot in such manner as the Senate may determine, shall hold their seats for two years and the second for four years, so that after the first election, one half of the senators shall be elected biennially."

Section 12 requires that a legislator be a resident of the district or county for "one year next preceding his election," and if he or she moves from that district or county, the seat "shall be thereby vacated." In *White v. Manchin* (1984), the West Virginia supreme court of appeals held that the word *election* referred to a general election, not a primary election. Sections 13 and 14 list a number of disqualifications for membership in the legislature, including "holding any other lucrative office or employment under this state, the United States, or any foreign government ..." and conviction "of bribery, perjury, or other infamous crimes...."

Section 17 exempts legislators from arrest during legislative sessions, as well as ten days before and after, except in cases of treason, felony, and breach of the peace; in addition, "for words spoken in debate, or any report, motion or proposition made in either house, a member shall not be questioned in any other place." Section 18 provides for regular sessions of the legislature, while section 19 allows the governor to convene special sessions by proclamation "whenever, in his opinion, the public safety or welfare should require it" or when requested in writing by three-fifths of the members of each house.

Section 24, as amended in 1970, specifies that a majority of the members of each house constitute a quorum, although "a smaller number may adjourn from day to day, and shall be authorized to compel the attendance of absent members...." Each house may determine its own rules; judge the election, returns, and qualifications of its members; and elect its officers: "The Senate shall choose, from its own body, a president; and the House of Delegates, from its own body, a speaker." Section 25 authorizes each house to "punish its own members for disorderly behavior, and with the concurrence of two thirds of the members elected thereto, expel a member...."

Section 28 states: "Bills and resolutions may originate in either house, but may be passed, amended or rejected by the other." Section 29 requires bills to be "fully and distinctly read, on three different days, in each house, unless in case of urgency, by a vote of four fifths of the members present, taken by yeas and nays on each bill, this rule is dispensed with: Provided, in all cases, that an engrossed bill shall be fully and distinctly read in each house." Section 30 provides in part that "[n]o act hereafter passed shall embrace more than one object, and that shall be expressed in the title.... And no act of the Legislature, except such as may be passed at the first session under this constitution, shall take effect until the expiration of ninety days after its passage, unless the Legislature shall by a vote of two thirds of the members elected to each house, taken by yeas and nays, otherwise direct." Section 31 prescribes the rules for amending a bill or joint resolution that has passed one house of the legislature.

Section 32 defines the phrase "'a majority of the members elected to either house of the Legislature,' or words to that effect" to mean "a majority of the whole number of members to which each house is, at the time, entitled, under the apportionment of representation, established by the provisions of this constitution." This definition could become important in cases where one or more seats are vacant in a particular house and thus the number of elected members is less than the number of seats to which that house is entitled.

Section 51B, added in 1918 and amended in 1968, mandates: "Within ten days after the convening of the regular session of the Legislature in odd-numbered years, unless such time shall be extended by the Legislature, and on the second Wednesday of January in even-numbered years, the governor shall submit to the Legislature a budget for the next ensuing fiscal year. The budget shall contain a complete plan of proposed expenditures and estimated revenues for the fiscal year...." The legislature may amend the budget "by increasing or decreasing any item therein" so long as a deficit is not created, although "no item relating to the judiciary shall be decreased" and "the salary or compensation of any public officer shall not be increased or decreased during his term of office...."

Section 39 enumerates cases in which local and special laws may not be passed, including granting divorces, locating county seats, and providing for the sale of church property; rather, "[t]he Legislature shall provide, by general laws, for the foregoing and in all other cases for which provision can be made...." In *State ex rel. Heck's, Inc. v. Gates* (1965), the West Virginia supreme court of appeals defined a "general" law as one that ideally would apply to everyone and every place in the state but recognized that it was not possible for all legislation to have such universal application.

Section 47 prohibits the granting of a "charter of incorporation ... to any church or religious denomination." **Section 49** requires the legislature to "pass such laws as may be necessary to protect the property of married women from the debts, liabilities and control of their husbands."

Executive Branch

Article VII, Executive Department, section 1, as amended in 1934 and 1958, declares in part: "The executive department shall consist of a governor, secretary of state, auditor, treasurer, commissioner of agriculture and attorney general, who shall be ex officio reporter of the court of appeals. Their terms of office shall be four years, and shall commence on the first Monday after the second Wednesday of January next after their election." **Section 4,** as amended in 1902 and 1970, stipulates that these executive officers may not hold any other office during their term of service; furthermore, "[a] person who has been elected or who has served as governor during all or any part of two consecutive terms shall be ineligible for the office of governor during any part of the term immediately following the second of the two consecutive terms." In *State ex rel. Maloney v. McCartney* (1976), the West Virginia supreme court of appeals indicated that term limitations for political office encourage vigorous competition for the position and thus further political pluralism.

Section 5 vests the chief executive power in the governor, "who shall take care that the laws be faithfully executed." Under **section 12,** the governor serves as commander in chief of the state's military forces, except when they are in the service of the United States, and "may call out the same to execute the laws, suppress insurrection and repel invasion."

Section 6 requires that "[t]he governor shall at the commencement of each session, give to the Legislature information by message, of the condition of the state, and shall recommend such measures as he shall deem expedient." Although this provision is fairly standard, throughout the document *Legislature* is capitalized while *governor* and *exec-*

utive department are not. **Section 7** authorizes the governor to convene the legislature "on extraordinary occasions ... at his own instance." **Section 14,** as amended in 1970, provides that the governor may veto bills passed by the legislature but that such vetoes may be overridden by "a majority of the members elected to" each house; however, a budget bill or supplementary appropriations bill requires "a vote of two thirds of the members elected to each house to become law notwithstanding the objections of the governor." Under **article VI, The Legislature, section 51D(11),** the governor may "disapprove or reduce items or parts" of budget and appropriations bills.

Article VII, Executive Department, sections 8, 9, and **10,** respectively, empower the governor to nominate and, with the advice and consent of the Senate, appoint "all officers whose offices are established by this constitution, or shall be created by law and whose appointment or election is not otherwise provided for"; to fill vacancies during the recess of the Senate; and to "remove any officer whom he may appoint in case of incompetency, neglect of duty, gross immorality, or malfeasance in office...." According to **section 18,** "The subordinate officers of the executive department and the officers of all the public institutions of the state, shall, at least ten days preceding each regular session of the Legislature, severally report to the governor, who shall transmit such report to the Legislature"; moreover, the governor may "require information in writing, under oath," from them relating to their offices.

Section 16, as amended in 1902 and 1958, provides: "In case of the death, conviction or impeachment, failure to qualify, resignation, or other disability of the governor, the president of the Senate shall act as governor until the vacancy is filled, or the disability removed...." In *State ex rel. McGraw v. Willis* (1984), the West Virginia supreme court of appeals declared that the president of the senate continues in that office until a successor is selected, even though that person's term as a senator has expired, thus ensuring that he or she is available to become the state's acting chief executive during this period, should the need arise. The speaker of the house of delegates is next in the line of succession. If a vacancy occurs in the governor's office during the first three years of the term, a new election for governor is to be held.

Article VIII, Judicial Power, concerning the judicial branch, was significantly revised by amendment in 1974.

Section 1 declares: "The judicial power of the state shall be vested solely in a supreme court of appeals and in the circuit courts, and ... magistrate courts as shall be hereafter established by the Legislature, and in the justices, judges and magistrates of such courts." **Section 2** specifies that the supreme court of appeals consists of five justices, a majority of whom constitute a quorum. The justices are elected for twelve-year terms, "unless sooner removed or retired as authorized in this article. The Legislature may prescribe by law whether the election of such justices is to be on a partisan or nonpartisan basis." Elections for justices of the supreme court of appeals are currently on a partisan basis. Section 2 continues in part: "Provision shall be made by rules of the supreme court of appeals for the selection of a member of the court to serve as chief justice thereof."

Section 3 outlines the jurisdiction of the supreme court of appeals. The court has original jurisdiction in proceedings in habeas corpus, mandamus, prohibition, and certiorari and appellate jurisdiction "in civil cases at law where the matter in controversy" is over a dollar amount that may be increased by the legislature; "in civil cases in equity; in controversies concerning the title or boundaries of land; in proceedings in quo warranto, habeas corpus, prohibition and certiorari; and in cases involving personal freedom or the constitutionality of a law." The court has appellate jurisdiction also "in criminal cases, where there has been a conviction for a felony or misdemeanor in a circuit court, and such appellate jurisdiction as may be conferred upon it by law where there has been such a conviction in any other court." In criminal proceedings relating to the public revenue, the state as well as the defendant may appeal. The court has other appellate jurisdiction "in both civil and criminal cases, as may be prescribed by law." Section 3 also provides that the supreme court of appeals has the power to promulgate rules "for all the courts of the state ..., which shall have the force and effect of law." The court has "general supervisory control over all intermediate appellate courts, circuit courts and magistrate courts." The chief justice is the administrative head of all the state courts.

Section 7 requires that all justices, judges, and magistrates be state residents and "commissioned by the governor" even though they are elected. Justices of the supreme court of appeals must have been "admitted to practice law for at least ten years prior to [their] election," while circuit court judges must have been "admitted to practice law for at least five years prior to [their] election." If a vacancy occurs in the office of a justice of the supreme court of appeals or a judge of a circuit court, the governor shall "issue a directive of election to fill such vacancy...."

Section 8 states in part: "Under its inherent rule-making power, which is hereby declared, the supreme court of appeals shall, from time to time, prescribe, adopt, promulgate and amend rules prescribing a judicial code of ethics, and a code of regulations and standards of conduct and performances for justices, judges and magistrates, along with sanctions and penalties for any violation thereof, and the supreme court of appeals is authorized to censure or temporarily suspend any justice, judge or magistrate ... for any violation" and may retire him or her for stated reasons. Section 8 further provides that a justice or judge may be removed "only by impeachment in accordance with the provisions of ... this constitution."

Impeachment

Article IV, Election and Officers, section 9, provides in part that officers of the state may be impeached for "maladministration, corruption, incompetency, gross immorality, neglect of duty, or any high crime or misdemeanor." The house of delegates has the sole power of impeachment, while the senate has the sole power to try impeachments. Conviction requires concurrence of two-thirds of the senators elected. **Section 6** also provides for the removal of "officers elected or appointed under this constitution" for "official misconduct, incompetence, neglect of duty, or gross immorality, in such manner as may be prescribed by general laws...."

Local Government

Article VI, section 39(a), added in 1936, states in part: "The Legislature shall provide by general laws for the incorporation and government of cities, towns and villages, and shall classify such municipal corporations, upon the basis of population, into not less than two nor more than five classes."

Article IX, County Organization, section 1, mandates that the voters of each county elect "a surveyor of lands, a prosecuting attorney, a sheriff, and one and not more than two assessors, who shall hold their respective offices for the term of four years."

Article X, Taxation and Finance, section 5, declares: "The power of taxation of the Legislature shall extend to provisions for the payment of the state debt, and interest thereon, the support of free schools, and the payment of the annual estimated expenses of the state; but whenever any deficiency in the revenue shall exist in any year, it shall, at the regular session thereof held next after the deficiency occurs, levy a tax for the ensuing year, sufficient with the other sources of income, to meet such deficiency, as well as the estimated expenses of such year."

Taxation and Finance

Article XII, Education, section 1, authorizes the legislature to provide, "by general law, for a thorough and efficient system of free schools." **Section 2,** as amended in 1958, directs that these schools be supervised by the state board of education, "which shall perform such duties as may be prescribed by law."

Education

Article XIV, Amendments, section 1, provides for the calling of a constitutional convention by a majority of the members of each house of the legislature and for ratification by the voters. **Section 2,** as amended in 1960 and 1972, notes that amendments may originate in either house of the legislature. If the proposal has been "read on three several days in each house" and "agreed to on its third reading, by two thirds of the members elected thereto …," it must be submitted for ratification by "a majority of the qualified voters" voting in that election. The amendment "shall be in force from the time of such ratification...."

Amendment Procedures

WISCONSIN

Wisconsin, the "Badger State," became the thirtieth state of the United States on May 29, 1848. Its capital is Madison. Bordered by Lake Superior and Michigan on the north, Lake Michigan on the east, Illinois on the south, and Iowa and Minnesota on the west, Wisconsin encompasses some 65,499 square miles. It ranks eighteenth among the states in population with approximately 5.1 millon residents. The state's principal industries include services, manufacturing, trade, and agriculture; among its chief crops are corn, soybeans, peas, and hay.

General Information

Government: The governor and lieutenant governor are elected for four-year terms on a single-party ticket. The legislature consists of thirty-three senators elected for four-year terms, one-half every two years, and ninety-nine members of the assembly elected for two-year terms. The supreme court is composed of a chief justice and six additional justices elected for ten-year terms.

Date of Constitution: 1848

Constitutional History

The territory that would become the state of Wisconsin was inhabited by the Ojibwa, or Chippewa, Winnebego, and Kickapoo peoples, among others, before the arrival of Europeans. The first of these was the Frenchman Jean Nicolet, who entered the region in 1634 during his quest for a northwest passage to India. Between 1658 and 1660 French fur traders came to the Wisconsin shores of Lake Superior, and French Jesuit priests established a mission at De Pere in 1672. On June 17, 1673, Louis Joliet and Father Jacques Marquette arrived at the Mississippi River by following the Fox River from Green Bay, which became the site of a French outpost in 1684.

At the end of the French and Indian War in 1763, all French possessions east of the Mississippi, including the Wisconsin region, were ceded to Great Britain, but British occupation of the area was minimal. The treaty ending the Revolutionary War in 1783 transferred jurisdiction over the Northwest Territory, which included Wisconsin, to the United States. Because Americans too were slow to settle the region, which became a part of the Indiana Territory in 1800, the influence of British Canada remained strong until after the War of 1812. During the war the first U.S. military post in Wisconsin, built in 1814, was captured by the British and then abandoned. In 1816 it was rebuilt as Fort Crawford.

In 1815 Nicolas Boilvin, an Indian agent and justice of the peace, reestablished formal American authority in the Wisconsin region, which had become a part of the Illinois Territory in 1809. To consolidate administration, in 1818 Wisconsin was attached to the Territory of Michigan and remained so until Michigan was on the verge of statehood. By the Territorial Act of 1836, Congress formally established a government for the separate Territory of Wisconsin. The state's name derives from the Chippewa word meaning "grassy place," used to describe land along the Wisconsin River.

On August 6, 1846, Congress passed an Act to Enable the People of Wisconsin Territory to Form a Constitution and State Government, and for Admission of Such State into the Union. Eager for statehood, the voters called a convention that drafted a constitution the same year, but it was decisively rejected for several reasons, including its grant of separate property rights for married women. A new constitutional convention met in Madison from December 15, 1847, to February 1, 1848, and its draft constitution was ratified by the voters on March 13, 1848. The document went into effect when Wisconsin became a state on May 29, 1848.

Only five current state constitutions are older than the 1848 Wisconsin constitution: those of Massachusetts (1780), New Hampshire (1784), Vermont (1793), Maine (1819), and Rhode Island (1842). Relatively short at some 15,531 words, the Wisconsin constitution was originally framed for a simple agricultural community by a sixty-nine-member convention of predominantly young Yankee farmers, all but eighteen of whom were originally from New York and New England. But it has evolved to effectively serve the people by means of 128 amendments as of January 1, 1998, which nevertheless have had little effect on the state's basic structure of government.

Home of Robert M. La Follette, U.S. senator and the Progressive Party's candidate for president in 1924, Wisconsin has been a pioneer in modern state government, enacting the first workable income tax, the first successful workers' compensation law, and an environmental protection program in 1911. U.S. Supreme Court Justice William O. Douglas once commented that the Court's decisions expanding individual liberties between 1953 and 1969 were "just trying to catch up with the Wisconsin Supreme Court."

The Wisconsin constitution creates a typical structure of state government with a bicameral legislature, an executive branch with a governor and lieutenant governor elected on a single ticket and three additional statewide elected officials, and an elected judiciary. Although it has no provision for the popular initiative or referendum, the document provides for recall of incumbent elected officials.

The Constitution

Preamble

The preamble to the 1848 Wisconsin constitution reads: "We, the people of Wisconsin, grateful to Almighty God for our freedom, in order to secure its blessings, form a more perfect government, insure domestic tranquility and promote the general welfare, do establish this constitution." This language obviously reflects that of the preamble to the U.S. Constitution.

Fundamental Rights

Article I, Declaration of Rights, section 1, as amended in 1986, declares: "All people are born equally free and independent, and have certain inherent rights; among these are life, liberty and the pursuit of happiness; to secure these rights, governments are instituted, deriving their just powers from the consent of the governed." The language of this section owes a debt to the Declaration of Independence. In *Matter of Guardianship of L.W.* (1992), the Wisconsin supreme court held that the state constitutional right to liberty includes the right to refuse unwanted life-sustaining medical treatment.

Sections 2, 3, and **4,** respectively, prohibit slavery, affirm freedom of speech and the press and truth as a defense to libel, and guarantee the right to peaceably assemble and petition the government. **Section 5,** as amended in 1922, guarantees trial by jury and states that "the legislature may, from time to time, by statute provide that a valid verdict, in civil cases, may be based on the votes of a specified number of the jury, not less than five-sixths thereof."

Section 6 prohibits excessive bail and cruel and unusual punishment; section 7 covers rights of the accused; and section 8, as amended in 1982, addresses prosecution, double jeopardy, self-incrimination, bail, and habeas corpus. Section 9 states: "Every person is entitled to a certain remedy in the laws for all injuries, or wrongs which he may receive in his person, property, or character; he ought to obtain justice freely, and without being obliged to purchase it, completely and without denial, promptly and without delay, conformably to the laws." A number of other state constitutions, including Rhode Island's, contain similar language guaranteeing the right of redress for wrongs or injuries. And section 9m, added in 1993, provides: "This state shall treat crime victims, as defined by law, with fairness, dignity and respect for their privacy. This state shall insure that crime victims have all of the following privileges and protections as provided by law: timely disposition of the case; the opportunity to attend court proceedings . . . ; reasonable protection from the accused . . . ; notification of court proceedings; the opportunity to confer with the prosecution; the opportunity to make a statement to the court at disposition; restitution; compensation; and information about the outcome of the case and the release of the accused. . . ."

Section 14 states in part: "All lands within the state are declared to be allodial, and feudal tenures are prohibited." Section 15 asserts that "[n]o distinction shall ever be made by law between resident aliens and citizens, in reference to the possession, enjoyment or descent of property." Section 16 prohibits imprisonment for debt, while section 17 provides: "The privilege of the debtor to enjoy the necessary comforts of life shall be recognized by wholesome laws, exempting a reasonable amount of property from seizure or sale for the payment of any debt or liability hereafter contracted."

Section 18, as amended in 1982, affirms freedom of worship, and section 19 prohibits religious tests for state office. Section 20 subordinates the military to civilian power. According to section 21, as amended in 1977, "(2) In any court of this state, any suitor may prosecute or defend his suit either in his own proper person or by an attorney of the suitor's choice."

Section 22 cautions that "[t]he blessings of a free government can only be maintained by a firm adherence to justice, moderation, temperance, frugality and virtue, and by frequent recurrence to fundamental principles." Section 23, added in 1967, provides: "Nothing in this constitution shall prohibit the legislature from providing for the safety and welfare of children by providing for the transportation of children to and from any parochial or private school or institution of learning." Similarly, section 24, added in 1972, states: "Nothing in this constitution shall prohibit the legislature from authorizing, by law, the use of public school buildings by civic, religious or charitable organizations during nonschool hours upon payment by the organization to the school district of reasonable compensation for such use."

Division of Powers

Like the U.S. Constitution and the constitutions of several other states, including New York, the Wisconsin constitution does not formally express the principle of the separation of powers of government. In *State ex rel. Friedrich v. Circuit Court for Dane County* (1995), the Wisconsin supreme court held that the separation of powers doctrine, while not expressly stated in the Wisconsin constitution, is implied in the division of government powers among the legislative, executive, and judicial branches.

Article IV, Legislative, section 1, declares: "The legislative power shall be vested in a senate and assembly." **Section 2** specifies that "[t]he number of the members of the assembly shall never be less than fifty-four nor more than one hundred" and "[t]he senate shall consist of a number not more than one-third nor less than one-fourth of the number of the members of the assembly."

Section 3, as amended in 1982, provides: "At its first session after each enumeration made by the authority of the United States, the legislature shall apportion and district anew the members of the senate and assembly, according to the number of inhabitants." This relatively simple provision regarding apportionment constrasts with the Hawaii constitution's detailed reapportionment provisions, which constitute an entire article with ten sections. In *State ex rel. Reynolds v. Zimmerman* (1964), the Wisconsin supreme court recognized the federalization of state reapportionment and its own power to grant some form of affirmative relief from malapportionment by the legislature.

Section 5, as amended in 1982, stipulates: "The senators shall be elected by single districts of convenient contiguous territory, at the same time and in the same manner as members of the assembly are required to be chosen; and no assembly district shall be divided in the formation of a senate district. The senate districts shall be numbered in the regular series, and the senators shall be chosen alternately from odd- and even-numbered districts for the term of 4 years." **Section 14** authorizes the governor to "issue writs of election to fill such vacancies as may occur in either house of the legislature."

Section 6 requires that for eligibility to the legislature a person be a state resident for one year and "a qualified elector in the district which he may be chosen to represent." **Section 13,** as amended in 1966, disqualifies from serving in the legislature "a member of congress, or [a person] holding any military or civil office under the United States...."

Section 7 allows each house to judge the election and qualifications of its members and defines a quorum as "a majority of each," although "a smaller number may adjourn from day to day and may compel the attendance of absent members...." **Section 8** authorizes each house to "determine the rules of its own proceedings, punish for contempt and disorderly behavior, and with the concurrence of two-thirds of all the members elected, expel a member"; however, "no member shall be expelled a second time for the same cause." **Section 15** exempts legislators from arrest, except in cases of treason, felony, and breach of the peace, and from civil action "during the session of the legislature, nor for fifteen days next before the commencement and after the termination of each session." **Section 16** provides: "No member of the legislature shall be liable in any civil action, or criminal prosecution whatever, for words spoken in debate."

Section 17, as amended in 1977, provides in part: "**(2)** No law shall be enacted except by bill ... [or] be in force until published. **(3)** The legislature shall provide by law for the speedy publication of all laws." **Section 19** permits bills to "originate in either house" and provides that "a bill passed by one house may be amended by the other."

Section 31, as amended in 1993, prohibits the legislature from passing special and private laws in certain cases, including "**(1)** ... changing the names of persons, constituting one person the heir at law of another or granting any divorce[;] **(3)** ... authorizing persons to keep ferries across streams at points wholly within the state[;] [and] **(7)** ... granting corporate powers or privileges, except to cities." **Section 32,** as amended in 1993, states: "The legislature may provide by general law for the treatment of any subject for which lawmaking is prohibited by section 31.... Subject to reasonable classifications, such laws shall be uniform in their operation throughout the state." In *Libertarian Party of Wisconsin v. State* (1996), the Wisconsin supreme court found that legislation is "general" if it contains classifications that are open, germane, and related to the true differences among the entities being classified.

Executive Branch

Article V, Executive, section 1, as amended in 1979, vests the state's executive power in "a governor who shall hold office for 4 years" and "a lieutenant governor [who] shall be elected at the same time and for the same term." In 1967 Wisconsin changed the term of office of its governor from two to four years. **Section 3,** as amended in 1967, requires that the governor and lieutenant governor "be chosen jointly, by the casting by each voter of a single vote applicable to both offices beginning with the general election in 1970." Pursuant to **section 2,** "No person except a citizen of the United States and a qualified elector of the state shall be eligible to the office of governor or lieutenant governor."

Section 4 discusses the governor's powers and duties, beginning: "The governor shall be commander in chief of the military and naval forces of the state." He or she may convene the legislature "on extraordinary occasions" and "in case of invasion, or danger from the prevalence of contagious disease at the seat of government, he may convene them at any other suitable place within the state." In addition, the governor "shall communicate to the legislature, at every session, the condition of the state, and recommend such matters to them for their consideration as he may deem expedient[;] transact all necessary business with the officers of the government, civil and military[;] expedite all such measures as may be resolved upon by the legislature; [and] take care that the laws be faithfully executed." **Section 6** empowers the governor to "grant reprieves, commutations and pardons, after conviction, for all offenses, except treason and cases of impeachment, upon such conditions and with such restrictions and limitations as he may think proper, subject to such regulations as may be provided by law relative to the manner of applying for pardons."

Section 7, as amended in 1979, deals with succession to the governorship: "**(1)** Upon the governor's death, resignation or removal from office, the lieutenant governor shall become governor for the balance of the unexpired term. **(2)** If the governor is absent from this state, impeached [or physically or mentally incapacitated], the lieutenant governor shall serve as acting governor [temporarily]." According to **section 8,** as amended in 1979, the secretary of state is next in the line of succession.

Section 10, as amended in 1990, addresses the governor's veto power: "**(1)(a)** Every bill which shall have passed the legislature shall, before it becomes a law, be presented to the governor. **(b)** If the governor approves and signs the bill, the bill shall become law...." The governor may veto appropriations bills in whole or in part but, pursuant to **section 10(1)(c)**, "may not create a new word by rejecting individual letters in the words of the enrolled bill." Before this particular restriction, the item veto power was the most extensive given to any state executive. In *State ex rel. Wisconsin Senate v. Thompson* (1988), the Wisconsin supreme court held that this section permitted the governor to veto phrases, digits, letters, and word fragments; to exercise partial veto power by striking digits resulting in reduction of appropriations; and even to change the meaning of legislation by selectively striking phrases and words within a sentence.

Section 10(2)(a) further provides: "If the governor rejects the bill, the governor shall return the bill, together with the objections in writing, to the house in which the bill orig-inated." The veto may be overridden by two-thirds of the members present. Vermont has the same requirement for overriding a veto, but other states have other requirements. Some, like Kentucky, require a majority of the members elected; some, like Rhode Island, require three-fifths of the members present and voting; and others, like Louisiana, require two-thirds of the members elected to the legislature.

Article VI, Administrative, section 1, as amended in 1979, states that "[t]he qualified electors of this state, at the times and places of choosing the members of the legislature, shall in 1970 and every 4 years thereafter elect a secretary of state, treasurer and attorney general who shall hold their offices for 4 years." **Section 2,** as amended in 1946, requires that the secretary of state "keep a fair record of the official acts of the legislature and executive department of the state" and "when required, lay the same and all matters relative thereto, before either branch of the legislature." In addition, the office holder performs "such other duties as shall be assigned him by law." **Section 3** notes that the powers and duties of the treasurer and attorney general "shall be prescribed by law."

Article VII, Judiciary, section 2, as amended in 1977, provides: "The judicial power of this state shall be vested in a unified court system consisting of one supreme court, a court of appeals, a circuit court, such trial courts of general uniform statewide jurisdiction as the legislature may create by law, and a municipal court [for any city, village, or town] if authorized by the legislature...."

Judicial Branch

Section 4, as amended in 1977, provides: "**(1)** The supreme court shall have 7 members who shall be known as justices of the supreme court. Justices shall be elected for 10-year terms of office ... [but] [o]nly one justice may be elected in any year. Any 4 justices shall constitute a quorum for the conduct of the court's business." Under **section 4(2)**, the justice with the longest continuous tenure on the court becomes the chief justice and as such, under **section 4(3)**, serves as "the administrative head of the judicial system" and exercises such administrative authority "pursuant to procedures adopted by the supreme court." **Section 9**, as amended in 1977, directs the governor to fill by appointment any vacancies that occur on the state supreme court or any other state court, and these appointments "shall continue until a successor is elected and qualified." The section adds: "There shall be no election for a justice or judge at the partisan general election for state or county officers, nor within 30 days either before or after such election."

Section 24, as amended in 1977, requires: "**(1)** To be eligible for the office of supreme court justice or judge of any court of record, a person must be an attorney licensed to practice law in this state … for 5 years immediately prior to election or appointment." **Section 24(2)** provides that no justice or judge may serve "beyond the July 31 following the date on which such person attains that age, of not less than 70 years, which the legislature shall prescribe by law," unless, as provided in **section 24(3)**, he or she is assigned temporary service by the chief justice.

Section 3, as amended in 1977, sets forth the supreme court's jurisdiction: "**(1)** The supreme court shall have superintending and administrative authority over all courts. **(2)** [It] has appellate jurisdiction over all courts and may hear original actions and proceedings … [and] may issue all writs necessary in aid of its jurisdiction. **(3)** [It] may review judgments and orders of the court of appeals, may remove cases from the court of appeals and may accept cases on certification by the court of appeals." The Wisconsin supreme court denied certification of *State v. Grawien* (1985) from the intermediate court of appeals and let stand a decision that, in accordance with the state supreme court's precedent, afforded stronger protection under the state's search and seizure provision than the comparable federal provision under subsequent U.S. Supreme Court precedents. The court of appeals certifying the case to the state supreme court held that its role in the Wisconsin judicial system was to correct errors made in lower courts and that the state supreme court's role was to declare the law.

Section 11 outlines disciplinary proceedings against justices and judges: "Each … shall be subject to reprimand, censure, suspension, removal for cause or for disability, by the supreme court pursuant to procedures established … by law.…" **Section 13** allows justices and judges to be removed from office "by address of both houses of the legislature, if two-thirds of all the members elected to each house concur therein.…" As elected officers, justices and judges are also subject to removal by recall procedures prescribed in **article XIII, Miscellaneous, section 12**, as amended in 1981.

Impeachment

Article VII, Judiciary, section 1, as amended in 1932, provides: "The court for the trial of impeachments shall be composed of the senate. The assembly shall have the power of impeaching all civil officers of this state for corrupt conduct in office, or for crimes and misdemeanors; but a majority of all the members elected shall concur in an impeachment." Conviction requires "concurrence of two-thirds of the members [of the senate] present." Judgment is restricted to "removal from office, or removal from office and disqualification to hold any office … under the state," although "the party impeached shall be liable to [other] punishment according to law."

Direct Democracy

Article XIII, Miscellaneous Provisions, section 12, as amended in 1981, states: "The qualified electors of the state, of any congressional, judicial or legislative district or of any county may petition for the recall of any incumbent elective officer after the first year of the term for which the incumbent was elected, by filing a petition with the filing officer with whom the nomination petition to the office in the primary is filed, demanding the recall of the incumbent." Pursuant to **section 12(1),** the petition must be signed by "electors equaling at least twenty-five percent of the vote cast for the office of governor at the last preceding election, in the state, county or district which the incumbent represents." A recall election is then held in which other candidates may run for the incumbent's office, and, according to section **12(5),** the person receiving the highest number of votes serves the remainder of the term. This recall procedure was originally adopted in 1926.

Article IV, Legislative, section 23, as amended in 1972, provides: "The legislature shall establish but one system of town government, which shall be as nearly uniform as practicable, but the legislature may provide for the election at large once in every 4 years of a chief executive officer in any county with such powers of an administrative character as they may from time to time prescribe in accordance with this section and shall establish one or more systems of county government." **Section 23a,** as amended in 1969, allows the chief executive officer to veto resolutions and ordinances passed by the county board.

Local Government

Article XI, Corporations, section 3, as amended in 1981, allows "**(1)** [c]ities and villages organized pursuant to state law [to] determine their local affairs and government, subject only to this constitution and to such enactments of the legislature of statewide concern as with uniformity shall affect every city or every village. The method of such determination shall be prescribed by the legislature."

Article VIII, Finance, section 5, states: "The legislature shall provide for an annual tax sufficient to defray the estimated expenses of the state for each year; and whenever the expenses of any year shall exceed the income, the legislature shall provide for levying a tax for the ensuing year sufficient, with other sources of income, to pay the deficiency as well as the estimated expenses of such ensuing year." **Section 6** authorizes: "For the purpose of defraying extraordinary expenditures the state may contract public debts (but such debts shall never in the aggregate exceed one hundred thousand dollars)."

Taxation and Finance

Section 8 requires: "On the passage in either house of the legislature of any law which imposes, continues or renews a tax, or creates a debt or charge, or makes, continues or renews an appropriation of public or trust money, or releases, discharges or commutes a claim or demand of the state, the question shall be taken by yeas and nays, which shall be duly entered on the journal; and three-fifths of all the members elected to such house shall in all such cases be required to constitute a quorum therein."

Article X, Education, section 1, as amended in 1982, declares: "The supervision of public instruction shall be vested in a state superintendent and such other officers as the legislature shall direct; and their qualifications, powers, duties and compensation shall be prescribed by law. The state superintendent shall be chosen by the qualified electors of the state at the same time and in the same manner as members of the supreme court, and shall hold office for 4 years. . . ."

Education

Amendment Procedures

Article XII, Amendments, section 1, states in part: "Any amendment or amendments to this constitution may be proposed in either house of the legislature, and if the same shall be agreed to by a majority of the members elected to each of the two houses, such proposed amendment or amendments shall be entered on their journals, with the yeas and nays taken thereon, and referred to the legislature to be chosen at the next general election...." If the proposed amendment or amendments are agreed to by "a majority of all the members elected to each house" at this election and by "a majority of the electors voting thereon," the amendment or amendments "shall become part of the constitution...."

Section 2 provides: "If at any time a majority of the senate and assembly shall deem it necessary to call a convention to revise or change this constitution, they shall recommend to the electors to vote for or against a convention at the next election for members of the legislature. And if it shall appear that a majority of the electors voting thereon have voted for a convention, the legislature shall, at its next session, provide for calling such convention."

Wyoming became the forty-fourth state of the United States on July 10, 1890. Cheyenne is the capital of the "Equality State." Some 97,818 square miles in area, Wyoming is bordered by Montana on the north, South Dakota and Nebraska on the east, Colorado and Utah on the south, and Utah and Idaho on the west. Wyoming ranks last among the states in population with approximately 480,000 inhabitants. The state's principal industries include mineral extraction, oil, natural gas, and tourism and recreation; its chief crops include wheat, beans, barley, and oats.

General Information

Government: The governor is elected for a four-year term and is limited by statute to serving no more than eight years of any sixteen-year period. There is no position of lieutenant governor. The legislature consists of thirty senators elected for four-year terms, with one-half elected every two years, and sixty members of the house of representatives elected for two-year terms. All legislators are limited by statute to serving twelve years of any twenty-four-year period. The supreme court includes a chief justice and four additional justices appointed by the governor from a list prepared by a judicial nominating commission; after the first year they stand for election for eight-year terms.

Date of Constitution: 1890

Constitutional History

Before the arrival of Europeans, the region that would become the state of Wyoming was inhabited by the Shoshone, Crow, Cheyenne, Ogala, and Arapaho peoples. In 1743, while on a fur trading expedition, Francis François and Louis La Vérendrye are reported to have sighted the Big Horn Mountains, a range that runs north and south from Montana into Wyoming. The state's name is derived from a Delaware people's word meaning "large or flat plain."

Meriwether Lewis and William Clark, commissioned by President Thomas Jefferson to explore the territory acquired from France under the terms of the 1803 Louisiana Purchase, missed the Wyoming region by sixty miles during their trek of 1804. The following summer, François Antoine Larocque, a Canadian fur trader, trained the local inhabitants of north-central Wyoming to prepare beaver pelts for the European fur trading market. In 1842 Jim Bridger, an American frontiersman and trapper, together with Louis Vásquez, a mountainman originally from St. Louis, built Fort Bridger in southwestern Wyoming, which they subsequently leased to the government. Under the terms of the 1848 Treaty of Guadalupe Hidalgo, which ended the Mexican War, the Wyoming territory that was not included in the Louisiana Purchase, along with vast expanses in the Southwest, became a part of the United States. A steady stream of Americans began passing through Wyoming en route to California after gold was discovered there in 1849.

The prospects for development were enhanced when in 1864 Congress granted the Union Pacific Company 4,582,520 acres of land in Wyoming to build part of the transcontinental railroad. Two years later, however, eighty U.S. soldiers were killed in the north-central part of the territory by a band of Sioux warriors led by Red Cloud and Crazy Horse. Nevertheless, on July 25, 1868, an act of Congress was approved "to provide a temporary government for the Territory of Wyoming." The population did not increase rapidly, however, impelling the territorial legislature to enhance the figures by granting voting rights to women in 1869. Wyoming thus was the first political jurisdiction in the world to extend suffrage to women. In 1893 New Zealand became the first country to do so, but in the United States women did not obtain the right to vote at the federal level until 1920, when the Nineteenth Amendment to the U.S. Constitution was adopted.

The U.S. census reported fewer than 10,000 nonindigenous residents in Wyoming in 1870 and just a little more than 20,000 in 1880. In September 1889, however, when the nonindigenous population had reached 60,000, a constitutional convention was convened in Cheyenne. By the end of the month it had drafted a constitution that was approved at the polls on November 5. On July 10, 1890, an act of Congress admitting Wyoming as a state of the Union was approved, and its constitution became effective on that day.

The Constitution

The 1890 Wyoming constitution was written in just twenty-five days in 1889, the same year in which constitutions were drafted in Idaho, Montana, North Dakota, South Dakota, and Washington. Of average length, with approximately 31,800 words, the document has been amended sixty-five times as of January 1, 1998. No fundamental changes have been made to the general structure of the government or the civil liberties included when the constitution was adopted, and the Wyoming supreme court has not actively sought to broaden its scope. Wyoming, along with Utah, included women's suffrage rights in its original constitution and was relatively progressive in other areas such as education and civil rights. But since those early days Wyoming has become less innovative and its constitution, accordingly, less remarkable.

The Wyoming constitution, like those of most other states, creates a plural executive branch including an elected governor, secretary of state, auditor, treasurer, and superintendent of public education. However, it makes no provision for an attorney general. It also creates a bicameral legislature and an elected judiciary. Similar to the constitutions of several other states whose economies rely heavily on mineral extraction, including Nevada, the Wyoming constitution contains provisions relating to mines and mining.

Preamble

The preamble to the 1890 Wyoming constitution reads: "We, the people of the State of Wyoming, grateful to God for our civil, political and religious liberties, and desiring to secure them to ourselves and perpetuate them to our posterity, do ordain and establish this Constitution."

Fundamental Rights

Article 1, Declaration of Rights, section 1, proclaims: "All power is inherent in the people, and all free governments are founded on their authority, and instituted for their peace, safety and happiness; for the advancement of these ends they have at all times an inalienable and indefeasible right to alter, reform or abolish the government in such manner as they may think proper." **Section 2** states: "In their inherent right to life, liberty and the pursuit of happiness, all members of the human race are equal."

Section 3 provides: "Since equality in the enjoyment of natural and civil rights is only made sure through political equality, the laws of this state affecting the political rights and privileges of its citizens shall be without distinction of race, color, sex, or any circumstance or condition whatsoever other than individual incompetency, or unworthiness duly ascertained by a court of competent jurisdiction."

Section 4 prohibits unreasonable searches and seizures; **section 5** bars imprisonment for debt, "except in cases of fraud"; **section 6** guarantees due process of law; and **section 7** declares: "Absolute, arbitrary power over the lives, liberty and property of freemen exists nowhere in a republic, not even in the largest majority." This last sentence recalls the words of the nineteenth-century English philosopher John Stuart Mill, who said that humankind would be no more justified in silencing one voice than a single person, if he or she had the power, would be in silencing all the rest of humankind.

Section 8 requires the courts to be open to every person and permits suits to be brought against the state in a prescribed manner. **Section 9,** as amended in 1980, guarantees trial by jury in criminal cases, and **section 10,** as amended in 1976, extends certain rights to those accused of a crime, including the right "to defend in person and by counsel, to demand the nature and cause of the accusation, to have a copy thereof, [and] to be confronted with the witnesses against him. . . ." **Section 11** prohibits self-incrimination and double jeopardy, and **section 12** prohibits any person from being "detained as a witness in any criminal prosecution longer than may be necessary to take his testimony or deposition, nor . . . confined in any room where criminals are imprisoned." **Section 14** guarantees bail "except for capital offenses when the proof is evident or the presumption great"; **section 15** requires that the "penal code shall be framed on the humane principles of reformation and prevention"; and **section 16** mandates: "No person arrested and confined in jail shall be treated with unnecessary rigor. The erection of safe and comfortable prisons, and inspection of prisons, and the humane treatment of prisoners shall be provided for." **Section 17** limits the suspension of the writ of habeas corpus.

Section 18 guarantees the "free exercise and enjoyment of religious profession and worship . . . ," while **section 19** forbids the state to give or appropriate money "to any sectarian or religious society or institution." **Sections 20** through **25,** respectively, guarantee freedom of speech and the press and establish truth as a defense in a libel suit; guarantee the right to peaceably assemble and petition; ensure protection for labor "through laws calculated to secure to the laborer proper rewards for his service"; recognize the "right of the citizens to opportunities for education"; guarantee the right to bear arms; and subordinate the military to civil power and limit the quartering of soldiers in private homes. **Section 26** defines treason, and **section 27** mandates: "Elections shall be open, free and equal, and no power, civil or military, shall at any time interfere to prevent an untrammeled exercise of the right of suffrage." **Section 28,** as amended in 1988, requires the consent of the people for taxation; and **section 29** guarantees equal treatment for aliens "as to the possession, taxation, enjoyment and descent of property."

Section 31 addresses the control of water. **Section 32** allows the use of private property for "private ways of necessity, and for reservoirs, drains, flumes or ditches on or across the lands of others for agricultural, mining, milling, domestic or sanitary purposes. . . ."; but **section 33** guarantees: "Private property shall not be taken or damaged for public or private use without just compensation." **Sections 34** through **37,** respectively, require that "[a]ll laws of a general nature shall have a uniform operation"; prohibit ex post facto laws and laws impairing the obligation of contracts; reserve rights of the people not enumerated in the constitution; and proclaim: "The State of Wyoming is an inseparable part of the federal union, and the constitution of the United States is the supreme law of the land."

Division of Powers

Article 2, Distribution of Powers, section 1, proclaims: "The powers of the government of this state are divided into three distinct departments: The legislative, executive and judicial, and no person or collection of persons charged with the exercise of powers properly belonging to one of these departments shall exercise any powers properly belong to either of the others, except as in this constitution expressly directed or permitted."

Legislative Branch

Article 3, Legislative Department, section 1, declares: "The legislative power shall be vested in a senate and house of representatives, which shall be designated 'the legislature of the State of Wyoming.'" **Section 2** provides in part: "Senators shall be elected for the term of four (4) years and representatives for the term of two (2) years. The senators elected at the first election shall be divided by lot into two classes as nearly equal as may be. The seats of senators of the first class shall be vacated at the expiration of the first two years, and of the second class at the expiration of four years." Senators must be not less than twenty-five years old, representatives at least twenty-one years old; all must be citizens of the United States and Wyoming and residents of their county or district for at least twelve months before the election. Wyoming has a statutory term limit for its legislators, restricting them to twelve years' service in the legislature during any twenty-four-year period.

Section 3 states in part: "Each county shall constitute a senatorial and representative district...." But this section has been held to be inconsistent with the federal requirement of "one man, one vote," and consequently the legislature may disregard this provision when apportioning either the senate or the house of representatives. **Section 8** notes: "No senator or representative shall, during the term for which he was elected, be appointed to any civil office under the state, and no member of congress or other person holding an office (except that of notary public or an office in the militia) under the United States or this state, shall be a member of either house during his continuance in office."

Section 10 allows the senate to elect a president and the house of representatives a speaker; moreover, "each house shall choose its other officers, and shall judge of the election returns and qualifications of its members." **Section 11** defines a quorum as a majority of each house, although "a smaller number may adjourn from day to day, and compel the attendance of absent members...." Under **section 12,** each house has the power to "determine the rules of its proceedings, and [to] punish its members or other persons for contempt or disorderly behavior in its presence; to protect its members against violence or offers of bribes or private solicitation, and with the concurrence of two-thirds, to expel a member, and shall have all other powers necessary to the legislature of a free state."

Section 14 directs: "The sessions of each house and of the committee of the whole shall be open unless the business is such as requires secrecy. . . ." Section 15 states: "Neither house shall, without the consent of the other, adjourn for more than three days, nor to any other place than that in which the two houses shall be sitting." According to section 16, "The members of the legislature shall, in all cases, except treason, felony, violation of their oath of office and breach of the peace, be privileged from arrest during their attendance at the sessions of their respective houses, and in going to and returning from the same; and for any speech or debate in either house they shall not be questioned. . . ."

Sections 20 through 36 address the passage of bills. Section 20 stipulates: "No law shall be passed except by bill, and no bill shall be so altered or amended on its passage through either house as to change its original purpose," while section 22 provides: "No bill for the appropriation of money, except for the expenses of the government, shall be introduced within five (5) days of the close of the session, except by unanimous consent of the house in which it is sought to be introduced." Section 33 requires that revenue bills originate in the house of representatives, although "the senate may propose amendments, as in [the] case of other bills." The constitutions of a number of other states, including New Hampshire, contain a similar limitation, which is also found in the U.S. Constitution; but those of other states do not. And section 36 notes: "No appropriation shall be made for charitable, industrial, educational or benevolent purposes to any person, corporation or community not under the absolute control of the state, nor to any denominational or sectarian institution or association."

Section 23 directs that "[n]o bill shall be considered or become a law unless referred to a committee, returned therefrom and printed for the use of the members." Section 24 requires: "No bill, except general appropriation bills and bills for the codification and general revision of the laws, shall be passed containing more than one subject, which shall be clearly expressed in its title; but . . . [if not], such act shall be void only as to so much thereof as shall not be so expressed." Pursuant to section 25, a bill becomes law only if approved by a majority of all the members elected to each house; the names of those voting are entered in the journal. Section 26 provides: "No law shall be revised or amended, or the provisions thereof extended by reference to its title only, but so much thereof as is revised, amended, or extended, shall be re-enacted and published at length."

Section 27 prohibits local and special laws in such cases as granting divorces, "changing or amending the charters of any cities, towns or villages," and "opening or conducting of any election or designating the place of voting. . . ." In *Mountain Fuel Supply Company v. Emerson* (1978), the Wyoming supreme court held that a state law voiding indemnity agreements (whereby a contractor agrees to hold a company harmless for its own negligence) only for well drilling and mining activities was a general law, although other occupations were equally dangerous.

Section 28 requires: "The presiding officer of each house shall, in the presence of the house over which he presides, sign all bills and joint resolutions passed by the legislature immediately after their titles have been publicly read. . . ." And section 41 directs:

"Every order, resolution or vote, in which the concurrence of both houses may be necessary, except on the question of adjournment, or relating solely to the transaction of the business of the two houses, shall be presented to the governor [for approval], or, being disapproved, be repassed by two-thirds of both houses as prescribed in the case of a bill."

Sections 43, 44, 45, and 46, respectively, address offers of bribes to officials of the legislative, executive, and judicial branches; witnesses to bribery charges; the offense of corrupt solicitation of government officials; and the requirements for a member "who has a personal or private interest in any measure or bill proposed or pending before the legislature." A further responsibility of the legislature, stated in article 4, Executive Department, section 14, as amended in 1990, is to "provide by law for examination of the accounts of [the] state treasurer, supreme court clerks, district court clerks, and all county treasurers, and treasurers of such other public institutions as the legislature may prescribe."

Executive Branch

Article 4, Executive Department, section 1, declares: "The executive power shall be vested in a governor, who shall hold his office for the term of four (4) years and until his successor is elected and duly qualified." Wyoming has a statutory term limit restricting the governor to serving eight years of any sixteen-year period. According to section 2, to be eligible to run for governor a person must be a U.S. citizen and a qualified elector of the state, at least thirty years old, and a resident of the state for five years before the election; he or she may not hold any other office during the term. In *State ex rel. Johnson v. Crane* (1948), the Wyoming supreme court held that because federal law controls the eligibility of members of Congress, a sitting governor is not precluded from running or being elected to Congress.

Section 4 outlines the governor's powers and duties: "The governor shall be commander-in-chief of the military forces of the state, except when they are called into the service of the United States, and may call out the same to execute the laws, suppress insurrection and repel invasion. He shall have power to convene the legislature on extraordinary occasions. He shall at the commencement of each session communicate to the legislature by message, information of the condition of the state, and recommend such measures as he shall deem expedient." The governor also transacts "all necessary business with the officers of the government, civil and military," expedites all legislative measures, and sees to it "that the laws be faithfully executed." Section 5 grants the governor "the power to remit fines and forfeitures, [and] to grant reprieves, commutations and pardons after conviction, for all offenses except treason and cases of impeachment," but the legislature may "regulate the manner in which the remission of fines, pardons, commutations and reprieves may be applied for." According to section 7, "When any office from any cause becomes vacant, and no mode is provided by the constitution or law for filling such vacancy, the governor shall have the power to fill the same by appointment."

Section 8 discusses the governor's role in the passage of bills: "Every bill which has passed the legislature shall, before it becomes a law, be presented to the governor. If he approve, he shall sign it; but if not, he shall return it with his objections to the house in which it originated. . . ." The veto may be overridden by "two-thirds of the members elected" to each house. Section 8 continues: "If any bill is not returned by the governor within three days (Sundays excepted) . . . , the same shall be a law, unless the legislature by its adjournment, prevents its return, in which case it shall be a law, unless he shall file the same with his objections in the office of the secretary of state within fifteen days of such adjournment." Under **section 9,** "The governor shall have power to disapprove of any item or items or part or parts of any bill making appropriations of money or property embracing distinct items, and the part or parts of the bill approved shall be the law, and [those] disapproved shall be void unless . . . [reconsidered by the legislature in the same manner] as is prescribed for the passage of bills over the executive veto."

Section 6 provides that "[i]f the governor be impeached, displaced, resign or die, or from mental or physical disease or otherwise become incapable of performing the duties of his office or be absent from the state, the secretary of state shall act as governor until the vacancy is filled or the disability removed." **Section 10** addresses bribery or coercion of or by the governor.

Section 11, as amended in 1982, states: "There shall be chosen by the qualified electors of the state . . . a secretary of state, auditor, treasurer, and superintendent of public instruction, who shall have attained the age of twenty-five (25) years respectively, shall be citizens of the United States, and shall have the qualifications of state electors. . . ." Wyoming's constitution, unlike the constitutions of most other states, makes no provision for an attorney general. Section 11 further states in part: "They shall severally hold their offices . . . for the term of four (4) years. . . . The legislature may provide for such other state officers as are deemed necessary." **Section 12** notes: "The powers and duties of the [state officers named under section 11] shall be as prescribed by law."

Article 5, Judicial Department, section 1, as amended in 1967, declares: "The judicial power of the state shall be vested in the senate, sitting as a court of impeachment, in a supreme court, district courts, and such subordinate courts as the legislature may, by general law, establish and ordain from time to time." Wyoming's constitution, like Oklahoma's, places the senate, as a court of impeachment, in the judicial branch of government.

Judicial Branch

Section 4, as amended in 1958, 1972, and 1976, provides in part: "**(a)** The supreme court of the state shall consist of not less than three nor more than five justices as may be determined by the legislature. The justices of the court shall elect one of their number to serve as chief justice for such term and with such authority as shall be prescribed by law. A majority of the justices shall constitute a quorum, and a concurrence of a majority of such quorum shall be sufficient to decide any matter." There are currently five justices on the Wyoming supreme court. Section 4 continues in part: "**(b)** A vacancy in the office of justice of the supreme court or judge . . . shall be filled by a qualified person appointed by the governor from a list of three nominees that shall be submitted by the judicial nominating committee. . . . **(f)** The terms of supreme court justices shall be eight years and the terms of district court judges shall be six years. **(g)** Each justice or judge selected under these provisions shall serve for one year after his appointment and until the first Monday in January following the next general election after the expiration of such year." A justice or judge then stands for election to continue in office for eight and six years, respectively; to remain in office the incumbent must again stand for election at the end of that term.

Section 8 sets forth the qualifications for a justice: "No person shall be eligible to the office of justice of the supreme court unless he be learned in the law, have been in actual practice at least nine (9) years, or whose service on the bench of any court of record, when added to the time he may have practiced law, shall be equal to nine (9) years, be at least thirty years of age and a citizen of the United States, nor unless he shall have resided in this state ... at least three years."

Sections 2 and **3** establish the supreme court's jurisdiction. **Section 2** provides that "[t]he supreme court shall have general appellate jurisdiction, co-extensive with the state, in both civil and criminal causes, and shall have a general superintending control over all inferior courts, under such rules and regulations as may be prescribed by law," while **section 3** states in part: "The supreme court shall have original jurisdiction in quo warranto and mandamus as to all state officers, and in habeas corpus. The supreme court shall also have power to issue writs of mandamus, review, prohibition, habeas corpus, certiorari, and other writs necessary and proper to the complete exercise of its appellate and revisory jurisdiction."

Section 5, as amended in 1972, directs the legislature to "provide for the voluntary retirement and compensation of justices and judges ... , on account of length of service, age and disability, and for their reassignment to active duty where and when needed. The office of every justice and judge shall become vacant when the incumbent reaches the age of seventy (70) years, as the legislature may prescribe...."

Section 6, as amended in 1918, 1972, and 1996, creates a commission on judicial ethics, which "**(d)** ... shall consider complaints of judicial misconduct against judicial officers and, to the extent permitted and as provided for by the code of judicial conduct, may: **(i)** [d]iscipline a judicial officer; or **(ii)** [r]ecommend discipline of a judicial officer to the supreme court or a special supreme court."

Section 16 states: "No duties shall be imposed by law upon the supreme court or any of the judges thereof, except such as are judicial, nor shall any of the judges thereof exercise any power of appointment except as herein provided." **Section 9** creates a clerk of the supreme court "who shall be appointed by the justices of said court and shall hold his office during their pleasure, and whose duties and emoluments shall be as provided by law."

Impeachment

Article 3, Legislative Department, section 17, provides in part: "The sole power of impeachment shall vest in the house of representatives; the concurrence of a majority of all the members being necessary to the exercise thereof. Impeachment shall be tried by the senate sitting for that purpose.... No person shall be convicted without a concurrence of two-thirds of the senators elected." **Section 18** provides: "The governor and other state and judicial officers except justices of the peace, shall be liable to impeachment for high crimes and misdemeanors, or malfeasance in office, but judgment … shall only extend to removal from office and disqualification [for any other state office]. The party … shall, nevertheless, be liable to … [any other] punishment according to law." **Section 19,** as amended in 1986, notes in part: "Except as hereafter provided, all officers not liable to impeachment shall be subject to removal for misconduct or malfeasance in office as provided by law."

Article 3, Legislative Department, section 52, as amended in 1968, sets forth in part: "**(a)** The people may propose and enact laws by the initiative, and approve or reject acts of the legislature by the referendum…. **(g)** The initiative shall not be used to dedicate revenues, make or repeal appropriations, create courts, define the jurisdiction of courts or prescribe their rules, enact local or special legislation, or enact that prohibited by the constitution for enactment by the legislature. The referendum shall not be applied to dedications of revenue, to appropriations, to local or special legislation, or to laws necessary for the immediate preservation of the public peace, health or safety."

Direct Democracy

Article 12, County Organization, section 4, directs the legislature to "provide by general law for a system of township organization and government, which may be adopted by any county whenever a majority of the citizens thereof voting at a general election shall so determine." **Article 13, Municipal Corporations, section 1,** as amended in 1972, provides in part: "**(b)** All cities and towns are hereby empowered to determine their local affairs and government as established by ordinance passed by the governing body, subject to referendum when prescribed by the legislature, and further subject only to statutes uniformly applicable to all cities and towns, and to statutes prescribing limits of indebtedness."

Local Government

Article 15, Taxation and Revenue, section 1, declares: "All lands and improvements thereon shall be listed for assessment, valued for taxation and assessed separately." **Section 3** provides: "All mines and mining claims from which gold, silver and other precious metals, soda, saline, coal, mineral oil or other valuable deposit, is or may be produced shall be taxed in addition to the surface improvements, and in lieu of taxes on the lands, on the gross product thereof, as may be prescribed by law; provided, that the product of all mines shall be taxed in proportion to the value thereof."

Taxation and Finance

Article 16, Public Indebtedness, section 2, mandates: "No debt in excess of the taxes for the current year, shall in any manner be created in the State of Wyoming, unless the proposition to create such debt shall have been submitted to a vote of the people and by them approved; except to suppress insurrection or to provide for the public defense."

Article 7, Education; State Institutions; Promotion of Health and Morals; Public Buildings, section 1, mandates: "The legislature shall provide for the establishment and maintenance of a complete and uniform system of public instruction, embracing free elementary schools of every needed kind and grade, a university with such technical and professional departments as the public good may require and the means of the state allow, and such other institutions as may be necessary."

Education

Environment

Article 8, Irrigation and Water Rights, section 1, states: "The water of all natural streams, springs, lakes or other collections of still water, within the boundaries of the state, are hereby declared to be the property of the state." **Section 2** creates a board of control "to be composed of the state engineer and superintendents of the water divisions; which shall, under such regulations as may be prescribed by law, have the supervision of the waters of the state and of their appropriation, distribution and diversion, and of the various officers connected therewith...." Similarly, because of the importance of land recovered from the sea, the constitution of the Netherlands also establishes water control boards.

Article 9, Mines and Mining, section 1, as amended in 1990, establishes the office of inspector of mines, and **section 3** directs: "The legislature shall provide by law for the proper development, ventilation, drainage and operation of all mines in this state."

Amendment Procedures

Article 20, Amendments, section 1, prescribes: "Any amendment or amendments to this constitution may be proposed in either branch of the legislature, and, if the same shall be agreed to by two-thirds of all the members of each of the two houses, voting separately, ... it shall be the duty of the legislature to submit such ... to the electors of the state at the next general election ..., and if a majority of the electors shall ratify the same, such amendment or amendments shall become a part of this constitution." In *State ex rel. White v. Hathaway* (1970) and several earlier cases, the Wyoming supreme court found that the term *electors* requires a majority of those voting in the election to approve an amendment, not simply a majority of those voting on the amendment.

Section 3 sets forth: "Whenever two-thirds of the members elected to each branch of the legislature shall deem it necessary to call a convention to revise or amend this constitution, they shall recommend to the electors to vote at the next general election for or against a convention, and if a majority of all the electors voting at such election shall have voted for a convention, the legislature shall at the next session provide by law for calling the same...." **Section 4** requires: "Any constitution adopted by such convention shall have no validity until it has been submitted to and adopted by the people."

Constitutions of U.S. Territories

American Samoa became a territory of the United States on February 20, 1929. Pago Pago is the capital of this island group. Approximately 55,000 inhabitants live on one major island and seven smaller ones, which together total about 90 square miles in area. American Samoa is located in the South Pacific Ocean some 40 miles southeast of Western Samoa and 2,300 miles southwest of Honolulu. The islands' principal industries include trade, services, and tourism; among their chief crops are vegetables, nuts, melons, and other fruits.

Government: The executive branch includes a governor and lieutenant governor elected jointly for four-year terms. The legislature, called the *Fono*, is composed of eighteen senators elected by county councils, in accordance with Samoan custom, for four-year terms and twenty members of the house of representatives elected for two-year terms. The supreme court, known as the high court, consists of a chief justice and seven associate justices appointed by the U.S. secretary of the interior for life (during good behavior).

Dates of Constitutions: 1960 and 1967

The Samoan islands were settled around 1000 B.C. by Polynesians. Jacob Roggeveen, a Dutchman, sailed near Samoa in 1722, and English missionaries arrived there in the 1830s. An agreement in 1899 with the United Kingdom and Germany gave the United States sovereignty over the eastern islands in the Samoan group; the remaining islands became known as Western Samoa, now an independent nation. The local chiefs began ceding their islands to the United States in 1900, but Congress did not formally accept the territory until February 20, 1929.

American Samoa, which once served as a strategic naval base for the United States, was administered by the U.S. Navy until 1951, when it was turned over to the U.S. Department of the Interior. The governor was appointed by the department even after the territory's first constitution was adopted in 1960 and its second took effect in 1967. Efforts by American Samoans to achieve greater control over their own affairs led to an amendment that in 1977 provided for an elected governor and an elected house of representatives for the first time.

Although American Samoa's 1967 constitution establishes a government structure similar to that of the states—an executive branch with a governor and lieutenant governor, a legislative branch with a bicameral legislature, and an independent judicial branch—there are a number of significant differences. For example, unlike a state governor, every year American Samoa's governor must "make an official report of the transaction of the Government of American Samoa to the Secretary of the Interior and the Legislature." In addition, judges of the territory's highest court are appointed by the secretary of the interior and, unlike any state or other territory, American Samoa is not within the geographic jurisdiction of a federal district court or court of appeals. As of January 1, 1998, the 6,000-word document has been amended seven times.

The last of six introductory paragraphs in the 1967 constitution of American Samoa reads: "Now, therefore, this revised Constitution having been ratified and approved by the Secretary of the Interior and having been approved by a Constitutional Convention

AMERICAN

SAMOA

General Information

Constitutional History

The Constitution

Preamble

of the people of American Samoa and a majority of the voters of American Samoa voting at the 1966 election, is established to further advance government of the people, by the people, and for the people of American Samoa."

Fundamental Rights

Article I, Bill of Rights, section 1, provides for separation of "church and government" and freedom of religion. **Section 2,** as amended in 1967, states: "No person shall be deprived of life, liberty, or property, without due process of law, nor shall private property be taken for public use without just compensation." **Section 3** asserts in part: "It shall be the policy of the Government of American Samoa to protect persons of Samoan ancestry against alienation of their lands and the destruction of the Samoan way of life and language...."

Sections 4 through **7,** respectively, guarantee respect for the dignity of the individual; prohibit unreasonable searches and seizures; extend rights to those accused of crimes; and guarantee that the writ of habeas corpus will be granted without delay or cost and suspended only "in the case of war, rebellion, insurrection, or invasion." **Section 8** limits the quartering of soldiers in private homes and subordinates the military to civilian authority; **section 9** prohibits imprisonment for debt except in cases of fraud; **section 10** bars slavery; and **section 11** defines treason in terms similar to those used in the U.S. Constitution. **Section 12** makes a "person who advocates, or who aids or belongs to any party, organization, or association which advocates the overthrow [of the government] by force or violence" ineligible for public office. **Section 13** prohibits bills of attainder, ex post facto laws, and the impairment of contractual obligations; **section 14** authorizes the enactment of laws relating to the health, safety, morals, and general welfare of the people; and **section 15** commits the government to operating "a system of free and non-sectarian public education." Declares **section 16** in part: "No law shall be made or enforced which shall abridge the privileges and immunities of the citizens of American Samoa."

Unlike the U.S. Constitution and most state constitutions, the constitution of American Samoa contains no guarantee of trial by jury. In *King v. Andrus* (1977), however, the U.S. District Court held, based on language used by the U.S. Court of Appeals in *King v. Morton* (1975), that the plaintiff, an American citizen and resident of American Samoa, was entitled to a trial by jury on criminal charges. The reasoning was that the government had failed to establish that a trial by jury, as required by the Sixth Amendment (1791) of the U.S. Constitution, would be "impractical or anomalous" in the unincorporated U.S. territory of American Samoa.

Division of Powers

Like the U.S. Constitution and some state constitutions, the constitution of American Samoa does not expressly set forth the principle of the separation of powers.

Legislative Branch

Article II, The Legislature, section 1, as amended in 1971, indicates that the legislature is to consist of a senate and house of representatives. The section further provides that legislation must not be inconsistent with "this Constitution or the laws of the United States applicable in American Samoa" and that appropriations may not exceed revenues. According to **section 2,** "The Senate shall consist of eighteen members, three from the

Manu'a District, six from the Western District, and nine from the Eastern District." In addition, the house of representatives "shall consist of twenty members elected from ... representative districts." The section notes that "[s]enators and representatives shall be reapportioned by law at intervals of not less than 5 years."

Section 3 states that a senator must be a U.S. national (a person who, although not a citizen of the United States, owes allegiance to it); at least thirty years of age at the time of election; and a resident of American Samoa at least five years "and ... a bona fide resident for at least 1 year next preceding his election." A senator, as distinguished from a representative, must also be "the registered matai [chief] of a Samoan family...." Senators are actually elected by a council of the county they are to represent. A representative must be a U.S. national, at least twenty-five years of age, and a resident for five years and "a bona fide resident of the district from which he is elected for at least 1 year next preceding his election." According to **section 6**, "Each senator shall hold office for a term of four years. Representatives ... shall each hold office for a term of two years."

Section 9 provides in part: "Every bill, having passed both Houses, shall be signed by the President of the Senate and the Speaker of the House...." Illinois and other states make a similar requirement. A bill "shall, before it becomes a law, be presented to the Governor for his approval. If he approves it, he shall sign it and it shall become a law, and he shall deposit it in the office of the Secretary of American Samoa." If the governor vetoes the bill, the legislature has fourteen months in which to override it "by a two-thirds majority of the entire membership of each House...." Section 9 also permits the governor to veto "items of appropriation of money." Pursuant to **section 10**, "A majority of all the members of each House, voting in the affirmative, shall be necessary to pass any bill or joint resolution." A quorum, according to **section 21**, is a "majority of each House."

Article IV, Executive Branch, section 1, which provided for the appointment of the governor and secretary of American Samoa, was superseded in 1977 by U.S. Department of the Interior Order no. 3009. **Section 2**, as amended by this order, states: "The Governor and the Lieutenant Governor of American Samoa shall, commencing with the first Tuesday following the first Monday of November in 1977, be popularly elected and serve in accordance with the laws of American Samoa." According to **section 3**, the secretary of American Samoa "may be referred to as Lieutenant Governor" and serves in the absence of the governor. **Section 4**, however, creates the position of secretary of Samoan Affairs, who "shall be appointed by the Governor from among the leading registered matais [chiefs]." The secretary's duties include heading the Department of Local Government and, in conjunction with the district governors, coordinating the administration of district, county, and village affairs and supervising ceremonial functions.

Sections 5 through **10** give the governor, among other responsibilities, the authority to call out the militia, supervise the executive department, grant pardons "after conviction for offenses against the laws of American Samoa," require the incumbent to "give the Legislature information on the state of the Government and recommend [to it] such measures as he may deem necessary and expedient."

Executive Branch

Judicial Branch   **Article III, Judicial Branch,** consists of only three sections that vest judicial power in "the High Court, the District Courts, and such other courts as may from time to time be created by law." They further mandate the judiciary's independence from the other two branches of government and empower the U.S. secretary of the interior to "appoint a Chief Justice of American Samoa and such Associate Justice[s] as he may deem necessary." The high court currently includes a chief justice and seven associate justices.

Amendment Procedures   **Article V, Miscellaneous, section 3,** states in part: "Any amendment to this Constitution may be proposed in either House of the Legislature, and if the same be agreed to by three-fifths of all members of each House … the governor shall then … submit [it] to the voters eligible to vote for members of the House of Representatives at the next general election. If a majority of the voters voting approve [it] the Governor shall … submit the same to the Secretary of the Interior for approval…." According to **section 4,** "In view of the changing conditions in American Samoa, the Governor shall appoint a new Constitutional Committee five years after the effective date of this Constitution to prepare amendments or a revised draft constitution …" to be submitted to the voters and the secretary of the interior for approval.

The Commonwealth of the Northern Mariana Islands became the most recent territory of the United States on November 4, 1986. The island of Saipan is its capital. With an area totaling about 189 square miles in the northern Pacific Ocean, the Northern Marianas are part of the island group known as Micronesia and lie about 125 miles north of the U.S. territory of Guam, 1,500 miles east of the Philippine Islands, and 3,300 miles west of Honolulu. More than 43,000 persons live on the territory's six inhabited islands. Its principal industries include trade, services, and tourism; among its chief crops are melons and other fruits, vegetables, and nuts.

Government: The governor and lieutenant governor are elected for four-year terms, and the governor is limited to two terms. The legislature consists of nine senators elected for four-year terms and eighteen members of the house of representatives elected for two-year terms. The supreme court includes a chief justice and two associate justices appointed by the governor with the advice and consent of the senate for an initial six-year term and a twelve-year term thereafter.

Date of Constitution: 1978

Descendants of settlers from Southeast Asia were living on the Mariana Islands when the Spanish navigator Ferdinand Magellan arrived there on March 6, 1521, on his first voyage around the world. Spanish sovereignty and priests followed in 1565. In 1899, however, Spain sold to Germany the northern Marianas, except for Guam, which had been occupied by the United States in 1898. In October 1914 Japan took possession of the northern Marianas and the rest of Micronesia, excluding Guam, and after World War I it continued possession first under the Treaty of Versailles of 1919 and later under a formal mandate from the League of Nations executed on December 17, 1920.

Although prohibited by the League mandate from doing so, Japan fortified the islands. After one of the bloodiest battles of World War II, the Battle of Saipan during the summer of 1944, U.S. military forces occupied the Mariana Islands. On July 18, 1947, the United States was given jurisdiction by the United Nations to administer the Mariana Islands and the rest of Micronesia under a "strategic" trusteeship agreement, which allowed military use of the islands. U.S. civilian administration went into effect on July 1, 1951. In 1973 the northern Marianas began negotiating with the United States separately from the rest of Micronesia—which includes other island groups such as Palau, Ponape, Yap, and the Marshall Islands—for post-trusteeship status. In 1975 a plebiscite in the northern Marianas approved commonwealth status with the United States. (The other Micronesian islands have variously chosen independence and free association with the United States.) Self-government began in the Commonwealth of the Northern Mariana Islands under its own constitution of January 9, 1978, and eligible residents became U.S. citizens. The U.S. trusteeship agreement, however, was not formally terminated by the United Nations until November 4, 1986, when the conditions for commonwealth status with the United States were fully satisfied.

The 1978 constitution of the Northern Mariana Islands, like those of all the states and territories except Nebraska, creates a bicameral legislature. The governor and lieutenant governor are the only territory-wide elected executive branch officials. As in several

NORTHERN MARIANA ISLANDS

NORTHERN MARIANA ISLANDS

Constitutional History

The Constitution

states including Delaware and Maine, judges are appointed by the governor with the advice and consent of the senate. An 11,000-word document, it has been amended fifty times as of January 1, 1998.

Because land is scarce and historically not easy to transfer, the Marianas constitution, like American Samoa's, restricts ownership of land to persons whose descent can be traced to native ancestors. In lieu of a nonvoting delegate to Congress, the document authorizes a resident representative to the United States, who is elected for four years to represent the commonwealth and perform duties provided by law. Once selected, the representative is certified by the governor to the U.S. secretary of state.

In *Borja v. Goodman* (1990), the Marianas supreme court declared that the Northern Mariana Islands is not a state within the meaning of the Fourteenth Amendment (1868) of the U.S. Constitution and that it did not enter into a political union with the United States on an equal footing with any state.

Preamble

The preamble to the 1978 constitution of the Commonwealth of the Northern Mariana Islands reads: "WE, THE PEOPLE OF THE NORTHERN MARIANA ISLANDS, GRATEFUL TO ALMIGHTY GOD FOR OUR FREEDOM, ORDAIN AND ESTABLISH THIS CONSTITUTION AS THE EMBODIMENT OF OUR TRADITIONS AND HOPES FOR OUR COMMONWEALTH IN POLITICAL UNION WITH THE UNITED STATES OF AMERICA."

Fundamental Rights

Article I, Personal Rights, section 1, states: "No law shall be made that is a bill of attainder, an ex post facto law, a law impairing the obligation of contracts, or a law prohibiting the traditional art of healing." The first part of this section contains language found in most state constitutions; however, the reason for selecting this language to begin the first section of the first article of the constitution is not self-evident, nor is the reference to "the traditional art of healing." **Section 2** guarantees freedom of religion, speech, the press, and "the right of the people peaceably to assemble and to petition the government for a redress of grievances." **Section 3** prohibits unreasonable searches and seizures, expressly including "wiretapping, electronic eavesdropping or other comparable means of surveillance," and states that a "person adversely affected by an illegal search or seizure has a cause of action against the government within limits provided by law."

Section 4 relates certain fundamental rights that are guaranteed in criminal prosecutions, including the rights of the accused; it also prohibits capital punishment. **Section 5** ensures due process of law; and **section 6** guarantees equal protection of the laws regardless of "race, color, religion, ancestry or sex." Added by amendment in 1985, **section 9** affirms the "right to a clean and healthful public environment," prohibiting, except as provided by law, "the storage of nuclear or radioactive material and the dumping or storage of any type of nuclear waste within the surface or submerged lands and waters of the Northern Mariana Islands." Aware of the long-term damage done to the environment by nuclear testing on Enewetok and Bikini in the Marshall Islands, many Pacific islands choose to bar nuclear materials. **Section 10** grants the right of privacy. Pursuant to other 1985 amendments, **section 11** provides restitution for victims of crime; and **section 12** states: "The abortion of the unborn child during the mother's pregnancy is prohibited in the Commonwealth of the Northern Mariana Islands, except as provided by law."

Like the U.S. Constitution and the constitutions of a number of states, the Northern Marianas constitution does not expressly mention the separation of government powers.

Article II, Legislative Branch, section 1, states: "The legislative power of the Commonwealth shall extend to all rightful subjects of legislation and shall be vested in a Northern Marianas Commonwealth legislature composed of a senate and a house of representatives." According to **section 2,** "The senate shall consist of nine members with three members elected at large from each of three senatorial districts.... [The] term of office for senator shall be four years...." A senator is required under the same section to be "qualified to vote in the Commonwealth, at least twenty-five years of age, and a resident and domiciliary of the Commonwealth for at least five years immediately" before taking office. Senatorial candidates must be registered to vote in their senatorial districts.

Section 3, as amended in 1985, provides that the "house of representatives shall consist of fourteen members [since increased to eighteen] ... [and their] term of office ... shall be two years." Representatives must be qualified to vote in the commonwealth, at least twenty-one years of age, and residents for three years before taking office. Candidates must be registered voters of the precinct in which they are standing for office.

Section 5, as amended in 1985, requires that appropriations and revenue bills be introduced in the house of representatives and that "a majority of the votes cast in each house" is necessary for passage of a bill. **Section 7,** as amended in 1985, authorizes the governor to veto a bill or an item in an appropriations bill, but the veto may be overridden by "two-thirds of the members in each house."

Section 6 permits exclusively local laws to be "enacted by the legislature or by the affirmative vote of a majority of the members representing that district." An unusual provision in **section 17,** added in 1985 and amended in 1989, establishes a legislative bureau in the legislature. The functions of the bureau include providing "all required services to the legislature in connection with duties and responsibilities during sessions and committee meetings. It shall maintain all records, files, library and other documents of the legislature."

Article XIX, Code of Ethics, section 1, added in 1985, calls on the legislature to "enact a comprehensive Code of Ethics which shall apply to appointed and elected officers and employees of the Commonwealth and its political subdivisions, including members of boards, commissions, and other instrumentalities." The code is to include a definition of proper conduct for legislators, require that conflicts of interest in the performance of official duties be avoided, and provide for punishment by fines and imprisonment.

Article III, Executive Branch, section 1, declares: "The executive power of the Commonwealth shall be vested in a governor who shall be responsible for the faithful execution of the laws." **Section 4,** as amended in 1985, mandates: "The governor and lieutenant governor shall be elected at large within the Commonwealth for a term of office of four years [and they] shall be elected jointly.... No person may be elected governor more than twice." According to **section 7**, as amended in 1985, and **section 8**, the lieutenant governor succeeds to the office of governor should it become vacant and becomes acting governor in the event of the governor's absence or disability.

Section 9, as amended in 1985, describes the executive duties of the governor, which include submitting a proposed budget annually to the legislature, reporting to the legislature "at least annually" regarding the affairs of the Commonwealth, and granting "reprieves, commutations and pardons after conviction for offenses after consultation with a board of parole. . . ." **Sections 11** through **13**, respectively, create the positions of attorney general, public auditor, and superintendent of education, who are appointed by the governor "with the advice and consent of the senate," except that the public auditor is appointed with the "advice and consent of each house of the legislature." Because the commonwealth has a sizable minority population of citizens whose families have migrated to the Mariana Islands from the Caroline Islands to the south, **section 18**, amended in 1985, provides in part: "**a)** The governor shall appoint an executive assistant for Carolinian affairs who is acceptable to the Carolinian community within the Commonwealth." Other executive branch officials, added in 1985, include a special assistant for women's affairs, under **section 22**, and a resident executive for indigenous affairs, under **section 23**.

Judicial Branch

Article IV, Judicial Branch, section 1, declares: "The judicial power of the Commonwealth shall be vested in a judiciary of the Northern Mariana Islands which shall include those trial and appeals courts established by the legislature under this article." Under **section 2**, as amended in 1985, "The Commonwealth trial court shall have original jurisdiction in all cases in equity and in all cases at law which involve land in the Commonwealth, and in all other civil actions. The court shall also have original jurisdiction in all criminal actions. **Section 3**, also amended in 1985, authorizes the legislature to create an appeals court, which is called the supreme court and consists of a chief justice and two associate justices.

Section 4, as amended in 1985, directs the governor to "appoint judges of the Commonwealth courts with the advice and consent of the senate. The term of office shall be six years and may be increased by law [which it has been] to not more than twelve years for judges who have served at least one term. A judge shall be at least thirty-five years of age, a citizen or national of the United States and possess other qualifications provided by law."

Impeachment

Article III, Executive Branch, section 19, states in part: "The governor and lieutenant governor are subject to impeachment . . . for treason, commission of a felony, corruption or neglect of duty." Under **article IV, Judicial Branch, section 6**, "Judges are [similarly] subject to impeachment. . . ." Pursuant to **article II, Legislative Branch, section 8**, "The legislature may impeach those executive and judicial officers of the Commonwealth subject to impeachment under this Constitution. The house of representatives may initiate impeachment proceedings by the affirmative vote of two-thirds of its members and the senate may convict after hearing by the affirmative vote of two-thirds of its members."

Article IX, Initiative, Referendum and Recall, outlines procedures for enacting laws by initiative under **section 1**; for rejecting laws by referendum under **section 2**; and for recalling elected officials under **section 3**.

Direct Democracy

Article XXII, Official Seal, Flag and Languages, section 3, added in 1985, states that the commonwealth's official languages are to be "Chamorro, Carolinian and English, as deemed appropriate and as enforced by the legislature. The legislature may provide that government proceedings and documents shall be in at least one of the three languages." It adds that the section "shall not be subject to judicial review."

Official Languages

Article XIV, Natural Resources, section 1, authorizes the legislature to manage, control, protect, and preserve the marine resources in waters off the Marianas coasts. **Section 2,** as amended in 1985, provides for a number of islands to be maintained as uninhabited cultural and natural resources. Under **section 3,** "Places of importance to the culture, traditions and history of the people of the Northern Mariana Islands shall be protected and preserved and public access to these places shall be maintained as provided by law. Artifacts and other things of cultural or historical significance shall be protected, preserved and maintained in the Commonwealth as provided by law."

Environment

Article XVIII, Constitutional Amendment, section 1, states: "Amendments to this Constitution may be proposed by constitutional convention, legislative initiative or popular initiative." According to **section 2,** as amended in 1985, the legislature "a) ... by the affirmative vote of a majority of the members of each house, may submit to the voters the question, 'Shall there be a constitutional convention to propose amendments to the Constitution?'" The question must be submitted "no later than ten years after the question was last submitted...." The question may also be proposed by an initiative petition, but in any case a convention must be approved by "two-thirds of the votes cast."

Amendment Procedures

Section 3 provides that the legislature "by the affirmative vote of three-fourths of the members of each house present and voting" may offer amendments, and under **section 4,** amendments may be proposed by popular initiative. Legislative proposals require "a majority of the votes cast" for ratification by the voters, while proposals by convention or initiative need "a majority of the votes cast and at least two-thirds of the votes cast in each of two senatorial districts."

PUERTO RICO

The Commonwealth of Puerto Rico became a territory of the United States on December 10, 1898, and a commonwealth *(Estado Libre Asociado* in Spanish) on July 25, 1952. San Juan is the capital of Puerto Rico, which at 3,508 square miles and with a population of approximately 3.8 million inhabitants is the largest American territory. Situated in the Caribbean Sea, it is the easternmost of the West Indies island group called the Greater Antilles and lies between the Virgin Islands to the east and Hispaniola to the west. The commonwealth's principal industry is manufacturing; its chief crops include coffee, plantains, and pineapples.

General Information

Government: The governor is elected for a four-year term. There is no position of lieutenant governor. The legislature, called the legislative assembly, consists of twenty-eight senators and fifty-four representatives elected for four-year terms. The supreme court includes a chief justice and six associate justices appointed by the governor and confirmed by the senate for life (during good behavior).

Date of Constitution: 1952

Constitutional History

When Christopher Columbus landed on what is now known as Puerto Rico on November 19, 1493, during his second voyage to the New World, the Arawak people called their home Boriquen. The Spanish began settling the island in 1508, and in 1511 the king of Spain, Ferdinand v, formally recognized it as a colony. In November 1897 Puerto Rico ("rich harbor" in Spanish) was granted a Charter of Autonomy, making it a Spanish dominion.

On February 15, 1898, the U.S. battleship *Maine* was blown up and sunk in Havana Harbor, allegedly by the Spanish. During the Spanish-American War that ensued, U.S. troops landed in Puerto Rico on July 25 and secured it by October 18. Under the Treaty of Paris signed on December 10, 1898, Spain ceded Puerto Rico to the United States, after which the Senate ratified the treaty on February 6, 1899. During World War I, 12,000 Puerto Ricans fought for the United States. Puerto Ricans gained U.S. citizenship on March 2, 1917, except that they are exempt from federal taxes and may not vote in presidential elections.

Women in Puerto Rico gained the right to vote for local officials and legislators in 1932; and in 1947 Congress accorded Puerto Ricans the right to vote for their governor, who was previously appointed by the president. Having campaigned in 1948 for a mandate to ask Congress for enabling legislation for a Puerto Rican constitution, after his election Governor Luis Muñoz Marin led a movement that resulted in a compact between the United States and Puerto Rico authorizing a constitutional convention. The convention convened in September 1951, and on July 25, 1952, after a vote of approval by the island's residents, Puerto Rico became a commonwealth with a constitution that went into effect on the same day. Congress made its approval of the Puerto Rican constitution conditional on deletion of a human rights provision, among other things.

The Constitution

Puerto Rico's relationship with the United States as a territory has been ambiguous. In *Downes v. Bidwell* (1901), known as one of the "insular cases," the U.S. Court of Appeals declared that Puerto Rico is not a part of the United States but is an unincorporated territory belonging to it; the court held that Congress thus is constrained only by the fundamental or natural rights of the inhabitants in dealing with the island. Federal authorities have sometimes regarded the island as a state, while on other occasions it has been treated either more or less favorably than a state of the United States. That Puerto Rico is designated a commonwealth and has its own constitution has not deterred the federal judiciary from maintaining jurisdiction over statutory matters dealing with it. There is also little doubt that Congress retains ultimate authority over the island's government affairs under the provision of the U.S. Constitution that gives it the "power to dispose of and make all needful rules and regulations respecting the territory or other property belonging to the United States."

In the space of six years, from 1950 to 1956, three territories of the United States—Hawaii, Puerto Rico, and Alaska—drafted constitutions. Each of these documents has been acclaimed as a model state constitution because of the balanced government structures they create—similar to New Jersey's constitution of 1947—and the clarity and brevity of their language. Puerto Rico's is the shortest of the three documents, consisting of only some 9,200 words, and, as of January 1, 1998, it has been amended only six times.

The untitled preamble to the 1952 Puerto Rican constitution reads in part: "We, the people of Puerto Rico, in order to organize ourselves politically on a fully democratic basis … do ordain and establish this Constitution for the commonwealth which, in the exercise of our natural rights, we now create within our union with the United States of America." **Preamble**

Article I, The Commonwealth, section 1, provides: "The Commonwealth of Puerto Rico is hereby constituted. Its political power emanates from the people and shall be exercised in accordance with their will, within the terms of the compact agreed upon between the people of Puerto Rico and the United States of America." **Fundamental Rights**

Article II, Bill of Rights, section 1, declares in part: "The dignity of the human being is inviolable. No discrimination shall be made on account of race, color, sex, birth, social origin or condition, or political or religious ideas." **Sections 2, 3, 4,** and **5,** respectively, guarantee among other things: "equal, direct and secret universal suffrage"; freedom of religion and separation of church and state; freedom of speech, the press, and the right "peaceably to assemble and to petition the government for a redress of grievances"; and "the right to an education. . . ." **Section 6** allows persons to organize freely, "except in military or quasi-military organizations"; and **section 7** states in part: "The right to life, liberty and the enjoyment of property is recognized. . . ." Other rights include a prohibition against unreasonable searches and seizures, rights of those accused of a crime, and certain rights of children. **Section 20,** which contained additional rights including the "right of every person to obtain work," was removed from the constitution as a condition for approval by Congress.

Like the U.S. Constitution and a number of state constitutions, the Puerto Rican constitution does not expressly acknowledge the separation of powers principle. **Division of Powers**

Article III, The Legislature, section 1, states: "The legislative power shall be vested in a Legislative Assembly, which shall consist of two houses, the Senate and the House of **Legislative Branch**

Representatives, whose members shall be elected by direct vote at each general election." According to **section 2**, the senate is to be composed of twenty-seven senators and the house of representatives of fifty-one members. It provides that these numbers may be increased, as set forth in **section 7**, if in any general election "more than two-thirds of the members of either house are elected from one political party or from a single ticket...." Currently there are twenty-eight senators and fifty-four representatives, all of whom serve four-year terms.

Section 3 provides in part that "Puerto Rico shall be divided into eight senatorial districts and forty representative districts. Each senatorial district shall elect two Senators and each representative district one Representative; [and there] shall also be eleven Senators and eleven Representatives elected at large." **Section 5** mandates: "No person shall be a member of the Legislative Assembly unless he is able to read and write the Spanish or English language and unless he is a citizen of the United States and of Puerto Rico and has resided in Puerto Rico at least two years immediately prior to the date of his election or appointment." Senators must be at least thirty years of age and representatives twenty-five.

Section 16 authorizes the legislative assembly "to create, consolidate or reorganize executive departments and to define their functions." Pursuant to **section 19**, "Every bill which is approved by a majority of the total number of members of which each house is composed shall be submitted to the Governor [for signature]." The governor may veto a bill, but it can be overridden "by two-thirds of the total number of members of ... each house." The governor also has the power to veto items in an appropriations bill.

Executive Branch

Article IV, The Executive, section 1, states: "The executive power shall be vested in a Governor, who shall be elected by direct vote in each general election." The governor's term is set under **section 2** at four years. **Section 3** requires that the governor be at least thirty-five years of age on the date of election and a citizen of the United States "during the preceding five years" and "a citizen and *bona fide* resident of Puerto Rico."

Section 4 provides that the governor is, among other things, to "execute the laws and cause them to be executed"; call the assembly or senate into special session "when in his judgment the public interest so requires"; make certain authorized appointments, some of which require "the advice and consent of the Senate or of both houses . . ."; be commander in chief of the militia; and have power to declare martial law. According to **section 5**, the governor "shall be assisted by Secretaries whom he shall appoint with the advice and consent of the Senate." This makes the governor more like the U.S. president in that he does not share executive power with other elected commonwealth officials as do many state governors. **Section 7** directs that when "a vacancy occurs in the office of Governor . . . , said office shall devolve upon the Secretary of State. . . ."

Judicial Branch

Article V, The Judiciary, section 1, declares: "The judicial power of Puerto Rico shall be vested in a Supreme Court, and in such other courts as may be established by law." In *Bonet v. Texas* (1940), the U.S. Court of Appeals held that the Puerto Rican courts should be accorded special deference in interpreting Puerto Rican laws and should not be overturned except when they are "inescapably wrong." **Section 2** notes that the "courts of Puerto Rico shall constitute a unified judicial system for purposes of jurisdiction, operation and administration." According to **section 3**, "The Supreme Court shall be the court of last resort ... and shall be composed of a Chief Justice and four Associate Justices. The number of Justices may be changed only by law upon request of the Supreme Court." Currently the Puerto Rican supreme court has seven members including the chief justice. Pursuant to **section 4**, as amended in 1960, "No law shall be held unconstitutional except by a majority of the total number of Justices of which the Court is composed...."

Section 8 states: "Judges shall be appointed by the Governor with the advice and consent of the Senate ... ; and shall hold their offices during good behavior." This provision is similar to the one in the U.S. Constitution governing the appointment of justices and judges; under many state constitutions judicial officials are elected for specified terms rather than appointed for life or during good behavior. **Section 9** requires that a supreme court justice be a citizen of the United States and Puerto Rico, be admitted to the practice of law in Puerto Rico at least ten years before the appointment, and reside in Puerto Rico at least five years. **Section 11** indicates that supreme court justices "may be removed for the causes and pursuant to the procedure [for impeachment]."

Impeachment

Article III, The Legislature, section 21, provides in part: "The House of Representatives shall have exclusive power to initiate impeachment proceedings and, with the concurrence of two-thirds of the total number of members ... to bring an indictment. The Senate shall have exclusive power to try and to decide impeachment cases.... No judgment of conviction ... shall be pronounced without the concurrence of three-fourths of the total ... members of ... the Senate...." Judgment is limited to removal from office, but a person may also be liable to other punishment according to law. "The causes of impeachment shall be treason, bribery, other felonies, and misdemeanors involving moral turpitude," it notes.

Taxation and Finance

Article VI, General Provisions, section 2, as amended in 1961, declares in part: "The power of the Commonwealth of Puerto Rico to impose and collect taxes and to authorize their imposition and collection by municipalities shall be exercised as determined by the Legislative Assembly...." **Section 3** mandates: "The rule of taxation in Puerto Rico shall be uniform." According to **section 7**, "The appropriations made for any fiscal year shall not exceed the total revenues ... for said fiscal year unless the imposition of taxes sufficient to cover said appropriations is provided by law."

Education

Article II, Bill of Rights, section 5, guarantees each person the right to an education, "which shall be directed to the full development of the human personality and to the strengthening of respect for human rights and fundamental freedoms." This section provides for a system of "free and wholly non-sectarian public education," adding that "[n]othing contained in this provision shall prevent the state from furnishing to any child non-educational services established by law for the protection or welfare of children."

Health and Welfare **Article II, Bill of Rights, section 15,** prohibits the "employment of children less than fourteen years of age in any occupation which is prejudicial to their health or morals or which places them in jeopardy of life or limb. . . ." It adds that children under sixteen years may not be kept in custody in a jail or penitentiary. Under **section 20,** which was eliminated at the request of Congress, the Puerto Rican constitution would have guaranteed the rights "to social protection in the event of unemployment, sickness, old age or disability" and "to a standard of living adequate for . . . health and well-being," including food, clothing, housing, medical care, "and necessary social services." It also would have ensured special care and assistance for mothers and children. **Article VI, General Provisions, section 19,** indicates that "within the limits of available resources," it is Puerto Rico's policy to provide "for adequate treatment of delinquents in order to make possible their moral and social rehabilitation."

Environment **Article VI, General Provisions, section 19,** asserts in part that it is the commonwealth's public policy "to conserve, develop and use its natural resources in the most effective manner possible for the general welfare of the community; [and] to conserve and maintain buildings and places declared by the Legislative Assembly to be of historic or artistic value. . . ."

Amendment Procedures **Article VII, Amendments to the Constitution, section 1,** provides in part: "The Legislative Assembly may propose amendments to this Constitution by a concurrent resolution approved by not less than two-thirds of the total number of members of which each house is composed." Amendments must be "ratified by a majority of the electors voting thereon" at either a general election or a special referendum.

Section 2 authorizes the legislature "by concurrent resolution approved by two-thirds of the total number of members" of each house to pose the question to the electors "of whether a constitutional convention shall be called to revise this Constitution." To call a convention, "a majority of the electors voting on this question" is necessary. **Section 3,** among other things, prohibits any amendment to the constitution that would "alter the republican form of government established by it or abolish its Bill of Rights."

Appendixes

U.S. Constitution

WE THE PEOPLE of the United States, in order to form a more perfect Union, establish justice, insure domestic tranquility, provide for the common defense, promote the general welfare, and secure the blessings of liberty to ourselves and our posterity, do ordain and establish this CONSTITUTION for the United States of America.

Section 1. All legislative powers herein granted shall be vested in a Congress of the United States, which shall consist of a Senate and House of Representatives.

Section 2. The House of Representatives, shall be composed of members chosen every second year by the people of the several states, and the electors in each state shall have the qualifications requisite for electors of the most numerous branch of the state legislature.

No person shall be a representative who shall not have attained to the age of twenty-five years, and been seven years a citizen of the United States, and who shall not, when elected, be an inhabitant of that state in which he shall be chosen.

Representatives and direct taxes shall be apportioned among the several states which may be included within this Union, according to their respective numbers, which shall be determined by adding to the whole number of free persons, including those bound to service for a term of years, and excluding Indians not taxed, three fifths of all other persons. The actual enumeration shall be made within three years after the first meeting of the Congress of the United States, and within every subsequent term of ten years, in such manner as they shall by law direct. The number of representatives shall not exceed one for every thirty thousand, but each state shall have at least one representative; and until such enumeration shall be made, the State of New Hampshire shall be entitled to choose three, Massachusetts eight, Rhode-Island and Providence Plantations one, Connecticut five, New York six, New Jersey four, Pennsylvania eight, Delaware one, Maryland six, Virginia ten, North Carolina five, South Carolina five and Georgia three.

When vacancies happen in the representation from any state, the executive authority thereof shall issue writs of election to fill such vacancies.

The House of Representatives shall choose their speaker and other officers; and shall have the sole power of impeachment.

Section 3. The Senate of the United States shall be composed of two Senators from each State, chosen by the legislature thereof, for six years; and each Senator shall have one vote.

Immediately after they shall be assembled in consequence of the first election, they shall be divided as equally as may be into three classes. The seats of the Senators of the first class shall be vacated at the expiration of the second year, of the second class at the expiration of the fourth year, and of the third class at the expiration of the sixth year, so that one-third may be chosen every second year; and if vacancies happen by resignation, or otherwise, during the recess of the Legislature of any State, the executive thereof may make temporary appointments until the next meeting of the legislature, which shall then fill such vacancies.

No person shall be a Senator who shall not have attained to the age of thirty years, and been nine years a citizen of the United States, and who shall not, when elected, be an inhabitant of that state for which he shall be chosen.

The Vice President of the United States shall be president of the Senate, but shall have no vote, unless they be equally divided.

The Senate shall choose their other officers, and also a president pro tempore, in the absence of the Vice President, or when he shall exercise the office of President of the United States.

The Senate shall have the sole power to try all impeachments. When sitting for that purpose, they shall be on oath or affirmation. When the President of the United States is tried, the Chief Justice shall preside: And no person shall be convicted without the concurrence of two thirds of the members present.

Judgment in cases of impeachment shall not extend further than to removal from office, and disqualification to hold and enjoy any office of honor, trust or profit under the United States; but the party convicted shall nevertheless be liable and subject to indictment, trial, judgment and punishment, according to law.

Section 4. The times, places and manner of holding elections for Senators and representatives, shall be prescribed in each state by the legislature thereof; but the Congress may at any time by law make or alter such regulations, except as to the places of choosing Senators.

The Congress shall assemble at least once in every year, and such meeting shall be on the first Monday in December, unless they shall by law appoint a different day.

Section 5. Each house shall be the judge of the elections, returns and qualifications of its own members, and a majority of each shall constitute a quorum to do business; but a smaller number may adjourn from day to day, and may be authorized to compel the attendance of absent members, in such manner, and under such penalties as each house may provide.

Each house may determine the rules of its proceedings, punish its members for disorderly behaviour, and, with the concurrence of two thirds, expel a member.

Each house shall keep a journal of its proceedings, and from time to time publish the same, excepting such parts as may in their judgment require secrecy; and the yeas and nays of the members of either house on any question shall, at the desire of one fifth of those present, be entered on the journal.

Neither house, during the session of Congress, shall without the consent of the other, adjourn for more than three days, nor to any other place than that in which the two houses shall be sitting.

Section 6. The Senators and representatives shall receive a compensation for their services, to be ascertained by law, and paid out of the treasury of the United States. They shall in all cases, except treason, felony and breach of the peace, be privileged from arrest during their attendance at the session of their respective houses, and in going to and returning from the same; and for any speech or debate in either house, they shall not be questioned in any other place.

No Senator or representative shall, during the time for which he was elected, be appointed to any civil office under the authority of the United States, which shall have been created, or the emoluments whereof shall have been increased during such time; and no person holding any office under the United States, shall be a member of either house during his continuance in office.

Section 7. All bills for raising revenue shall originate in the House of Representatives; but the Senate may propose or concur with amendments as on other bills.

Every bill which shall have passed the House of Representatives and the Senate, shall, before it becomes a law, be presented to the President of the United States; if he approve he shall sign it, but if not he shall return it, with his objections to that house in which it shall have originated, who shall enter the objections at large on their journal, and proceed to reconsider it. If after such reconsideration two thirds of that house shall agree to pass the bill, it shall be sent, together with the objections, to the other house, by which it shall likewise be reconsidered, and if approved by two thirds of that house, it shall become a law. But in all such cases the votes of both houses shall be determined by yeas and nays, and the names of the persons voting for and against the bill shall be entered on the journal of each house respectively. If any bill shall not be returned by the President within ten days (Sundays excepted) after it shall have been presented to him, the same shall be a law, in like manner as if he had signed it, unless the Congress by their adjournment prevent its return, in which case it shall not be a law.

Every order, resolution, or vote to which the concurrence of the Senate and House of Representatives may be necessary (except on a question of adjournment) shall be presented to the President of the United States; and before the same shall take effect, shall be approved by him, or being disapproved by him, shall be repassed by two thirds of the Senate and House of Representatives, according to the rules and limitations prescribed in the case of a bill.

Section 8. The Congress shall have power to lay and collect taxes, duties, imposts and excises, to pay the debts and provide for the common defense and general welfare of the United States; but all duties, imposts, and excises shall be uniform throughout the United States;

To borrow money on the credit of the United States;

To regulate commerce with foreign nations, and among the several states and with the Indian tribes;

To establish an uniform rule of naturalization, and uniform laws on the subject of bankruptcies throughout the United States;

To coin money, regulate the value thereof, and of foreign coin, and fix the standard of weights and measures;

To provide for the punishment of counterfeiting the securities and current coin of the United States;

To establish post offices and post roads;

To promote the progress of science and useful arts, by securing for limited times to authors and inventors the exclusive right to their respective writings and discoveries;

To constitute tribunals inferior to the Supreme Court;

To define and punish piracies and felonies committed on the high seas, and offenses against the law of nations;

To declare war, grant letters of marque and reprisal, and make rules concerning captures on land and water;

To raise and support armies, but no appropriation of money to that use shall be for a longer term than two years;

To provide and maintain a navy;

To make rules for the government and regulation of the land and naval forces;

To provide for calling forth the militia to execute the laws of the Union, suppress insurrections and repel invasions;

To provide for organizing, arming, and disciplining the militia, and for governing such part of them as may be employed in the service of the United States, reserving to the states respectively, the appointment of the officers, and the authority of training the militia according to the discipline prescribed by Congress;

To exercise exclusive legislation in all cases whatsoever, over such district (not exceeding ten miles square), as may, by cession of particular states, and the acceptance of Congress, become the seat of the government of the United States, and to exercise like authority over all places purchased by the consent of the legislature of the state in which the same shall be, for the erection of forts, magazines and arsenals, dock yards, and other needful buildings;—And

To make all laws which shall be necessary and proper for carrying into execution the foregoing powers, and all other powers vested by this Constitution in the government of the United States, or in any department or officer thereof.

Section 9. The migration or importation of such persons as any of the states now existing shall think proper to admit, shall not be prohibited by the Congress prior to the year one thousand eight hundred and eight, but a tax or duty may be imposed on such importation, not exceeding ten dollars for each person.

The privilege of the writ of habeas corpus shall not be suspended, unless when in cases of rebellion or invasion the public safety may require it.

No bill of attainder or ex post facto law shall be passed.

No capitation, or other direct, tax shall be laid, unless in proportion to the census or enumeration hereinbefore directed to be taken.

No tax or duty shall be laid on articles exported from any state.

No preference shall be given by any regulation of commerce or revenue to the ports of one state over those of another; nor shall vessels bound to, or from, one state, be obliged to enter, clear, or pay duties in another.

No money shall be drawn from the treasury, but in consequence of appropriations made by law; and a regular statement and account of the receipts and expenditures of all public money shall be published from time to time.

No title of nobility shall be granted by the United States; and no person holding any office of profit or trust under them, shall without the consent of the Congress, accept of any present, emolument, office, or title of any kind whatever from any king, prince or foreign state.

Section 10. No state shall enter into any treaty, alliance or confederation; grant letters of marque and reprisal; coin money, emit bills of credit; make any thing but gold and silver coin a tender in payment of debts; pass any bill of attainder, ex post facto law or law impairing the obligation of contracts, or grant any title of nobility.

No state shall, without the consent of the Congress, lay any imposts or duties on imports or exports, except what may be absolutely necessary for executing its inspection laws; and the net produce of all duties and imposts, laid by any state on imports or exports, shall be for the use of the treasury of the United States; and all such laws shall be subject to the revision and control of the Congress.

No state shall, without the consent of Congress, lay any duty of tonnage, keep troops, or ships of war in time of peace, enter into any agreement or compact with another state, or with a foreign power, or engage in war, unless actually invaded, or in such imminent danger as will not admit of delay.

Section 1. The executive power shall be vested in a President of the United States of America. He shall hold his office during the term of four years, and, together with the Vice President, chosen for the same term, be elected, as follows

Each state shall appoint, in such manner as the legislature thereof may direct, a number of electors, equal to the whole number of Senators and representatives to which the state may be entitled in the Congress; but no Senator or representative, or person holding an office of trust or profit under the United States, shall be appointed an elector.

The electors shall meet in their respective states, and vote by ballot for two persons, of whom one at least shall not be an inhabitant of the same state with themselves. And they shall make a list of all the persons voted for, and of the number of votes for each; which list they shall sign and certify, and transmit sealed to the seat of the government of the United States, directed to the President of the Senate. The President of the Senate shall, in the presence of the Senate and House of Representatives, open all the certificates, and the votes shall then be counted. The person having the greatest number of votes shall be the President, if such number be a majority of the whole number of electors appointed; and if there be more than one who have such majority, and have an equal number of votes, then the House of Representatives shall immediately choose by ballot one of them for President; and if no person have a majority, then from the five highest on the list the said house shall in like manner choose the President. But in choosing the President, the votes shall be taken by states, the representation from each state having one vote; a quorum for this purpose shall consist of a member or members from two thirds of the states, and a majority of all the states shall be necessary to a choice. In every case after the choice of the President, the person having the greatest number of votes of the electors shall be the Vice President. But if there should remain two or more who have equal votes, the Senate shall choose from them by ballot the Vice President.

The Congress may determine the time of choosing the electors, and the day on which they shall give their votes; which day shall be the same throughout the United States.

No person except a natural born citizen, or a citizen of the United States, at the time of the adoption of this Constitution, shall be eligible to the office of President; neither shall any person be eligible to that office who shall not have attained to the age of thirty-five years, and been fourteen years a resident within the United States.

In case of the removal of the President from office, or of his death, resignation, or inability to discharge the powers and duties of the said office the same shall devolve on the Vice President, and the Congress may by law provide for the case of removal, death, resignation or inability, both of the President and Vice President, declaring what officer shall then act as President, and such officer shall act accordingly, until the disability be removed, or a President shall be elected.

The President shall, at stated times, receive for his services, a compensation, which shall neither be increased or diminished during the period for which he shall have been elected, and he shall not receive within that period any other emolument from the United States, or any of them.

Before he enter on the execution of his office, he shall take the following oath or affirmation:—"I do solemnly swear (or affirm) that I will faithfully execute the office of President of the United States, and will to the best of my ability, preserve, protect and defend the Constitution of the United States."

Section 2. The President shall be commander-in-chief of the Army and Navy of the United States, and of the militia of the several states, when called into the actual service of the United States; he may require the opinion, in writing, of the principal officer in each of the executive departments, upon any subject relating to the duties of their respective offices, and he shall have the power to grant reprieves and pardons for offenses against the United States, except in cases of impeachment.

He shall have power, by and with the advice and consent of the Senate, to make treaties, provided two thirds of the Senators present concur; and he shall nominate, and by and with the advice and consent of the Senate, shall appoint ambassadors, other public ministers and consuls, judges of the Supreme Court, and all other officers of the United States, whose appointments are not herein otherwise provided for, and which shall be established by law; but the Congress may by law vest the appointment of such inferior officers, as they think proper, in the President alone, in the courts of law, or in the heads of departments.

The President shall have power to fill up all vacancies that may happen during the recess of the Senate, by granting commissions which shall expire at the end of their next session.

Section 3. He shall from time to time give to the Congress information of the state of the Union, and recommend to their consideration such measures as he shall judge necessary and expedient; he may, on extraordinary occasions, convene both houses, or either of them and in case of disagreement between them, with respect to the time of adjournment, he may adjourn them to such time as he shall think proper; he shall receive ambassadors and other public ministers; he shall take care that the laws be faithfully executed, and shall commission all the officers of the United States.

Section 4. The President, Vice President and all civil officers of the United States, shall be removed from office on impeachment for, and conviction of, treason, bribery, or other high crimes and misdemeanors.

Section 1. The judicial power of the United States, shall be vested in one Supreme Court, and in such inferior courts as the Congress may from time to time ordain and establish. The judges, both of the Supreme and inferior courts, shall hold their offices during good behavior, and shall, at stated times, receive for their services, a compensation, which shall not be diminished during their continuance in office.

Section 2. The judicial power shall extend to all cases, in law and equity, arising under this Constitution, the laws of the United States, and treaties made, or which shall be made, under their authority;—to all cases affecting ambassadors, other public ministers and consuls;—to all cases of admiralty and maritime jurisdiction;—to controversies to which the United States shall be a party;—to controversies between two or more states;—between a state and citizens of another state;—between citizens of different states;—between citizens of the same state claiming lands under grants of different states, and between a state, or the citizens thereof, and foreign states, citizens or subjects.

In all cases affecting ambassadors, other public ministers and consuls, and those in which a state shall be party, the Supreme Court shall have original jurisdiction. In all the other cases before mentioned, the Supreme Court shall have appellate jurisdiction, both as to law and fact, with such exceptions, and under such regulations as the Congress shall make.

The trial of all crimes, except in cases of impeachment, shall be by jury; and such trial shall be held in the state where the said crimes shall have been committed; but when not committed within any state, the trial shall be at such place or places as the Congress may by law have directed.

Section 3. Treason against the United States, shall consist only in levying war against them, or in adhering to their enemies, giving them aid and comfort. No person shall be convicted of treason unless on the testimony of two witnesses to the same overt act, or on confession in open court.

The Congress shall have power to declare the punishment of treason, but no attainder of treason shall work corruption of blood, or forfeiture except during the life of the person attainted.

Section 1. Full faith and credit shall be given in each state to the public acts, records, and judicial proceedings of every other state. And the Congress may by general laws prescribe the manner in which such acts, records and proceedings shall be proved, and the effect thereof.

Section 2. The citizens of each state shall be entitled to all privileges and immunities of citizens in the several states.

A person charged in any state with treason, felony, or other crime, who shall flee from justice, and be found in another state, shall on demand of the executive authority of the state from which he fled, be delivered up, to be removed to the state having jurisdiction of the crime.

No person held to service or labor in one state, under the laws thereof, escaping into another, shall, in consequence of any law or regulation therein, be discharged from such service or labor, but shall be delivered up on claim of the party to whom such service or labor may be due.

Section 3. New states may be admitted by the Congress into this Union; but no new state shall be formed or erected within the jurisdiction of any other state; nor any state be formed by the junction of two or more states, or parts of states, without the consent of the legislatures of the states concerned as well as of the Congress.

The Congress shall have power to dispose of and make all needful rules and regulations respecting the territory or other property belonging to the United States; and nothing in this Constitution shall be so construed as to prejudice any claims of the United States, or of any particular state.

Section 4. The United States shall guarantee to every state in this Union a republican form of government, and shall protect each of them against invasion; and on application of the legislature, or of the executive (when the legislature cannot be convened) against domestic violence.

Article V

The Congress, whenever two thirds of both houses shall deem it necessary, shall propose amendment to this Constitution, or, on the application of the legislatures of two thirds of the several states, shall call a convention for proposing amendments, which, in either case, shall be valid to all intents and purposes, as part of this Constitution, when ratified by the legislatures of three fourths of the several states, or by conventions in three fourths thereof, as the one or the other mode of ratification may be proposed by the Congress: Provided that no amendment which may be made prior to the year one thousand eight hundred and eight shall in any manner affect the first and fourth clauses in the ninth section of the first article; and that no state, without its consent, shall be deprived of its equal suffrage in the Senate.

Article VI

All debts contracted and engagements entered into, before the adoption of this Constitution, shall be as valid against the United States under this Constitution, as under the Confederation.

This Constitution, and the laws of the United States which shall be made in pursuance thereof; and all treaties made, or which shall be made, under the authority of the United States, shall be the supreme law of the land; and the judges in every state shall be bound thereby, anything in the Constitution or laws of any state to the contrary notwithstanding.

The Senators and representatives before mentioned, and the members of the several state legislatures, and all executive and judicial officers, both of the United States and of the several states, shall be bound by oath or affirmation, to support this Constitution; but no religious tests shall ever be required as a qualification to any office or public trust under the United States.

The ratification of the conventions of nine states shall be sufficient for the establishment of this Constitution between the states so ratifying the same.... **Article VII**

Amendments to the Constitution

Congress shall make no law respecting an establishment of religion, or prohibiting the free exercise thereof; or abridging the freedom of speech, or of the press; or the right of the people peaceably to assemble, and to petition the government for a redress of grievances. [ratified 1791] **Article I**

A well regulated militia, being necessary to the security of a free state, the right of the people to keep and bear arms, shall not be infringed. [ratified 1791] **Article II**

No soldier shall, in time of peace be quartered in any house, without the consent of the owner, nor in time of war, but in a manner to be prescribed by law. [ratified 1791] **Article III**

The right of the people to be secure in their persons, houses, papers, and effects, against unreasonable searches and seizures, shall not be violated, and no warrants shall issue, but upon probable cause, supported by oath or affirmation, and particularly describing the place to be searched, and the persons or things to be seized. [ratified 1791] **Article IV**

No person shall be held to answer for a capital, or otherwise infamous crime, unless on a presentment or indictment of a grand jury, except in cases arising in the land or naval forces, or in the militia, when in actual service in time of war or public danger; nor shall any person be subject for the same offense to be twice put in jeopardy of life or limb; nor shall he be compelled in any criminal case to be a witness against himself, nor be deprived of life, liberty, or property, without due process of law; nor shall private property be taken for public use, without just compensation. [ratified 1791] **Article V**

In all criminal prosecutions, the accused shall enjoy the right to a speedy and public trial, by an impartial jury of the state and district wherein the crime shall have been committed, which district shall have been previously ascertained by law, and to be informed of the nature and cause of the accusations; to be confronted with the witnesses against him; to have compulsory process for obtaining witnesses in his favor, and to have the assistance of counsel for his defense. [ratified 1791] **Article VI**

In suits at common law, where the value in controversy shall exceed twenty dollars, the right of trial by jury shall be preserved, and no fact tried by a jury, shall be otherwise re-examined in any court of the United States, than according to the rules of the common law. [ratified 1791] **Article VII**

Article VIII	Excessive bail shall not be required, nor excessive fines imposed, nor cruel and unusual punishments inflicted. [ratified 1791]
Article IX	The enumeration in the Constitution, of certain rights, shall not be construed to deny or disparage others retained by the people. [ratified 1791]
Article X	The powers not delegated to the United States by the Constitution, nor prohibited by it to the states, are reserved to the states respectively, or to the people. [ratified 1791]
Article XI	The judicial power of the United States shall not be construed to extend to any suit in law or equity, commenced or prosecuted against one of the United States by citizens of another state, or by citizens or subjects of any foreign state. [ratified 1798]
Article XII	The electors shall meet in their respective states, and vote by ballot for President and Vice President, one of whom, at least, shall not be an inhabitant of the same state with themselves; they shall name in their ballots the person voted for as President, and in distinct ballots the person voted for as Vice President, and they shall make distinct lists of all persons voted for as President, and of all persons voted for as Vice President, and of the number of votes for each, which lists they shall sign and certify, and transmit sealed to the seat of the government of the United States, directed to the President of the Senate;—The President of the Senate shall, in the presence of the Senate and House of Representatives, open all the certificates and the votes shall then be counted;—The person having the greatest number of votes for President, shall be the President, if such number be a majority of the whole number of electors appointed; and if no person have such majority, then from the persons having the highest numbers not exceeding three on the list of those voted for as President, the House of Representatives shall choose immediately, by ballot, the President. But in choosing the President, the votes shall be taken by states, the representation from each state having one vote; a quorum for this purpose shall consist of a member or members from two thirds of the states, and a majority of all the states shall be necessary to a choice. And if the House of Representatives shall not choose a President whenever the right of choice shall devolve upon them, before the fourth day of March next following, then the Vice President shall act as President, as in the case of the death or other constitutional disability of the President. The person having the greatest number of votes as Vice President, shall be the Vice President, if such number be a majority of the whole number of electors appointed, and if no person have a majority, then from the two highest numbers on the list, the Senate shall choose the Vice President; a quorum for the purpose shall consist of two-thirds of the whole number of Senators, and a majority of the whole number shall be necessary to a choice. But no person constitutionally ineligible to the office of President should be eligible to that of Vice President of the United States. [ratified 1804]
Article XIII	**Section 1.** Neither slavery nor involuntary servitude, except as a punishment for crime whereof the party shall have been duly convicted, shall exist within the United States, or any place subject to their jurisdiction.

Section 2. Congress shall have power to enforce this article by appropriate legislation. [ratified 1865]

Section 1. All persons born or naturalized in the United States, and subject to the jurisdiction thereof, are citizens of the United States and of the state wherein they reside. No state shall make or enforce any law which shall abridge the privileges or immunities of citizens of the United States; nor shall any state deprive any person of life, liberty, or property, without due process of law; nor deny to any person within its jurisdiction the equal protection of the laws.

Section 2. Representatives shall be apportioned among the several states according to their respective numbers, counting the whole number of persons in each state, excluding Indians not taxed. But when the right to vote at any election for the choice of electors for President and Vice President of the United States, representatives in Congress, the executive and judicial officers of a state, or the members of the legislature thereof, is denied to any of the male inhabitants of such state, being twenty-one years of age, and citizens of the United States, or in any way abridged, except for participation in rebellion, or other crime, the basis of representation therein shall be reduced in the proportion which the number of such male citizens shall bear to the whole number of male citizens twenty-one years of age in such state.

Section 3. No person shall be a Senator or representative in Congress, or elector of President and Vice President, or hold any office, civil or military, under the United States, or under any state, who, having previously taken an oath, as a member of Congress, or as an officer of the United States, or as a member of any state legislature, or as an executive or judicial officer of any state, to support the Constitution of the United States, shall have engaged in insurrection or rebellion against the same, or given aid or comfort to the enemies thereof. But Congress may by a vote of two-thirds of each house, remove such disability.

Section 4. The validity of the public debt of the United States, authorized by law, including debts incurred for payment of pensions and bounties for services in suppressing insurrection or rebellion, shall not be questioned. But neither the United States nor any state shall assume or pay any debt or obligation incurred in aid of insurrection or rebellion against the United States, or any claim for the loss or emancipation of any slave; but all such debts, obligations and claims shall be held illegal and void.

Section 5. The Congress shall have power to enforce by appropriate legislation, the provisions of this article. [ratified 1868]

Section 1. The right of citizens of the United States to vote shall not be denied or abridged by the United States or by any state on account of race, color, or previous condition of servitude.

Section 2. The Congress shall have power to enforce this article by appropriate legislation. [ratified 1870]

| Article XVI | The Congress shall have power to levy and collect taxes on incomes, from whatever source derived, without apportionment among the several states, and without regard to any census or enumeration. [ratified 1913] |

Article XVII

The Senate of the United States shall be composed of two Senators from each state, elected by the people thereof, for six years; and each Senator shall have one vote. The electors in each state shall have the qualifications requisite for electors of the most numerous branch of the state legislatures.

When vacancies happen in the representation of any state in the Senate, the executive authority of such state shall issue writs of election to fill such vacancies: *Provided,* That the legislature of any state may empower the executive thereof to make temporary appointment until the people fill the vacancies by election as the legislature may direct.

This amendment shall not be so construed as to affect the election or term of any Senator chosen before it becomes valid as part of the Constitution. [ratified 1913]

Article XVIII

Section 1. After one year from the ratification of this article the manufacture, sale, or transportation of intoxicating liquors within, the importation thereof into, or the exportation thereof from the United States and all territory subject to the jurisdiction thereof for beverage purposes is hereby prohibited.

Section 2. The Congress and the several states shall have concurrent power to enforce this article by appropriate legislation.

Section 3. This article shall be inoperative unless it shall have been ratified as an amendment to the Constitution by the legislatures of the several states, as provided in the Constitution, within seven years from the date of the submission hereof to the states by the Congress. [ratified 1919; repealed 1933]

Article XIX

The right of citizens of the United States to vote shall not be denied or abridged by the United States or by any state on account of sex.

Congress shall have power to enforce this article by appropriate legislation. [ratified 1920]

Article XX

Section 1. The terms of the President and Vice President shall end at noon on the 20th day of January, and the terms of Senators and representatives at noon on the 3rd day of January, of the years in which such terms would have ended if this article had not been ratified; and the terms of their successors shall then begin.

Section 2. The Congress shall assemble at least once in every year, and such meeting shall begin at noon on the 3rd day of January, unless they shall by law appoint a different day.

Section 3. If, at the time fixed for the beginning of the term of the President, the President elect shall have died, the Vice President elect shall become President. If a President shall not have been chosen before the time fixed for the beginning of his term, or if the President elect shall have failed to qualify, then the Vice President elect shall act as President until a President shall have qualified; and the Congress may by law provide for the case wherein neither a President elect nor a Vice President elect shall have qualified, declaring who shall then act as President, or the manner in which one who is to act shall be selected, and such person shall act accordingly until a President or Vice President shall have qualified.

Section 4. The Congress may by law provide for the case of the death of any of the persons from whom the House of Representatives may choose a President whenever the right of choice shall have devolved upon them, and for the case of the death of any of the persons from whom the Senate may choose a Vice President whenever the right of choice shall have devolved upon them.

Section 5. Sections 1 and 2 shall take effect on the 15th day of October following the ratification of this article.

Section 6. This article shall be inoperative unless it shall have been ratified as an amendment to the Constitution by the legislatures of three-fourths of the several states within seven years from the date of its submission. [ratified 1933]

Section 1. The eighteenth article of amendment to the Constitution of the United States is hereby repealed.

Article XXI

Section 2. The transportation or importation into any state, territory, or possession of the United States for delivery or use therein of intoxicating liquors, in violation of the laws thereof, is hereby prohibited.

Section 3. This article shall be inoperative unless it shall have been ratified as an amendment to the Constitution by conventions in the several states, as provided in the Constitution, within seven years from the date of the submission hereof to the states by the Congress. [ratified 1933]

Section 1. No person shall be elected to the office of the President more than twice, and no person who has held the office of President, or acted as President, for more than two years of a term to which some other person was elected President shall be elected to the office of the President more than once. But this article shall not apply to any person holding the office of President when this article was proposed by the Congress, and shall not prevent any person who may be holding the office of President, or acting as President, during the term within which this article becomes operative from holding the office of President or acting as President during the remainder of such term.

Article XXII

Section 2. This article shall be inoperative unless it shall have been ratified as an amendment to the Constitution by the legislatures of three-fourths of the several states within seven years from the date of its submission to the states by the Congress. [ratified 1951]

Section 1. The District constituting the seat of Government of the United States shall appoint in such manner as the Congress may direct:

Article XXIII

A number of electors of President and Vice President equal to the whole number of Senators and Representatives in Congress to which the District would be entitled if it were a State, but in no event more than the least populous State; they shall be in addition to those appointed by the States, but they shall be considered, for the purposes of the election of President and Vice President, to be electors appointed by a State; and they shall meet in the District and perform such duties as provided by the twelfth article of amendment.

Section 2. The Congress shall have power to enforce this article by appropriate legislation. [ratified 1961]

Article XXIV

Section 1. The right of citizens of the United States to vote in any primary or other election for President or Vice President, for electors for President or Vice President, or for Senator or Representative in Congress, shall not be denied or abridged by the United States or any State by reason of failure to pay any poll tax or other tax.

Section 2. The Congress shall have power to enforce this article by appropriate legislation. [ratified 1964]

Article XXV

Section 1. In case of the removal of the President from office or of his death or resignation, the Vice President shall become President.

Section 2. Whenever there is a vacancy in the office of the Vice President, the President shall nominate a Vice President who shall take office upon confirmation by a majority vote of both houses of Congress.

Section 3. Whenever the President transmits to the President pro tempore of the Senate and the Speaker of the House of Representatives his written declaration that he is unable to discharge the powers and duties of his office, and until he transmits to them a written declaration to the contrary, such powers and duties shall be discharged by the Vice President as acting President.

Section 4. Whenever the Vice President and a majority of either the principal officers of the executive departments or of such other body as Congress may by law provide, transmit to the President pro tempore of the Senate and the Speaker of the House of Representatives their written declaration that the President is unable to discharge the powers and duties of his office, the Vice President shall immediately assume the powers and duties of the office as acting President.

Thereafter, when the President transmits to the President pro tempore of the Senate and the Speaker of the House of Representatives his written declaration that no inability exists, he shall resume the powers and duties of his office unless the Vice President and a majority of either the principal officers of the executive department or of such other body as Congress may by law provide, transmit within four days to the President pro tempore of the Senate and the Speaker of the House of Representatives their written declaration that the President is unable to discharge the powers and duties of his office. Thereupon Congress shall decide the issue, assembling within forty-eight hours for that purpose if not in session. If the Congress, within twenty-one days after receipt of the latter written declaration, or, if Congress is not in session, within twenty-one days after Congress is required to assemble, determines by two-thirds vote of both houses that the President is unable to discharge the powers and duties of his office, the Vice President shall continue to discharge the same as acting President; otherwise, the President shall resume the powers and duties of his office. [ratified 1967]

Article XXVI

Section 1. The right of citizens of the United States, who are eighteen years of age or older, to vote shall not be denied or abridged by the United States or by any State on account of age.

Section 2. The Congress shall have power to enforce this article by appropriate legislation. [ratified 1971]

Article XXVII

No law, varying the compensation for the services of the Senators and Representatives, shall take effect, until an election of Representatives shall have intervened. [ratified 1992]

Note

This text, except for capitalization and spelling, follows the arrangement of the reprint of the Constitution of the United States (5th edition, 1952), published by the Library of Congress.

Table of Cases

Applicable states and territories are indicated in brackets.

Abercrombie v. McClung, 525 P.2d 594 (1974) [Hawaii]

Adams v. Bolin, 247 P.2d 617 (1952) [Ariz.]

Advisory Opinion to the Governor, In re, 688 A.2d 288 (1997) [R.I.]

Alaskans for Legislative Reform v. State, 887 P.2d 413 (1994) [Alaska]

Alexander v. State, 441 So.2d 1329 (1983) [Miss.]

Allen, People v., 42 N.Y. 378 (1870) [N.Y.]

Allied Stores of Ohio, Inc. v. Bowers, 358 U.S. 522 (1959) [Ohio]

Amador Valley Joint Union High School Dist. v. State Bd. of Equalization,
    583 P.2d 1281 (1978) [Calif.]

American Fork City v. Crosgrove, 701 P.2d 1069 (1985) [Utah]

Americans United v. Rogers, 538 S.W.2d 711 (1976) [Mo.]

Anderson, People v., 493 P.2d 880 (1972) [Calif.]

Anderson v. Ritterbusch, 98 P. 1002 (1908) [Okla.]

Andrews, State v., 186 A.2d 546 (1962) [Conn.]

Apkin v. Treasurer & Receiver General, 517 N.E.2d 141 (1988) [Mass.]

Application of Nelson, 163 N.W.2d 533 (1968) [S.D.]

Arnett v. Meredith, 121 S.W.2d 36 (1938) [Ky.]

Attorney General v. Waldron, 426 A.2d 929 (1981) [Md.]

Auditor of Public Accounts, Ex parte, 609 S.W.2d 682 (1980) [Ky.]

Austin v. New Hampshire, 420 U.S. 656 (1975) [N.H.]

Austin, Nichols & Co. v. Okl. Cty. Bd., etc., 578 P.2d 1200 (1978) [Okla.]

Baehar v. Lewin, 852 P.2d 44 (1993) [Hawaii]

Baker v. Carr, 369 U.S. 186 (1962) [Fla., Mich., and Tenn.]

Barnes v. New Haven, 98 A.2d 523 (1953) [Conn.]

Barron v. Baltimore, 32 U.S. 243 (1833) [Md.]

Batchelder v. Allied Stores International, Inc., 445 N.E.2d 590 (1983) [Mass.]

Beals v. Washington Int'l., Inc., 386 A.2d 1156 (1978) [Del.]

Becker, State v., 287 A.2d 580 (1972) [Vt.]

Beirkamp v. Rogers, 293 N.W.2d 577 (1980) [Iowa]

Belmont Fire Protection District, In re, 489 N.E.2d 1385 (1986) [Ill.]

Biggs v. State Dept. of Retirement Systems, 622 P.2d 1301 (1981) [Wash.]

Blue v. State, 558 P.2d 636 (1977) [Alaska]

Bonet v. Texas Co., 308 U.S. 463 (1940) [Puerto Rico]

Bonomo v. Louisiana Downs, Inc., 337 So.2d 553 (1976) [La.]

A Book Named "John Cleland's Memoirs of a Woman of Pleasure" v. Attorney General of
    Commonwealth of Massachusetts, 383 U.S. 413 (1966) [Fla.]

Boomer v. Olsen, 10 N.W.2d 507 (1943) [Neb.]

Borja v. Goodman, 1 N. Mar. I. 63 (1990) [Northern Marianas]

Bradner v. Hammond, 553 P.2d 1 (1976) [Alaska]

Brickell v. Board of Education, 508 P.2d 996 (1973) [Kans.]

Brown v. Board of Education of Topeka, 347 U.S. 483 (1954) [Kans., Ky., Miss., and Mo.]

Brown v. City of Galveston, 75 S.W. 488 (1903) [Tex.]

Brown v. State, 358 So.2d 16 (1978) [Fla.]

Busik v. Levine, 307 A.2d (1973) 571 [N.J.]

Calder v. Bull, 3 Dallas 386 (1798) [Conn.]

Capitol Distrib. Co. v. Redwine, 57 S.E.2d 578 (1950) [Ga.]

Cardiff v. Bismarck Public School District, 263 N.W.2d 105 (1978) [N.D.]

Carrillo, Matter of, 542 S.W.2d 105 (1976) [Tex.]

Cassidy v. Willis, 323 A.2d 598 (1974) [Del.]

Chenault v. Carter, 332 S.W.2d 623 (1960) [Ky.]

Chisolm v. Georgia, 2 Dallas 419 (1793) [Ga.]

City of ____ (see name of city)

Clarke v. Growe, 461 N.W.2d 385 (1990) [Minn.]

Class, People v., 494 N.E.2d 444 (1986) [N.Y.]

Coalition for Political Honesty v. State Board of Elections, 359 N.E.2d 138 (1976) [Ill.]

Coe, State v., 679 P.2d 353 (1984) [Wash.]

Colorado v. Nunez, 465 U.S. 324 (1984) [Colo.]

Commonwealth v. ____ (see opposing party)

Commonwealth ex rel. v. ____ (see opposing party)

Conard v. State, 16 A.2d 121 (1940) [Del.]

Constitutionality of House Bill No. 222, In re, 90 S.W.2d 692 (1936) [Ky.]

Couch v. Delmarva Power & Light Co., 593 A.2d 554 (1991) [Del.]

County of ____ (see name of county)

Cox v. New Hampshire, 312 U.S. 569 (1941) [N.H.]

Crandall v. Nevada, 6 Wallace 35 (1868) [Nev.]

C. S., In the Interest of, 516 N.W.2d 851 (1994) [Iowa]

Cudihee v. Phelps, 136 P. 367 (1913) [Wash.]

Culotta, State v., 343 So.2d 977 (1976) [La.]

Dade County, State ex rel. v. Dickinson, 230 So.2d 130 (1969) [Fla.]

Delaware v. Van Arsdall, 475 U.S. 673 (1986) [Del.]

DKM Richmond Assoc. v. City of Richmond, 457 S.E.2d 76 (1995) [Va.]

Doak v. Milbauer, 343 N.W.2d 751 (1984) [Neb.]

Douglas, State ex rel. v. Sporhase, 305 N.W.2d 614 (1981) [Neb.]

Downes v. Bidwell, 182 U.S. 244 (1901) [Puerto Rico]

Duggan v. Beerman, 334 N.W.2d 68 (1996) [Neb.]

Duncan v. Louisiana, 391 U.S. 145 (1968) [La.]

Edgewood Independent School District v. Kirby, 777 S.W.2d 391 (1989) [Tex.]

Evans v. Tuttle, 613 N.E.2d 854 (1993) [Ind.]

Ex parte ____ (see name of party)

Farmington, Township of, Oakland County, v. Scott, 132 N.W.2d 607 (1965) [Mich.]

Ferguson v. Watkins, 448 So.2d 271 (1984) [Miss.]

Flora v. White, 692 F.2d 53 (1982) [Ark.]

Jefferson v. State, 527 P.2d 37 (1974) [Alaska]

Johanson v. Fischer, 808 P.2d 1083 (1991) [Utah]

Johnson, State ex rel. v. Crane, 197 P.2d 864 (1948) [Wyo.]

Julius v. Callahan, 65 N.W. 267 (1895) [Minn.]

Kadan v. Board of Supervisios of Elections of Baltimore County, 329 A.2d 702 (1974) [Md.]

Kahalekai v. Doi, 590 P.2d 543 (1979) [Hawaii]

Kaiser v. Whitehall, 718 P.2d 1341 (1986) [Mont.]

Kalodimos v. Village of Morton Grove, 470 N.E.2d 266 (1984) [Ill.]

Kansas v. Colorado, 206 U.S. 46 (1907) [Kans.]

Kansas Malpractice Coalition v. Bell, 757 P.2d 251 (1988) [Kans.]

Kelly v. Kalodner, 181 A. 598 (1935) [Del.]

Kempf's Will, In re, 252 App. Div. 28 (N.Y.) (1937) [N.Y.]

King v. Andrus, 452 F.Supp. 11 (1977) [American Samoa]

King v. Morton, 520 F.2d 1140 (1975) [American Samoa]

Lance v. Board of Educ., 170 S.E.2d 783 (1969) [W. Va.]

Leonardis, State v., 375 A.2d 607 (1977) [N.J.]

Levin v. Whalen, 349 N.E.2d 820 (1976) [N.Y.]

Libertarian Party of Wisconsin v. State, 546 N.W.2d 424 (1996) [Wis.]

Lochner v. New York, 198 U.S. 45 (1905) [N.Y.]

Lopez Tijerina v. Henry, 48 F.R.D. 274 (1969) [N.M.]

Loring v. Young, 132 N.E. 65 (1921) [Mass.]

Loving v. Virginia, 388 U.S. 1 (1967) [S.C.]

Lucas v. People of the State of Michigan, 420 F.2d 259 (1970) [Mich.]

Luker v. Curtis, 136 P.2d 978 (1943) [Idaho]

Luther v. Borden, 7 Howard 1 (1849) [R.I.]

Lyons v. Spaeth, 20 N.W.2d 481 (1945) [Minn.]

Mabuti, State v., 807 P.2d 1264 (1991) [Hawaii]

Maddox v. Fortson, 172 S.E.2d 595 (1970) [Ga.]

Magnolia Bar Ass'n, Inc. v. Lee, 793 F.Supp. 1386 (1992) [Miss.]

Maloney, State ex rel. v. McCartney, 223 S.E.2d 607 (1976) [W. Va.]

M.A.P., State v., 281 N.W.2d 334 (1979) [Minn.]

Mapp v. Ohio, 367 U.S. 643 (1961) [Ohio]

Marbury v. Madison, 1 Cranch 137 (1803) [Conn.]

Marks v. Vehlow, 671 P.2d 473 (1983) [Idaho]

Marquardt, Matter of, 778 P.2d 241 (1989) [Ariz.]

Martin, State v., 213 A.2d 459 (1965) [Conn.]

Mathieu v. Bath Iron Works, 667 A.2d 862 (1995) [Maine]

Matter of _____ (see name of party)

Matthews, State v., 153 S.E.2d 791 (1967) [N.C.]

Mattson, State ex rel. v. Kiedrowski, 391 N.W.2d 777 (1986) [Minn.]

McClusky v. Hunter, 266 P. 18 (1928) [Ariz.]

McGraw, State ex rel. v. Willis, 323 S.E.2d 600 (1984) [W. Va.]
McInnis v. Cooper Communities, Inc., 611 S.W.2d 767 (1981) [Ark.]
McLaurin v. Oklahoma State Regents, 339 U.S. 637 (1950) [Okla.]
McLeod, State ex rel. v. McLeod, 243 S.E.2d 446 (1978) [S.C.]
Mears v. Hall, 569 S.W.2d 91 (1978) [Ark.]
Meredith, Commonwealth ex rel. v. Hall, 126 S.W.2d 1056 (1939) [Ky.]
Metropolitan Development and Housing Agency v. Leech, 591 S.W.2d 427 (1979) [Tenn.]
Meyer v. Grant, 486 U.S. 414 (1988) [Colo.]
Meyer v. Nebraska, 262 U.S. 390 (1923) [Neb.]
Michigan v. Long, 463 U.S. 1032 (1983) [Mich.]
Miers, Ex parte, 64 S.W.2d 778 (1933) [Tex.]
Miller, State v., 630 A.2d 1315 (1993) [Conn.]
Miller v. State, 555 S.W.2d 563 (1977) [Ark.]
Miller v. State, 471 P.2d 213 (1970) [Nev.]
Miranda v. Arizona, 384 U.S. 436 (1966) [Ariz.]
Missouri v. Holland, 252 U.S. 416 (1920) [Mo.]
Missouri v. Iowa, 7 Howard 861 (1849) & 10 Howard 1 (1850) [Iowa]
Missouri ex rel. Gaines v. Canada, 305 U.S. 337 (1938) [Mo.]
Mitchem v. State ex rel. Schaub, 250 So.2d 883 (1971) [Fla.]
Monaco v. Mississippi, 292 U.S. 313 (1934) [Miss.]
Montana v. Jackson, 460 U.S. 1030 (1983) [Mont.]
Moodie, State ex rel. v. Bryan, 39 So. 929 (1905) [Fla.]
Moore v. Shanahan, 486 P.2d 506 (1971) [Kans.]
Moore v. Sumter County Council, 387 S.E.2d 455 (1990) [S.C.]
Morgan, State v., 48 N.W. 314 (1891) [S.D.]
Morris, State v., 378 N.E.2d 708 (1978) [Ohio]
Mountain Fuel Supply Company v. Emerson, 578 P.2d 1351 (1978) [Wyo.]
Municipal Suffrage to Women, In re, 36 N.E. 488 (1894) [Mass.]
Munn v. Illinois, 94 U.S. 113 (1877) [Ill.]

Nantucket Conservation Foundation, Inc. v. Russell Management, Inc.,
    402 N.E.2d 501 (1980) [Mass.]
National Hearing Aid Centers, Inc. v. Smith, 376 A.2d 456 (1977) [Maine]
Near v. Minnesota, 283 U.S. 697 (1931) [Minn.]
Nebbia v. New York, 291 U.S. 502 (1934) [N.Y.]
Nicholson v. Judicial Retirement and Removal Comm., 562 S.W.2d 306 (1978) [Ky.]
North Ridge General Hospital, Inc. v. City of Oakland Park, 374 So.2d 461 (1979) [Fla.]

Olsen v. Nebraska, 313 U.S. 236 (1941) [Neb.]
Oneida, County of v. Berle, 404 N.E.2d 133 (1980) [N.Y.]
Opinion of the Justices, 379 So.2d 939 (1980) [Ala.]
Opinion of the Justices, 261 A.2d 58 (1970) [Maine]
Opinion of the Justices, 81 So.2d 881 (1955) [Ala.]
Opinion of the Justices, 125 N.E. 849 (1920) [Mass.]
Opinion to the Governor, In re, 178 A. 433 (1935) [R.I.]

Oregon v. Kennedy, 456 U.S. 667 (1982) [Ore.]
Otto v. Buck, 295 P.2d 1028 (1956) [N.M.]

Pacific States Telephone and Telegraph Co. v. State of Oregon, 223 U.S. 118 (1912) [Ore.]
Paisner v. Atty. Gen., 458 N.E.2d 734 (1983) [Mass.]
Palka v. Walker, 198 A.2d 265 (1938) [Conn.]
Pate v. State, 429 P.2d 542 (1967) [Okla.]
Pawtucket, City of v. Sundlun, 662 A.2d 40 (1995) [R.I.]
Pennsylvania Labor Relations Bd., Commonwealth v., 388 A.2d 736 (1978) [Pa.]
People v. ____ (see opposing party)
People ex rel. v. ____ (see opposing party)
Peoples, In re, 250 S.E.2d 890 (1978) [N.C.]
Peper v. Princeton, 389 A.2d 465 (1978) [N.J.]
Perry v. Decker, 457 A.2d 357 (1983) [Del.]
Pinana v. State, 352 P.2d 824 (1960) [Nev.]
Pinnick v. Cleary, 271 N.E.2d 592 (1971) [Mass.]
Plumb v. Christie, 30 S.E. 759 (1898) [Ga.]
Prentis v. Atlantic Coast Line, 211 U.S. 210 (1908) [Va.]
Priest, People v., 99 N.E. 547 (1912) [N.Y.]

Ravin v. State, 537 P.2d 494 (1975) [Alaska]
Reapportionment of Towns of Hartland, Windsor and West Windsor, In re, 624 A.2d 323 (1993) [Vt.]
Reed, State v., 811 P.2d 1163 (1991) [Kans.]
The Regents of the University of Michigan v. State, 235 N.W.2d 1 (1975) [Mich.]
Reynolds, State ex rel. v. Zimmerman, 126 N.W.2d 551 (1964) [Wis.]
Reynolds v. Sims, 377 U.S. 533 (1964) [Tenn.]
Reynolds v. State Election Board, 233 F.Supp. 323 (1964) [Okla.]
Right to Choose v. Byrne, 450 A.2d 925 (1982) [N.J.]
Robinson v. Cahill, 303 A.2d 273 (1973) [N.J.]
Roeschlein v. Thomas, 280 N.E.2d 581 (1972) [Ind.]
Roman v. Sincock, 377 U.S. 695 (1964) [Del.]
Romer v. Colorado General Assembly, 840 P.2d 1081 (1992) [Colo.]
Romer v. Evans, 116 S.Ct. 1620 (1996) [Colo.]

San Antonio Independent School District v. Rodriguez, 411 U.S. 1 (1973) [N.J.]
Sanstead, State ex rel. v. Freed, 251 N.W.2d 898 (1977) [N.D.]
Schowgurow v. Maryland, 213 A.2d 475 (1965) [Md.]
Scudder v. Smith, 200 A. 601 (1938) [Pa.]
Sego, State ex rel. v. Kirkpatrick, 524 P.2d 975 (1974) [N.M.]
Serrano v. Priest, 557 P.2d 929 (1976) [Calif.]
Shaheed v. Winston, 885 F.Supp 861 (1995) [Va.]
Shields v. Gerhart, 658 A.2d 924 (1995) [Vt.]
Simon, People ex rel. v. Bradley, 101 N.E. 766 (1913) [N.Y.]

Slate v. Jewett, 500 A.2d 233 (1985) [Vt.]

Smith, State ex rel. v. Gore, 143 S.E.2d 791 (1965) [W. Va.]

Smith v. Davis, 426 S.W.2d 827 (1968) [Tex.]

Sneed v. Greensboro City Bd. of Ed., 264 S.E.2d 106 (1980) [N.C.]

South Dakota v. North Carolina, 192 U.S. 286 (1904) [N.C.]

South Dakota Association of Tobacco and Candy Distributors v. State by and through Department of Revenue, 280 N.W.2d 662 (1979) [S.D.]

Spire, State ex rel. v. Conway, 472 N.W. (1991) [Neb.]

Springer v. Government of the Philippine Islands, 277 U.S. 189 (1928) [N.J.]

Standard Drug Co. v. General Electric, 117 S.E.2d 289 (1960) [Va.]

Stanley v. Darlington County School Dist., 879 F.Supp 1341 (1995) [S.C.]

Stanton v. Stanton, 421 U.S. 7 (1975) [Utah]

Staples v. Gilmer, 33 S.E.2d 49 (1945) [Va.]

State v. ____ (see opposing party)

State ex rel. v. ____ (see opposing party)

Steady, In re, 641 A.2d 117 (1994) [Vt.]

Stevenson, State ex rel. v. Tufly, 12 P. 835 (1887) [Nev.]

Sutton, State v., 816 P.2d 518 (1991) [N.M.]

Succession of Brown, 388 So.2d 1151 (1980) [La.]

Sweeny v. Otter, 804 P.2d 308 (1990) [Idaho]

Taylor v. Worrell Enterprises, Inc., 409 S.E.2d 136 (1991) [Va.]

Tennessee v. Davis, 100 U.S. 257 (1879) [Tenn.]

Todd, State v., 468 N.W.2d 462 (1991) [Iowa]

Towns v. Suttles, 69 S.E.2d 742 (1952) [Ga.]

Township of ____ (see name of township)

Travelers' Insurance Co. v. Marshall, 76 S.W.2d 1007 (1934) [Tex.]

Trenton, City of v. New Jersey, 262 U.S. 182 (1923) [N.J.]

Trombetta v. State of Florida, 353 F.Supp 575 (1973) [Fla.]

Tucker v. State, 35 N.E.2d 270 (1941) [Ind.]

Tucson Elec. Power Co. v. Apache County, 912 P.2d 9 (1996) [Ariz.]

Tusculum College v. State Board of Equalization, 600 S.W.2d 739 (1980) [Tenn.]

UMW v. Parsons, 305 S.E. 343 (1983) [W. Va.]

U.S. Term Limits, Inc. v. Thornton, 115 S.Ct. 1842 (1995) [Colo. and S.D.]

Van Bergen v. State of Minn., 59 F.3d 1541 (1995) [Minn.]

Vermont Educational Buildings Financing Agency v. Mann, 247 A.2d 68 (1968) [Vt.]

Vogel, State ex rel. v. Garaas, 261 N.W.2d 914 (1978) [N.D.]

Voss, State ex rel. v. Davis, 418 S.W.2d 163 (1967) [Mo.]

Wagner v. Secretary of State, 663 A.2d 564 (1995) [Maine]

Walker v. Baker, 196 S.W.2d 324 (1946) [Tex.]

Washburn v. Thomas, 616 A.2d 495 (1992) [N.H.]

Wein v. State of New York, 347 N.E.2d 586 (1976) [N.Y.]

Glossary

Ad valorum (Latin: "according to value"). Taxation based on the value of an item.

Address. A legislature's formal request that a chief executive perform an act such as removing a judge or justice.

Allodial. Land that is free of obligation; the opposite of feudal tenure.

Appeal. A legal proceeding in which a superior court is asked to review and change a decision of an inferior court.

Attainder. Under English law, punishment that extinguished civil rights and required forfeiture of property by a person found guilty of a felony or treason.

Body corporate. A corporation.

Breach of the peace. A violation of public tranquility and order, often by riotous, forcible, or unlawful acts.

Cabinet. The heads of government departments. In parliamentary governments, as in the United Kingdom, cabinet members, known as ministers, are chosen from the parliament; their approval is required for major actions by the prime minister. In the United States, a federal government, heads of departments in the executive branch are chosen by the president and confirmed by the Senate; heads of executive branch departments in the states may be elected statewide when the governor is elected or appointed by the governor or the legislature.

Casting vote. The privilege of the presiding officer of a legislature to cast a vote when the votes are equally divided.

Censure. Reprimand, expulsion, or other action taken by a legislature against a member for improper behavior. Originally, the sentence of disgrace imposed by a Roman censor on a citizen for disreputable conduct.

Certiorari (Latin: "to be informed of"). A writ or legal instrument issued by a superior court to an inferior court to send a matter to the superior court for review.

Chancery. *See* Equity

Common law. A legal tradition developed in Great Britain in which legal precedent derives from decisions of courts of law, rather than from equity law or civil code law.

Commutation. The reduction of a sentence after conviction.

Contempt. An improper act or a refusal to follow an order of a court or legislature that may form the basis for punishment.

Conviction. A final judgment of a court that a person has been found guilty of a crime.

Corruption of the blood. The deprivation of a person's right to pass title to property or to sue in court; a result of attainder.

Council of state. A body that advises the head of a government; an executive council.

Disseized. To be deprived of possession of real property.

Domicile. A person's legal or permanent residence.

Emolument. Profit or gain from an office or employment.

En banc. *See* In banc

Entailment. Interference with ordinary inheritance procedures by limiting how property is to descend.

Equity. A system of law that developed in the English chancery courts (also called equity courts) in which remedies not available under common law could be granted on the basis of fairness.

Ex parte (Latin: "of the one part"). A legal proceeding in which there is only one party.

Ex post facto law (Latin: "after the occurrence"). A law passed after an act has been committed that makes the act illegal.

Ex rel (Latin: "upon information from"). A legal proceeding by a state official at the instigation of an interested private party.

Feudal tenure. An entitlement to real property based on rights and responsibilities between a property holder and the feudal lord.

Frame of government. The structure and procedures of government; a constitution establishing a system of government.

Freehold. The ownership of real property for an uncertain duration as determined by the document conveying rights to it; not a leasehold. For example, the deed or title document may specify "in fee simple" or "for the life of the grantee" or another person.

Good behavior. Proper conduct. Judges and justices who hold office "during good behavior" have no fixed term of office.

Grand jury. A panel consisting of twelve to twenty-three persons who decide, on the basis of evidence presented to them, whether a person should be indicted for a crime. *See also* Petit jury

Habeas corpus (Latin: "you have the body"). A writ or legal instrument developed in England to bring an imprisoned person to court and explain the legal basis for the person's detention.

Hereditary emolument. Payment for an office or employment that can be inherited.

High crimes and misdemeanors. Serious unlawful acts that technically do not constitute a felony; more serious and aggravated misdemeanors.

Honoraria. Payments to professionals in lieu of fees that are legally or traditionally required.

In banc (Latin: "in the bench"). Sitting as a full bench or court of all the judges.

Indefeasible. Something that cannot be defeated, revoked, or voided.

Indictment. A formal statement from a grand jury charging a person with the commission of a crime.

Information. A written set of accusations, such as an indictment, filed by a prosecutor directly charging a person with the commission of a crime.

Injunction. A writ prohibiting an action.

Interlocutory. Temporary; not final.

Joint resolution. A measure, other than a law, passed by both houses of a bicameral legislature.

Judicatories. Courts of law or justice.

Law of descent. The legal rules for succession of ownership of an estate on the death of the owner.

Letters patent. A grant by a sovereign under seal and delivered open, rather than closed to avoid inspection.

Magistracy. Broadly, a body of public officials; more narrowly, officials charged with the application and execution of the laws.

Majority. More than half. In an election with two candidates, the one who receives the most votes has a majority. In elections of three or more candidates, the candidate with more than one-half is said to have the majority of the votes; a candidate with the most votes but less than one-half has a plurality of the votes. A simple majority consists of at least one-half plus one of the votes cast. An absolute majority requires no fewer than one-half plus one of all the votes possible, even if some votes are not cast. A supermajority is a majority greater than one-half plus one of the votes.

Malfeasance. The execution of an act without the right to do so. *See also* Misfeasance

Mandamus (Latin: "we command"). A writ or legal instrument from a court of superior jurisdiction directed to a public or private official, commanding that an act be done.

Misdemeanor. In criminal law, a lesser criminal offense than a felony.

Misfeasance. The improper performance of a rightful act. *See also* Malfeasance

Money bill. A legislative act raising revenue or making an appropriation.

Moral turpitude. A base, vile, or depraved act that is contrary to accepted moral principles of society.

Non compos mentis (Latin: "not sound of mind"). Insane.

Of counsel. An attorney associated with the principal attorney retained by a client to handle a particular matter.

Ordinance. A rule or law; more specifically, the enactment of a municipal legislative body. Also, an enactment that serves as an organic law but does not have the status of a constitution.

Parliament. The legislature in a parliamentary system of government, composed of elected representatives who fill one or two houses or chambers; the lower house is generally the more representative and has the greater power. A parliamentary system also includes a cabinet of ministers and a prime minister who is approved by the parliament as head of government. A parliament is theoretically the supreme branch of government, whereas a congress is one of at least three coequal branches of government.

Perpetuities. Procedures that keep property from being disposable at any time and therefore violate public policy. Rules against perpetuities bar an interest in property from coming into existence twenty-one years after the death of a living person.

Petit jury. The jury in a trial, generally consisting of fewer members than a grand jury. *See also* Grand jury

Plenary. Full or complete. Plenary power is complete power; a plenary session is one that all members attend.

Plural executive branch. An executive branch of government in which the governor and usually a lieutenant governor must share power with other elected officials such as a secretary of state and an attorney general.

Pocket veto. A refusal by a chief executive to endorse a measure passed by the legislature or to return it with a formal veto before adjournment. The action prevents the legislature from overriding the veto and ensures the measure's failure.

Poll tax. A tax on registered voters, regardless of the amount of a person's property, used in some states at one time to preclude poor persons, especially blacks, from voting.

Precedent. A judicial decision used as the basis of a future judicial decision.

Presentment. An informal report by a grand jury on an investigation of a public official's action or a report by a grand jury based on an offense derived from the jurors' own knowledge; not a formal indictment.

Primogeniture. The superiority or exclusive right of a first-born son.

Privy council. A body that advises a head of state or monarch, particularly in the United Kingdom, where the term originated.

Pro tempore (Latin: "for the time being"). A member of a body who acts temporarily in the absence of the legally designated presiding officer—for example, a member of a state senate who acts in place of the constitutionally designated president of that body, the lieutenant governor.

Procedendo (Latin: "to be proceeded in"). A writ or legal instrument issued by a superior court to an inferior court in a matter previously removed to the superior court by a writ of certiorari. It returns the matter and directs the inferior court to proceed to determine the matter.

Procedural rules and laws. Regulations and acts that prescribe how substantive rules or laws are to be administered. *See also* Substantive rules and laws

Prorogue. To direct that a legislative session be terminated.

Quasi-judicial. A function or body that is not judicial but that is similar to a judicial function or body.

Quo warranto (Latin: "by what authority"). A writ by which the government inquires into the right of a person or legal entity to hold office or exercise a franchise.

Quorum. The minimum number of members of a body necessary to transact business, usually a majority.

Remand. The return of a decision by a superior court to a lower court for further action.

Remonstrance. A representation to a court or legislative body showing why something should not be done.

Right of property in man. A concept in some pre-1865 state constitutions used to legitimize slavery.

Rule making. Determining the accepted procedures for an activity. Courts and government agencies possess rule-making, as opposed to law-making, authority.

Sanguinary laws. Literally, "bloodthirsty" laws. Ones that freely impose the death penalty.

Selectmen. Certain elected officials in some New England municipalities.

Sine die (Latin: "without a day"). The final adjournment of a legislative session, without another day set to reconvene.

Sovereign immunity. The legal principle that a monarch or an independent political entity cannot be sued in court without providing consent.

Statute. A written law enacted by a legislature.

Substantive rules and laws. Regulations and acts that are to be applied by courts. *See also* Procedural rules and laws

Unified court system. A judicial system in which all the courts of law are under the government's highest court for purposes of administration.

Vicinage (French: "neighborhood"). The jurisdiction in which a crime was committed and the trial held.

Writ. In law, a written command or formal order issued by a court to enforce obedience to its authority. An appellate court may issue a writ of error to a trial court to obtain the record of a matter to be reviewed, or a superior court may issue a writ of prohibition to an inferior court to prohibit further action on a matter. More rarely, a warrant to hold an election or certify election returns. Some writs, including mandamus and quo warranto, are called prerogative writs, meaning that they are an exercise of a court's extraordinary power, as opposed to writs of right.

Constitutional references used in the preparation of this book include state constitutions, state law codes, and related materials supplied by state governments. General references consulted were Michael L. Shore and Abigail O'Donnell, eds., *Constitutions of the United States: National and State* (Dobbs Ferry, N.Y.: Oceana Publications, 1997); William F. Swindler, ed., *Sources and Documents of United States Constitutions* (Dobbs Ferry, N.Y.: Oceana Publications, 1973–79); *The Book of the States,* vols. 31 and 32 (Lexington, Ky.: Council of State Governments, 1996 and 1998); Henry Steele Commager, ed., *Documents of American History* (New York: Appleton-Century-Crofts, 1968); Samuel E. Morison, Henry S. Commager, and Edward W. Leuchtenburg, *The Growth of the American Republic* (New York: Oxford University Press, 1980); and state constitutions available at http://www.louisville.edu/groups/library–www/ekstrom/govpubs// goodsources/history/constitution.

References providing citations to cases (in addition to state law codes) were Robert F. Williams, comp., *State Constitutional Law: Cases and Materials,* with 1990–91 supplement (Washington, D.C.: Advisory Commission on Intergovernmental Relations, 1990); Thomas C. Marks and John F. Cooper, *State Constitutional Law* (St. Paul, Minn.: West, 1988); Paul C. Bartholomew, *Summaries of Leading Cases on the Constitution,* 4th ed. (Paterson, N.J.: Littlefield, Adams, 1962); Jennifer Friesen, *State Constitutional Law: Litigating Individual Rights, Claims, and Defenses* (New York: Matthew Bender, 1992); G. Alan Tarr, ed., *Constitutional Politics in the States: Contemporary Controversies and Historical Patterns* (Westport, Conn.: Greenwood Press, 1996).

General information on states came from *The World Almanac and Book of Facts: 1997* (Mahwah, N.J.: World Almanac Books, 1996); and Joseph N. Kane, Steven Anzovin, and Janet Podell, *Facts About the States* (New York: H. W. Wilson, 1992).

In addition to the sources listed above, the following materials were consulted:

Sources

Stewart, William H., Jr. *The Alabama Constitutional Commission: A Pragmatic Approach to Constitutional Revision.* University, Ala.: University of Alabama Press, 1975.

Alabama

———. *The Alabama State Constitution: A Reference Guide.* Westport, Conn.: Greenwood Press, 1994.

McBeath, Gerald A. *The Alaska State Constitution: A Reference Guide.* Westport, Conn.: Greenwood Press, 1997.

Alaska

Naske, Claus-M. *Alaska: A History of the 49th State.* 2d ed. Norman: University of Oklahoma Press, 1987.

———. *A History of Alaskan Statehood.* Lanham, Md.: University Press of America, 1985.

Henderson, Roger C. "Tort Reform, Separation of Powers, and the Arizona Constitutional Convention of 1910." *Arizona Law Review* 35 (fall 1993): 535–619.

Arizona

Leshy, John D. *The Arizona State Constitution: A Reference Guide.* Westport, Conn.: Greenwood Press, 1993.

Arkansas	Freyer, Tony A. *The Little Rock Crisis.* Westport, Conn.: Greenwood Press, 1984.
	Goss, Kay C. *The Arkansas State Constitution: A Reference Guide.* Westport, Conn.: Greenwood Press, 1993.
California	Grodin, Joseph R., Calvin R. Massey, and Richard B. Cunningham. *The California State Constitution: A Reference Guide.* Westport, Conn.: Greenwood Press, 1993.
	Witkin, B. E. *Summary of California Law,* vol. 7. 9th ed. San Francisco: Bancroft-Whitney, 1988.
Connecticut	Bysiewicz, Shirley. *Sources of Connecticut Law.* Boston: Butterworth Legal Publishers, 1987.
	Horton, Wesley W. *The Connecticut State Constitution: A Reference Guide.* Westport, Conn.: Greenwood Press, 1993.
Delaware	Federal Writers' Project. *Delaware: A Guide to the First State.* 1938. Reprint, New York: Hastings House, 1948.
	Munroe, John A. *Colonial Delaware.* Millwood, N.Y.: KTO Press, 1978.
	Rubenstein, Harvey B., ed. *The Delaware Constitution of 1897: The First One Hundred Years.* Wilmington: Delaware State Bar Association, 1997.
Florida	D'Alemberte, Talbot. *The Florida State Constitution: A Reference Guide.* Westport, Conn.: Greenwood Press, 1991.
	Gannon, Michael. *Florida: A Short History.* Gainesville: University Press of Florida, 1993.
Georgia	Coleman, Kenneth. *Colonial Georgia: A History.* New York: Scribner, 1976.
	Frech, Mary L., ed. *Chronology and Documentary Handbook of the State of Georgia.* Dobbs Ferry, N.Y.: Oceana Publications, 1973.
	Hill, Melvin B., Jr. *The Georgia State Constitution: A Reference Guide.* Westport, Conn.: Greenwood Press, 1994.
Hawaii	Bunge, Frederica M., and Melinda W. Cook. *Oceania: A Regional Study.* Arlington, Va.: U.S. Department of the Army, 1985.
	Lee, Ann F. *The Hawaii State Constitution: A Reference Guide.* Westport, Conn.: Greenwood Press, 1993.
Idaho	Colson, Dennis C. *Idaho's Constitution: The Tie That Binds.* Moscow, Idaho: University of Idaho Press, 1991.

Crowley, Donald, and Florence Heffron. *The Idaho State Constitution: A Reference Guide.* Westport, Conn.: Greenwood Press, 1994.

Burman, Ian D. *Lobbying at the Illinois Constitutional Convention.* Urbana: University of Illinois Press, 1973.

Carrier, Lois. *Illinois: Crossroads of a Continent.* Urbana: University of Illinois, 1993.

Keefe, John, and Neal R. Peirce. *The Great Lake States of America.* New York: W. W. Norton, 1980.

McLauchlan, William P. *The Indiana State Constitution: A Reference Guide.* Westport, Conn.: Greenwood Press, 1996.

Heller, Francis H. *The Kansas State Constitution: A Reference Guide.* Westport, Conn.: Greenwood Press, 1992.

Channing, Steven A. *Kentucky: A Bicentennial History.* New York: W. W. Norton, 1977.

Kilbourne, Richard H. *A History of the Louisiana Civil Code: The Formative Years, 1803–39.* Baton Rouge: Louisiana State University, 1987.

Symeonides, Symeon. *Louisiana Civil Law System.* 4th ed. Baton Rouge: Herbert Law Center, Louisiana State University, 1988.

Taylor, Joe G. *Louisiana: A Bicentennial History.* New York: W. W. Norton, 1976.

Clark, Charles E. *Maine: A Bicentennial History.* New York: W. W. Norton, 1977.

Tinkle, Marshall J. *The Maine State Constitution: A Reference Guide.* Westport, Conn.: Greenwood Press, 1992.

Bode, Carl. *Maryland: A Bicentennial History.* New York: W. W. Norton, 1978.

Tolley, Michael C. *State Constitutionalism in Maryland.* New York: Garland, 1992.

Wheeler, John P., Jr., and Melissa Kinsey. *Magnificent Failure: The Maryland Constitutional Convention of 1967–68.* New York: National Municipal League, 1970.

Gross, Robert A. *The Minutemen and Their World.* New York: Hill and Wang, 1976.

Labaree, Benjamin W. *Colonial Massachusetts: A History.* Millwood, N.Y.: KTO Press, 1979

Peters, Ronald M., Jr. *The Massachusetts Constitution of 1780.* Amherst: University of Massachusetts Press, 1974.

Illinois

Indiana

Kansas

Kentucky

Louisiana

Maine

Maryland

Massachusetts

Michigan	Catton, Bruce. *Michigan: A Bicentennial History.* New York: W. W. Norton, 1976.
Mississippi	Cobb, James C. *The Most Southern Place on Earth: The Mississippi Delta and the Roots of Regional Identity.* New York: Oxford University Press, 1992.
	Skates, John R. *Mississippi: A Bicentennial History.* New York: W. W. Norton, 1979.
	Winkle, John W. *The Mississippi State Constitution: A Reference Guide.* Westport, Conn.: Greenwood Press, 1993.
Missouri	Nagel, Paul C. *Missouri: A Bicentennial History.* New York: W. W. Norton, 1977.
Montana	Spence, Clark C. *Montana: A Bicentennial History.* New York: W. W. Norton, 1978.
Nebraska	Creigh, Dorothy W. *Nebraska: A Bicentennial History.* New York: W. W. Norton, 1977.
	Miewald, Robert D., and Peter J. Longo. *The Nebraska State Constitution: A Reference Guide.* Westport, Conn.: Greenwood Press, 1993.
Nevada	Bowers, Michael W. *The Nevada State Constitution: A Reference Guide.* Westport, Conn.: Greenwood Press, 1993.
	Bushnell, Eleanore. *The Nevada Constitution.* Reno: University of Nevada, 1977.
	Laxalt, Robert. *Nevada: A Bicentennial History.* New York: W. W. Norton, 1977.
New Hampshire	Morison, Elizabeth F. *New Hampshire: A Bicentennial History.* Nashville, Tenn.: American Association for State and Local History, 1976.
New Jersey	Connors, Richard J. *The Process of Constitutional Revision in New Jersey: 1940–47.* New York: National Municipal League, 1970.
	Fleming, Thomas J. *New Jersey: A Bicentennial History.* New York: W. W. Norton, 1984
	Williams, Robert F. *The New Jersey State Constitution: A Reference Guide.* Westport, Conn.: Greenwood Press, 1990.
New Mexico	Simmons, Marc. *New Mexico: A Bicentennial History.* New York: W. W. Norton, 1977.
	Smith, Chuck. *The New Mexico State Constitution: A Reference Guide.* Westport, Conn.: Greenwood Press, 1996.
New York	Bliven, Bruce. *New York: A Bicentennial History.* New York: W. W. Norton, 1981.

Breuer, Ernest H. *Constitutional Developments in New York, 1777–1958.* Albany: University of the State of New York, 1958.

Carter, Robert A. *New York State Constitution: Sources of Legislative Intent.* Littleton, Colo.: Fred B. Rothman, 1988.

Galie, Peter J. *Ordered Liberty: A Constitutional History of New York.* New York: Fordham University Press, 1996.

Johnson, Herbert A. *Essays on New York Colonial Legal History.* Westport, Conn.: Greenwood Press, 1981.

Weinstein, Jack B., et al. *Essays on the New York Constitution.* South Hackensack, N.J.: Fred B. Rothman, 1966.

Exum, James G., Jr. *The North Carolina State Constitution: A Reference Guide.* Westport, Conn.: Greenwood Press, 1993.   **North Carolina**

Boughey, Lynn M. "An Introduction to North Dakota Constitutional Law: Content and Methods of Interpretation." *North Dakota Law Review* 63, no. 2 (1987): 152–300.   **North Dakota**

Wilkins, Robert P. *North Dakota: A Bicentennial History.* New York: W. W. Norton, 1977.

Havighurst, Walter. *Ohio: A Bicentennial History.* New York: W. W. Norton, 1976.   **Ohio**

Morgan, Howard W. *Oklahoma: A Bicentennial History.* New York: W. W. Norton, 1977.   **Oklahoma**

Stone, Robert L. "Nine Articles of the Constitution of the State of Oklahoma of 1907 and Comparative Constitutional Law." *Oklahoma City University Law Review* 17, no. 1 (spring 1992): 89–129.

Dodds, Gordon B. *Oregon: A Bicentennial History.* New York: W. W. Norton, 1977.   **Oregon**

Cochran, Thomas C. *Pennsylvania: A Bicentennial History.* New York: W. W. Norton, 1978.   **Pennsylvania**

Wolf, George D. *Constitutional Revision in Pennsylvania: The Dual Tactic of Amendment and Limited Convention.* New York: National Municipal League, 1969.

Conley, Patrick, T. *Democracy in Decline: Rhode Island's Constitutional Development, 1777–1841.* Providence: Rhode Island Historical Society, 1977.   **Rhode Island**

Cornwell, Elmer E., Jr., and Jay S. Goodman. *The Politics of the Rhode Island Constitutional Convention.* New York: National Municipal League, 1969.

McLoughlin, William G. *Rhode Island: A Bicentennial History.* New York: W. W. Norton, 1978.

South Carolina   Wright, Louis B. *South Carolina: A Bicentennial History.* Nashville, Tenn.: American Association for State and Local History, 1976.

South Dakota   Milton, John R. *South Dakota: A Bicentennial History.* New York: W. W. Norton, 1977.

Tennessee   Dykeman, Wilma. *Tennessee: A Bicentennial History.* Nashville, Tenn.: American Association for State and Local History, 1975.

Laska, Lewis L. *The Tennessee State Constitution: A Reference Guide.* Westport, Conn.: Greenwood Press, 1990.

Texas   Braden, George D., et al. *The Constitution of the State of Texas: An Annotated and Comparative Analysis.* Austin: Texas Advisory Commission on Intergovernmental Affairs, 1977.

Frantz, Joe B. *Texas: A Bicentennial History.* New York: W. W. Norton, 1984.

May, Janice C. *The Texas State Constitution: A Reference Guide.* Westport, Conn.: Greenwood Press, 1996.

Utah   Peterson, Chares S. *Utah: A Bicentennial History.* New York: W. W. Norton, 1977.

Vermont   Morrissey, Charles T. *Vermont: A Bicentennial History.* New York: W. W. Norton, 1981.

Virginia   Howard, A. E. Dick. *Commentaries on the Constitution of Virginia.* Charlottesville: University Press of Virginia, 1974.

Morris, Thomas R., and Larry J. Sabbato, eds. *Virginia Government and Politics: Readings and Comments.* Virginia Chamber of Commerce. 3d rev. ed. Charlottesville: Center for Public Service, University of Virginia, 1990.

Sutton, Robert P. *Revolution to Succession: Constitution Making in the Old Dominion.* Charlottesville: University Press of Virginia, 1989.

Washington   Clark, Norman H. *Washington: A Bicentennial History.* New York: W. W. Norton, 1976.

Schwantes, Carlos A. *The Pacific Northwest.* Lincoln: University of Nebraska Press, 1989.

Snure, Brian. "A Frequent Recurrence to Fundamental Principles: Individual Rights, Free Government and the Washington State Constitution." *Washington Law Review* 67, no. 3 (July 1992): 669–90.

Bastress, Robert M. *The West Virginia State Constitution: A Reference Guide.* Westport, Conn.: Greenwood Press, 1995.

Williams, John A. *West Virginia: A Bicentennial History.* New York: W. W. Norton, 1976.

Stark, Jack. *The Wisconsin State Constitution: A Reference Guide.* Westport, Conn.: Greenwood Press, 1997.

Keiter, Robert B., and Tim Newcomb. *The Wyoming State Constitution: A Reference Guide.* Westport, Conn.: Greenwood Press, 1992.

Laughlin, Stanley K., Jr. *The Law of the United States Territories and Affiliated Jurisdictions.* Danvers, Mass.: Lawyers Cooperative, 1995.

West Virginia

Wisconsin

Wyoming

U.S. Territories

Index

318, 387, 398, 406, 454

vs. amendment, 43

See also Amendments

Revolutionary War, 55, 71, 81, 107, 117, 143, 151, 159–60, 169, 178, 185, 194, 202, 221, 261, 279, 307, 335, 372, 397, 405, 421, 430

Ricker, Marilla, 252

Right to work, 29, 365, 461

Rights. *See* Fundamental rights

Riley, Bennet, 36

Roman Catholics, 168, 281

Roman Senate, xv

Roosevelt, Theodore, 186, 318

Rousseau, Jean-Jacques, 211, 252

S

Safety, committees of, 81, 251, 354

Same-sex marriages, 91

Sanguinary laws, 161

Saunders, Alvin, 232

Schools

acts relating to, passage of, 312

boards of education, advisory role of, 193

buildings, private use of, 432

financing of constitutionality, 267–68, 287, 386

"literary fund," 411

school funds, 78, 124, 133, 176, 210, 219, 305, 419

student fees, 297

taxes, 61, 267

town responsibility, 167

religion in, 205, 424

segregation of, xii, 141–42, 144, 150, 184, 203, 219, 262, 319, 358

state aid to private schools, 308–9

superintendents of education, 5, 20, 76, 102, 106, 135, 156, 225, 239, 249, 294, 302, 322, 331, 339, 360, 369, 416, 437, 445, 458

teacher training, bilingual, 277

transportation to, 432

Searches and seizures

admissibility of evidence, 187, 309

and Fourth Amendment, 74, 271, 281, 309, 365, 436

"fruit of the poison tree" doctrine, 365

warrant for, validity of, 153

Seat of government, reasons for moving, 122

Secession

prohibited, 204, 291, 423

use of force to prevent, 243

Secessionist constitutions, 2, 26, 72, 81, 152, 203, 290, 354, 381, 406

Secessionists, re-enfranchisement of, 2, 169, 422

Second Continental Congress, 261, 335

Secret political societies prohibited, 291

Secretaries of state

acts valid during governor's absence, 20

appointed by governor, 174

functions of, 57–58

records of acts, 59

service as lieutenant governor, 12

Secretary of civil and military affairs, 402

Segregation

of military forces, 262

of schools, xii, 142, 144, 150, 184, 203, 219, 262, 319, 358

Selectmen, 184

Self-incrimination

breathalyzer test, 390

refusal to testify, 320

Senators. *See* Legislators

Sentences, mandatory minimum, 105

Separation of powers, xviii–xix, 74, 121, 128, 137, 145, 162, 171, 187–88, 206, 214, 263

cooperation not precluded, 263

delegation of legislative powers, 57, 234, 375

formal vs. real, 196

implied in state organization, 432–33

legislative and judicial powers combined, 407

legislature's influence on supreme court, 403

no overlap acknowledged, 356

not expressly stated, 10, 64, 90, 92, 137, 282, 300, 309, 337, 415, 432, 452, 457, 461

structural separation, 261–62

unconstitutional infringement, 38, 244, 366

Sequoya, 317

Sergeant, Jonathan Dickinson, 261

Seward, William H., 9

Sexual discrimination

exemption from jury duty, 214

in child support, 391

in college admissions, 36

in voting, 252

prohibited, xii, 10, 38, 47, 57, 91, 110, 153, 171, 179, 223, 262, 272, 337, 346, 382, 391, 407, 415, 440–41, 456, 461

See also Women

Sexual offenses not bailable, 233

Slavery, xii

outside equal protection of the law, 56

right to own slaves, 145

See also Compromise of 1850; Missouri Compromise

Slum clearance, 96

Smith, John, 250

The Social Contract (Rousseau), 252

Solid waste management, 318

Sovereign immunity

in suit by foreign nation, 205

voided for personal injuries, 224

waiver of, 83
Sovereignty, popular, xv,
    252, 406
Spanish-American War,
    460
Special laws
  allowable if not expressly
      prohibited, 75
  permissible in place of
      general laws, 225
  prohibited but not
      enumerated, 112,
      164, 189
  types prohibited, 48, 65,
      102, 121, 130, 141,
      173, 200, 274, 293,
      321, 358, 367, 416,
      426, 434, 443
Speech and the press,
    freedom of
  political activities on
      private property,
      336–37
  prior restraint of publica-
      tion, 195
  state guarantees vis-à-vis
      U.S. Constitution,
      413–14
The Spirit of the Laws
    (Montesquieu), xviii,
    196
St. Lusson, Simon
    Daumont, sieur de,
    185
Stamp Act, 177
State constitutions
  concept of state con-
      stitutionalism, 327
  differences among
      states, xvii
  first (N.H.), xi, xiv,
      251
  innovations, xii–xiii
  oldest in force (Mass.),
      xi, xv, 178, 398

vis-à-vis U.S. Constitu-
    tion, xvi–xvii, xx,
    xxii–xxiii. See also
    U.S. Constitution
Statehood
  definition of, 456,
      460–61
  vis-à-vis federal statutes,
      15
Stevens, John Paul, 68
Student loans, 383
Suffrage. See Voting rights
Suicides, estates of, 46,
    145, 214, 224
Superintendents of
    education, 5, 20,
    76, 102, 106, 135,
    156, 225, 239, 249,
    294, 302, 322, 331,
    339, 360, 369, 416,
    437, 445, 458
Supermajority votes
  for amendments, xxii,
      201
  for legislative quorum,
      120, 255, 283, 329,
      375–76, 383
  to create additional
      courts, 191
  to override appro-
      priations bills, 11,
      427
  to pass revenue bills,
      283, 330, 437
  to raise taxes, 401
Supreme courts
  chief justices. See Chief
      justices
  composition of, xxi
  control over inferior
      courts and agencies,
      324
  jurisdiction of, xxi
  amendments, challenges
      to, 314

laws on governor's
    ability to serve, 113
local vs. state, 78
not expressly stated,
    165
prescribed by law, 346,
    350–51
similar to British high
    court of chancery,
    69
legislature's authority
    over, 417
majorities required, 41,
    51, 77, 104, 114,
    156, 175, 227, 237,
    276, 304, 313, 324,
    360, 378, 385, 394,
    410, 417, 445, 463
qualifications for, xxi
quorums required, 69,
    77, 86, 104, 114,
    122, 131, 175, 208,
    209, 237, 265, 276,
    304, 313, 324, 360,
    385, 417, 427, 435,
    445
removal of judges,
    191, 332
rule-making authority,
    32, 131, 403
specified location of
    sessions, 140
term limits. See Term
    limits
trial by jury prohibited,
    199
See also Judges and
    justices; Judiciary
Surveillance, types pro-
    hibited, 456
Sutter, John, 35

T
Taft, William Howard,
    17, 270, 318

Tax and budget reform
    commissions, 79, 95,
    98–99, 124
Tax exemptions
  as the exception, 411
  charitable, 379
  for checking and savings
      accounts, 379
  for factories, 149
  for mines, 249
Taxes
  assessment for, 130
  capitation, 249, 297
  collection of, 173
  commuter, 258
  income, 70, 96, 115,
      152, 184, 267, 431
  on aircraft, 201
  on forest products,
      200–201
  on hazardous substances,
      267
  on mines, 447
  payments suspended,
      386
  poll, 2, 72, 144, 150,
      170, 258, 297
  property, 7, 42–43, 105,
      124, 149–50, 184,
      258, 267, 277, 315,
      362
  not to defray state
      expenses, 305
  relief for retired
      property owners, 419
  rates, 277
  school, 61, 267
  uniformity of, 70
Taxpayers
  rights of, xii, 52, 74
  power to sue state or
      county, 219
Telephone and telegraph
    communications,
    interception of, 281